SEXUAL DEVIANCE AND SOCIETY

In a society where sexualized media has become background noise, we are frequently discouraged from frank and open discussions about sex and offered few tools for understanding sexual behaviors and sexualities that are perceived as being out of the norm. This book encourages readers to establish new ways of thinking about stigmatized peoples and behaviors, and to think critically about gender, sex, sexuality and sex crimes.

Sexual Deviance and Society uses sociological theories of crime, deviance, gender and sexuality to construct a framework for understanding sexual deviance. This book is divided into four units:

- Unit I, *Sociology of Deviance and Sexuality*, lays the foundation for understanding sex and sexuality through sociological frameworks of deviance.
- Unit II, *Sexual Deviance*, provides an in depth dialogue to its readers about the sociological constructions of sexual deviance with a critical focus on contemporary and historical conceptualizations.
- Unit III, *Deviant Sexual Acts*, explores a variety of deviant sexual acts in detail, including sex in public, fetishes, and sex work.
- Unit IV, *Sex Crimes and Criminals*, examines rape and sexual assault, sex crimes against children, and societal responses to sex offenders and their treatment within the criminal justice system.

Utilizing an integrative approach that creates a dialogue between the subjects of gender, criminology and deviance, this book is a key resource for students interested in crime and deviance, gender and sexuality, and the sociology of deviance.

Meredith Gwynne Fair Worthen is as an Associate Professor of Sociology and elected faculty member of the Women's and Gender Studies Program at the University of Oklahoma, USA.

"Meredith Worthen's Sexual Deviance and Society is the sort of book I've been looking forward to for some time. The author has intelligently organized the relevant topics, and she and her colleagues have discussed and analyzed them with great insight and imagination. Every sociologist of deviance should consider adopting this volume and every one of our students will be enlightened by reading it. I loved it and so will they."

Erich Goode, *Sociology Professor Emeritus,*
Stony Brook University

"Drawing from both sociological and criminological perspectives, Sexual Deviance and Society offers a thoughtful, nuanced, and comprehensive examination of sexual deviance. Worthen's analysis is both theoretically grounded and empirically supported, and provides readers with a thorough understanding of the complex and ever-evolving societal attitudes toward human sexual behavior."

Amanda Burgess-Proctor, *Associate Professor of*
Criminal Justice, Oakland University

"Meredith Worthen serves the reader with a very sophisticated analysis of one of the most complicated and dynamic topics facing society. The topics in Sexual Deviance and Society are schemed and analyzed with great insight and creativity. Students in Deviance classes will be informed by its content and more progressive in thinking about sexual deviance. Human sexual behavior is probably the most exciting topic in sociology and Meredith takes it a step beyond. Worthen proves that deviance is alive, well, and exciting. A great text and research tool. Worthen bares and explores all the topics."

Craig J. Forsyth, *Professor of Sociology, University of Louisiana,*
Lafayette, and editor of Deviant Behavior

"This book fills an important niche in the sociological study of deviant behavior. Worthen has structured the book to allow the reader to set aside preconceived heteronormative ideas about what is and is not 'normal' sexual behavior, framed in both historical and theoretical frameworks, focusing on the social construction of defining acts or individuals as deviant. She gently challenges the reader to understand the differences between statistical deviance and the often politicized labeling of behaviors as deviant, focusing on the role of power structures, location and time, emphasizing the ever-evolving definitions of what is (and is not) considered deviant. Because some of the material may tap into past trauma, she incorporates suggestions for self-care in the text. Replete with well-crafted figures and illustrations, the book is ideal for a course on this topic as well as informative for any student of human sexuality. It is a must-have for those whose interests fall under the umbrella of the sociology of deviance."

Susan F. Sharp, *David Ross Boyd Professor of Sociology,*
University of Oklahoma

SEXUAL DEVIANCE AND SOCIETY

A sociological examination

Meredith G. F. Worthen

LONDON AND NEW YORK

First published 2016
by Routledge
2 Park Square, Milton Park, Abingdon, Oxon OX14 4RN

and by Routledge
711 Third Avenue, New York, NY 10017

Routledge is an imprint of the Taylor & Francis Group, an informa business

British Library Cataloguing-in-Publication Data
A catalogue record for this book is available from the British Library

Library of Congress Cataloging in Publication Data
Names: Worthen, Meredith Gwynne Fair, editor.
Title: Sexual deviance and society: a sociological approach / edited by
Meredith G. F. Worthen.
Description: First Edition. | New York: Routledge, 2016. | Includes
bibliographical references and index.
Identifiers: LCCN 2015050286 | ISBN 9781138819061 (hardback) | ISBN
9781138819078 (pbk.) | ISBN 9781315744858 (ebook)
Subjects: LCSH: Paraphilias. | Sex crimes. | Public sex.
Classification: LCC HQ71.S4119 2016 | DDC 364.15/3–dc23
LC record available at http://lccn.loc.gov/2015050286

ISBN: 978-1-138-81906-1 (hbk)
ISBN: 978-1-138-81907-8 (pbk)
ISBN: 978-1-315-74485-8 (ebk)

Typeset in Bembo
by Sunrise Setting Ltd, Brixham, UK

Printed and bound in the United States of America by Publishers Graphics,
LLC on sustainably sourced paper.

To anyone who has ever felt "normal"
and to anyone who has ever felt "deviant."
This book is for you.

CONTENTS

FIGURES

IMAGES

TABLES

BOXES

ABOUT THE AUTHOR

Meredith Gwynne Fair Worthen, Ph.D. (the University of Texas at Austin, 2009), is an Associate Professor of Sociology, elected faculty member of the Women's and Gender Studies Program, and faculty affiliate of the Center for Social Justice at the University of Oklahoma. Her main interests are in the sociological constructions of deviance and stigma, gender, sexuality, and LGBTQ identities, as well as feminist and queer criminology. She is the author of dozens of articles and currently serves as an associate editor of *Deviant Behavior*. Dr. Worthen has received multiple awards for her work including the Irene Rothbaum Outstanding Assistant Professor award given to a model teacher recognized for dedication, effectiveness, and ability to inspire students to high levels of achievement, the Robert D. Lemon Social Justice Award given to those who demonstrate courage, compassion, and leadership while working to eliminate discrimination, oppression, and injustice locally and globally, and the Jill Irvine Leadership Award given to a faculty member who exemplifies collaborative spirit, expansive vision, commitment to advancing women's and LGBTQ issues, service to campus, and dedication to leadership.

In addition to her work in academia, Dr. Worthen is also the creator of The Welcoming Project, a non-profit organization that promotes LGBTQ-friendly businesses, organizations, churches, and health care providers by providing "All Are Welcome" rainbow signs to post in their windows and on their websites. She is also a regular contributor to Bio.com. As a researcher, teacher, and activist, Dr. Worthen's work dissects multiple dimensions of prejudice in efforts to cultivate understanding, empathy, and social change.

ABOUT THE CONTRIBUTORS

Paul D. C. Bones, Ph.D. (the University of Oklahoma, 2015), is an Assistant Professor of Sociology at Texas Woman's University in Denton, TX. He is interested in disability studies, the ecological predictors of crime, and victimology. His recent publications have appeared in the *Journal of Quantitative Criminology* and *Deviant Behavior*. Dr. Bones' contribution is Box 3.4 in chapter 3.

Danielle Dirks, Ph.D. (the University of Texas at Austin, 2011), is a sociologist, professor, and author. She is the author of *Confronting Campus Rape: Legal Landscapes, New Media, and Networked Activism* (Routledge 2016) and co-author of *How Ethical Systems Change: Lynching and Capital Punishment* (Routledge 2011). Her work has been featured in the *New York Times, National Public Radio, Gawker, Ms. Magazine, Chronicle of Higher Education*, and a handful of feature-length documentaries. Dr. Dirks' co-authored contribution is chapter 5.

Amanda E. Fehlbaum, Ph.D. (the University of Oklahoma, 2014), is an Assistant Professor of Sociology at Youngstown State University in Youngstown, OH. She is interested in gender, feminism, sex education, body and embodiment, and qualitative methods. Her current research focuses on sexual assault prevention on college campuses. Dr. Fehlbaum's contribution is chapter 8.

Trenton M. Haltom, M.A. (the University of Houston, 2015), is a Ph.D. student at the University of Nebraska-Lincoln in the Department of Sociology. Specializing in men and masculinities, his research focuses on men in effeminized or effeminately stigmatized spaces as well as men's health and sexuality. Haltom's contribution is Box 10.6 in chapter 10.

Melissa S. Jones, M.A. (the University of Oklahoma, 2014), is a Ph.D. student at the University of Oklahoma in the Department of Sociology. She is interested in gender, family, and victimology. Her current research focuses on the linkages between adverse events in childhood, adult victimization, mental illness, and substance abuse. Jones' contribution is chapter 13.

Sister Libby Rayshun is a member of the Tulsa chapter of the Sisters of Perpetual Indulgence. As his secular self, he is a doctoral candidate in the Department of Educational Leadership and Policy Studies at the University of Oklahoma. His dissertation work is an educative history of same-sex sexualities in Tulsa, Oklahoma. His research interests include the historical and sociological foundations of sexuality education, research methods, as well as exploring the usage of transformative learning theory in educational contexts. Sister Libby's contribution is Box 10.5 in chapter 10.

Chauntelle A. Tibbals, Ph.D. (the University of Texas at Austin, 2010), is a public sociologist and author. Her research has been published in numerous scholarly journals, including the *Stanford Law and Policy Review* and *Sexualities*. Dr. Tibbals is committed to the accessibility of rigorous research, as well as demystifying the scholarship process. As such, she is a regular contributor to *Men's Health*, *Playboy*, and various other news outlets including CNBC, NBC News, VICE, MTV, and Al Jazeera. Her book, *Exposure: A Sociologist Explores Sex Society and Adult Entertainment* (2015) is available from Greenleaf Press. Dr. Tibbals' contribution includes chapter 11 and Box 13.2 in chapter 13.

Samantha A. Wallace, M.A. (the University of Oklahoma, 2015), is a Ph.D. student at the University of Oklahoma in the Department of Sociology and the Director of Philanthropy for The Welcoming Project, an LGBTQ advocacy nonprofit. She is interested in deviance, sexuality, and education/pedagogy. She frequently guest lectures on drug deviance, human sexuality, and educational stratification. Wallace's contribution is the SM content in chapter 10.

PREFACE

The conceptualization of this textbook began when I was an undergraduate sociology student. In my senior year, I was enrolled in a criminology course that provided an investigation into the nature of criminal events including rape, homicide, property crimes, and white-collar crimes. Armed with three years of previous work in a broad range of courses including those focused on deviance and gender, I was eager to learn about the complexities involved in sex crime. I envisioned an in-depth discussion of the gendered power dynamics that contribute to rape and a sociocultural investigation of norms, values, and belief systems that interact to generate the alarming statistics I had heard about rape on college campuses. Specifically, that one in five women will experience sexual assault in her lifetime. A number that left me both concerned for my own well-being and motivated to learn more so that I could help change it.

However, much to my disappointment, I was not presented with this type of knowledge. Quite the contrary, we spent a total of one lecture dedicated to the topic of sex crime in which I was provided not only with inadequate information but also, I was taught false, that is to say non-factual, fallacies about rape. There was no attention drawn to the systemic power imbalances involved in sex crime and there was no explanation as to why rape was a problem on college campuses—including our own. Needless to say, I was utterly dissatisfied and a bit upset. I was both under-informed and under-educated about something that I believed should be central to an undergraduate experience—both for students in general who deserve to learn about how sex crime affects their lives and especially for those students focused on sociology and criminology as I was. Along with my peers, I was missing a basic fundamental building block in my educational experience. But unlike most of my peers, I was aware of this injustice and the potentially long-term ramifications resultant from being misinformed about such important issues.

So I began to strategize. I planned to gain the knowledge I needed and I began to think about how to share that knowledge with others. And in my last year of graduate school, I finally had that chance. I was offered the opportunity to develop and teach my very own specialty course and I knew what it would be: *Sexual Deviance and Society*. I shaped this course to fill the gaps in my own undergraduate education as well as to encourage students to think critically about gender, sex, sexuality, and sex crimes—all framed in a discourse about the norms that shape them. I taught this course every semester from fall 2008 to fall 2015 without an appropriate textbook and finally, post-tenure, I was able to work with Routledge and a handful of close colleagues to create this textbook.

Along this journey and in this textbook, I have chosen to review a spectrum of "deviant" identities and activities—many of which are heavily politicized. Some may question, for example, my inclusion of gay and bisexual people in a discussion of "sexual deviance." Some may think I am downright politically incorrect for doing so. But before you misjudge my motives, know this: just as others have done before me, "I choose to use [the word deviant] in the same way some gay people now use the word 'queer'—as a badge of pride and as a sign of defiance against the forces of sexual conformity" (Gates 2000:8). Thus, to me, deviance can be a signifier of difference *and* defiance. Deviance need not (but frequently does) come with a negative, bad, or categorically "evil" connotation. It can be associated with empowerment and it can be conflated with imprisonment. Perhaps most in line with the goals of this textbook, studying deviance can create a space for self-reflection and it can help establish a new way of thinking about stigmatized people and behaviors. Thus, in considering the social construction of deviance as a whole and sexual deviance in particular, both the content and language utilized in this textbook are designed to be reflective and culturally interactive.

Overall, I see this textbook both as an invitation to learn, to think, and to evolve; to arm yourself with knowledge and/or to arm your students with awareness. As you take this trip through sexual deviance, it is my sincere hope that you will be challenged, reassured, titillated, inspired, and alarmed and that this textbook builds a bridge between wherever you were to wherever you want to go.

Reference

Gates, Katharine. 2000. *Deviant Desires: Incredibly Strange Sex*. New York, NY: Juno Books.

1

INTRODUCTION AND SELF-CARE

Could a sexy cereal get you in the mood? New muesli claims to be full of ingredients that will boost sexual desire, United Kingdom[1]
Melissa Nelson: Dental assistant fired for being "irresistible," United States[2]
Australian loses compensation case for sex injury, Australia[3]
I had consensual sex with elderly aunt, claims rape accused, Ireland[4]
Larry Collum paid Rhonda Kelley for sex with a roll of quarters, police say, United States[5]
This teen just auctioned her virginity for about $27,000, Russia[6]
Man who has had sex with 999 cars, ready to commit to VW Beetle, United States[7]
Ania Lisewska's 100,000-man sex marathon angers Egyptian Islamists, Poland[8]

While we are often bombarded with salacious headlines as the above news stories from around the world suggest, the opportunity to critically examine the ways societies construct sex and sexuality may escape us. What is more, we may even be discouraged from having frank and open discussions about sex because, interestingly, many cultures are plagued with sexualized media but offer little room for understanding sexual behaviors and sexualities that are perceived as anything out of the norm. In doing so, we may find ourselves with a lack of understanding of *sexual diversity*—or worse—we may allow or actively support judgmental or even damaging laws and policies that punish those who do not behave or identify within culturally established and regulated norms about sex and sexuality.

Sexual diversity is an umbrella term for the wide spectrum of sexual behaviors and identities that exist in society. Considering sexual behaviors and identities on a continuum provides a space for acknowledging the fluidity, complexity, and variability inherent in human beings. Sexual diversity encompasses sexual behaviors and identities perceived as normative and those that are perceived as deviant or outside of the established norms in a particular society. In this way, examining sexual diversity necessarily encompasses a critical discussion of *sexual deviance*, sexual behaviors, and identities perceived as non-normative, and therefore, deviant in a particular society.

Introducing sexual deviance

To best understand sexual deviance, we must first acknowledge that what is perceived as sexually deviant is both complex and variable. Indeed, as French sociologist Émile Durkheim stated, "today's deviance can become tomorrow's morality" (1964 [1895]:71). Simply put: what is considered to be deviant at one time and place can be perceived as both acceptable and normative in another time and place. For example, interracial marriage was once an illegal and criminal act in the United States and it was not until 1967, in the landmark civil rights Supreme Court case, *Loving v. Virginia,* that the laws prohibiting interracial marriage were declared to be unconstitutional. Not only have laws changed, but also, perceptions of interracial marriage as deviant have also changed over time. United States public opinion Gallup Poll data collected since the late 1950s indicate a marked increase in approval of Black-White marriages. Indeed, as seen in Figure 1.1, 2013 data show that 87 percent of Americans support marriage between Blacks and Whites, up from a scant 4 percent in 1958, representing one of the largest shifts of public opinion in Gallup history (Newport 2013). Today we can reflect upon this

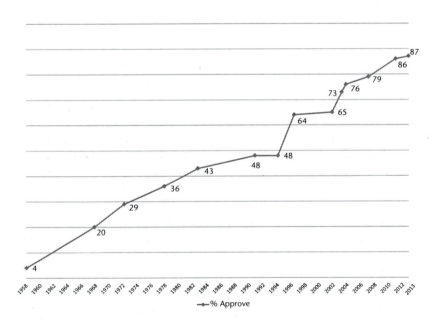

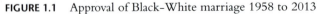

FIGURE 1.1   Approval of Black-White marriage 1958 to 2013

Notes: Data adapted from U.S. Gallup's Minority Rights and Relations poll 1958 to 2013; 1958 wording: "Do you approve or disapprove of marriages between white and colored people?"; 1968–78 wording: "… whites and nonwhites?"; 1978–2013 wording: "… Blacks and Whites?"

significant change and see that what is identified as criminal and perceived as deviant certainly varies across time but is also influenced by cultural values that may be unique to a particular society, in this case, the United States. Sexual deviance is therefore a process related to norms about sex, sexuality, race, culture, law, and criminal culpability.

Integrating sexual deviance

Understanding the construction of sexual deviance necessitates a dialogue that integrates three major areas of study in sociology: criminology, deviance, and gender (which often encompasses the sub-disciplines of sex and sexuality).

Criminology

Criminology investigates the causes, consequences, and prevention of criminal behavior (formal violations of laws) in both the individual and society. Criminological theory has evolved over time, beginning in the mid-eighteenth century with the Classical School, which emerged in the wake of the desire to reform the criminal justice and penal systems. Italian philosopher Cesare Beccaria (1738–1794) and British philosopher Jeremy Bentham (1748–1832) were both Classical criminologists and emphasized free will as part of the causes of criminal behavior and deterrence as an effective prevention mechanism (e.g., Beccaria 2013 [1764]; Bentham 2009 [1791]). The Positivist School followed and emphasized a more deterministic approach. For example, utilizing biological determinism, Italian researcher Cesare Lombroso (1835–1909) attempted to identify criminals through the physiological traits of men's faces (1972 [1911]). This archaic and highly disputed process has been rejected by a majority of criminologists today. The Chicago School arose in the early twentieth century and shifted the focus of criminology to the investigation of ecological and social structures. For example, American criminologists Clifford Shaw (1895–1957) and Henry McKay (1899–1980) examined neighborhood contexts in inner-city Chicago, Illinois (U.S.) to understand the relationship between social disorganization and juvenile delinquency (Shaw and McKay 1942). Cultural theories emerged out of the ideas that subcultures of violence can arise in certain settings and can inculcate a socially learned value system of deviance (see Ronald Akers' 1998 and Edwin Sutherland's 1939 work on social learning and differential association). The field of Criminology now includes diverse frameworks that examine involvement in crime as related to individual characteristics such as self-control (see Gottfredson and Hirschi 1990), while others emphasize ecological characteristics as in the case of Routine Activity Theory (Cohen and Felson 1979). We have also seen the integration of Marxist Conflict Theory, Feminist Theory (see Daly and Chesney-Lind 1988), and Life-Course Theory (see Sampson and Laub 1993) into modern explanations of crime (Lilly *et al.* 2007). While the theoretical mechanisms for explaining the causes, consequences, and prevention of criminal behavior may differ, these are some of the established criminological foundations that underscore the significance of understanding crime and criminals from a theoretical standpoint (see more in chapter 3).

Deviance

The sociological field of deviance investigates non-normative beliefs, behaviors, and identities in efforts to understand how norms are created, reinforced, and violated in a particular society. Variations in what constitutes a "norm violation" are emphasized through a critical and cultural lens. The theoretical field of deviance is a complicated terrain and often overlaps—either fully or partially—with criminological theories. While the division between what constitutes a "crime theory" and what constitutes a "deviance theory" remains relatively unclear, there are some distinctions in theoretical discussions of deviance worth noting. Durkheim (1858–1917) is often cited as a deviance theorist because his work critically examined the maintenance and organization of society from a functionalist perspective that emphasized the value in all non-normative behavior. Specifically, Durkheim's work posited that deviance is universal and that all societies contain deviance because moral boundaries are maintained and reified through the process of defining deviance. Durkheim's research on suicide (1951 [1897]) also contributed to the emergence of labeling theories that underscore the significance of society's responses to certain behaviors as condemnatory. In this way, attaching a deviant label to a particular behavior or identity necessarily defines behaviors and identities as deviant. The negative social stigma that accompanies a deviantly labeled behavior or identity is a key part of understanding deviance in society. Canadian sociologist Erving Goffman's (1922–1982) work on stigma (1963) provides great theoretical insight into our understandings of how people manage their stigmatized identities through passing, covering, and double-living processes. Theories about deviance show us that becoming deviant (see Matza 1969) is a complex process that involves the violation of socially constructed norms and the recognition, labeling, and condemnation of that norm violation as deviant. In addition to crime theories that inform our understandings about violations of formally enacted law, theorizing about deviance can teach us about informal violations of social norms. In this way, crime and deviance theories work together to explain how social norms and formally enacted laws affect the stigma that often accompanies identities and/or involvement in behaviors that are perceived as criminal and/or deviant (see more in chapter 3).

Gender

From a sociological standpoint, *gender* is a social construct that is related to the ways a culture organizes people and labels characteristics and visual cues into dichotomous identities of "men" and "women." Often gender is described as distinct from *sex*, which is typically confined to the labels of "male" or "female" based on biological markers such as the external appearances of genitalia and to a lesser extent, chromosomes. Presentations of gender are also frequently categorized dichotomously (i.e., feminine and masculine). While many cultures often view both sex and gender as binary concepts, sociologists emphasize the social construction of gender as existing within a spectrum that acknowledges variance in the expression and social attributes of an individual's gender identity. American sociologists Candace West (born in 1950) and Don Zimmerman (born in 1937) further developed the concept of gender in their 1987 seminal article "Doing Gender" suggesting that gender is a routine accomplishment embedded in daily life (West and Zimmerman 1987). Through social interactions, we embody, display, and communicate messages about our gender and, in turn, others perceive us as "men" or as "women." These processes are coded in ways that not only reinforce norms about gender, but also, norms about sexuality. When we actively perform gender, we also send messages about our sexualities. Recent scholarship has argued that the processes of "doing gender" are intimately related to presumptions of heterosexuality such that "doing gender" is also "doing heteronormativity" (Schilt and Westbrook 2009). *Heteronormativity* is the assumption that it is "normal" to be heterosexual. Just as norms about gender dictate either "man" or "woman," in many cultures, norms about sexuality dictate "heterosexual" as normative. Overall, sociologists emphasize the variance of gender and sexualities as existing on a spectrum, while also acknowledging the cultural existence of strict norms that reinforce rigid parameters of "appropriate" expressions of gender and sexuality (see more in chapters 4 and 5).

Sexual deviance

Together, sociological theories of crime, deviance, gender, and sexuality allow us to build a framework for understanding sexual deviance. Criminological theories show us that crimes are violations of formally enacted laws that depend on cultural values. Furthermore, individual, ecological, and social conditions contribute to involvement in criminal activity. Thus, sex crimes should be understood in a context that recognizes the ways a society both defines sex crimes and punishes criminals that engage in illegal sexual acts. Incorporating a deviance perspective, informal violations of socially constructed norms should be examined through a process that recognizes, labels, and stigmatizes certain norm violations as deviant. Both formal and informal violations of norms about sexual behavior, gender, and sexuality fit within the realm of sexual deviance. Thus, the study of sexual deviance should be understood through an integrative framework that incorporates sociological traditions and theoretical frameworks from criminology, deviance, gender, and sexuality.

Outline

This book provides a dialogue to its readers about the sociological constructions of sex and sexuality with a critical focus on deviance by integrating theories of crime, deviance, gender and sexuality. It is organized into four units: I. Sociology of deviance and sexuality; II. Sexual deviance; III. Deviant sexual acts; and IV. Sex crimes and criminals.

I. Sociology of deviance and sexuality

This unit lays the foundation for understanding sex and sexuality through socio-logical frameworks of deviance. Chapters 2 and 3 provide an overview of the various ways deviance has been theorized about, beginning with a discursive description of deviance followed by detailed discussions of both historical and modern theories of crime and deviance. Chapter 4 offers basic foundations for understanding the definitions of gender, sex, and sexual identities. The processes behind these socially constructed categories are also discussed as they fit into perspectives about social power. Chapter 5 outlines the ways in which gender is highly performative and intimately tied to heterosexual ideals. Using a sociological focus, norms about heterosexuality, gender identity, genitalia, and heteronormativity are critically analyzed in the context of deviance.

II. Sexual deviance

This unit provides an in-depth dialogue to its readers about the sociological constructions of sexual deviance with a critical focus on contemporary and historical conceptualizations. In chapter 6, sexual deviance is defined through myriad examples that illustrate "statistical" sexual normalcy and deviance using global samples. Chapter 7 historically and culturally situates sexual deviance by tracing changes in perspectives about sexual imagery, the sale of sex, same-sex sexual behavior, and sexual pleasure over time through ancient civilizations in Egypt, China, India, Greece, and Italy up to Western cultures in the Middle Ages, the Renaissance, the Victorian era, the twentieth century, and modern society. In Chapter 8, adolescent sexuality is discussed and both virginity and abstinence are highlighted as culturally significant labels that symbolize normative and deviant teen sexuality. Through incorporating a perspective that recognizes historical, global, and age-related constructs, this unit continues to scrutinize the complexities of sexual deviance.

III. Deviant sexual acts

This unit examines several deviant sexual acts in detail, beginning with sex in public in chapter 9. Various examples (including tearooms, gym locker rooms, and bathhouses) are highlighted and the significance of sex in public as deviant is situated in the context of the historically intense criminal investigation of men who have sex with other men (MSM) in public spaces. In chapter 10, three categories of fetishes are reviewed: "object"-specific fetishes (podophilia, retifism, agalmatophilia, pygmalionism, balloon fetishes, objectophilia, mechaphilia), "animal"-specific fetishes (zoophilia, formicophilia, bestiality, furry fandom, plushies, bronies, cloppers), and Dom/sub role-play (bondage, discipline, sadomasochism, SM). The stigma that fetishists experience is highlighted alongside the commonality of "deviant" sexual fantasies. The final chapter of this unit investigates sex work. Two forms of sex work are discussed in depth: prostitution (street prostitution, escorting, brothel prostitution, and sugar dating) as well as pornography production and performance. The legal and social regulations of sex work are critically discussed alongside the stigma allocated to all those involved in these industries. Overall, the third unit of this textbook considers sexually deviant acts as well as the actors who participate in them through situating them within a socio-cultural and legal context.

IV. Sex crimes and criminals

The final unit of this text considers sex crimes and criminals. Chapter 12 focuses on rape and sexual assault. In addition to defining rape and consent, this chapter emphasizes cultural variations in laws about rape, crime statistics about rape, and problems with estimating rape prevalence with special attention to reasons for under-reporting. In addition, *rape myths*, social misconceptions about rape, are described and the university environment is critically examined as a context for rape. In particular, the roles of alcohol, "hooking up," and campus party culture are detailed. Motivations of men who rape (i.e., power and control) and rape survivors' experiences, including survivor empowerment, are also provided. Chapter 13 discusses sex crimes against children by examining pedophilia, incest, and child sexual abuse in sex-related media (CSAM). Illustrative examples are provided including NAMBLA (North American Man/Boy Love Association) and sexting. The final chapter of this unit examines sex offenders as a highly stigmatized group and the social consequences associated with the "sex offender" label (employment, housing, victimization) as well as sex offender treatment (cognitive behavioral therapy, chemical and surgical castration) and its relationship to recidivism.

Self-care

The topics covered in this book range from fun, exciting, and even titillating to disturbing and difficult. Some issues discussed in this text are likely to evoke uncomfortable feelings and may even trigger intense emotional responses. Most of us have some personal experiences with sexual deviance whether they be from our own lives or through those around us. If you are a survivor of a sex crime, some chapters may be especially difficult for you to read. Furthermore, you may discover things about yourself while reading this text that may be upsetting to you. As a result, it is important to engage in self-care as you read this book. Self-care involves actions and behaviors that both prioritize and nurture the self in efforts to maintain overall mental, physical, and emotional health. Self-care is essential when encountering difficult experiences.

Recommended steps of self-care for reading this textbook

As seen in Figure 1.2, the first step of the self-care process while reading this textbook involves checking in periodically in order to gauge your emotional responses

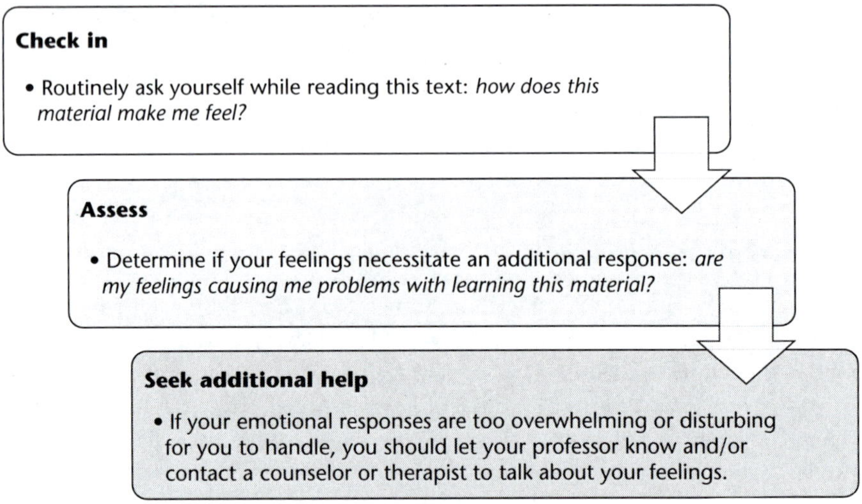

> **Check in**
> • Routinely ask yourself while reading this text: *how does this material make me feel?*

> **Assess**
> • Determine if your feelings necessitate an additional response: *are my feelings causing me problems with learning this material?*

> **Seek additional help**
> • If your emotional responses are too overwhelming or disturbing for you to handle, you should let your professor know and/or contact a counselor or therapist to talk about your feelings.

FIGURE 1.2   Recommended steps of self-care for reading this textbook

to this material. How does this material make you feel? After checking in, assess your feelings (step two). Are you having difficulties reading about this subject matter? Assessing your feelings is an important part of this process because feeling especially upset can mean that additional self-care steps may be needed. While assessing your feelings, determine if you need to respond. Are your feelings causing problems with learning this material? If your emotional responses to this subject matter are too overwhelming or disturbing for you to handle, you may need to seek additional help (step three). If you are reading this textbook as a part of a course or seminar, consider letting your professor know about the difficulties you are having. You may also consider contacting a counselor or therapist to talk about your feelings. Above all, it is important to remember that all students engage with this material differently so it is essential to engage in self-care steps when learning about sexual deviance.

Notes

1   July 21, 2013. Retrieved from: http://www.dailymail.co.uk/news/article-2372893/SexCereal-Could-sexy-cereal-mood.html#ixzz2joEwHGiO
2   December 23, 2012. Retrieved from: http://abcnews.go.com/blogs/headlines/2012/12/melissa-nelson-dental-assistant-fired-for-being-irresistible-is-devastated/
3   October 30, 2013. Retrieved from: http://abcnews.go.com/International/wireStory/australian-loses-compensation-case-sex-injury-20722132
4   June, 13, 2013. Retrieved from: http://www.breakingnews.ie/ireland/i-had-consensual-sex-with-elderly-aunt-claims-rape-accused-597406.html
5   August 19, 2013. Retrieved from: http://www.huffingtonpost.com/2013/08/19/larry-collum-paid-for-sex-roll-of-quarters_n_3780260.html
6   November 5, 2013. Retrieved from: http://www.huffingtonpost.com/2013/11/05/siberia-virginity-auction-shatuniha-27000_n_4219720.html?ref=topbar

7   October 15, 2013. Retrieved from: http://www.huffingtonpost.com/2013/10/15/
    edward-smith_n_4098886.html?utm_hp_ref=weird-sex
8   September 13, 2013. Retrieved from: http://www.huffingtonpost.com/2013/09/13/
    ania-lisewska-_n_3901889.html?utm_hp_ref=weird-sex

References

Akers, Ronald L. 1998. *Social Learning and Social Structure: A General Theory of Crime and Deviance*. Boston, MA: Northeastern University Press.

Beccaria, Cesare. 2013 [1764]. *On Crimes and Punishments*. Boston, MA: Branden Books.

Bentham, Jeremy. 2009 [1791]. *Panopticon: Or the Inspection House*. Whitefish, MT: Kessinger Publishing.

Cohen, Lawrence and Marcus Felson. 1979. "Social Change and Crime Rate Trends: A Routine Activity Approach." *American Sociological Review* 44(4):588–608.

Daly, Kathleen and Meda Chesney-Lind. 1988. "Feminism and Criminology." *Justice Quarterly* 5:497–538.

Durkheim, Émile. 1951 [1897]. *Suicide: A Study in Sociology*. New York, NY: Free Press.

Durkheim, Émile. 1964 [1895]. *The Elementary Forms of Religious Life*. New York, NY: Free Press.

Goffman, Erving. 1963. *Stigma: Notes on the Management of Spoiled Identity*. Englewood Cliffs, NJ: Prentice-Hall.

Gottfredson, Michael R. and Travis Hirschi. 1990. *A General Theory of Crime*. Stanford, CA: Stanford University Press.

Lilly, J. Robert, Francis T. Cullen, and Richard A. Ball. 2007. *Criminological Theory: Context and Consequences*, Fourth Edition. Thousand Oaks, CA: Sage Publications.

Lombroso, Cesare. 1972 [1911]. *Criminal Man, According to the Classification of Cesare Lombroso*. New York, NY: Putnam.

Loving v. Virginia, 388 U.S. 1 (1967).

Matza, David. 1969. *On Becoming Deviant*. Englewood Cliffs, NJ: Prentice Hall.

Newport, Frank. 2013. "In U.S., 87% Approve of Black-White Marriage, vs. 4% in 1958." *Gallup Poll*. Retrieved from: http://www.gallup.com/poll/163697/approve-marriage-blacks-whites.aspx.

Sampson, Robert and John Laub. 1993. *Crime in the Making: Pathways and Turning Points through Life*. Cambridge, MA: Harvard University Press.

Schilt, Kristen and Laurel Westbrook. 2009. "Doing Gender, Doing Heteronormativity: 'Gender Normals', Transgender People, and the Social Maintenance of Heterosexuality." *Gender & Society* 23:440–64.

Shaw, Clifford R. and Henry D. McKay. 1942. *Juvenile Delinquency in Urban Areas*. Chicago, IL: University of Chicago Press.

Sutherland, Edwin. 1939. *Principles of Criminology*. Philadelphia, PA: J.B. Lippincott.

West, Candace and Don H. Zimmerman. 1987. "Doing Gender." *Gender and Society* 1(2):125–51.

UNIT I

SOCIOLOGY OF DEVIANCE AND SEXUALITY

Unit I introduction

People are often fascinated by crime and criminals. In fact, you may have enrolled in a deviance course because of your interest in the dangerous, unsavory, or downright criminal behaviors that humans engage in. But how do sociologists examine deviance? The first step in our investigation is to explore the concept of deviance itself. What is it? What does it entail? How do we define it as sociologists? The purpose of the first unit of this textbook is to provide you with a broad basis for understanding sex and sexuality through sociological frameworks of deviance. In doing so, each chapter offers a critical examination of foundational concepts in the sociology of deviance and sexuality.

Chapter 2 provides an in-depth discussion of defining deviance as a social construct that is derived from behaviors, identities, and beliefs that are perceived as norm-violations. Specifically, the process underlying deviance is described as (i) ever changing, (ii) culturally dependent, and (iii) temporally relative. Furthermore, the differences between social and criminal deviance are highlighted in the context of William Graham Sumner's (1907) distinction between everyday norms based on manners, customs, and decorum (which he identified as *folkways*) and norms about moral values (which he identified as *mores*). The spectrum of deviance is further expanded upon with a discussion of positive and negative deviance. Heckert and Heckert's (2002) wider scope of deviance (i.e., rate-busting and deviance admiration) is also included and a new concept (*deviance fascination*) is provided to further develop their typology. Cultural variations in deviance are emphasized through illustrative examples, including global differences in attitudes toward cigarette smoking. In addition, moral panics (Cohen 1972) are described in the context of the 1980s "War on Drugs." Finally, students are encouraged to understand their own deviance.

Chapter 3 offers an overview of various ways of thinking about crime and deviance. This chapter begins with a summary of Marx, Weber, and Durkheim's contributions to theories of crime and deviance. Next, the beginnings of criminology are traced through the Classical School, the Positivist School, and the Chicago School. Then, a sampling of criminology theories is provided including Anomie/Strain Theory, Differential Association Theory, Techniques of Neutralization, Social Control/Social Bond Theory, Routine Activity Theory, Feminist Criminology, Self-Control Theory, General Strain Theory, Age-Graded Theory of Informal Social Control, and Social Learning Theory. Perspectives highlighting the significance of understanding and theorizing about deviance are examined in the context of symbolic interactionism and labeling theories. Stigma and its accompanying typologies are discussed using the work of Goffman (1963) and others (Falk 2001; Link and Phelan 2001). Overall, the theoretical discussions offered here frame crime and deviance as social constructs.

Chapter 4 discusses how social power shapes our understandings of gender, sex, and sexuality, and thus, defines some as deviant and others as normative. The chapter begins with a critical discussion of the concepts of gender, sex, and sexual identity as social constructs. Gender is described as a master status related to social interactions, norms, life expectancy, educational attainment, career success, and family life. The complex relationships between sexual identity and sexual behavior are also outlined. Alfred Kinsey and colleagues' work (Kinsey *et al.* 1948, 1953) is provided as a historical example while Edward Laumann and colleagues' (Laumann *et al.* 1994, 1999) research is highlighted as contemporary research on sexual behavior. Recent research investigating prejudices toward sexual identity and behavior (in terms of social attitudes) is contextualized alongside a discussion of homophobia, sexual prejudice (as defined by Gregory Herek 2000, 2004), and concludes with an emphasis on the importance of considering LGBT stigmas as separate, but related, phenomena. Finally, social power, gender, sex, and sexuality are examined through two case examples: the Netherlands and Yemen.

In Chapter 5, gender is discussed as both highly performative and intimately tied to heterosexual ideals drawing from West and Zimmerman's (1987) seminal piece "Doing Gender." Furthermore, an intersectional approach to understanding so-called deviant sexualities is provided and the ways in which individuals challenge restrictive gender binaries in favor of more expansive and fluid ideas about gender are discussed. Using a sociological focus, norms about heterosexuality, gender identity, genitalia, and heteronormativity are critically examined in the context of deviance. The overarching goal of this chapter is to consider gender as a curiously complicated social construct embedded in norms that are so pervasive, their deconstruction often remains elusive. By examining gender through the lens of deviance, the intricacies involved in both normative and deviant conceptualizations of gender, sex, and sexuality are revealed. This chapter also includes a critical and historical discussion of whiteness as root for a bigenderist, racialized system that sets the stage for a heteronormativity by drawing on the work of American Black feminist scholars Kimberle Crenshaw (1991) and Patricia Hill Collins (1991) and other race scholars such as Richard Fung (2008). Overall, a wide range of performances, identities, and sexualities are discussed as embodying "doing gender deviance" and the impossibility of being a "gender normal" is highlighted.

Overall, the first unit of this textbook provides an initial dialogue to its readers about the sociological constructions of sex and sexuality with a critical focus on deviance by integrating theories of crime, deviance, gender, and sexuality. Through this discussion a framework for understanding sexual deviance is built. Incorporating a deviance perspective, this book argues that both formal and informal violations of socially constructed norms should be examined through a process that recognizes, labels, and stigmatizes certain norm violations as deviant.

References

Cohen, Stanley. 1972. *Folk Devils and Moral Panics*. London: Routledge.

Collins, Patricia Hill. 1991. *Black Feminist Thought: Knowledge, Consciousness, and the Politics of Empowerment*. New York, NY: Routledge.

Crenshaw, Kimberle. 1991. "Mapping the Margins: Intersectionality, Identity Politics, and Violence against Women of Color." *Stanford Law Review* 43(6):1241–99.

Falk, Gerhard. 2001. *Stigma: How We Treat Outsiders*. Amherst, NY: Prometheus Books.

Fung, Richard. 2008. "Looking for My Penis: The Eroticized Asian in Gay Video Porn." Pp. 235–53 in *A Companion to Asian American Studies*, edited by Kent Ono. New York, NY: John Wiley.

Goffman, Erving. 1963. *Stigma: Notes on the Management of Spoiled Identity*. Englewood Cliffs, NJ: Prentice-Hall.

Heckert, Alex and Druann Maria Heckert. 2002. "A New Typology of Deviance: Integrating Normative and Reactivist Definitions of Deviance." *Deviant Behavior* 23:449–79.

Herek, Gregory. 2000. "The Psychology of Sexual Prejudice." *Current Directions in Psychological Science* 9:19–22.

Herek, Gregory. 2004. "Beyond Homophobia: Thinking about Sexual Prejudice and Stigma in the Twenty-First Century." *Sexuality Research & Social Policy* 1:6–24.

Kinsey, Alfred, Wardell Pomeroy, and Clyde Martin. 1948. *Sexual Behavior in the Human Male*. Philadelphia, PA: W.B. Saunders Company.

Kinsey, Alfred, Wardell Pomeroy, Clyde Martin and Paul Gebhard. 1953. *Sexual Behavior in the Human Female*. Philadelphia, PA: W.B. Saunders Company.

Laumann, Edward O., John H. Gagnon, Robert T. Michael, and Stuart Michaels. 1994. *The Social Organization of Sexuality*. Chicago, IL: University of Chicago Press.

Laumann, Edward O., Anthony Paik, and Raymond C. Rosen. 1999. "Sexual Dysfunction in the United States." *JAMA: The Journal of the American Medical Association* 281(6):537–44.

Link, Bruce and Jo Phelan. 2001. "Conceptualizing Stigma." *Annual Review of Sociology* 27:63–85.

Sumner, William G. 1907. *Folkways: A Study of the Sociological Importance of Usages, Manners, Customs, Mores, and Morals*. Boston, MA: Ginn & Company Publishers.

West, Candace, and Don H. Zimmerman. 1987. "Doing Gender." *Gender & Society* 1(2):125–51.

2
DEFINING DEVIANCE

What is deviance?

Norms and deviance

Most of us have heard the term "deviance" before. Outside of academia, what is viewed as deviant most often has a negative connotation. For example, common synonyms for deviance include "bad," "threatening," "offensive," "illegal," or even "criminal." In the field of sociology, however, deviance is understood within the context of cultural norms. *Norms* are established standards of behavior and beliefs maintained by a particular society. Norms are communicated and reinforced in our daily lives. Few are even aware of the complex happenings in norm construction and maintenance, yet every person in every culture is a part of the ongoing processes involving norms and their violations. There is also no universality to norms or norm violations:

> for we live in a world of 'cultural reality'... Caviar is not a delicacy to the general. Cows are not food to the Hindu. Mohammed is not the prophet of God to me. To an atheist God is not God at all.
>
> *(Ellsworth 1937:150–1)*

In relationship to norms, *deviance* is a sociological field that investigates non-normative beliefs, behaviors, and identities in an effort to understand how norms are created, reinforced, and violated in a particular society. As a result, deviance is a relative phenomenon based on an interpretative analysis: what is considered "deviant" in one time and place may or may not be considered deviant in another time and place (Geertz 1973; Orcutt 1983; Walzer 1987; Ben-Yehuda 1990). Just like norms, there is also no universality to deviance: "so deviance, like beauty, is in the eyes of the beholder ... almost every conceivable human characteristic of activity is pariah in somebody's eyes ... there is nothing inherently deviant to any human act" (Simmons 1969:4).

Furthermore, prominent deviance scholars Patricia Adler (born in 1951) and Peter Adler (born in 1952) note that "people can be labeled deviant as the result of the ABCs of deviance: their attitudes, behaviors, or conditions" (2012:13). For example, perspectives about a variety of issues (including abortion, gay and lesbian relations, sex between teenagers, birth control, pornography, and polygamy to name a few) have been considered quite contentious in American culture. However, attitudes toward these issues have shifted over time with some becoming significantly more positive. Thus, normative beliefs about a particular issue and normative responses to those engaging in a particular behavior can (and do) shift over time. For example, U.S. Gallup Polls on the moral acceptability of abortion, polygamy, and gay/lesbian relations from 2003 to 2014 indicate that Americans' views on the morality of gay/lesbian relations have undergone a significant transition from less than half (44 percent) viewing gay/lesbian relations as "acceptable" in 2003 to majority support since 2010 (see Figure 2.1). Such findings suggest that acceptance of gay and lesbian rights is becoming significantly more normative. As a result, those who are in the minority (those who do not support gay and lesbian rights) are becoming more and more deviant in the United States. Furthermore, even highly stigmatized deviant behaviors, such as polygamy (defined by Gallup as "when a married person has more than one spouse at the same time"), are becoming less morally repugnant. The moral acceptability of polygamy was amongst the lowest of any of the issues Gallup inquired about in their U.S. Values and Beliefs poll from 2003 to 2014. In 2006, only 5 percent of

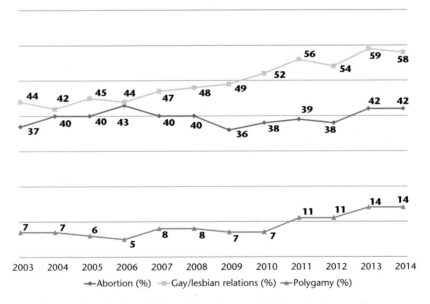

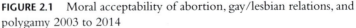

FIGURE 2.1 Moral acceptability of abortion, gay/lesbian relations, and polygamy 2003 to 2014

Data adapted from U.S. Gallup's Values and Beliefs poll 2003 to 2014.

Americans viewed polygamy as morally acceptable (just slightly higher than the meager 4 percent who viewed married men and women having an affair as morally acceptable). However, the acceptability of having multiple spouses increased nearly three-fold with 14 percent viewing polygamy as morally acceptable in 2014. This sharp rise in support (and by contrast decrease in stigma) could be attributed to the increase in media presence of polygamist families on television shows (e.g., HBO's *Big Love*, Olsen and Scheffer 2006–2011) (Riffkin 2014a). By contrast, Americans' perspectives about the moral acceptability of married men and women having an affair remains low (7 percent in 2014). In addition, abortion attitudes continue to be relatively stable, varying only a few percentage points from 2003 to 2014. Thus, for some issues, especially gay and lesbian issues, what (and who) is considered "deviant" is currently being redefined with swings in majority opinion shifting the entire politics of deviance in the current U.S. climate. For example, from 2004 to 2015, the U.S. went from having only one state that granted same-sex couples the right to marry (Massachusetts) to legalizing same-sex marriage for all. For other issues, including abortion, Americans' perspectives have remained somewhat resolute.

Deviance as process

Defining deviance in juxtaposition to norms is only one part of the story. It is important to remember that what is seen as deviant is forever changing and developing out of human interactions. Indeed, deviance is entirely a social construct, thus, it is culturally dependent and temporally relative. Deviance emerges out of a process that is embedded in the intricacies of daily life that are so minute, most of us are unaware of the incredibly vibrant activity that hums below the surface of human interaction. If we were to take a metaphorical microscope and place a slide of social goings on underneath the lens, we would see a myriad of activity involving the policing and monitoring of what people wear, how we act, what we say to one another, how we identify, and what we believe. Consequently, the processes of daily life necessarily entail the construction and maintenance of how a society defines deviance and deviants. Because this defining deviance process is ongoing and ever-changing, the dynamics of what is seen as deviant are inherently time and place dependent (see Figure 2.2). That is to say that "deviance" can change in the blink of an eye because it is part of the colorful fabric of human existence and emerges only through social interactions that reinforce certain beliefs, behaviors, and identities as "normal" and thus define others as "deviant." As a result, the process of "deviantization" is fluid, negotiable, and perpetual (Ben-Yehuda 1990:231).

The spectrum of deviance

Social and criminal deviance

When defining deviance, it is important to understand the qualitative distinction between social and criminal deviance. *Social deviance* is a violation of a cultural norm, such as picking your nose in public, eating spaghetti with your fingers,

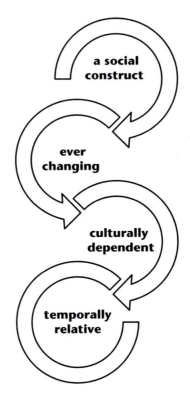

FIGURE 2.2   Sociological foundations of deviance

talking on the phone loudly in a movie theatre, or wearing an evening gown to school. While socially deviant behaviors may be seen as unpleasant or unusual, they are not typically highly problematic occurrences. You might view a person who does these things as strange or odd, but it is unlikely that you would read much more into these deviant behaviors. Such norm violations can be further understood in the context of folkways and mores. William Graham Sumner (1840–1910) taught the first American "Sociology" course at Yale University in 1875. Amongst other things, Sumner (1907) identified a distinction between everyday norms based on manners, customs, and decorum (which he identified as *folkways*) and norms about moral values (which he identified as *mores*). Unlike folkway violations that have little to no large consequences (someone is not likely to utterly despise you simply because you choose to dress in attire that is deemed unusual), violations of mores evoke a greater emotional response because they threaten the larger structure of a society's value system. For example, as noted earlier in this chapter, adultery is viewed as morally wrong by the vast majority of U.S. society (ranging from 87 percent to 93 percent) (Riffkin 2014a). Engaging in adultery is a violation of the social norm that married couples should be in honest and monogamous sexual relationships. But adulterers are seen as more than just norm violators, indeed, many would view those who engage in extramarital affairs as despicable or abhorrent.

This is because adultery threatens the family structure on which American culture is based (i.e., marriage). Thus, adultery represents a violation of mores and adulterers are seen as deviants. In contrast to folkway violations that are less likely to be tied to moral outrage, mores violations are of greater magnitude and mores themselves have greater social significance. Indeed, Sumner tells us that "mores define the limits which make right and wrong" (1907:521). In this way, upholding mores (and defining those who do not as deviant) reinforces a social value system that contributes to the normative/deviant structure of a given society. In summary, folkways distinguish *refined* from *rude*, while mores tell us what is *right* and *wrong*. Some folkway and mos violations can be considered as social deviance whereas some can be defined as criminal deviance.

Unlike social deviance, criminal deviance is, by definition, illegal. To engage in *criminal deviance* is to violate a society's formally enacted law. Although laws may change over time, and they are likely to do so because they are grounded in norms regarding social deviance (see Box 2.1), the connection between criminal deviance and law makes criminal deviance somewhat easier to identify. While social deviance is defined from norms, customs, and morals that are for the most part unwritten, criminal deviance is based on violations of formal written laws. Thus, someone could read a "what to do" and "what not to do" list of laws to avoid engaging in criminal deviance. Those who violate laws, and thus engage in criminal deviance, risk formal punishments from institutions of social control such as the criminal justice system.

BOX 2.1 DEFINING CRIME

Why are some behaviors "criminal" and others are not? Any behavior can be defined as a crime; it need only violate a formally enacted law to do so. Thus, the process of defining a crime is actually the companion to the process of creating and enforcing a law. Because laws reflect a society's value system in that they are based on the norms that the dominant group desires to uphold, what is defined as a "crime" is also a reflection of the norms and values in a particular community. As a result, the process of defining crime is inherently sociological because it is dependent on social norms, laws, and their violations.

The emergence of a sociological discussion of defining crime can be traced back to Durkheim's early work. In *The Rules of the Sociological Method*, Durkheim posited that crime is normal and universal:

> Crime is present not only in the majority of societies of one particular species but in all societies of all types. There is no society that is not confronted with the problem of criminality. Its form changes; the acts thus characterized are not the same everywhere; but, everywhere and

always, there have been men who have behaved in such a way as to draw upon themselves penal repression . . . What is normal, simply, is the existence of criminality, provided that it attains and does not exceed, for each social type, a certain level, which it is perhaps not impossible to fix in conformity with the preceding rules.

(Durkheim 1938 [1895]:65)

According to Durkheim, because all functioning societies have a need for crime, all societies must also decide what behaviors are defined as criminal. And going about deciding what is a "crime" is dependent on cultural norms. That is to say that what is identified as a crime in one community may not be in another. Durkheim offers the example of a "society of saints." He tells us that even a community of "perfect" individuals will need to define some behaviors as crimes and thus, criminals will always exist:

Imagine a society of saints, a perfect cloister of exemplary individuals. Crimes, properly so called, will there be unknown; but faults which appear venial to the layman will create there the same scandal that the ordinary offense does in ordinary consciousnesses. If, then, this society has the power to judge and punish, it will define these acts as criminal and will treat them as such. For the same reason, the perfect and upright man judges his smallest failings with a severity that the majority reserve for acts more truly in the nature of an offense.

(Durkheim 1938 [1895]: 68–9)

Crime then, emerges even in a "perfect" society of saints. Small variances in behaviors are magnified and those engaging in such deviant acts are deemed to be criminals. Even in societies in which it would appear that no crimes could exist, crimes and criminals will emerge through formal punishment of norm violations.

Durkheim's discussion of the universality of crime even within a society of saints, albeit quite engaging, is purely theoretical. His ideas have inspired modern day sociologists to see how his theory might play out in real life. In the 1960s, American sociologist Kai Erikson (born in 1931) conducted an historical investigation of the Puritan Quakers of Massachusetts Bay. His study showed that within this community of Puritans who were devoutly religious and embodied an "exaggeration of conventional values" but lived in a constant fear of sin (Erikson 2005 [1966]:45), there was still evidence of three crime waves in the 1600s. From his analysis of these patterns, Erikson determined that these seemingly large upsurges of crime within Quaker society, did not, in fact, represent an increase in the actual volume of crime at these times. Rather, what was perceived and defined as criminal is what changed and thus, the crime waves represented a shift in what types of deviance were of most concern to the Puritans. Erikson's (2005 [1966]) work shows us (as Durkheim posited), that even seemingly "perfect" societies will define behaviors as criminal and these patterns are indicative of shifts in norms and *not* shifts in actual variances in behaviors.

A few decades later, Daniel Patrick Moynihan (1927–2003) further expanded on these ideas in his influential article "Defining Deviancy Down" (1993). Drawing from Durkheim's (1938 [1895]) and Erikson's (2005 [1966]) work, Moynihan tackles the concept of the stability of crime. He suggests that societies can tolerate only so much crime and as a result, when they become overloaded with crime, norms will shift and societies will actually redefine formerly egregious behavior as tolerable. When we define deviance down, we normalize the crime level and as a result, our judgments of certain behaviors become more favorable. This redefinition of negatively stigmatized behaviors into normal day-to-day happenings ensures a smoothly operating functional society.

As with defining deviance, defining crime is dependent on norms, but unlike deviance, what is seen as a crime is also dependent on violations of formally enacted laws. Both are a part of a sociological process that varies across time and culture. Furthermore, Durkheim (1938 [1895]) and his contemporaries (i.e., Moynihan 1993; Erikson 2005 [1966]) show us that while the existence of crime is universal, what is perceived and defined as criminal is what changes over time.

However, as seen in Figure 2.3, the relationship between social and criminal deviance is not black and white. That is to say that what is socially deviant may or may not be criminally deviant and what is criminally deviant may or may not be socially deviant. For example, in almost all jurisdictions around the world, a teacher firing a gun at a student in a school classroom is both socially and criminally deviant because it violates a formally enacted law and a socially defined norm. This occurrence squarely fits the criteria of both criminal and social deviance, thus, the overlap between these types of deviance is evident for this particular situation. Conversely, there are some crimes that criminals can engage in while risking little (if any) social ramifications. Take, for instance, the crime of jaywalking (crossing the street on foot in violation of traffic law, especially outside of designated pedestrian crosswalks usually delineated by diagonally painted lines at traffic intersections). Jaywalking is a crime worthy of fines in the United States, as well as in other countries including Australia, Canada, China, Germany, the Philippines, and Singapore (Lewis 2014). While walking across the street outside of a designated pedestrian area is a violation of criminal law, most who do so are not thought of as social deviants. In fact, jaywalking laws are rarely enforced and pedestrians frequently flout them. Thus, the jaywalker is a criminal

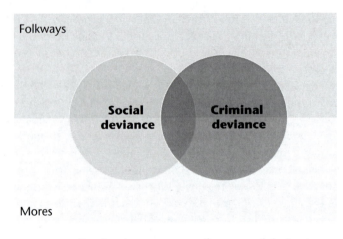

FIGURE 2.3 Overlapping constructs of norms and deviance

deviant but is not a social deviant. In this example, criminal deviance and social deviance are separate social constructs.

Positive and negative deviance

The spectrum of deviance is not complete without a discussion of positive and negative deviance. As noted earlier in this chapter, the colloquial understanding of deviance is negative, bad, or criminal. From a sociological perspective, however, deviance can be conceptualized with a more neutral tone (as a norm violation). Even so, it is true that some behaviors evoke strongly adverse reactions (e.g., murder) while others arouse a pleasurable response (e.g., a concert symphony performed by child musicians). While both of these examples can be defined as deviant because they violate norms (most people are not murderers and most children are not highly skillful musicians), these behaviors can also be understood as different types of deviance. Murder represents an underconformity or nonconformity to norms that carries a negative connotation, or in other words, *negative deviance*. Formally, murderers receive severe punishment from the criminal justice system. For example, the crime of murder is the only crime in the United States for which individuals have been put to death since 1977 (Death Penalty Information Center). Informally, murderers are viewed as a detestable group because they are seen as devaluing the sanctity of human life. Even if released from prison and exonerated for their crimes, they continue to experience severe hardships while coping with life after death row (Westervelt and Cook 2012). For those convicted of murder, their negative deviance becomes a *master status*, a defining characteristic of who they are. Furthermore, being an ex-prisoner carries a very palpable stigma. *Stigma* is "an attribute that is deeply discrediting" that diminishes the bearer "from a whole and usual person to a tainted, discounted one" (Goffman 1963:3). Those who are stigmatized are seen as socially undesirable and they may experience negative

stereotyping, discrimination, devaluation, and denigration as a result of their deviant status. Those who engage in negative deviance risk stigmatization.

In contrast to negative deviance, positive deviance typically evokes more favorable responses. Positive deviance can be conceptualized as exceeding norms, surpass-
ing expectations, and achieving idealized standards (Dodge 1985; Heckert and
Heckert 2002). For example, a concert symphony performed by child musicians is
positive deviance, or overconformity to norms that carries a positive connotation.
Exceptionally talented child musicians are celebrated and lauded for their skills.
They are described as prodigies and viewed as prestigious members of society. As a
result, positive deviants receive special treatment including admiration, praise,
honors, gifts, and awards for their valued qualities. In these ways, positive deviance
is the counterpart to negative deviance.

Negative deviance has been (and remains) the customary focus of the field of
deviance. Indeed, a survey of topics discussed in contemporary deviance courses
and texts will yield a host of negatively evaluated subjects including drug addiction,
eating disorders, and mental illness. Less discussed, however, are examples of positive
deviance. Although alluded to by Durkheim (1938 [1895]) in the sense that deviance is functional and can promote positive changes in society and further emphasized as an important area of focus by Lemert (1951), positive deviance remains on
the periphery of sociological discourse and empirical study (see also Dodge 1985;
Ben-Yehuda 1990; Heckert and Heckert 2002).

While positive and negative deviance can be considered two sides of the same
coin, some scholars have envisioned a wider scope of deviance. *Rate-busting* is similar to positive deviance in that it involves overconformity to norms, however, unlike
positive deviance, rate-busting carries a negative connotation. Exceptionally gifted
and talented students who are negatively stereotyped as "nerds" or "geeks" are rate-
busters. Furthermore, even though these "nerds" are positively deviant due to their
extraordinary intellectual skills, they are often additionally negatively stereotyped as
anti-social "four-eyes" who lack a keen fashion sense and make inadequate romantic partners. Thus, they are positive deviants with a negative reputation (i.e., rate-
busters). By contrast, *deviance admiration* is underconformity to norms that carries an
extremely positive connotation. Deviance admiration occurs when negative deviance
is celebrated and sometimes idolized. Deviants such as Billy the Kid, Jesse James,
Butch Cassidy, Al Capone, and Bonnie (Parker) and Clyde (Barrow) are often
admired for their abilities to evade the law as both notorious and successful criminals (Heckert and Heckert 2002). In addition to deviance admiration, the current
landscape of reality television reflects a culture of *deviance fascination*, or underconformity to norms that carries a somewhat positive connotation (albeit less positive
than deviance admiration). Deviance fascination is one step below deviance admiration and can clearly be seen as a dominant force in contemporary media. For
example, *COPS*, an unscripted U.S.-based reality series that first aired in 1989, is a
wildly successful television show due to our utter fascination with crime and criminals. *COPS* has filmed over 1,000 episodes in five countries (Bolivia, China, Russia,
the United Kingdom, and the United States) and it has been released in English,

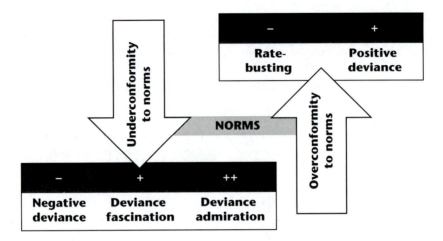

FIGURE 2.4 Adaptation of Heckert and Heckert's (2002) Typology of Deviance

Spanish, German, and Russian (Langley and Barbour 1989–present). The show features on-location real time footage of police officers' daily activities that include both vice arrests and narcotics stings. Often, the criminals featured on *COPS* are belligerent and their crimes are petty (such as public intoxication, simple assault, possession of marijuana). Our desire to watch *COPS* and other shows like it demonstrates our captivation with crime. As seen in Figure 2.4, our interest in deviance reflects both positive and negative evaluations of norm breaking, from fascination and admiration of criminals to negative judgments of overachievers.

Cultural variations in deviance

As emphasized elsewhere, cultural dependence is key to defining deviance. That is to say that what may be viewed as deviant at one time and place may be entirely normal in another. Take for example, smoking cigarettes. In the United States, cigarette use rates reached their peak in 1964 and have been declining since 1975. Put another way, while close to half of men and women were cigarette smokers in the U.S. in the 1960s, those numbers have been cut in half over the past several decades with less than a quarter of American adults currently smoking cigarettes (Cummings and Proctor 2014). Alongside a significant decrease in cigarette smoking behavior, we have seen an increase in the stigma associated with smoking. Gallup's 2014 Consumption Habits Survey showed that 56 percent of Americans saw smoking cigarettes as something that should be banned from all public places (up from 31 percent in 2003) and 19 percent of Americans believed cigarette smoking should be totally illegal in the United States (slightly up from 16 percent in 2003) (Riffkin 2014b). Thus, cigarette smoking in the U.S. is seen as a deviant activity worthy of quarantine by a slight majority and total banishment by a sizeable minority. Furthermore, beyond the general stigmatization of smoking behavior, a study of 816 current and former smokers revealed that cigarette smoking carried a very real stigma. As seen in Figure 2.5, fully 81 percent believed that socially distancing children from smokers is normative and 21 percent viewed smoking as a sign of personal failure (Stuber *et al.* 2008). Such overtly negative judgments demonstrate the profound stigma that smoking carries. Overall, while cigarette smoking was once the norm for Americans in the 1960s, today, being a smoker in the U.S. is a deviant activity and smokers themselves are stigmatized for their deviance.

Beyond the United States, however, there are important cultural differences in cigarette smoking that are worth noting. While American cigarette consumption is at an all-time low because of increased regulations of smoking behavior and aware-ness of the health risks associated with cigarette use, smoking rates are increasing in many developing nations because tobacco companies have focused their marketing campaigns on emerging economies (Cummings and Proctor 2014). As a result, across the globe, tobacco use continues to be the leading cause of preventable death, killing approximately 6 million people every year (World Health Organization 2013). For example, in China, nearly 3,000 people die each day from smoking-related illnesses and estimates indicate that that by 2050, more than 8,000 Chinese deaths could be attributed to cigarette consumption. This phenomenon is a cul-tural artifact. Indeed, in some parts of Asia, it is commonplace for men to smoke and deemed to be both a social norm and a rite of passage for boys (Cummings and Proctor 2014). The normativity of cigarette smoking in China, however, is limited to men. Data from Gallup indicate that 60 percent of Chinese men smoke while only 3 percent of Chinese women report using cigarettes (Ott and Srinivasan 2011).

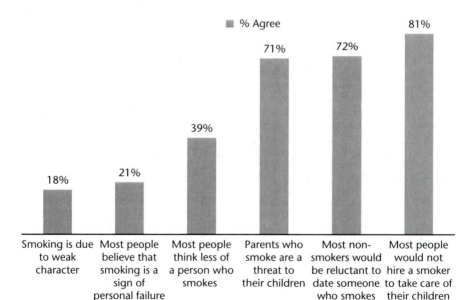

FIGURE 2.5 Smoker–related stigma

Data adapted from Stuber *et al.* (2008).

Thus, cigarette smoking is a normative behavior for Chinese men and a deviant behavior for Chinese women. Other cross-cultural comparative data show us that the majority of Canadians, Americans, and Australians believe that, generally, society disapproves of smoking while significantly fewer support this perspective in Malaysia (Hosking *et al*. 2009). Thus, the deviance of cigarette smoking is culturally dependent.

Insiders and outsiders

Deviance not only varies cross-culturally, but also, what is defined as deviant can vary within a particular culture, depending on who has the "insider" status and who is designated as the "outsider." Put simply, "insiders" are those that support main-stream norms and "outsiders" are those that depart from mainstream norms or in other words, break the rules of the dominant culture and embrace their own values and norms. For example, members of certain motorcycle clubs in the U.S. (such as the Hells Angels, Bandidos, and Outlaws) embody a "biker" lifestyle that is often characterized as criminal, hyper-masculine, and nonconformist (Quinn and Forsyth 2009). In contrast to "insiders" (i.e., non-bikers), bikers support an anti-mainstream lifestyle, and thus, are seen as "outsiders" in comparison to dominant culture. In this way, bikers in the Hells Angels, for example, are members of a *counterculture* (a sub-group whose values and norms are at odds with the dominant culture). Members of countercultures are often viewed as deviant outsiders.

However, it is important to note that who is thought of as the "insider" and who is thought of as the "outsider" depends on whose perspective is being examined. An individual who is perceived by dominant culture as an "outsider" might feel like those who are judging him (those in mainstream culture) are actually the ones who should be seen as the "outsiders" (Becker 1963). For example, consider an inner city youth who engages in violence to defend his turf. As American sociologist Elijah Anderson (born in 1943) shows us, young urban men embrace a "code of the street," whereby physicality, ruthlessness, and violence are normalized (1999). From the inner city youth's perspective, his violence is normal; it is even expected and rewarded. To those around him, such as teachers and police officers, however, his violence may be seen as delinquent and criminal. Within his peer network, the young man's violence is normative and he is seen as an "insider" because he oper-ates within the rules of his group, however, within mainstream culture, he is viewed as an "outsider." Thus, he can be viewed as an "insider" or an "outsider" depending on the frame of reference by which he is judged.

But who decides what rules should be enforced and what rule-breaking should be perceived as deviant? Or, in other words, who decides who are the "insiders" and who are the "outsiders"? The ability to both create and enforce particular types of norms, rules, and laws is a reflection of social power. Our identities and social posi-tions shape our abilities to become rule-enforcers. The inner city youth may feel that the norms of dominant culture do not resonate with his experiences and thus, he is being forced to follow rules that he never agreed to; however, for the most part, he is subject to the prevailing mainstream cultural norms and as a result, he will most often be seen as a deviant "outsider." These complexities can be further elucidated as follows:

> People are in fact always *forcing* their rules on others, applying them more or less against the will and without the consent of those others ... The middle class makes rules the lower class must obey—in the schools, the courts, and elsewhere ... Distinctions of age, sex, ethnicity, and class are all related to differences in power, which accounts for differences in the degree to which groups so distinguished can make rules for others.
>
> *(Becker 1963:17–18)*

For both the Hells Angels biker and the urban youth, their deviant status is relative. Within their groups, their violence is normal. Outside of their group, however, their violence is deviant. Thus, depending on whose frame of reference is being examined, they can be perceived as either "insiders" or "outsiders." Overall, both cross- and within-cultural relativity are important to consider when defining deviance. But above all, social power plays a significant role in who decides who are the "insiders" and who are the "outsiders," and as a result, those who are most often seen as "deviants" operate outside of (or counter to) mainstream cultural norms.

Moral panics

What is defined as deviant can also be influenced by the political climate. For example, when U.S. President Richard Nixon identified drug issues as "public enemy number one" in 1971 (Nixon 1972:755), he set off a firestorm of activity that shifted political and cultural concern that would continue for the better part of two decades. Indeed, prior to Nixon's declaration that a "War on Drugs" was necessary to counteract the social atrocities of the world (Johnson *et al.* 1996:182), drug abuse was not even considered to be one of the most important issues facing the country. But by September 1989, a *New York Times*/CBS News poll found that a surprisingly high number (64 percent) of respondents indicated drug abuse as the most important problem in the U.S. (Goode and Ben-Yehuda 1994). Contemporary deviance scholars note that Americans were intensely preoccupied with drug abuse issues in the 1980s (Goode and Ben-Yehuda 1994). However, by the 1990s, drug issues became increasingly less prominent in the prevailing political climate and since 2001, U.S. public opinion polls continue to indicate similar trends. While more than half (58 percent) of Americans stated that they worried a great deal about drug use in 2001, only about a third (34 percent) reported drug use as a highly worrisome issue in 2014 (Gallup 2014). In fact, in response to the open-ended question "What do you think is the most important problem facing this country today?" recent Gallup poll data reveal that "the economy" (14 percent) and "dissatisfaction with the government" (17 percent) are the most significant concerns of the American public while only 1 percent of Americans indicated that "drugs" are an important social problem (Gallup 2015).

Why were Americans so engrossed with drug issues in the 1980s and just a short time later deeming them to be relatively insignificant? In short, the state of "national emergency" declared by Nixon in the 1970s (Johnson *et al.* 1996:182) festered and blossomed into a full blown moral panic in the 1980s. South African-born British sociologist Stanley Cohen (1942–2013) described moral panics as:

> A condition, episode, person or group of persons emerges to become defined as a threat to societal values and interests; its nature is presented in a stylized and stereotypical fashion by the mass media; the moral barricades are manned by editors, bishops, politicians and other right-thinking people; socially accredited experts pronounce their diagnoses and solutions; ways of coping are evolved or (more often) resorted to; the condition then disappears, submerges or deteriorates and becomes more visible. Sometimes the object of the panic is quite novel and at other times it is something which has been in existence long enough, but suddenly appears in the limelight. Sometimes the panic passes over and is forgotten, except in folklore and collective memory; at other times it has more serious long-lasting repercussions and might produce such changes as those in legal and social policy or even in the way society conceives itself.
>
> *(Cohen 1972:1)*

Cohen (1972) further identifies a moral panic as a battle between moral entrepreneurs and folk devils. *Moral entrepreneurs* crusade to combat what they see as social evils and work to eradicate or convert deviants to their ways of acting and thinking. By contrast, *folk devils* are the scapegoats; they are the groups who are blamed for the shortcomings (and deviance) in a particular society. In a moral panic, the conflict between the moral entrepreneurs and the folk devils ensues only under certain circumstances. Specifically, there are five specific conditions of a moral panic (Goode and Ben-Yehuda 1994:33–9):

1. *Concern*: there is awareness that the behavior, group, or idea/belief system in question is likely to have a negative impact on society.
2. *Hostility*: there is intense opposition against those engaging in the behavior (or representing the idea/belief system) of concern.
3. *Consensus*: there is widespread acceptance that the behavior, group, or idea/belief system of concern poses a very real threat to the dominant culture's societal values and interests.
4. *Disproportionality*: the action(s) taken against the behavior, group, or idea/belief system of concern are disproportionate to the actual threat posed by them and the amount of harm they have (or will) impart upon the dominant culture's societal values and interests.
5. *Volatility*: the action(s) taken against the behavior, group, or idea/belief system of concern disappear as quickly as they appeared.

The 1980s distress about drug abuse in the U.S. can be thought of as a moral panic because public opinion polls reflected great *concern* about drug issues and the palpable stigma of drug use in the 1980s demonstrated a general *hostility* directed toward drug users. Furthermore, the fact that the majority of the American public viewed drug abuse as the most important problem in the U.S. in the 1980s shows us that there was widespread *consensus* that drug issues posed a very real threat to American societal values and interests. The criminal justice system's response to the drug panic in the 1980s was also extreme. For example, in the U.S. state of California, prison admissions for drug offenses rose 635 percent from 1982 to 1987 (Austin and McVey 1989) while evidence indicates that the use of illicit drugs during the 1980s actually dropped [e.g., 34 percent of high school seniors reported using illicit drugs (other than marijuana) in 1981 and by 1992, only 15 percent indicated illicit drug use (Johnston *et al.* 1999)]. Thus, the dramatic increase in arrests for drug offenses seen in the 1980s did not match up with a similar increase in the use of illicit drugs, in fact, the opposite occurred. In other words, there was a *disproportionate* response to drug abuse such that as illicit drug use rates were on a significant decline, arrests for drug offenses skyrocketed in the 1980s. Finally, the patterns of public opinion polls (reviewed above) that reveal significant public preoccupation with drug issues in the 1980s followed by sharp decreases in the 1990s and 2000s demonstrate the *volatility* evident in the 1980s drug panic. Thus, U.S. responses to drug issues in the 1980s can be classified as a moral panic (Goode and Ben-Yehuda 1994).

Moral panics (and their accompanying political and cultural climates) have the power to shape what is viewed as deviant. For example, during the 1980s, drug users were generally abhorred and public attitudes toward illicit drug use was significantly unfavorable. However, the drug panic waned and Americans began to view illicit drug use differently. Take, for example, the case of marijuana. In the 1980s, only one quarter of Americans believed that marijuana should be legalized. Fast forward three decades and 58 percent of Americans support marijuana legalization (Swift 2013) and a handful of states have actually legalized recreational marijuana use. As a result, what was once viewed as a highly deviant activity in the 1980s (marijuana use), is now, perhaps, becoming more normative with the majority supporting the legalization of this (mostly) illicit drug. No doubt the drug panic of the 1980s shaped the predominantly negative attitudes toward marijuana in the past and paved the way for majority support for legalization of marijuana in the U.S. today. Such evidence supports Durkheim's eloquent anecdote: "today's deviance can become tomorrow's morality" (1964 [1895]:71).

Understanding your own deviance

Thus far, we have defined deviance as an ever changing social construct that is both culturally and temporally relative to norms in a particular society. We have discussed the processes behind defining the spectrum of deviance and we have emphasized its cultural and political dependence. However, before we go further on our deviance journey, it is important to take this time to think about your own deviance. We are all deviant in some way. We all engage in behaviors that break norms at most on a regular basis or at least occasionally. We all have a unique overlap of identities and beliefs that places us somewhere on the spectrum of deviance. You may not think of yourself as a deviant, but rest assured, others do, at least some of the time. To understand how you may be seen as deviant, consider Charles Horton Cooley's (1902) concept of the looking-glass self. Cooley suggests that our interpretation of our own self concept is based on how we think others perceive us: "the thing that moves us to pride or shame is not the mere mechanical reflection of ourselves, but an imputed sentiment, the imagined effect of this reflection upon another's mind" (Cooley 1902:184). In other words, when we look into a mirror, we see what we think others see. The looking-glass self has three elements: (i) we imagine how we appear to others; (ii) we imagine the judgment of that appearance; and (iii) we develop our self through the judgments of others. When we envision ourselves through others' eyes, we can begin to understand our own deviant identities. We may begin to think of ourselves as deviant if we think others are doing so. This means that understanding our own deviance is part of both self-reflection and social interpretation.

So how are you deviant? Research indicates that college students engage in a wide variety of deviant behaviors. For example, in a study of 1,753 American undergraduate students, 36 percent reported "binge drinking" in the last week (drinking five or more alcoholic beverages in one sitting) and 18 percent report cheating on college work at least once per semester. As seen in Figure 2.6, other less

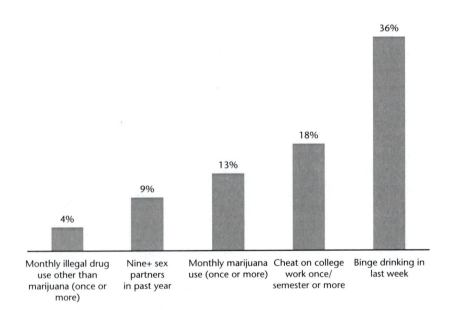

FIGURE 2.6   College student deviance

Data adapted from Koch *et al.* (2010).

common deviant behaviors among college students include marijuana use (13 percent) and other illegal drug use (4 percent), as well as high numbers of sexual partners (9 percent reported nine or more sex partners in the past year) (Koch *et al*. 2010). Thus, it is clear that college students engage in deviance.

But these examples only provide evidence of deviant behaviors. As we have learned, sometimes our identities and values can be perceived as deviant. As a result, it is also important to consider how your identities and beliefs may be labeled as deviant and perhaps even stigmatized. For example, not believing in a god carries a strong stigma in American culture. In a U.S. study of 2,081 Americans, atheists were significantly less likely to be socially accepted when compared to other minority groups and were more likely to be seen as amoral, valueless, and un-American (Edgell *et al*. 2006). Atheism not only carries a negative stigma in the U.S., it is also relatively uncommon. According to the Global Index of Religiosity and Atheism (WIN-Gallup International 2012) measuring beliefs of more than 50,000 people in 57 countries across the globe, only 5 percent of Americans report that they are "convinced atheists" compared to 13 percent worldwide. However, it is important to note that elsewhere, for example in Japan, the Czech Republic, and France, nearly one in three identify as atheists and in China, close to half (47 percent) report they are convinced atheists (see Figure 2.7). Education level also plays a significant role. Globally, those with a university education are more likely to report atheist beliefs (19 percent) compared to those with only secondary school education levels (10 percent) and those reporting little to no education (7 percent). Thus, for example,

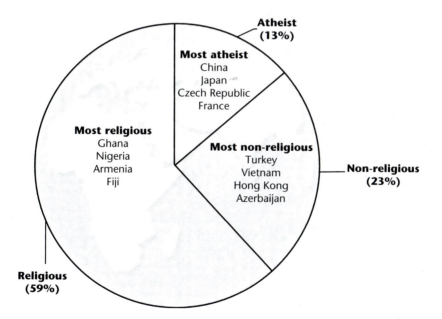

FIGURE 2.7   Global religiosity and atheism

Data adapted from WIN-Gallup International Global Index of Religiosity and Atheism (2012).

being an atheist college student in China is quite normative. While atheism among American college students is more common when compared to non-college graduates in the U.S., atheism is still an overall deviant and stigmatized belief system in America.

Empathy and deviance

Why is it important to understand your own deviance? What does understanding your own deviance provide you with? In short: empathy. If we can begin to understand how we are "deviant," we can empathize with others who are "deviant," even if they occupy a different deviant status other than our own. Having a personal awareness of our own deviance provides us with a better understanding of who we are and how others perceive us.

References

Adler, Patricia A. and Peter Adler. 2012. *Constructions of Deviance: Social Power, Context, and Interaction*, Seventh Edition. Belmont, CA: Wadsworth.

Anderson, Elijah. 1999. *Code of the Street: Decency, Violence, and the Moral Life of the Inner City*. New York, NY: W. W. Norton & Company.

Austin, James and Aaron D. McVey. 1989. *The 1989 NCCD Prison Population Forecast: The Impact of the War on Drugs*. San Francisco, CA: National Council on Crime and Delinquency.

Becker, Howard. 1963. *Outsiders: Studies in the Sociology of Deviance*. New York, NY: The Free Press.

Ben-Yehuda, Nachman. 1990. "Positive and Negative Deviance: More Fuel for a Controversy." *Deviant Behavior* 11(3):221–43.

Cohen, Stanley. 1972. *Folk Devils and Moral Panics*. London: Routledge.

Cooley, Charles Horton. 1902. *Human Nature and the Social Order*. New York, NY: Scribner's.

Cummings, K. Michael and Robert Proctor. 2014. "The Changing Public Image of Smoking in the United States: 1964–2014." *Cancer Epidemiology, Biomarkers & Prevention* 23(1):32–6.

Death Penalty Information Center. (n.d.) "Death Penalty for Offenses Other Than Murder." Retrieved from: http://www.deathpenaltyinfo.org/death-penalty-offenses-other-murder

Dodge, David. 1985. "The Over-Negativized Conceptualization of Deviance: A Programmatic Exploration." *Deviant Behavior* 6(1):17–37.

Durkheim, Émile. 1938 [1895]. *The Rules of the Sociological Method*. New York, NY: Free Press.

Durkheim, Émile. 1964 [1895]. *The Elementary Forms of Religious Life*. New York, NY: Free Press.

Edgell, Penny, Joseph Gerteis, and Douglas Hartmann. 2006. "Atheists As 'Other': Moral Boundaries and Cultural Membership in American Society." *American Sociological Review* 71(2):211–34.

Ellsworth, Faris. 1937. *The Nature of Human Nature*. New York, NY: McGraw-Hill.

Erikson, Kai. 2005 [1966]. *Wayward Puritans: A Study in the Sociology of Deviance*. Boston, MA: Pearson.

Gallup. 2014. "Crime: Illegal Drugs." *Gallup Poll*. Retrieved from: http://www.gallup.com/poll/1657/illegal-drugs.aspx

Gallup. 2015. "Trends A–Z: Most Important Problem." *Gallup Poll*. Retrieved from http://www.gallup.com/poll/1675/most-important-problem.aspx

Geertz, Clifford. 1973. *The Interpretation of Cultures*. New York, NY: Basic Books.

Goffman, Erving. 1963. *Stigma: Notes on the Management of Spoiled Identity*. Englewood Cliffs, NJ: Prentice-Hall.

Goode, Erich and Nachman Ben-Yehuda. 1994. "The American Drug Panic of the 1980s." Pp. 205–23 in *Moral Panics: The Social Construction of Deviance*. Oxford: Wiley-Blackwell.

Heckert, Alex and Druann Maria Heckert. 2002. "A New Typology of Deviance: Integrating Normative and Reactivist Definitions of Deviance." *Deviant Behavior* 23:449–79.

Hosking, Warwick, Ron Borland, Hua-Hie Yong, Geoffrey Fong, Mark Zanna, Fritz Laux, James Thrasher, Wonkyong Beth Lee, Buppha Sirirassamee and Maizurah Omar. 2009. "The Effects of Smoking Norms and Attitudes on Quitting Intentions in Malaysia, Thailand and Four Western Nations: A Cross-Cultural Comparison." *Psychology & Health* 24:95–107.

Johnson, Thomas, Wayne Wanta, Timothy Boudreau, Janet Blank-Libra, Killian Schaffer, and Sally Turner. 1996. "Influence Dealers: A Path Analysis Model of Agenda Building During Richard Nixon's War on Drugs." *Journalism & Mass Communication Quarterly* 73(1):191–4.

Johnston, Lloyd, Patrick O'Malley, and Jerald Bachman. 1999. *National Results on Drug Use from The Monitoring of the Future Study, 1975-1998. Volume 1: Secondary School Students*. Bethesda, MD: National Institute on Drug Abuse.

Koch, Jerome R., Alden E. Roberts, Myrna L. Armstrong, and Donna C. Owen. 2010. "Body Art, Deviance, and American College Students." *The Social Science Journal* 47: 151–61.

Langley, John and Malcolm Barbour (Creators). 1989–Present. *COPS*. United States: Fox Broadcasting.

Lemert, Edwin. 1951. *Social Pathology*. New York, NY: McGraw-Hill.

Lewis, Aidan. 2014. "Jaywalking: How the Car Industry Outlawed Crossing the Road." *BBC News*, February 11. Retrieved from: http://www.bbc.com/news/magazine-26073797

Moynihan, Daniel Patrick. 1993. "Defining Deviancy Down." *The American Scholar* 62(1):17–30.

Nixon, Richard. 1972. *Public Papers of the President of the United States: Richard Nixon, 1971*. Washington, D.C.: GPO.

Olsen, Mark and Will Scheffer (Creators). 2006–2011. *Big Love*. [Television Series]. United States: HBO.

Orcutt, James D. 1983. *Analyzing Deviance*. Homewood, IL: The Dorsey Press.

Ott, Bryant and Rajesh Srinivasan. 2011. "Three in 10 Chinese Adults Smoke." *Gallup Poll*. Retrieved from: http://www.gallup.com/poll/152546/Three-Chinese-Adults-Smoke.aspx

Quinn, James and Craig Forsyth. 2009. "Leathers and Rolexes: The Symbolism and Values of the Motorcycle Clubs." *Deviant Behavior* 30:235–65.

Riffkin, Rebecca. 2014a. "New Record Highs in Moral Acceptability: Premarital Sex, Embryonic Stem Cell Research, Euthanasia Growing in Acceptance." *Gallup Poll*. Retrieved from: http://www.gallup.com/poll/170789/new-record-highs-moral-acceptability.aspx

Riffkin, Rebecca. 2014b. "Americans Favor Ban on Smoking in Public, but Not Total Ban." *Gallup Poll*. Retrieved from: http://www.gallup.com/poll/174203/americans-favor-ban-smoking-public-not-total-ban.aspx?utm_source=smoking&utm_medium=search&utm_campaign=tiles

Simmons, J. L. 1969. *Deviants*. Berkeley, CA: The Glendessary Press.

Stuber, Jennifer, Sandro Galea, and Bruce G. Link. 2008. "Smoking and the Emergence of a Stigmatized Social Status." *Social Science & Medicine* 67:420–30.

Sumner, William G. 1907. *Folkways: A Study of the Sociological Importance of Usages, Manners, Customs, Mores, and Morals*. Boston, MA: Ginn & Company Publishers.

Swift, Art. 2013. "For First Time, Americans Favor Legalizing Marijuana." *Gallup Poll*. Retrieved from: http://www.gallup.com/poll/165539/first-time-americans-favor-legalizing-marijuana.aspx?utm_source=legalize marijuana&utm_medium=search&utm_campaign=tiles

Walzer, Michael. 1987. *Interpretation and Social Criticism*. Cambridge, MA: Harvard University Press.

Westervelt, Saundra D. and Kimberly J. Cook. 2012. *Life After Death Row: Exonerees' Search for Community and Identity*. New Brunswick, NJ: Rutgers University Press.

WIN-Gallup International. 2012. "Global Index of Religiosity and Atheism." Press Release. Retrieved from: http://www.wingia.com/web/files/news/14/file/14.pdf

World Health Organization. 2013. *WHO Report on the Global Tobacco Epidemic*. Geneva, Switzerland: WHO Press. Retrieved from: http://www.who.int/tobacco/global_report/2013/en/

3

THEORIES OF CRIME AND DEVIANCE

Foundations

The beginnings of sociology are often credited to three[1] innovative philosophers: Karl Marx (1818–1883), Maximilian "Max" Karl Emil Weber (1864–1920), and Émile Durkheim (1858–1917). During the 1800s, these men helped craft an academic field that examined society in new and exciting ways. Specifically, Marx, Weber, and Durkheim developed theoretical paradigms that contributed toward the systematic and scientific study of society and social behavior. In addition to their discussions of social stratification, religion, inequality, and culture, Marx, Weber, and Durkheim contributed to the sociology of deviance and crime.

Marx

Marx's theoretical focus was on power, conflict, and social inequality. He viewed society as organized into social classes based on their relationships to economic production (ruling/bourgeoisie and working/proletariat) as a part of the capitalist superstructure. Marx believed that the distribution of social power is perpetually uneven and as a result, conflict between the classes is an ever present part of society. In perhaps his most famous book, Marx joined with fellow German philosopher, Friedrich Engels (1820–1895), and published *The Communist Manifesto* in 1848 (originally published in German as *Manifest der kommunistischen Partei*). Like his other projects, *The Communist Manifesto* emphasized class conflict as the major source of social problems. This work, as well as others by the duo, shaped what has become known as *Marxism*, a perspective that emphasizes class struggle and societal conflict to critique capitalism and argue for social change. The Social Conflict Approach emerged out of this tradition. Although Marx had little to say about crime and deviance specifically, applying a Marxian Social Conflict Approach emphasizes crime and deviance as inherently tied to social inequality that places those with little social power at risk of being labeled as deviant and the powerful as dictators of norms and norm-breaking behavior (for example, see Box 3.1). In other words, the powerful "rule-makers" (bourgeoisie) decide who are the "rule-breakers" (deviants). This macro-level approach considers large social structures as they relate to both the causes and solutions to social inequality, crime, and deviance.

BOX 3.1 THE U.S. POWDER AND CRACK COCAINE 100-TO-1 SENTENCING RATIO

In the midst of the "War on Drugs" (see chapter 3 for a further discussion of this) and the increase in the use of crack cocaine in the 1980s (sometimes described as the "crack epidemic"), the Anti-Drug Abuse Act of 1986 effectively initiated a sentencing disparity between crack and powder cocaine violations that would last for nearly 25 years. Specifically, the Anti-Drug Abuse Act created a 100-to-1 sentencing ratio, whereby those convicted of possession of a single gram of crack received the exact same punishment as those convicted of possession of 100 grams of powder cocaine. This vast sentencing disparity remained unchanged from 1986 to 2010 (although multiple attempts to change it were made) and resulted in high levels of punishment for crack offenders, most of whom were African American (Beaver 2010). For example, as shown in Figure 3.1, the 2009 U.S. Sentencing Commission's Report found that 79 percent of the individuals sentenced for crack possession under the 100-to-1 ratio were African American, while only 10 percent were white and 10 percent were Hispanic. By contrast, racial disparity in sentencing was not quite as extreme for powder cocaine convictions (17 percent of these offenders were white, 28 percent were African American, and 53 percent were Hispanic) (Kurtzleben 2010). Research shows that these racial disparities in sentencing are *not* artifacts of racial differences in crack cocaine use. While African American defendants account for 79 percent of those arrested for crack-related offenses, public health data indicate that only 25 percent of crack cocaine users are African American (SAMHSA 2010). With African Americans nearly eight times more likely to be sentenced for crack cocaine violations when compared to whites, these racial differences in sentencing disparities have had large effects on the prison population as well. For example, the 2009 average sentence for cocaine offenses was 87 months, while it was 115 months for crack offenses. As a result, African Americans have been imprisoned for longer amounts of time and at higher rates than whites and Hispanics (Kurtzleben 2010).

There is no doubt that African Americans experienced the greatest hardships as a result of the 100-to-1 sentencing ratio. What has been debated about, however, is why. Applying a Marxian Social Conflict Approach to this phenomenon suggests that because African Americans have less social power than

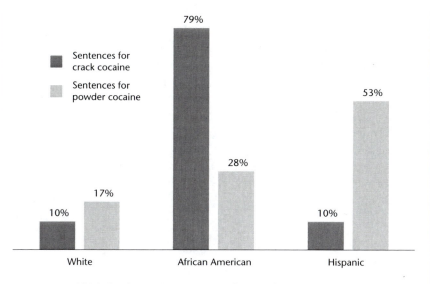

FIGURE 3.1 2009 Crack cocaine sentences by race/ethnicity

Data adapted from U.S. Sentencing Commission Report (2010).

whites in U.S. culture, they are at a higher risk of being labeled as deviant. By contrast, whites are the "ruling class" and as a result, they have the authority to determine who is deviant. Thus, powder cocaine users (who are perceived as more likely to be white) are punished less severely than crack cocaine users (who are perceived as more likely to be African American). In this way, what is seen as a crime and who is seen as a criminal are both inherently tied to social inequalities.

The 100-to-1 sentencing ratio (and the accompanying disparate sentences for crack and powder cocaine violations) remained in effect until the Fair Sentencing Act (Public Law 111-220) was signed into law by U.S. President Barack Obama on August 3, 2010. Although sentences for crack and powder cocaine violations were not equalized, the Fair Sentencing Act reduced the disparity from a 100-to-1 sentencing ratio to an 18-to-1 sentencing ratio. While this is a step in the right direction, many still view this disparity as another draconian exercise against people of color, as noted by the American Civil Liberties Union:

> The [Fair Sentencing Act] was a step toward fairness, but the 18:1 ratio was a compromise and it still reflects outdated and discredited assumptions about crack cocaine. Because crack and powder cocaine are two forms of the same drug, there should not be *any* disparity in sentencing between crack and powder cocaine offenses – the only truly fair ratio is 1:1.
>
> *(American Civil Liberties Union 2014)*

Weber

Weber also emphasized class conflict, but unlike Marx, he took a more pluralistic view of social inequality as determined by a nexus of experiences involving class (wealth), status (prestige), and power (the imposing ability to dominate others) (Walsh and Ellis 2006:147). Utilizing a perspective that emphasizes diversity in class inequality, a Weberian theoretical stance highlights the existence of systems of social stratification beyond inequities of economic production. Specifically, Weber's work shows us that class divisions occur because societies are hierarchically organized into systems of domination and subordination across various groups (e.g., Weber 2004 [1905]). Social conflict, crime, and deviance emerge as a result of inequalities based on class, gender, race/ethnicity, religion, age, sexuality (and many other characteristics).

Durkheim

Unlike Marx and Weber, who emphasized deficiencies in social organization, Durkheim was predominately concerned with societal efficiencies. One of Durkheim's major paradigm contributions to sociology is a Structural Functionalist Approach to understanding society. Durkheim viewed all existing parts of society as integral and functional to its continued survival. Just like gears in a clock, each moving part is necessary and useful; otherwise, it would cease to exist. For example, utilizing a structural functionalist approach, we can see that even behaviors that carry extreme stigma and are often described as "social evils," such as prostitution, can be viewed as functional to society (See Box 3.2).

Overall, a Durkheimian Structural Functionalist Approach to crime and deviance can be summarized through four tenets. First, deviance and crime are basic and universal to social organization. That is to say that all societies contain deviance because it is useful; if deviance was not functional, it would not thrive (recall also Durkheim's discussion of deviance in a society of saints from chapter 2). Second, crime and deviance affirm cultural values and norms by clarifying moral boundaries. Individuals come to understand what is appropriate (and by contrast what is inappropriate) through deviance and crime. Without crime and deviance, such morals, values, and norms are difficult to conceptualize. Third, crime and deviance promote social unity. Through mutual agreement of what is "right" and what is "wrong," individuals join closer together and bond against social and criminal deviance. As a result, norms are further solidified, moral boundaries are refined, and social bonds are reinforced. Fourth, deviance can encourage social change. The condemnation of certain behaviors and beliefs as amoral, deviant, and even criminal can actually pave the way toward paradigm shifts.

In just a few short decades, many behaviors that were once viewed as deviant and even criminal have become more normative and accepted. For example, in the U.S., racial segregation in public schools was deemed to be unconstitutional in 1954 (*Brown v. Board of Education*), interracial marriage was legalized in 1967 (*Loving v. Virginia*), abortion was legalized in 1973 (*Roe v. Wade*), "homosexuality" was declassified

BOX 3.2 PROSTITUTION AS FUNCTIONAL?

In 1937, American sociologist Kingsley Davis (1908–1997) posed a series of questions about prostitution (Davis 1937:744):

- Why is it that a practice so thoroughly disapproved, so widely outlawed in Western civilization, can yet flourish so universally?
- Prostitution is a veritable institution, thriving even when its name is so low in public opinion as to be synonymous with "the social evil." How, then, can we explain its vitality?

Davis went on to offer a functionalist response to these queries. Specifically, he described three features of prostitution that contribute to both the vitality and continued existence of prostitution as (likely) permanent fixtures in modern society:

- Prostitution (sex for the exchange of money, goods, or services) serves a specific function that differs from other types of sex (e.g., sex between marital partners).
- For both the prostitute and the customer, the exchange of sex for money, goods, or services is merely a means to end. For the prostitute, it is the payment of money, goods, or services and for the customer, it is bodily gratification.
- There will always be a system of social dominance that provides both a motive for selling sex and a scale of attractiveness which creates the need for purchasing sex.

Through his analysis, Davis determines that prostitution serves a specific function in modern society, one which no other institution fully performs. In doing so, he attributes the "permanence" of prostitution to the functions it serves.

Contemporary scholars who investigate prostitution as sex work (e.g., Chapkis 1997) have built upon Davis' (1937) analysis of prostitution and acknowledge that in "the wider debates surrounding the notion of sex work as a form of labour, prostitution cannot simply be analysed through an economic lens, because of the global moral condemnation to which women who sell sex are subject" (Sanders 2005:321). Thus, although sex work serves a function in society, it is sex workers themselves who are often stigmatized, labeled, and subject to criminal prosecution, while their customers are frequently able to avoid these social and criminal risks. As a result, when considering "prostitution as functional," it is necessary to acknowledge the inherent power differentials that continue to organize most sex work in a hierarchical system of exploitation (see more in chapter 11).

as a "mental disorder" in the Diagnostic and Statistical Manual of Mental Disorders (DSM) in 1973 (first printed in the 1974 edition of the DSM-II), sodomy was decriminalized in 2003 (*Lawrence v. Texas*), and same-sex marriage was legalized in 2015 (*Obergefell v. Hodges*). But these changes did not just happen overnight. The shift in attitudes toward these issues was gradual and began with small groups of activists, many of whom were deemed as social pariahs in the beginning and some were jailed for their efforts toward promoting beliefs that were viewed as deviant. However, we can see that although the beginnings of the U.S. Civil Rights Movement, for example, were met with extreme hostility, over time, supporting racial equality has become much more accepted. Put another way, looking back we can see that ideas and beliefs that were once viewed as deviant are now quite normative. As Durkheim would say: "today's deviance can become tomorrow's morality" (1964 [1895]:71).

Early criminology

Criminology investigates the causes, consequences, and prevention of criminal behavior (formal violations of laws) in both the individual and society. The beginnings of criminology can be organized into three schools of thought: the Classical School, the Positivist School, and the Chicago School.

The Classical School

Emerging in the wake of the desire to reform the criminal justice and penal systems during the mid-eighteenth century, the Classical School emphasized free will as part of the causes of criminal behavior and deterrence as an effective prevention mechanism. Italian philosopher Cesare Beccaria (1738–1794) and British philosopher Jeremy Bentham (1748–1832) were both classical criminologists. In the Classical School, criminals are thought of as rational actors and crime occurs when people choose to engage in criminal behavior. Because individuals are presumed to be inherently pain-avoidant, pleasure-seeking, and hedonistic, the prevention of crime must be tied to a particular type of punishment—one that outweighs the pleasures that a crime provides (Burke 2009). For example, Beccaria (2013 [1764]) believed that in order to deter people who are naturally inclined to engage in hedonistic behavior from engaging in criminal acts, punishments should be proportional to the seriousness of the crime.[2] For Beccaria (2013 [1764]) and Bentham (2009 [1791]), this could be accomplished through lengthy imprisonment. In fact, in 1791, Bentham designed an idealized institutional building to allow for maximum reconnaissance, referred to as the *Panopticon*. The circular edifice is positioned around a single central tower from which a watchman can observe all the inmates of an institution. The idea behind the Panopticon is to promote constant surveillance so that chains and other restraints become entirely superfluous (Burke 2009). Although the Panoptican, in its strict interpretation, was never built, some prisons adopted the circular design that can be seen in Kilmainham Gaol's East Wing, for example (see Image 3.1).

IMAGE 3.1   Kilmainham Gaol's east wing in Dublin, Ireland

The east wing of Kilmainham Gaol located in Dublin, Ireland opened in 1864 and it has been described as panoptic in design. ©Shutterstock, Matthi.

The Positivist School

The Positivist School followed and utilized a deterministic approach. In contrast to the Classical School's emphasis on free will and rational choice, the Positivist School examined individual characteristics that were believed to pre-determine criminal behavior. In other words, people were thought to have little or no control over their crime involvement—some humans are simply predestined to be criminals. Early biological determinist criminologists, namely Cesare Lombroso (1835–1909), Enrico Ferri (1856–1929), and Raffaele Garofalo (1852–1934), or the Italian School as they are sometimes described, believed that "criminals" could be identified through physical typologies. For example, Lombroso (1972 [1911]) used traits of men's faces (e.g., large sloping foreheads, odd-shaped ears, receding chins, and crooked noses) to detect criminality. This archaic practice has been rejected by a majority of contemporary criminologists, indeed, most would find this process to be "highly simplistic and even laughable by the standards of today" (Burke 2009:65).

The Chicago School

The Chicago School arose in the early twentieth century and shifted the focus of criminology away from individual characteristics to the examination of ecological and social structures. Literally borne out of the very first sociology department in the United States founded at the University of Chicago in 1892, the Chicago School is often credited with the development of urban sociology. Viewing the "city as a social laboratory" (Park 1952:73), Chicago School researchers observed humans in their "natural habitat" and contributed to complex and innovative criminological theory development. For example, utilizing the work of Robert Park (1864–1944) and Ernest Burgess (1886–1966),[3] who identified a concentric zone model to explain urban social organization (Park *et al.* 1925), American criminologists Clifford Shaw (1895–1957) and Henry McKay (1899–1980) investigated neighborhood contexts in inner-city Chicago, Illinois (U.S.) to understand juvenile delinquency. Shaw and McKay (1942) determined that it was not individual traits, but rather it was neighborhood characteristics that affected crime involvement. Specifically, cities are structured in such a way that some areas are more crime prone while others are less likely to have high levels of crime. This foregrounds Social Disorganization Theory: certain areas in the city with deteriorating housing, dilapidated factories, and abandoned buildings are the least desirable to live in (described as "zones of transition" in Park *et al.* 1925) and it is within these areas that both family and communal ties are weakened, resulting in social disorganization. Dominant norm and value systems are replaced and youth growing up in socially disorganized inner city slum areas are socialized to value crime. Social Disorganization Theory has received a great deal of empirical support (e.g., Sampson and Groves 1989) and continues to foreground contemporary criminological theory development. Overall, the Chicago School's lasting legacy has had a profound effect on criminology. Indeed, most would agree that the groundwork for many criminology theories lies in the Chicago School.

Criminology theories

On the shoulders of early criminologists, from the mid-1900s onward, criminological theory development flourished. Some theorists have created multiple perspectives (e.g., Travis Hirschi), while others have expanded upon existing theory (e.g., Robert Agnew). Below, a sampling of criminology theories is provided. This is not intended to be an exhaustive list; rather those provided here represent an overview of some major paradigms in criminological theory. They are presented in chronological order.

Merton and Anomie/Strain Theory

American sociologist Robert Merton (1910–2003) utilized Durkheim's work on anomie (see Box 3.3) to develop a theory to explain why individuals engage in deviant behavior. Central to his argument is the importance of a learned value system and the existence of social structural limitations (or strains) that individuals encounter that limit their ability to achieve culturally valued goals. Specifically, Merton (1938) developed a typology to explain how individuals adapt to this system of cultural norms when they lack the means to achieve culturally valued goals that includes: conformity, innovation, ritualism, retreatism, and rebellion (see Table 3.1). According to Merton (1938), conformity to cultural goals through socially accepted means is by far the most common and conversely retreatism (rejection of both cultural goals and socially accepted means by which to achieve them) is the least common. In this way, the majority of society is comprised of "conformists" while "retreatists" are relatively uncommon, or in other words, deviant. Other methods of adaptation, however, are important to consider. For example, "innovators" continue to value dominant cultural goals but they go about achieving these goals through deviant (sometimes illegal) means. By contrast, "ritualists" are accepting of legitimate means but are not interested in achieving or supporting normative cultural goals. "Rebellion" represents a departure from traditional culture that includes both a rejection of normative cultural goals/legitimate means and a substitution of a new set of goals and means by which to achieve them. Because of its focus on hardships that preclude individuals from achieving culturally valued goals, Merton's work is sometimes referred to as Strain Theory (although he himself questions this label, see Cullen and Messner 2011). Agnew (1992) later expanded upon these ideas with General Strain Theory (see below).

BOX 3.3 DURKHEIM AND ANOMIE

Durkheim conceptualized anomie in his doctoral dissertation, *The Division of Labor in Society* (in French: *De la division du travail social*), first published in 1893. In this work, Durkheim constructed an analysis of collective guild labor and the transition from primitive to advanced industrial societies. Specifically, he believed that *mechanical solidarity* is exhibited in small primitive societies where people feel connected through their homogeneity (e.g., they have similar work, educational, and religious experiences). By contrast, *organic solidarity* emerges when societal demands require specializations in the workplace. As a result, modern industrialized societies depend on complementarities between people (rather than similarities) to strengthen and solidify society. Through the increasing industrialization of society, divisions of labor create societies that exhibit organic solidarity.

One side-effect of the transition from primitive to advanced (i.e., mechanical to organic solidarity) is anomie. When societies are in flux, individuals have difficulties grasping onto collective norms and values. In a sense, the "dominant" norm system is unclear during societal transitions (this is sometimes described as normlessness). There may even be discrepancies between individuals and groups as to what should (and should not) become the dominant norm system. As a result, individuals experience *anomie*, social instability that emerges from normlessness caused by the modernization of society.

Durkheim further discussed this concept in his highly influential book *Suicide: A Study in Sociology* (1951 [1897]). Durkheim theorized that suicidal patterns could be attributed to symptoms of anomie. Specifically, Durkheim identified four types of suicide as emergent from social conditions related to varying extremes of social integration and social regulation. Altruistic suicide occurs when individuals experience high levels of social integration and its opposite, egoistic suicide, is the lack of social integration. Fatalistic and anomic suicide are also opposites. While the former is too much social regulation, the latter is a lack of social regulation. Of particular interest here, anomic suicide is described by Durkheim as resultant from: "man's activity lacking regulation and his consequent sufferings . . . In anomic suicide, society's influence is lacking in the basically individual passions, thus leaving them without a check-rein" (Durkheim 1951 [1897]:258). Thus, when individuals are still socially integrated and connected to one another but lack any guidance or clear delineation of norms and expectations (i.e., social regulation), they experience anomie and anomic suicide can result.

Merton's (1938) work builds on Durkheim's concept of anomie by identifying crime and deviance as repercussions that result from discrepancies between culturally valued goals and the legitimate means to attain those goals. By examining anomie, both Merton (1938) and Durkheim (1997 [1893], 1951 [1897]) acknowledge societal structures as part of the causes of deviance. Moreover, these scholars recognize a symbiotic relationship between these concepts:

> anomie and deviance . . . are mutually reinforcing. The weakening of institutionalized norms initially allows a limited number of people to violate socially approved standards. But such deviance, once completed successfully and observed by others poses a concrete challenge to the norms' legitimacy.
>
> *(Lilly et al. 2007:58)*

As a result, anomic conditions breed crime and deviance.

TABLE 3.1 Merton's typology of adaptation

	Culturally valued goals	*Socially accepted means*
Conformity	+	+
Innovation	+	−
Ritualism	−	+
Retreatism	−	−
Rebellion	+/−	+/−

Adapted from Merton (1938:40).

Sutherland and Differential Association Theory

Edwin Sutherland (1883–1950) was an American sociologist who emphasized social learning. Sutherland argued that deviance and crime emerge through interactions with deviants/criminals, or in other words "differential associations." Sutherland (1939) believed that anyone could be socialized into crime because criminal values are learned and flourish within certain groups (such as gangs). In this way, crime and deviance are more about "who you hang out with" and less about individual characteristics.[4] Specifically, Sutherland (1947:6–7) identified nine tenets of Differential Association Theory:

- Criminal behavior is learned.
- Criminal behavior is learned in interaction with other persons in a process of communication.
- The principal part of the learning of criminal behavior occurs within intimate personal groups.
- When criminal behavior is learned, the learning includes techniques of committing the crime, which are sometimes very complicated, sometimes very simple, and the specific direction of motives, drives, rationalizations, and attitudes.
- The specific direction of motives and drives is learned from definitions of the legal codes as favorable or unfavorable.
- A person becomes delinquent because of an excess of definitions favorable to violation of law over definitions unfavorable to violation of the law.
- The process of learning criminal behavior by association with criminal and anti-criminal patterns involves all of the mechanisms that are involved in any other learning.
- Although criminal behavior is an expression of general needs and values, it is not explained by those general needs and values, because non-criminal behavior is an expression of the same needs and values.
- Differential association varies in frequency, duration, priority, and intensity. The most frequent, longest running, earliest and closest influences will be most efficacious or determinant of learned behavior.

Differential Association Theory is a major paradigm contribution to criminology. Indeed, many have emphasized the importance of peer behavior in understanding juvenile delinquency (e.g., Giordano *et al.* 1986; Warr 2002). Sutherland's Differential Association Theory is the foreground for Akers' (1998) Social Learning Theory (see below).

Sykes and Matza's Techniques of Neutralization[5]

American criminologists Gresham Sykes (1922–2010) and his former student David Matza (born in 1930) argued that most people (even criminals) generally adhere to predominant norm and value systems. Sykes and Matza (1957) believed that juvenile delinquents do experience guilt as a result of their criminal behavior but they manage to justify their engagement in crime. To understand why people can continue to commit deviant acts despite adherence to mainstream norms, Sykes and Matza (1957) developed five Techniques of Neutralization that criminals/deviants/delinquents use to justify their crimes. They are:

- *Denial of responsibility.* The individual asserts that the delinquent acts are beyond his control; he is a "billiard ball ... helplessly propelled into new situations" (667).
- *Denial of injury.* The individual feels that his delinquent behavior did not cause any great harm despite the fact that it was against the law (668).
- *Denial of the victim.* The individual insists that even if his delinquent act resulted in injury or hurt, the injury is not wrong in light of the circumstances: "the injury, it may be claimed, is not really an injury; rather, it is a form of rightful retaliation or punishment" (668).
- *Condemnation of the condemners.* The individual shifts the attention away from his own delinquency to those who are disapproving of his behaviors. He may claim that his condemners are "hypocrites, deviants in disguise, or impelled by personal spite" (668).
- *Appeal to higher loyalties.* The individual feels that he must sacrifice the demands of the larger society for the demands of a smaller social group (such as his peer network). For example, delinquent acts may be necessary to help out a friend: "the delinquent may see himself as caught up in a dilemma that must be resolved, unfortunately, at the cost of violating the law" (669).

Later, in chapter 13, we will see how Sykes and Matza's (1957) Techniques of Neutralization have been applied to a highly stigmatized group supportive of adult sex with children (the North American Man/Boy Love Association, otherwise known as NAMBLA).

Hirschi and Social Control/Social Bond Theory

Travis Hirschi (born in 1935) is an American criminologist who theorized that the strengths of various types of social bonds can deter involvement in crime and deviance. Stronger ties to pro-social people, values, and institutions will result in stronger adherence to pro-social norms, and as a result, individuals will be less likely to engage in crime/deviance. Put another way, Hirschi (1969) states: "delinquent acts result when an individual's bond to society is weak or broken" (16). Specifically, Hirschi (1969) identified four types of social bonds that can curtail criminal/deviant behavior:

- *Attachment.* When individuals form close, strong, personal attachments to others, they are typically interested in preserving those relationships. If those attachments are to pro-social people, the desire to maintain those relationships by adhering to pro-social norms will likely follow, especially in the case of relationships with continuing intimacy, such as family, friends, and romantic partners.

- *Commitment.* When individuals have strong ties to others, they invest in the social norms and rules that are collectively valued. For most, this investment results in a desire to maintain a strong commitment to pro-social rules and thus, crime is unlikely because when contemplating a deviant act, an individual "must consider the costs of this deviant behavior, the risk he runs of losing the investment he has made in conventional behavior" (20). In other words, because individuals with pro-social commitments have a powerful stake in conformity, they are unlikely to risk rupturing those ties by engaging in crime and deviance.
- *Involvement.* When individuals are involved in socially legitimate activities they are less likely to participate in crime. The sheer amount of time that individuals spend engaging in non-criminal acts precludes them from engaging in crime and deviance. In this way, Hirschi's (1969) concept of involvement reflects the old adage "idle hands are the devil's workshop" (Lilly *et al.* 2007:105).
- *Belief.* When individuals agree with the dominant values within a society, they are likely to conform to laws. Social reinforcements encourage individuals to believe in the integrity of laws and norms, and as a result, criminal/deviant behavior is deterred.

Hirschi's emphasis on the importance of social bonding in the curtailment of crime and deviance has influenced many contemporary criminologists but interestingly, Hirschi largely abandoned this theory in favor of Self-Control Theory (see below).

Cohen and Felson's Routine Activity Theory

American criminologists Lawrence Cohen (born in 1945) and Marcus Felson (born in 1947) developed a theoretical standpoint that shaped a new era of criminology. Namely, they created Routine Activity Theory that focuses on everyday life circumstances. Rather than emphasizing offender characteristics as done in most previous criminological work, the theory stipulates three necessary conditions that shape the likelihood of direct-contact predatory crime, defined as illegal acts in which "someone definitely and intentionally takes or damages the person or property of another" (Glaser 1971:4). According to Cohen and Felson (1979:580), the following three circumstances must converge in time and space to create the opportunities for a direct-contact predatory crime to occur:

- *A motivated offender.* A successful direct-contact predatory crime minimally requires an offender with both criminal inclinations and the ability to carry out those inclinations.
- *A suitable target.* A person or object providing a suitable target for the offender must also be present. Target suitability is likely to reflect such things as value (i.e., the material or symbolic desirability of a personal or property target for offenders), physical visibility, access, and the inertia of a target against illegal treatment by offenders (including the weight, size, and attached or locked

features of property inhibiting its illegal removal and the physical capacity of personal victims to resist attackers with or without weapons).

• *The absence of a capable guardian.* Those capable of preventing violations must be absent. Direct-contact predatory crimes are less likely to occur in spaces where guardianship is enhanced (such as within the home).

Cohen and Felson further argue that "the lack of any one of these elements is sufficient to prevent the successful completion of a direct-contact predatory crime" (Cohen and Felson 1979:589). Thus, these "routines" shape the opportunity structure for both legitimate and illegitimate activities. By considering the importance of everyday circumstances rather than assuming that "predatory crime is simply an indicator of social breakdown" (Cohen and Felson 1979:605), Routine Activity Theory emphasizes a pragmatic approach to crime and crime prevention. Routine Activity Theory paved the way for other approaches including Rational Choice Theory (Cornish and Clarke 1986), which argues that criminals are not "empty vessels" but rather calculated decision makers. Both theories argue that direct-contact predatory crime can (and should) be prevented through situational crime prevention measures by reducing opportunities to commit crime (Clarke 1992). The focus on situational factors (rather than individual criminal characteristics) offers yet another criminological perspective that continues to shape contemporary criminology, especially through innovative new crime mapping technologies that allow researchers to identify crime hot spots using Geographic Information Systems (GIS) as described in Box 3.4.

BOX 3.4 GEOGRAPHIC INFORMATION SYSTEMS AND MAPPING NEIGHBORHOOD CRIME

Paul D. C. Bones

Geographic Information Systems (GIS) are a category of techniques used to study the relationship between variables and physical space (Chainey and Ratcliffe 2005). Some examples of GIS studies include plotting exact locations of crimes, the dispersion of neighborhood variables in a city, tracking movements across cities, and changes in areas over time. GIS can be useful for law enforcement officials who want to track crime as well as scholars who wish to explain why crime occurs in certain areas.

Police officers and other law enforcement agents typically use GIS to track existing crime or to predict future crimes. In any geographic area, crime tends to cluster in a handful of locations. These areas of high criminal activity are referred to as "hotspots" (Ratcliffe 2004). Hotspots can be divided into two categories. Hotpoints are small areas that contain a high volume of criminal offenses and are relatively stable over time. Hotbeds are larger areas that spread

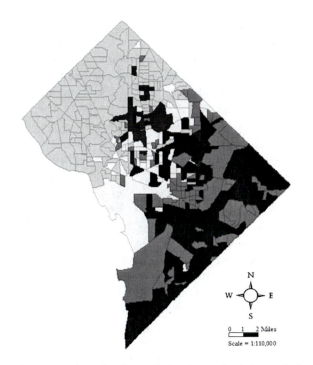

FIGURE 3.2 Concentration of police calls for domestic violence during a weekday night in Washington, D.C. 2005 to 2006

Data adapted from Roman (2009). Figure used with permission from Paul D.C. Bones.

out from a hot point (Ratcliffe and McCullagh 1999). Figure 3.2 shows a map of the dispersion of police reports of domestic violence occurring on a weekday night in Washington, D.C. during 2005 and 2006. The black areas show parts of the city where crime significantly clustered while the light gray shows areas with little to no crime. As you can see from the map, the northern and western parts of D.C. are mostly crime free, while the south and east have much larger clusters of domestic violence. Officers can use maps like this to determine where to focus their patrols and to track changes in crime patterns over time.

Law enforcement districts, particularly large police districts such as Washington, D.C. and New York City, often track hotspots by using Complaint Statistics (COMPSTATS), which are weekly tabulations of arrests, summons, calls to police, and reports from police patrols (Weisburd *et al.* 2002). Districts take these reports and use GIS to determine the best way to handle any patterns they see.

When law enforcement officials use GIS, they are mostly interested in where crime is occurring but academics are more often concerned with why crime is taking place in one area and not another. Scholarly studies of how neighborhoods influence crime tend to focus on either compositional or contextual effects. Compositional effects are products of the kinds of people living in an area, while contextual effects involve aspects of the neighborhood itself. Concentrated Disadvantage is an example of a compositional effect. According to scholars, neighborhoods that have extremely high rates of poverty, single-mother households, and unemployment have high crime rates because these life circumstances trigger intense strains (Sampson and Raudenbush 1999). In addition, these neighborhoods often have few controls in place to discourage offending. Concentrated Disadvantage does not say that all impoverished people will commit crime, but rather crime is much more likely to occur when neighborhood dynamics reach a certain tipping point. Neighborhoods with abandoned buildings, broken windows, graffiti, drug paraphernalia, and other physical signs of disinvestment increase the risk of crime because they broadcast to offenders that they will not be punished if they offend in this area (because the residents and police are not engaged in the community). Open air drug markets, visible prostitution, loitering, and clusters of bars also send social messages that a neighborhood is open for crime (Sampson and Raudenbush 1999, 2004). Academics track disorder by driving through neighborhoods and taking detailed notes about what they see, which they then turn into maps that can be compared to crime in an area.

GIS has the potential to aid law enforcement and academia by providing an easy to understand visual depiction of exactly what is going on in neighborhoods and how it can be addressed. It is most effective when it combines both law enforcement practices and academic theory, as most crime remedies involve police intervention and a social component to address why an area had a high crime rate in the first place.

Daly, Chesney-Lind, and Feminist Criminology

In their highly influential piece titled "Feminism and Criminology" (1988), American criminologists Kathleen Daly (born in 1948) and Meda Chesney-Lind (born in 1947) build upon other feminist scholarly work (e.g., Adler 1975) to incorporate feminist thought into criminology, effectively bringing the interdisciplinary field of Feminist Criminology to the forefront of emerging criminological thinking. In doing so, scholars emphasize that "feminism" is not a monolithic topic but rather concerns diverse frameworks (see Box 3.5). Specifically, Daly and Chesney-Lind (1998:504) identify five elements of feminist thought that they believe distinguish it from other types of social and political thought:

- Gender is not a natural fact but a complex social, historical, and cultural product; it is related to, but not simply derived from, biological sex difference and reproductive capacities.

- Gender and gender relations order social life and social institutions in fundamental ways.
- Gender relations and constructs of masculinity and femininity are not symmetrical but are based on an organizing principle of men's superiority and social and political-economic dominance over women.
- Systems of knowledge reflect men's views of the natural and social world; the production of knowledge is gendered.
- Women should be at the center of intellectual inquiry, not peripheral, invisible, or appendages to men.

BOX 3.5 FIVE FEMINIST PERSPECTIVES AND CRIMINOLOGY

It is important to recognize that "feminism" is not monolithic. While all feminists believe that equality between men and women is important, feminists differ in the ways they see both the emergence of gender inequality and solutions to it. There are five major feminist perspectives that are commonly cited in feminist literature (Burgess-Proctor 2006; Daly and Chesney-Lind 1988) and each offers a different contribution to criminology:

- *Liberal feminists* view gender differences (and the inequalities that result from them) as emergent from socialization patterns (i.e., women are socialized to be passive while men are socialized to be aggressive). In criminology, liberal feminists stress these socialization patterns as the source of gender differences in crime and deviance.
- *Radical feminists* conceive gender inequality as rooted in patriarchal social organization. Likewise, radical feminist criminologists examine patriarchy as the reason for women's involvement in crime and deviance.
- *Marxist feminists* identify women's subordinate class status within capitalist societies as the source of gender inequality. In criminology, Marxist feminists theorize that women are driven to engage in crime to support themselves economically.
- *Socialist feminists* view gender inequality as resultant from both sex- and class-based inequalities. Socialist feminist criminologists thus believe that women's crime and deviance occur because of sex- and class-based oppression.
- *Postmodern feminists* question the existence of permanent fixed categories in favor of multiple conceptualizations of sex and gender. In criminology, postmodern feminists "interrogate the social construction of concepts such as 'crime,' 'justice,' and 'deviance' and challenge accepted criminological truths" (Burgess-Proctor 2006:29).

Although all feminists critically examine gender inequality, feminist perspectives diverge in their identification of the causes of women's oppression. Similarly, feminist criminologists are united in their desire to understand links between gender, crime, and justice but differ in their explanations for women's involvement in crime and deviance. As a result, both feminism and feminist criminology encompass diverse perspectives about gender and crime.

Utilizing the feminist framework they describe, Daly and Chesney-Lind (1988) argue that criminologists can (and should) reflect on the androcentrism of the discipline and appreciate feminist inquiry in examinations of crime and justice. Specifically, they suggest that bringing feminist thought to criminology allows for (i) sophistication in thinking about gender relations; (ii) support for the study of women's and men's lives and the structural and social contexts for their behavior; and (iii) awareness that the majority of criminological theory (especially prior to the 1980s) is a product of white, economically privileged men's experiences. Although they acknowledge that a single feminist analysis across crime and justice issues is not possible, their seminal work paved the way for a focus on gender within criminology and more specifically, a space for Feminist Criminology to develop. And that is precisely what has happened. In 2014, The Division of Women and Crime, the unit of the American Society of Criminology whose members are dedicated to feminist criminology, celebrated its 30th anniversary and its affiliates (as well as others) have produced a plethora of research highlighting the complexities of the nexus that gender and crime exist within. Overall, many contemporary scholars (e.g., Burgess-Proctor 2006; Button and Worthen 2014) have heeded the call that Daly and Chesney-Lind succinctly articulated: "feminist theories and research should be part of any criminologist's approach to the problems of crime and justice" (Daly and Chesney-Lind 1988:507).

Gottfredson and Hirschi's Self-Control Theory

In *A General Theory of Crime* (1990), American criminologists Michael Gottfredson (born in 1951) and Travis Hirschi (born in 1935) boldly put forth a theory that they claim will explain *all* individual differences in the propensity to commit crime (which they describe as acts of force and fraud) that focuses exclusively on self-control. Unlike many other criminological theories, Self-Control Theory posits that an individual's level of self-control is set early in life and due to low levels of self-control, would-be criminals are effectively seduced into various forms of deviance. Gottfredson and Hirschi (1990) place the blame squarely on parents: the predominant source of low self-control is the failure of parents to recognize and punish children with conduct issues. By contrast, those with parents who are effective at punishing misconduct are more likely to develop a sense of self-control that will prevent them engaging in crime. Thus, the propensity to commit crime is fixed in childhood and stable throughout the life course.

Their theory focuses on the following six well-known realities about the nature of the majority of criminal behavior (Lilly *et al.* 2007:108):

- Crime provides short-term gratification such as excitement, small amounts of money, and relief from situational aggravations.
- People who engage in crime also engage in analogous behaviors that furnish short-term gratification such as smoking, substance abuse, speeding in automobiles, gambling, and irresponsible sexual behaviors.
- Criminals do not plan their conduct.
- Crimes are not specialized or sophisticated but rather are responses to whatever easy illegal opportunities present themselves.
- Criminals fail in other social domains (such as school, work, marriage) that also require planning, sustained effort, and delayed gratifications.
- Involvement in crime is stable: children manifesting behavioral problems tend to grow into juvenile delinquents and eventually into adult offenders.

Gottfredson and Hirschi (1990) concede that Self-Control Theory is the logical explanation for involvement in crime based on these six established facts. Indeed, empirical tests utilizing the six dimensions of self-control that Gottfredson and Hirschi (1990) offer to explain criminal involvement (impulsivity, a preference for simple tasks, risk-seeking, the favoring of physical over mental activities, self-centeredness, and a bad temper) are fairly supportive of Self-Control Theory. These scholars make no qualms about their assertions. Indeed, Gottfredson and Hirschi (1990) maintain that self-control "explains all crime, at all times, and, for that matter many forms of behavior that are not sanctioned by the state" (117) and is "for all intents and purposes, *the* individual-level cause of crime" (232, emphasis in original). Other criminologists (Tittle *et al.* 2004:166), however, have pointed out the "conceptual incompleteness" of self-control by highlighting the fact that the capacity and desire for self-control differ across individuals, and thus, self-control may not be as universally explanative as Gottfredson and Hirschi (1990) claim.

Robert Agnew's General Strain Theory

In 1992, American criminologist Robert Agnew (born in 1953) reconceptualized strain theory into General Strain Theory (GST). GST focuses on individuals' immediate social environments by examining strenuous life circumstances as a central cause of negative, delinquent, and criminal behavior. While previous strain theories viewed the inability to achieve goals as highly criminogenic (e.g., Merton 1938), Agnew (1992) expanded on these ideas by further identifying three types of strainful experiences that may lead to deviant behavior:

- The actual or anticipated failure to achieve positively valued goals (examples include poor academic performance, failed romantic relationships, and losing employment).

- The actual or anticipated removal of positively valued stimuli (examples include loss of a boyfriend/girlfriend, the death or serious illness of a friend, moving to a new school district, the divorce/separation of one's parents, and suspension/expulsion from school).
- The actual or anticipated presentation of negative or noxious stimuli (examples include child abuse and neglect, criminal victimization, physical punishment, negative relations with parents, peers, and/or romantic partners, and adverse or negative school experiences).

When these stressful events are seen as unjust, greater in magnitude or size, and are more recent, longer in duration, and clustered in time, they are more likely to result in a range of negative emotions including anger, disappointment, despair, depression, and fear. According to GST, anger is highly significant because it is the emotion that is most likely to result in blame and the desire for revenge (emotions that are conducive to deviance and crime). Thus, GST posits that strainful events lead to negative emotions and this may lead individuals to engage in deviance and crime in order to alleviate strain (and its accompanying negativity). However, not all who experience strain engage in criminogenic coping. Those who have access to social support as well as cognitive, behavioral, and/or emotional pro-social coping strategies are less likely to engage in maladaptive, deviant, or criminal behaviors (Agnew 1992). Building on the work of Merton (1938), Agnew (1992) successfully revitalized strain theories into GST, effectively inspiring contemporary researchers to reconsider this foundational theory in the context of modern criminology (e.g., Broidy and Agnew 1997; Button and Worthen 2014).

Sampson and Laub's Age-Graded Theory of Informal Social Control

American criminologists Robert Sampson (born in 1956) and John Laub (born in 1953) developed an integrated theory that incorporates Hirschi's (1969) Social Control/Social Bond Theory (by emphasizing attachment) with frameworks that acknowledge the importance of understanding changes during the life course. Their Age-Graded Theory of Informal Social Control (shortened to Age-Graded Theory of Crime) posits that changes in social bonds throughout the life course lead to desistence from crime. As peers become less important after adolescence and significant life events such as marriage, family formation, and career development occur during early adulthood, desistance from criminal behavior is likely. In other words, social bonds change throughout the life course and these changes explain shifts in criminal involvement. As marital partners replace best friends, our social networks shift, our social bonds strengthen and mature, and crime is less likely. In this way, informal social control is "age-graded" because the salience of different types of bonds changes throughout life (Sampson and Laub 1993). Their theory can be illustrated through what has been termed the *age-crime curve*, a depiction

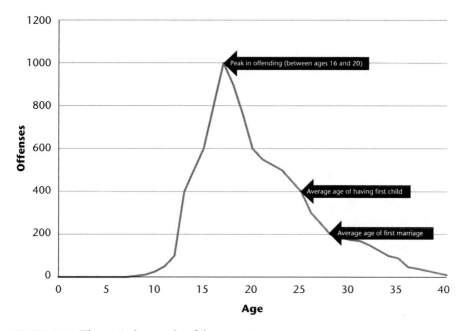

FIGURE 3.3   Theoretical example of the age-crime curve

This figure utilizes fictional data and U.S. average ages of significant life course transitions to illustrate Sampson and Laub's (1993) Age-Graded Theory of Crime.

of the age distribution of crime that plots the age of the offender and a particular criminal act against one another. The age-crime curve shows us that the majority of crimes are most prevalent during mid to late adolescence (about ages 16 to 20) and then crime involvement decreases with age in adulthood (Hirschi and Gottfredson 1983). The Age-Graded Theory of Crime supports the age-crime curve and further suggests that social bonding changes throughout the life course can explain the well-known patterns of age and the distribution of crime (see Figure 3.3). Indeed, in 1986 when Sampson and Laub stumbled upon 60 cartons of data on 500 delinquents and 500 non-delinquents from childhood to adulthood (Glueck and Glueck 1950) that had been stored in the basement of the Harvard Law School, they had the fodder to create an ideal dataset to develop, analyze, and ultimately support their Age-Graded Theory of Crime. By integrating established theory with contemporary perspectives, Sampson and Laub (1993) effectively demonstrated the importance of continued criminological theory development.

Akers' Social Learning Theory

American criminologist Ronald Akers (born in 1939) expanded upon Sutherland's Differential Association Theory (1939, 1947) to develop Social Learning Theory. Like Sutherland, Akers emphasized the importance of differential association, but his theory also offers three additional mechanisms by which criminal behavior is learned (Akers and Jennings 2009):

- *Differential association.* When individuals are exposed to pro-criminal norms, values, and definitions through "differential associations" within intimate personal groups, the probability of engaging in deviant or criminal behavior is likely.
- *Definitions.* When individuals have pro-criminal "definitions" (personal orientations and attitudes toward a given behavior) that are general (religious, moral, etc.) and/or specific (particular to a situation) in nature, they are likely to engage in crime and deviance.
- *Differential reinforcement.* When individuals anticipate and/or experience rewards for criminal behavior, they are likely to engage in crime and deviance. Conversely, if individuals experience punishments as a result of their criminal/deviant acts, they are less likely to continue engaging in crime.
- *Imitation.* When individuals observe criminal behavior (either directly or indirectly), they are likely to model that criminal behavior.

Among the four components of Social Learning Theory, Akers has argued that "imitation is most salient in the initial acquisition and performance of a novel or new behavior" (Akers and Jennings 2009:327). Through this expansion of Sutherland's (1939, 1947) Differential Association Theory, Akers' Social Learning Theory offers important contributions to contemporary criminology. For example, Akers (1998) extended his own work into Social Structure and Social Learning Theory, which emphasizes the indirect effect of certain types of social structural factors on criminal involvement.

Deviance versus criminology

While tracing the development of criminological theory allows for clear delineations between schools of thought, identifying theories of deviance is a more difficult task. We have already discussed various ways deviance has been defined in chapter 2. Here we learn more about the theoretical underpinnings of the work of deviance scholars. But before we do, a little discussion about the "disciplines" of criminology and deviance is warranted.

While the interdisciplinary field of criminology has an established home in academia spanning sociology, criminal justice, and criminology departments and programs, the academic field of deviance has always been a complicated terrain. In the first place, many do not distinguish between criminology and deviance but instead blend the two together offering little (if any) discussion about differences and similarities between them. As scholars have noted: "it is difficult for students and in some cases professors to clearly differentiate between courses entitled 'deviance,' 'social problems,' 'criminology' and 'sociology of mental disorders'" (Liska and Messner 1999:3). For example, in a study of topics covered in popular deviance and criminology textbooks, deviance textbooks were found to be more likely to discuss alcohol abuse, homosexuality, mental disorders, and suicide, but both criminology and deviance textbooks had similar coverage of white collar/corporate crime, rape, drug abuse, prostitution, family violence, and pornography (Bader *et al.* 1996). Thus, it is sometimes unclear what falls under "deviance" and "criminology." As a result, the nuances embedded in academic discussions of deviance are sometimes obscured. As we learned in chapter 2, the key to defining deviance is understanding social norms and their violations. In comparison to criminology, which focuses on a narrower subset of violations of criminal law, the study of deviance encompasses a wider range of behaviors that are not necessarily criminal. As a result, deviance is an inherently unwieldy academic field.

Second, there are no collectively agreed upon deviance "theories." Indeed, most discussions of "theories of deviance" will overlap either partially or entirely with theories that were built on understanding crime. Although the criminology theories reviewed above sometimes discuss deviance, most examined crime and/or delinquency in their development and few branch into the realm of examining behavior that is deviant, but not criminal. As a result, identifying deviance "theory" and deviance "theorists" is a challenge. Even so, there are some theoretical discussions that lend themselves well to understanding deviance. These are reviewed below.

Theorizing deviance

Most early criminologists focused explicitly on crime and criminals. Deviance, if discussed, was mentioned in the same breath as crime. Indeed, "crime" and "deviance" were often used interchangeably. Starting in the 1930s, however, perspectives highlighting the significance of understanding deviance began to emerge. Although not often explicitly identified as "theories of deviance," these theoretical stances offer a more nuanced understanding of the spectrum of both crime and deviance by emphasizing the social processes behind the construction of deviant behavior, identities, and beliefs.

Symbolic interactionism

American philosopher George Herbert Mead (1863–1931) contributed toward the development of the symbolic interactionist approach (Mead 1934). Symbolic interactionists generally believe that "reality" is a social construct developed through human interaction and modified through interpretation. Thus, feedback from society members affects how an individual defines him/herself. Through communication and interaction, an individual's self-concept emerges. It is only through such a process that "reality" comes to exist.

Applying a symbolic interactionist approach to deviance shows us that nothing is inherently deviant, but rather what is seen as deviant is interpreted through social interaction and communicated through symbols. As a result, for symbolic interactionists, understanding deviance becomes more about the response to certain behaviors rather than the characteristics of the actor himself [also, recall Cooley's (1902) concept of the looking-glass self from chapter 2]. In this way, deviance is socially dependent and culturally variant. Responses to deviance (rather than the deviant behaviors themselves) are also at the heart of labeling and stigma theories (reviewed below).

Labeling theories

In line with the symbolic interactionist approach, labeling theorists (e.g., Tannenbaum 1938; Lemert 1951; Becker 1963) propose that behaviors are only seen as deviant when others label them as such. The basic underlying process of labeling and its social consequences is as follows:

- Individuals who support the dominant norms in a culture interpret certain behaviors/identities/beliefs as deviant.
- After a behavior/identity/belief is viewed as deviant, a deviant label is attached; this effectively distinguishes between deviance and non-deviance.
- Individuals who are deviantly labeled sometimes internalize this label and behave in ways consistent with their assigned deviant status.
- Often (but not always), a stigma accompanies the deviant label.

The significance of labeling in the deviantization process can be summarized as follows:

> Social groups create deviance by making the rules whose infraction constitutes deviance, and by applying those rules to particular people and labeling them as outsiders. Deviance is NOT a quality of the act the person commits but rather a consequence of the application by others of rules and sanctions to be an offender. The deviant is the one to whom that label has been applied; deviant behavior is behavior that people so label.
>
> *(Becker 1963:9)*

In this way, attaching a deviant label to a particular behavior or identity necessarily defines behaviors and identities as deviant. Thus, the process and significance of applying the label is at the crux of labeling theories.

American sociologist Edwin Lemert (1912–1996) offered a significant contribution to labeling theory in 1951. Specifically, he identified what he described as primary and secondary deviance:

- *Primary deviance* is a behavior that departs from a social norm yet causes no long-term consequences for the offender. This lack of consequence may be because the initial deviation prompts no reaction or, if the deviance does prompt a reaction, that reaction is not particularly negative or stigmatizing. Primary deviance does not lead to a permanent label from external observers or to a deviant self-identity on the part of the offender.
- *Secondary deviance* is not simply a violation of social norms, but a violation of social norms that results in a realignment of an individual's self-concept either

with the deviance itself or with a subgroup that is considered deviant in relation to the social norms. Secondary deviance often leads to a permanent label
from external observers (Rosenberg 2010).

- *Tertiary deviance* is a concept later developed by Japanese American sociologist
John Kitsuse (1923–2003). Tertiary deviance refers to "the deviant's confrontation, assessment, and rejection of the negative identity imbedded in secondary
deviation, and the transformation of that identity into a positive and viable
self-conception" (Kitsuse 1980:9). Through tertiary deviance, individuals celebrate their "deviant" identities.

These three forms of deviance reflect an escalating significance of the deviant label.
While there is no label in the case of primary deviance, secondary deviance results
in a deviant label that continues to follow an individual, perhaps in conjunction
with an accompanying stigma. While episodes of norm violations are common (and
thus, so is primary deviance), secondary deviance only occurs when observers
begin to "make something" of the norm violations, and thus, label them as deviant.
Individuals who have been deviantly labeled may embrace their deviant status
(in the case of tertiary deviance) and revel in their deviant group membership. As
a result, the deviant label moves from non-existent (primary deviance) to status
changing (secondary deviance) to celebrated (tertiary deviance). Labeling, then, is
an integral part of the deviantization process.

Internalizing labels

The deviant label itself can have social consequences; in some cases, it can change
an individual's *master status*, or defining characteristic of who they are. For example,
labeling theorists (Tannenbaum 1938; Lemert 1967) suggest that norm violators
may experience more than just a new label. Specifically, deviantly labeled individuals can encounter:

- Differential treatment from "normal" members of society.
- Deviant group placement, by social definition if not by physical location, with
other individuals who have the same label.
- Barriers to reintegration into the dominant social group.
- New social identities as deviant.
- Internalized deviant labels.

Because of their deviant label and deviant group placement, individuals are sepa-
rated from the dominant social group. Now viewed as different from the "normal"
members of society, labeled individuals may start to internalize their deviant label
and their accompanying new social status. In summary:

> The process of making the criminal, therefore, is a process of tagging, defin-
> ing, identifying, segregating, describing, emphasizing, [and] making conscious

and self-conscious; it becomes a way of stimulating, suggesting, emphasizing, and evoking the very traits that are complained of ... The person becomes the thing he is described as being.

(Tannenbaum 1938:20)

Thus, by internalizing a deviant label, individuals may come to see themselves as deviant and both embody a deviant identity and engage in deviant behaviors. The deviant label also changes how people respond to the deviantly labeled individual (see Box 3.6). In short, a deviant label can have powerful impacts on an individual.

BOX 3.6 DEVIANCE AND MEDICALIZATION

Deviant behavior has become increasingly identified and relabeled as a medical issue. For example, "extreme forms of deviant drinking (now called alcoholism) have been defined as sin, moral weakness, crime, and most recently illness" (Conrad and Schneider 1980:32–3). Other deviantly identified behaviors have also been treated under the medical model including drug addiction, hyperactivity in children, obesity, and learning problems, to name a few. With such variance in what is viewed as deviant and what is treated as a medical issue, we are often left wondering: *"is it sin, crime, or sickness?"* (Conrad and Schneider 1980:36).

To answer this question, we must first examine how something gets defined as sickness in the first place. Sickness and disease are social constructions. That is to say that what becomes conceived of as illness or disease is based on human judgment and this varies over time and cross culturally: "in some fashion, illness, like beauty (and deviance), is in the eye of the beholder" (Conrad and Schneider 1980:31). But labeling something as an illness has social consequences. Thus, secondly, we must acknowledge that "a disease designation is a moral judgment, for to define something as a disease or illness is to deem it undesirable" (Conrad and Schneider 1980:36). As a result, the "disease" label carries its own set of social scripts.

In 1951, American sociologist Talcott Parsons (1902–1979) discussed these ideas in his conceptualization of the "sick role." A person who is identified and labeled as suffering from illness or disease experiences a shift in both his social responsibilities and social obligations; in essence he/she takes on a new "role" in society, one of a "sick" person. Specifically, the "sick role" has four components (Conrad and Schneider 1980:32):

- Exemptions:

    o The sick person is exempt from normal social responsibilities.
    o The sick person is not held responsible for his/her condition and is not expected to recover by any act of will.

- Obligations:

  - The sick person should recognize that being ill is undesirable and must want to recover.
  - The sick person should seek competent treatment (i.e., medical intervention) and should cooperate with medical professionals.

Third, once we recognize that sickness is a social construct with social scripts that come with social consequences, we must examine how sickness differs from deviance. As we have learned, however, this is merely a case of semantics. Anything can be labeled as deviant and anything can be labeled as illness because the labeling process "takes place on a moral, or more properly, immoral continuum" (Conrad and Schneider 1980:271) and morals/values vary culturally and temporally. Scholars note, however, that perceived culpability may distinguish these two concepts: "deviance considered *willful* tends to be defined as crime; when it is *unwillful* it tends to be defined as illness" (Conrad and Schneider 1980:32, emphasis in original). Thus, when asking "*is it sin, crime, or sickness?*" societal responses to behaviors and perceptions of responsibility may be key to defining both deviance and illness.

American medical sociologists Peter Conrad (born in 1945) and Joseph Schneider (born in 1943) developed a theoretical model in their book, *Deviance and Medicalization: From Badness to Sickness* (1980), to further understand these ideas. In their view, the medicalization of deviant behavior is "the defining and labeling of deviant behavior as a medical problem, usually, an illness, and mandating the medical profession to provide some type of treatment for it" (Conrad and Schneider 1980:29). Specifically, they offer a five stage sequential model of the medicalization of deviance:

- A behavior is first defined as deviant *prior to* the emergence of a medical definition.
- The behavior is then announced as a "medical issue" in the realm of medicine.
- Moral entrepreneurs follow by actively making claims for this behavior to be identified as a medical issue and *not* deviance.
- Laws and courts acknowledge this behavior as medical issue and secure its legitimacy in the realm of medicine.
- Finally, medical deviance is institutionalized through codification (as in the case of being listed in the DSM) and bureaucratization (as in the establishment of organizations such as the National Institutes of Mental Health – NIMH).

Through this process, deviant behavior is re-codified as a medical issue. As a result, the deviant is now viewed as "sick" and the "the social response to deviance is 'therapeutic' rather than punitive" (Conrad and Schneider 1980:34). Specifically, the medicalization of deviance affects (i) who responds, (ii) how people respond, and (iii) the personal competence of the deviant person. With the medicalization of deviance, medical professionals (rather than legal authorities) respond to deviance. In addition, because people view the individual as in need of medical attention, they are less likely to see the individual as personally responsible for his/her condition. As a result, the stigma attached to deviance is lessened or entirely ameliorated when deviance is medicalized. Finally, an individual who is labeled as "medically deviant" may begin to see him/herself differently, perhaps as less blameworthy for his/her social condition as a result of the medical attention and sympathetic societal response to his/her deviant behavior. Together, these experiences demonstrate the significance of the medical "label" and its impact on societal response to deviant behavior.

Labeling and stigma

Theories of stigma are companions to labeling theories. Once a behavior, identity, or belief is labeled as deviant, a negative social stigma often follows. Recall from chapter 2 that those who are stigmatized are seen as socially undesirable and they may experience negative stereotyping, discrimination, devaluation, and denigration as a result of their deviant status. It is important to note that a stigma, similar to a deviant label, is also an entirely socially constructed concept: societal response is necessary for both labeling and stigmatization processes to occur. Because a stigma follows from a deviant label, one cannot exist without the other. In other words, stigma is dependent on a deviant label.

Canadian sociologist Erving Goffman (1922–1982) is perhaps the most notable "stigma" scholar whose work continues to shape contemporary research. His book, *Stigma: Notes on the Management of Spoiled Identity* (1963) provides great theoretical insight into our understandings of stigma. For example, according to Goffman (1963:4) there are three types of social stigma:

1. Abominations of the body (including various physical deformities).
2. Blemishes of individual character (including weak will, dishonesty, and treacherous beliefs).
3. "Tribal stigmas" are associated with race, nationality or religion (these may be transmitted through family lineages).

He further elaborates on these ideas by offering the concept of *courtesy stigma* that occurs when "individuals are stigmatized simply for being close to a stigmatized individual" (Goffman 1963:30). Thus, an individual need not possess negatively-valued characteristics to be stigmatized because a stigma can be applied to those who are affiliated with other stigmatized people.

Beyond offering one of the first typologies of stigma, Goffman (1963) also discussed how people manage their "spoiled identities" through covering and double living strategies. For example, *covering* is an effort to conceal stigma from other parties through reducing visibility and obtrusiveness of a stigmatizing quality (Goffman 1963). Those who choose to "cover" their stigmatized identity, behavior, or belief do not want others to be aware of their potentially deviant status. By contrast, other people may choose to engage in a *double living* strategy whereby they keep their deviance secret from one group of persons while systematically exposing themselves as deviant to other groups of persons (Goffman 1963). In other words, they are "covering" in one realm and exposing their deviance in another. As a result, their "spoiled identities" are sometimes hidden. In any case, a stigma and its accompanying label must be managed through social interaction.

Existential stigma and achieved stigma

While Goffman's work contributed to the early theoretical underpinnings of stigma, more contemporary scholarship by German-born sociologist and historian Gerhard Falk (born in 1924) further identified two distinct categories of stigma (Falk 2001:11):

- *Existential stigma* is derived from a condition which the target either did not cause or over which he has little control.
- *Achieved stigma* is derived from conduct and/or individual contribution to attainment of the stigma in question.

By clarifying a division between existential and achieved stigma, Falk (2001) effectively offers an important contribution to theories of stigma. From this typology, we can see that not all stigma is avoidable, indeed, some are "born" into stigmatized identities as in the case of some physically disabled, facially disfigured, and mentally impaired individuals. While stigma remains a social construct (indeed, the stigma these individuals face is based on social responses to these perceived abnormalities), the concept of "choice" to embody a stigmatized identity is not applicable for some (as in the case of existential stigma) but may be an active decision for others (as in the case of achieved stigma). This much-needed clarification allows for the concept of "stigma" to remain relevant to contemporary sociology.

Conceptualizing stigma

To respond to criticisms about the vagueness of the concept of stigma, scholars have offered a new "conceptualization" of stigma. Specifically, American socio-medical researchers Bruce Link (born in 1949) and Jo Phelan (born in 1953) (2001:367) define stigma as part of a process that results when the following interrelated components converge:

- *Labeling*: people distinguish and label human differences.
- *Stereotyping*: dominant cultural beliefs link labeled persons to undesirable characteristics—to negative stereotypes.

- *Separation*: labeled persons are placed in distinct categories so as to accomplish some degree of separation of "us" from "them."
- *Status loss and discrimination*: labeled people experience status loss and discrimination that lead to unequal outcomes.
- *Power dependence*: stigmatization is entirely contingent on access to social, economic, and political power that allows the identification of differentness, the construction of stereotypes, the separation of labeled persons into distinct categories, and the full execution of disapproval, rejection, exclusion, and discrimination.

Through defining stigma in ways that highlight both individual experiences and societal responses, Link and Phelan (2001) effectively move this concept forward. Their work contributes not only to a new definition of stigma but also considers stigma as a matter of degree. They suggest that labeling can be more or less significant because labels can lead to many stereotypes or none at all. As a result, some individuals experience more stigma than others. Thus, stigma is truly variant. Together, Link and Phelan's ideas show us that stigma is a "persistent predicament" because powerful groups continue to forcefully label and extensively stereotype less powerful groups (2001:379). Overall, contemporary scholarly development of the stigma concept allows us to recognize the significance of both labeling and the accompanying societal responses to it.

Thinking about theories of crime and deviance

This chapter has offered an overview of various ways of thinking about crime and deviance. While no theory can fully explain the complicated terrain of criminal and deviant behavior, learning about theories of crime and deviance offers a diverse framework from which to consider the sociological significance of norm violations. In doing so, we have discussed crime theories that inform our understandings about violations of formally enacted law and we have learned about informal violations of social norms through theoretical discussions of deviance. In this way, we can see that crime and deviance theories work together to explain how social norms and formally enacted laws affect the stigma that often accompanies crime and deviance. Overall, the theoretical discussions offered here show us that crime and deviance are social constructs and thus, efforts to explain them are necessarily sociological.

Notes

1   Others have also been described as central to the development of sociology including: Auguste Comte, W.E.B. Du Bois, Georg Simmel, Herbert Spencer, William Graham Sumner, Alexis de Tocqueville, and Ferdinand Tönnies.
2   Contemporary deterrence theorists have investigated the proportionality perspective put forth by classical criminologists by examining the principles of certainty, severity, and swiftness in the administration of criminal justice (e.g., Zimring and Hawkins 1973).
3   Park and Burgess wrote what has been regarded as the first comprehensive text of sociology as a scientific discipline, *Introduction to the Science of Sociology*, in 1921.

4   Some have questioned whether there is a self-selection effect in delinquent peer networks. For example, individuals could choose to be friends with other delinquents because they themselves are already engaging in (or interested in) delinquent behavior. This process is sometimes described as "birds of a feather flock together." Haynie (2002), however, found quite the contrary. She found that peer networks are actually quite heterogeneous. Although there is some evidence that delinquents cluster together, most adolescents have both delinquent and non-delinquent friends in their networks of close acquaintances.

5   In 1964, Matza further developed these ideas into Drift Theory in which he argued that delinquency occurs because of "subterranean convergence" between techniques of neutralization and authority figures' emphasis on moral order.

References

Adler, Freda. 1975. *Sisters in Crime: The Rise of the New Female Criminal*. New York, NY: McGraw-Hill.

Agnew, Robert. 1992. "Foundation for a General Strain Theory of Crime and Delinquency." *Criminology* 30:47–87.

Akers, Ronald L. 1998. *Social Learning and Social Structure: A General Theory of Crime and Deviance*. Boston, MA: Northeastern University Press.

Akers, Ronald and Wesley Jennings. 2009. "Social Learning Theory." Pp. 323–32 in *21st Century Criminology: A Reference Handbook*, edited by J. Mitchell Miller. Thousand Oaks, CA: Sage Publications.

American Civil Liberties Union. 2014. "Fair Sentencing Act." Retrieved from: https://www.aclu.org/fair-sentencing-act

Bader, Christopher, Paul Becker, and Scott Desmond. 1996. "Reclaiming Deviance as a Unique Course from Criminology." *Teaching Sociology* 24(3):316–20.

Beaver, Alyssa. 2010. "Getting a Fix on Cocaine Sentencing Policy: Reforming the Sentencing Scheme of the Anti-Drug Abuse Act of 1986." *Fordham Law Review* 78(5):2531–75.

Beccaria, Cesare. 2013 [1764]. *On Crimes and Punishments*. Boston, MA: Branden Books.

Becker, Howard. 1963. *Outsiders*. New York, NY: Free Press.

Bentham, Jeremy. 2009 [1791]. *Panopticon: Or the Inspection House*. Whitefish, MT: Kessinger Publishing.

Broidy, Lisa and Robert Agnew. 1997. "Gender and Crime: A General Strain Theory Perspective." *Journal of Research in Crime and Delinquency* 34(3):275–306.

Brown v. Board of Education, 347 U.S. 483 (1954).

Burgess-Proctor, Amanda. 2006. "Intersections of Race, Class, Gender, and Crime: Future Directions for Feminist Criminology." *Feminist Criminology* 1(1):27–47.

Burke, Roger. 2009. *An Introduction to Criminological Theory*, Third Edition. Portland, OR: Willan Publishing.

Button, Deeanna and Meredith G. F. Worthen. 2014. "General Strain Theory for LGBQ and SSB Youth: The Importance of Intersectionality in the Future of Feminist Criminology." *Feminist Criminology* 9(4):270–97.

Chainey, Spencer and Jerry Ratcliffe. 2005. *GIS and Crime Mapping*. Chichester: John Wiley & Sons.

Chapkis, Wendy. 1997. *Live Sex Acts: Women Performing Erotic Labor*. New York, NY: Routledge.

Clarke, Ronald. 1992. *Situational Crime Prevention: Successful Case Studies*. New York, NY: Harrow & Heston.

Cooley, Charles Horton. 1902. *Human Nature and the Social Order*. New York, NY: Scribner's.

Cohen, Lawrence and Marcus Felson. 1979. "Social Change and Crime Rate Trends: A Routine Activity Approach." *American Sociological Review* 44(4):588–608.

Conrad, Peter and Joseph W. Schneider. 1980. *Deviance and Medicalization: From Badness to Sickness*. London: The C.V. Mosby Company.

Cornish, Derek and Ronald Clarke. 1986. *The Reasoning Criminal: Rational Choice Perspectives on Offending*. New York, NY: Springer.

Cullen, Francis and Steven Messner. 2011. "The Making of Criminology Revisited: An Oral History of Merton's Anomie Paradigm." Pp. 89–120 in *The Origins of American Criminology: Advances in Criminological Theory, Volume 16*, edited by Francis Cullen, Cheryl Jonson, Andre Myer, and Freda Adler. London: Transaction Publishers.

Daly, Kathleen and Meda Chesney-Lind. 1988. "Feminism and Criminology." *Justice Quarterly* 5:497–538.

Davis, Kingsley. 1937. "The Sociology of Prostitution." *American Journal of Sociology* 2(5):744–55.

Durkheim, Émile. 1951 [1897]. *Suicide: A Study in Sociology*. New York, NY: Free Press.

Durkheim, Émile. 1964 [1895]. *The Elementary Forms of Religious Life*. New York, NY: Free Press.

Durkheim, Émile. 1997 [1893]. *The Division of Labor in Society*. New York, NY: Free Press.

Fair Sentencing Act of 2010, Public Law 111–220.

Falk, Gerhard. 2001. *Stigma: How We Treat Outsiders*. Amherst, NY: Prometheus Books.

Giordano, Peggy, Stephen Cernkovich, and M. D. Pugh. 1986. "Friendships and Delinquency." *American Journal of Sociology* 91(5):1170–202.

Glaser, Daniel. 1971. *Social Deviance*. Chicago: Markham.

Glueck, Sheldon and Eleanor Glueck. 1950. *Unraveling Juvenile Delinquency*. New York, NY: The Commonwealth Fund.

Goffman, Erving. 1963. *Stigma: Notes on the Management of Spoiled Identity*. Englewood Cliffs, NJ: Prentice-Hall.

Gottfredson, Michael R. and Travis Hirschi. 1990. *A General Theory of Crime*. Stanford, CA: Stanford University Press.

Haynie, Dana. 2002. "Friendship Networks and Delinquency: The Relative Nature of Peer Delinquency." *Journal of Quantitative Criminology* 18(2):99–134.

Hirschi, Travis. 1969. *The Causes of Delinquency*. Berkeley, CA: University of California Press.

Hirschi, Travis and Michael Gottfredson. 1983. "Age and the Explanation of Crime." *American Journal of Sociology* 89(3):552–83.

Kitsuse, John. 1980. "Coming Out All Over: Deviants and the Politics of Social Problems." *Social Problems* 28:1–13.

Kurtzleben, Danielle. 2010. "Data Show Racial Disparity in Crack Sentencing." *U.S. News & World Report*, August 3. Retrieved from: http://www.usnews.com/news/articles/2010/08/03/data-show-racial-disparity-in-crack-sentencing

Lawrence v. Texas, 539 U.S. 558 (2003).

Lemert, Edwin. 1951. *Social Pathology*. New York, NY: McGraw-Hill.

Lemert, Edwin. 1967. *Human Deviance, Social Problems, and Social Control*. Englewood Cliffs, NJ: Prentice Hall.

Lilly, J. Robert, Francis T. Cullen, and Richard A. Ball. 2007. *Criminological Theory: Context and Consequences*, Fourth Edition. Thousand Oaks, CA: Sage Publications.

Link, Bruce and Jo Phelan. 2001. "Conceptualizing Stigma." *Annual Review of Sociology* 27:63–85.

Liska, Allen and Steven Messner. 1999. *Perspectives on Crime and Deviance*. Upper Saddle River, NJ: Prentice Hall.

Lombroso, Cesare. 1972 [1911]. *Criminal Man, According to the Classification of Cesare Lombroso*. New York, NY: Putnam.

Loving v. Virginia, 388 U.S. 1 (1967).

Marx, Karl and Friedrich Engels. 1848. *Manifest der kommunistischen Partei*. London: Bishopgate.

Matza, David. 1964. *Delinquency and Drift*. New York, NY: John Wiley.

Mead, George H. 1934. *Mind, Self and Society*. Chicago, IL: University of Chicago Press.

Merton, Robert. 1938. "Social Structure and Anomie." *American Sociological Review*. 3: 672–82.

Obergefell v. Hodges, 576 U.S. Nos. 14-556, 14-562, 14-571, 14-574 (2015).

Park, Robert E. 1952. *Human Communities: The City and Human Ecology*. Glencoe, IL: The Free Press.

Park, Robert E. and Ernest W. Burgess. 1921. *Introduction to the Science of Sociology*. Chicago, IL: The University of Chicago Press.

Park, Robert E., Ernest W. Burgess and Roderick McKenzie. 1925. *The City*. Chicago, IL: The University of Chicago Press.

Parsons, Talcott. 1951. *The Social System*. New York, NY: The Free Press.

Ratcliffe, Jerry H. 2004. "The Hotspot Matrix: A Framework for the Spatio-Temporal Targeting of Crime Reduction." *Police Practice and Research* 5(1): 5–23.

Ratcliffe, Jerry H. and Michael. J. McCullagh. 1999. "Hotbeds of Crime and the Search for Spatial Accuracy." *Geographical Systems* 1(4): 385–98.

Roe v. Wade, 410 U.S. 113 (1973).

Roman, Caterina Gouvis. 2009. "Alcohol Availability, Type of Alcohol Establishment, Distribution Policies, and Their Relationship to Crime and Disorder in the District of Columbia, 2000-2006." ICPSR25763-v1. Ann Arbor, MI: Inter-university Consortium for Political and Social Research [distributor].

Rosenberg, Michael. 2010. "Lemert, Edwin M.: Primary and Secondary Deviance." Pp. 550–2 in *Encyclopedia of Criminological Theory*, edited by Francis T. Cullen and Pamela K. Wilcox. Thousand Oaks, CA: Sage.

SAMHSA. 2010. "Crack Use in Lifetime, Past Year, and Past Month among Persons Aged 12 or Older, by Demographic Characteristics." Table 1.43A in *2010 National Survey on Drug Use and Health, Population Estimates*. Washington, D.C.: Substance Abuse and Mental Health Services Administration.

Sampson, Robert and W. Byron Groves. 1989. "Structure and Crime: Testing Social-Disorganization Theory." *The American Journal of Sociology* 94(4):774–802.

Sampson, Robert and John Laub. 1993. *Crime in the Making: Pathways and Turning Points through Life*. Cambridge, MA: Harvard University Press.

Sampson, Robert J. and Stephen W. Raudenbush. 1999. Systematic Social Observation of Public Spaces: A New Look at Disorder in Urban Neighborhoods. *American Journal of Sociology* 105(3): 603–51.

Sampson, Robert J. and Stephen W. Raudenbush. 2004. "Seeing Disorder: Neighborhood Stigma and the Social Construction of 'Broken Windows.'" *Social Psychology Quarterly* 67(4): 319–42.

Sanders, Teela. 2005. "'It's Just Acting': Sex Workers' Strategies for Capitalizing on Sexuality." *Gender, Work and Organization* 12(4):319–42.

Shaw, Clifford R. and Henry D. McKay. 1942. *Juvenile Delinquency in Urban Areas*. Chicago, IL: University of Chicago Press.

Sutherland, Edwin. 1939. *Principles of Criminology*. Philadelphia, PA: J.B. Lippincott.

Sutherland, Edwin. 1947. *Principles of Criminology*, Fourth Edition. Philadelphia, PA: J.B. Lippincott.

Sykes, Gresham M. and David Matza. 1957. "Techniques of Neutralization." *American Sociological Review* 22: 664–70.

Tannenbaum, Frank. 1938. *Crime and the Community*. New York, NY: Columbia University Press.

Tittle, Charles R., David A. Ward and Harold G. Grasmick. 2004. "Capacity for Self-Control and Individuals' Interest in Exercising Self-Control." *Journal of Quantitative Criminology* 20:143–72.

Walsh, Anthony and Lee Ellis. 2006. *Criminology: An Interdisciplinary Approach*. Thousand Oaks, CA: Sage Publications.

Warr, Mark. 2002. *Companions in Crime: The Social Aspects of Criminal Conduct*. New York, NY: Cambridge University Press.

Weber, Max. 2004 [1905]. *The Protestant Ethic and the Spirit of Capitalism*. New York, NY: Routledge.

Weisburd, David, Stephen D. Mastrofski, Ann Marie McNally, and Rosann Greenspan. 2002. "Reforming to Preserve: Compstat and Strategic Problem Solving in American Policing." *Criminology & Public Policy* 2: 421.

Zimring, Franklin and Gordon Hawkins. 1973. *Deterrence*. Chicago, IL: University of Chicago.

4

SOCIAL POWER AND GENDER, SEX, AND SEXUALITY

Gender and sex

Recall from chapter 1 that sociologists define *gender* as a social construct that is related to the ways a culture organizes people and labels characteristics and visual cues into dichotomous identities of "men" and "women." Often gender is described as distinct from *sex*, which is typically confined to the labels of "male" or "female" based on biological markers such as the external appearances of genitalia and to a lesser extent, chromosomes. Presentations of gender are also frequently categorized dichotomously (i.e., feminine and masculine). While most cultures often view both sex and gender as binary concepts, sociologists emphasize the social construction of gender as existing within a spectrum that acknowledges variance in the expression and social attributes of an individual's gender identity.

Any broadly recognized gender system, however, is built from prevailing perspectives about gender. As a result, what is perceived as "masculine" or "feminine" is a reflection of social power whereby societal norms about gender emerge from the dominant group. Thus, individuals who test the boundaries of gender are often marginalized and sometimes deviantized (see more about this in chapter 5). As a result, both the construction of and adherence to gender norms are inherently tied to social power.

Gender as a master status

Although we know that gender is a social construct, the processes behind the creation of "gender" in society are so hidden, most are completely unaware of the complexities involved. Furthermore, experiences and expressions of gender are so pervasive, they impact almost every interaction in our daily lives. This is because gender is a master status. In most cultures, individuals are identified and classified into "man" or "woman" on a daily basis. Based on perceptions of physical appearances and behaviors, judgments of "masculine" or "feminine" are made, and as a result, we are immediately put into a gender category in all social interactions. Such rigid forms of categorization lead to "gender deviants" that will be discussed further in chapter 5. Because gender is a master status, our gender identity dominates our other social identities (such as father, teacher, author, etc.) and thereby determines our general position within society. Gender, then, is more than just an identity, it organizes social interactions.

In addition, gender permeates almost every section of our lives. Our gender affects how we interact with people including our family members, romantic partners, friends, and workplace associates. Norms about gender are reinforced through cultural messages in advertising, media, and even our daily language. Indeed, popular culture has the power to shape our identities:

> Sexual statuses, populations, behaviors, and so on, all get processed through popular culture. Some become visible in it, others are rendered invisible; some are celebrated or treated as legitimate, others are denigrated or delegitimated. So popular culture affects who and what gets on the cultural map in the first place.
>
> *(Gamson 2011:27)*

In this way, our gender identity is created and reproduced through dominant cultural norms.

Furthermore, researchers have long recognized that our gender (being a man or a woman) also has significant impacts on life expectancy, educational attainment, career success, and family life (Hochschild 1997; DiPrete and Buchmann 2006; Gorman and Read 2007; Williams 2013). For example, the U.S. National Equal Pay Task Force report released by the White House in 2013 found that full-time working women only earn 77 percent of what their male counterparts earn, despite 50 years after the passage of the Equal Pay Act of 1963, which "established a basic labor standard requiring employers to pay women and men the same wages when performing jobs that are equal, or substantially equal, in content" (White House 2013:5). The gender pay gap is even further complicated by race/ethnicity with African-American women earning 64 cents and Hispanic women earning 56 cents for every dollar earned by a non-Hispanic white man. Over the last 50 years, women have gone from earning 60 percent of men's pay in 1963, down to 57 percent in 1973, back up to 60 percent in 1980, 72 percent by 1990, 74 percent by 2000, and in 2013, women earned 77 cents for every dollar a man earned in the U.S. (White House 2013). While this is a move in the right direction, gender inequality continues to be a systemic part of society. To put it succinctly:

> Ultimately, no matter how you look at the data, a persistent pay gap remains. Decades of research shows a gender gap in pay even after factors such as the type of work performed and qualifications (education and experience) are

taken into account. These studies consistently conclude that discrimination likely explains at least some of the remaining difference.

(White House 2013:23)

As we can see, a person's gender has far-reaching effects on his/her daily interactions and broader social standing. Because gender is a master status, how you present yourself and how others interpret your gender identity impacts your life in a variety of ways. What's more, dominant norms dictate what being a "man" and being a "woman" entails. As a result, our gender identity can sometimes become less about how we feel and more about how dominant social stereotypes define our behaviors and appearances. Because gender systems typically identify certain types of people as "normal" and others as "deviant," the ways our gender is perceived can sometimes lead to deviantization (see chapter 5). In these ways, gender is a social construct shaped by social power.

Sexual behavior and sexual identity

Sexual behavior

Sex can be many things: it can be a source for pleasure (and pleasure can be viewed as sinful, romantic, or adventurous), it can be intimate and caring, it can be about power and control, it can be an expression of love, it can be a casual experience, it can be a rite of passage, and it can be a means to start a family (Seidman *et al.* 2011). But above all, sexual behavior is often considered a "private" matter. Even so, researchers have frequently examined sexual behavior in efforts to better understand human interactions. Emerging from some of the earliest systematic studies of sexual behavior, including Alfred Kinsey's work in the 1940s (see Box 4.1), we continue to learn a great deal about the diversity of human sexual experiences through continued research. For example, the General Social Survey (GSS) has been conducted since 1972 and it has contributed to our basic understandings of American society. In the realm of sexual deviance, findings from the GSS show that about one in five Americans has had an extra-marital affair but paying for sex is relatively uncommon (2 percent report paying for sex in the past year) (Smith *et al.* 2013).

BOX 4.1 ALFRED KINSEY

Sometimes described as the father of American sexology (the scientific study of human sexuality), Alfred Kinsey (1894–1956) performed a series of studies on human sexual behavior with more than 10,000 subjects from 1938 to 1953. Kinsey sought to accumulate "an objectively determined body of fact about sex which strictly avoids social or moral implications" (Kinsey *et al.* 1948:5).

TABLE 4.1 Selections from Alfred Kinsey's Research

	Males	Females
Masturbatory behavior	92%	62%
Experienced nocturnal orgasm	83%	37%
Engaged in pre-marital sex	68%	50%
Erotic response to being bitten	50%	55%
Preference for sex activities in lighted room	40%	19%
At least one same-sex sexual experience	37%	13%
At least one extramarital sex partner	28%	21%
Erotic response to sadomasochism	22%	12%
First intercourse by age 16	21%	6%
Time to orgasm less than 2 minutes	18%	23%
First orgasm through coitus	13%	27%
Performed oral sex prior to marriage	10%	19%

Data adapted from Kinsey *et al.* (1948) and Kinsey *et al.* (1953).

His findings were extensive and challenged what people viewed as "normal" sexual behavior. For example, data reported in his most popular books, *Sexual Behavior in the Human Male* (1948) and *Sexual Behavior in the Human Female* (1953), demonstrated a vast range of sexual fantasies, behaviors, and erotic feelings (see Table 4.1).

Although not without controversy (see Jones 2004), Kinsey's findings had the power to shape (and change) norms about sexual behavior because his research was so widely recognized and lauded as scientifically credible. His lasting legacy remains in the massive amount of research still being conducted at the Kinsey Institute for Research in Sex, Gender, and Reproduction founded in 1947 by Kinsey himself at the University of Indiana.

In the 1990s, American sociologist Edward Laumann (born in 1938) and several colleagues provided us with the first population-based in-depth assessment of sexual behavior in the 40 years since Kinsey's (1948; 1953) work in their book *The Social Organization of Sexuality* (1994). In an interview with Steven Seidman (born in 1948), a prominent sexualities scholar, Laumann discussed what he believed to be the most significant and surprising findings from his research with over 3,000 American men and women (Laumann 2011). First, Laumann notes that while 75 percent of men and women in the U.S. have had oral sex in their lives, only one in four engage in oral sex on a regular basis. He surmises that oral sex "is a practice that is likely to happen early on in a relationship, but does not remain a strong preference over the long haul of a relationship" (Laumann 2011:22). Second, Laumann's research revealed that ongoing, mutually monogamous sexual partnerships are more emotionally and physically satisfying than concurrent or overlapping sexual

partnerships. He believes this finding is related to the significance of trust and commitment, both of which are socially valued characteristics of romantic relationships
and are most common in mutually monogamous relationships. Third, Laumann
sees the most surprising finding of his research to be the remarkable presence of
sexual dysfunction in men and women throughout the life course. Overall, his
research showed that sexual dysfunction (defined as lack of interest for sex, arousal
difficulties, inability to achieve climax, anxiety about sexual performance, climaxing
too early, physical pain during intercourse, and not finding sex pleasurable) was
quite common but was found to be more prevalent for women (43 percent) than
men (31 percent). Furthermore, the most commonly reported sexual dysfunction
for women was a lack of interest in sex (32 percent), while men most frequently
mentioned climaxing too early (31 percent) (Laumann *et al.* 1999). Overall, Laumann
and his colleagues (1994, 1999) have had significant impacts on shaping our awareness and understandings of American sexual behavior.

Other research on sexual behavior has focused on sexual health and sexually
transmitted infections. For example, the Centers for Disease Control and Prevention
(CDC) indicates that U.S. HIV infection diagnoses in 2013 were highest among
persons aged 25 to 29 years followed by persons aged 20 to 24 years (CDC 2013).
Thus, CDC findings show us that young people are at a particular risk for contract-
ing HIV. Additional contemporary research has found that young Black gay men
are disproportionately impacted by HIV (Arnold *et al.* 2014). In this way, it is clear
that gathering data about sexual behavior has important implications for public
health. Sociologists, however, are often more interested in the links between sexual
behavior and other social identities, such as sexual identities.

Sexual identity

A *sexual identity*, sometimes also described as a sexual orientation or sexual preference, is an individual's self-identification of his/her romantic, sexual, emotional,
intellectual, and/or spiritual attraction to others based on the ways a culture organizes people and labels characteristics and visual cues into socially constructed identities. Sexual identity labels include lesbian, bisexual, heterosexual, gay, and pansexual
to name a few. Although identity development processes are often delegated to the
realm of psychology (e.g., Cass 1979; D'Augelli 1994), the importance of social
experiences in shaping sexual identity is often emphasized in sociological discussions. For example, American sociologist Steven Seidman's (2003) work focuses on
how sexualities are created and solidified through social interactions. In this viewpoint, sex and sexual identities are predominantly social because "it is social forces
which determine . . . which desires and acts become the basis of identities, and what
social norms regulate behavior and intimacies" (Seidman *et al.* 2011:xvi).

With this perspective in mind, sexual identity is socially constructed. That is to say
that like other concepts we have discussed previously (i.e., gender, sex, and deviance),
sexual identity is dependent on culture, is temporally relative, and is ever-changing. For
example, as we will discuss in chapter 7, behaviors that would today be described as

deviant, criminal, homosexual, and hebephilic, were quite normative in some Ancient societies. Thus, "sexual identity formation must be reconceptualized as a process of describing one's social location within a changing social context" (Rust 1993:50).

However, it is also important to note that sexual identity is constructed within the confines of prevailing social norms and dominant discourses of social power. In most cultures, a heterosexual identity is so normative that it is often the "default" category of sexual identity. In this way, heteronormativity is the overarching social system that organizes some sexual identities as "normal" and others as "deviant." As a result, in most cultures, heterosexual or straight-identified individuals occupy a superior status to all other people who identify otherwise. To summarize:

> Today, the leading edge of scholarship views sex as fundamentally social. We're born with bodies but it is society that determines which parts of the body and which pleasures and acts are sexual. And, the classification of sex acts as good and bad or acceptable and illicit is a product of social power; the dominant sexual norms express the dominant social groups . . . specific groups impose social norms.
>
> *(Seidman 2011:12)*

Linking sexual behavior and sexual identity

The relationships between certain sexual behaviors and the adoption of a particular sexual identity can be quite complex. While an individual may report involvement in sexual behaviors with others who identify within the same gender category, this may or may not result in the adoption of a gay, lesbian, or bisexual identity. In fact, sometimes sexual behaviors have little to do with sexual identities. For example, in a large U.S. population-based survey of high school students, researchers found that a sizeable majority (61.7 percent) identify as heterosexual even though they indicate that their only sexual partners have been those of the same sex (Kann *et al.* 2011). In other words, as seen in Figure 4.1, only a minority of those who have had same-sex sexual contact actually identify as gay, lesbian, bisexual, or "unsure." Furthermore, among those reporting sexual contact with both men and women, only about half (50.9 percent) indicate a bisexual identity. Thus, sexual identity and sexual behavior may be related to one another most of the time, but at least some of the time, these two constructs operate in unexpected ways.

Why might an individual choose to identify as "heterosexual" if he/she has had sexual contact with partners of the same sex? There are many possible answers to this question. Most of which speak to how we create sexual identity. Because our sexual identity is socially constructed (as noted earlier), we are influenced by many factors when considering how we identify and how others may identify us. Some possible variables that individuals might contemplate when thinking about their sexual identity are:

- Romantic, sexual, emotional, intellectual, and/or spiritual attraction to certain types of people.
- Relationships (either short or long in duration) with certain types of people.

- Involvement in certain types of sexual behaviors with certain types of people.
- Enjoyment of certain types of sexual behaviors with certain types of people.
- Social responses (from family, friends, sexual partners, etc.) to certain types of sexual behaviors and people.
- Unofficial societal responses (mores and folkways, stereotypes, stigma, etc.) to certain types of sexual behaviors and people.
- Official societal responses (laws, policies, protections, etc.) to certain types of sexual behaviors and people.
- Social, political, and/or cultural allegiances to certain types of sexual behaviors, people, and/or groups.

As we can see, sexual identity is more than just a label associated with our sexual behavior. It is a socially constructed concept that is dependent on interpretations of behavior, identity, relationships, politics, and much more. As a result, when considering the links between sexual behavior and sexual identity, it is important to understand the complexity between these cultural constructs. But as we will learn below, societal responses (especially in terms of social attitudes and official laws) affect our own understandings of sexual identity and behavior because they are deeply embedded in systems of social power.

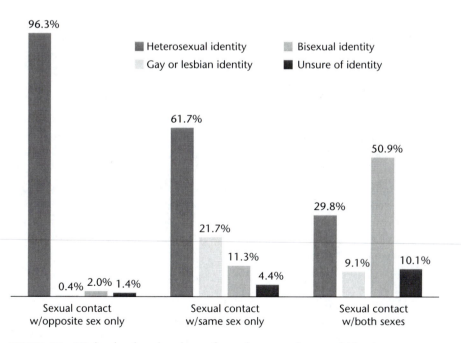

FIGURE 4.1   High school students' sex of sexual contacts by sexual identity

Data adapted from the median values in Table 4 in the Youth Risk Behavior Surveillance System Report 2001 to 2009 (Kann *et al.* 2011).

Attitudes toward non-heterosexuality

Attitudes toward those who are not heterosexual have been consistently variant both temporally and cross-culturally as we will discuss further in chapter 7. In today's cultural climate (in most places across the globe), the stigma that goes along with identifying as non-heterosexual and/or engaging in non-heterosexual behavior is significant (see Box 4.2 for a discussion of the term "homosexual"). For example, in a recent survey of 39 countries conducted by the Pew Research Center's Global Attitudes Project (2013), when asked "should society accept homosexuality?" overall, 55 percent responded "no." However, opinions varied widely by region. As seen in Figure 4.2, individuals in Africa and the Middle East were significantly less accepting of "homosexuality" when compared to those in Europe and North America,

---

BOX 4.2 THE DECLINE AND FALL OF THE "H WORD"

The term "homosexual" has historically been used to describe those who have romantic, sexual, emotional, intellectual, and/or spiritual attraction to those of the same sex and/or gender identity. However, things have changed in the past several decades and there has been a backlash against the "H word" because "for many gays and lesbians, the term 'homosexual' is flinch-worthy . . . more pejorative" (Peters 2014). In fact, the Gay and Lesbian Alliance Against Defamation (GLAAD) includes "homosexual" on its list of offensive terms and many major media outlets including *The New York Times, The Washington Post,* and *The Associated Press* have restricted the use of "homosexual" opting for terms such as "gay" or "lesbian" instead. Why? GLAAD summarizes these issues in their media reference guide as follows:

> **Offensive:** "homosexual" (n. or adj.)
> **Preferred:** "gay" (adj.); "gay man" or "lesbian" (n.); "gay person/people"
> Please use gay or lesbian to describe people attracted to members of the same sex. Because of the clinical history of the word "homosexual," it is aggressively used by anti-gay extremists to suggest that gay people are somehow diseased or psychologically/emotionally disordered – notions discredited by the American Psychological Association and the American Psychiatric Association in the 1970s. Please avoid using "homosexual" except in direct quotes.

Put simply, the use of the word "homosexual" is outdated and derogatory. As George Chauncey (born in 1954), a Yale Professor of history and author who studies gay and lesbian culture states: "'homosexual' has the ring of 'colored' now, in the way your grandmother might have used that term" (Peters 2014). Overall, the "H word" is no longer politically correct.

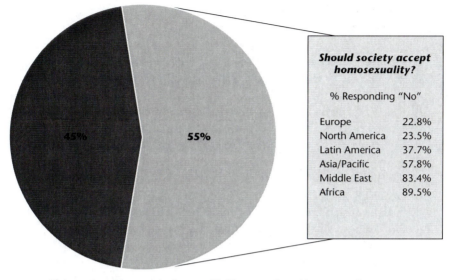

Should society accept homosexuality?	
% Responding "No"	
Europe	22.8%
North America	23.5%
Latin America	37.7%
Asia/Pacific	57.8%
Middle East	83.4%
Africa	89.5%

■ Accepting of homosexuality   ▨ Not accepting of homosexuality

FIGURE 4.2   Global attitudes toward homosexuality

Data adapted from the Pew Research Center's Global Attitudes Project (2013).

while Latin Americans and Asians were in between these two extremes. Thus, it is clear that "homosexuality" is a contested issue across the globe; however, attitudes are diverse and culturally dependent. While such studies provide us with important information about global opinions, simply asking individuals to respond to one survey question about these issues does not adequately capture the diversity embedded within attitudes toward non-heterosexuality. To better understand how non-heterosexuals are deviantized, scholars have developed sophisticated tools, some of which are reviewed below.

Homophobia

Homophobia can be defined as fear and dislike of homosexuality. While contemplating the strongly negative personal reactions directed toward gay men and lesbian women that he observed, American psychologist George Weinberg (born in 1935) created this term in the late 1960s (see Weinberg 1972). He detailed its initial emergence as follows:

> I coined the word homophobia to mean it was a phobia about homosexuals ... It was a fear of homosexuals which seemed to be associated with a fear of contagion, a fear of reducing the things one fought for—home and family. It was a religious fear and it had led to great brutality as fear always does.
>
> *(Herek 2004:7)*

BOX 4.3 RIDDLE HOMOPHOBIA SCALE

Dorothy Irene Riddle (born in 1944) is an American-Canadian psychologist whose work has focused on women's studies, psychology, and spiritual growth. In the 1970s, Riddle was appointed to the American Psychological Association Task Force on the Status of Lesbian and Gay Male Psychologists that led to the removal of homosexuality from the DSM and began a shift away from viewing gay and lesbian people as mentally ill. Following this appointment, Riddle continued to focus on gay and lesbian issues in her research. Based on her observations of differing attitudes toward gay and lesbian people, Riddle developed the Riddle Homophobia Scale (summarized in Figure 4.3), which is currently utilized as a resource in many LGBT ally training programs throughout the United States and Canada (Broido 1999).

The Riddle Homophobia Scale considers prejudice on a spectrum. There are four levels of homophobic attitude (repulsion, pity, tolerance, acceptance) and four levels of positive attitude (support, admiration, appreciation, nurturance). What is unique about this scale is that attitudes such as "tolerance" and "acceptance," which we generally associate with positivity, are considered "homophobic" because they convey negativity (albeit less severe than repulsion and pity) toward gay and lesbian identities (Broido 1999). By placing attitudes on a scale ranging from repulsion to nurturance, the Riddle Homophobia Scale effectively captures the complexity of attitudes toward gay and lesbian people. Specifically, examining opinions in this way allows for not only a better understanding of our own perspectives, but also, the Riddle Homophobia Scale helps us to see how we might begin to effectively work toward changing homophobic attitudes.

Homophobic levels of attitude   *Positive levels of attitude*

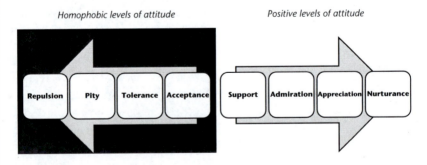

FIGURE 4.3   Riddle Homophobia Scale

Repulsion
Homosexuality is pathological and immoral, and as such, any method is appropriate to eradicate it.

Support
Homophobia is wrong. People in this stage have a basic awareness of homophobia's existence, although they may not yet be comfortable with lesbians and gays.

Pity
Heterosexuality is the only right or normal sexual orientation, and those who are unable to be or become heterosexual should be pitied.

Admiration
It is difficult to be lesbian or gay. People in this stage are willing to examine their own homophobia.

Tolerance
Lesbian and gay identities are merely an adolescent phase, which individuals will or should grow out of. Lesbians and gays are therefore to be treated as children.

Appreciation
People in this stage recognize the contributions of lesbian and gay men, and see them as an important part of the human community. These people are willing to address their own homophobia and that of others.

Acceptance
It's OK if I don't have to see it or know about it. Homosexuality is something distasteful which must be accepted, but it is not to be embraced.

Nurturance
People in this stage genuinely and fully embrace lesbians and gay men. They are willing to be advocates for lesbian and gay issues.

Adapted from Broido (1999).

This "fear" of homosexuality has sparked decades of continuing research about attitudes toward non-heterosexuals. In fact, many scholars have gone on to criticize, contextualize, and expand upon "homophobia" in contemporary research (see, for example, Box 4.3). But the significance of Weinberg's work should not be lost: "by giving a simple name to that hostility and helping to identify it as a problem for individuals and society, he made a profound and lasting contribution" (Herek 2004:9).

Beyond homophobia to sexual prejudice

Published studies measuring "homophobic" attitudes began around the same time Weinberg's public discussion of "homophobia" became widely recognized. In 1971, one of the first scales of its kind was designed to measure negative or fearful responses to "homosexuality" and included yes/no responses to statements such as "homosexuals should be allowed to hold government positions" and "I find the thought of homosexual acts disgusting" (Smith 1971). Since then, researchers have suggested that "homophobia" may be an outdated concept because identifying prejudices directed toward gay and lesbian people as "phobias" indicates that they are simply manifestations of individual psychopathology (Herek 2000). Instead, many contemporary scholars have suggested that these prejudicial attitudes are more about socially reinforced concepts regarding stigma and sexuality (e.g., Herek 2000, 2004; Worthen 2013).

Specially, American psychologist Gregory Herek (born in 1954) developed the concept of sexual prejudice to encompass these ideas in a more thoughtful way. Herek (2000, 2004) defines *sexual prejudice* as a negative attitudinal evaluation of an individual because of her/his sexual orientation that is based on emotional, cognitive, and behavioral information. While anyone can be the target of sexual prejudice, Herek (2000, 2004) notes that sexual prejudice is most commonly directed at people who engage in same-sex sexual behavior or label themselves gay, lesbian, or bisexual. In other words, because heterosexuals have more social power, sexual minorities (i.e., non-heterosexuals) are at a higher risk for sexual prejudice and deviantization. By conceptualizing negative attitudes directed toward people because of their non-heterosexual identity as evidence of sexual prejudice (rather than homophobia), Herek (2004) effectively situates this concept within the larger framework of scholarship on prejudicial attitudes. In doing so, it is clear that most people who are described as "homophobic" are not, in strict terms, suffering from "a debilitating fear of homosexuality" but rather they are exhibiting sexual prejudices by being hostile toward gay, lesbian, and bisexual people and communities (Herek 2004:17).

Attitudes toward LGBT individuals

Scholarship investigating "homophobia" has come a long way in the last four decades. Along with expansions and revision to the initial concept, including the introduction of new conceptualizations of these ideas as in the case of Herek's (2000, 2004) discussion of sexual prejudice, there is also evidence that stereotypes about lesbian women, gay men, bisexual men and women, trans women (also described as male-to-female or MtF individuals) and trans men (also described as female-to-male FtM individuals) may vary substantially because our prejudices directed toward these groups may have different roots and may operate in systematically different ways. Put another way, our feelings about gay men are not the same as our feelings about bisexual women, for example. As a result, it is especially important to consider LGBT stigmas as separate, but related, phenomena.

Starting in the 1970s, researchers began to offer separate explorations of attitudes toward gay men and lesbian women (e.g., MacDonald *et al.* 1973; Herek 1984; Raja and Stokes 1998) as well as perspectives about bisexual men and women in the 1990s (e.g., Rust 1995; Ochs 1996; Eliason 1997; Mohr and Rochlen 1999; Herek 2002). Furthermore, studies began to emerge that specifically investigated attitudes toward transgender individuals (Leitenberg and Slavin 1983; Hill and Willoughby 2005; Nagoshi *et al.* 2008), although most previous work in this area has neglected to explore differences in attitudes toward trans men and women. Overall, research continually provides evidence of differences in perspectives toward LGBT people, however, the roots behind these prejudices have yet to be fully uncovered.

To speak to this issue, emerging scholarship has recognized the need for separate analyses of attitudes toward LGBT individuals. In particular, a discussion that highlights prejudicial attitudes as they vary by the target of prejudice (who is being stigmatized) and the respondents' characteristics (who is doing the stigmatizing) with special attention to how the intersections of gender and sexual identity affect attitudes toward LGBT individuals is necessary. For example, six patterns of heterosexual men's and women's LGBT prejudices have been established in prior research (Worthen 2013):

- Heterosexual men are significantly more prejudiced toward "homosexuals" when compared to heterosexual women (D'Augelli and Rose 1990; Hinrichs and Rosenberg 2002; Negy and Eisenman 2005).
- Heterosexual men have more negative attitudes toward "gays" and more positive attitudes toward "lesbians," while heterosexual women report similar attitudes toward "gays" and "lesbians" (Herek 1988; Eliason 1997; Kite and Whitley 1998) [although in some research, heterosexual women had more negative attitudes toward lesbians and more positive attitudes toward gay men, see Raja and Stokes (1998)].
- Heterosexual men are much more likely than heterosexual women to agree with negative stereotypes about "bisexuals" (i.e., bisexuals are more likely to have more than one sexual partner at a time than heterosexuals; bisexuals are gays/lesbians who are afraid to admit they are gay; and bisexuals spread AIDS to lesbians and heterosexuals) (Eliason 1997; Mohr and Rochlen 1999).
- When asked specifically about their attitudes toward bisexual men and bisexual women, heterosexual men have more negative attitudes toward bisexual men and more positive attitudes toward bisexual women (Eliason 1997; Mohr and Rochlen 1999).
- Heterosexual men (compared to heterosexual women) report higher levels of hostility toward "transgender" individuals (Leitenberg and Slavin 1983; Hill and Willoughby 2005; Nagoshi et al. 2008).
- Heterosexual men (compared to heterosexual women) are more violent toward trans women than they are toward trans men (Serano 2007; Schilt and Westbrook 2009; Gerhardstein and Anderson 2010).

Overall, these studies point to different roots of prejudices and suggest if we cluster "LGBT" individuals into one group, we would likely mask these important differences. Furthermore, because we see that these attitudinal patterns differ by both the gender and sexual identity of the respondent and of the target of prejudice, it is important to consider the theoretical reasons why we would expect to see these differences.

Scholars offer six theoretical reasons to explain the well-documented "gender gap" in attitudes whereby heterosexual men (compared to heterosexual women) have been found to be overwhelmingly less supportive of LGBT individuals: (i) conflation of gays, bisexual men, and transgender individuals with HIV/AIDS;

(ii) fear of sexual advances; (iii) sexualization of lesbians and bisexual women; (iv) "coveting" of gays by heterosexual women; (v) gender nonconformity prejudice; and (vi) heterosexism, sexism, and cisnormativity. As seen in Table 4.2, these theoretical explanations for LGBT prejudices work differently for heterosexual men and women. In particular, heterosexual men are more inclined to support negative stereotypes about gay, bisexual, and transgender men while heterosexual women are more likely to be accepting toward all LGBT people (Worthen 2013). Even so, heterosexual women may view lesbian and bisexual women negatively because they may perceive them as "competitors" in the sexual marketplace, while heterosexual men are more likely to objectify and sexualize lesbian and bisexual women (Hamilton 2007; Rupp and Taylor 2010). Furthermore, sexism, *gender nonconformity prejudice*, or differential treatment and/or negative attitudes toward individuals whose gender expression does not follow traditional stereotypical gender roles and/or norms (Gordon and Meyer 2007), *heterosexism*, or the bias that heterosexuality is "the only way to be" and those that are not heterosexual are somehow "wrong," and *cisnormativity*, or the assumption that it is "normal" to be *cisgender* (a match between an individual's sex assigned at birth, his/her body, and personal gender identity) (Schilt and Westbrook 2009) are all perspectives more commonly held among straight men. Overall, by considering who is being stigmatized and who is doing the stigmatizing, important patterns about heterosexual men's and women's attitudes toward LGBT individuals are revealed.

While there are certainly arguments in the literature that have focused on heterosexual men's and women's opinions about LGBT individuals, few studies have examined gays' and lesbians' attitudes about these issues. We do know, however, that just as straight people stereotype LGBT people, gays have prejudices about lesbians and lesbians have prejudices about gays. For example, lesbians may stereotype gays as "over-sexed," "promiscuous," and may even see them as poor relationship partners. Conversely, gays may stereotype lesbians as "man-haters," "overeager to jump into a serious relationship" or otherwise known as "U-Haul lesbians" who are victims of the "urge to merge" (Gordon 2006; Eliason 2010). Furthermore, in her article entitled "GL vs. BT," Jillian Weiss clearly points out that "heterosexism against bisexuals and transgender [people] exists not only in the straight community, but in the gay and lesbian community as well" (Weiss 2004:27). Although the LGBT community is often thought of as "monolithic," it is certainly true that gays and lesbians may see bisexual and transgender individuals and the issues that they face as entirely separate from their own (Weiss 2004).

Bisexual people also have distinct prejudicial experiences. For example, bisexual men and women feel a double-stigmatization in which they are rejected from both heterosexual and gay/lesbian communities (Ochs 1996; Mulick and Wright 2002; Brewster and Moradi 2010). Such negative attitudes include (i) verbal accusations that bisexual men and bisexual women are "traitors" to the gay and lesbian movement (Hutchins and Ka'ahumanu 1991; Rust 1995; Ault 1996; Burleson 2005); (ii) bisexuals are "colluders" in promoting heterosexist relationship norms (Stone 1996); and (iii) bisexual men and bisexual women are just "junior members" of the

TABLE 4.2 Theoretical explanations for heterosexual men's and women's attitudes toward LGBT individuals

	Conflation of gay and bisexual men with HIV/AIDS	Fear of sexual advances	Sexualization of lesbian and bisexual women	"Coveting" of gays by heterosexual women	Gender nonconformity prejudice	Heterosexism, sexism, and cisnormativity
Heterosexual men	Associate HIV and AIDS with men who have sex with men Blame bisexual men for transmission of HIV to straight people Perceive all LGBT people as "vectors" of disease	Fear sexual advances from gay, bisexual, and trans men because they fear being thought of as "gay" Worry that they may send out a "gay vibe" that threatens their masculinity Violent toward trans women when their birth sex is revealed	Enjoy eroticization of lesbian and bisexual women in pornography and other media Sexually titillated by bisexual women because not only will they kiss women, they may also kiss men	Do not view gay men as a threat to their sexual relationships with straight women View media attention focused on the gay man/heterosexual woman couple configuration as socially acceptable	Strict in their own gender role expressions Desire high levels of conformity to strict gender roles for all Condemnatory of those who they perceive as gender-role violators (likely LGBT people)	Hold traditional perspectives about relationships Believe all relationships should be straight couplings of opposite cisgender individuals View straight cisgender men as superior to all
Heterosexual women	Greater concern about contracting HIV from bisexual men	Fear sexual advances from lesbian, bisexual, and trans women because fear they will be thought of as "lesbian" themselves and may no longer be viewed as a potential dating partner for heterosexual men	May kiss other women to attract the attention of heterosexual men because they know it is a sexual turn-on to them May encourage sexual fluidity among women	Comfortable around gay men because they feel least threatened by them sexually Desire to be a part of the popular media concept of gay man/straight woman duo (i.e., *Will and Grace*)	More fluid in their own expressions of gender and sexuality Accepting of diversity in gender expression and gender nonconformity (likely in LGBT people)	Perceive lesbian, bisexual, and trans women as "incomplete" or "insufficient" Judge lesbian, bisexual, and trans women negatively on the grounds that they are not "real" women

Adapted from Worthen (2013).

gay and lesbian population who are "bi now, gay later" (Burleson 2005; see Brewster and Moradi 2010:452).

Together, it is clear that attitudes and prejudices toward non-heterosexuals are culturally dependent. Furthermore, opinions vary by who is being stigmatized and who is doing the stigmatizing. As a result, our understandings of sexual identity vary by our own experiences and others' perspectives. What is also clear, however, is that some people are much more likely to retain dominant social positions within most cultures and others are not. As a result, in most societies, heterosexuals retain social power and LGBT people remain secondary and deviant.

Examining social power, gender, sex, and sexuality: the Netherlands and Yemen as two case examples

In thinking about how social power shapes the social construction of gender, sex, and sexuality, it is helpful to consider how demographic measures and societal laws affect this dynamic. Take, for example, the Netherlands. According to several demographic measures of gender equality including women's health, women's education, women in politics, and women in the labor force as seen in Table 4.3, the Netherlands consistently ranks among the top ten best countries across the globe for equal rights between men and women. In addition, the Netherlands was the first country in the world to legalize same-sex marriage in 2001. Thus, both demographic measures and societal laws in the Netherlands reflect gender equality and support equal rights for gay, lesbian, and bisexual individuals.

By contrast, Yemen was ranked dead last in both the 2012 and 2013 Gender Inequality Index Report based on a composite measure of women's reproductive health, empowerment and participation in the labor market. Yemen consistently has very high rates of pregnancy-related deaths, high rates of births to women ages 15 to 19, as well as low levels of women's involvement in politics, the labor force, and secondary education (see Table 4.3). In addition, same-sex marriages are not legally recognized and same-sex sexual behavior is punishable by death in some circumstances. As a result, the socio-legal context of Yemen does not reflect gender equality or rights for non-heterosexual people. Overall, the "dominant Arab, Muslim, tribal, male, and heterosexual character of Yemeni society" poses difficulties for all women and LGBT people in Yemen (Walters 1996:63).

By examining two very different countries (the Netherlands and Yemen), we can see that not only are women and LGBT people treated differently in these locations, but also, the cultural scripts for these groups vary widely. For example, in the Netherlands, gender equality is reflected not only in official measures (as seen in Table 4.3) but also through things such as family-friendly policies with generous maternity leave (16 weeks of 100 percent paid leave for all women employees; den Dulk 2014) and increased focus on women's labor force participation (Haas 2003). There is also great inertia behind the continued improvement of LGBT rights in the Netherlands. Although discrimination on grounds of sexual orientation has already been established as prohibited under the General Equal Treatment Act

TABLE 4.3 Measures of gender equality in selected countries

	Gender Inequality Index rank	Maternal mortality ratio	Adolescent birth rate	Women in parliament	Women's secondary education	Women's labor force participation rate	Criminalization of same-sex sexual behavior	Legalized same-sex marriage
Netherlands	7	6	6.2	37.8	87.7	79.9	No	Yes
Australia	19	7	12.1	29.2	94.3	58.8	No	No
Japan	25	5	5.4	10.8	87.0	48.1	No	No
United States	47	21	31.0	18.2	95.1	56.8	No	Yes
Brazil	85	56	70.8	9.6	51.9	59.5	No	Yes
Egypt	130	66	43.0	2.8	43.4	23.6	17 years in prison	No
Yemen	152	200	47.0	0.7	7.6	25.2	Death penalty	No

Gender Inequality Index (2013). A composite measure reflecting inequality in achievement between women and men in three dimensions: reproductive health, empowerment and the labor market. Maternal mortality ratio (2010). Number of deaths due to pregnancy-related causes per 100,000 live births. Adolescent birth rate (2010/2015). Number of births to women ages 15 to 19 per 1,000 women ages 15 to 19. Women in parliament (2013). Proportion of seats held by women in a lower/single house or/and an upper house/senate expressed as percentage of total seats. For countries with bicameral legislative systems, the share of seats is calculated based on both houses. Women's secondary education (2005–2012). Population percentage of women ages 25 and older who have reached (but not necessarily completed) a secondary level of education. Women's labor force participation rate (2012). Proportion of a country's working-age population (women aged 15 and older) that engages in the labor market, either by working or actively looking for work, expressed as a percentage of the working-age population. Criminalization of same-sex sexual behavior (2015). Countries where same-sex sexual behavior is illegal; maximum punishment described. Legalized same-sex marriage (2015). Countries where same-sex marriage has been legalized. Data adapted from: Human Development Reports, see http://hdr.undp.org/en/content/table-4-gender-inequality-index; Human Rights Campaign, see http://hrc-assets.s3-website-us-east-1.amazonaws.com//files/images/issues/WorldMarriageMap–030315.pdf and http://hrc-assets.s3-website-us-east-1.amazonaws.com//files/assets/resources/Criminalization_Map_12-17-14.pdf.

(in Dutch: *Algemene wet gelijke behandeling*), the LGBT and Gender Equality Policy Plan recommendations for 2015 focus on other issues such as:

- Lesbian couples will no longer need to go to court to establish the legal parenthood of two mothers.
- For men, sexual contact with other men will no longer lead to life-long exclusion from donating blood.
- The sterilization requirement for changing the official sex of a person as indicated on birth certificates will be removed.

Overall, the socio-legal context of the Netherlands is supportive of women[1] and LGBT people and their government policies position the Dutch as "the global vanguard in terms of the social acceptance and protection of the rights of LGBT people" (LGBT and Gender Equality Policy Plan 2011–2015:26). By promoting gender and sexuality-based systems of equality, the Netherlands empowers women and LGBT people. Not only are they protected by legal and social norms, but also, the current political climate reflects continued dedication to the improvement of their lives. Within this system, social power is not only designated to heterosexual men but rather shared amongst diverse groups.

In Yemen, gender inequity is visible not only in official measures (as seen in Table 4.3) but also through cultural scripts that dictate Yemeni women's subservient position in society. A predominantly Muslim country (see Image 4.1), Yemen is a sex-segregated society where a woman's reputation is based on her ability to please her father and after marriage, her husband (Basha 2005; Walters 1996). Because women are devalued, many families deny their daughters the right to education (65 percent of Yemeni women aged 15 to 24 are illiterate) and most Yemeni girls are married as teenagers (14 percent of girls are married before age 15 and 52 percent before age 18) to a single man while a man is allowed to be married to up to four women at one time in Yemen (Basha 2005; Ministry of Health and Population and UNICEF 2008). Official laws in Yemen are also highly restrictive of women's rights (Basha 2005):

- A woman in Yemen is not recognized as a full person before the court; the testimony of two women equals the testimony of one man.
- A husband can divorce his wife at any time without providing any justification, whereas a woman must litigate in court and present adequate justification in order to have the marriage contract nullified.
- There are no legal protections for women who suffer from domestic violence; marital rape is not criminalized in Yemen.
- No laws protect women from sexual harassment in the workplace in Yemen.

For LGBT individuals, the situation in Yemen is quite dire. The cultural context is one of denial of access to information about LGBT issues, the existence of LGBT people, and LGBT rights. For example, OpenNet Initiative (ONI), an organization that has been documenting internet filtering globally since 2003, found that the Yemen government engages in extensive censorship of webpages with LGBT information (ONI 2009). In fact, of the 74 countries investigated in 2012, Yemen is amongst the 21 countries found to be pervasively filtering websites (in terms of both breadth and depth) based on content perceived to be socially offensive (covering issues such as sexuality, gambling, and illegal drugs). This may have an extremely large impact on global accessibility to LGBT issues and information. ONI estimates that over 960 million, or 47 percent of all internet users, are affected by pervasive filtering and censorship of webpages (ONI 2012).

Furthermore, LGBT people continue to be effectively closeted in Yemen. For example, activist Alaa Jarban (born in 1990) came out as one of Yemen's first publicly non-heterosexual men on his blog in 2013 and his simple two-word announcement, "I'm Queer," sparked both controversy and backlash because of the anti-LGBT Yemeni political atmosphere. In fact, through the use of his blog as a platform, the invisibility of LGBTQ people in Yemen has been highlighted. As one anonymous blog commentator noted: "I asked friends where is the gay community, and people said there are no gays in Yemen" (BBC 2013). While obviously a hyperbole, the idea

IMAGE 4.1   Muslim woman in Sanaa, Yemen

A Muslim woman in a traditional abaya (a simple loose-fitting garment that covers the entire body except for the face, feet, and hands) and a niqāb (a face veil that covers all but the eyes) walks past traditional Yemeni houses in Sanaa, Yemen. ©Shutterstock, Robert Paul Van Beets

that "there are no gays in Yemen" certainly sends a strong message. This statement tells Yemeni people that if you are gay and/or if you participate in same-sex sexual behavior, you need to remain closeted. Official laws reflect this mentality. As of 2015, Yemen is one of only ten countries in the world where consensual sexual acts between adults of the same sex are punishable with the death penalty.[2] According to the Yemen National Penal Code, official punishment for "homosexuality" is quite extreme (Itaborahy and Zhu 2013:66):

- Article 264. "Homosexuality between men is defined as penetration into the anus. Unmarried men shall be punished with 100 lashes of the whip or a maximum of one year of imprisonment, married men with death by stoning."
- Article 268. "Homosexuality between women is defined as sexual stimulation by rubbing. The penalty for premeditated commission shall be up to three years of imprisonment; where the offence has been committed under duress, the perpetrator shall be punishable with up to seven years detention."

Overall, in Yemen, women and LGBT people struggle. Their limited access to social power means that they are continually denied equality both in official capacities (through law, for example) and unofficial capacities (through social norms, stereotypes, and stigma). As a result, the cultural climate of Yemen outlines rigid terms for women and LGBT people. Within this system, social power is designated only to heterosexual men while women are faced with legal and social barriers to equality and LGBT people remain politically invisible and deviantized.

Social power and sexual deviance

In this chapter, we have learned that your gender, sex, and sexual identity can create situations where others define you as deviant. Furthermore, both social attitudes and legal policies can shape individual experiences and broader cultural contexts. As a result, systems of social power designate some groups as more powerful than others and those patterns vary cross-culturally and temporally. Thus, what is viewed as deviant is shaped by broad political, social, and cultural norms. In the next chapter, we will learn more about how those who step beyond dominant norms about gender can experience both stigma and empowerment.

Notes

1 Some have criticized the Dutch gender equality policies as especially problematic for migrant Muslim women (Roggeband and Verloo 2007). Thus, "gender equality" should be understood in a cultural context.
2 According to the Human Rights Campaign, in 2015, same-sex sexual behavior was punishable by death in 10 countries: Mauritania, Sudan, Nigeria, Somalia, Brunei, Iran, Qatar, Saudi Arabia, United Arab Emirates, and Yemen. See http://hrc-assets.s3-website-us-east-1.amazonaws.com//files/assets/resources/Criminalization-Map-042315.pdf.

References

Arnold, Emily, Gregory Rebchook, and Susan Kegeles. 2014. "'Triply Cursed': Racism, Homophobia and HIV-Related Stigma are Barriers to Regular HIV Testing, Treatment Adherence and Disclosure among Young Black Gay Men." *Culture, Health & Sexuality: An International Journal for Research, Intervention and Care* 16(6):710–22.

Ault, Amber. 1996. "Ambiguous Identity in an Unambiguous Sex/Gender Structure: The Case of Bisexual Women." *The Sociological Quarterly* 37:449–63.

Basha, Amal. 2005. "Yemen." Pp. 335–54 in *Women's Rights in the Middle East and North Africa: Citizenship and Justice*, edited by Sameena Nazir and Leigh Tomppert. Oxford: Freedom House.

BBC. 2013. "Alaa Jarban: One of Yemen's First Openly Gay Men." *BBC News: Middle East*, June 18, 2013. Retrieved from: http://www.bbc.com/news/world-middle-east-22893341.

Brewster, Melanie and Bonnie Moradi. 2010. "Perceived Experiences of Antibisexual Prejudice: Instrument Development and Evaluation." *Journal of Counseling Psychology* 57:451–68.

Broido, Ellen. 1999. "Ways of Being an Ally to Lesbian, Gay, and Bisexual Students." Pp. 345–69 in *Toward Acceptance: Sexual Orientation Issues on College Campus*, edited by Vernon Wall and Nancy Evans. Lanham, MD: American College Personnel Association.

Burleson, William. 2005. *Bi America: Myths, Truths, and Struggles of an Invisible Community*. New York, NY: Harrington Park Press.

Centers for Disease Control and Prevention (CDC). 2013. "Diagnoses of HIV Infection in the United States and Dependent Areas." *HIV Surveillance Report* 25:1–82.

Cass, Vivienne. 1979. "Homosexuality Identity Formation: A Theoretical Model." *Journal of Homosexuality* 4(3):219–35.

den Dulk, Laura. 2014. "Netherlands Country Note" in *International Review of Leave Policies and Research 2014*, edited by Peter Moss. Retrieved from: http://www.leavenetwork.org/lp_and_r_reports/.

D'Augelli, Anthony R. 1994. "Identity Development and Sexual Orientation: Toward a Model of Lesbian, Gay, and Bisexual Development." Pp. 312–33 in *Human Diversity: Perspectives on People in Context*, edited by Edison J. Trickett, Roderick J. Watts, and Dina Birman. San Francisco, CA: Jossey-Bass.

D'Augelli, Anthony R. and M. Rose. 1990. "Homophobia in a University Community: Attitudes and Experience of White Heterosexual Freshmen." *Journal of College Student Development* 31: 484–91.

DiPrete, Thomas and Claudia Buchmann. 2006. "Gender-Specific Trends in the Value of Education and the Emerging Gender Gap in College Completion." *Demography* 43(1):1–24.

Eliason, Michele. 1997. "The Prevalence and Nature of Biphobia in Heterosexual Undergraduate Students." *Archives of Sexual Behavior* 26:317–26.

Eliason, Michele. 2010. "A New Classification System for Lesbians: The Dyke Diagnostic Manual." *Journal of Lesbian Studies* 14:401–14.

Gamson, Joshua. 2011. "Popular Culture Constructs Sexuality." Pp. 27–31 in *Introducing the New Sexuality Studies*, Second Edition, edited by Steven Seidman, Nancy Fisher, and Chet Meeks. New York, NY: Routledge.

Gerhardstein, Kelly and Veanne Anderson. 2010. "There's More than Meets the Eye: Facial Appearance and Evaluations of Transsexual People." *Sex Roles* 62:361–73.

GLAAD. n.d. "GLAAD Media Reference Guide - Terms To Avoid." *Gay & Lesbian Alliance Against Defamation*. Retrieved from http://www.glaad.org/reference/offensive.

Gordon, Liahna E. 2006. "Bringing the U-Haul: Embracing and Resisting Sexual Stereotypes in a Lesbian Community." *Sexualities* 9:171–92.

Gordon, Allegra and Ilan Meyer. 2007. "Gender Nonconformity as a Target of Prejudice, Discrimination and Violence against LGB Individuals." *Journal of LGBT Health Research* 3:55–71.

Gorman, Bridget and Jen'nan Ghazal Read. 2007. "Why Men Die Younger than Women." *Geriatrics and Aging* 10(3):182–91.

Haas, Linda. 2003. "Parental Leave and Gender Equality: Lessons from the European Union." *Review of Policy Research* 20(1):89–114.

Hamilton, Laura. 2007. "Trading on Heterosexuality: College Women's Gender Strategies and Homophobia." *Gender & Society* 21:145–72.

Herek, Gregory. 1984. "Beyond 'Homophobia': A Social Psychological Perspective on Attitudes toward Lesbians and Gay Men." *Journal of Homosexuality* 10:1–21.

Herek, Gregory. 1988. "Heterosexuals' Attitudes toward Lesbians and Gay Men: Correlates and Gender Differences." *The Journal of Sex Research* 25:451–77.

Herek, Gregory. 2000. "The Psychology of Sexual Prejudice." *Current Directions in Psychological Science* 9:19–22.

Herek, Gregory. 2002. "Heterosexuals' Attitudes toward Bisexual Men, and Bisexual Women in the United States." *The Journal of Sex Research* 39:264–74.

Herek, Gregory. 2004. "Beyond Homophobia: Thinking about Sexual Prejudice and Stigma in the Twenty-First Century." *Sexuality Research & Social Policy* 1:6–24.

Hill, Darryl and Brian Willoughby. 2005. "The Development and Validation of the Genderism and Transphobia Scale." *Sex Roles* 53(7/8):531–44.

Hinrichs, Donald and Pamela Rosenberg. 2002. "Attitudes toward Gay, Lesbian, and Bisexual Individuals among Heterosexual Liberal Arts College Students." *Journal of Homosexuality* 43:61–84.

Hochschild, Arlie. 1997. *The Time Bind: When Work Becomes Home and Home Becomes Work.* New York, NY: Henry Holt & Company.

Hutchins, Loraine and Lani Ka'ahumanu, editors. 1991. *Bi Any Other Name: Bisexual People Speak Out.* Boston, MA: Alyson.

Itaborahy, Lucas Paoli and Jingshu Zhu. 2013. *State Sponsored Homophobia Report.* International Lesbian, Gay, Bisexual, Trans and Intersex Association. Retrieved from http://old.ilga.org/Statehomophobia/ILGA_SSHR_2014_Eng.pdf.

Jones, James H. 2004. *Alfred C. Kinsey: A Life.* New York, NY: W.W. Norton & Company.

Kann, Laura, Emily O'Malley Olsen, Tim McManus, Steve Kinchen, David Chyen, William A. Harris, Howell Wechsler. 2011. "Sexual Identity, Sex of Sexual Contacts, and Health-Risk Behaviors Among Students in Grades 9–12, Youth Risk Behavior Surveillance, Selected Sites, United States, 2001–2009." *CDC MMWR* 60(1):1–133.

Kinsey, Alfred, Wardell Pomeroy, and Clyde Martin. 1948. *Sexual Behavior in the Human Male.* Philadelphia, PA: W.B. Saunders Company.

Kinsey, Alfred, Wardell Pomeroy, Clyde Martin, and Paul Gebhard. 1953. *Sexual Behavior in the Human Female.* Philadelphia, PA: W.B. Saunders Company.

Kite, Mary and Bernard Whitley, Jr. 1998. "Do Heterosexual Women and Men Differ in Their Attitudes Toward Homosexuality? A Conceptual and Methodological Analysis." Pp. 39–61 in *Psychological Perspectives on Lesbians and Gay Issues: Vol 4. Stigma and Sexual Orientation*, edited by Gregory Herek. Thousand Oaks, CA: Sage.

Laumann, Edward. 2011. "Surveying Sex." Pp. 20–3 in *Introducing the New Sexuality Studies*, Second Edition, edited by Steven Seidman, Nancy Fisher, and Chet Meeks. New York, NY: Routledge.

Laumann, Edward O., John H. Gagnon, Robert T. Michael, and Stuart Michaels. 1994. *The Social Organization of Sexuality.* Chicago, IL: University of Chicago Press.

Laumann, Edward O., Anthony Paik, and Raymond C. Rosen. 1999. "Sexual Dysfunction in the United States." *JAMA: The Journal of the American Medical Association* 281(6):537–44.

Leitenberg, Harold and Lesley Slavin. 1983. "Comparison of Attitudes toward Transsexuality and Homosexuality." *Archives of Sexual Behavior* 12:337–46.

LGBT and Gender Equality Policy Plan of the Netherlands 2011–2015. *Ministry of Education, Culture and Science.* Retrieved from: https://www.government.nl/documents/leaflets/2012/01/10/lgbt-and-gender-equality-policy-plan-of-the-netherlands-2011-2015.

MacDonald, A. P., Jim Huggins, Susan Young, and Richard Swanson. 1973. "Attitudes toward Homosexuality: Preservation of Sex Morality or the Double Standard?" *Journal of Consulting and Clinical Psychology* 40:161.

Ministry of Health and Population and UNICEF. 2008. "Yemen: Monitoring the Situation of Children and Women." *Multiple Indicator Cluster Survey 2006, Final Report.* Retrieved from http://www.childinfo.org/files/MICS3_Yemen_FinalReport_2006_Eng.pdf.

Mohr, Jonathan and Aaron Rochlen. 1999. "Measuring Attitudes Regarding Bisexuality in Lesbian, Gay Male, and Heterosexual Populations." *Journal of Counseling Psychology* 46:353–69.

Mulick, Patrick and Lester Wright, Jr. 2002. "Examining the Existence of Biphobia in the Heterosexual and Homosexual Populations." *Journal of Bisexuality* 2:45–64.

Nagoshi, Julie, Katherine Adams, Heather Terrell, Eric Hill, Stephanie Brzuzy, and Craig Nagoshi. 2008. "Gender Differences in Correlates of Homophobia and Transphobia." *Sex Roles* 59:521–31.

Negy, Charles and Russell Eisenman. 2005. "A Comparison of African American and White College Students' Affective and Attitudinal Reactions to Lesbian, Gay, and Bisexual Individuals: An Exploratory Study." *The Journal of Sex Research* 42:291–8.

Ochs, Robyn. 1996. "Biphobia: It Goes More than Two Ways." Pp. 217–39 in *Bisexuality: The Psychology and Politics of an Invisible Minority*, edited by Beth A. Firestein. Thousand Oaks, CA: Sage Publications.

ONI. 2009. "Yemen." August 7, 2009. Retrieved from https://opennet.net/research/profiles/yemen.

ONI. 2012. "Global Internet Filtering in 2012 at a Glance." April 3, 2012. Retrieved from https://opennet.net/blog/2012/04/global-internet-filtering-2012-glance.

Peters, Jeremy. 2014, March 21. "The Decline and Fall of the 'H' Word." *New York Times: Fashion & Style.* Retrieved from: http://www.nytimes.com/2014/03/23/fashion/gays-lesbians-the-term-homosexual.html?_r=0.

Pew Research Center. 2013. "The Global Divide on Homosexuality." *Global Attitudes Project.* June 4, 2013. Retrieved from: http://www.pewglobal.org/2013/06/04/the-global-divide-on-homosexuality/.

Raja, Sheela and Joseph Stokes. 1998. "Assessing Attitudes toward Lesbians and Gay Men: The Modern Homophobia Scale." *Journal of Gay, Lesbian, and Bisexual Identity* 3:113–34.

Roggeband, Conny and Mieke Verloo. 2007. "Dutch Women are Liberated, Migrant Women are a Problem: The Evolution of Policy Frames on Gender and Migration in the Netherlands." *Social Policy & Administration* 41(3):271–88.

Rupp, Leila and Verta Taylor. 2010. "Straight Girls Kissing." *Contexts* 9:28–32.

Rust, Paula. 1993. ""Coming Out" In the Age of Social Constructionism: Sexual Identity Formation among Lesbian and Bisexual Women." *Gender & Society* 7(1):50–77.

Rust, Paula C. 1995. *Bisexuality and the Challenge to Lesbian Politics: Sex, Loyalty and Revolution.* New York, NY: NYU Press.

Schilt, Kristen and Laurel Westbrook. 2009. "Doing Gender, Doing Heteronormativity: 'Gender Normals', Transgender People, and the Social Maintenance of Heterosexuality." *Gender & Society* 23:440–64.

Seidman, Steven. 2003. *The Social Construction of Sexuality.* New York, NY: W.W. Norton & Company.

Seidman, Steven. 2011. "Theoretical Perspectives." Pp. 1–12 in *Introducing the New Sexuality Studies*, Second Edition, edited by Steven Seidman, Nancy Fisher, and Chet Meeks. New York, NY: Routledge.

Seidman, Steven, Nancy Fisher, and Chet Meeks. 2011. *Introducing the New Sexuality Studies*, Second Edition. New York, NY: Routledge.

Serano, Julia. 2007. *Whipping Girl: A Transsexual Woman on Sexism and the Scapegoating of Femininity*. Berkeley, CA: Seal Press.

Smith, Kenneth. 1971. "Homophobia: A Tentative Personality Profile." *Psychological Reports* 29:1091–4.

Smith, Tom W., Peter Marsden, Michael Hout, and Jibum Kim. 2013. *General Social Surveys, 1972–2012* [machine-readable data file]/Principal Investigator, Tom W. Smith; Co-Principal Investigator, Peter V. Marsden; Co-Principal Investigator, Michael Hout; Sponsored by National Science Foundation. NORC ed. Chicago, IL: National Opinion Research Center [producer]; Storrs, CT: The Roper Center for Public Opinion Research, University of Connecticut [distributor].

Stone, Sharon. 1996. "Bisexual Women and the 'Threat' to Lesbian Space: Or What if All the Lesbians Leave?" *Frontiers: A Journal of Women Studies* 16:101–16.

Walters, Dolores. 1996. "Cast among Outcastes: Interpreting Sexual Orientation, Racial, and Gender Identity in the Yemen Arab Republic." Pp. 58–69 in *Out in the Field: Reflections of Lesbian and Gay Anthropologists*, edited by Ellen Lewin and William Leap. Champaign, IL: University of Illinois Press.

Weiss, Jillian. 2004. "GL vs. BT: The Archaeology of Biphobia and Transphobia within the U.S. Gay and Lesbian Community." *Journal of Bisexuality* 3(3/4):25–55.

White House. 2013. "Fifty Years After the Equal Pay Act." *National Equal Pay Task Force*. Washington, D.C.: The White House. Retrieved from: https://www.whitehouse.gov/sites/default/files/equalpay/equal_pay_task_force_progress_report_june_2013_new.pdf.

Weinberg, George. 1972. *Society and the Healthy Homosexual*. New York, NY: St. Martin's.

Williams, Christine. 2013. "The Glass Escalator, Revisited: Gender Inequality in Neoliberal Times." *Gender & Society* 27:609–29.

Worthen, Meredith G. F. 2013. "An Argument for Separate Analyses of Attitudes Toward Lesbian, Gay, Bisexual Men, Bisexual Women, MtF and FtM Transgender Individuals." *Sex Roles: A Journal of Research* 68(11/12):703–23.

5

GENDER AND DEVIANCE[1]

Meredith G. F. Worthen and Danielle Dirks

On June 29, 2008, Thomas Beatie gave birth to his first child, Susan Juliette Beatie, in an Oregon hospital. The announcement received intense coverage and scrutiny, because unlike millions of other expecting women, Thomas was considered by multiple media outlets to be the world's very first "pregnant man" (Beatie 2009). Indeed, *Guinness World Records* (2010), named Thomas Beatie the "World's First Married Man to Give Birth" (Glenday 2010:110). With his then wife, Nancy Gillespie (married in 2003, divorced in 2015), Thomas, a self-identified transgender man who transitioned from female-to-male with "top" surgery involving chest reconstruction and the change of his sex marker from female to male on all of his state and federal documents in 2002 and "lower" surgery involving the creation of a functioning penis in 2012, conceived his first daughter (and two subsequent children) through artificial insemination. Because of his self-identification as male/masculine/man, Beatie's pregnancy exploded in media outlets throughout the world and challenged ideas about sex, gender, biology, and sexuality. Both uninformed and informed critics questioned his identity and his motives. Even a gender scholar wrote on a popular sociological blog, "I'm not sure what to make, sociologically, of the attention that Thomas' pregnancy is receiving in the mass media, but it is ripe for analysis" (Wade 2008). Thomas Beatie's widely publicized persona as the first "pregnant man" demonstrates society's fascination with blurred lines when it comes to gender. Thomas himself actively challenges the social construction of gender through his website and T-shirt company, both emblazoned with the critical inquisitive title: "Define Normal." Examining "gender" in the context of "normalcy" and "deviance" is a daily, albeit mostly unrecognized, practice. Even so, little deviance scholarship has examined gender with a critical, intersectional lens.

Contemporary sociologists, including sociologists of deviance, have developed a critically informed viewpoint of both gender and sexuality as socially and politically constructed, pushing forth sophisticated theoretical frameworks for understanding gender that includes systems of heterosexism (Collins 1991), heteronormativity (Ingraham 1994), and compulsory heterosexuality (Rich 1980). Furthermore, the emergence of Queer Theory (Seidman 1994; Stein and Plummer 1994) has created another conceptual push to envision gender and sexualities as both fluid and dynamic, and representative of, and intricately entwined with, social power and relations. This "queering" of sociology has set out to deconstruct monolithic notions of "male" and "female" and "heterosexual" and "homosexual" as rigid organizing categories that do very little to explain the diverse range of attitudes, behaviors, or conditions of individuals' experiences within these categories. Individuals on the "outs" of these exclusive groups seek to challenge such restrictive boundaries by disrupting strict interpretations of male and female, gay and straight. Relatedly, scholars have taken up questions focusing on the intersection of gender and sexuality, with a focus on the ways in which race and class complicate our understandings of identity, lived experiences, and oppression. To adequately examine gendered deviance, such a critical and intersectional approach is necessary.

In this chapter, gender is discussed as both highly performative and intimately tied to heterosexual ideals. Furthermore, an intersectional approach to understanding so-called deviant sexualities is provided and the ways in which individuals challenge restrictive gender binaries in favor of more expansive and fluid ideas about gender are discussed. Using a sociological focus, norms about heterosexuality, gender identity, genitalia, and heteronormativity are critically examined in the context of deviance. The overarching goal of this chapter is to consider gender as a curiously complicated social construct embedded in norms that are so pervasive, their deconstruction often remains elusive. By examining gender through the lens of deviance, the intricacies involved in both normative and deviant conceptualizations of gender, sex, and sexuality are revealed.

Doing gender deviance? Doing gender and doing heteronormativity

As noted in chapter 1, West and Zimmerman's (1987) work shows us that norms governing gender are communicated in everyday interactions. For example, when we engage in behaviors and displays that are coded as expressions of masculinity and femininity, we are "doing gender." Furthermore, "doing gender is unavoidable" (West and Zimmerman 1987:137): it is an integral part of human social interaction. Because gender is very much a social construct, there is a great deal of work that goes into being a "gendered" person in society. That is to say that to be "gendered" is to participate in interactions that reflect a particular culture's norms about masculinity and femininity. In doing so, most individuals follow these generally accepted "rules of gender," or gender norms (Bornstein 1994:46):

- There are two and only two genders.
- One's gender is invariant.
- Genitals are the essential signs of gender.

- Any exceptions are not serious.
- There are no transfers from one gender to another except ceremonial ones.
- Everyone is one gender or the other.
- The M/F dichotomy is a "natural" one.
- Membership in one gender or the other is "natural".

Together, these rules enforce a system of "bigenderism"—a gender system that "does not permit or allow for variations, exceptions, and/or deviations from the norm" (Gilbert 2009:95).

In many cultures, such norms are often presumed to be "natural" whereby persons who are assigned to the male sex category at birth (typically based on the visual appearance of their biological genitalia) are to behave in masculine ways and persons who are assigned to the female sex category at birth are to behave in feminine ways. However, in the majority of social circumstances, presumptions are made about both gender and biological genitalia. For example, for the most part, biological genitalia are hidden from public view, yet we continue to see and do gender (even without seeing and exposing our biological genitals). In this way, gender attribution is based on *cultural genitals* whereby an individual's masculine and feminine performances and displays dictate gender and it is only a presumption that such behaviors "match" an individual's biological genitals (Kessler and McKenna 1978:153). This presumption is built on *cisnormativity*, or the assumption that it is "normal" to be cisgender—a label for individuals who have a match between the sex they were assigned at birth, their bodies, and their personal gender identity (Schilt and Westbrook 2009; Worthen 2013).

Cultural genitalia, then, is key to understanding gender norms, and conversely, gender deviance. In a normative performance of gender, for example, an individual's cultural genitalia "matches" his or her biological genitalia. A deviant performance of gender, then, could occur if an individual's cultural genitalia does not "match" his or her biological genitalia; however, this might only be recognized if we are made aware of a person's biological genitals. For example, "transgender people—people who live with a social gender identity that differs from the gender they were assigned at birth—can successfully do masculinity or femininity without having the genitalia that are presumed to follow from their outward appearance" (Schilt and Westbrook 2009:443). In this way, cultural genitalia and cisnormativity most often dominate the prescription of gender norms: those who behave as masculine are perceived as men and as having male biological genitalia while those who behave as feminine are perceived as women and as having female biological genitalia.

How can we understand deviant performances of gender? Deviant performances of gender occur when a "mismatch" between cultural genitalia and biological genitalia is revealed and this may be most heightened in sexual or sexualized encounters. In some extreme situations, the exposure of a deviant gender performance can result in fatal violence. Media accounts of murders of transgender people demonstrate extreme punishment for gender norm violations that can occur when perpetrators of violence feel "tricked", or "deceived" (Schilt and Westbrook 2009:454). For example, the New Jersey *Star-Ledger* reported the following 2010 incident:

> Maplewood, New Jersey police indicated that one Victoria Carmen White was murdered after Alshram Chambers, age 24, a man she met in a nightclub, discovered her transgender status. White, 28, a lingerie model, had sex reassignment surgery nine years earlier. Investigators believe Chambers shot White after learning she was a transgender female.
>
> *(Friedman 2011)*

This violent act demonstrates an extreme consequence of deviant gender performance. Victoria Carmen White identified as a woman, engaged in feminine gender performances, and had biological female genitalia (though not from birth), thus both her cultural and biological genitals were female/feminine/woman. Even so, the reveal of her transgender status enraged her murderer so much that he engaged in fatal violence. Because of her transgender status, conventional norms define Victoria Carmen White's gender performance as deviant; therefore, these norms dictated she deserved harsh punishment.

Condemnation for deviant gender performance is inextricably tied to the performance of sexuality. Thus, deviant gender performances also reflect deviant sexual performances. For example, *compulsory heterosexuality* whereby "heterosexuality is presumed as a 'sexual preference' of 'most women,' either implicitly or explicitly" (Rich 1980:633) shows us that "deviant" gender performances run against presumed norms about heterosexuality: those with biologically female genitals should behave and identify as "feminine," "woman," and "heterosexual." Furthermore, *heteronormativity* as "the view that institutionalized heterosexuality constitutes the standard for legitimate and prescriptive sociosexual arrangements" (Ingraham 1994:204) tells us that heterosexuality is a taken-for-granted norm that is presumed in social interactions. Specifically, heteronormativity is produced through the presumptions that heterosexuality, gender performance, and gender identity follow from biological genitalia, as shown in Figure 5.1. Together, these concepts illustrate that normative gender performances also reflect normative (hetero)sexual performances whereby "doing gender" is also "doing heteronormativity" (West and Zimmerman 1987; Schilt and Westbrook 2009).

Because of the multiple moving parts involved in "doing gender," "doing gender deviance" is linked to violations of heteronormativity (presumptions about gender performance, gender identity, and heterosexuality). This means a wide range of performances, identities, and sexualities can embody "doing gender deviance." For example, in line with the concept of heteronormativity, *heteromasculinity* describes a type of masculinity (gender performance) that is closely entwined with the stereotypes associated with men (gender identity) and heterosexuality. Men express their heteromasculinity to reinforce the fact that they are heterosexual (Worthen 2014). In many ways, the male competitive athlete embodies idealized heteromasculinity because stereotypes associated with the male competitive athlete (i.e., strong,

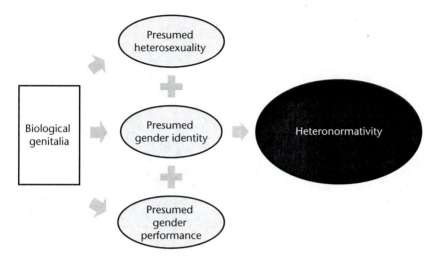

FIGURE 5.1   The relationships between heterosexuality, gender identity, genitalia, and heteronormativity

masculine, good-looking, and hyper-heterosexual) reinforce hegemonic heteromasculinity (Messner 1992; Anderson 2008). Thus, when those with male biological genitalia identify as heterosexual men and perform heteromasculinity, they maintain heteronormativity. By contrast, varying one or more of these elements results in "doing gender deviance."

Because sports in Western cultures are highly gendered activities, when men participate in "feminized" sports, they experience challenges to their heterosexuality, gender identity, and gender performance. The involvement of men in ballet can serve as a departure from heteromasculinity due to the feminized context of ballet and the association of male ballet dancers with homosexuality. As a result, male ballet dancers are often aware that they are "doing gender deviance" and they compensate through stigma management techniques. For example, research shows that in order to reinforce their heteromasculine identities and deemphasize their gender deviance, male ballet dancers engage in a "making it macho" strategy (Fisher 2007:46). This strategy plays up the heteromasculine characteristics of ballet (for instance, performances that seem especially athletically masculine and resolutely heterosexual) and downplays the feminine characteristics (such as the frilly costumes and classical music) as part of an attempt to make ballet acceptable for men in the Western world (Fisher 2007) as "America demands masculinity more than art" (Foulkes 2001:113). Others (Haltom and Worthen 2014) have found that heterosexual male ballet dancers use stigma management techniques to emphasize their heteromasculine identities and downplay their gender deviance (see Image 5.1). Specifically, some men highlight their heterosexual privilege through describing how their experiences in ballet allow them to have access to women, as one male ballet dancer noted, "look, I get to touch these women, probably more women

(a)   (b)

IMAGE 5.1 Two depictions of male ballet dancers

Male ballet dancers juxtaposed: the image on the left (a) depicts a male ballet dancer in a stereotypically feminized ballet costume while the image on the right (b) depicts a male ballet dancer in much more masculine attire in a heteromasculine pose with a female partner. ©Shutterstock, Filatova Liubov, ayakovlevcom

than these guys that were making fun of me or whatever get to touch in their life" (Haltom and Worthen 2014:767).

Other qualitative work with male cheerleaders has shown that access to women—that is, "compensatory hypermasculinity," the explicit assertion of hetero-sexuality in the face of a "discrediting" fact (Grindstaff and West 2006:511)—is a strategy that men use to de-stigmatize their involvement in feminized sports. For example, a male cheerleader in one study stated, "I'm hanging around with some of the hottest, in-shape young ladies that the school has to offer. I'm touching them and holding them in places you can only dream about" (Grindstaff and West 2006:511). Because of their participation in a feminized sport, these men violate the presumptions of heteronormativity by engaging in feminine gender performances. As a result, male ballet dancers and male cheerleaders experience challenges to both their gender identities as men and their heterosexualities. By engaging in stigma management techniques, these men are "doing heteronormativity" to compensate for "doing gender deviance."

Western intersectionalities: race, gender, and sexuality

Scholars who examine the nexus between gender performance, gender identity, and heterosexuality note that heteronormativity is embedded in racialized cultural systems (Bérubé 2001; Ferguson 2004; Carter 2007). That is to say that idealized gender performances are not only conceived within strict norms about gender, sex, and sexuality, but that such performances are also intimately connected to race and racial identity. Such a view reflects an intersectional approach to understanding how various identities and oppressions overlap and interlock to produce different lived experiences. Intersectionality, theorized by American Black feminist scholars such as Kimberlé Crenshaw (born in 1959) and Patricia Hill Collins (born in 1948), developed out of a critique of earlier feminist writings that presented a monolithic view of women and womanhood (Collins 1991; Crenshaw 1991). These scholars exposed the fact that previous work invoking discussions of "women" was almost always solely referring to the experiences, lives, and sisterhood of white women. In so doing, they called for a more inclusive scholarship that examines and theorizes how women's experiences are differentially and profoundly shaped by their race, ethnicity, sexuality, nationality, ability, age, status, and other markers of difference.

As an analytical tool, intersectionality elucidates the complexities within single-identity categories such as "woman" or "heterosexual." Inherent in its use is an understanding of power and how power differentially shapes individuals' identities, experiences, and lives. Since its inception, intersectionality has provided scholars with new venues for understanding the production of deviance as it relates to gender, sex, and sexuality. For example, scholars have been invited to "sharpen their analytical lenses, to grow sensitized to the discursive production of sexual identities, and to be mindful of the insidious force of heteronormativity as a fundamental organizing principle throughout the social order" (Green 2002:521). Intersectional scholarship holds the promise of providing a fundamentally more complex and comprehensive understanding of the myriad ways in which gender, sex, and sexuality are influenced by other forms of oppression, such as racial domination. Through intersectionality, we can understand that the lived experience of a poor, Latina bisexual woman will differ greatly from the experience of a middle-class, white lesbian woman. Such a view provides insight into how their "deviant" sexual identities are not read in the same manner, as whiteness is privileged across various categories of difference.

In the following section, an intersectional approach in understanding the ways in which gender and deviance are inextricably linked to ideas about race and sexuality is utilized. First, an historical view of racialized gender identities rooted in white, Western ideals of masculinity and femininity is provided. This bigenderist, racialized system sets the stage for a heteronormativity that is coded as white, while any deviance from gender and sexuality norms are coded as "nonwhite" (Ferguson 2004). Next, white heteronormativity is discussed as it relates to racialized sexualities for persons of color in the United States in tandem with impossible ideals of whiteness—ones that render nearly everyone "deviant." Lastly, the ways these ideals shape racialized sexualities and the social and political consequences of such interlocking systems of oppression are highlighted.

As we have seen, the Western bigenderist system provides strict prescriptions for masculinity and femininity and "gender rules" individuals must follow to properly accomplish such performances (Gilbert 2003, 2009). Taking an intersectional approach, we can understand the ways in which the roots of masculinity and femininity ideals in Western societies developed out of a racist system that favors whiteness. Thus, white masculinity and white femininity are "identity norms" that serve as the standards by which everyone's accomplishment of gender is measured. As described by Goffman, identity norms are shared beliefs about how individuals ought to be—ideals for individuals to attain—behaviorally and otherwise. Thus, identity norms are key to understanding normal and deviant identities. In explaining what he referred to as "hegemonic masculinity" he wrote:

> There is only one complete unblushing male in America: a young, married, white, urban, northern, heterosexual, Protestant, father, of college education, fully employed, of good complexion, weight and height, and a recent record of sports. Any male who fails to qualify in any one of these ways is likely to view himself—during moments at least—as unworthy, incomplete, and inferior.
> *(Goffman 1963:128)*

This hegemonic view of masculinity is articulated in a way that defines it as an ideal rooted in whiteness, one that must be defined against its difference from—primarily, women—but those constructed as "Other" (Connell 1987). That constructed Other is a racialized Other—one that is constructed "opposite" of white in order to give both constructed meaning through their difference (Hall 1991, 1997; Gasche 1994). To be clear, Otherness can only be constructed through its "representative of the normal," and vice versa (Ferguson 1998:68). As such, those exemplifying whiteness, masculinity, and heterosexuality ideals are signified as the "really, really normal subject" (Ward 2008a).

If white, heterosexual masculinity is the ideal by which everyone is measured, what does the "really, really normal subject" look like today? Masculinity scholars define masculinity as the ascendency to claim power over others (Connell 1995; Kimmel 2005). Others note it is deeply rooted in homophobia (Kimmel 1994, 2005, 2008) and is a repudiation of femininity (Schippers 2007) and gay masculinities (Connell and Messerschmidt 2005). This "guy code" for masculinity for young, white men in America encourages them to be "strong, tough, and violent" and "not back down to threats" (Kalish and Kimmel 2010:458). Thus, this code requires that young men demonstrate their masculinity and heterosexuality on a daily basis. If we understand white to be normative, then white masculinity demonstrates that masculinity is hierarchical on more than one plane (Pascoe 2007, Dean 2013). As such, white masculinity is foregrounded against women, people of color, and the non-heteronormative ("deviant Others"), in many white men's attempts to maintain privilege and material benefits of whiteness and masculinity within the United States today (Kimmel 2013).

Such theorizing on difference and deviance leads to questions about white masculinity's direct opposite – white femininity. Historically, white femininity has been understood by scholars as rooted in the "cult of true womanhood," or, the "cult of domesticity" (Welter 1966). Dating back to nineteenth-century America, the terms refer to a system among upper- and middle-class white women whose social value was determined through their successful achievements related to their roles restricted to the home and family. Proponents of the "cult of domesticity" were "primarily white and Protestant, with roots in New England and the Northeast" who promoted this ideal version of womanhood to everyone despite the fact that few could actually accomplish it (Lindley 1996:56). These proponents delineated an ideal value system for white women to uphold four "cardinal virtues" in their roles as wives and mothers: piety, purity, domesticity, and submissiveness (Welter 1966). Thus, these ideals dictated what it meant to be a woman—fostering a distinctive understanding of white women's feminine, domestic roles in comparison to white men's public spheres of social, political, and economic power. These boundaries set forth rules for white women's roles and participation within the cult of domesticity. White women were to be moral and asexual while at the same time dependent and submissive to their husbands. Interestingly, many of the women who espoused the values of the "cult of domesticity" were themselves deviants within the very system they promoted—as unmarried or widowed white women (Lindley 1996).

The cult of domesticity and its rigid gendered boundaries created additional deviants as well, given its class and race dimensions because "the cult of true womanhood was not only geared toward white women, but white women of means. This ideal of womanhood placed certain white women on a pedestal" (Patton 2000:30). That pedestal had no room for poor women, immigrants, or women of color, whose work outside of the home to provide for their families blocked them from leisure opportunities or domestic duties provided to white women who could adhere to the ideals of the cult of domesticity (Lindley 1996), thus marking broad swaths of women as deviant. Thus, Black women—like poor women, immigrants, and other women of color—were directly cast as deviant given the "cult of true womanhood" ideal that favored white women over anyone lacking the proper class or race privilege to be able to meet these ideals. This pedestal was a moral one that delineated notions about women's sexuality during slavery and the antebellum period that continue to shape troubling narratives about women's sexuality along lines of class and race that persist today. Furthermore:

> Antebellum ideas about women's sexuality, classifying all women as either good or evil, crossed lines of race and class but also stereotyped women based on race and class. While middle-class white women were placed on a moral pedestal and depicted as pure, physically fragile symbols of "good" womanhood, black and poor white women shared the stigma of "bad" womanhood.
>
> *(Yee 1992:41)*

White women's frailty stood in stark contrast to Black women's treatment during slavery, which served to masculinize Black women. For example, as American cultural critic bell hooks (born in 1958) describes, "the black female was exploited as a laborer in the fields, a worker in the domestic household, a breeder, and as an object of white male sexual assault" during slavery (hooks 1981:22). Thus, the ideals represented by the cult of white womanhood stood as antithetical to the unthinkably harsh realities of Black women's experiences of racism and sexism during slavery. The negative images and ideologies that served to buttress white men's degradation of Black women continue today in the form of negative stereotypes that depict Black women as hypersexual in contrast to white women's presumed purity. This juxtaposition laid the foundation for controlling images of gender, sex, and sexuality that persist today for women of color.

Gender norms within the United States are rooted in the history of "normality" in early twentieth-century America that outlined "appropriate" forms of sexuality (Nagel 2000; Carter 2007). Whiteness, heterosexuality, and monogamy were foundational for what it meant to be an "acceptable American" in the early 1900s. For example, instructional marital and sex education guides between 1880 and 1940 discursively set forth white superiority and marriage as what it meant to be civilized and "normal" at the time (Carter 2007). Collectively, these materials encouraged what was seen as "normal behavior" as critical to the perpetuation of the white race (Sargent 2009). From these discourses, we can see the underpinnings of racist dialogues that treated anyone but whites as "lower-order animals" whose sexuality was pathologized under this regime (Collins 1991). Indeed, "any divergences from the social norms of marriage, domesticity, and the nuclear family have brought serious accusations of savagery, pathology, and deviance upon Black people" (Richardson 2003:64). These early restrictions would serve to further distance people of color away from the ability to accomplish "normal" sexuality in myriad ways.

These normalizing discourses surrounding whiteness and sexuality were codified into law in order for ruling whites to lay claim to appropriate gender and sexuality practices. For example, in the post-slavery era, lawmakers worked overtime to ensure that the perceived "nonheteronormative" practices of slaves' intimate and familial arrangements (for instance, "abroad" marriages—where married partners lived on separate plantations, engaged in polyamory, and so on) would end with the formal end of slavery (Stevenson 1996). If newly emancipated slaves wished to become citizens, they would need to be monogamous and married to be considered for the full rights and benefits of American citizenship (Ferguson 2004). Around the same time, California lawmakers targeted South Asian and Chinese men for allegedly importing "unnatural sexual practices" such as sodomy, statutory rape, and vagrancy (Shah 2005). Such policing and punishment upheld clear distinctions between normality and degeneracy that were clearly racialized in targeting individuals whose race, ethnicity, or nationality did not meet the standards of whiteness and heterosexuality set forth for American citizenship. Whites in power designed antimiscegenation laws that prevented "race mixing" through romantic relationships or marriage, out of fear that whites would be marked as deviant by contagion. For example, until 1931, white women could lose their citizenship if they married a man of Asian descent (Haney-Lopez 1996). In a very real sense, nonwhites were deviantized: "in the racial logic of the state, immigrants and native-born nonwhites were racialized as the antithesis of heteropatriarchal ideals" (Ferguson 2005:55).

As such, anyone who failed to meet "a valorized sexuality between biologically born male-female couples who belong to the dominant racial-ethnic group and the middle class" was designated as deviant and undeserving of the rights of person-hood or citizenship (Luibhéid 2008:171). These restrictive ideologies and practices continue today in shaping ideas about sexuality, as we discuss further below.

Patricia Hill Collins' books *Black Feminist Thought* (1991) and *Black Sexual Politics* (2004) have been most influential in laying out a theoretical framework for under-standing racialized sexualities, particularly as they relate to African Americans. Collins demonstrates the ways whites have constructed Black heterosexuality as pathological or abnormal, providing a historical view of negative and controlling gendered images of Blackness that persist today. Such images include Black men as rapacious "Black brutes" and Black women as highly sexualized "jezebels," images that helped to justify whites' horrific treatment of African Americans during and after the formal end of slavery in the United States. These stereotypes continue today to denigrate Black love and sexuality, which she cogently argues is a form of "sexualized racism." For example, she cites Black women's contemporary popular cultural portrayals as "golddiggers" and "sexualized bitches" who like to "get a freak on" as updated forms of the jezebel (Collins 2004). Collins' work encourages us to think about the "sexual politics of Black womanhood" to understand the processes and mechanisms by which the sexualities of people of color are called into question, designated deviant, or pathologized as abnormal.

This sexualized racism targets members of other marginalized groups, in meas-uring their identities against white, heteronormative ideals that are impossible to achieve. Sexualized racism provides the ideological groundwork for homophobia and heterosexism and the gross stereotyping that portrays the gender and sexuality of people of color as deviant. Popular cultural images serve to denigrate the sexual-ity of women of color in troubling ways (Dirks and Mueller 2007). For example, women of Asian descent are slotted into the "dragon lady/lotus blossom" dichot-omy that fetishizes them as childlike, submissive, and eager to sexually please (Fung 2008). Such controlling images include Asian women's depictions as "China Dolls—servile, submissive, exotic, sexually available, mysterious, and guiding" or "Dragon Ladies—steely and as cold as Cruella de Vil, lacking in the emotions of or the neuroses of real women" (Prasso 2005:xiii). As such, women of Asian descent are routinely stereotyped as "exotic Orientals," while men of Asian descent are emas-culated through a "desexualized Zen asceticism" (Fung 2008). Such heteronorma-tive and racist stereotyping denies persons of Asian descent a full range of gender and sexual identities.

Similar to normalizing practices that erased LGBTQ persons historically, such restrictive portrayals and views of people of color continue to silence and erase "nonconforming" individuals (Moore 2011). For example, there is a fascinating his-tory of slaves (such as that of Clarissa Davis who "arrived in male attire") wearing drag to hide their gender identity but their Underground Railroad escapes to free-dom have yet to be told (Still 2005 [1872]). As some scholars have pointed out, people of color are afraid to even speak about the diversity of their experiences with gender, sex, and sexuality for fear of being further labeled deviant (Richardson 2003). Under this system, persons of color are caught in a double-bind: their gender and sexuality is coded as deviant because they do not meet white ideals of gender and heterosexuality, but also because they do not fulfill the denigrating and restrictive stereotypes for their racial or ethnic group. Thus, presenting as "normal" is a tool of resistance for fighting against sexism, racism, and homophobia. There are significant social and political consequences for a white-dominant system that casts the gender and sexuality of people of color as deviant, no matter their beliefs or practices.

Using white ideals for gender and sexuality has severe consequences for persons of color who are labeled as deviants. For example, hypersexual stereotypes of women of color may prevent them from being able to be properly viewed as "sympathetic victims" of sexual violence (Jimenez and Abreu 2003). This view of women of color, Native, or indigenous women may then translate to fewer legal protections for them against various forms of violence (Deer 2004; Chief Elk 2014). Additionally, the view that women of color are sexually promiscuous has led to deeply troubling public health policies that restrict the reproductive rights of women. Such examples include the forced sterilization and sterilization abuse of Chicana women (Davis 1982), Puerto Rican women (Rodriguez-Trias 1978; Lopez 1987), Native American women (Lawrence 2000; Torpy 2000), and African American women (Nsiah-Jefferson 1989; Roberts 1991) well into the twentieth century (Ekland-Olson 2011; Hansen and King 2013). Conveniently, these policies and practices have been tied up in eugenicist policies that deem children of color as deviant "undesirables" (Trombley 1988). In school settings, the sexuality of young men of color may be policed and disciplined more harshly, even when it is more liberatory than young white men's violent homophobia (Pascoe 2007). Together, these examples demonstrate the perniciousness of white-dominated gender and sexuality ideals and the treatment of persons of color as "deviants."

Whites' marginalization of people of color occurs even within gender and sexuality liberation movements against "deviant" designations (Ward 2008b). For example, "it's not just the media, both straight and gay, that robs gay men of color of equal representation, the gay 'community' is no less to blame. Gay organizations themselves promote and reinforce the 'whiteness of gay life'" (Han 2007:53). Such views translate to queer political organizing that "sells whiteness" at the expense of including people of color, or as "gay rights for gay whites" as it has been described (Hutchinson 2000). Racism within these movements (Yoshino 2006; Moore 2010) is compounded by the fact that much organizing for gay rights is fractured by biphobia and transphobia as well (Weiss 2008). In the same way that bigenderism restricts the freedom and rights of gender variant individuals, strict notions about what it means to be gay serve to marginalize people who do not fit neatly into "gay" or "lesbian" categories. Advocates argue that hypocritically marginalizing "deviants" within these liberation movements will hurt this cause immensely, as it has done in previous social movements (Weiss 2008).

Here, we have elucidated the historical underpinnings of the racialized nature of gender and sexuality norms within contemporary American society. White, Western ideals of masculinity and femininity are rooted in ideals of whiteness that prescribe and proscribe a specific set of gendered and heteronormative boundaries and requirements. From these examples, it is clear that white gender and sexuality ideals are impossible to achieve for most—if not all—individuals. This becomes particularly true if we consider whiteness as a discursive identity that is complicated by the intersections of gender, class, sexuality, ability, age, status, location, and temporality (Terry and Urla 1995). Such tenuous ideas of what is set forward as "normal" raises questions about how such forms of idealized whiteness become sites where domination and white supremacy reign in regimes of "normal." In other words, "how does this conflation of the categories white and black function to reproduce white privilege and domination in ways that white people 'colonize' the definition of normal?" (Haymes 1995:111).

Recall that the bigenderist system prescribes specific ways to accomplish how to be a man and how to be a woman. Those who fail to accomplish this specific set of criteria for ideal notions of masculinity and femininity—or those who reject this system—are considered deviants. This racialized system labels people of color, trans people, and gender variant individuals as outsiders (Gilbert 2009). Such a racialized, bigenderist system, with its tightly prescribed standards, ensures that nearly everyone—save certain privileged cisgender whites who practice hypermasculinity or hyperfemininity—do not fit these impossible ideals. Thus, this system ensures that nearly everyone is deviant. Yet, individuals whose gender, racial, ethnic, or sexual identities place them even further outside of these highly rigid categories of "normal" are more likely to suffer punishment, ridicule, or attack. Consequently, "bigenderism, by codifying the distinction between male and female, man and woman, masculine and feminine, creates a virulently sexist, heterosexist, and transphobic culture just because of the valuation of the sexes" (Gilbert 2009:103). If we are all deviant in such a rigid system and the stakes are so high, how can we imagine a system wherein anyone is considered "gender normal" then?

Breaking the binaries through gender deviance

A great deal of scholarship demonstrates gender deviance as violations of binaries whereby there are two categories of gender (man and woman), two categories of sex (male and female), and two categories of gender performance (masculine and feminine). Therefore "gender normals" are not only cisgender (Garfinkel 1967), but also, "gender normals" perform gender in ways that reflect their cisgender status. Thus, *gender normals* are masculine men with male genitals and feminine women with female genitals. However, theorists caution against such binary divisions and promote the deconstruction of gender, sex, and gender performance (Butler 1990, 2004; Lorber 1996). If we deconstruct such binaries, both "gender deviants" and "gender normals" are revealed as a part of the same social fabric.

One such way to challenge gender binaries is to consider intersexuality. Judith Butler (born in 1956) situates her deconstruction of the sex and gender binary with the proclamation that the "sex = biological and gender = sociological" argument is inherently flawed (Butler 1990, 2004). In fact, Butler believes that what Western cultures have conceived of as "sex" has really been "gender all along" (Kitzinger 1999:498). Every baby is born with somewhat ambiguous genitalia—no two genitals are alike—and it is up to medical professionals to dictate "male" and "female" designations based on socially constructed conceptualizations of "sex" identity. Similarly, the designation of "intersex identity" is also a reflection of social constructs [although Western medical culture would lead us to erroneously believe that "hermaphroditism" is an easily defined birth defect based on the visual appearance of the genitals as phallic—or not (Dreger 2000)]. In this way, our "biological" definitions of both sex and gender are socially constructed, and thus, the number of categories that comprise sex and gender are dependent on sociocultural beliefs.

Gender deviants, then, fall outside of socially constructed norms about sex, gender, and gender performance but gender deviance may not always represent a "binary mismatch." For example, using socially situated Western cultural concepts, Figure 5.2 depicts numerous labels of sexual identity, gender performance, gender identity, and sex identity moving beyond binary conceptualizations. From this

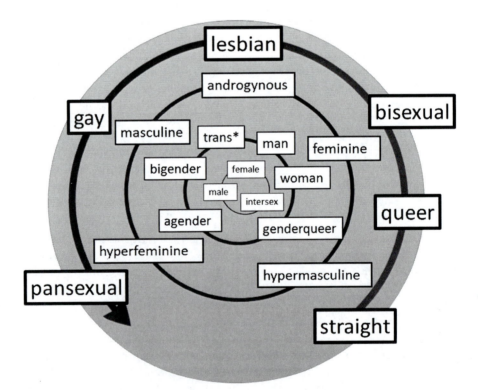

FIGURE 5.2 Multiple conceptualizations of sexual identity, gender performance, gender identity, and sex identity

Image used with permission from Kasey Catlett.

representation, it is clear that there are various ways that an individual may identify, and thus, there are multiple ways an individual can embody gender deviance. However, even though many conceptualizations of sex, gender, and gender performance exist outside of binaries, breaking the binaries is in and of itself, gender deviance.

Individuals who violate the binaries have been defined (and sometimes identify themselves) in various ways such as gender misfits, gender benders, genderqueer, pangender, agender, and gender fluid to name a few. Beyond identity labels, breaking the gender binaries can exemplify identity politics, that is to say that gender deviance can operate as a political decision. *Genderfuck* is an identity politics movement based on gender performance that actively disrupts the gender binaries. As explained in "Genderfuck and Its Delights," one cultural critic stated:

> I want to criticize and poke fun at the roles of women and of men too. I want to try and show how not-normal I can be. I want to ridicule and destroy the whole cosmology of restrictive sex roles and sexual identification.
>
> *(Lonc 1974/1991)*

There are highly visible media instances of performing genderfuck seen in cinema (e.g., Dr. Frank-N-Furter from the movie, *Rocky Horror Picture Show*) and in the music industry (e.g., Boy George, Prince, Marilyn Manson).

Beyond this, drag kings and drag queens embody genderfuck and gender deviance in their performances (see Image 5.2). Drag kings and queens challenge the presumptions that gender is "natural" by revealing that gender is constructed through performance (Butler 1993) and for some, drag performance can have highly politicized motives (Munoz 1999; Shapiro 2007; Rupp *et al.* 2010). For example, the 801 Girls, a drag queen troupe of self-identified gay men in Key West, Florida, challenge gender, sex, and sexual identity categories in their drag performances (Rupp and Taylor 2003). Drag king group Disposable Boy Toys, a political feminist collective in Santa Barbara, California, shows us that drag can "unbraid gender and sex," and "destabilize hegemonic gender, sex, and sexuality" (Shapiro 2007:258, 267). Both the 801 girls and Disposable Boy Toys contest binary gender and heteronormativity through drag (Rupp *et al.* 2010). In this way, both drag kings and queens deconstruct gender on stage through performances of gender deviance. In doing so, their political motivations are revealed: both drag troupes impact the ways their audiences think about sex, gender, and sexuality, breaking the gender binaries through gender deviance.

Beyond strategic performances of gender that break the binaries, other cultures have relatively fixed identities outside of the binary system. For example, in South Asia, *Hijras*, who are typically born and identified as male based on the appearance of their genitalia, form the third gender category (Monro 2007). As members of the third gender category deemed to have mystical powers, Hijras are both revered and marginalized. Their existence challenges the binary system but because of their typically low social caste, their gender is highlighted as deviant (Monro 2007).

IMAGE 5.2 Drag attire

Eric H. in drag queen performance attire (a) and in business attire (b).

In North American Native American communities, *two-spirit people* occupy a third gender category as well. They are sometimes described as simultaneously embodying both a masculine and a feminine spirit. Two-spirit people often receive a spiritual calling to transform into the third gender category; as two-spirits, their status is typically associated with mystical powers and fortune-telling abilities. However, due to the enforcement of Western cultural ideas that most North American Native American communities have experienced, the two-spirit people have experienced oppression (Jacobs *et al.* 1997). Thus, it is clear that breaking the binaries is a form of gender deviance that is culturally dependent.

Concluding remarks: gender normals?

On February 13, 2014, the social networking site Facebook rolled out a new feature for users who navigate the site in English—56 "custom" gender options such as "androgynous," "gender variant," and "non-binary," for users who choose to identify as something other than one of the two the previously restrictive responses of "male" or "female" (see Table 5.1 for a complete list). Users were also given the new options of not responding or keeping their gender private as well as selecting between three pronouns: "he/him," "she/her," or "they/their" (Goldman 2014). While the move was hailed by LGBTQ advocates who assisted with the development of the site's new expansive list of gender identities, others were not as excited. As one Fox News reporter mocked, but "what if you identify as a pine cone?" (Maza 2014). Such dismissiveness is reflective of other points in history where

TABLE 5.1 Gender, relationship, and "interested in" options for English platform Facebook users in 2015

Gender options ★ *(56)*

Agender	Cisgender Male	Male to Female	Transgender Male
Androgyne	Cisgender Man	MtF	Transgender Man
Androgynous	Cisgender Woman	Neither	Transgender Person
Bigender	Female to Male	Neutrois	Transgender Woman
Cis	FtM	Non-binary	Transmasculine
Cisgender	Gender Fluid	Other	Transsexual
Cis Female	Gender Nonconforming	Pangender	Transsexual Female
Cis Male	Gender Questioning	Trans	Transsexual Male
Cis Man	Gender Variant	Trans★	Transsexual Man
Cis Woman	Genderqueer	Trans Female	Transsexual Person
Cisgender Female	Intersex	Trans★ Female	Transsexual Woman
		Trans Male	Two-Spirit
		Trans★ Male	
		Trans Man	
		Trans★ Man	
		Trans Person	
		Trans★ Person	
		Trans Woman	
		Trans★ Woman	
		Transfeminine	
		Transgender	
		Transgender Female	

Relationship options (12)

Divorced	In a domestic partnership	It's complicated	Separated
Engaged	In a relationship	Married	Single
In a civil union	In an open relationship	Not specified	Widowed

"Interested in" options (2)

Women	Men

★ In 2014, Facebook revealed 56 gender options. In 2015, Facebook launched a new platform that allowed users to write in up to ten custom gender terms on personal profiles. Adapted from Cohen (2014), Goldman (2014), and Kellaway (2015).

challenges to gender systems have been made. In one action, Facebook effectively invited close to 160 million American members, 1.23 billion worldwide members, and countless non-members viewing the wide-range of news coverage about this topic to rethink a bigenderist system that insists upon two rigid categories. Such a move begins to normalize "gender deviants," and both dismantles such a restrictive means of categorizing identity and forces recognition that a bigenderist system simply does not account for everyone. As the reader may be quick to point out after perusing this chapter, even a 50-plus gender system may not reflect the vast diversity of how individuals choose to identify their gender. In 2015, Facebook responded to these concerns and now allows users to write in up to ten custom gender terms on their personal profiles to further describe themselves (Kellaway 2015). In addition, Facebook now has 12 options to describe relationship statuses (Cohen 2014) but only two options ("men" or "women") to describe who you are interested in, as of 2015 (see Table 5.1). As a result, this social media giant has offered an ever-evolving list of self-description options for its users but these options remain inadequate in capturing the complexity of gender and sexuality diversity evident in today's cultural climate. In addition, the fact that these categories are only available to users who navigate the site in English limits the global impact of these innovations.

Throughout this chapter, we have shown that such challenges to our notions of "deviancy" reveal cracks in the system and beg questions about the legitimacy of the category of "gender deviants." There are a variety of ways to conceptualize gender deviance. However, most discussions of deviance have operated in tandem with a discussion of gender normals. Thus, "gender normals" represent an ideal type, and consequently, an impossible goal to achieve. In a sense, we are all stigmatized, although in varying degrees, for our inability to adhere to the requirements of being "gender normals," and thus, we are all gender deviants. As Goffman proposes:

> The stigma involves not so much a set of concrete individuals who can be separated into two piles: the stigmatized and the normal, as a pervasive two-role social process in which every individual participates in both roles at least in some connections and in some phases in life. The normal and the stigmatized are not persons but rather perspectives.
>
> *(Goffman 1963:138)*

Since the time of Goffman's writing, we have witnessed remarkable shifts in scholarly and popular thinking on the processes of creating gender normals and gender deviants. That categorizing has troubled advocates who argue that the creation and maintenance of gender deviants comes at a great cost to all of us. To break free of such a divisive and unnecessary process, we join advocates in the call to engage in the work of normalizing such "deviance." In closing:

> A non-genderist world is not around the corner. In the meantime, anything that can be done to reduce the tyranny of bigenderism is a forward move.

Anything that aids in defeating bigenderism is progressive and liberating. Those activities and creeds that work toward this end include feminism, transgenderism, homosexuality, and heterosexuality devoid of heterosexism, all of which violate gender rules.

(Gilbert 2009:109)

In performing the everyday praxis of resistance to bigenderism, we can imagine new gender and sexuality systems that work to eliminate sexism, heterosexism, homophobia, and transphobia.

Note

1   The majority of this chapter has been reproduced with permission: Worthen, Meredith G. F. and Danielle Dirks. 2015. "Gender and Deviance." Pp. 277–97 in *Handbook of Deviance*, edited by Erich Goode. Hoboken, NJ: Wiley.

References

Anderson, Eric. 2008. "'Being Masculine is Not about Who You Sleep with . . . :' Heterosexual Athletes Contesting Masculinity and the One-time Rule of Homosexuality." *Sex Roles* 58(1/2):104–15.

Beatie, Thomas. 2009. *Labor of Love: The Story of One Man's Extraordinary Pregnancy*. Berkeley, CA: Seal Press.

Bérubé, Allan. 2001. "How Gay Stays White and What Kind of White it Stays." Pp. 234–65 in *The Making and Unmaking of Whiteness*, edited by Birgit B. Rasmussen, Irene Nexica, Eric Klinenberg, and Matt Wray. Durham, NC: Duke University Press.

Bornstein, Kate. 1994. *Gender Outlaw: On Men, Women, and the Rest of Us*. New York, NY: Routledge.

Butler, Judith. 1990. *Gender Trouble: Feminism and the Subversion of Identity*. New York, NY: Routledge.

Butler, Judith. 1993. *Bodies that Matter: On the Discursive Limits of Sex*. New York, NY: Routledge.

Butler, Judith. 2004. *Undoing Gender*. New York, NY: Routledge.

Carter, Julian B. 2007. *The Heart of Whiteness: Normal Sexuality and Race in America, 1880–1940*. Durham, NC: Duke University Press.

Chief Elk, Lauren. 2014, February 3. "There is No 'We': V-Day, Indigenous Women and the Myth of Shared Gender Oppression." *Model View Culture*. Retrieved from: http://modelviewculture.com/pieces/there-is-no-we-v-day-indigenous-women-and-the-myth-of-shared-gender-oppression

Cohen, David. 2014, March 3. "More Relationship Status Options Added To Core Audiences In Facebook's Ads Manager, Power Editor." Retrieved from: http://www.adweek.com/socialtimes/relationship-status-core-audiences/432928

Collins, Patricia Hill. 1991. *Black Feminist Thought: Knowledge, Consciousness, and the Politics of Empowerment*. New York, NY: Routledge.

Collins, Patricia Hill. 2004. *Black Sexual Politics*. New York, NY: Routledge.

Connell, R.W. 1987. *Gender and Power*. Sydney: Allen and Unwin.

Connell, R.W. 1995. *Masculinities*. Cambridge: Polity Press.

Connell, R.W. and James W. Messerschmidt. 2005. "Hegemonic Masculinity: Rethinking the Concept." *Gender & Society* 19(6):829–59.

Crenshaw, Kimberle. 1991. "Mapping the Margins: Intersectionality, Identity Politics, and Violence against Women of Color." *Stanford Law Review* 43(6):1241–99.

Davis, Angela. 1982. *Women, Race, and Class.* New York, NY: Random House.

Dean, James Joseph. 2013. "Heterosexual Masculinities, Anti-Homophobias, and Shifts in Hegemonic Masculinity: The Identity Practices of Black and White Heterosexual Men." *The Sociological Quarterly* 54(4):534–60.

Deer, Sarah. 2004. "Toward an Indigenous Jurisprudence of Rape." *Kansas Journal of Law and Public Policy* 14(1):121–54.

Dirks, Danielle and Jennifer C. Mueller. 2007. "Racism and Popular Culture." Pp. 115–29 in *Handbook of the Sociology of Racial and Ethnic Relations*, edited by Joe R. Feagin and Hernan Vera. New York, NY: Springer.

Dreger, Alice Domurat. 2000. *Hermaphrodites and the Medical Invention of Sex.* Cambridge, MA: Harvard University Press.

Ekland-Olson, Sheldon. 2011. *Who Lives, Who Dies, Who Decides? Abortion, Neonatal Care, Assisted Dying, Capital Punishment.* New York, NY: Routledge.

Ferguson, Roderick A. 1998. *Representing "Race": Ideology, Identity and the Media.* London: Arnold.

Ferguson, Roderick A. 2004. *Aberrations in Black: Toward a Queer of Color Critique.* Minneapolis, MN: University of Minnesota Press.

Ferguson, Roderick A. 2005. "Race-ing Homonormativity: Citizenship, Sociology, and Gay Identity." Pp. 21–51 in *Black Queer Sociology: A Critical Anthology*, edited by E. Patrick Johnson and Mae G. Henderson. Durham, NC: Duke University Press.

Fisher, Jennifer. 2007. "Make it Maverick: Rethinking the 'Make it Macho' Strategy for Men in Ballet." *Dance Chronicle* 30(1):45–66.

Foulkes, Julia L. 2001. "Dance is for American Men: Ted Shawn and the Intersection of Gender, Sexuality, and Nationalism in the 1930s." Pp. 113–46 in *Dancing Desires: Choreographing Sexualities On and Off the Stage*, edited by Jane Desmond. Madison, WI: University of Wisconsin Press.

Friedman, Alexi. 2011, June 20. "Newark Man Indicted on Murder and Intimidation of Transgender Woman." *The Star-Ledger.* Retrieved from: http://www.nj.com/news/ index.ssf/2011/06/newark_man_indicted_on_murder.html

Fung, Richard. 2008. "Looking for My Penis: The Eroticized Asian in Gay Video Porn." Pp. 235–53 in *A Companion to Asian American Studies*, edited by Kent Ono. New York, NY: John Wiley.

Gasche, Rodolphe. 1994. *Inventions of Difference: On Jacques Derrida.* Cambridge, MA: Harvard University Press.

Garfinkel, Harold. 1967. *Studies in Ethnomethodology.* Englewood Cliffs, NJ: Prentice Hall.

Gilbert, Miqqi A. 2003. "Bigenderism." *Transgender Tapestry* 102(1):16–17.

Gilbert, Miqqi A. 2009. "Defeating Bigenderism: Changing Gender Assumptions in the Twenty-first Century." *Hypatia* 24(3):93–112.

Glenday, Craig. 2010. *Guinness World Records.* New York, NY: Random House.

Goffman, Erving. 1963. *Stigma: Notes on the Management of Spoiled Identity.* Englewood Cliffs, NJ: Prentice-Hall.

Goldman, Russell. 2014, February 13. "Here's a List of 58 Gender Options for Facebook Users." Retrieved from: http://abcnews.go.com/blogs/headlines/2014/02/heres-a-list-of-58-gender-options-for-facebook-users/

Green, Adak I. 2002. "Gay but Not Queer: Toward a Post-Queer Study of Sexuality." *Theory and Society* 31(4):521–45.

Grindstaff, Laura and Emily West. 2006. "Cheerleading and the Gendered Politics of Sport." *Social Problems* 53(4):500–18.

Hall, Stuart. 1991. "Ethnicity: Identity and Difference." *Radical America* 23(4):9–20.

Hall, Stuart, editor. 1997. *Representation: Cultural Representations and Signifying Practices* (Vol. 2). Thousand Oaks, CA: Sage.

Haltom, Trenton and Meredith G. F. Worthen. 2014. "Male Ballet Dancers and Hetero-masculinity." *Journal of College Student Development* 55(8): 757–78.

Han, Chong-suk. 2007. "'They Don't Want to Cruise Your Type': Gay Men of Color and the Racial Politics of Exclusion." *Social Identities* 13(1):51–67.

Haney-Lopez, Ian. 1996. *White by Law: The Legal Construction of Race*. New York, NY: NYU Press.

Hansen, Randall, and Desmond King. 2013. *Sterilized by the State: Eugenics, Race, and the Population Scare in the Twentieth-Century North America*. Cambridge, UK: Cambridge University Press.

Haymes, Stephen N. 1995. "White Culture and the Politics of Racial Difference." Pp. 105–28 in *Multicultural Education, Critical Pedagogy, and the Politics of Difference*, edited by Christine E. Sleeter and Peter McLaren. Albany, NY: SUNY Press.

hooks, bell. 1981. *Ain't I a Woman: Black Women and Feminism* (Vol. 3). Boston, MA: South End Press.

Hutchinson, Darren L. 2000. "Gay Rights for Gay Whites: Race, Sexual Identity, and Equal Protection Discourse." *Cornell Law Review* 85(5):1358–91.

Ingraham, Chrys. 1994. "The Heterosexual Imaginary: Feminist Sociology and Theories of Gender." *Sociological Theory* 12(2):203–19.

Jacobs, Sue-Ellen, Wesley Thomas, and Sabine Lang. 1997. *Two-spirit People: Native American Gender Identity, Sexuality, and Spirituality*. Urbana, IL: University of Illinois.

Jimenez, Jorge A. and José M. Abreu. 2003. "Race and Sex Effects on Attitudinal Perceptions of Acquaintance Rape." *Journal of Counseling Psychology* 50(2):252–6.

Kalish, Rachel and Michael Kimmel. 2010. "Suicide by Mass Murder: Masculinity, Aggrieved Entitlement, and Rampage School Shootings." *Health Sociology Review* 19(4):451–64.

Kellaway, Mitch. 2015, February 27. "Facebook Now Allows Users to Define Custom Gender." Retrieved from: http://www.advocate.com/politics/transgender/2015/02/27/facebook-now-allows-users-define-custom-gender

Kessler, Suzanne and Wendy McKenna. 1978. *Gender: An Ethnomethodological Approach*. Chicago, IL: University of Chicago Press.

Kimmel, Michael. 1994. "Masculinity as Homophobia: Fear, Shame and Silence in the Construction of Gender Identity." Pp. 119–41 in *Theorizing Masculinities*, edited by Harry Brod and Michael Kaufman. Thousand Oaks, CA: Sage Publications.

Kimmel, Michael. 2005. *The Gender of Desire*. Albany, NY: SUNY Press.

Kimmel, Michael. 2008. *Guyland*. New York, NY: HarperCollins.

Kimmel, Michael. 2013. *Angry White Men: American Masculinity at the End of an Era*. New York, NY: Nation Books.

Kitzinger, Celia. 1999. "Intersexuality: Deconstructing the Sex/Gender Binary." *Feminism & Psychology* 9(4):493–8.

Lawrence, Jane. 2000. "The Indian Health Service and the Sterilization of Native American Women." *The American Indian Quarterly* 24(3):400–19.

Lindley, Susan Hill. 1996. *You Have Stept Out of Your Place: A History of Women and Religion in America*. Louisville, KY: Westminster John Knox Press.

Lonc, Christopher. 1974/1991. "Genderfuck and Its Delights." Pp. 223–336 in *Gay Roots: Twenty Years of Gay Sunshine*, edited by Winston Leyland. San Francisco, CA: Gay Sunshine Press.

Lopez, Iris. 1987. "Sterilization among Puerto Rican Women in New York City: Public Policy and Social Constraints." Pp. 269–91 in *Cities of the United States: Studies in Urban Anthropology*, edited by Leith Mullings. New York, NY: Columbia University Press.

Lorber, Judith. 1996. "Beyond the Binaries: Depolarizing the Categories of Sex, Sexuality, and Gender." *Sociological Inquiry* 66(2):143–60.

Luibhéid, Eithne. 2008. "Queer/Migration: An Unruly Body of Scholarship." *GLQ: A Journal of Lesbian and Gay Studies* 14(2):169–90.

Maza, Carlos. 2014, February 14. "Fox News Isn't Comfortable with these New Facebook Gender Options." *Media Matters*. Retrieved from: http://mediamatters.org/blog/2014/02/14/fox-news-isnt-comfortable-with-these-new-facebo/198057

Messner, Michael. 1992. *Power at Play: Sports and the Problem of Masculinity*. Boston, MA: Beacon.

Monro, Surya. 2007. "Transmuting Gender Binaries: the Theoretical Challenge" *Sociological Research Online* 12(1): doi:10.5153/sro.1514.

Moore, Mignon. 2010. "Articulating a Politics of (Multiple) Identities: LGBT Sexuality and Inclusion in Black Community Life." *Du Bois Review* 7(2):1–20.

Moore, Mignon. 2011. *Invisible Families: Gay Identities, Relationships, and Motherhood among Black Women*. Berkeley, CA: University of California Press.

Munoz, José Esteban. 1999. *Disidentifications: Queers of Color and the Performance of Politics*. Minneapolis, MN: University of Minnesota Press.

Nagel, Joane. 2000. "Ethnicity and Sexuality." *Annual Review of Sociology* 26(1):107–33.

Nsiah-Jefferson, Laurie. 1989. "Reproductive Laws, Women of Color, and Low-income Women." Pp. 23–67 in *Reproductive Laws for the 1990s*, edited by Sherrill Cohen and Nadine Taub. Clifton, NJ: Humana Press.

Pascoe, C.J. 2007. *Dude, You're a Fag: Masculinity and Sexuality in High School*. Berkeley, CA: University of California Press.

Patton, Venetria. 2000. *Women in Chains: The Legacy of Slavery in Black Women's Fiction*. Albany, NY: SUNY Press.

Prasso, Sheridan. 2005. *The Asian Mystique: Dragon Ladies, Geisha Girls, and Our Fantasies of the Exotic Orient*. New York, NY: PublicAffairs.

Rich, Adrienne. 1980. "Compulsory Heterosexuality and Lesbian Existence." *Signs* 5(4):631–60.

Richardson, Mattie Udora. 2003. "No More Secrets, No More Lies: African American History and Compulsory Heterosexuality." *Journal of Women's History* 15(3):63–76.

Roberts, Dorothy. 1991. "Punishing Drug Addicts Who Have Babies: Women of Color, Equality, and the Right to Privacy." *Harvard Law Review* 104(7):1419–81.

Rodriguez-Trias, Helen. 1978. "Sterilization Abuse." *Women & Health* 3(3):10–15.

Rupp, Leila J. and Verta Taylor. 2003. *Drag Queens at the 801 Cabaret*. Chicago, IL: University of Chicago Press.

Rupp, Leila J., Verta Taylor, and Eve Shapiro. 2010. "Drag Queens and Drag Kings: The Difference Gender Makes." *Sexualities* 13(3):275–94.

Sargent, Andrew. 2009. "*The Heart of Whiteness: Normal Sexuality and Race in America, 1880–1940* (review)." *College Literature* 36(2):152–5.

Schilt, Kristen, and Laurel Westbrook. 2009. "Doing Gender, Doing Heteronormativity: 'Gender Normals', Transgender People, and the Social Maintenance of Heterosexuality." *Gender & Society* 23(4):440–64.

Schippers, Mimi. 2007. "Recovering the Feminine Other: Masculinity, Femininity, and Gender Hegemony." *Theory and Society* 36(1):85–102.

Shah, Nayan. 2005. "Between 'Oriental Depravity' and 'Natural Degenerates': Spatial Borderlands and the Making of Ordinary Americans." *American Quarterly* 57(3): 703–25.

Shapiro, Eve. 2007. "Drag Kinging and the Transformation of Gender Identities." *Gender & Society* 21(2):250–71.

Seidman, Steven. 1994. "Queer-ing Sociology, Sociologizing Queer Theory: An Introduction." *Sociological Theory* 12(2):166–77.

Stein, Arlene and Ken Plummer. 1994. "'I Can't Even Think Straight' 'Queer' Theory and the Missing Revolution in Sociology." *Sociological Theory* 12(2):178–87.

Stevenson, Brenda. 1996. *Life in Black and White: Family and Community in the Slave South.* New York, NY: Oxford University Press.

Still, William. 2005 [1872]. *The Underground Rail Road.* Philadelphia, PA: Porter & Coates. Retrieved from: http://www.gutenberg.org/files/15263/15263-h/15263-h.htm

Terry, Jennifer and Jacqueline Urla, editors. 1995. *Deviant Bodies: Critical Perspectives on Difference in Science and Popular Culture.* Bloomington, IN: Indiana University Press.

Trombley, Stephen. 1988. *The Right to Reproduce: A History of Coercive Sterilization.* London: Weidenfeld & Nicholson.

Torpy, Sally J. 2000. "Native American Women and Coerced Sterilization: On the Trail of Tears in the 1970s." *American Indian Culture and Research Journal* 24(2):1–22.

Wade, Lisa. 2008, April 4. "Thomas Beatie, the Pregnant Man, in the Public Sphere." *Sociological Images.* Retrieved from: http://thesocietypages.org/socimages/2008/04/04/thomas-beatie-the-pregnant-man-in-the-public-sphere/

Ward, Jane. 2008a. "Dude-Sex: White Masculinities and Authentic Heterosexuality Among Dudes Who Have Sex With Dudes." *Sexualities* 11(4):414–34.

Ward, Jane. 2008b. "White Normativity: Cultural Dimensions of Whiteness in a Racially Diverse LGBT Organization." *Sociological Perspectives* 51(3):563–86.

Weiss, Jillian Todd. 2008. "The Archaeology of Biphobia and Transphobia within the US Gay and Lesbian Community." *Journal of Bisexuality* 3(3–4):25–55.

Welter, Barbara. 1966. "The Cult of True Womanhood: 1820–1860." *American Quarterly* 18(2):151–74.

West, Candace and Don H. Zimmerman. 1987. "Doing Gender." *Gender & Society* 1(2):125–51.

Worthen, Meredith G. F. 2013. "An Argument for Separate Analyses of Attitudes toward Lesbian, Gay, Bisexual Men, Bisexual Women, MtF and FtM Transgender Individuals." *Sex Roles: A Journal of Research* 68(11/12):703–23.

Worthen, Meredith G. F. 2014. "Blaming the Jocks and the Greeks? Identifying the Underlying Constructs of Collegiate Athletes' and Fraternity/Sorority Members' Attitudes toward LGBT Individuals." *Journal of College Student Development* 55(2):168–95.

Yee, Shirley J. 1992. *Black Women Abolitionists: A Study in Activism, 1828–1860.* Knoxville, TN: University of Tennessee Press.

Yoshino, Kenji. 2006. *Covering: The Hidden Assault on Our Civil Rights.* New York, NY: Random House.

UNIT II
SEXUAL DEVIANCE

Unit II introduction

So far we have learned that deviance is a complex culturally embedded concept that is temporally variant. We have also learned that to best understand sexual deviance, which of course is the goal of this textbook, we must also understand the relationships between social power, gender, sex, and sexuality. By investigating theoretical stances on deviance and gender in the first part of this textbook, we have built a foundation for understanding the sociology of deviance and sexuality. Now it is time to clearly identify what is meant by sexual deviance with both a modern and historical lens. The overarching purpose of the second unit of this textbook is to provide you with a deep understanding of sexual deviance through sociological and historical frameworks that consider the cultural and temporal significance of defining this complex subject. In doing so, the myriad nuances entrenched within sexual deviance are uncovered and explored.

Chapter 6 builds on previous discussions of "defining deviance" (which were particularly described in chapter 2) by offering various ways to understand sexual deviance. Specifically, "statistical" sexual normalcy and deviance are discussed using data from the World Health Organization, the Global Study of Sexual Attitudes and Behaviors, and nationally representative samples. Next, "cultural" sexual normalcy and deviance are evaluated based on data investigating cultural perceptions and understandings of relationships and sexual behaviors. Using the National Health and Social Life Survey, attitudes and preferences toward sexual behaviors, orgasm, and sexual satisfaction are highlighted. A critical discussion of what types of sexual behaviors are regarded as "sex" is offered in the context of the 1998 Clinton-Lewinsky oral sex scandal in the United States. To clarify sexual deviance, American serial killer, rapist, and necrophiliac, Ted Bundy, is offered as an exemplar. Finally, sexual deviance is defined.

Chapter 7 offers a discussion of historical variance of perspectives on four topics (i) sexual imagery, (ii) the sale of sex, (iii) same-sex sexual behavior, and (iv) sexual pleasure. Starting with early humans, the evolution of sexual deviance is highlighted through ancient civilizations in Egypt, China, India, Greece, and Italy up to Western cultures in the Middle Ages, the Renaissance, and the Victorian Era. Modern-day perspectives about sexual deviance are also provided in a cultural context. From Paleolithic cave art, to chastity belts, to the World Wide Web, historical examples illustrate the complexity behind contemporary perspectives about sex. Overall, this chapter offers an in-depth exploration of aspects about sexuality that have been considered both normal and deviant throughout history. By using a lens that is both historically and culturally sensitive, the evolution of sexual deviance is illuminated and readers can learn how to situate their own perspectives about these issues.

Chapter 8 provides an investigation into the ways sexual deviance is defined during adolescence. The chapter begins by exploring what adolescent sexuality is and what sexual behaviors adolescents participate in while also looking at how adolescents negotiate the dominant teen tropes of virginity and abstinence. Next, it examines how adolescents are taught about sexuality from school, parents, and peers. Last, because not all cultures hold the same attitudes, we will learn how the Netherlands compares to the United States in their treatment of adolescent sexuality. By looking at the difference in normative expectations about teen sex versus their actual behavior, the nature of deviance itself is called into question.

Overall, the second unit of this textbook provides an in-depth dialogue to its readers about the sociological constructions of sexual deviance with a critical focus on contemporary and historical conceptualizations of this concept. In addition, adolescent sexual deviance is explored as it relates to norms about virginity and abstinence. Through examples of variations in sexual norms throughout history, the temporal significance of sexual deviance is highlighted. Furthermore, through the juxtaposition of modern-day norms with historical illustrations, a framework for understanding sexual deviance is built. By incorporating a perspective that recognizes the historical, global, and age-related variance of sexual deviance, this unit continues to dissect the underpinnings of sexual norms and the complexities of sexual deviance.

6
DEFINING SEXUAL DEVIANCE

"Whatever is forbidden is eroticized."
Valerie Steele, Fetish: Fashion, Sex, and Power *(1996:195)*

Thus far, we have discussed many socially constructed concepts including gender, sexuality, crime, and deviance, to name a few. We have also emphasized their ever-changing cultural and temporal variance and the importance of social power in their construction. In doing so, we have built a framework for understanding sexual deviance. A close reader may wonder why we have not yet fully discussed a definition of sexual deviance until now, especially because "sexual deviance" is in the title of this textbook. This is because we must first understand the complexities within gender, sexuality, crime, and deviance in order to do so. *Sexual deviance* can be defined as sexual behaviors and identities perceived as deviant in a particular society. Almost any sexual behavior can, and may, in some societies or cultures, be considered a forbidden act or one that deserves criminal sanction. For example, pornography, premarital sex, and prostitution have all been defined as deviant and criminal, and by contrast, they have also been viewed as normative. Sexual deviance, then, is a social construct—one that is created not only through social interactions, but also, through perceptions:

> All societies create sexual hierarchies that establish boundaries between good and bad or legitimate and illicit sexualities. Societies classify certain desires, acts, and identities as normal, respectable, good, healthy, and moral; other forms of sexuality are classified as unhealthy, abnormal, sinful, and immoral. Societies support and privilege "normal and good" forms of sexuality and punish those defined as "abnormal and bad" through law, violence, ridicule, or stigma ... American society considers heterosexuality, monogamy, marriage, and reproductive sex to be good and normal; it defines and treats S/M

(sadism and masochism), commercial, public, and multiple-partner sex as bad ...
Those who engage in such behaviors, regardless of gender, will be stigmatized
and subject to ridicule and at times criminalization.

(Seidman et al. 2011:7–8)

As a result, perceptions foreground deviance, and thus, if we are to understand sexual
deviance as sexual behaviors and identities that are perceived as deviant, then we
need to understand what sexual behaviors and identities are perceived as normal.

Defining "normative" sexual behavior

Recall from chapter 2 that the process of defining norms and deviance is complex.
This is because deviance is defined in opposition to social norms that vary temporally and culturally. Consider the nuances we have previously discussed:

- There is no universality to norms or norm violations.
- Norm construction is an ongoing process dependent on cultural realities.
- Normative beliefs about a particular issue and normative responses to those
  engaging in a particular behavior can (and do) shift over time.

These patterns remain when it comes to defining sexual norms and sexual deviance.
Thus far, myriad sexual norms have been reviewed throughout the first unit of this
textbook. We have considered temporal and cultural variations in the moral acceptability of abortion, adultery, polygamy, and gay/lesbian relationships. We have also discussed how norms shape our continually evolving understandings of gender and sexual
identity. Overall, when considering how to define "normative" sexual behavior, sexual
normalcy (and by default, sexual deviance) can be evaluated in five ways (Tiefer 2004):

- *Clinical*: normal means medically functional. In an interview with *Time* magazine, American sexologist Alfred Kinsey once stated: "the only unnatural sex
  act is that which you cannot perform" (Time 1966). However, because medical
  diagnoses change as social perceptions change, as in the case of the DSM
  declassification of "homosexuality" as a "mental disorder" in 1973, clinical
  evaluations of normalcy are not as scientifically infallible as they are often
  thought to be (see also Box 3.6 in chapter 3).
- *Idealistic*: normal means perfect. An idealized sense of sexual normalcy is based
  on coveted (often childlike) imagery of the perfect relationship (as in fairy
  tales) and the perfect sex that should take place within it (as in romance novels).
  Idealistic notions such as "some day my prince will come" and the frequently
  described scenario of being "swept away" by true love have been found to
  negatively affect women's sexual development (Lieberman 1972) and reduce
  their likelihood of using condoms (Diekman *et al.* 2000).
- *Subjective*: normal means the same as others. Subjective sexual normalcy can be
  summarized as: *my sex life is normal so anyone who is the same as me (sexually) is*

normal also. Overall, 95 percent of American men and women perceive their own sex practices as "completely normal" or "normal" (Janus and Janus 1993). Of course, in order to judge sexual normalcy subjectively, you must know (or at least think you know) what type of sex others around you are engaging in; and this is often not the case.

- *Statistical*: normal means frequent. Statistical sexual normalcy implies that the sexual behaviors that most regularly occur are normal. We will discuss statistical sexual "normativity" and "deviance" in depth throughout this chapter but as we will learn later, most of us are not fully aware of the statistical breakdown of participation in certain types of sexual behaviors in our cultures.
- *Cultural*: normal means commonly positively evaluated. Cultural sexual normalcy is based on cultural perceptions and understandings of particular types of people, relationships, and sexual behaviors as "normal." We most commonly use cultural evaluations when considering sexual normalcy and deviance. Cultural sexual "normativity" and "deviance" will also be discussed at length in this chapter.

Statistical sexual "normativity" and "deviance"

Starting with Kinsey and colleagues' research in the 1940s to 1950s, there has been a prominent interest in the examination of human sexual behavior in the United States. For example, as previously discussed in chapter 4, Laumann and his colleagues (1994, 1999) conducted the first population-based in-depth assessment of sexual behavior in the 40 years since Kinsey's work (1948, 1953) and their findings have continued to shape our understandings of American sexual behavior. Such research provides statistics, or in other words, actual frequencies of behaviors, that give us information that we perceive as "authentic" data about sex and sexuality. In a sense, statistical data is judged as "scientific," "true," or even "irrefutable" evidence. As a result, there is a great deal of reliance on surveys of human sexual behavior as indicative of "real" patterns about sex. We can (and often do) use such data to support our ideas that certain sexual behaviors and identities are normal (because they are highly prevalent) and others are deviant (because they rarely occur). In doing so, we are relying on statistical evidence to support our understandings of sexual "normativity" and "deviance."

Statistically speaking, what is "normal sex"?

Sexual behaviors

According to nearly all surveys of sexual behavior, there is a wide range of diversity within human sexual experiences. Using data from 59 countries, the World Health Organization indicates that there is substantial variety in sexual behavior by world region and there is no universality in sexual intercourse patterns (Wellings *et al.* 2006). The National Survey of Sexual Health and Behavior (NSSHB) found that among a nationally representative sample of Americans ages 14 to 94 (N = 5,865;

93 percent of whom identified as heterosexual), there are more than 40 combinations of sexual activity described by participants. For example, in an analysis of partnered sexual events reported by 3,990 American adults (ages 18 to 59; 92 percent of whom identified as heterosexual), men and women most commonly indicated participation in penile-vaginal sex (80 percent of men; 86 percent of women) as well as receiving oral sex (44 percent of men; 31 percent of women), giving oral sex (37 percent of men; 37 percent of women), and partnered masturbation (29 percent of men; 24 percent of women) (Herbenick *et al.* 2010a). Furthermore, sexual behavior varies cross-culturally (see Table 6.1). In a stratified sample of 1,752 Slovenians aged 18 to 49, men and women also frequently reported vaginal intercourse (90 percent of men and 91 percent of women indicated penile-vaginal sex in the past year) but oral sex was much more common than in the U.S.: 75 percent of men and 70 percent of women in Slovenia reported oral sex in the past year (Klavs *et al.* 2009). Among a stratified sample of 11,161 British residents, vaginal intercourse and oral sex were also common (73 percent of men and 76 percent of women indicated vaginal sex in the past month; 78 percent of men and 77 percent of women indicated oral sex in the past year) (Johnson *et al.* 2001). As a result, these data show us that "statistically speaking" penile-vaginal sex is common and oral sex may also be quite normative as well. Of course, these patterns are built on data that is comprised from overwhelmingly heterosexual samples; thus, statistical normality within non-heterosexual sex experiences likely differs significantly (see Box 6.1 later in this chapter for a more in-depth discussion of these ideas).

Orgasm and sexual satisfaction

There are also marked differences in orgasm experiences and overall sexual satisfaction. For example, among a nationally representative sample of Americans (92 percent of whom identified as heterosexual), 92 percent of men reported that they experienced orgasm in their most recent sexual encounter and they also indicated that 85 percent of their partners experienced orgasm. By contrast only 64 percent of women reported that they experienced orgasm in their most recent sexual encounter but they indicated that 92 percent of their partners experienced orgasm. Furthermore, men were more likely to report orgasm as resultant from participation in vaginal intercourse while women were more likely to report orgasm as resultant from a variety of sex acts (Herbenick *et al.* 2010a). These data show us that while penile-vaginal sex is the most frequently reported sexual event among predominantly heterosexual samples, orgasm may not be a common occurrence, especially for women. Indeed, the Global Study of Sexual Attitudes and Behaviors involving 13,882 women and 13,618 men aged 40 to 80 years in 29 countries found that sexual satisfaction is highly variant cross culturally, as seen in Figure 6.1. For example, 91.1 percent of women in Austria indicated that they were "sexually satisfied" compared to only 39.7 percent of women in Japan. For men, the highest levels of sexual satisfaction were also reported in Austria (91.4 percent indicated they were sexually satisfied) and lowest among men in Taiwan (60 percent reported

TABLE 6.1 Frequencies of selected sexual behaviors in three countries across age groups

	U.S. adults (ages 18–59)		British adults (ages 16–44)		Slovenian adults (ages 18–49)		U.S. teens (ages 14–17)		U.S. older adults (ages 50+)	
	Male	Female	Male	Female	Male	Female	Male	Female	Male	Female
Penile–vaginal sex	80%	86%	73%	76%	90%	91%	20%	21%	54%	42%
Oral sex (received)	44%	31%	—	—	—	—	22%	17%	39%	26%
Oral sex (gave)	37%	37%	—	—	—	—	13%	19%	37%	26%
Oral sex (unspecified)	—	—	78%	77%	75%	70%	—	—	—	—
Anal sex	—	4%, receptive	12%	11%	19%	14%	4%	4%	8%	4%
	2%, receptive 7%, insertive									

U.S. adult data come from Herbenick et al. (2010a); data describe percentages reporting particular sex from most recent sexual event within the past year. Anal sex was specified as receptive or insertive in this survey only. British data come from Johnson et al. (2001); penile–vaginal sex data describe percentages reporting particular sex act in the past month and oral/anal sex data describe percentages reporting particular sex act in the past year. Slovenian data come from Klavs et al. (2009); data describe percentages reporting particular sex act in the past year. U.S. teens data come from Fortenberry et al. (2010); data describe percentages reporting particular sex act in the past year. U.S. older adults data come from Schick et al. (2010); data describe percentages reporting particular sex act in the past year.

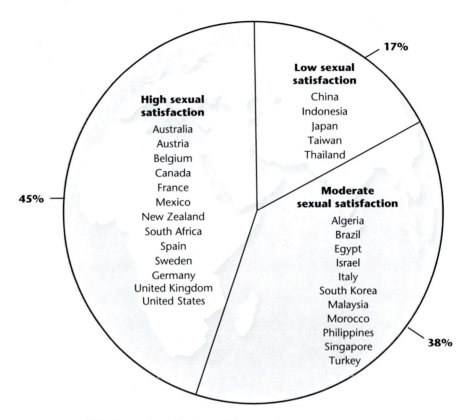

FIGURE 6.1 Global sexual satisfaction in 29 countries

Data adapted from Laumann *et al.* (2006).

sexual satisfaction) (Laumann *et al.* 2006). This means that sexual behaviors (and their likelihood of leading to orgasm) differ by both gender and cultural context. For example, it is relatively normative for Japanese women to be sexually dissatisfied while this is quite uncommon for Austrian women (Laumann *et al.* 2006). Thus, both the actual sexual behaviors individuals engage in and the feelings elicited during sex acts can contribute to our understandings of normality within sexual experiences. What is normal in one culture (for example, sexual satisfaction for women) may not be normal in another. As a result, "normal" sex is all about perception. There is no set of behaviors that will always be perceived as "normal" because normality and deviance are created from how we experience sex as well as how we view sex acts and who is engaging in them.

Sex among teens and elders

We may perceive certain sexual behaviors as normative, but only, for example, among those we think of as the "appropriate" age to be sexually active, namely young and middle-aged adults. Data shows, however, that both teenagers and the elderly are sexually active (see Table 6.1). For example, a nationally representative U.S. study found that 8 percent of young men and 6 percent of young women aged 14 to 15 as well as 16 percent of young men and 21 percent of young women aged 16 to 17 report engaging in penile-vaginal sex in the past month (see more about adolescent sexual behavior in chapter 8). Among the elderly, 28 percent of adult men and 12 percent of adult women aged 70+ report engaging in penile-vaginal sex in the past month (Herbenick et al. 2010b). Results from an Australian longitudinal study of 2,783 men found that 40 percent of men aged 75 to 79 were sexually active in the previous year as well as 27 percent of men aged 80 to 84, 19 percent of men aged 85 to 89, and 11 percent of men aged 90 to 95 (Hyde et al. 2010). Although sex among the elderly may be less common in comparison to men and women aged 25 to 29 [74 percent of whom report engaging in penile-vaginal sex in the past month (Herbenick et al. 2010b)], these data show us that sexual activity takes place through-out the life course including both during the teenage years and the golden years of life. While we know that the frequency of sexual behavior may change over our lifetimes, we also know that our perceptions of a "normative" frequency of sexual behavior also vary by age. Studies show us that many older adults continue to have active pleasurable sex lives and report a range of different behaviors and partner types (Schick et al. 2010) but our cultural understandings of sex often limit our abilities to view sex among the elderly as normative. As a result, "normal" sex is qualified by both the particulars of the sexual act and who is participating.

Statistically speaking, what is "deviant sex"?

Statistically speaking, deviant sexual acts can be identified as those that are relatively uncommon occurrences. When examining surveys of sexual behavior, sometimes such deviant sexual acts can be revealed. In a nationally representative study of sexual experiences reported by 3,990 American adults (92 percent of whom identi-fied as heterosexual), anal intercourse was amongst the least common sex act reported. Only 7 percent of men indicated participation in insertive anal inter-course in their most recent sexual experience and receptive anal intercourse was also very uncommon (2 percent of men and 4 percent of women indicated par-ticipation in receptive anal intercourse) (Herbenick et al. 2010a). However, as we have discussed at length, what is viewed as "deviant" sexual behavior varies cross-culturally. For example, anal sex has been found to be more common in Slovenian samples: 19 percent of men and 14 percent of women indicated anal sex in the past year (Klavs et al. 2009) and British samples: 12 percent of men and 11 percent of women indicated anal sex in the past year (Johnson et al. 2001) (see Table 6.1). In addition, in a European Sex Survey[1] of 14,371 men and women from 13 coun-tries, individuals indicated a wide range of involvement in various sexual behaviors (see Figure 6.2). While viewing porn was relatively frequent (39 to 63 percent indicated watching pornography), the use of sex toys (e.g., vibrators) was highly variant across the 13 countries surveyed. Only 12 percent of Italians indicated using

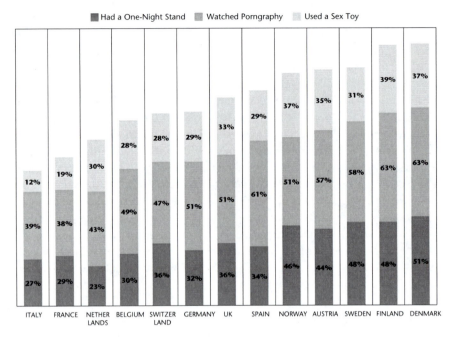

■ Had a One-Night Stand ▨ Watched Porngraphy ▨ Used a Sex Toy

FIGURE 6.2 Sexual behaviors in 13 European countries

Data adapted from European Sex Survey (2013).

sex toys compared to 39 percent of Finnish. In addition, reports of having a "one-night stand," where individuals engaged in sexual contact with a partner for one night only, also differed cross-culturally with more than half (51 percent) of the Danes indicating a one-night stand in their sexual histories compared to only a quarter (23 percent) of the Dutch (European Sex Survey 2013). Because of this cultural variance, identifying a list of "sexually deviant" behaviors is a challenging task. To adequately speak to the question *what is deviant sex?* we must move beyond statistical frequencies to examine cultural context.

Cultural perceptions of sexual "normativity" and "deviance"

Thus far we have examined statistics—that is to say that we have looked at frequencies of involvement in particular sexual behaviors by reviewing various findings from global sex survey research. While this certainly gives us important information about "normative" and "deviant" sex, it is only part of the story. In particular, most of us do not examine bar charts and percentage breakdowns of sexual behavior (in general) and furthermore, most of us do not use such statistical data to inform our understandings of particular sexual behaviors as normative or deviant. Instead, most people determine what they see as normative or deviant sexual behavior from cultural observations. That is to say that how we define sex acts emerges from our cultural understandings and perceptions.

Culturally speaking, what is "normal" and "deviant" sex?

Sexual behaviors

Previously in this chapter, we learned that oral sex is a relatively common sexual experience among Americans, Britons, and Slovenians (Johnson *et al.* 2001; Klavs *et al.* 2009; Herbenick *et al.* 2010a). But these statistical data do not allow us to embed these experiences within cultural context. When we examine attitudes toward oral sex among Americans as seen in Table 6.2, we see that a little over half (59 percent of men and 55 percent of women) indicate that "oral sex is very normal." Both giving and receiving oral sex is more appealing to men (33.5 percent of men and 16.5 percent of women enjoy giving oral sex and 45 percent of men and 28.8 percent women enjoy receiving oral sex) while women are more likely to indicate that they prefer to achieve orgasm through oral sex (18 percent of women and 10 percent of men prefer oral sex orgasms) (Janus and Janus 1993; Laumann *et al.* 1994). These attitudes and preferences tell us that oral sex is likely both a common sexual experience (statistically) and also a culturally normative sexual act (for more about cultural perceptions of oral sex, see Box 6.1).

BOX 6.1 WOULD YOU SAY YOU "HAD SEX" IF . . .?

In addition to being a relatively normative sexual experience, oral sex is also part of the complex cultural definition of "sex." And some might point to the Bill Clinton (then American President) and Monica Lewinksy (then White House intern) sex scandal that exploded into public discourse in 1998 as the catalyst that triggered an intense "*is oral sex actually sex?*" debate that reached across global news outlets and family dinner tables. Allegedly, multiple sexual encounters took place between the then 49-year-old President and the 22-year-old intern, which was shocking enough to the American public, but President Bill Clinton's response to Miss Lewinksy's claims set off an additional firestorm of activity. After the scandal hit media outlets, in his public address to the people on January 26, 1998, Clinton stated:

> I want to say one thing to the American people. I want you to listen to me. I'm going to say this again: *I did not have sexual relations with that woman*, Miss Lewinsky. I never told anybody to lie, not a single time; never. These allegations are false.
>
> *(Clinton 1998)*

This sentiment was reinforced when it was later revealed in court that Clinton believed that the sex acts that did occur between the two (receipt of oral sex by Clinton) did not meet the definition of "sexual relations." The general public was divided: did oral sex, in fact, qualify as sexual relations? Had Clinton, in fact, "had sex" with Lewinsky? There was no clear answer to these questions. Accordingly, in a study conducted by the Kinsey Institute in the 1990s, close to half of men (about 44 percent) and about 37 percent of women believed that oral-genital contact counted as "having sex" (Sanders and Reinisch 1999). Additional American studies throughout the 1990s continued to indicate support for the "oral sex = sex" debate (for a review, see Remez 2000). However, about a decade later, opinions shifted.

In a 2007 study, only one-fifth of straight men and women (about 20 percent) believed that oral-genital contact qualifies as "having sex" (see Figure 6.3). Compared to the research in the 1990s, studies in the 2000s showed a marked and significant decrease in support for the idea that oral sex is synonymous with having "had sex." Specifically, percentages were cut in half, with about 40 percent of men and women viewing "oral sex = sex" in the 1990s and only about 20 percent with similar beliefs in the 2000s (Hans *et al.* 2010).

Furthermore, researchers also began to critically investigate the meanings of "sex" for LGBT people. This line of inquiry is especially significant because while it was expected that gay and lesbian individuals might be more likely to view both penile-anal intercourse and oral-genital contact as having "had sex" to a much greater degree than straight-identified individuals, there was no empirical support to back this idea up until relatively recently. A handful of studies have shown that the standards of what constitutes "sex" may differ for same-sex as opposed to opposite-sex sexual experiences (e.g., Carpenter 2005;

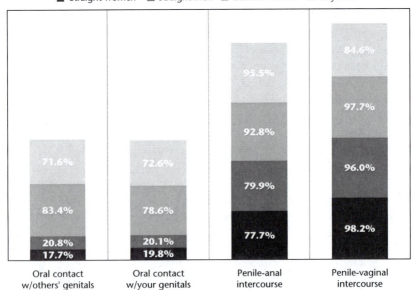

FIGURE 6.3 Straight, gay, and lesbian perceptions of what "counts" as sex

Data for straight men and women are from Hans *et al.* (2010).
Data for gay men are from Hill *et al.* (2010).
Data for lesbian women are from Horowitz and Spicer (2013).

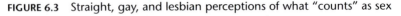

Hill *et al.* 2010; Horowitz and Spicer 2013; Averett *et al.* 2014). For example, when examining gay men's attitudes toward sex, we learn that gay men are more likely than straight men and women to indicate that anal intercourse, rather than vaginal intercourse, constitutes "sex" (Hill *et al.* 2010). Specifically, nearly all gay men (95.5 percent) considered anal sex as having "had sex" while only 84.6 percent thought the same about vaginal sex (see Figure 6.3). Similar to gay men, nearly all lesbian women (92.8 percent) viewed anal sex as "sex" and only about 80 percent of straight men and women thought the same (see data for lesbian women in Figure 6.3). In addition, both gay men and lesbian women are significantly more likely to evaluate oral-genital contact as "sex" (ranging from about 72 to 84 percent) while only about 20 percent of straight men and women count oral sex as "sex." Lesbian women are also more likely to view the use of sex aids on the genitals (e.g., strap-ons, vibrators, etc.) and manual stimulation of the genitals as having "had sex" when compared to straight men and women (Horowitz and Spicer 2013). There is additional research that indicates that LGBT people are more likely than straight men and women to view oral sex and anal sex as "virginity loss" (Carpenter 2005; Averett *et al.* 2014). Indeed, in a study of LGBT people, one man succinctly described the variability of defining sex across sexual and gender identities:

> What I am trying to get across to you is that there are so many differences in our own community that you have to define it a little further . . . I mean, like for lesbians, it's going to be different than bisexual people than to gays, than to transgender people who do not fit any of those boxes.
>
> *(Averett et al. 2014:270)*

As a result of this previous work, it is clear that gay men and lesbian women view both anal sex and oral sex differently than straight men and women. In particular, LGBT people may view these sex acts (oral-genital contact and anal intercourse) as having "had sex" to a much greater degree than straight men and women. Thus, defining sex can be a challenging endeavor. It is also important to note that for teens, these issues maybe even more complex. As we will discuss further in chapter 8, teenage cultural scripts regarding oral sex can be entwined with the desire to preserve "technical virginity" (when young people substitute non-penile-vaginal sexual activities in place of vaginal intercourse, see Uecker *et al.* 2008). As a result, we know that what counts as "sex" depends on:

- What the sex act is (vaginal, anal, oral, or something else).
- Who the sex partners are (in particular, the gender and sexual identities of the participants).
- What the cultural expectations about the participants' behaviors are (especially in regards to age and other social identities).

By contrast, we also learned earlier in this chapter that anal sex is a relatively uncommon sexual experience among Americans, Britons, and Slovenians (see Table 6.1). Attitudes toward anal sex among Americans further support this activity as non-normative with only 8 percent of men and 5 percent of women indicating that "anal sex is very normal." Furthermore, both giving and receiving anal sex was universally unappealing to men and women (only 5.6 percent of men and 4.1 percent of women enjoy giving anal stimulation and 6.2 percent of men and 2.4 percent women enjoy receiving anal stimulation) and a preference for achieving orgasm through anal sex was also uncommon (2 percent of men prefer anal sex orgasms, no data for women's preferences toward anal orgasms were provided) (see Table 6.2). Such findings show us that anal sex is a statistically uncommon sexual experience and may also be a culturally non-normative sex act. As we will see below, however, such preferences may also be related to our social attitudes about who is engaging in particular sex acts.

Who is having sex?

As previously discussed in chapter 2, attitudes toward same-sex sexual relations have varied overtime with the majority of Americans supporting gay and lesbian relationships only recently (since 2010) (Riffkin 2014). Cross-culturally, attitudes toward "homosexuality" also vary (see also, chapter 4). For example, in a study of 40 nations across the globe, 98 percent of Ghanaians indicated that "homosexuality" is morally unacceptable compared to only 6 percent of Spaniards. Furthermore, when examining these attitudes by world region, those in Australia were most supportive of homosexuality (only 18 percent indicated that homosexuality is morally unacceptable) while 82 percent of those in the Middle East and Africa viewed homosexuality as immoral (see Figure 6.4). Although this survey inquired explicitly about attitudes toward "homosexuality," these data are also likely tapping into attitudes toward "homosexual" sex. In other words, when asking people about "homosexuality" we

TABLE 6.2 Attitudes and preferences toward selected sexual behaviors

	Men	Women
Oral Sex		
Oral sex is very normal★★	59%	55%
I find giving oral sex to be appealing★	33.5%	16.5%
I find receiving oral sex to be appealing★	45.0%	28.8%
I prefer to achieve orgasm through oral sex★★	10%	18%
Anal Sex		
Anal sex is very normal★★	8%	5%
I find giving anal stimulation to be appealing★	5.6%	4.1%
I find receiving anal stimulation to be appealing★	6.2%	2.4%
I prefer to achieve orgasm through anal sex★★	2%	—

★ National Health and Social Life Survey (Laumann *et al.* 1994).
★★ Janus Report (Janus and Janus 1993).

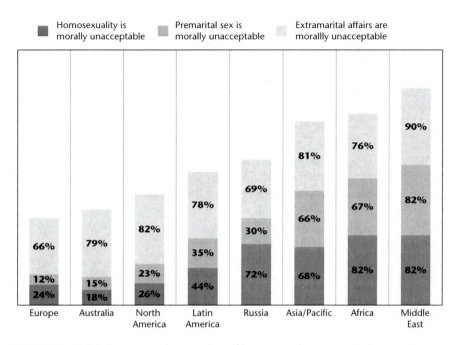

■ Homosexuality is
  morally unacceptable

■ Premarital sex is
  morally unacceptable

Extramarital affairs are
moralIly unacceptable

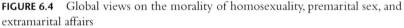

FIGURE 6.4 Global views on the morality of homosexuality, premarital sex, and extramarital affairs

Data adapted from Pew Research Center (2014a, 2014b, 2014c).

are also indirectly asking people about what they perceive to be "homosexual" sex. Many think about same-sex sexual behavior as involving anal sex (although of course opposite sex partners can engage in anal sex and same-sex sexual behavior may not entail anal sex at all, especially in the case of sex between two women). Even so when people are formulating their attitudes toward "homosexuality" they may be using their opinions about anal sex in their evaluation. Some research indicates that anal sex, in general, is viewed quite negatively, especially when it is between two men (compared to anal sex between a man and a woman) (Heflick 2010). Because people may have a general aversion toward anal sex and a specific aversion toward anal sex between two men, they may also have an aversion toward "homosexuality." As a result, when considering opinions toward "homosexuality," there may be an implied bias against anal sex. Thus, anal sex may be viewed as culturally deviant at least partially because it is presumed that gay men (who are also viewed as deviant) are the most frequent participants in this particular sex act. In other words, who is perceived to be having anal sex is closely entwined with our evaluation of that particular sex act as deviant. Accordingly, it is not the sex act *per se*, but rather it is those who are engaging in it who are seen as deviant.

In addition, other judgments of deviance may also be based on who is engaging in sex rather than the sex act itself. For example, research indicates that there is a wide variation in global attitudes toward premarital sex. Across all major world regions using data from 40 countries, premarital sex was viewed most unfavorably in the Middle East (82 percent indicated that premarital sex is morally unacceptable) while only 12 percent of Europeans viewed premarital sex as immoral (see Figure 6.4). Indonesians were most likely to view premarital sex as immoral (97 percent indicated as such) while French and Germans were least likely to indicate that premarital sex is morally unacceptable (only 4 percent indicated as such) (Pew Research Center 2014b). Some have suggested that changes in religious trends and increasing secularization evident in European and North American cultures have contributed to a decline in the perceptions of premarital sex as immoral (Petersen and Donnenwerth 1997; Scott 1998). By contrast, intense religious doctrines that dictate honor as inherently linked to premarital female virginity and sex as appropriate only within marriage remain firm in other parts of the world including in the Middle East and Sub-Saharan Africa (Dunne 1998). As a result, premarital sex is perceived as deviant in some cultures but quite normative in others. From these findings, we see that again, such evaluations of deviance are more about who is having sex (in this case, those who do so prior to marriage) as opposed to what sex acts they are engaging in.

Globally, there is relatively high congruence in judgments of married people having an affair, ranging from 66 percent of Europeans to 90 percent of Middle Easterners viewing sex outside of marriage as immoral (see Figure 6.4). Out of the 40 countries surveyed, extramarital affairs were viewed most unfavorably in Palestinian Territories and Turkey (94 percent indicated sex outside of marriage as immoral) and least unfavorably in France (47 percent similarly indicated extra-marital affairs as immoral) (Pew Research Center 2014c). Research indicates that attitudes toward extramarital affairs are strongly influenced by religion with more secularized cultures being more willing to tolerate adultery, although in general, most are condemnatory of extramarital affairs (Scott 1998). Compared to other behaviors that have been increasingly less deviantized in some cultures (such as "homosexuality" and premarital sex), sex outside of marriage remains quite deviant across the globe. Such attitudes show us that the particulars of the sexual behaviors may not be as important as who is engaging in sex; it is rather the context, in this case sex outside of marriage, that dictates perceptions of deviance.

Overall, our evaluations of sexual deviance emerge from our cultural under-standings and perceptions. What we see as the "appropriate" context for sexual behavior including what the sex and gender identities of the sex partners are, if they are married to each other, and whether or not the sex took place outside of mar-riage can dictate what is perceived as normative and what is perceived as deviant. Thus, judgments of sexual deviancy can sometimes be more about the people engaging in sex and not the particular sex act *per se*.

Sexual deviance defined

In this chapter, we have discussed wide global variance in perceptions of sexual devi-ance. In fact, you may (again) be wondering how we can even begin to define sexual deviance in any comprehensive way. There are some undeniably sexually deviant

BOX 6.2 TED BUNDY

Theodore Robert "Ted" Bundy (1946–1989) was an American serial killer whose violent rampage in the 1970s resulted in the murders of at least 30 young women across seven states. Bundy has been frequently described as a handsome man who was able to successfully lure his victims to their deaths using his charisma and charm. To facilitate many of his murders, he feigned injury (using crutches and/or homemade casts) and requested assistance from young college women.

In his homicides, Bundy beat, strangled, and bludgeoned his victims. Beyond being a murderous criminal, Bundy was also a sexual deviant. He raped and sodomized the majority of his victims and was also a necrophiliac (he received sexual arousal from corpses). In some cases, he would continue to engage in necrophilic sex acts with his victims' dead bodies until putrefaction and/or destruction by wild animals rendered their bodies decayed beyond identification. Because some of his victims were found with clothing items, hair styles, jewelry, and nail polish that were not identified by their family members as their own, it is believed that Bundy would revisit his victim's dead bodies and continue to groom their cadavers well after their deaths. Bundy also kept mementos from his homicides including Polaroid photos of his victims' dead bodies, and sometimes, their decapitated heads. His criminal and sexual deviance can only be surmised as purely sadistic. Indeed, in a biography about Ted Bundy, he was described as "a sadistic sociopath who took pleasure from another human's pain and the control he had over his victims, to the point of death, and even after" (Rule 2009:xiv).

Bundy was arrested in 1975 in Utah after failing to pull over for a routine traffic stop. Upon investigation of his vehicle, the police officer found a disturbing "kit" of items including a ski mask, a mask fashioned from pantyhose, handcuffs, trash bags, rope, an orange electrical cord, a crowbar, a red-handled ice pick, a flashlight, a woman's belt, and two right-handed gloves (see Image 6.1). These items were later determined to be Bundy's "hunting tools" that he would bring along with him to facilitate his murders. After multiple convictions and two successful escapes from prison (during which he murdered three young women), Bundy was ultimately recaptured in Florida in 1978. His trials were widely publicized both in the U.S. and abroad. In fact, his 1979 trial was one of the first U.S. trials to be televised nationally. In the end, Bundy received three death sentences in two separate trials. He was executed via the electric chair at Raiford Prison in Starke, Florida on January 24, 1989 (Murray 2009; Rule 2009; Sullivan 2009).

Ted Bundy was a murderer, a serial killer, and a sexual deviant. His behaviors are regarded as abhorrent, disgusting, and horrific by nearly all people in nearly all societies. As a result, Ted Bundy can be described as an entity that fully embodies sexual deviance. Because of his blatant disregard for human life and his involvement in multiple sadistic murderous rapes and necrophilic sex acts, Ted Bundy is the universal exemplar of sexual deviance.

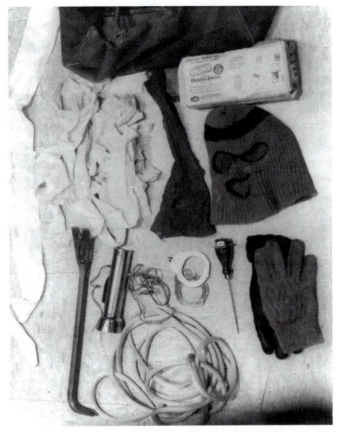

1975 POLICE PHOTO OF TED BUNDY ITEMS

IMAGE 6.1 Items found in Ted Bundy's car in his 1975 arrest

Photo used with permission from Salt Lake City, Utah Sheriff's Office and King County Archives: 20.1-25-496 [leather bag, masks, gloves, cord, flashlight, pry bar, etc.: evidence?], 1970s, investigative files, Series 954, Department of Public Safety, Box 35, Folder 11, King County Archives, Seattle, Washington, USA.

acts. For example, American serial killer, rapist, and necrophiliac Ted Bundy is an exemplar of sexual deviance (see Box 6.2). But for the most part, sexual deviance is highly variant. What is defined as sexual deviance depends on perceptions of:

- Particular types of behaviors (and their frequency).
- Particular types of people.
- Particular types of relationships.

Together, sexual deviance emerges from opinions about particular people in particular types of relationships engaging in particular behaviors. Furthermore, as we will see in chapter 7, perceptions of sexual deviance have a great deal of historical variance as well. As a result, defining sexual deviance is built from perceptions and because almost any sexual behavior can, and may, in some societies, be considered forbidden, it is essential to consider both historical and cultural context when learning about sexual deviance.

Note

1   This survey was collected by YouGov, an international internet-based market research firm founded in the UK with 25 offices worldwide across the UK, United States, Europe, Nordics, the Middle East, and Asia Pacific. YouGov operates an online panel of over 3 million panelists across 33 countries. Using a statistical weighting process, YouGov creates nationally representative samples weighted to the national profile of all adults aged 18+ (including people without internet access) by age, gender, social class, region, party identity, and the readership of individual newspapers. Some have questioned its validity; however, as Twyman (2008) points out, YouGov has provided accurate forecasts of the results of several major elections, thus, its validity should be recognized.

References

Averett, Paige, Amy Moore, and Lindsay Price. 2014. "Virginity Definitions and Meaning Among the LGBT Community." *Journal of Gay & Lesbian Social Services* 26(3):259–78.

Carpenter, Laura. 2005. *Virginity Lost: An Intimate Portrait of First Sexual Experiences.* New York, NY: NYU Press.

Clinton, Bill. 1998, January 26. "Response to the Lewinsky Allegations." *Miller Center of Public Affairs.* Retrieved from: http://millercenter.org/president/speeches/speech-3930

Diekman, Amanda, Mary McDonald, and Wendi L. Cardner. 2000. "Love Means Never Having to be Careful: The Relationship Between Reading Romance Novels And Safe Sex Behavior." *Psychology of Women Quarterly* 24:179–88.

Dunne, Bruce. 1998. "Power and Sexuality in the Middle East." *Middle East Report* 206:8–11+37.

European Sex Survey. 2013. "European Sex Survey." *YouGov* Retrieved from http://cdn. yougov.com/cumulus_uploads/document/mkyaii2h6k/YouGov-Survey-European-Omnibus-Sex-Research-130621.pdf

Fortenberry, J. Dennis, Vanessa Schick, Debby Herbenick, Stephanie A. Sanders, Brian Dodge, and Michael Reece. 2010. "Sexual Behaviors and Condom Use at Last Vaginal Intercourse: A National Sample of Adolescents Ages 14 to 17 Years." *The Journal of Sexual Medicine* 7(Supplement 5):305–14.

Hans, Jason, Martie Gillen, and Katrina Akande. 2010. "Sex Redefined: The Reclassification of Oral-Genital Contact." *Perspectives on Sexual and Reproductive Health* 42(2):74–78.

Heflick, Nathan. 2010, February 6. "EWWW. . . . Anal Sex is Icky! Men, Women and Anal Sex." *Psychology Today.* Retrieved from: https://www.psychologytoday.com/blog/the-big-questions/201002/ewwwanal-sex-is-icky

Herbenick, Debby, Michael Reece, Vanessa Schick, Stephanie A. Sanders, Brian Dodge, and J. Dennis Fortenberry. 2010a. "An Event-Level Analysis of the Sexual Characteristics and Composition Among Adults Ages 18 to 59: Results from a National Probability Sample in the United States." *The Journal of Sexual Medicine* 7(Supplement 5):346–61.

Herbenick, Debby, Michael Reece, Vanessa Schick, Stephanie A. Sanders, Brian Dodge, and J. Dennis Fortenberry. 2010b. "Sexual Behavior in the United States: Results from a National Probability Sample of Men and Women Ages 14–94." *The Journal of Sexual Medicine* 7(Supplement 5):255–65.

Hill, B. J., Q. Rahman, D. A. Bright, and S. A. Sanders. 2010. "The Semantics of Sexual Behavior and their Implications for HIV/AIDS Research and Sexual Health: US and UK Gay Men's Definitions of Having 'Had Sex.'" *AIDS Care* 22(10):1245–51.

Horowitz, Ava and Louise Spicer. 2013. "'Having Sex' as a Graded and Hierarchical Construct: A Comparison of Sexual Definitions among Heterosexual and Lesbian Emerging Adults in the U.K." *Journal of Sex Research* 50(2):139–50.

Hyde, Zoë, Leon Flicker, Graeme J. Hankey, Osvaldo P. Almeida, Kieran A. McCaul, S.A. Paul Chubb, and Bu B. Yeap. 2010. "Prevalence of Sexual Activity and Associated Factors in Men Aged 75 to 95 Years A Cohort Study." *Annals of Internal Medicine* 153(11):693–702.

Janus, Samuel and Cynthia Janus. 1993. *The Janus Report on Sexual Behavior*. New York, NY: John Wiley & Sons, Inc.

Johnson, Anne, Catherine Mercer, Bob Erens, Andrew Copas, Sally McManus, Kaye Wellings, Kevin Fenton, Christos Korovessis, Wendy Macdowall, Kiran Nanchahal, Susan Purdon, and Julia Field. 2001. "Sexual Behaviour in Britain: Partnerships, Practices, and HIV Risk Behaviours." *Lancet* 358:1835–42.

Klavs, Irena, Laura C. Rodrigues, Kaye Wellings, Helen A. Weiss, and Richard Hayes. 2009. "Sexual Behaviour and HIV/Sexually Transmitted Infection Risk Behaviours in the General Population of Slovenia: A Low HIV Prevalence Country in Central Europe." *Sexually Transmitted Infections* 85:132–8.

Kinsey, Alfred, Wardell Pomeroy, and Clyde Martin. 1948. *Sexual Behavior in the Human Male*. Philadelphia, PA: W.B. Saunders Company.

Kinsey, Alfred, Wardell Pomeroy, Clyde Martin, and Paul Gebhard. 1953. *Sexual Behavior in the Human Female*. Philadelphia, PA: W.B. Saunders Company.

Laumann, Edward O., John H. Gagnon, Robert T. Michael, and Stuart Michaels. 1994. *The Social Organization of Sexuality*. Chicago, IL: University of Chicago Press.

Laumann, Edward O., Anthony Paik, and Raymond C. Rosen. 1999. "Sexual Dysfunction in the United States." *JAMA: The Journal of the American Medical Association* 281(6):537–44.

Laumann, Edward O., Anthony Paik, Dale B. Glasser, Jeong-Han Kang, Tianfu Wang, Bernard Levinson, Edson D. Moreira, Jr., Alfredo Nicolosi, and Clive Gingell. 2006. "A Cross-National Study of Subjective Sexual Well-Being Among Older Women and Men: Findings From the Global Study of Sexual Attitudes and Behaviors." *Archives of Sexual Behavior* 35(2):145–61.

Lieberman, Marcia R. 1972. "'Some Day My Prince Will Come': Female Acculturation through the Fairy Tale." *College English* 34(3):383–95.

Murray, William. 2009. *Serial Killers*. London: Canary Press.

Petersen, Larry and Gregory V. Donnenwerth. 1997. "Secularization and the Influence of Religion on Beliefs about Premarital Sex." *Social Forces* 75(3):1071–88.

Pew Research Center. 2014a. "Global Views on Morality – Homosexuality." *Pew Research Center*. Retrieved from: http://www.pewglobal.org/2014/04/15/global-morality/table/homosexuality/

Pew Research Center. 2014b. "Global Views on Morality – Premarital Sex." *Pew Research Center*. Retrieved from: http://www.pewglobal.org/2014/04/15/global-morality/table/premarital-sex/

Pew Research Center. 2014c. "Global Views on Morality – Extramarital Affairs." *Pew Research Center*. Retrieved from: http://www.pewglobal.org/2014/04/15/global-morality/table/extramarital-affairs/

Remez, Lisa. 2000. "Oral Sex Among Adolescents: Is It Sex or Is It Abstinence?" *Family Planning Perspectives* 32(6): 298–304.

Riffkin, Rebecca. 2014. "New Record Highs in Moral Acceptability: Premarital Sex, Embryonic Stem Cell Research, Euthanasia Growing in Acceptance." *Gallup Poll*. Retrieved from: http://www.gallup.com/poll/170789/new-record-highs-moral-acceptability.aspx

Rule, Ann. 2009. *The Stranger Beside Me*. New York, NY: Pocket Books.

Sanders, Stephanie and June Reinisch. 1999. "Would you say you "had sex" if . . . ?" *Journal of the American Medical Association* 281(3):275–7.

Schick, Vanessa, Debby Herbenick, Michael Reece, Stephanie A. Sanders, Brian Dodge, Susan E. Middlestadt, and J. Dennis Fortenberry. 2010. "Sexual Behaviors, Condom Use, and Sexual Health of Americans Over 50: Implications for Sexual Health Promotion for Older Adults." *The Journal of Sexual Medicine* 7(Supplement 5):315–29.

Scott, Jacqueline. 1998. "Changing Attitudes to Sexual Morality: A Cross-National Comparison." *Sociology* 32(4):815–45.

Seidman, Steven, Nancy Fisher, and Chet Meeks. 2011. *Introducing the New Sexuality Studies, Second Edition*. New York, NY: Routledge.

Steele, Valerie. 1996. *Fetish: Fashion, Sex, and Power*. New York, NY: Oxford University Press.

Sullivan, Kevin. 2009. *The Bundy Murders: A Comprehensive History*. Jefferson, NC: McFarland & Company.

Tiefer, Leonore. 2004. *Sex is Not a Natural Act & Other Essays*. Boulder, CO: Westview Press.

Time. 1966, January 21. "Essay: The Homosexual in America." *Time Magazine*. New York, NY. Retrieved from: http://content.time.com/time/magazine/article/0,9171,835069,00.html

Twyman, Joe. 2008. "Getting It Right: YouGov and Online Survey Research in Britain." *Journal of Elections, Public Opinion and Parties* 18(4):343–54.

Uecker, Jeremy, Nicole Angotti, and Mark D. Regnerus. 2008. "Going Most of the Way: 'Technical Virginity' among American Adolescents." *Social Science Research* 37(4):1200–15.

Wellings, Kaye, Martine Collumbien, Emma Slaymaker, Susheela Singh, Zoé Hodges, Dhaval Patel, and Nathalie Bajos. 2006. "Sexual Behaviour in Context: A Global Perspective." *The Lancet Sexual and Reproductive Health Series* 368(9548):1706–28.

7

HISTORICAL PERSPECTIVES ON SEXUAL DEVIANCE

Examining historical perspectives about any subject allows us to trace the evolution of contemporary views about particular issues. This is especially true for sex, sexuality, and of special interest for this textbook, sexual deviance. This is because we often think that our own perceptions about what is "normal" and what is "deviant" as far as sex goes are indisputable facts. It frequently surprises us to find out, for example, that modern-day foods such as Graham crackers and Kellogg's cornflakes got their start during The Age of Masturbatory Insanity or that adult men having sex with teenage boys was not only normative, but celebrated in Ancient Greece. For these reasons among others, it is essential that we consider cultural context when examining historical perspectives. We must be careful not to inappropriately emblazon our modern-day understandings onto past societal practices. We must keep an open mind. We must exercise *cultural relativism* and acknowledge that "although for every culture some moral judgements are valid, no moral judgement is universally valid. Every moral judgment is culturally relative" (Tilley 2000:505). By using a lens that is both historically and culturally sensitive, we can learn about the evolution of sexual deviance as well as our connections to, and departures from, past perspectives.

Thus, the examination of the historical evolution of sexual deviance is a relativistic endeavor. As a result, "when we try to figure out what sexuality means to us today, it is useful to see what was important to past societies: what behaviors were praised or condemned, tolerated or criticized, assumed as natural or rejected as unnatural" (Kuefler 2007:67). In this chapter, just a small sampling of sexual perspectives that have been thought of as both normal and deviant throughout history is offered. This sample is not intended to cover all cultures, all of history, or all aspects of sexual deviance—in fact, quite the contrary. The examples provided in this chapter were chosen to highlight cultural diversity in sexual deviance throughout time. Specifically, this chapter offers an historical discussion of perspectives on four topics: (i) sexual imagery, (ii) the sale of sex, (iii) same-sex sexual behavior, and (iv) sexual pleasure. As we will see the "deviance" of each of these subjects varies not only over time, but also, cross-culturally.

Sexual imagery

Man/woman-created imagery has always been a part of human existence. But how we have come to understand what images are "sexual," "erotic," "pornographic," and/or "deviant" is very much a modern day discussion. Likewise, our analysis of certain images as representative of any of these categories is also filtered through our own cultural experiences. When we look at a cave drawing of what appears to be two humans engaged in a sex act, for example, we may see this in any number of ways, "the same visual material might be deemed suggestive, titillating, erotic, pornographic, or obscene ... There is really no word that is completely neutral to describe this imagery – even the word 'sexual' itself suggests associations that may or may not be accurate" (Easton 2008:1). As a result, an historical discussion of "sexual imagery" should be tempered by the fact that the modern day scholar is attempting to invoke the past by claiming that some types of images are "sexual" or "pornographic" and others are not—essentially drawing conclusions that some imagery is/was socially acceptable and some is/was deviant. The truth is that we do not really know if any of the historical artifacts created prior to the invention of writing could truly be accurately labeled as "erotica." Even the term "pornography" (although derived from the Greek word *pornographos* literally "the writing of prostitutes") did not exist until relatively recently in time (Bullough and Bullough 1977:159). Today's "definition" of pornography (albeit highly dubious) seems to informally go by U.S. Supreme Court Justice Potter Stewart's infamous claim in an obscenity case in 1964, "*I know it when I see it*" (Gewirtz 1996:1023). But this rhetorical phrase is obviously simply another way of evoking the culturally relativistic nature of any social artifact. As a result, examining "sexual" imagery throughout time is a process that necessarily entails cultural and historical sensitivity. Below, the terms "sexual," "erotic," and "pornographic" are used to explain these images recognizing that these descriptions in and of themselves are imprinted with modern cultural context. Likewise, whether or not this type of imagery was viewed as "normative" or "deviant" is also speculated based on contemporary interpretations of ancient (and some not-so ancient) human creations. Even so, a journey through the human history of "sexual" imagery yields at the very least—humanity's long-term fascination with the human body and sex practices and at the very most—humanity's undeniable pleasure-seeking, sensuous, and sexually celebratory nature.

Early humans

Sexual imagery has existed as long as humans have been able to create it. Evidence shows that Neanderthals, an extinct group of humans who lived between about 30,000 and 130,000 years ago, were likely as advanced as modern humans in areas such as tool-making (Szalay 2013), and as a result, they may have created the very first depictions of human sexuality (what may be categorized as erotic art in modern terms). Paleolithic cave paintings and carvings dating back to 40,000 years ago are some of the oldest known surviving examples of sexual imagery and possibly, erotica. They consist of nude humans, human genitalia, and humans engaged in sexual behavior. Small statuettes of the female form, sometimes collectively described as "Venus figurines" are amongst the earliest works of art known to man. Venus figurines typically have small faceless heads and exaggerated feminine features including swollen bellies, wide hips, thighs and buttocks, large breasts, and/or engorged vulva (see Image 7.1). To date, hundreds of ancient Venus figurines have been unearthed, most of them dating back from 22,000 to 28,000 years ago (Soffer *et al.* 2000). But in 2008, archaeologists from the University of Tübingen in Germany discovered a 40,000-year-old figurine, later named Venus of Hohle Fels for the cave in southwestern Germany where it was found, representing the earliest Venus figurine known in existence. Venus figurines have been described as symbolic art, spiritual artifacts, fertility statues, and even "prehistoric porn" (Curry 2012). While their purpose is unknown, it is clear that at least some early humans celebrated the female form and this may be a link to our earliest erotic art.

Ancient Egypt

Sexual imagery from more than 5,000 years ago has been credited to Ancient Egyptian cultures. For example, the Turin Erotic Papyrus is the only known surviving erotic scroll-painting in existence and it dates back to 1150 B.C.E. It is quite

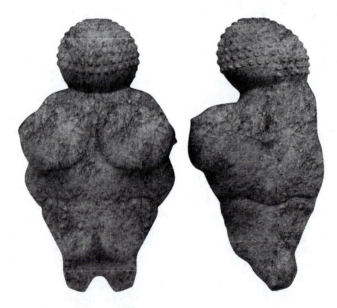

IMAGE 7.1 Paleolithic era Venus figurine

Example of Paleolithic era Venus figurine. ©Shutterstock, 3drenderings.

large, measuring 8.5 feet (2.6 m) by 10 inches (25 cm), and contains 12 erotic vignettes depicting various sexual positions. Although its purpose is unknown and it may have not actually been pornographic in nature, it has been jokingly described as "the world's first men's mag" (Gioia 2015:20). Other examples of sexualized imagery have been located in ancient Egyptian temples and tombs. For example, depictions of the erect penis generally thought to symbolize fertility are evident in Egyptian artifacts (see Image 7.2). Such sexual imagery can also be viewed as erotic art. Thus, it is clear that illustrations of sex, what we may see as "pornography," were a significant part of ancient Egyptian sexual life (Manniche 1987).

Ancient Pompeii

The ancient city of Pompeii was founded in 700 to 600 B.C.E. and later buried under 20 feet of ash when Mount Vesuvius erupted in 79 C.E. This catastrophe destroyed the city and its inhabitants (an estimated 11,000 people) but also preserved many artifacts, including sexualized imagery often described as "erotic art" in the lost city of Pompeii. For example, the Pompeii public bath house for bathing, the Suburban Baths, contained seven frescos depicting various sexual acts including both group sex and oral sex (Clarke 1998). Because of their location in the public baths, these erotic scenes must have been a topic of conversation for those who came to bathe and may even have served pornographic purposes. These frescos show us that overt expressions of sexuality were commonplace in Ancient Pompeii, and as a result, pornographic imagery was likely not viewed as deviant.

(a)   **(b)**

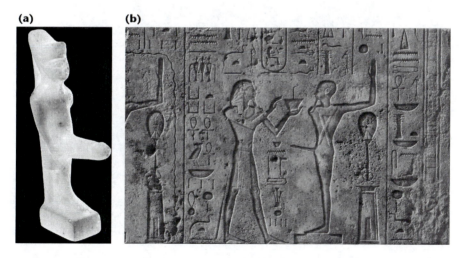

IMAGE 7.2   Depictions of Ancient Egyptian God Min

Ancient Egyptian fertility god Min is often depicted in an ithyphallic (with an erect phallus) style, shown here both in (a) statuette form and in (b) sunk relief form at the great ancient Egyptian temple of Amun at the Karnak Temple, Luxor, Egypt. ©Shutterstock, Anton Kudelin, mountainpix.

Ancient India

Perhaps one of the most extensive collections of ancient sexual imagery is exhibited in hundreds of architectural sculptures dedicated to Hinduism and to Jainism at the Khajurāho temples in Madhya Pradesh, India built between 950 and 1050 c.e. by the Chandela Dynasty. There were originally close to 100 temples spread over 20 square kilometers in the Khajurāho temple complex but only about 25 temples have survived. The remaining temples display intricately carved statues depicting various practices of everyday human life. They are most well-known, however, for the sexual scenes located on non-prominent spaces that cover only a small fraction (most estimates indicate less than 10 percent) of the temples (see Image 7.3).

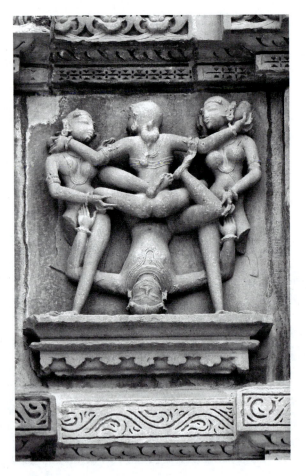

IMAGE 7.3 North wall of the Kaṇḍāriya Mahādeva temple at Khajurāho

Detail image of the north wall of the Kaṇḍāriya Mahādeva temple at Khajurāho in Madhya Pradesh, India. ©Shutterstock, Guillermo Garcia.

Although the depictions of sexual acts on Khajurāho temples are sometimes described as erotic art, even pornographic in nature, most historians believe that they were more than likely demonstrative of daily life (Zannas and Auboyer 1960). As a result, sexuality was viewed as commonplace—a normative human experience in ancient Indian art and daily life.

Western Europe in the Middle Ages

During the Middle Ages, sometimes described as the Dark Ages, the Roman Catholic Church impeded on the dominant social structure in Western Europe. Almost every aspect of life was organized around Christianity, and that included artistic expression. While some have suggested that this meant that there was no sexual imagery produced in the Middle Ages (because all public art was commissioned by the church and therefore it was religious and non-sexual), others have discovered erotic undertones as well as overt but hidden expressions of sexuality in medieval art. For example, the myriad images of bare-breasted virgin martyrs with long flowing hair typical of medieval art who are often described as "ideal women" elicit both religious and erotic responses (Easton 2008:6). This type of artistic expression whereby religious figures are somewhat paradoxically erotically presented has been described as "religious pornography" (Miles 1989:156) because both purity and sexuality are highlighted in such imagery. Some suggest that "religious pornography" was common in the art of the Middle Ages. Other medieval art is more overtly sexual, but hidden. For example, thirteenth century misericords, small shelves underneath church seating on which church-goers could lean during long periods of prayer, display a wide variety of salacious carvings including "lovers, bare-breasted sirens and mermaids, men exposing their buttocks and genitals and naked women astride animals" (Easton 2008:14-15). Because of their placement, these erotic images are rather well hidden, despite the fact that they are within the walls of the church. Churches are also the home to twelfth century Sheela-na-gigs, architectural grotesque sculptures of women squatting and pulling back the lips of their vaginas, which can be found on the exteriors of Romanesque churches, especially in Ireland and Great Britain (see Image 7.4). Sheela-na-gigs have been connected to themes of eroticism, lust, sexuality, birth, death, life, and fertility (Easton 2008). While it is clear that sexual and even erotic imagery existed during the Middle Ages, whether or not these images functioned as what we conceive of as "pornography" remains a mystery. It is also most likely the case that because these sexual images were often hidden, their construction may in itself fit within the realm of deviance. In other words, both the creation and display of sexual art in the Middle Ages were deviant endeavors. Even so, during a time when the Catholic Church controlled nearly all aspects of everyday life, people still found a way to express sexuality through erotic art.

IMAGE 7.4 Twelfth century Sheela-na-gig

A twelfth century Sheela-na-gig on the south side of Kilpeck Church near Hereford, England. Photo used with permission from John Harding, www.sheelanagig.org.

Western Europe in the Renaissance

The Renaissance was a period of rebirth and rediscovery of the classical past that celebrated sexuality (in contrast to the repressive Dark Ages). Renaissance artists were emboldened by this period of enlightenment and created an astonishingly vast amount of sculpture, paintings, and architecture. Artistic expression during the Renaissance celebrated courtly love and the nude form. Beyond these romantic themes, sex and sexuality thrived in Renaissance art as well. There is even a secret room, the Stuffeta di Bibbiena, in the Vatican (not open for public viewing) in which Renaissance master Raphael painted erotic imagery in the early 1500s that includes depictions of masturbation and cavorting naked deities (Perrottet 2011; McCall *et al.* 2013). What is more, the invention of the mechanical printing press in the late 1400s also meant that sexual imagery could be easily produced, transported, and shared. Prior to this, nearly all art existed in public spaces and within churches— hardly practical viewing locations for pornographic purposes. With the ability to mass print pamphlets with erotic imagery and writings, the Western world could now view "pornography" at a whim. In fact, scholars have noted the rise of the printing press during the Renaissance as central to the early (and continued) success of pornography (Coopersmith 1998). For example, the late fifteenth century pornographic copper printing plate image *Allegory of Copulation* (depicting a man and a woman sexually embracing with a large bird in the form of a penis nearby) was so popular that the original plate was re-engraved and heavily used again, so much so that none of the original impressions printed, which are believed to be in the hundreds, have survived (Levinson and Oberhuber 1973). With erotic material now accessible to the general public, the business of pornography was on the front-lines during the Renaissance and its controversial success continues today.

Western Europe in the Victorian era

What modern-day contemporaries conceive of as "pornography" can be traced to the Victorian era. Despite the fact that the Victorian era is well known as the age of sexual repression (Foucault 1978), some have claimed that the porn "industry" actually originated at this time (Marcus 1964). Beyond the erotic prints, pamphlets, and literature that had previously existed, the Victorian era saw the emergence of new communication technologies that were seemingly instantly "sexualized":

> Each and every instrument of communication that has been devised to date by man ... has been almost immediately turned to the service of what the culture in which it was invented called 'pornography ... ' regardless of so-called 'public attitudes' at the time or law.
>
> *(Gordon 1980:33)*

The rapid growth of technologies during the Victorian era no doubt shaped the availability and popularity of pornography. By the late 1800s, pornography was a booming market that included:

- *Photographs.* Emerging in the 1840s, the first practical photography method for mass production (the calotype process) single-handedly created a trade industry centered around erotic photography. Many viewed Paris, France, as the hub of this industry because in 1848 there were only 13 photography studios but by 1870, there were more than 350, most of which received the majority of their revenue from the sale of erotic photos. The press described this as a "pandemic of obscene pictures" as early as 1851 (Barss 2010:65).
- *Magazines.* Another technological advancement, the invention of halftone printing in the 1880s, paved the way for pornographic images to be produced in gentlemen's magazines. They made their first appearance in France and

featured nude models, many of whom were burlesque dancers. While most modern interpreters of these photos would describe these photos as "softcore" imagery, the blatant display of nudity in these magazines was seen as not only risqué, but also, obscene (Barss 2010).

- *Moving pictures.* First emerging in the late 1800s, most erotic films were short and rather crude in production. Prior to the genre collectively known as "stag films" (discussed below), the typical pornographic film was black and white with no sound and was about 10 minutes in length. These primitive "dirty" films often depicted women participating in various mundane activities such as undressing and bathing and viewers were voyeurs "peeping" in to watch them in the nude (Barss 2010).

Alongside the growth and availability of multiple media forms of pornography was the emergence of laws criminalizing porn—a unique Victorian construct that drew clear lines between "normative" and "deviant" sexuality and sexual expression. Two significant laws emerged during this time, one that applied to the United Kingdom and Ireland (the Obscene Publications Act of 1857 also known as Lord Campbell's Act) and one in the United States (the Comstock Act of 1873). Both Acts targeted pornography by deeming "obscene" material illegal (although neither offered a clear definition of obscenity at the time[1]). In the case of Lord Campbell's Act, any material found to be "obscene" could be destroyed by a magistrate or justice of the peace. The Comstock Act made it illegal to use the U.S. Postal Service to transport any "obscene" materials (which ran the gamut from pornography and sex toys to contraceptives and even some anatomy textbooks) (Foster 1957). For perhaps the first time in recent history, pornography was unmistakably delineated as "criminal."

Early American twentieth century

Beginning in the twentieth century, a genre collectively described as "stag films" emerged alongside the successes of the erotic photography trade. Early stag films were very primitive; in fact, most were shot anonymously. Unlike the "softcore" pornographic imagery of the 1800s, stag films offered close-up, hardcore graphic shots of genital, oral, and anal sex acts. For example, one of the earliest known American stag films, *A Free Ride* (produced in 1915), depicts a motorist who picks up two women from the roadside and the three of them participate in multiple sex acts (including oral sex and sexual intercourse) with one another. This 9-minute black-and-white silent film is characteristic of early pornographic films due to its rudimentary nature and its use of "crude humor" in its fictional opening credits with the director listed as "A. Wise Guy" and the photographer credited to "Will B. Hard" (Williams 2007:62). Because of the prevailing obscenity laws, *A Free Ride*, similar to other pornographic films of that era, was an underground vice, most likely shown only in brothels and gentlemen's clubs (Williams 2007). While viewing stag films was most definitely a deviant act in the early twentieth century, today these films are priceless historical artifacts, with one of the largest known collections of historical stag films (close to 1,700 films) housed in the Kinsey Institute in Indiana.

American mid-to-late twentieth century

Porn "mags"

Erotic photography experienced a boost in revenue in the 1940s when "pin ups" were popularized by World War II U.S. soldiers who tore pictures of semi-nude women from men's magazines and calendars and "pinned" them "up" on their lockers and barracks' walls. By the 1950s, Marilyn Monroe's curvaceous figure became the icon of erotic imagery. In fact, she was pictured on the cover of the inaugural edition of *Playboy* (released in December 1953) and her nude centerfold is rumored to be the source of the enormous success of the first issue, which sold out in just a few short weeks at 50 cents per copy. Since then, millions of *Playboy* magazines have been sold in over 50 different countries worldwide featuring hundreds of famous film, television, music, and sports celebrities as well as models in the buff [although in 2016, *Playboy* abandoned the publication of totally nude, pornographic images opting to showcase women in "provocative poses" (Vokes-Dudgeon 2015)]. *Penthouse* followed in 1956 (released in the United States in 1969) and offered more explicit close-up shots of female genitalia, and in 1974, *Hustler* magazine became one of the first pornographic magazines to depict hardcore themes including penetration and group sex (Semonche 2007). The market for these magazines is predominately heterosexual men and although they were soaring in popularity during the 1970s amongst this group, the possession and viewing of porn "mags" was (and sometimes still is) considered to be at its worst "dirty" and "deviant" but at the very least, a clandestine activity. For example, accounts of youthful experiences with pornography during this time describe young men finding illicit magazines at home and at the homes of friends and family, and subsequently, "stashing" porn mag collections in secret locations such as underneath mattresses and even in the woods (Paasonen *et al.* 2015). Whether, hiding and collecting porn "mags" or openly displaying "pin ups" from them, the simultaneous feelings of shame and excitement characterize "porn mag" experiences during this time and perhaps still do today.

The adult film industry

In the 1960s, film technology was advancing and pornographers got rich: this was the beginning of the first "golden age of pornography" (Barss 2010:78). Interestingly, the real money started with stand-alone booths called "peeps," which were popular in the 1960s to 1970s. Patrons would go into a small booth, lock the door, and pay 25 cents to watch two minutes of an 8 mm pornographic film. One need only drop in more quarters to watch more of the film—and that is exactly what they did. These peeps, which started out as an innovative way to show stag films in a public setting but to private viewers, were enormously successful. Due to the unprecedented demand for new peep films, between 50 and 75 new peep "loops" of film were released each week. Profits were staggering: at a cost of $8 to make a loop, revenues could be between $2,000 and $10,000 per week and it is estimated that over $2 billion worth of coins were dropped in peep booths during the 1970s alone. As a result of the need for new and exciting stag films to show in peep booths, porn actors and actresses were in high demand. In essence, peeps generated a full-blown "adult film industry" (Barss 2010:79).

The adult film industry would continue to flourish with Denmark becoming the first country in the world to abolish all laws related to the production and consumption of pornography in 1969. In the United States, the controversial multimillion-dollar success of the first *almost* mainstream X-rated hardcore American film, *Deep Throat*, in 1972, marked the emergence of plotlines within porn movies. By the 1980s, videocassette recorders (VCRs) became popular and people could now watch pornography in the comfort of their own homes. As a result, the adult film industry continued to thrive via videotape. In fact, some evidence shows that X-rated movies constituted over 50 percent of the sales of videotapes during this time (Ford 1999; Semonche 2007; Barss 2010). In the 1990s, DVDs continued to offer a convenient at-home option for porn viewers, but perhaps the most significant innovation to the porn industry during this time was the bulletin board system, or BBS, a primitive form of what we know as the world wide web. The BBS allowed users to "dial up" and connect to the online system using a terminal program and upload/download software and data, exchange messages, and engage in online chatroom discussions. Porn distributors grabbed onto this technology immediately and the internet became a new permanent home for pornography and the porn trade in general. Estimates indicate that by 1992, there were 45,000 BBSs in the U.S., servicing 12 million computers and grossing nearly $1 billion in revenue (with close to $850 million of that to local phone companies) (Lane 2001). Because of this, "pornography was paying for the infrastructure of the information age" (Barss 2010:122). More about pornography in the twenty-first century is discussed in chapter 11.

Summary: historical perspectives on sexual imagery

Overall, the overtly sexual art evident throughout history shows us that humans have been fascinated by sexual behavior since the beginning. From Paleolithic cave drawings to sculptures, copper printing plates, peep booths, and porn mags, "pornographic" images have never been too hard to find. However, perspectives about imagery that is representative of the nude form or even graphic sex have varied from supportive and celebratory to deviant and criminal. One need only take a snapshot of human history to see the complex emotions evoked from erotic visual expression. In doing so, we can see not only the historical variance in depictions of sexual imagery—but also, the diversity in attitudes toward erotic art. This journey through time shows us that our own perspectives about pornography are both culturally and historically embedded in ways that are not so easily understood without careful sociological examination.

Sale of sex

The exchange of sex acts for some form of remuneration is evident throughout history in nearly all societies. Although there is more historical evidence of women selling sexual favors to men (in comparison to other arrangements such as men selling sex to men or women), both men and women have participated in the lucrative business of selling sex throughout time. Indeed, perspectives about gender and sexuality shaped the business of sex within the earliest of human civilizations. Even so, contemporary examinations of "sex for sale" are built from interpretations of historical norms and behaviors. The words "prostitute" and "prostitution" did not make their way into modern language until relatively recently, and as a result, an historical examination of selling sex should be tempered by the fact that present-day perspectives about "prostitution" are both temporally and culturally dependent. For example, the commonly held modern-day American view of "sex for sale" as both deviant and criminal has not always been the norm—in fact, quite the contrary. Over time, selling sex has been both normative and celebrated as well as deviantized and criminalized. Thus, as we examine the sale of sex over time it is important to be both culturally and historically sensitive. Below, the terms "prostitute" and "prostitution" are used to explain the business of selling sex recognizing that these words are fixed within a modern cultural milieu. Similarly, whether or not this type of behavior was viewed as "normative" or "deviant" is also speculated based on historical accounts. Even so, a journey through the human history of "sex for sale" demonstrates the complex relationships between sex, money, gender, and power throughout time.

Ancient Mesopotamia

It is unknown precisely when humans began exchanging sexual services for remuneration; however, we can look to ancient artifacts to trace the emergence of "prostitution" as an occupation. For example, prostitution has been found on ancient Sumerian lists of professions generated in approximately 2400 B.C.E. The Sumerian word for female prostitute, *kar.kid*, occurs in these lists in conjunction with *kur-garru*, a male prostitute or entertainer. On the same ancient lists, we find other women's occupations such as "lady doctor," "scribe," "barber," and "cook." Thus, despite the old adage that "prostitution is the world's oldest profession" we have clear evidence that "while it is a very old profession, is not the oldest" (Lerner 1986:236, 245). Prostitution continued to be seen as an occupation throughout the Middle Babylonian period. Historians believe that in ancient Mesopotamia, sex was both pleasing to the gods and normative to society. During this time, both religious sexual services connected to spiritual ceremony (sometimes described as sacred or cultic prostitution[2]) existed alongside commercial prostitution (Lerner 1986). However, commercial female prostitution became much more common in conjunction with military conquests in the third millennium B.C.E. that led to the enslavement of women and the sale of female slaves as prostitutes. Slave masters began to set up brothels and harems and possession of these captive women quickly became a symbol of power for aristocrats, bureaucrats, and wealthy men (Lerner 1983). Women were also sold into prostitution by their impoverished family members and husbands (a practice we still see today).

By most historical accounts, commercial prostitution was considered a "social necessity for meeting the sexual needs of men" (Lerner 1986:247) during this time. It was not until the enactment of Middle Assyrian Law (MAL) 40 in approximately 1115 to 1077 B.C.E. that the "respectability" of these women was formally called into question. MAL 40 legislated the practice of veiling[3] to only certain types of women and in doing so, effectively created a hierarchical rank order system for the social status of women. Married women and unmarried daughters were at the top of respectability and were required to wear veils when in public, married concubines were ranked next and although they had a lower status, they were still required to veil themselves, and at the bottom were unmarried prostitutes who were the least respected type of women who were not afforded the social status of wearing a veil. Historians speculate that this is one of the first of many laws throughout human history that would both regulate prostitution and visually designate those involved in prostitution, especially prostitutes themselves, as social deviants and criminals. In this case, this deviantization process was obvious to all because prostitutes were the only women walking the streets without veils (Lerner 1986).

Ancient China

Historians believe that the "*ying-chi*" ("camp harlots") were amongst the first women who worked in commercial prostitution in China during the Western Han Dynasty (140 to 87 B.C.E.) (Ruan 1991). Courtesanship, which is believed to have originated in China in approximately 772 to 481 B.C.E., became a form of government-regulated prostitution during the T'ang Dynasty (618 to 907 C.E.). *Courtesans* were professionally trained female performers who entertained men with music and dance but also provided sexual pleasure. House courtesanship was so commonplace during the T'ang Dynasty that courtesans were regularly housed by high-ranking government officials as both entertainers and in some cases, prostitutes. In fact, emperors throughout the T'ang Dynasty including Chung-tsung (r. 705 to 709), Hsuan-tsung (r. 712 to 756), Te-tsung (r. 780 to 805), and Mu-tsung (r. 821 to 824) were all highly supportive of courtesan culture. In addition, most major cities in ancient China had brothels, which are believed to have formally emerged in approximately 635 to 689, where private courtesans worked. Overall, the T'ang Dynasty celebrated both sexuality and opulence and as a result, successful courtesanship (both in government and private industry) reflected a thriving culture of prostitution in ancient China (Yao 2002).

Ancient Greece

In general, prostitution was well tolerated in ancient Greece, and in fact, brothels were introduced by lawmakers (i.e., Solon) and regulated in approximately 638 to 558 B.C.E. This organized system of female prostitution was hierarchical and included dicteriades, auletrides, and hetairae. The dicteriades occupied the lowest status among prostitutes in ancient Greek society and although they charged small amounts for their sexual services, they were immensely popular. The auletrides ("flute-players") were "middle class" status prostitutes who frequently worked as musicians and dancers at banquets and feasts both as entertainment and providers of sexual pleasure. The hetairae, who have been described as the "queens of courtesans in Greece" (Adămuț 2009:15), were well-respected women. They were highly educated (unlike most other women of ancient Greece) and could serve as intellectual companions to men in addition to providing them with sexual services, although only the wealthy could gain sexual access to the hetairae (Adămuț 2009). As a result, relationships with hetairae were viewed as high status.

Young men also worked as prostitutes in ancient Greece. As we will discuss later in this chapter, adolescent boys were highly eroticized in Greece in approximately 600 to 500 B.C.E. Indeed, pederastic love affairs between adult men and adolescent boys were both institutionalized as normal and idealized. As a result of this culture, some young men worked as prostitutes with adult men as their primary clientele. However, these young male prostitutes were, for the most part, of low social standing. In fact, they were deprived of certain citizenship rights in adulthood as a result of their transgressions. Even so, while they occupied a deviant status, it was not unusual to find young men working as prostitutes during this time. Furthermore, because many adolescent boys were given gifts by their adult male lovers, the precise line between what was defined as "prostitution" and what was viewed as a socially valued pederastic love affair between men and boys in ancient Greece was not entirely clear (Ormand 2009; Lanni 2010).

Ancient Pompeii

Prostitution continued to thrive in ancient Roman culture. One of the oldest surviving brothels located in the Pompeii ruins, the Lupanar, was preserved in time after the eruption of Mount Vesuvius in 79 C.E. Although scholars have debated about the number of brothels in the ancient city of Pompeii, most agree that the Lupanar is the only structure that operated solely as a place where the sale of sex occurred because of (i) evidence of a masonry bed, (ii) the presence of sexually explicit frescos, and (iii) the presence of graffiti believed to have been inscribed by the clientele of prostitutes describing the sex acts that occurred on the premises (Wallace-Hadrill 1995). The Lupanar contains five small rooms with carved masonry "beds" with "pillows," which are believed to have functioned as places where the exchange of sex for remuneration occurred. Evidence shows that the Lupanar was located in a bustling part of the city in close proximity to major streets and popular public establishments including the Forum and the Stabian Baths. Because of this, it is believed that the brothel was a business just like any other in ancient Rome, although the brothel itself was not an upper-class establishment. For example, the prostitutes working in Pompeii, both women and men, were relatively inexpensive and their clients were also relatively poor. The series of erotic frescos on the walls of the Lupanar depicting a man and woman in various forms of sexual activity (see Image 7.5) are far more luxurious than the Lupanar itself, thus these paintings were likely designed to be enticing fantasies to the Lupanar's lower-class patrons (Clarke 1998). Even so, the Lupanar's well-positioned location and apparent lucrative success indicates that prostitution was commonplace in ancient Rome. In addition, because no laws explicitly defined prostitution as illegal in ancient Rome, visiting prostitutes was likely perceived as normative. Although it may have been frowned upon by some, prostitution was not criminalized or severely deviantized in ancient Rome (Ormand 2009).

Western Europe in the Middle Ages

Throughout medieval society in Western Europe, public attitudes toward prostitution shifted dramatically. For example, during the twelfth and thirteenth centuries, the domination of the Christian church meant that prostitution was tolerated as a necessary evil because seeing a prostitute deterred from greater sins such as rape and masturbation. The social organization during this time placed men's desires above the economic exploitations of women working as prostitutes: "the underlying assumptions were that men had sexual needs, and that providing 'safe' women to fulfill them was important for civil order. The economic vulnerability of poor women meant that some were always available to sell their sexual services" (Crawford 2007:173). By the fourteenth and fifteenth centuries, prostitution became

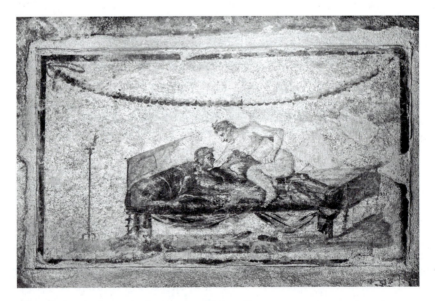

IMAGE 7.5 Erotic fresco in the Lupanar, Pompeii

Erotic fresco picturing a man and woman in Pompeii's brothel, the Lupanar [located at VII, 12, 18–20]. ©Shutterstock, Boris Stroujko.

institutionalized and government-sanctioned in Western Europe. For example, many countries including England, France, and Germany created ordinances that set aside certain streets where prostitution was tolerated. In fact, a popular euphemism for hiring a prostitute, "to pluck a rose," comes from the fact that streets with the word "rose" in them were commonly designated for prostitution in England during this time (Bullough 1982:182). While prostitution was tolerated by society and law, prostitutes themselves were considered deviant and this was made clear to all members of society through clothing requirements. To alert others to their deviant status, prostitutes were required to wear distinctive attire, which varied by city ordinance as follows (Richards 1994; Crawford 2007):

- Milan, Italy: black cloaks.
- Florence, Italy: gloves and bells on hats.
- Southeastern France: red armbands.
- Germany: red hats.

But by the sixteenth century, the rules had changed and prostitution became a relatively universally punishable offense. Nearly all brothels were shut down throughout Western Europe and no government-sanctioned prostitution remained (Crawford 2007). Some see this tightening of prostitution laws as resultant from the public response to new knowledge about infectious diseases, specifically the bubonic plague and syphilis. In the fourteenth century, the "Black Death" killed an estimated 75 to 200 million people, including 30 to 60 percent of the European population. About 150 years later, the first recorded syphilis outbreak occurred in Naples, Italy, from 1494 to 1495, and it quickly spread across Europe. Perhaps due to the need for scapegoating, some blamed prostitutes for the syphilis outbreak, viewing these women and their clients as "vectors of disease" (this notion is also evident in WWII propaganda as we will discuss later in this chapter) (Bullough and Bullough 1977). Others have noted the stronghold of the Christian church at this time as the source of severe punishment for prostitution. For example, Louis XIV of France (1638 to 1718), described as "God's Most Christian King" (Riley 2001:8), ordered incarceration of all prostitutes on the grounds that they were sinful in April of 1684. In fact, because of Louis XIV's edict, by 1697, the French prison, La Salpêtrière, was filled with more than 4,000 women, the majority of whom were believed to have been arrested for prostitution and in need of "reformation" (Andrews 1994). As a result, prostitution by the end of the Middle Ages was both deviant and criminal.

Western Europe in the Victorian era

The sale of sex during the Victorian era continued to be seen as deviant and criminal, although three major events shaped new cultural perceptions about prostitution. First, British medical doctor William Acton's (1813–1875) research in 1857 found that there were between 9,409 (an estimate from the police) to more than 80,000 (an estimate from the Bishop of Exeter) prostitutes in London alone. This alarming study defined prostitution as a major social and moral problem that needed to be addressed. Accordingly, the second event during the Victorian era that shaped public attitudes toward prostitution was a noticeable concentrated effort to house these "fallen women" in Magdalene Institutions, especially in the late 1800s. Although convents and reformatories for "incorrigible" women in the name of the biblical figure, Mary Magdalene (who is often characterized as a reformed prostitute), emerged much earlier, hundreds of Magdalene Institutions were founded during the Victorian era in Australia, Canada, England, Ireland, Scotland, and the United States. Magdalene Institutions have been described both as places of salvation (i.e., reformatories and shelters) and as places of punishment (asylums, prisons and forced-labor penitentiaries) for any women who "might cause moral damage to the community" (McCarthy 2010:163). Although Magdalene Institutions originally emerged as places to protect prostitutes and other "fallen women" (unwed mothers, troublemakers, and other "undesirables") from the dangers of being on the street, most ended up effectively imprisoning and exploiting these women for cheap labor, especially in the case of the Magdalene laundries in Dublin, Ireland, in which thousands of Irish women were forced to work as laundresses for no pay (McCarthy 2010:8). Even so, the public attitude toward prostitution during the Victorian era was that these women needed to be housed in "reformatories" due to their immoral and deviant participation in the sale of sex.

The third event that shaped public attitudes toward prostitution in Western Europe during the Victorian era was the introduction of the Contagious Diseases (CD) Acts of 1864, 1866, and 1869 in the United Kingdom. The CD Acts were originally created to monitor the spread of venereal diseases among military personnel. In practice, however, the CD Acts effectively required any woman believed to be a "common prostitute" (a vague description that police used to harass women that did not meet the pious standards of Victorian society) to be subjected to compulsory examinations for venereal disease (Smith 1990:197). Women could be stopped on the street by policemen if suspected to be soliciting the sale of sex and required to submit to an internal gynecological exam. If the woman was diagnosed with any venereal disease (such as syphilis or gonorrhea), she could be detained within a "lock hospital" (a hospital with special wards for women with venereal diseases) for up to one year. As a result, thousands of suspected prostitutes found to have venereal diseases were effectively imprisoned; they had no right of appeal and no recourse to habeas corpus (Smith 1990). The idea behind the CD Acts was to protect men, especially military men, from venereal disease. Because they were socialized by the military to avoid marriage, masturbation, and same-sex sexual behavior, prostitution was considered a necessary evil. So while the CD Acts locked up women for their venereal disease status, no men were reprimanded; in fact, there were no examinations or inquisitions of prostitutes' clientele of any kind. This "double standard" (in which women were judged harshly for participating in the sale of sex while their clients went unpunished) became the center of debate amongst one of the first organized feminist collectives. Led by Josephine Butler, the Ladies National Association for the Repeal of the Contagious Diseases Acts brought charges against the Acts in 1869 claiming them to be generally "cruel and degrading" specifically noting that "the Act brutalizes and violates women" (Smith 1990:198). Because of their efforts, the CD Acts were repealed in 1886, although similar laws emerged about 100 years later in the United States (see more about how the HIV/ AIDS crisis shaped prostitution legislation later in this chapter).

As a result of these three events and accompanying debate about them, prostitution became a widely discussed issue in Western Europe during the 1800s. For the first time in a long while, prostitutes' rights were at the center of this discourse and the social control of prostitution was no longer the only goal of legislation. Even so prostitution remained a deviant, criminal, and dangerous profession[4] during the Victorian era.

Early American twentieth century

In the early American twentieth century, prostitution was illegal in all states (48 at the time; Alaska and Hawaii would later follow when they became states and so would subsequent U.S. territories and insular areas) with few exceptions.[5] Even so, prostitution flourished. Starting in the early 1900s, widespread use of telephones created an organized system where prostitutes no longer had to remain in brothels or work the streets to gain clients. "Call girls" could simply hand out their telephone numbers and arrange meetings with clients off the streets and away from law enforcement agencies. Although prostitution remained illegal, it was not hard to find sex for sale in early twentieth century America.

However, the cultural landscape would largely change during World War II (1939 to 1945). During this time, women around the world were forced into prostitution at alarming rates. In Germany, it is estimated that close to 35,000 European women were forced to serve as prostitutes during the German occupation in addition to the thousands of women working in German concentration camp brothels (Herbermann et al. 2000). Furthermore, hundreds of thousands of women from Korea, Taiwan, China, the Philippines, Indonesia, and other countries were forced into prostitution by the Japanese military. Described as "comfort women," girls as young as 12 years old were forced to engage in multiple sex acts with military men (including American soldiers) on a daily basis in military-controlled "comfort stations" (Hicks 1997). Beyond forced prostitution, many women were living in poverty due to the economic conditions during the War and as a result, prostitution became a viable opportunity to make money (especially with the influx of soldiers who were often eager clientele). The rampant prostitution during WWII was not a secret. In fact, the U.S. government issued a variety of colorful posters urging military men to resist the temptations of the "disease-ridden" prostitutes they would likely encounter and their message was clear and simple: "abstain from illicit sexual contact because it is unpatriotic, lethal, or detrimental to one's health, and shameful to one's spouse, girlfriend, or family back home" (Mungia et al. 2014:20). These propaganda posters focused on three key areas: (i) demonizing ladies of the night/prostitutes/pickups/ good time girls and women in general; (ii) highlighting the peril/danger/maladies/

guilt/career damage associated with sex with these "evil women" (and the likely accompanying exposure to venereal diseases); and (iii) the importance of protecting yourself via prophylaxis (i.e., condoms and penicillin if needed) (Mungia *et al.* 2014). In all, however, these posters used laughable gimmicks such as:

- "She may look clean–BUT . . . Pick-ups, good time girls, prostitutes . . . SPREAD SYPHILIS AND GONORRHEA. You can't beat the Axis if you get VD" (Mungia *et al.* 2014:26).
- "LOADED. *Don't take chances with pickups!* Loose women may also be LOADED with disease!" (Mungia *et al.* 2014:19, 47). (Note that there are two versions of the ad, both featuring a picture of a gun emblazoned across the top.)
- "V.D. WORST OF THE THREE" (Mungia *et al.* 2014:50). (Note that this ad features three people locked arm and arm strolling happily with one another: Hitler, Hirohoto, and a woman in a sexy red dress with a skeleton face.)
- "VD can be cured, but there's no medicine for *REGRET*" (Mungia *et al.* 2014:31).
- "Most *Promiscuous women* have **VENEREAL DISEASE**! *Don't take a chance* . . . Take a *Pro*" (Mungia *et al.* 2014:35. (Note that this ad includes a detailed map with six prophylactic stations in the Tacloban area of the Philippines where soldiers could go to get condoms.)
- "**NO** is the best tactic, the next, **PRO**PHYLACTIC!" (Mungia *et al.* 2014:38, 39).

From these ads, it is clear that prostitutes and other "loose women" were blamed for venereal diseases and that military men were instructed to resist these temptresses at all costs. Although this ad campaign may seem comical to the contemporary viewer, it was likely a reaction to the loss of nearly 18,000 men that were discharged for venereal diseases during WWI (Mungia *et al.* 2014). With the visibility of wartime prostitution heightened, these women were labeled as "vectors of disease" and generally deviantized.

American mid-to-late twentieth century

Although prostitution remained illegal in the majority of the U.S., four events would shape the landscape of prostitution during the latter half of the twentieth century. First, Mustang Ranch became Nevada's first licensed brothel in 1971 and paved the way for future successful brothel franchises in Nevada, many of which still remain operable today (Albert 2002). Second, the Sex Workers Rights Movement[6] emerged in the 1970s. One of the first and most well-known groups advocating for prostitutes in the United States, COYOTE "Call Off Your Old Tired Ethics," was founded by former prostitute Margo St. James in 1973. COYOTE calls for (Jenness 1990:403):

- The repeal of all existing prostitution laws.
- The reconstitution of prostitution as a credible service occupation.
- The protection of prostitutes' rights as legitimate workers.

COYOTE leaders promote a revision of contemporary views of prostitution. Specifically, they envision a world where prostitution is free from stigma and garners the same respect as other voluntarily chosen service work: "a rather profound misconception that people have about prostitution is that it is 'sex for sale,' or that a prostitute is selling her body. In reality, a prostitute is being paid for her time and skill" (St. James and Alexander 1977:n.p.). Overall, COYOTE sees the stigma, violence, inadequate health care, and denial of protection by and under the law that most prostitutes face as major civil rights issues: "from COYOTE's perspective, as workers prostitutes should be afforded equal protection under the law and should be free of violations of their civil rights" (Jenness 1990:406). Continuing in line with sex workers' rights, former prostitute turned activist Carol Leigh (a.k.a. the "Scarlot Harlot") coined the term "sex worker" in 1978 (Nagle 1997:13). With both a firm footing in a civil rights organization (COYOTE) and the discourse to legitimize prostitution as "work," prostitution was at the center of a feminist activism movement and the 1970s general public was challenged to consider this new set of perspectives about sex work. As a result, the "deviance" of prostitution was actively being called into question.

The third event that triggered yet another reconceptualization of prostitution in the late twentieth century was the onset of HIV/AIDS in the 1980s. Sometimes referred to as "The AIDS Epidemic," during just a few short years (from 1981 to 1992), nearly a quarter of a million Americans were diagnosed with HIV and diseases related to complications from HIV/AIDS had claimed the lives of more than 90 percent of these people by the early nineties (CDC 2001). In addition, many had the erroneous perception that only gay men could contract HIV/AIDS and the virus was negatively referred to as "the gay plague" and even briefly labeled as "gay-related immune deficiency (GRID)" by medical professionals (Dowsett 2009:130, 136). To respond to this devastating crisis and increasing misinformation, an educational pamphlet about HIV/AIDS was mailed by post to all 107 million households in the United States in 1988. This pamphlet was designed to educate the public about HIV/AIDS and specifically noted that (i) HIV/AIDS is transmitted through oral, anal, and vaginal intercourse (as well as sharing drug needles and syringes with an infected person) and (ii) condoms are the best preventive measure against AIDS (besides not having sex) (NIH 1988). As a result, the majority of the American public became aware that HIV/AIDS was associated with unprotected sex. This radically altered perspectives about prostitution and new laws began to emerge that harkened back to the CD Acts of the late 1800s (previously reviewed in this chapter). For example, the state of California passed a harsh law in 1988 that once again targeted prostitutes (not their clients) as "carriers of disease" (Shepard 2006:427). Specifically, the law

- mandated statewide HIV testing of all convicted prostitutes;
- required HIV test results to be placed on the permanent records of all prostitutes; and
- shifted prostitution charges from a misdemeanor to a felony with required jail time.

These punitive penalties were enacted *despite* the fact that the CDC had reported that prostitutes were *more likely* than the general population to use condoms and there was no evidence that prostitutes are more likely to have HIV/AIDS than the general public (Shepard 2006). Even so, as a result of the AIDS epidemic and accompanying panic, prostitutes were once again further deviantized and more harshly criminalized.

Finally, the 1990s ushered in a new wave of internet-enabled solicitation. Both individual sex workers and brothels could now virtually advertise their services and clients could contact them with the click of a mouse. As discussed previously in this chapter, the relationship between the sex industry and the internet has been synergistic from the beginning (Barss 2010). As the world wide web began to develop, so did the online home for the sale of sex. This new world expanded opportunities for prostitutes and changed sex work forever. More about prostitution in the twenty-first century is discussed in chapter 11.

Summary: historical perspectives on sex for sale

Overall, evidence of the business of selling sex throughout history shows us that humans have been interested in the exchange of sex for some form of remuneration since the beginning of civilization. From ancient Mesopotamia to the world wide web, "prostitution" has never been very well hidden. However, perspectives about selling sex have been diverse ranging from commonplace tolerance to deviant and criminal. By examining these attitudinal shifts over time, we can see that our own feelings about selling sex are both culturally and historically embedded in ways that are deeply codified by our understandings of sex, gender, money, and power. Our frequent modern-day labeling of "prostitution" as "deviant," is built from a complex history of varying attitudes toward sex for sale.

Same-sex sexual behavior

Sex acts between two people of the same sex date back to the earliest of humans. And although such behavior has been around since the beginning of humanity, today's identity labels such as "gay" or "lesbian" are very recent developments. Thus, our modern-day understanding of same-sex sexual behavior as linked to gay and lesbian identities should be understood with both cultural and historical sensitivity. As we examine the history of same-sex sexual desire, it is important to recognize that same-sex sexual experiences have often been excluded from historical writings, biographies, literature, and art because many societies have viewed same-sex sex acts as deviant and criminal. As a result, same-sex sexual desire has been completely overlooked in some cases. In particular, women with romantic interests in other women have been largely ignored throughout history because "sex between women defied the dominant heteronormativity differently than did sex between men, in part because what women did was considered something of a mystery" (Crawford 2007:190). As a result, the majority of what we know about same-sex desire throughout history is built from accounts of men's sexual and/or romantic interest in other men. Furthermore, because there were no identity constructs that could be tied to this behavior until very recently, it is important to avoid labeling behaviors (and people) based on the use of the modern-day terms such as "gay" or "lesbian." In general, same-sex sexuality was celebrated and normalized until the West was dominated by Christian ideals. Throughout the past several hundred years, same-sex desire has shifted from punishable by death to a complex modern-day milieu of activism in the West. Thus, contemporary perspectives about the deviance of same-sex sexuality are embedded in historical belief systems that have varied significantly over time.

Early humans

Since the beginning of humanity, those of the same sex have engaged in sexual behaviors with one another. During the Paleolithic era, early humans created artifacts that demonstrated this appreciation of same-sex eroticism. Some examples can be seen in ancient cave art such as an etched drawing of two men apparently engaged in anal intercourse found in the French cave of La Marche dated back to 14,000 B.C.E. and a plate carving of two women touching one another's breasts found in the Cave of Gönnersdorf, Germany, dated back to more than 12,000 years ago. Spanish scholars in charge of the 2011 "Sex in Stone" exhibition of these artifacts (Marcos García Díez and Javier Angulo) argue that historians, archeologists, and other academics have frequently hidden or silenced much evidence of same-sex sexual behavior throughout human history (Oviedo 2011). These ancient artifacts (along with countless others) are strong indicators that same-sex sexual behavior was a common practice among early humans.

Ancient China

One of the oldest and best documented traditions of same-sex sexuality can be traced throughout ancient Chinese history. Awareness and acceptance of same-sex sexual relationships in ancient China are evident in the political ideologies, philosophies, and religious teachings from the earliest Chinese dynasties dating back to the Zhou Dynasty (1046 B.C.E. to 256 B.C.E.). For example, Ming Dynasty (1368 to 1644) literature portrays both love and marital relationships between men in Fujian noting that this southeastern area of China represented "the region foremost in passion for men" (Neill 2011:259). Writings from the Song Dynasty (960 to 1279) also demonstrate support for same-sex sexuality between men: "all the gentlemen and officials esteemed it. All men in the realm followed this fashion to the extent that husbands and wives were estranged. Resentful unmarried women became jealous" (Neill 2011:247). Evidence of women involved in same-sex activity is not as commonly found in ancient Chinese writings, although some Han Dynasty (206 B.C.E. to 220 C.E.) literature makes reference to love between women. However, as Western attitudes expanded into the Far East, particularly during the Qing Dynasty (1644 to 1912), negative moral judgements about the deviance of same-sex sexual behavior began to dominate Chinese culture (Neill 2011).

Ancient Greece

Some of the earliest known Western artifacts concerning same-sex sexual relationships have come from ancient Greece. In particular, sexual relationships between men were commonly depicted in literature, art, and poetry. Greeks celebrated a social system that contemporary scholars have described as "pederasty" (derived from Greek meaning "boy-love") in which mutual loving relationships between adult men and teenage boys were socially sanctioned and normalized (Kuefler 2007:68). Adult men were expected to participate in mentorships with boys in order to introduce them to the general social order of men. The sexual component was deemed to be a natural part of these relationships as "*most* Athenian men . . . found boys to be attractive sexual objects" (Ormand 2009:57). Adult men would even compete for the most attractive young boys by showering them with gifts (sometimes even blurring the line between pederasty and prostitution) (Lanni 2010). Although modern-day interpreters might view this behavior as hebephilic, homosexual, and most certainly deviant (even criminal), the love affair between adult men and teenage boys was not only a common experience in ancient Greece, but also, it was a highly celebrated relationship. However, there were proscriptions in this relationship: the sexual nature of these mentorships was expected to end when the boy reached manhood and married (although the older man and his protégé would remain intellectual companions) (Ormand 2009).

Same-sex sexuality between women of ancient Greece is less overt and certainly less understood. One often looks to the Greek lyric poet Sappho (612 B.C.E. to ~570 B.C.E.) who was born on the island of Lesbos in the North Aegean Sea (the island from which we have derived our modern word "lesbian") to get a glimpse of understanding about ancient sexual relationships between women (Ormand 2009:38). Although much about Sappho's life and her writings is unclear, her poetry teaches us that Greeks—both men and women—were enthusiastic about sex. She writes of pleasure and delight and of the joys of sensuality but contrary to modern folklore, she rarely speaks about same-sex sexual behavior or "lesbianism" in the modern sense. Even so, contemporary scholars have extrapolated that "Sappho the Beautiful" (as Socrates called her), as well as other women of ancient Greece, loved and desired women (Ormand 2009; Neill 2011:161). Thus, ancient Greece marked both same-sex sexual behavior and heterosexual sexual behavior as celebratory acts of human nature.

Ancient Rome

Unlike the socially sanctioned system of pederasty common in ancient Greece, the Romans disapproved of sexual relationships of adult men with younger *citizen* boys. In fact, sexual penetration of citizen boys was frowned upon and at times, deemed to be illegal. This disapproval was due to the fact that Romans were much more concerned about citizenship than Greeks were—they regarded sexual relations with citizen boys on par with sexual relations with unmarried women. As a result of these restrictions, the system of mentorship, sex, and friendship that was so common between adult men and teenage boys in ancient Greece largely dissipated and same-sex sexual desire was no longer an institutionalized part of Roman society. In particular, rules about passivity became socially paramount and Roman law dictated that those who took the passive (i.e., penetrated) role in a sex act between two men could lose their citizenship rights (Ormand 2009). As a result, deviance within same-sex sexual relationships became more clearly defined. Images (c. 62 C.E. to 79 C.E.) from the preserved ancient city of Pompeii reflect this shift with nearly all depictions of sexuality being between men and women (contrary to the myriad sexual images of men engaged in sex acts with other men, especially boys, in ancient Greek art). Sex between women was also rarely referenced in Roman art and literature (although at least one image from the Pompeii Suburban Baths depicts two women copulating) (Clarke 1998). Even though same-sex sexual behaviors were becoming more restricted (and more deviant) during this time, a dramatic shift in attitudes occurred when Constantine the Great (272 C.E. to 337 C.E.) became the first Christian Roman emperor and Christian ideals took over the West. For the first time in antiquity, same-sex sexual behaviors (i.e., sodomy) became punishable by death (Neill 2011). The dominance of the Christian church in the West continues to shape contemporary attitudes toward same-sex sexuality as deviant.

Western Europe in the Middle Ages

Throughout the Middle Ages in the Western World, the governance of Christianity meant that same-sex sexual behavior was generally condemned as deviant and criminal. Specifically, "sodomy" (an umbrella term that applied to a range of sexual behaviors including masturbation, sex between two women or two men, sex acts with animals or any non-procreative sex act) was deemed to be illegal and punishable by death in some cases. Along with these harsh criminal sanctions, social norms about sex became so rigid, so intolerant, and so extreme, that some have described late medieval society as a place of mass hysteria and paranoid panic (Neill 2011). People were constrained in nearly all aspects of life. Indeed, the rules of the church were so complex it seemed that any semblance of pleasure was condemned from the pulpit. In addition, the so-called birth of a criminal class of "crimes against nature" would draw a firm line between appropriate "natural" sex (i.e., between a man and a woman for the purposes of procreation) and "unnatural" sex (anything else) (Crawford 2007:155). As a result, same-sex sexuality was not only deviant in the High Middle Ages, but punishable by burning, beheading, hanging, and dismemberment (Crawford 2007).

Western Europe in the Renaissance

Following the restrictive Dark Ages, condemnatory attitudes toward same-sex sexuality were challenged during the Renaissance's rebirth of knowledge. Art, literature, and poetry began to openly allude to same-sex desire and the medieval moral sex panic began to wane. Even so, sodomy remained a capital offense and as a result, public displays of same-sex sexuality were hidden. For example, in eighteenth century London, there was an active underground subculture whereby gay men met in taverns (comparable to modern gay bars). These so-called "molly houses" were inconspicuous on the outside but were known to men who enjoyed the company of other men ("mollies") to be places where they could meet others like themselves (Crawford 2007; Neill 2011). The Renaissance marked a complicated time whereby same-sex sexuality was evident in art and literature, but still deviantized and criminalized. Sodomy would remain punishable by death in the Western world until the late 1700s when Italy and France became the first to decriminalize sodomy, followed by the majority of Western European countries in the nineteenth and twentieth centuries, although some countries still invoke the death penalty for acts of same-sex sexual behavior (see chapter 4, footnote 2).

Western Europe in the Victorian era

The Victorian era is well known for its highly sexually repressive mores (Foucault 1978). Sexual prudery was the norm and sex itself was shameful. Many sex acts were considered deviant including masturbation, adultery, and even sexual pleasure. Beyond this, laws dictated the criminality of same-sex sexual behaviors in many Western countries. For example, sodomites could be sentenced to death by gallows in nineteenth century England. Due to its unspeakable nature, "homosexuality" in Victorian society was locked up and hidden away in what contemporary theorists have described as "the closet," a place where same-sex desire is kept secret (Cocks 2003). Hiding same-sex sexuality in "the closet" became a normative strategy for those who had sexual interest in others of the same sex in Victorian society (Sedgwick 1990). Indeed, by 1900, "the continual refusal to acknowledge the existence of legitimacy of same-sex desire had turned it into *the* sexual secret" (Cocks 2003:3). People knew it was possible that some Victorians had interests in those of the same sex, but it was publicly condemned as both deviant and criminal.

Even so, same-sex sexual desire was not completely hidden in Victorian society. In fact, notable Victorian literary figures, such as Irish author, playwright and poet Oscar Wilde (1854–1900) (who was imprisoned for his involvement in same-sex sexual behavior in the late 1800s) made discussions of "homosexuality" abuzz in Victorian society. And although such behavior was still considered to be deviant, all the while people were not only participating in homoerotic sex, they were also beginning to understand their desires as more than just lustful urges. Indeed, the Victorian era marks the emergence of a discourse that recognized those attracted to others of the same sex as having their own identity that differed from heterosexual identities. Prior to this, there was no parallel to our modern understandings of gay and lesbian identities; but Victorian literature offered a means to communicate these ideas. Oscar Wilde himself has been described as the "originator of the homosexual identity" (Cocks 2003:159) because of his unique ability to discuss gay identity in his Victorian literary creations. Thus, just as Victorian society is known for its sexually repressive norms, it is also known for its clandestine management of secretive same-sex desire and the emergence of gay identity constructs.

Early American twentieth century and WWII

In the early twentieth century, "homosexuality" continued to be a deviant and punishable vice. For example, in 1903, New York City police raided the Ariston Hotel Baths (a gay bathhouse) and arrested 26 men, 12 of whom were charged with sodomy and 7 of whom received sentences ranging from 4 to 20 years in prison. This was just the first in a stream of gay bathhouse and gay bar raids by police officers that would occur over the next 50 years. Even so, activism for gay and lesbian rights was bubbling up through the mire of anti-gay politics in early American society. For example, in the early 1900s, Emma Goldman (1869–1940) began publicly speaking about gay and lesbian rights and this earned her a spot on the Federal Bureau of Investigation's radar as "the most dangerous woman in America for her views on equality, gay rights, and anarchy" (Myers 2013:xxxv). Others were also organizing for equality. Henry Gerber (1892–1972) founded the very first gay rights organization in the United States in 1924, the Society for Human Rights, and although it quickly disbanded and Gerber himself was arrested on moral charges for publishing the organization's newsletter, *Friendship and Freedom*, he continued to work as an activist until his death. And just a few years later, *The New York Times* became the first major American publication to use the word "homosexuality" in 1926 (Myers 2013:xxxv).

In the 1930s to 1940s, however, gay and lesbian people suffered greatly, especially in the context of WWII. Under Adolf Hitler's desire for Aryan racial and social purity, people deemed to be "deviant" were targeted and placed into concentration camps by the thousands—and this included those suspected of or known to be engaging in same-sex sexual behavior: "socially unacceptable" women were required to wear black triangles on their prison uniforms and gay men were required to wear pink triangles (a symbol that was later reclaimed and adopted as a modern-day emblem of gay rights activism) as part of a system of identification of "deviants" in Nazi concentration camps (Myers 2013:xxxvi). Although exact numbers are unknown, estimates indicate that between 1939 and 1945 more than 15,000 gay and lesbian individuals were imprisoned in Nazi Germany. Beyond the unmistakably gruesome and abhorrent treatment of all prisoners in the concentration camps, "homosexuals" were targeted: lesbian women were raped and gay men were beaten daily. Even when Nazi concentration camps were liberated by the Allied forces in 1945, those interned for "homosexuality" were not freed, but instead, they were required to serve out the full term of their sentences because they were still classified as criminals.[7] The Holocaust marks an especially horrific time for many and these events dramatically affected the lives of gay and lesbian people.

But even amidst these horrendous circumstances, historians have found that the events of WWII allowed young soldiers (both men and women) to comingle in ways they never had before. Serving in the Armed Forces meant that young people were away from the watchful eyes of their parents and they had the freedom to explore their sexual desires with others like themselves (D'Emilio 2002). Unfortunately, most of society was not ready for these changes and during the 1940s, the U.S. Military began to screen potential soldiers for "homosexual" tendencies, issuing "blue discharges" for recruits and subjecting current military personnel suspected of same-sexual desire to dishonorable discharges and even imprisonment (Myers 2013:267). The military continued to enforce anti-homosexuality policies such as the Department of Defense's simple statement: "homosexuality is incompatible with military service" in 1982 and the more complex directive "Don't Ask, Don't Tell (Don't Pursue)" (DADT) (1993), which continued to closet gay, lesbian, and bisexual servicemen and women until it was repealed in 2010 and lifted by all branches in 2011 (Myers 2013:267).

American mid-to-late twentieth century and beyond

Gay and lesbian activism bourgeoned in the middle of the twentieth century. Amongst many other happenings that were central to the growth of gay and lesbian rights that were occurring across the globe, three major events shaped the American gay and lesbian rights movement: (i) the founding of the first sustainable gay and lesbian organization, the Mattachine Society in 1950, (ii) the Stonewall Riots in 1969, and (iii) the removal of "homosexuality" from the DSM's list of mental disorders in 1973.

The Mattachine Society

The Mattachine Society was established by Harry Hay (1912–2002) in Los Angeles, California in 1950 and is one of the oldest American national gay rights organizations. It is well-known for its 1955 to 1961 publication of the *Mattachine Review* that highlighted important political issues for gay rights activism. Chapters across the United States (first in San Francisco, then New York, Washington, D.C., Chicago, and other locations) emerged throughout the 1960s and although the national chapter disbanded, the Mattachine Society is recognized as one of the first organized collectives of the gay and lesbian movement (Myers 2013).

The Stonewall Riots

In late June of 1969, four plainclothes New York City policemen raided a Manhattan gay bar (The Stonewall Inn) in search of those believed to be violating laws against "homosexuality" in public and private businesses that were active at the time. Police raids on gay bars were frequent—but this time was different. This event triggered a riot after several gay patrons were handcuffed and arrested for their "crimes." Violence escalated and angry protesters soon lined the streets of Greenwich Village in open rebellion. This was a demonstration: an uprising against unfair treatment of gay men and lesbian women. Although the riots dissipated after three uproarious days and nights, these events led to the very first American Gay Pride March in New York City just a few days later on July 2, 1969. The Stonewall Riots are widely described as the event that effectively triggered the contemporary gay liberation movement in the United States (Myers 2013). Today, a bar in part of the building where the original Stonewall Inn was located still exists in Greenwich Village and the building is listed on the federal National Register of Historic Places.

"Homosexuality" in the DSM

Published by the American Psychiatric Association (APA), the *Diagnostic and Statistical Manual of Mental Disorders* (DSM) is widely recognized as the preeminent source of both language and criteria for the classification of mental disorders. In its inaugural addition (DSM-I 1952), "homosexuality" was classified as "a sociopathic personality disturbance" and in the next edition (DSM-II 1968), "homosexuality" was listed as a "nonpsychotic mental disorder" (Myers 2013:59). Needless to say, this "diagnosis" meant that gays and lesbians were viewed as mentally ill deviants who could be forced into mental institutions and even required to undergo electric shock treatments and lobotomies to be rid of their disorder. It was not until a secretive group of APA members (known as the GAY-PA) offered a proposal to change this language that "homosexuality" was officially declassified as a "mental disorder" in 1973 and first printed as such in the 1974 edition of the DSM-II (Myers 2013). This event meant that medical professionals would no longer be able to use the DSM to define "homosexuals" as mentally disordered individuals. And as we learned in chapter 3, this reverse process of "medicalization" declassified same-sex sexual desire as deviant in the eyes of the medical community (although this did not happen overnight). Even so, slowly society began to recognize that "homosexuality" was not a disease, but rather an identity. Although the DSM has been criticized as culturally and superficially biased, because it is so widely recognized and consulted as *the* resource to understand mental disorders, the declassification of "homosexuality" as a "mental disorder" marked a continued increase in support of gay and lesbian individuals.

Beyond this, some other notable events continued to shape the landscape of gay and lesbian rights in the latter half of the twentieth century and beyond (Myers 2013):

- *1958.* In *One, Inc. v. Olesen*, the U.S. Supreme Court ruled in favor of the continued publication of the first openly gay/lesbian publication, *One Magazine*, upholding the First Amendment and marking the very first instance of the Supreme Court's involvement in a case focused on gay issues.
- *1961.* Illinois became the very first U.S. state to decriminalize sodomy.
- *1977/1978.* Harvey Milk (1930–1978) became the first openly gay person to be elected to a public office (the San Francisco Board of Supervisors in 1977) and was assassinated in 1978 along with San Francisco Mayor George Mascone. The murderer, Dan White, was said to be suffering from diminished capacity as a result of his depression, which his lawyers blamed on a diet of sugary junk foods (which worked because even though he gunned down two men, he only served five years in prison). This so-called "Twinkie defense" has become a symbol of injustice for gay rights.

- *1978.* Gilbert Baker (born in 1951) designed the very first gay pride flag comprised of eight colorful stripes representing diversity: hot pink (sexuality), red (life), orange (healing), yellow (sun), green (nature), blue (art), indigo (harmony), and violet (human spirit). Baker hand-dyed each fabric and hand-stitched the first two flags that flew in the San Francisco Gay Freedom Day Parade on June 25, 1978. However, after the assassination of Harvey Milk, demand for the rainbow flag greatly increased and the shortage of hot pink fabric meant that the flag was reduced to seven stripes, later to be reduced again to six stripes (red, orange, yellow, green, blue, and violet). The current six-striped rainbow pride flag symbolizes the diversity of the LGTBQ community and is displayed globally[8] as an emblem of LGBTQ support (Moore 2001).
- *1979.* The first National Lesbian and Gay Pride March on Washington, D.C. was held with more than 100,000 participants.
- *1990.* The Immigration and Nationality Act of 1952 that banned lesbian and gay people from entering the U.S. was repealed.
- *1993.* The United States Military enacted the "Don't Ask, Don't Tell (Don't Pursue)" policy that banned gay, lesbian, and bisexual servicemen and women from serving openly in the Armed Forces, effectively closeting thousands of current military members and precluding thousands more from joining the armed forces (later repealed in 2010 and lifted by all branches in 2011).
- *1996.* The U.S. Congress passed the Defense of Marriage Act (DOMA) defining marriage solely as the union between a man and a woman under federal law.
- *1998.* Openly gay University of Wyoming student Matthew Shepard (1976–1998) is severely beaten and later dies as a result of his vicious attack. Shepard's sexual identity is believed to have played a role his victimization. His murder (and surrounding activism) led to the creation of the Matthew Shepard and James Byrd, Jr. Hate Crimes Prevention Act (2009) (see below).
- *2003.* The U.S. Supreme Court case *Lawrence v. Texas* struck down all remaining state sodomy laws, effectively legalizing same-sex sexual behavior in the U.S. for the very first time in recent history.
- *2004.* Massachusetts became the first state (and only the sixth jurisdiction in the world after the Netherlands, Belgium, Ontario, British Columbia, and Quebec) to issue marriage licenses to same-sex couples.
- *2009.* The Matthew Shepard and James Byrd, Jr. Hate Crimes Prevention Act updated the FBI's definitions of sexual orientation, race, and ethnicity and officially expanded the federal hate crime laws to include violence directed at transgender and gender nonconforming people.
- *2013.* In *United States v. Windsor*, the U.S. Supreme Court ruled DOMA to be unconstitutional and the federal government recognized legal marriages of same-sex couples for the purpose of federal laws or programs. Individual states, however, remained independently capable of determining the recognition of same-sex marriage at the state level.
- *2013.* Barack Obama became the first U.S. president to publicly announce support for same-sex marriage.

- *2015.* In *Obergefell v. Hodges*, the U.S. Supreme Court rules in favor of same-sex couples' right to marry nationwide, striking down all remaining state-wide marriage bans.

The flurry of activity regarding gay and lesbian rights is evident in recent American history. And while this list is just a sampling of events that have occurred as of late, it is clear that the gay and lesbian movement has had a stronghold since the 1990s. Indeed, historians note: "gay issues in this period became a permanent part of the world of politics and public policy, and gay people became a regularly visible part of American cultural and social life" (D'Emilio 2002:91). Today, Americans are increasingly supportive of gay and lesbian rights. Even so, the "deviance" of non-heterosexuality remains a fixture in American society.

Summary: historical perspectives on same-sex sexual behavior

Overall, the existence of same-sex sexual behavior since the beginning of humanity shows us that these activities are quite normative. Early civilizations both normalized and celebrated same-sex sexual desire, especially between men. However, same-sex sexuality was both deviantized and criminalized in the West when the Christian church began to dominate public discourse. This was further enhanced by the sexually repressive discourse that characterized Victorian society (Foucault 1978). These events dramatically shifted our understandings about both sex and desire, and as a result, the complexity behind contemporary perspectives about same-sex sexual behavior can be linked to these early religious and social patterns. By tracing this evolution, we can see the cultural and historical entrenchment of religious and Victorian beliefs in modern-day attitudes toward same-sex sexual behavior.

Sexual pleasure

Both enjoyment and fulfillment from sexual behavior are uniquely human experiences. However, specifically defining and identifying sexual pleasure has always been a complex process. For men, sexual pleasure is often confined to erection and ejaculation (although these actions are not always considered to be pleasurable). Women's sexual pleasure has been frequently entwined with fertility rituals in ancient societies and evidence of female orgasm and awareness of the clitoris as a source of sexual pleasure is rather limited. Indeed, as we continue to see today, historical perspectives about gender and sex strongly shaped sexual pleasure within the earliest of human civilizations. As a result, present-day examinations of "sexual pleasure" are constructed from interpretations of historical norms and behaviors. The commonly held contemporary view that sex should bring pleasure to all willing participants is a modern-day creation. In particular, the idea that women could (and should) be sexually satisfied has not always been the norm. Over time, sexual pleasure has been both normative and celebrated as well as deviantized and ignored. Thus, both cultural and historical sensitivity are necessary as we examine sexual pleasure throughout time. Below, sexual pleasure is discussed in the context of ancient art and historical writings, as well as in modern representations of human interest in sexual gratification, recognizing that these examples are now fixtures within contemporary society. By examining variations in perspectives about sexual pleasure over time, we can see that the modern-day relationship between shame and sexual gratification has historical roots—but this has not always been the case.

Early humans

It is clear that from the start, humans have been curious about sex. As discussed earlier in this chapter, Paleolithic cave paintings dating back to 40,000 years ago depict sexual imagery created by some of the earliest human descendants. Exploring sexual pleasure may also have been intertwined with tool-making among Neanderthals. Archaeologists have unearthed ancient stone phalluses carved by early humans, some of which are believed to have been sexual-aid devices. The oldest of these is the Hohle Fels Phallus, discovered in 2005 in southwestern Germany (recall that this cave is also the site of the oldest known Venus figurine as discussed earlier in this chapter). Measuring 19.2 centimeters long (approximately 7.5 inches) and 2.8 centimeters wide (approximately 1.1 inches) and dated back to 28,000 years ago, this siltstone object could very well be the very first "dildo" ever created by humans. Researchers speculate that its highly polished finish and clearly recognizable phallic shape with etched rings around one end combined with its anatomically correct size demonstrate its obvious sexual purposes to prehistoric sexual pleasure (Amos 2005). It is hard to imagine the sex drive of early humans as anything but primal but recent research suggests that *Homo sapiens* (the modern human species) interbred not only with Neanderthals in Eurasia but also with other archaic species including *Homo erectus* and *Homo habilis* in Africa (Hammer *et al.* 2011). Additional genetic evidence shows that *Homo sapiens* also had sex with another ancient human ancestor, Denisovans, and possibly other hominids (Callaway 2013). This interbreeding behavior clearly demarcates the emergence of modern humans but may also be our earliest evidence of sexual pleasure between human-like species of various types. With such a great deal of sex activity taking place between multiple archaic humans, one can only imagine that pleasure may have at least played some role in these early sex acts.

Ancient Egypt

Beyond the obvious depictions of sexual pleasure in the erotic imagery of ancient Egypt described earlier in this chapter, there is also ample evidence that sex as a source of enjoyment was commonplace in ancient Egyptian culture. For example, the ankh (see Image 7.6) has been described as a symbol of fertility, love, creation, and as the combination of both male and female sex organs with both yonic and phallic representation (Wolberg 1944). The sexual unity within this symbol of ancient Egypt likely represents genuine positivity surrounding sexual pleasure during this time. Furthermore, masturbation, a solitary form of sexual pleasure, was also

IMAGE 7.6   Egyptian ankh

Ancient Egyptian ankh at the Karnak Temple, Luxor, Egypt. ©Shutterstock, ArTDi101.

celebrated in ancient Egypt. For example, according to myth, Egyptian gods were created through masturbation (Bullough 2002). Even the revered Egyptian Pharaoh Cleopatra (69 B.C.E. to 30 B.C.E.) is rumored to have utilized one of the first primitive vibrators—a gourd filled with bees placed near her genitals for vibrating sexual stimulation. Overall, ample evidence shows us that sexual pleasure was both normalized and celebrated in ancient Egypt.

Ancient India

The sensual pleasures of ancient India are also evident in visual depictions as reviewed in the discussion of the Khajurāho temples earlier in this chapter. Beyond this, the *Kama Sutra* (aphorisms of love) written by Hindu philosopher Vātsyāyana between the first and sixth centuries (C.E.) is a treatise that guides the virtuous through life and love. Although Dharma (virtue or religious merit), Artha (wealth and property), and Kama (love, pleasure, and sensual gratification) are each discussed as spiritual goals within the text, the *Kama Sutra* is most well-known for its descriptions of sexual pleasure. Numerous sex acts are detailed including kissing, scratching, clawing, biting, and striking as well as various sexual positions that are said to maximize spiritual sexual union. The *Kama Sutra's* emphasis on sensual gratification in the context of spiritual guidance emphasizes the cultural significance of sexual pleasure in ancient India and the clear demarcation of the celebratory nature of sexuality (Burton 2008).

Ancient Rome

In ancient Rome, bathing took place in public facilities that housed pools that were supplied with water from an aqueduct or adjacent river or stream. Nearly all Roman cities had at least one public bathing facility and most had several. The Roman bathhouse served many purposes. Beyond its practicality (i.e., a location for cleanliness), the bathhouse of ancient Rome was also a center for social and recreational activity and even informal business transactions. This meant that public nudity was not only normalized, but it was also commonplace to see your comrades naked while bathing in public. The sexual themes evident in the frescos surrounding public baths, such as in the Suburban Baths at Pompeii, suggest that the Roman bath might also have served a sexual purpose. Some note that the socializing within the baths may have been a prelude to sexual trysts (Fagan 2002). While the precise relationship between nudity, public bathing, and sex in ancient Rome is not entirely known, it is likely that the wide-spread acceptance of public nude bathing practices resulted in sexual pleasures between many bathers. In fact, sexual pleasure was highly valued and viewed as a normal part of humanity to be enjoyed in ancient Rome. However, a significant shift in the celebration of sexual pleasure (or at least the overt expressions of it) came about when Constantine the Great (272 C.E. to 337 C.E.) became the first Christian Roman emperor. During this time, the West saw an overarching transition to public norms in which "sex" was synonymous with "sin" and "controlling desire was the Christian goal" (Crawford 2007:234). Constantine's Christian legacy continued to dominate Western Europe throughout subsequent centuries and some still argue that today's attitudes toward sexual pleasure are rooted in this religious and social shift.

Western Europe in the Middle Ages

Because the Roman Catholic church organized the dominant social structure in Western Europe during the Middle Ages, medieval sexual pleasure was hidden—but not non-existent. While the "purest" men and women were those that remained chaste, single, and devoted to god, when it came to sex, the message from the church was loud and clear: sex should be in the context of marriage and only for the utilitarian purposes of procreation because "sex was a shameful, sordid business" (Brundage 1987:81). Even sex between married persons included vehement restrictions (Brundage 1987):

- Sex was forbidden during Lent, vigils, major feast days, and on Sundays throughout the year as well as during menstrual periods, pregnancy, and after childbearing years.
- Newly married couples were required to refrain from sex on their wedding night and were forbidden to enter the church for 30 days following their wedding.
- Marital sex for enjoyment was considered to be sinful (although wives were required to submit to sex with their husbands if requested to do so as part of the marital contract).

Beyond this, the list of sins (and accompanying penances, the most extreme of which was punishment by death) was also lengthy (Brundage 1987):

- *Sexual positions.* Only "missionary" position sex acts (for procreative purposes) were acceptable.
- *Sexual pleasure.* Pleasure from sex was a sin; individuals were encouraged to make the sign of the cross and pray to god that they would not experience pleasure during sex.
- *Oral/anal sexual acts.* Sex acts of any kind that did not involve penetration of the vagina by the penis between man and wife were sinful.
- *Same-sex sexual behavior.* Sex acts between two men or two women were considered moral sins, especially acts of sodomy.
- *Adultery.* Sex between unmarried persons as well as extramarital sex among married persons went against the church.
- *Incest.* Marital contracts between those who were related by blood and previous marriage were sinful.
- *Prostitution.* Sex with prostitutes was a moral sin and prostitutes themselves sinned each time they engaged in a sex act with a client (although turning to a prostitute was viewed as a "necessary evil" and was considered to be *less* sinful than masturbation).
- *Masturbation.* Sexual pleasure through manual stimulation was a serious sin (on par with adultery).
- *Spontaneous nocturnal omissions.* Unstimulated ejaculations (especially during sleep) were considered serious social problems because they demonstrated high frequencies of erotic dreams (an indication of lustful tendencies) that were also deserving of punishment.
- *Sexual imagery or theatrical demonstrations of sexual themes.* Obscene spectacles that led to sexual sin and were thus sinful in themselves.

Despite the stronghold of the Christian church and its extensive list of "dos and don'ts," in practice, sexual pleasure still made its way into medieval society. For example, medieval sex manuals from the thirteenth and fourteenth centuries depicted acts of sexual pleasure (although somewhat modestly in most cases) (Easton 2008). Even so, the Middle Ages marked an era of sexual repression. Although attitudes during the Western Renaissance shifted norms about sexuality to those that were significantly more permissible, the Christian legacy of the Middle Ages has had a long-lasting impact on contemporary views of sex, especially in thinking about certain kinds of sex as "sinful."

Western Europe in the Renaissance

The Renaissance was a time of awakening of sexuality not only in artistic expression (as discussed earlier in this chapter) but also in terms of sexual norms and discourse. During the Renaissance, courtly love became a common social experience and couples were encouraged to develop an emotional connection with one another prior to marriage. Beyond the "wooing" of men attempting to entice women as suitors through romantic poetry, sonnets, and songs, open discussions about sex were also relatively socially permissible. In fact, pamphlets rampant with advice on how and when to have sex were readily available during the Renaissance thanks to the invention of the printing press in the late 1400s. Such pamphlets illustrated sexual positions as well as important tips about conception, pregnancy, childbirth, child rearing, and marital relations. One of the most salacious erotic texts of the Renaissance, *I Modi* (The Ways), offered detailed depictions of 16 different sexual positions to heighten lovemaking pleasure. Its sexual imagery not only caught the eye of the average citizen who treasured his/her copy, but also, Pope Clement VII's. Almost immediately, the Italian Pope ordered all copies of *I Modi* to be burned and made replication of any related materials (including the book in its entirety) to be punishable by death. Even the illustrator of the woodcut images, Giulio Romano, was imprisoned for his participation in the creation of *I Modi*. But in 1527 (three years after the first edition), a second addition of *I Modi* was released—this time with the inclusion of 16 highly graphic sonnets. Counterfeit versions followed for years to come and scholars generally agree that *I Modi* sexually enticed both readers and future authors/illustrators of erotica during the Renaissance (Bell 1999). Thus, in the midst of being a deviant and illegal vice, sources of sexual pleasure were highly valued commodities.

Western Europe and America in the Victorian era

If the Renaissance represented a rebirth and awakening of sexual pleasure following the Dark Ages, the Victorian era symbolized a retreat back into sexual repression. In Western Europe, "respectability" was characterized by restraint from all bodily lustful urges. Upper class families showed their refinement by not having children, and thus, not having sex. Sex was considered to be utilitarian (for the purposes of reproduction only) and members of Victorian society generally believed that sexual repression was a sign of good breeding (Foucault 1978). Women were especially targeted by this social norm. In fact, the most revered women were passionless and devoid of all sexual appetite: "lustfulness was simply uncharacteristic" for the Victorian woman (Cott 1978:220). The Victorian woman was encouraged to be modest, demure, sexually passive, pious, chaste, submissive and even asexual, although not all women succumbed to these restrictive stereotypes (see Box 7.1). In particular, Victorian women's chastity became "the archetype for human morality" (Cott 1978:223). Restrictions on women's behavior were severe. Take, for example, the 1870s advice of Dr. John Cowan from his laughably titled book *The Science of a New Life*, in which he states:

> Constricting the waist and abdomen by corsets, girdles, and waistbands, prevents the return of the venous blood to the heart, and the consequent overloading of the sexual organs, and, as a result, the unnatural excitement of the sexual system. In the mode of wearing the hair, it is observable that the majority of women, adoring followers of the goddess Fashion, wear the hair in a large, heavy knot on the back part of the head . . . This great pressure of hair on the small brain produces great heat in the part, and causes an unusual flow of blood to amativeness, and if persisted in, a chronic inflammation of the organ and a chronic desire for its sexual exercise.
>
> *(Cowan 1870:99–100)*

Other than clothing and hairstyle restrictions, Cowan lists additional daily activities that should be moderated including idleness, novel-reading, gossip, and even certain foods (i.e., oysters, eggs, fish, salt, pepper, spices, gravies, beer, porter, cider, wine, and other alcoholic liquors, tobacco, tea, coffee, chocolate, salted meats, pies, bread made from fine white flour) because "all these things have a direct influence on the abnormal exercise of the sexual system" (Cowan 1870: 98).

BOX 7.1 DR. CLELIA DUEL MOSHER

Dr. Clelia Duel Mosher (1863–1940) (see Image 7.7) conducted the first-ever American study on Victorian sexuality, and most surprisingly, all her subjects were women. While most have described the Victorian Era as a sexually repressive and constrictive space, Dr. Mosher's work shows us that at least some Victorian women had enjoyable sex lives and valued sexual pleasure. Unfortunately, her exciting findings were not published until the 1970s when Pulitzer Prize-winning historian Carl Degler (1921–2014) unearthed an old collection of files while digging through the archives at Stanford University. His astonishing finding revealed not only never-before-seen nuanced details about the sex lives of Victorian women, but also, the existence of the oldest sex survey in American history predating Kinsey's well-known research (Kinsey *et al.* 1953) by several decades (Degler 1974, 1980; D'Emilio and Freedman 1997).

Mosher's fascination with human physiology started at an early age and throughout her academic career at Stanford University, her research successfully challenged "the entrenched view of women as weak beings" by "exploding the

IMAGE 7.7 Dr. Clelia Duel Mosher
Clelia Duel Mosher (1896). Photo used with permission from Stanford University Archives.

cliches that limited women's lives" (Degler 1980:xv). Her master's research at Stanford confirmed that women, just like men, breathe from the diaphragm. She subsequently concluded that women's supposed "monthly disability" was due to constrictive clothing, inactivity, and the general assumption that pain was an inevitable accompaniment to menstruation. She even invented a set of exercises, commonly known as "Moshering," to counteract menstrual pain and improve women's health (Coolidge 1941:638). Overall, her research supported women's exercise, the abandonment of restrictive corsets, and an overall cultural shift toward women's empowerment.

The Mosher Sex Survey

Perhaps the most fascinating part of Mosher's research profile is a survey she conducted on Victorian women's sex lives that was not published until after her death. In fact, she may never have conducted the survey at all if it were not for her mentor, Mary Roberts (Smith) Coolidge's (1860–1945) suggestion that she learn about the sex lives of women as part of her desire to practice "woman-centered" medicine (Tunc 2010:132). From 1892 to 1920, she interviewed 45 women all born before 1890 (the majority of whom were highly educated middle- and upper-middle-class women) asking them about their sexual attitudes and practices—and this was the very first time any scientific researcher had done so (Rosenberg 1982). What is more surprising is what she found. Overall, this particular sample of Victorian women were sexual beings who reported engaging in sex with their husbands an average of five times per month (Reiss 1982). Specifically, Mosher (1980) found:

- 78 percent felt desire for sexual intercourse independent of their husband's interest.
- 76 percent experienced vaginal orgasm and 36 percent said they "always" or "usually" had vaginal orgasms during sexual intercourse.
- 53 percent thought that the purpose of sex was pleasure for both men and women (only one thought sex was exclusively a pleasure for men).
- 84 percent used at least one method of fertility control (withdrawal, rhythm method, or a device such as a cervical cap).

It is clear from Mosher's findings that these women did not match the sexually repressed stereotype of the Victorian era that is so commonly referred to by contemporaries (D'Emilio and Freedman 1997). In fact, Carl Degler (who fortuitously happened upon Mosher's sex surveys over 30 years after her death and rescued the forgotten file from the Stanford archives) believes that "among these women sexual relations were neither rejected nor engaged in with distaste or reluctance. In fact for them sexual expression was a part of healthy living and frequently a joy" (Degler 1974:1488). Mosher herself acknowledges the power of her own research in her introduction to the collection of surveys: where she wrote "this material, which represents experience of 47[1] women, has given the investigator a priceless knowledge for a practicing physician and teacher; a background sufficiently broad to avoid prejudice in her work with women" (Mosher 1980:3).

Although the historical value of Mosher's sex survey is undeniable, because this sample was quite small and comprised only of highly educated women, her results should not be presumed to be descriptive of all women of the time, and some suggest quite the contrary (Seidman 1990). Even so, Mosher's findings show us that not all Victorian women fit the archetype of frigid, sexless beings, in fact, the majority of her sample enjoyed sex. As a result, Mosher's research adds to the complex picture of Victorian women's sexuality in ways that continue to challenge modern stereotypes.

Note

[1][Although there are remnants of 47 surveys, historians have determined that there are only 45 usable surveys (one survey is incomplete and two were completed by the same woman) (Mosher 1980).]

As a result of these types of restrictions, Victorian women were repressed—to say the least—and at most—suffering from physical ailments including but not limited to fainting, edema, nervousness, insomnia, sensations of heaviness in the abdomen, muscle spasms, shortness of breath, loss of appetite for food or for sex with the approved male partner, and a "tendency to cause trouble" (Maines 1999:23). The diagnosis for women exhibiting these symptoms was often "hysteria" (a catch-all term for female difficulties) but contemporaries generally recognize that sexual frustration was a likely cause for these ailments. In fact, manual genital massage until "hysterical paroxysm" (orgasm) as a treatment to relieve hysteria was recommended as early as the second century by Greek physician Galen of Pergamon (129 to 200 C.E.) and remained the main source of treatment for hysteria throughout the following centuries (Maines 1999; Bullough 2002).

In the Victorian era, diagnoses of female hysteria were reaching epidemic proportions. In fact, hysteria in women was one of the most frequently diagnosed diseases in history until its removal from the American Psychological Association's list of disorders in 1952. To treat hysteria, self-masturbation was not recommended (as it was considered to be a highly deviant activity, see Box 7.2). Instead, physicians generally believed that women suffering from symptoms of hysteria should be relieved through manual stimulation of the genitals until orgasm. Contrary to contemporary perspectives about a male physician rubbing a woman's genitals to the point of climax, the general lack of understanding about women's sexuality (including the utter ignorance about the existence and purpose of the clitoris) meant that this activity was not seen as sexual. Because it was believed that penetration was the only way to fully sexually satisfy women, manual stimulation of the genitals was neither sexual nor immoral. In fact, it was generally considered to be a tedious and time-consuming task. As a result, physicians and other inventors began developing new technologies to rid themselves from "the job nobody wanted" and to relieve women suffering from symptoms of hysteria (Maines 1999:1). In just a short time (150 years or so), physician-assisted paroxysm would become antiquated:

- *1752.* Hydrothreaphy and hydriatic massage (bursts of water stimulating the genitals of women bathers) are introduced in English and British spas.
- *1830s to 1840s.* German physician Vicenz Priessnitz treats hysteria patients with a direct stream of water (douche) directed at women's genitals.
- *1869.* American physician George Taylor invents the first steam powered massage and vibratory apparatus.
- *1880.* English physician Joseph Mortimer Granville patents the first electromechanical battery-powered vibrator with several interchangeable vibratodes.
- *1905.* Dozens of convenient portable handheld vibrators become amongst the first in-home electronic devices available for purchase, preceded only by the sewing machine, fan, teakettle, and toaster.

Needless to say, by the early 1900s, vibrators were a wildly successful commodity. Numerous advertisements in reputable magazines including *Sears, Roebuck & Company* and *Good Housekeeping* depicted a variety of home portable vibrators as "very useful and satisfactory for home service" (Maines 1999:105).With the help of the hand-held vibrator, women could relieve their hysteria symptoms in the comfort of their own homes without the help of the doctor.While contemporary readers might simply see the success of the hand-held vibrator as an indicator of general support for masturbatory aids during the Victorian era, the vibrator was primarily viewed as a medical instrument to cure symptoms of hysteria and this perspective remained intact until the 1920s (Maines 1999). In general, masturbation was viewed as a deviant practice during the Victorian era and sexual restraint was regarded as the most acceptable behavior. Sexual pleasure was simply not socially acceptable.

BOX 7.2 THE AGE OF MASTURBATORY INSANITY

Starting with the domination of the Christian church in the West, masturbation was considered to be shameful and unnatural. Indeed, it was so deviant and so sinful, masturbatory behavior was punishable with extreme penalties (in some cases death). While these attitudes were commonly held throughout the Middle Ages, the organization of these ideas under a "medical" umbrella brought the dangers of masturbation out of church doctrine and into the hands of prominent physicians in the 1700s. In fact, it was Swiss physician Samuel Auguste Tissot (1728–1797) who labeled all non-procreative sexual activity as "*onanism*" in 1766 (Tissot 1766). But beyond coining a term for this type of behavior, Tissot supplied society with a detailed graphic and gruesome list of side effects believed by many to result from masturbatory activity that included (Bullough 2002:29):

- Cloudiness of the mind (or even madness).
- Decay of bodily powers (and subsequent coughs, fevers, and other ailments).
- Acute headaches, rheumatic pains, and aching numbness.
- Pimples, blisters, and painful itching.
- Impotence, premature ejaculation, gonorrhea, priapism, and tumors in the bladder.
- Intestinal disorders, constipation, and hemorrhoids.

Others warned of the dangers of masturbation including prominent American physician, Benjamin Rush (1746–1813), who argued that masturbation could lead to a host of negative outcomes including impotence, vertigo, epilepsy, loss of memory, and even death (Rush 1794–1798). Due to these extreme risks and the association of onanism with madness, this period in time was adequately nicknamed "The Age of Masturbatory Insanity" (Bullough 2002:28).

In the nineteenth century, advice about how to avoid becoming victim to this evil pleasure was rampant. Beyond the thousands of books and pamphlets dedicated to the subject, the continued heightening of the fear of solitary sex made its way into the sustenance marketplace. For example, American Reverend Sylvester Graham (1794–1851) promoted the Graham Diet, a regimen of bland foods designed to suppress unhealthy carnal urges. To align with his recommendations, Graham actually invented the modern-day graham cracker (which was made from plain unsweetened flour at the time) as a snack that he believed could curb masturbatory desires. Similarly, American physician John Harvey Kellogg (along with his brother) invented the mild-in-flavor Kellogg's cornflakes cereal to prevent chronic masturbation (Laqueur 2003).

So worrisome was the idea that children could get involved in this self-indulgent evil, parents looked to the "experts" for advice. At the most extreme, physicians recommended horrific things that included (Bullough 2002):

- For boys:
  - Insertion of rings into the foreskin of the penis.
  - Castration or complete amputation of the penis.
- For girls:
  - Burning of the clitoris or girls' thighs (with a hot iron).
  - Clitoridectomies and/or the removal of labia.

Beyond these gruesome medically assisted methods of masturbation prevention, other parents simply purchased devices to dissuade their children from fondling themselves. There are hundreds of U.S. patents from this time—most of which were designed to "cage" or "house" the wearer's genitalia so that urination was still possible but any touching was not. For men, this was typically an iron housing that fit closely around the shaft of the penis. For women, this was an iron belt (sometimes referred to as a chastity belt) that covered the vulva and had a tooth-sawed opening allowing for urination (see Image 7.8). Other methods to prevent this self-indulgence focused on bedtime behaviors because this was the time of day where children were believed to be most prone to self-induced sexual gratification due to their lack of adult supervision and the possibility of their imaginations "running wild" as they drifted off to sleep. To prevent bedtime masturbation, some parents required their children to wear special gloves that made sexual touching unpleasant and there was even a device installed on children's beds that prevented linens from brushing over their genitals as a result of a nighttime breeze through an open window or movement while the child slept (Bullough 2002). The need to prevent children from masturbating was a strong indicator that this evil pleasure was considered to be a truly deviant activity.

It really was not until the twentieth century that people began to disassociate masturbation with "disease." Changes in modern research and a better understanding of the ways many diseases are spread (i.e., Germ Theory) meant that most doctors no longer believed that self-indulgent sexual gratification led to physical ailments. As a result, people began to think about masturbation as more of a social vice (and not a medical problem). However, when Kinsey's

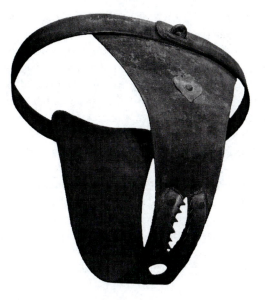

IMAGE 7.8   Anti-masturbation "chastity" belt
Example of a "chastity" belt designed to prevent female involvement in any sexual activity (especially masturbation). ©Shutterstock, shalunts.

research revealed that over 90 percent of men and over 60 percent of women participated in masturbatory behavior, this began to lift the veil on "deviant" solitary sex (Kinsey *et al.* 1948, 1953). Accompanying other significant cultural shifts in perspectives toward sexual pleasure amidst the sexual revolution, society was beginning to be more open-minded to the idea that people might pleasure themselves, however, it was (and is) considered to be a very private and somewhat socially deviant behavior. For example, in a 1975 study, only about half of men and women thought that masturbation was a "normal" sexual activity (Abramson and Mosher 1975). Thus, even though we knew that *most* people did it, we still thought of masturbation as non-normative. A few decades later, U.S. Surgeon General Joycelyn Elders (born in 1933), suggested at a 1994 U.N. Conference that masturbation was a healthy alternative to risky sexual activity and that children should be taught to pleasure themselves as one method to prevent STIs (indeed, solitary sex is the safest form of sex any person can engage in). This controversial perspective (i.e., masturbation is a healthy activity for kids) did not go over well and a few weeks later, she was forced to resign by the then U.S. President Bill Clinton. Elders' forced resignation demonstrates the continued lingering deviance associated with masturbation.

Today, examinations of social attitudes show us that modern-day boundless access to sexual pleasure and self-gratification is still a moral and sometimes a religious issue. The association of masturbatory behavior with impurity, evil, self-indulgence, and deviance is still evident. Indeed, contemporary research indicates that religious people tend to be less supportive of masturbation and tend to associate solitary sex with guilt, shame, and even deviance (Laqueur 2003). There is also a very real gendered process at work here. While most people generally accept that men masturbate, female masturbation is definitely more taboo. For example, in a 2010 study, when asked if masturbation was a "normal" sexual activity, gender differences were very prominent. In fact, while 84 percent of men and 78 percent of women agreed that masturbation is normal for men, only 67 percent of men and 55 percent of women agreed that masturbation is normal for women, demonstrating that when it comes to solitary sex, it may still be considered "deviant," especially for women (see Figure 7.1). What is also interesting is that women are more likely than men to view female masturbation as non-normative. As a result, we can see that evaluating contemporary attitudes toward solitary sex is a complex process. And although masturbation is very common in both men and women [87 percent of women and 95 percent of men aged 14 to 69 report engaging in masturbatory behavior (Herbenick *et al.* 2010)], its religious, moral, and gendered contexts sometimes deem it to be a deviant behavior.

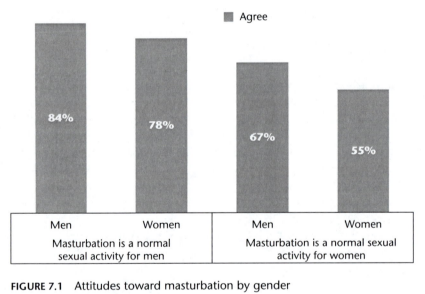

FIGURE 7.1 Attitudes toward masturbation by gender
Data adapted from Worthen (2010).

Early American twentieth century

The Roaring Twenties gave birth to a new outlook on women and sexuality, and in particular, the flapper—the short-skirted red-lipped unruly sexual icon of the 1920s. With their bobbed haircuts, short hemlines, deep cleavage, and the complete rejection of the lady's quintessential undergarment of the Victorian era (the corset), flappers were known as rebels who pushed the social envelope by challenging Victorian gender stereotypes. Not only did some work outside the home, some partook in "unladylike" activities including smoking, joyriding, drinking, and visiting speakeasies. Beyond this, flappers challenged the sexual conservativism of previous generations. They were more open about their interests in sex and they even went to "petting parties" where "making out" was the main event (Zeitz 2006:44). This new view on "sex rights"—"the right of women to a frank enjoyment of the sensuous side of the sex relation" rang true with social commentators who claimed it was "Sex o'clock in America." "Everywhere one turned in the mid-1920s, sex was on the brain. When Americans weren't having it, they were thinking about it or reading about it" (Zeitz 2006:106; 23; 115) and even watching it in cartoons such as Betty Boop (a caricature of a Jazz age flapper) who, unlike previous female cartoon characters, represented a sexualized woman complete with a flaming red short mini-dress, high heels, a garter, and contoured bodice that showed cleavage. With a newly earned right to vote, women of the 1920s were well-poised for this sexual revolution and by all accounts, the flapper's social presence meant changes to style, romance, courtship, and sex. However, the sexual openness of the Roaring Twenties declined after the Stock Market Crash in 1929 and the hedonistic indulgent lifestyle popularized during this decade shifted toward conservatism during the Great Depression and WWII (Zeitz 2006).

American mid-to-late twentieth century

The next major sexual revolution in the U.S. began in the mid-twentieth century. Although Kinsey's wildly popular 1950s book, *Sexual Behavior in the Human Female*, revealed to all its captivated readers that sexual pleasure was a common experience [in particular about three-fourths of married women experienced orgasm during sex with their husbands according to Kinsey *et al.* (1953)], the public shift in attitudes toward openness about sex did not pick up speed until the 1960s to 1970s when several events reshaped the sexual culture of America yet again. These included:

- The mass market integration of highly effective pregnancy prevention methods including the birth control pill and copper intrauterine devices (IUDs).
- The legalization of abortion, via *Roe v. Wade* (1973).
- The Stonewall Riots of 1969 and the start of the American gay liberation movement (see more earlier in this chapter).
- The emergence of Second-Wave Feminism that broadened the First-Wave Feminist Movement (which primarily focused on suffrage) to include a wider range of issues such as reproductive rights, gender inequality in the workplace, domestic violence, marital rape, women in the domestic sphere, among others.

Within this swirling cultural change, many were viewing sex much differently than before. Having easier access to tools to prevent pregnancy and thriving in a political culture that acknowledged both gender and sexuality inequalities, the sexual liberalization of the 1960s to 1970s shaped public discourse and sexual practices. Youth embracing a lifestyle rejecting the mores of mainstream America (known as "hippies") heralded a new ethos of "free love." Among hippies, a common unabashedly hedonistic pleasure-oriented attitude was "if it feels good, then do it as long as it doesn't hurt anyone else" (Miller 2011:5). With millions of young people preaching the power of love and the beauty of sex as a natural part of ordinary life, the discourse surrounding sexual pleasure was generally positive (Miller 2011).

But beyond the hippie counterculture sentiments, in general, people were more open to diversity in sexual experiences. For example, American Gallup Poll data tells us that in 1969, 68 percent viewed premarital sex as "wrong" but by 1973, that number had dropped to 47 percent (Gallup 2003). In addition, revealing clothing styles were more popular than ever before with women's wear including the miniskirt and the even shorter version, the micromini, as well as short shorts (hot pants), crop tops (baring the midriff), and backless halter tops that eliminated the need for a bra (Niven 2011). The change from the generally "covered up" fashion of the 1950s (and before) to one of bare skin coincided with the sexual revolution of the 1960s to 1970s. In addition, sexual pleasure was openly discussed and even promoted through enormously popular books such as *Sex and the Single Girl* (Brown 1962), *The Way to Become a Sensuous Woman* (Garrity 1969), *Everything You Always Wanted to Know About Sex (But Were Afraid to Ask)* (Rueben 1969), and *The Joy of Sex* (Comfort 1972). It is clear that the 1960s to 1970s evoked a celebration of sex and sexual pleasure in multiple ways.

These attitudes, however, were affected by the AIDS crisis in the 1980s. People were scared, and in particular, they were scared of sex. Although international HIV/AIDS education campaigns alerted the general public that much of the risk associated with sex could be reduced by the use of condoms, some saw the AIDS epidemic as "the price of free love," blaming the permissive pleasure-focused practices of the sexual revolution as the cause of the AIDS outbreak. Research during the 1980s indicated that people's sex lives were altered and sexual pleasure suffered. For example, a study of straight British college students revealed that many changed their sexual habits following the British government's AIDS education campaign. Specifically, they engaged in "safer sex" practices by cutting down on casual sex, restricting sex acts to one partner only, refraining from anal sex, and using condoms "all the time" (*New Scientist* 1987:26). Additional research shows that Australian gay and bisexual men also modified their sex practices; many gave up the sexual behaviors they enjoyed and others had little if any sex at all because of their fears of HIV transmission during the AIDS crisis (Connell and Kippax 1990). It is clear that sexual pleasure was sacrificed, at least for some, because of HIV/AIDS. Even so, with prolifically widespread internet access to pornography gaining ground in the 1990s, sexual self-pleasure (albeit a bit tempered from the "free love" of the 1970s) has been dramatically amplified (Barss 2010). Contemporary perspectives about sexual pleasure exist within a nexus of unlimited access to sexual media, social power discourse that acknowledges how gender, sexuality, and other identities affect sexual pleasure, and even a multibillion dollar sex toy industry.

Summary: historical perspectives on sexual pleasure

Overall, sexual pleasure has had its place in human interaction since the beginning. Early civilizations both normalized and celebrated sexual gratification, evidenced in ancient art and literature. However, just as seen in the shifts in attitudes toward prostitution, same-sex sexuality, and sexual imagery, the domination of the Christian church in the West contributed toward a shameful and deviant discourse surrounding sexual pleasure, especially among women. Even so, starting in the latter half of the twentieth century, sexual gratification entered mainstream culture (again) and people were overtly interested in conversations about satisfying themselves and their sexual partners. Today, there is a multibillion dollar industry built on sexual pleasure. As with other forms of sexual deviance, historical variations in attitudes toward sexual pleasure illustrate the complexity behind contemporary perspectives about sex. When we examine these shifts over time, we can see the importance of cultural and historical sensitivity in understanding both past and modern attitudes toward sexual desire.

Sexual deviance: then and now

This journey through time has shown us that sexual deviance is a truly socially embedded concept: "we need only look at the past and its customs and prohibitions about sex, to see how bound up in culture sexuality is" (Kuefler 2007:70). Just as sex is a permanent fixture in society, so is sexual deviance. As a result, we must be careful to understand the historical and cultural variations in both sex and sexual deviance. When we practice such cultural relativism, we can uncover a "hidden history" that reveals important things about sexuality, including historical celebrations of deviance that can have the power to change our own perspectives about deviance today (Kuefler 2007:402).

Notes

1   Although neither the Obscene Publications Act of 1857 nor the Comstock Act of 1873 offered a definition of "obscenity" in their original conceptualization, later tests would come to define obscenity. In the United Kingdom, the Hicklin Test became the parameter for legal obscenity, established in *Regina v. Hicklin* (1868). The justice Lord Cockburn decided that "the test of obscenity is whether the tendency of the matter charged as obscenity is such as to deprave and corrupt those whose minds are open to such immoral influences and into whose hands a publication of this sort might fall" (Foster 1957:248). In the United States, the Hicklin Test was utilized until the Roth Test became the prevailing parameter of defining legal obscenity in 1957. The Supreme Court ruled in *Roth v. United States* (1957) that the Hicklin test was inappropriate, opting for a new definition whereby obscene was defined as "erotic material, pandering to prurient interests" (Foster 1957:254). In 1973, the U.S. Supreme Court changed the legal statutes for obscenity yet again in *Miller v. California* (1973). The three-prong Miller Test for obscenity includes an evaluation of a given work as: (i) whether "the average person, applying contemporary community standards" would find that the work, taken as a whole, appeals to the prurient interest; (ii) whether the work depicts or describes, in a patently offensive way, sexual conduct specifically defined by the

applicable state law; and (iii) whether the work, taken as a whole, lacks serious literary, artistic, political, or scientific value (Main 1986/1987).

2 In ancient Mesopotamia, "sacred" or "cultic" prostitution included sexual rituals within the context of religious worship. Often, such sexual services were offered to the gods as part of fertility ceremonies. Commercial prostitution existed alongside sacred prostitution; however, the two should not be considered the same or even similar practices (as they are often confused with one another) (Lerner 1986).

3 The practice of veiling in this context was instituted an indicator of respectability (most frequently related to the sexual histories of women); although other instances of veiling have been more closely entwined with specific religious practices of modesty (Lerner 1986).

4 Near the end of the nineteenth century, a series of murders took place in the Whitechapel district of East London. The majority of the victims were women working as street prostitutes. These homicides are generally attributed to the unidentified serial killer named only as "Jack the Ripper." The murders were widely publicized and as a result, society was alerted to the dangers associated with prostitution during the Victorian era (Sugden 2012).

5 In Rhode Island, a loophole allowed prostitution to be legal from 1980 to 2009—as long as it was behind closed doors. Currently, only certain counties in Nevada have legalized prostitution. Even so, prostitution continues to be a thriving (but largely criminal) industry across the United States.

6 Alongside COYOTE, WHISPER (Women Hurt in Systems of Prostitution Engaged in Revolt) emerged in the early 1980s. Contrary to COYOTE who seeks to empower prostitutes and legitimize prostitution as work, WHISPER's primary objective is the total and complete abolition of prostitution. WHISPER sees prostitutes as powerless, helpless victims who need to be rescued from the streets. The schism between COYOTE and WHISPER was a defining factor of the sex workers' rights movement in the early 1980s (Jenness 1990).

7 Paragraph 175 was a provision of the German Criminal Code active from 1871 to 1994 that criminalized acts of sodomy. Both East and West Germany continued to enforce Paragraph 175 until it was amended in 1968/1969 to include only sodomy acts engaged in with minors and it was fully repealed in 1994 upon the reunification of Germany (Myers 2013).

8 In 1994, Baker was commissioned to create a mile-long (30 feet wide) rainbow pride flag utilizing the basic six colors to be carried by 10,000 people in a New York City parade in honor of the 25th anniversary of the Stonewall Riots. In 2003, to commemorate the 25th anniversary of the flag itself, Baker again created a giant rainbow pride flag. This time the mile-and-a-quarter-long flag (2 km) utilized the original eight colors. Following both occasions, the giant flags were cut up and disseminated to over a hundred cities worldwide.

References

Abramson, Paul R. and Donald Mosher. 1975. "Development of a Measure of Negative Attitudes toward Masturbation." *Journal of Consulting and Clinical Psychology* 43(4):485–90.

Acton, William. 1857. *Prostitution, Considered in Its Moral, Social, and Sanitary Aspects, in London and Other Large Cities and Garrison Towns, with Proposals for the Mitigation and Prevention of Its Attendant Evils*. London: John Churchill & Sons.

Adămuț, Anton. 2009. "On the Domestic Space for Greeks (and on other spaces)." *Philosophy, Social and Human Disciplines* 1:11–21.

Albert, Alexa. 2002. *Brothel: Mustang Ranch and its Women*. New York, NY: Random House, Inc.

Amos, Jonathan. 2005, July 25. "Ancient Phallus Unearthed in Cave." *BBC News*. Retrieved from: http://news.bbc.co.uk/2/hi/science/nature/4713323.stm

Andrews, Richard Mowery. 1994. *Law, Magistracy, and Crime in Old Regime Paris, 1735–1789.* Cambridge: Cambridge University Press.

Barss, Patchen. 2010. *The Erotic Engine: How Pornography Has Powered Mass Communication from Gutenberg to Google.* Toronto: Anchor Canada.

Bell, Rudolph. 1999. *How To Do It: Guides for Good Living for Renaissance Italians.* Chicago, IL: University of Chicago Press.

Brown, Helen Gurley. 1962. *Sex and the Single Girl.* New York, NY: Bernard Geis Associates

Brundage, James. 1987. *Law, Sex, and Christian Society in Medieval Europe.* Chicago, IL: University of Chicago Press.

Bullough, Vern. 1982. "Prostitution in the Later Middle Ages." Pp. 176–86 in *Sexual Practices and the Medieval Church,* edited by Vern L. Bullough and James Brundage. Buffalo, NY: Prometheus Books.

Bullough, Vern. 2002. "Masturbation: A Historical Overview." *Journal of Psychology & Human Sexuality* 14(2/3):17–33.

Bullough, Vern and Bonnie Bullough 1977. *Sin, Sickness, and Sanity: A History of Sexual Attitudes.* London: Garland Publishing.

Burton, Richard. 2008. *The Kama Sutra of Vatsyayana.* St Petersburg, FL: Red and Black Publishers.

Callaway, Ewen. 2013, November 19. "Mystery Humans Spiced Up Ancients' Sex Lives." *Nature.* Retrieved from: http://www.nature.com/news/mystery-humans-spiced-up-ancients-sex-lives-1.14196

CDC. 2001, June 1. "HIV and AIDS — United States, 1981–2000." *Morbidity and Mortality Weekly Report* 50(21):430–4. Retrieved from: http://www.cdc.gov/mmwr/PDF/wk/mm5021.pdf

Clarke, John. 1998. *Looking at Lovemaking. Constructions of Sexuality in Roman Art, 100 B.C. to A.D. 250.* Berkeley, CA: University of California Press.

Cocks, H. G. 2003. *Nameless Offences: Homosexual Desire in the 19th Century.* London: I. B. Tauris & Company, Limited.

Comfort, Alex. 1972. *The Joy of Sex.* New York, NY: Crown Publishers.

Connell, R. W. and Susan Kippax. 1990. "Sexuality in the AIDS Crisis: Patterns of Sexual Practice and Pleasure in a Sample of Australian Gay and Bisexual Men." *The Journal of Sex Research* 27(2):167–98.

Coolidge, Mary Roberts. 1941. "Clelia Duel Mosher, the Scientific Feminist." *The Research Quarterly of the American Association for Health, Physical Education, and Recreation* 12(3):633–45.

Coopersmith, Johnathan. 1998. "Pornography, Technology, and Progress." *Icon* 4:94–125.

Cott, Nancy. 1978. "Passionlessness: An Interpretation of Victorian Sexual Ideology, 1790–1850." *Signs* 4(2):219–36.

Cowan, John. 1870. *The Science of a New Life.* New York, NY: Cowan & Company Publishers.

Crawford, Katherine. 2007. *European Sexualities: 1400–1800.* New York, NY: Cambridge University Press.

Curry, Andrew. 2012, March. "The Cave Art Debate." Retrieved from: http://www.smithsonianmag.com/history/the-cave-art-debate-100617099/

DADT. Public Law 103-160, 10 U.S.C. § 654. 1993. *Don't Ask, Don't Tell.*

Degler, Carl. 1974. "What Ought To Be and What Was: Women's Sexuality in the Nineteenth Century." *The American Historical Review* 79(5):1467–90.

Degler, Carl. 1980. "Introduction." Pp. xi–xix in *The Mosher Survey: Sexual Attitudes of 45 Victorian Women,* by Clelia Duel Mosher. New York, NY: Arno Press.

D'Emilio, John. 2002. *The World Turned: Essays on Gay History, Politics, and Culture.* Durham, NC: Duke University Press.

D'Emilio, John and Estelle Freedman. 1997. *Intimate Matters: A History of Sexuality in America*, Second Edition. Chicago, IL: University of Chicago Press.

DOMA. Public Law No. 104–199, 110 Stat. 2419. 1996. *The Defense of Marriage Act.*

Dowsett, Gary. 2009. "The Gay Plague Revisited: AIDS and its Enduring Moral Panic." Pp.130–56 in *Moral Panics, Sex Panics: Fear and the Fight over Sexual Rights*, edited by Gilbert Herdt. New York, NY: NYU Press.

Easton, Martha. 2008. "Was it good for you too? Medieval Erotic Art and Its Audiences." *Different Visions: A Journal of New Perspectives on Medieval Art* 1. Retrieved from: http://differentvisions.org/issue1PDFs/Easton.pdf

Fagan, Garrett. 2002. *Bathing in Public in the Roman World*. Detroit, MI: University of Michigan Press.

Ford, Luke. 1999. *A History of X: 100 Years of Sex in Film*. Amherst, NY: Prometheus Books.

Foster, Henry. 1957. "Comstock Load: Obscenity and the Law." *Journal of Criminal Law and Criminology* 48(3):245–58.

Foucault, Michel. 1978. *The History of Sexuality, Volume I: An Introduction*. New York, NY: Vintage Books.

Gallup, George. 2003, June 24. "Current Views on Premarital, Extramarital Sex." *Gallup: Religion and Social Trends*. Retrieved from: http://www.gallup.com/poll/8704/current-views-premarital-extramarital-sex.aspx

Garrity, Joan. 1969. *The Way to Become a Sensuous Woman*. New York, NY: Dell Publishing.

Gewirtz, Paul. 1996. "On 'I Know It When I See It'." *The Yale Law Journal* 105(4):1023–47.

Gioia, Ted. 2015. *Love Songs: The Hidden History*. Oxford: Oxford University Press.

Gordon, George. 1980. *Erotic Communications: Studies in Sex, Sin, and Censorship*. New York, NY: Hastings House.

Hammer, Michael, August Woerner, Fernando Mendez, Joseph Watkins, and Jeffery Wall. 2011. "Genetic Evidence for Archaic Admixture in Africa." *Proceedings of the National Academy of Sciences* 108(37):15123–8.

Herbenick, Debby, Michael Reece, Vanessa Schick, Stephanie A. Sanders, Brian Dodge, and J. Dennis Fortenberry. 2010. "Sexual Behavior in the United States: Results from a National Probability Sample of Men and Women Ages 14–94." *The Journal of Sexual Medicine* 7(Supplement 5):255–65.

Herbermann, Nanda, Hester Baer, and Elizabeth Roberts Baer. 2000. *The Blessed Abyss: Inmate #6582 in Ravensbruck Concentration Camp for Women*. Detroit, MI: Wayne State University Press.

Hicks, George. 1997. *The Comfort Women: Japan's Brutal Regime of Enforced Prostitution in the Second World War*. New York, NY: W. W. Norton & Company.

Immigration and Nationality Act of 1952. Public Law 82–414, 66 Stat. 163, (June 27, 1952).

Jenness, Valerie. 1990. "From Sex as Sin to Sex as Work: COYOTE and the Reorganization of Prostitution as a Social Problem." *Social Problems* 37(3):403–20.

Kinsey, Alfred, Wardell Pomeroy, and Clyde Martin. 1948. *Sexual Behavior in the Human Male*. Philadelphia, PA: W.B. Saunders Company.

Kinsey, Alfred, Wardell Pomeroy, Clyde Martin, and Paul Gebhard. 1953. *Sexual Behavior in the Human Female*. Philadelphia, PA: W.B. Saunders Company.

Kuefler, Matthew. 2007. *The History of Sexuality Sourcebook*. Ontario. Broadview Press.

Lane, Frederick. 2001. *Obscene Profits: The Entrepreneurs of Pornography in the Cyber Age*. London: Routledge.

Lanni, Adriaan. 2010. "The Expressive Effect of the Athenian Prostitution Laws." *Classical Antiquity* 29(1):45–67.

Laqueur, Thomas. 2003. *Solitary Sex: A Cultural History of Masturbation*. New York, NY: Zone Books.

Lawrence v. Texas, 539 U.S. 558 (2003).

Lerner, Gerda. 1983. "Women and Slavery." *Slavery and Abolition: A Journal of Comparative Studies* 4(3):173–98.

Lerner, Gerda. 1986. "The Origin of Prostitution in Ancient Mesopotamia." *Signs* 11(2):236–54.

Levinson, Jay A. and Konrad Oberhuber. 1973. *Early Italian Engravings from the National Gallery of Art.* Washington, D.C.: National Gallery of Art.

McCall, Timothy, Sean Roberts, and Giancarlo Fiorenza. 2013. *Visual Cultures of Secrecy in Early Modern Europe.* Kirksville, MO: Truman State University Press.

McCarthy, Rebecca. 2010. *Origins of the Magdalene Laundries: An Analytical History.* Jefferson, NC: McFarland & Company, Inc.

Main, Edward John. 1986/1987. "The Neglected Prong of the Miller Test for Obscenity: Serious Literary, Artistic, Political, or Scientific Value." *Southern Illinois University Law Journal* 11:1159–78.

Maines, Rachel. 1999. *The Technology of Orgasm: "Hysteria," Vibrators and Women's Sexual Satisfaction.* Baltimore, MD: Johns Hopkins University Press.

Manniche, Lise. 1987. *Sexual Life in Ancient Egypt.* London: KPI Ltd.

Marcus, Steven. 1964. *The Other Victorians: A Study of Sexuality and Pornography in Mid-Nineteenth Century England.* New York, NY: Basic Books.

Miles, Margaret. 1989. *Carnal Knowing: Female Nakedness and Religious Meaning in the Christian West.* Boston, MA: Beacon Press.

Miller, Timothy. 2011. *The Hippies and American Values.* Knoxville, TN: University of Tennessee Press.

Miller v. California, 413 U.S. 15 (1973).

Moore, Clive. 2001. *Sunshine and Rainbows: The Development of Gay and Lesbian Culture in Queensland.* St. Lucia: University of Queensland Press.

Mosher, Clelia Duel. 1980. *The Mosher Survey: Sexual Attitudes of 45 Victorian Women*, edited by James MaHood and Kristine Wenburg. New York, NY: Arno Press.

Mungia, Ryan, Jim Heimann, Jessi Jillo, Nemuel DePaula, and Cindy Vance 2014. *Protect Yourself: Venereal Disease Posters of World War II.* Los Angeles, CA: Boyo Press.

Myers, JoAnne. 2013. *Historical Dictionary of the Lesbian and Gay Liberation Movements.* Lanham, MD: Scarecrow Press, Inc.

Nagle, Jill. 1997. *Whores and Other Feminists.* New York, NY: Routledge.

Neill, James. 2011. *The Origins and Role of Same-Sex Relations in Human Societies.* Jefferson, NC: McFarland & Company, Inc.

New Scientist. 1987, September 3. "Fear of AIDS Alters Sex Behaviour." *New Scientist* 1115: 26.

NIH. 1988. "Understanding AIDS: A Message from the Attorney General." Retrieved from: http://profiles.nlm.nih.gov/ps/access/QQBDRL.pdf

Niven, Felicia. 2011. *Fabulous Fashions of the 1970s.* Berkeley Heights, NJ: Enslow Publishing, Inc.

Obergefell v. Hodges, 576 U.S. Nos. 14-556, 14-562, 14-571, 14-574 (2015).

One, Inc. v. Olesen, 355 U.S. 371 (1958).

Ormand, Kirk. 2009. *Controlling Desires: Sexuality in Ancient Greece and Rome.* London: Praeger.

Oviedo, M. 2011. "Sexo en el Paleolítico." Retrieved from: http://www.lne.es/sociedad-cultura/2010/08/05/sexo-paleolitico/951386.html

Paasonen, Susanna, Katarinna Kyrölä, Kaarina Nikunen, and Laura Saarenmaa. 2015. "'We Hid Porn Magazines in the Nearby Woods': Memory-Work and Pornography Consumption in Finland." *Sexualities* 18(4): 394–412.

Perrottet, Tony. 2011. "Inside the Vatican's Pornographic Bathroom." *Slate.* Retrieved from: http://www.slate.com/articles/life/welltraveled/features/2011/vatican_inside_the_secret_city/vatican_guide_the_pope_s_pornographic_bathroom.html

Regina v. Hicklin, 16 L.R. 3 Q.B. 360 (1868).

Reiss, Ira. 1982. "Review of *The Mosher Survey: Sexual Attitudes of 45 Victorian Women* by Clelia Duel Mosher." *Journal of Marriage and Family* 44(1): 251–3.

Richards, Jeffrey. 1994. *Sex, Dissidence and Damnation: Minority Groups in the Middle Ages*. New York, NY: Routledge.

Riley, Philip. 2001. *A Lust for Virtue: Louis XIV's Attack on Sin in Seventeenth-century France*. Westport, CT: Greenwood Publishing.

Roe v. Wade, 410 U.S. 113 (1973).

Rosenberg, Rosalind. 1982. *Beyond Separate Spheres: Intellectual Roots of Modern Feminism*. New Haven, CT: Yale University Press.

Roth v. United States, 354 U.S. 476 (1957).

Ruan, Fang Fu. 1991. *Sex in China: Studies in Sexology in Chinese Culture*. New York, NY: Plenum Press.

Rueben, David. 1969. *Everything you Always Wanted to Know About Sex (But Were Afraid to Ask)*. New York, NY: Random House, Inc.

Rush, Benjamin. 1794–1798. *Medical Inquiries and Observations*, Volumes 1-5. Philadelphia, PA: Dobson.

Sedgwick, Eve. 1990. *The Epistemology of the Closet*. Berkeley, CA: University of California Press.

Seidman, Steven. 1990. "The Power of Desire and the Danger of Pleasure: Victorian Sexuality Reconsidered." *Journal of Social History* 24(1): 47–67.

Semonche, John. 2007. *Censoring Sex: A Historical Journey Through American Media*. Washington, D.C.: Rowman & Littlefield Publishers.

Shepard, Benjamin. 2006. "Scapegoating." Pp. 245–430 in *Encyclopedia of Prostitution and Sex Work*, Volume 2, edited by Melissa Hope Ditmore. Westport, CT: Greenwood Publishing.

Smith, F.B. 1990. "The Contagious Diseases Acts Reconsidered." *The Society for the Social History of Medicine* 3(2): 197–215.

Soffer, O., J. M. Adovasio, and D. C. Hyland. 2000. "The 'Venus' Figurines: Textiles, Basketry, Gender, and Status in the Upper Paleolithic." *Current Anthropology* 41(4):511–37.

St. James, Margo and Priscilla Alexander. 1977. "Prostitution: The Feminist Dilemma." *City Magazine*, October/November.

Sugden, Philip. 2012. *The Complete History of Jack the Ripper*. London: Constable & Robinson Ltd.

Szalay, Jessie. 2013, March. 19. "Neanderthals: Facts About Our Extinct Human Relatives." *Live Science*. Retrieved from: http://www.livescience.com/28036-neanderthals-facts-about-our-extinct-human-relatives.html

Tilley, John. 2000. "Cultural Relativism." *Human Rights Quarterly* 22(2):501–47.

Tissot, Samuel Auguste. 1766. *Onanism: Or a Treatise Upon the Disorders of Masturbation*. London: K. Pridden.

Tunc, Tanfer Emin. 2010. "Talking Sex: Deciphering Dialogues of American Female Sexuality in the Mosher Survey, 1892–1920." *Journal of Women's History* 22(1):130–53.

United States v. Windsor, 570 U.S. 12-307. (2013).

Vokes-Dudgeon, Sophie. 2015, October 13. Playboy Magazine Abandons Nude Photos: "It's So Passe." *US Weekly*. Retrieved from http://www.usmagazine.com/celebrity-news/news/playboy-magazine-to-drop-nude-pictures-20151310

Wallace-Hadrill, Andrew. 1995 "Public Honour and Private Shame: The Urban Texture of Pompeii." Pp. 39–62 in *Urban Society in Roman Italy*, edited by T.J. Cornell and Kathryn Lomas. London: UCL Press.

Williams, Linda. 2007. *Hard Core: Power, Pleasure, and the "Frenzy of the Visible."* Berkeley, CA: University of California Press.

Wolberg, L. R. 1944. "Phallic Elements in Primitive, Ancient and Modern Thinking." *Psychiatric Quarterly* 18(2):278–97.

Worthen, Meredith G. F. 2010. College Student Survey. Unpublished report.

Yao, Ping. 2002. "The Status of Pleasure: Courtesan and Literati Connections in T'ang China (618–907)." *Journal of Women's History* 14(2):26–53.

Zannas, Eliky and Jeannine Auboyer. 1960. *Khajurāho*. Berlin, Germany: Mouton & Co., Publishers.

Zeitz, Joshua. 2006. *Flapper: A Madcap Story of Sex, Style, Celebrity, and the Women Who Made America Modern*. New York, NY: Broadway Books.

8

ADOLESCENT SEXUAL DEVIANCE

Amanda E. Fehlbaum

"The best sex education for kids is when Daddy pats Mommy on the fanny when he comes home from work."

William H. Masters, 1971 (Chirban 2012:37)

In Mississippi schools, teachers are forbidden from giving any demonstration of how to use condoms. Instead, the majority of teachers are required to stress abstinence from sexual intercourse until marriage. Although teen birth and pregnancy rates have dropped to historic lows across the United States, Mississippi ranks at 47th in the nation with 42.6 births per 1,000 teen girls and 49th in the nation with 76 pregnancies per 1,000 teen girls (Kost and Henshaw 2014; Martin *et al.* 2015). Compared to other developed countries, the U.S. continues to have higher rates of teen births, as seen in Figure 8.1 (United Nations Department of Economic and Social Affairs 2014; Martin *et al.* 2015).

There is no doubt that these two issues are correlated. When teens are not provided with information about safer sex practices, they are *more* likely to engage in unprotected sex and they are *more* likely to have unintended pregnancies (Kohler *et al.* 2008). Schools are often viewed as the institution that should be primarily responsible for educating teens about sex, but in an environment that forbids condom demonstrations, how can safer-sex practices be taught? Sometimes, you have to get creative.

Take, for example, Sanford Johnson's YouTube approach. Johnson is the deputy director of Mississippi First, an organization that advocates for comprehensive sex education. Because of Mississippi's prohibition on condom demonstrations, Johnson (2012) decided to post a video on YouTube entitled, "How to Put on a Sock." He explains at the beginning of the video, "we're going to teach teens how to use condoms correctly and consistently; however, we cannot do condom demonstrations." Instead, Johnson instructs viewers in how to put on a sock:

> If you're going to be engaged in a sock activity, whether you're wearing an athletic shoe, or whether you're using a dress shoe – doesn't matter – as long

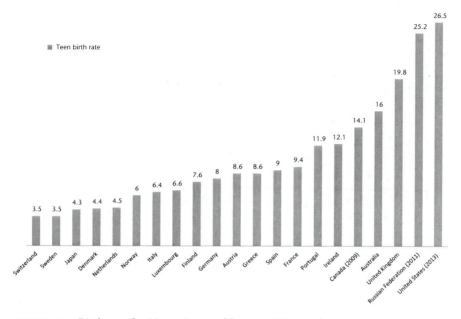

FIGURE 8.1 Birth rate for 15 to 19 year olds per 1,000 population

Data adapted from United Nations Department of Economic and Social Affairs (2014) and Martin *et al.*
2015. All data are from 2012 unless otherwise noted.

as your foot is protected. I want to make sure that you have on a sock. So, when I'm putting on a sock, what I do is that I start with the sock and I pinch out the air in the tip of the sock because I want to make sure that there's room for my toes before engaging in shoe activity. Then I take the sock, put it on the top of my foot, then all I do is just roll it down . . . You want to roll it all the way down your foot, and then you can put it inside your shoe and you're ready to engage in a shoe activity.

(Johnson 2012)

By talking about "sock activity" and demonstrating the appropriate and safe way to put on, remove, and dispose of "socks," Johnson is rather successful in educating about condom use without actually using condoms. In fact, his YouTube video has been viewed over 1.5 million times. Johnson's creative approach underscores the extent to which sex education advocates are willing to go to provide teens with helpful information about sex and sexuality.

Recall from chapter 4 that sociologists define sexual behavior as encompassing many things. Sex is not just about procreation, but can also be about pleasure, intimacy, power, love, and/or maturity. However, people often think that sex is an activity that is reserved only for adults. In fact, in the majority of the Western world, it is illegal for adolescents to engage in sexual behaviors if they are under the age of consent dictated by law (see Box 12.2 in chapter 12). Overall, adolescent sexuality is a very sensitive, complex issue, in part, because it acknowledges that teens are sexual beings that will have sex someday, if they are not doing so already. Some wish to protect teens from such realities, while others accept that sex can, and does, happen between teens.

This chapter begins by exploring what adolescent sexuality is and what sexual behaviors adolescents are participating in while also examining how adolescents negotiate the dominant teen tropes of virginity and abstinence. Next, we look at how adolescents are taught messages about sexuality from school, parents, and peers. Last, because not all cultures hold the same attitudes toward teen sex, we will learn how the Netherlands compares to the United States in their treatment of adolescent sexuality. The overarching goal of this chapter is to demonstrate that ideas about what teens should be doing and what teens are actually doing in terms of sex do not always match up. By looking at the difference between normative expectations about teen sex in comparison to their actual behavior, the nature of deviance itself is called into question.

The concept of adolescent sexuality

Advances in nutrition and, in some cases, over nutrition have meant that teenagers reach sexual maturity at earlier ages than they did a century ago (Karlberg 2002). For example, in 1860, the average age of menarche was around age 16, in 1920 it was about 14, it dropped another year by 1950 to age 13, and by the 1990s, the average age of menarche was 12.5 (Herman-Giddens *et al.* 1997). Today, most girls and boys show onset of pubertal development between the ages of 9 and 10 and reach reproductive maturity by age 17 (Herman-Giddens 2006). Thus, the gap between when someone reaches sexual maturity and when that person has earned the social status of adulthood has grown. Not only are teenagers going through the physical changes that accompany puberty, but also, they are experiencing psychological and cognitive shifts in how they analyze and interpret their relationships, their bodies, and the cultural scripts surrounding sexuality (Tolman and McClelland 2011). In the U.S., tropes abound glamorizing youthful sexuality while at the same time showing concern about teenage hormones running wild. Adolescent sexuality is constructed as a social problem and restrictions are put in place through public policies in an effort to keep teens "safe" and "innocent" or in other words, restrict teen sexual behavior and deviantize teen sexual activity (Russell 2005).

In fact, adolescence has always been intimately tied to the control of sexuality. Until 1904, the term "adolescence" did not exist as a label to describe the period between childhood and adulthood, instead, being considered an adult had more to do with economic measures rather than age. The inventor of "adolescence," G. Stanley Hall, linked the new concept with that of sexual control:

> Hall placed chastity and self-denial directly at the center of his interpretation. Indeed, adolescence was precisely that period of chastity between puberty, or sexual awakening, and marriage, when the young man or woman's sexual

impulses could finally be expressed. Without the demand for sexual repression and sublimation, the modern concept of adolescence made no sense at all.

(Moran 2000:14–15)

Thus, "adolescence" was (and still is) entwined with expectations of sexual repression and chastity. Contemporary perspectives continue to represent these archetypes while simultaneously describing any teen involvement in sexual activity as "risky" and sometimes "deviant."

However, adolescent sexuality research in the twenty-first century has seen a shift away from the conceptualization of sexuality as dangerous and deviant and toward a new vision of teen sexuality as a normative part of adolescent development (Tolman and McClelland 2011). This aligns with the recommendations of the Sexuality Information and Education Council of the United States (SIECUS), which advocates that young people be taught that exploring their sexuality is part of the process of becoming sexually mature (2004). It is also an implicit acknowledgement that, despite strictures against adolescent sexuality, teens are having sex. Research indicates that most U.S. high school students have had penile-vaginal intercourse (PVI) and the average age of virginity loss (i.e., the age at which individuals first had PVI) is 17.2 years for women and 16.8 years for men (Kann *et al.* 2014; CDC 2015). By the time Americans reach age 18, over half of young men and women have had PVI, as shown in Figure 8.2. Similar patterns are evident across the globe—overall, PVI tends to first occur between the ages of 15 and 19; however, regional variations are evident by age and gender. For example, in Nigeria, the median age at first PVI is 15 for women and 39 percent of women have had sex prior to age 15. For Nigerian men, however,

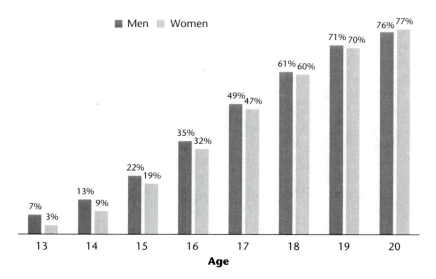

FIGURE 8.2   Percentage of Americans who have had penile-vaginal intercourse by age
Data adapted from Finer and Philbin (2013).

the median age at first PVI is 20 and only 6 percent of men have had sex prior to age 15. In contrast in Australia, the median age at first PVI is the same for men and women (17.5) (Wellings *et al.* 2006). Thus, while the concept of "adolescence" is just over a century old, our conceptualizations of deviant sexual activity among teenagers are ever-changing cultural constructs that are linked to our ideas about gender, sex, and appropriate teenage behavior.

Adolescent sexual behavior

When understanding adolescent sexual behavior, it is important to consider how teens view and describe their sexual activities. For example, some teens may consider PVI as sex, while oral and anal intercourse and other non-coital sexual activities may not be considered sex. And as we will learn, teens' perspectives about sex are linked to cultural stereotypes about "deviant" and "normative" adolescent sexual behavior and perceptions of virginity.

Abstinence and virginity: oral sex versus PVI

Overall, oral sex is very common among adolescents (and adults, see chapter 6). For example, a survey of 2,271 U.S. adolescents found that more than half have ever had oral sex (Lindberg *et al.* 2008). Researchers have determined that, compared to PVI, adolescents perceive oral sex to be more acceptable, less risky, less of a threat to their belief systems, and more common among their peers (Halpern-Felsher *et al.* 2005). Furthermore, compared to those who had PVI, adolescents who engaged in *only* oral sex (and not PVI) were less likely to feel guilty or used, fear pregnancy and sexually transmitted infections (STIs), get in trouble with their parents, and have their relationship with their intimate partner worsen (Brady and Halpern-Felsher 2007).

Some teens engage in oral sex in lieu of PVI to maintain abstinence, or "technical virginity." While there are many reasons that one might wish to remain a "technical virgin," sociologists have linked this concept to religiosity, morality, and the desire to stay "pure." However, interestingly, these have not been amongst the most important reasons teens have described as to why they are interested in maintaining their technical virginity. In fact, most technical virgins are motivated by risk reduction, that is, wanting to avoid pregnancy and/or STIs. Thus, technical virginity is not always about religiosity or having signed an abstinence pledge; instead, the desire to preserve one's technical virginity may actually be an active choice to avoid perceived risks associated with PVI (such as unintended pregnancy) that may not accompany other types of sexual behaviors (Uecker *et al.* 2008). Because oral sex is commonplace and thus rather normative among teens, this type of sexual behavior may be a choice some teens make to avoid the "deviant" label of "sexually active" teen (which is often assigned to teens who have engaged in PVI).

The links between the concepts of "sexually active," "abstinent," and "virgin," are rather complex because some adolescents do not consider abstinence and sexual activity to be opposing constructs and some "virgins" participate in sexual behaviors. In other words, some teens who engage in non-coital (not PVI) behaviors may be defined as "sexually active virgins" who are technically abstinent from PVI. For example, in a study of 2,271 American adolescents, between 13 and 21 percent have given or received oral sex but have not engaged in PVI (Lindberg *et al.* 2008). In another study of 2,026 American heterosexual adolescents, none of whom have engaged in PVI, about one-third engaged in partner masturbation and about one in ten indicated participation in oral sex, as shown in Figure 8.3 (Schuster *et al.* 1996). Overall, these "virgins" who are "abstinent" (i.e., not engaging in PVI) are actually quite sexually active. In fact, total and complete abstention from any sexual activity (whether coital or not) may have more to do with lack of a willing partner than with intentions to be abstinent. For example, in a study of 205 American 18 to 21-year-olds, those virgins who totally abstained from any sexual activity were found to have had fewer social and dating opportunities and lacked viable relationships (Woody *et al.* 2000).

In summary, it is obvious that most adolescents engage in sexual activity of some kind. Whether or not such activity is coded as "sex" or "virginity loss" depends not only on how teens define sex, but also what they perceive as "abstinence." What is clear is that adolescent sexual behavior is slowly turning away from being viewed as dangerous and deviant toward a normative and healthy part of the development process (Tolman and McClelland 2011). Even so, teens who are defined as "sexually active" can risk being labeled as sexual deviants.

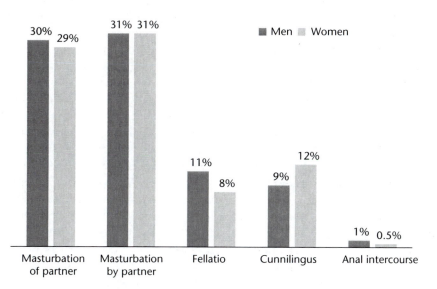

FIGURE 8.3 Sexual activities of American heterosexual adolescent "virgins"

"Virgins" are defined by the researchers as those who have not engaged in PVI. Data adapted from Schuster *et al.* (1996).

Sex and identity

As discussed in chapter 4, over 60 percent of U.S. high school students identified as heterosexual though their only sexual partners were those of the same sex (Kann *et al.* 2011). Furthermore, researchers have determined that teens often have a changing and unstable sexual self-identification (Savin-Williams 2005; Diamond 2008). In other words, in the first decade of the twenty-first century, many teens have shifted from gay- or lesbian-identified to "an extremely diverse group who may at times adopt a gay, lesbian, bisexual, or no specific identity, may be actively questioning their identity, may engage in same-sex sexual activities, and/or may report same-sex attractions" (Tolman and McClelland 2011:246). This shift underscores how adolescence is a time when one's sexual selfhood, or an individual's image of himself or herself having intimate relations and/or experiencing sexual pleasure, is developed. As a result, sexual behaviors during adolescence can be an exploration of sexual identity and sexual pleasure that may involve oral, anal,[1] or vaginal sex with different partners. Sometimes teens may perceive such activities as "sex" and other times, they may not. Because of the association of teen sex with deviance, adolescents may also be motivated to avoid labeling their own behaviors as "sex" and may also be interested in maintaining "virginity" and "abstinence" to fit the normative stereotype that teens should not be sexual beings. This may be further exacerbated by teens engaging in non-normative sex that may be coded as "gay" or "lesbian" sexual behavior.

Adolescent sexual socialization

Thinking about sex, certain sexual behaviors, virginity, and abstinence are all a part of being a normal teenager in today's society. But where do our perceptions about these concepts come from? By mid-adolescence, teens have the cognitive ability to understand as well as challenge and accept sexual scripts that shape sexuality in the society around them (Russell *et al.* 2012). In other words, by the age of 14 or so, teens are beginning to reflect about their own experiences with sexual socialization. *Sexual socialization* is the process in which adolescents learn about sex and how to be sexual individuals from their social contexts. The way that society views adolescent sexuality and how it either enables or constrains sexual development has repercussions for expressions of sexuality throughout adulthood. Although there is agreement among the general U.S. population that adolescents need to know about certain topics related to sex, there is disagreement about what they are and who should teach them (National Public Radio *et al.* 2003). Much of this disagreement lies in fundamental differences in beliefs about the purposes of sex education and the morality of sex itself. In the United States, the vast majority of high schools require some form of sex education; however, this education has been influenced at the national and local levels by religious conservative movements that mobilize to ensure that an abstinence-only approach is emphasized and information about condoms and contraception is limited (Kendall 2008). Although much of the popular debate about sex education is situated in schools, as we will learn below, lessons about adolescent sexuality come from many sources, including school, but also parents and peers.

BOX 8.1 TYPES OF SEX EDUCATION

The Sexuality Information and Education Council of the United States (n.d.) describes four broad types of sexuality education programs:

- *Comprehensive sexuality education*. These programs include age-appropriate, medically accurate information on a broad set of topics related to sexuality including human development, relationships, decision-making, abstinence, contraception, and disease prevention. Comprehensive sex education emphasizes science through provision of the facts with which to make one's own decision, being critical of sexist portrayals of women and/or negative stereotypes about LGBT people, and feeling free in the triumph of reason over tradition and of personal decision-making over mandates.
- *Abstinence-based*. These programs emphasize the benefits of abstinence and include information about sexual behavior other than PVI as well as contraception and disease-prevention methods. These programs are also referred to as "abstinence-plus" or "abstinence-centered."
- *Abstinence-only/abstinence-only-until-marriage*. These programs emphasize abstinence from all sexual behaviors outside of marriage. Either the programs do not include information about contraception or disease prevention methods or if they are discussed, they tend to emphasize failure rates. They often present marriage as the only morally correct context for sexual activity. Abstinence-only curriculum emphasizes feeling sure and not confused, feeling safe by not engaging in sexual behaviors or interacting with sexually active teenagers, and feeling in control by knowing the consequences of premarital sex and what constitutes a good partner.
- *Fear-based*. This includes abstinence-only and abstinence-only-until-marriage programs that are designed to control young people's sexual behavior by instilling fear, shame, and guilt. They rely on negative messages about sexuality, distort information about condoms and STIs, and promote biases based on gender, sexual identity, marriage, family structure, and pregnancy options.

Lessons from school

Most American teenagers encounter at least some form of sexual education while in school; however, the type received is not the same (see Box 8.1). The Centers for Disease Control (CDC) recommends that health education curricula cover a wide range of topics including STIs and pregnancy prevention methods. However, the extent to which states cover such topics varies widely. For students in grades 9, 10, 11 and 12 (Demissie *et al.* 2013):

Nearly all (85 to 90 percent) states cover these topics:
- How HIV and other STIs are transmitted (95.3 percent).

- How to prevent HIV, other STIs, and pregnancy (94.9 percent).
- The benefits of being sexually abstinent (94.8 percent).
- Health consequences of HIV, other STIs, and pregnancy (94.3 percent).
- The differences between HIV and AIDS (94.2 percent).
- The relationship between alcohol and other drug use and risk for HIV, other STIs, and pregnancy (93.3 percent).
- The relationship among HIV, other STIs, and pregnancy (92.6 percent).
- How HIV and other STIs are diagnosed and treated (92 percent).
- The influences of media, family, and social and cultural norms on sexual behavior (91.8 percent).
- How to create and sustain healthy and respectful relationships (91.3 percent).
- How to access valid and reliable health information, products, and services related to HIV, other STIs, and pregnancy (90.7 percent).
- Communication and negotiation skills related to eliminating or reducing the risk for HIV, other STIs, and pregnancy (89.9 percent).
- Goal-setting and decision-making skills related to eliminating or reducing risk for HIV, other STIs, and pregnancy (88.6 percent).

A large percentage (70 to 80 percent) of states cover these topics:
- Efficacy of condoms, that is, how well condoms work and do not work (80.2 percent).
- Compassion for persons living with HIV or AIDS (76.5 percent).
- The importance of using condoms consistently and correctly (70.9 percent).

About half of states cover these topics:
- Importance of using a condom at the same time as another form of contraception to prevent both STIs and pregnancy (63.2 percent).
- Importance of using contraceptive methods, other than condoms, consistently and correctly (63.2 percent).
- How to obtain condoms (52.9 percent).
- How to obtain contraceptives other than condoms (52.6 percent).
- How to correctly use contraceptives other than condoms (52.3 percent).

Less than half of states cover these topics:
- How to correctly use a condom (45.1 percent).
- All 22 topics (32.3 percent).

It is important to note, however, that many sexually experienced teens do not receive formal instruction about contraception before they have sex for the first time (Mueller *et al.* 2008). In fact, in a nationally representative survey of 498 American adults between the ages of 18 and 19, 41 percent reported knowing little or nothing about condoms and 75 percent reported knowing little or nothing about birth control pills (Kaye *et al.* 2009). Furthermore, such messages that teens get about sex differ by gender. As seen in Figure 8.4, both young men and women are similarly likely to receive sex education in American schools about STIs and

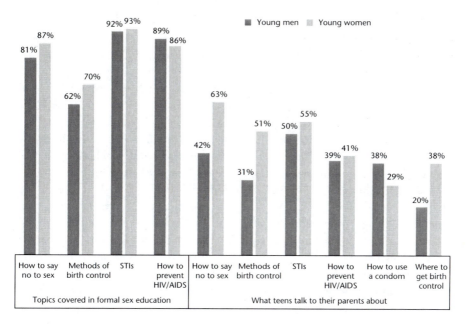

FIGURE 8.4   Topics covered in formal sex education and what teens talk to their parents about by gender

Data adapted from Martinez *et al.* (2010).

how to prevent HIV/AIDS, however, young women are more likely than young men to learn about how to say no to sex and methods of birth control (Martinez *et al.* 2010). Thus, sex education is widely variant.

The impacts of abstinence messages

No matter what type of sex education curricula is utilized at school, most American high school students are exposed to the overwhelmingly strong ideal of abstinence. In fact, the majority of U.S. high school health textbooks used in sex education curriculum indicate that marriage is the only appropriate context for people to have sex. In addition, U.S. high school health textbooks also aim to instruct teens on how to make responsible decisions, how to evade engaging in deviant behavior, and stress that sex is. a high-risk activity that teens should avoid in favor of abstinence (Fehlbaum 2014). However, these messages do not resonate with the typical high school student because the majority engage in sexual behaviors of some sort while in high school and more than half will engage in PVI before graduating (Finer and Philbin 2013). By sending the message that abstinence is the only healthy, non-deviant, and socially acceptable choice for teens, an abstinence-only sex education curriculum systematically:

• Denies the possibility of healthy, responsible sexual-decision making other than abstinence.
• Uses scare tactics to evoke fear and shame surrounding any sexual behavior.

- Ignores teens that have had sex, labeling them as failures and deviants.
- Fails to address specific reproductive health needs of sexually active teens.
- Overlooks victims of sexual violence who have had unwanted sexual experiences.
- Disregards how non-heterosexually identified teens understand sex and abstinence.

In all, both textbooks and their accompanying abstinence-focused sex education curriculum do not adequately prepare individuals to navigate their sex lives as adults. By sending strong messages about abstinence and limiting knowledge about sex, teens are deprived of basic information about their bodies, the bodies of their sexual partners, sexual relationships, and sexual behaviors and how these things will change as they age. As a result, this engenders sexual illiteracy among youth and consequently, adults (di Mauro and Joffe 2007; Fehlbaum 2014).

There is no evidence to suggest that abstinence-only education effectively delays the onset of sexual activity. Indeed, compared to students who receive no sexual education, students who complete abstinence-only-until-marriage programs are identical in terms of their age of first sex and numbers of sexual partners (Trenholm *et al.* 2007). In other words: abstinence-only programs are ineffective at changing behaviors. Furthermore, abstinence-only strategies actually *deter* contraceptive use among sexually active teens, increasing their risk of unintended pregnancies and STIs (Kirby 2007; Underhill *et al.* 2007; Lindberg and Maddow-Zimet 2012). Thus, abstinence-only focused dialogues do not result in teens being sexually abstinent but they do result in teens engaging in risky sex practices without contraceptives.

The impacts of more comprehensive messages

What happens when we do tell teens about sex? There are many positive results of comprehensive sex education programs including (Kirby 2007):

- Delaying or reducing sexual activity.
- Reducing number of sexual partners.
- Increasing condom or contraceptive use.
- Being effective for all youth populations across sex categories, major ethnic categories, different settings, different communities, and for sexually experienced and inexperienced teens.

And these impacts can be long lasting. For example, a study of British university students found that exposure to formal sex education as a teen reduces both risky sexual behavior and the likelihood of STI contraction in sexually active young adults (Vivancos *et al.* 2013). Thus, more comprehensive sex education curricula can have positive impacts on both teens' and young adults' sex lives.

So then, why abstinence-only in US schools?

The American Medical Association, American Nurses Association, American Academy of Pediatrics, American College of Obstetricians and Gynecologists, the American Public Health Association, the Institute of Medicine, and the Society for Adolescent Health and Medicine all support comprehensive approaches to sex education. So why is the United States so dedicated to the abstinence-only approach? It comes down to panic and control.

Sex panics, or hostilities that break out in communities debating sex education programs, have regularly occurred since the 1960s (Irvine 2006) (recall also our discussion of moral panics in chapter 2). Such sex panics are part of a political initiative by some social and religious conservatives to control sexual knowledge and, in doing so, protect young people and preserve sexual morality. Generally, they believe that all sex should be confined to marriage and discussions of sex should be controlled so as to not entice youth to immoral thoughts or behaviors. In the view of such conservatives, discussion of both sex and contraceptives has led to high levels of adolescent sexual activity, teenage pregnancy, and STIs (Irvine 2006). The best approach to sexual health then, in their opinion, is to teach youth to abstain from all sexual behavior until they are married (and furthermore, this is expected to be a heterosexual, monogamous marriage). As a result, more than $1.7 billion dollars have been poured into abstinence-only initiatives since 1982, culminating with the enactment of Title V, Section 510 of the Personal Responsibility and Work Opportunity Reconciliation Act in 1996. Title V funds are offered to states who teach abstinence-only education, as defined in Box 8.2. For the first five years of the Title V initiative, every state but California participated in the program. Today, however, only about half of U.S. states continue to receive and pursue Title V funding for abstinence-only education, and the majority of those states are concentrated in the south.

This southern regional concentration of funding for abstinence-only education is notable for two reasons. First, these states tend to be considered amongst the most religious and the most conservative (Newport 2014, 2015). Given what we know about the ties of social and religious conservative perspectives to sex panics, it makes sense that these states would have a high concentration of Title V funding. However, there are consequences for the reliance on abstinence-only education. In addition to being the states with the highest concentration of abstinence-only education, many of these same states also have the highest teen birth rates (see Table 8.1). In other words, there is significant overlap between religiousness, conservativeness, abstinence-only education, and high teen birth rates. Furthermore, compared to their counterparts in the rest of the country, more southern youth engage in risky sexual behaviors such as having four or more sexual partners and not using contraceptives if they are currently sexually active (Djamba *et al.* 2012; Kann *et al.* 2014). Thus, the lack of comprehensive sex education in the south can have problematic effects on teens' lives.

Overall, it is clear that the type of sex education a student receives in school has consequences on their sexual behavior. Abstinence-only education has been shown to be ineffective at substantially delaying the onset of sexual activity. In addition, those who received abstinence-only education are more likely to take risks, such as not using

---

BOX 8.2 ABSTINENCE EDUCATION GUIDELINES UNDER TITLE V

Under Section 510, abstinence education is defined as an educational or motivational program that:

(A) has as its exclusive purpose, teaching the social, psychological and health gains to be realized by abstaining from sexual activity;

(B) teaches abstinence from sexual activity outside of marriage as the expected standard for all school age children;

(C) teaches that abstinence from sexual activity is the only certain way to avoid out-of-wedlock pregnancy, STDs and other associated health problems;

(D) teaches that a mutually faithful monogamous relationship in the context of marriage is the expected standard of human sexual activity;

(E) teaches that sexual activity outside of the context of marriage is likely to have harmful psychological and physical effects;

(F) teaches that bearing children out of wedlock is likely to have harmful consequences for the child, the child's parents, and society;

(G) teaches young people how to reject sexual advances and how alcohol and drug use increases vulnerability to sexual advances;

(H) teaches the importance of attaining self-sufficiency before engaging in sexual activity.

Data adapted from Social Security Act (1998).

TABLE 8.1 Top 10 U.S. states by religiousness, political conservativeness, and teen birth rates

Most religious	Most conservative	Highest teen birth rates
Alabama★	Alabama★	Alabama★
Arkansas★	Arkansas★	Arkansas★
Georgia★	Idaho	Kentucky★
Louisiana★	Louisiana★	Louisiana★
Mississippi★	Mississippi★	Mississippi★
North Carolina★	Montana	New Mexico
Oklahoma★	Oklahoma★	Oklahoma★
South Carolina★	South Carolina★	Texas★
Tennessee★	Tennessee★	Tennessee★
Utah★	Utah★	West Virginia★

Data adapted from Newport (2014, 2015) and Martin et al. (2015).
★State received Title V funding in 2011.

condoms, than those who receive comprehensive sex education. By construing sex as a deviant behavior that should only be done within the confines of marriage, abstinence–only education advocates negatively impact adolescent sexual socialization.

Lessons from parents

Although schools are often looked to as the main source of sex education, teens' preferred source of sex education is their parents, specifically their mothers (Jordan *et al.* 2000; Somers and Surmann 2004). Teenagers do talk to their parents about a number of sexual topics, as seen in Figure 8.4, although girls learn more about sex from their parents than boys do, especially how to say "no" to sex and about various methods of birth control and where to get them (Martinez *et al.* 2010). Accordingly, most parents believe that their role in sex education is crucial; however, their effectiveness in providing sex education is questionable. Part of the issue is that most parents are not sure what to discuss in their conversations with teens about sex. For example, some parents want their children to be informed about sex but worry that too much knowledge would rob sex of its mystery (Elliot 2012). Another problem is that parents themselves are often uncomfortable with their own sexualities. As parents are expected to explain sex to their teens, their feelings of embarrassment and discomfort mean that conversations tend to be infrequent (Elliot 2010). Yet another issue is that parents may have inaccurate or incomplete knowledge about sexual health topics, such as underestimating the effectiveness of condoms for preventing pregnancy and sexually transmitted infections (perhaps because they received inadequate sex education when they were young) (Eisenberg *et al.* 2004). Together, this means that while most parents want to talk to their teens about sex, conversations are complicated by feelings of uneasiness from both teens and parents.

In addition to their own experiences with their teens, parents' concerns about the sexualization of adolescents are intensified by the ways that teen sexual activity is discussed in the media. For example, teens are often described as highly over-sexualized beings that are at risk for involvement in deviant sexual behavior such as in the case of sensationalized stories about sex bracelets, rainbow parties, and group sex parties that are widely spread across news outlets (see Box 8.3). However, heightened concerns about these extreme forms of sexual deviance say more about what adults fear than what most teens are actually doing. Messages from the media and images from popular culture reinforce the idea that teens are having sex at increasingly younger ages and they are participating in incredibly dangerous, promiscuous, and reckless sexual behaviors. However, the consensus of most research indicates that such claims about teens and sex are grossly exaggerated (Best and Bogle 2014).

Parents and the purity movement

Parents sometimes choose to discuss sex with their children using a purity-focused dialogue. Thus, conversations are not about contraceptives or sexual pleasure, but rather focus on encouraging abstinence through purity pledges. A purity pledge is a family ritual in which the child (or parent of a child speaking for him/her) signs a formal, social agreement to remain sexually abstinent or "pure" until marriage. Many of those who have signed such pledges wear a "promise," "chastity," or "purity" ring

---

BOX 8.3 SEX BRACELETS, RAINBOW PARTIES, AND GROUP SEX PARTIES – OH MY!

Media representations of teen sexuality tends to cause alarm among parents—especially when these stories are headlines on the nightly news. Starting in the early 2000s, several news media outlets picked up stories about teen sexual deviance that sparked a great deal of controversy.
These included:

- *Sex bracelets.* In 2003, reports came out that linked these colorful fashion accessories (also known as gel bracelets or jelly bracelets) to sexual behavior, with the color of each band representing a different sexual act (e.g., orange = kissing, black = sexual intercourse). Stories differed as to the bracelets' meanings. One claim was that the color of the bracelet indicated what sex act the wearer had already participated in while others claimed that the color of the bracelet alerted others to what sex acts the wearer was willing to engage in. Other reports described games like *Snap!* that involved pulling on each other's bracelets and if one broke, the wearer had to perform the sexual act associated with that color with the person who broke it (Best and Bogle 2014).
- *Rainbow parties.* Tales of these gatherings started in the early 2000s. At rainbow parties, teen girls wear different shades of lipstick and, as they take turns fellating teen boys, create a rainbow on the boys' penises (Best and Bogle 2014). Little evidence exists that these parties actually take place, although an episode of *Law & Order: Special Victims Unit* ("Granting Immunity," 2015) depicts such an event.
- *Group sex parties.* Teen gatherings have always caused concern; however, the media alerted us to the fact that some parties were no longer places where the furthest teens might go is a kiss with "spin the bottle" or "seven minutes in heaven." In one example, boys would line up on one side of the room as girls worked their way down the "train," fellating each one as they went (Best and Bogle 2014).

While it is unknown exactly how many teens participate in these forms of extreme sex, the media coverage in the 2000s was enough to strike fear into the hearts of many parents who were frightened about the risky sex their teens might be engaging in. And while this is certainly not a new pattern (parents are frequently shocked by the sexual escapades of their children), these particular forms of sexual deviance play into parents' fears that not only are their child's peers deviant, but that teens are in need of protection from such unsavory behavior.

---

on their wedding finger (i.e., left ring finger) to indicate this vow will later be replaced by a wedding band. Most often, parents promote purity pledges for their children in the context of Christian perspectives that view adolescent sex as amoral and deviant. To protect their children from the dangerous sin of sex before marriage, Christian parents (and churches) promote purity pledges and reinforce their value by emphasizing how premarital sex leads to STIs, pregnancy, and public shame. In this way, parents move beyond what is taught in the schools (even if it is abstinence) by entwining their interest in abstinence with religious and family value systems (Manning 2014). Some purity pledge organizations include the Silver Ring Thing and True Love Waits (DeRogatis 2015; Moslener 2015). The Silver Ring Thing program was created in 1995 in Yuma, Arizona, and it has expanded to nine countries (Silver Ring Thing 2015). True Love Waits was founded in 1993 in Nashville, Tennessee, and it now has international presence in the Philippines and parts of Africa and South America (True Love Waits Project History). Each program offers a way to vow your commitment to abstinence until marriage whether it be through public declarations, signing a pledge, or ring ceremonies. For example, True Love Waits offers pledge cards to sign either online or to be mailed into their organization dictating the following commitment:

> Believing true love waits, I make a commitment to God, myself, my family, my friends, my future mate and my future children, to a lifetime of purity including sexual abstinence from this day until I enter a Biblical marriage relationship.
>
> *(True Love Waits Project)*

Young women's chastity (as opposed to young men's[2]) is often the main focal point of purity pledges. This is evident in the case of purity balls. The purity ball movement started in the 1990s when Randy Wilson, an employee of the Family Research Council,[3] founded the organization Generations of Light and organized the first formal dinner and dance where daughters could pledge their chastity to their fathers and to god (Oppenheimer 2012). Since then, thousands of purity balls occur across the United States every year. Many of the purity balls, especially in Arizona, are sponsored by the New Life Pregnancy Centers[4] (DeRogatis 2015). These events are highly ritualized and religious:

> After daughters sign their chastity pledge documents, or otherwise silently commit to chastity via a ritual of laying a white rose on a cross, each father signs another document as a witness and guardian who promises to help his daughter 'honor God with her body.'
>
> *(Fahs 2010:132)*

In essence, fathers are signing a pledge to guard their daughters' chastity as their own property. For example, the father's purity pledge from Generations of Light reads as follows:

> I, (daughter's name)'s father, choose before God to cover my daughter as her authority and protection in the area of purity. I will be pure in my own

life as a man, husband and father. I will be a man of integrity and account-
ability as I lead, guide and pray over my daughter and my family as the high
priest in my home. This covering will be used by God to influence generations to come.

(Generations of Light 2007a)

The purity movement in general takes away the agency of teens, especially daughters in the case of purity balls. By signing over your sexual decision-making to god,
your father, or both, this public declaration demonstrates a lack of trust in yourself
to make your own choices about sex. In doing so, the purity movement reinforces
both the idea that teen sex is deviant and that teen sexual decision-making is both
problematic *and* deviant if it does not involve abstinence. As far as their effectiveness
(i.e., if virginity pledges actually delay sexual activity until marriage), this is discussed below.

In summary, both teens and their parents believe that parents should play a vital
role in adolescents' sexual socialization; however, parents' ideas about what is appropriate for their teens differ widely. Some parents feel insecure about their own
knowledge about sex, while others have been influenced by stories in the media.
Evangelical Christian parents may try to control their child's sexuality by having
their daughter (or son) pledge to maintain their virginity until marriage. As you will
learn below, though, such pledges are not very effective.

Lessons from peers

Beyond schools and parents, peers in general, and especially friends, have a strong
impact on teenagers' lives. Overall, adolescent sexual activity and sexual risk-taking
behavior are influenced by sexual peer norms (van de Bongardt *et al.* 2014). Sexual
peer norms fall into three categories: those regarding actual or perceived behavior,
those regarding actual or perceived attitudes, and peer pressure. Norms about peer
sexual behavior include having sexual experience, age at sexual onset, number of
partners, and frequency of sexual activity. Norms about peer sexual attitudes involve
whether there would be approval or disapproval of sexual activity. Peer pressure is
an active and explicit encouragement from peers to engage in a behavior. Teens are
motivated to conform to their peers' expectations due to desire for potential social
gains or fear of potential social losses.

Researchers have found that adolescent sexual activity and sexual risk-taking
behavior is more strongly related to what they think their peers do than what they
think their peers approve of (van de Bongardt *et al.* 2014). Ultimately, teens who
perceive their peers as more sexually active, as more approving of having sex, and as
exerting more pressure on them to be sexually active tend to be more sexually
active themselves. The same can be said for engaging in sexual risk-taking behavior:
if teens believe that their friends are doing risky sexual behaviors, they are more
likely to engage in such behaviors themselves.

Peer pressure and sex

The age-old notion of "peer pressure" and the strong influence that teens have on each other's behavior is evident when it comes to sexual decision-making. For example, in a U.S. survey of 483 adolescents, 29 percent of 15 to 17 year-olds reported feeling pressure to have sex, which was comparable to the pressure they felt to use drugs or smoke cigarettes. Notably, compared to their peers who had not already had sex, sexually active teens were twice as likely to report feeling pressure to have sex (National Public Radio *et al.* 2003). In addition, even if they are not currently having sex, when teens think that their classmates (and friends in particular) are having sex, they are more likely to report their desire and intent to have sex soon (Miranda-Diaz and Corcoran 2012). Although it would appear that perhaps teens are "pressuring" each other to have sex, there is no indication that shaming non-sexually active teens for their virginity status is commonplace. In other words, teens might have sex to feel like they fit in among their sexually active peers; however, the extent to which they are pressured from others to do so is not as frequent as is generally thought.[5]

However, although they are not pressuring others to have sex or publicly shaming those who are not, teens are often judgmental about their peers' involvement in sexual behavior, especially if members of their social group are perceived as more sexually permissive than others in terms of premarital, casual, or group sex, early sexual debut, or nonverbal cues such as wearing provocative clothing. Indeed, teens that are perceived as sexually permissive due to one or more of these factors are at a higher risk of social rejection and aggression from their peers, including those who are sexually permissive themselves (Vrangalova *et al.* 2014). Teens can be cruel—especially when it comes to others and their perceived sexual promiscuity. Those who are labeled as "slutty" or "whorish" risk a ruined reputation, loss of respect, and public shaming. This is especially true for young women. Adolescent girls who have had more than eight sexual partners report fewer friends, however, adolescent boys who have had more than eight sexual partners report more friends (Kreager and Staff 2009). This sexual double standard shows us that teen sexual deviance is a highly gendered construct. As a result, peer perceptions about sexual promiscuity create sexually deviant statuses among some teens but not others.

Peer groups and purity pledges

Millions of adolescents in the United States have taken virginity pledges (Kantor *et al.* 2008). Beyond a simple vow of sexual inactivity, those who take purity pledges see their oath as a way to positively tie themselves to a community of friends and family and they rely upon influential people within their support system—parents, close friends, church members—to help hold them accountable to their pledge. In fact, the most successful virginity pledgers (i.e., the pledgers that are more likely to maintain their virginity for longer periods of time) are embedded in social networks that support their oath to remain abstinent until marriage.

For example, making a purity pledge at an abstinence event, such as one with lights, spiritual music, and personal testimonies, typically involves large numbers of like-minded teenagers who can help each other feel that their decision to remain abstinent is both normative and socially valuable (although in some instances, these events may result in teens feeling pressured into making a commitment they do not actually believe in) (Gardner 2015).

Purity pledges, however, are not found to be that effective at helping teens maintain abstinence until marriage. In fact, pledging has only been found to be associated with a (short) delay in first sexual intercourse (PVI) for those between the ages of 15 to 17 and *only if* there are few other pledgers within their schools. Pledging has no effect on transition to first sex in schools where more than 30 percent of students are pledgers and in schools where there are a small number of pledgers, their delay to first sexual intercourse is only about 18 months compared to non-pledgers (Brückner and Bearman 2005). Overall, sociologists have found that nearly all (88 percent) of those who take virginity pledges do not wait until marriage to have sexual intercourse (Bearman and Brückner 2001). However, pledgers differ from non-pledgers in that they:

- initiate sex (PVI) at older ages (18-month delay for pledgers);
- get married at earlier ages (52 percent of pledgers are married by age 25, compared to 34 percent of non-pledgers);
- have fewer lifetime sexual partners (on average, pledgers report 1 to 2 lifetime partners compared to 2 to 3 lifetime partners for non-pledgers);
- are significantly less likely to have used a condom at first PVI (55 percent of pledgers used condoms at first PVI compared to 60 percent of non-pledgers);
- are more likely to report having had only oral sex (not PVI) (13 percent of pledgers report only oral sex compared to 2 percent of non-pledgers).

In addition, pledgers and non-pledgers have similar rates of STIs, which is not surprising given pledgers' lower rates of condom use and the substitution of oral sex for vaginal sex (Brückner and Bearman 2005). In other words, pledges are overwhelmingly ineffective at preventing sex until marriage and what they are successful in doing is increasing riskier sex practices (i.e., reducing the likelihood of using contraceptives when sex does occur). Because pledgers are under the impression that they will abstain from sex, they are not likely to be mentally prepared when it does happen and furthermore, they are very unlikely to have condoms on hand and know how to use them. Overall, peer networks have an effect on virginity pledges but virginity pledges themselves are unlikely to prevent sexual intercourse until marriage.

In summary, peers are an important agent of sexual socialization as they help set the boundaries of both expected and acceptable behavior for each other. For example, having sex might be normative within a peer group, but having sex with too many people may be considered deviant for teen girls and positive for teen boys. In addition, virginity pledges are often introduced by parents and churches but are frequently reinforced, at least socially, by peers. Even so, virginity pledges do not substantially delay the onset of sex. Thus, the relationship between peer norms and sexual behavior is more often about teens wanting to feel like they fit in among their sexually active peers.

Adolescent sexuality in the Netherlands: an international comparative example

Although the United States and the Netherlands have similar levels of economic development, the parents in each country have drastically different attitudes toward teens and sexual behavior. For example, compared to Americans' conservative and restrictive attitudes toward adolescent sexual behavior, in the Netherlands, sexuality is seen "as a part of life that should be governed by self-determination, mutual respect, frank conversation, and the prevention of unintended consequences" (Schalet 2014:231). And this perspective has been institutionalized in the Dutch health care system and schools as well as in the general public. For example, access to contraception is widespread and the sex education curriculum emphasizes a holistic approach that addresses issues rarely mentioned in American sex education such as women's sexual pleasure, masturbation, and gay and lesbian sexuality, as well as the importance of mutual respect and consent in sexual relationships. In the Netherlands, sexuality education starts as early as age 4, but the content is designed to be age appropriate, such as learning about kinds of intimacy that feel good and do not feel good, different types of families, and body awareness (de Melker 2015).

Dutch parents themselves downplay the difficult and dangerous aspects of teenage sexuality and instead tend to normalize sex as part of being a teen. For example, because they want to respect their teens' sexuality, even as sex becomes part of their children's lives, it is common for Dutch teenagers with steady girlfriends or boyfriends to be allowed to spend the night with them in their rooms—behind closed doors (something that is highly frowned upon by the vast majority of American parents). Notably, teens in the Netherlands do not have sex at earlier ages than those in other European countries or the United States. However, Dutch teens are different from American teens in that:

- Dutch teens are more likely to use reliable methods of contraception from first intercourse onward (Schalet 2011).
- Dutch teens report their first sexual experiences as "well-timed, wanted, and fun" (Schalet 2011:S5).
- The Dutch have easy access to contraception. Condoms are available in vending machines and the birth control pill is free for anyone under age 21 (de Melker 2015).
- Dutch teens are among the top users of the birth control pill (Currie *et al.* 2012).

Instruction about safe sex practices in northern European countries is more liberal compared to elsewhere in Europe and across the globe:

> In the Netherlands, a popular television news program for children staged a condom demonstration on a model of an erect penis; a Danish cartoon book showed "Oda and Ole" making love using a condom; Finnish authorities sent a sex education leaflet and a condom to all adolescents on their sixteenth birthdays; and in Sweden, teachers passed around condoms in class and urged students to experiment with them.
>
> (Zimmerman 2015:120)

The straightforward way in which condom instruction takes place in these countries is striking in comparison to the way that Americans, such as Sanford Johnson from the beginning of this chapter, must use metaphors and coded messages to talk about sex and condoms in the United States. The radical difference between American and Dutch perspectives about adolescent sexuality is related to higher levels of Christian religiosity among Americans (which tends to emphasize abstinence until marriage) (Schalet 2014). As we can see, although the United States and the Netherlands are both economically developed countries, their approaches and attitudes toward sexuality differ dramatically. This international comparative example illustrates the cultural variance both in attitudes toward normative adolescent sexuality and how deviance varies cross-culturally.

Are "sexually active" adolescents deviant?

In this chapter, we have learned that what adolescents are told they should do and what they actually do in terms of their sexual behavior do not always match. This raises the question—are sexually active adolescents deviant? To the extent that sexuality is a normative part of adolescent development and most teens engage in some form of sexual behavior, sexually active adolescents are not deviant. However, given that American social attitudes toward adolescent sexuality sanction sexual behavior as dangerous, deviant, and risky, while simultaneously urging teens to wait until they are married to engage in sex, sexually active adolescents are viewed as deviants. And while these perspectives may be slowly shifting, "teens and sex" is a scary combination for most American adults.

Notes

1 Anal sex among adolescents is significantly less common. Only 11 percent of American adolescents between the ages of 15 to 19 have ever engaged in heterosexual anal sex (Leichliter *et al.* 2007).
2 Although boys do not typically take pledges at purity balls, Generations of Light (2007b), the first organization to establish purity balls, encourages fathers to have a manhood ceremony called "Brave Heart of a Warrior" when their sons turn 12 years old. At the ceremony, sons are presented with a purity ring as well as a large sword so that they may stand as warriors of god.

3   The Family Research Council (FRC) is an American conservative Christian group and lobbying organization formed in the United States in 1981. Randy Wilson serves as FRC's National Field Director for Church Ministries.
4   New Life Pregnancy Centers are a type of crisis pregnancy center. Such centers are typically run by pro-life Christian groups and are established to discourage women from seeking abortions. Some provide non-medical assistance in the form of counseling, Bible study, and material resources (diapers, bottles).
5   Peer pressure, while an overt and direct sexual peer norm, is actually difficult to measure reliably and consistently, especially as it may be difficult for teens to recognize that they were vulnerable to peer pressure when making their decisions (van de Bongardt *et al.* 2014).

References

Bearman, Peter and Hannah Brückner. 2001. "Promising the Future: Virginity Pledges and First Intercourse." *American Journal of Sociology* 106:859–912.

Best, Joel and Kathleen A. Bogle. 2014. *Kids Gone Wild.* New York, NY: NYU Press.

Brady, Sonya S. and Bonnie L. Halpern-Felscher. 2007. "Adolescents' Reported Consequences of Having Oral Sex Versus Vaginal Sex." *Pediatrics* 119(2):229–36.

Brückner, Hannah and Peter Bearman. 2005. "After the Promise: The STD Consequences of Adolescent Virginity Pledges." *Journal of Adolescent Health* 36:271–78.

CDC. 2015. *Vaginal Sexual Intercourse.* Centers for Disease Control Retrieved from: http://www.cdc.gov/nchs/nsfg/key_statistics/s.htm#vaginalsexual

Chirban, John. 2012. *How to Talk with Your Kids about Sex: Help Your Children Develop a Positive, Healthy Attitude Toward Sex and Relationships.* Nashville, TN: Thomas Nelson.

Currie, Candace, Cara Zanotti, Antony Morgan, Dorothy Currie, Margaretha de Looze, Chris Roberts, Oddrun Samdal, Otto R.F. Smith, and Vivian Barnekow. 2012. *Social Determinants of Health and Well-Being Among Young People.* Copenhagen: WHO Regional Office for Europe.

de Melker, Saskia. 2015. "The Case for Starting Sex Education in Kindergarten." *PBS Newshour.* May 27, 2015. http://www.pbs.org/newshour/updates/spring-fever/

Demissie, Zewditu, Nancy D. Brenner, Tim McManus, Shari L. Shanklin, Joseph Hawkins, and Laura Kann. 2013. *School Health Profiles 2012: Characteristics of Health Programs Among Secondary Schools.* Atlanta, GA: Centers for Disease Control and Prevention.

DeRogatis, Amy. 2015. *Saving Sex: Sexuality and Salvation in American Evangelicalism.* New York, NY: Oxford University Press.

Diamond, Lisa M. 2008. *Sexual Fluidity: Understanding Women's Love and Desire.* Cambridge, MA: Harvard University Press.

di Mauro, Diane and Carole Joffe. 2007. "The Religious Right and the Reshaping of Sexual Policy: An Examination of Reproductive Rights and Sexuality Education." *Sexuality Research and Social Policy: Journal of NSRC* 4(1):67–92.

Djamba, Yanyi K., Theresa C. Davidson, and Mosisa G. Aga. 2012. *Sexual Health of Young People in the U.S. South: Challenges and Opportunities.* Montgomery, AL: Center for Demographic Research.

Eisenberg, Marla E., Linda H. Bearinger, Renee E. Sieving, Carolyne Swain, and Michael D. Resnick. 2004. "Parents' Beliefs about Condoms and Oral Contraceptives." *Perspectives on Sexual and Reproductive Health* 36(2):50–7.

Elliot, Sinikka. 2010. "Talking to Teens About Sex: Mothers Negotiate Resistance, Discomfort, and Ambivalence." *Sexuality Research and Social Policy: Journal of NSRC* 7:310–22.

Elliot, Sinikka. 2012. *Not My Kid: What Parents Believe About the Sex Lives of Their Teenagers.* New York, NY: NYU Press.

Fahs, Breanne. 2010. "Daddy's Little Girls: On the Perils of Chastity Clubs, Purity Balls, and Ritualized Abstinence." *Frontiers* 31(3):116–42.

Fehlbaum, Amanda. 2014. *Sex Ex Libris: Abstinence Messages in High School Health Textbooks Cultivate Sex Negativity Among Teens.* PhD diss. Norman: The University of Oklahoma.

Finer, Lawrence B. and Jesse M. Philbin. 2013. "Sexual Initiation, Contraceptive Use, and Pregnancy among Young Adolescents." *Pediatrics* 131(5):1–6.

Gardner, Christine J. 2011. *Making Chastity Sexy: The Rhetoric of Evangelical Abstinence Campaigns.* Oakland, CA: University of California Press.

Generations of Light. 2007a. "The Pledge." Retrieved from: https://generationsoflight.com/html/thepledge.html

Generations of Light. 2007b. "What About Boys." Retrieved from: http://generationsoflight.com/html/boys.html

Halpern-Felsher, Bonnie L., Jodi L. Cornell, Rhonda Y. Kropp, and Jeanne M. Tschann. 2005. "Oral Versus Vaginal Sex Among Adolescents: Perceptions, Attitudes, and Behavior." *Pediatrics* 115(4):845–51.

Herman-Giddens, Marcia E. 2006. "Recent Data on Pubertal Milestones in United States Children: The Secular Trend Toward Earlier Development." *International Journal of Andrology* 29:241–6.

Herman-Giddens, Marcia E., Eric J. Slora, Richard C. Wasserman, Carlos J. Bourdony, Manju V. Bhapkar, Gary G. Koch, and Cynthia M. Hasemeier. 1997. "Secondary Sexual Characteristics and Menses in Young Girls Seen in Office Practice: A Study from the Pediatric Research in Office Settings Network." *Pediatrics* 99(4):505–12.

Irvine, Janice M. 2006. "Emotional Scripts of Sex Panics." *Sexuality Research and Social Policy: Journal of NSRC* 3(3):82–94.

Johnson, Sanford. 2012. "How To Put On A Sock." Retrieved August 30, 2015. https://www.youtube.com/watch?v=06kT9yfj7QE

Jordan, Timothy R., James H. Price, and Shawn Fitzgerald. 2000. "Rural Parents' Communication with Their Teenagers About Sexual Issues." *Journal of School Health* 70(8):338–44.

Kann, Laura, Emily O'Malley Olsen, Tim McManus, Steve Kinchen, David Chyen, William A. Harris, and Howell Wechsler. 2011. "Sexual Identity, Sex of Sexual Contacts, and Health Risk Behaviors Among Students in Grades 9–12, Youth Risk Behavior Surveillance, Selected Sites, Unites States, 2001–2009." *CDC MMWR* 60(1):1–133.

Kann, Laura, Steve Kinchen, Shari L. Shanklin, Katherine H. Flint, Joseph Hawkins, William A. Harris, Richard Lowry, Emily O'Malley Olsen, Tim McManus, David Chyen, Lisa Whittle, Eboni Taylor, Zewditu Demissie, Nancy Brener, Jemekia Thornton, John Moore, and Stephanie Zaza. 2014. "Youth Risk Behavior Surveillance – United States, 2013." *CDC MMWR* 63(4):1–172.

Kantor, Leslie, John Santelli, Julien Teitler, and Randall Balmer. 2008. "Abstinence-only Policies and Programs: An Overview." *Sexuality Research & Social Policy* 5(3):6–17.

Karlberg, Johan. 2002. "Secular Trends in Pubertal Development." *Hormone Research* 57:19–30.

Kaye, Kelleen, Katherine Suellentrop and Corinna Sloup. 2009. *The Fog Zone.* Washington, D.C.: The National Campaign to Prevent Teen and Unplanned Pregnancy.

Kendall, Nancy. 2008. "Sexuality Education in an Abstinence-Only Era: A Comparative Case Study of Two U.S. States." *Sexuality Research and Social Policy: Journal of NSRC* 5(2):23–44.

Kirby, Douglas. 2007. "Abstinence, Sex, and STD/HIV Education Programs for Teens: Their Impact on Sexual Behavior, Pregnancy, and Sexually Transmitted Disease." *Annual Review of Sex Research* 18(1):143–77.

Kohler, Pamela K., Lisa E. Manhart, and William E. Lafferty. 2008. "Abstinence-Only and Comprehensive Sex Education and the Initiation of Sexual Activity and Teen Pregnancy." *Journal of Adolescent Health* 42:344–51.

Kost, Kathryn and Stanley Henshaw. 2014. *U.S. Teenage Pregnancies, Births, and Abortions, 2010: National Trends by Age, Race, and Ethnicity.* New York, NY: Guttmacher Institute.

Kreager, Derek A. and Jeremy Staff. 2009. "The Sexual Double Standard and Adolescent Peer Acceptance." *Social Psychological Quarterly* 72(2):143–64.

Law & Order: Special Victims Unit. "Granting Immunity." Directed by Holly Dale. Written by Brianna Yellen and A. Zell Williams. Wolf Films. April 8, 2015.

Leichliter, Jami S., Anjani Chandra, Nicole Liddon, Kevin A. Fenton, and Sevgi O. Aral. 2007. "Prevalence and Correlates of Heterosexual Anal and Oral Sex in Adolescents and Adults in the United States." *The Journal of Infectious Diseases* 196(12):1852–9.

Lindberg, Laura Duberstein and Issac Maddow-Zimet. 2012. "Consequences of Sex Education on Teen and Young Adult Sexual Behavior and Outcomes." *Journal of Adolescent Health* 51:332–8.

Lindberg, Laura Duberstein, Rachel Jones, and John S. Santelli. 2008. "Noncoital Sexual Activities Among Adolescents." *Journal of Adolescent Health* 43:231–8.

Manning, Jimmie. 2014. "Paradoxes of (Im)Purity: Affirming Heteronormativity and Queering Heterosexuality in Family Discourses of Purity Pledges." *Women's Studies in Communication* 38(1):99–117.

Martin, Joyce A., Brady E. Hamilton, Michelle J. K. Osterman, Sally C. Curtin, and T.J. Matthews. 2015. "Births: Final Data for 2013." *National Vital Statistics Report* 64(1):1–68.

Martinez, Gladys, Joyce Abma, and Casey Copen. 2010. "Educating Teenagers about Sex in the United States." *NCHS Data Brief, no. 44.* Hyattsville, MD: National Center for Health Statistics.

Miranda-Diaz, Miriam and Kevin Corcoran. 2012. "'All My Friends Are Doing It:' The Impact of the Perception of Peer Sexuality on Adolescents' Intent to Have Sex." *Journal of Evidence-Based Social Work* 9:260–4.

Moran, Jeffrey P. 2000. *Teaching Sex.* Cambridge, MA: Harvard University Press.

Moslener, Sara. 2015. *Virgin Nation: Sexual Purity and American Adolescence.* New York, NY: Oxford University Press.

Mueller, Trisha E., Lorrie E. Gavin, and Aniket Kulkarni. 2008. "The Association Between Sex Education and Youth's Engagement in Sexual Intercourse, Age at First Intercourse, and Birth Control Use at First Sex." *Journal of Adolescent Health* 42:89–96.

National Public Radio, Kaiser Family Foundation, John F. Kennedy School of Government. 2003. *Sex Education in America.* Washington, D.C.: National Public Radio.

Newport, Frank. 2014. "Mississippi Most Religious State, Vermont Least Religious." *Gallup.* February 3, 2014. Retrieved from: http://www.gallup.com/poll/167267/mississippi-religious-vermont-least-religious-state.aspx

Newport, Frank. 2015. "Mississippi, Alabama, and Louisiana Most Conservative States." *Gallup.* February 6, 2015. Retrieved from: http://www.gallup.com/poll/181505/mississippi-alabama-louisiana-conservative-states.aspx

Oppenheimer, Mark. 2012. "'Purity Balls' Get Attention, but Might Not Be All They Claim." *The New York Times.* July 20, 2012. Retrieved from: http://www.nytimes.com/2012/07/21/us/purity-balls-local-tradition-or-national-trend.html?_r=0

Russell, Stephen T. 2005. "Conceptualizing Positive Adolescent Sexuality Development." *Sexuality Research & Social Policy* 2(3):4–12.

Russell, Stephen T., Kali S. Van Campen, and Joel A. Muraco. 2012. "Sexuality Development in Adolescence." Pp. 70–87 in *Sex for Life: From Virginity to Viagra, How Sexuality Changes Throughout Our Lives,* edited by Laura M. Carpenter and John DeLamater. New York, NY: NYU Press.

Savin-Williams, Ritch C. 2005. *The New Gay Teenager*. Cambridge, MA: Harvard University Press.

Schalet, Amy T. 2011. "Beyond Abstinence and Risk: A New Paradigm for Adolescent Sexual Health." *Women's Health Issues* 21(3):S5–S7.

Schalet, Amy T. 2014. "Sex, Love, and Autonomy in the Teenage Sleepover." Pp. 229–34 in *Sex Matters: The Sexuality & Society Reader*, Fourth Edition, edited by Mindy Stombler, Dawn M. Baunach, Wendy Simons, Elroi J. Windsor, and Elisabeth O. Burgess. New York, NY: W.W. Norton.

Schuster, Mark A., Robert Bell, and David E. Kanouse. 1996. "The Sexual Practices of Adolescent Virgins: Genital Sexual Activities of High School Students Who Have Never Had Vaginal Intercourse." *American Journal of Public Health* 86 (11):1570–6.

Sexuality Information and Education Council of the United States (SIECUS). 2004. *National Guidelines Task Force: Guidelines for Comprehensive Sexuality Education*, Third Edition. Washington, D.C.

Sexuality Information and Education Council of the United States (SIECUS). n.d. "Sexuality Education Q & A." Retrieved from: http://siecus.org/index.cfm?fuseaction=page.viewpage&pageid=521&grandparentID=477&parentID=514

Silver Ring Thing. 2015. *What Is Silver Ring Thing*. Retrieved from: http://www.silverringthing.com/what-is-silver-ring-thing

Social Security Act. 1998. *Separate Program for Abstinence Education. Title V*. Retrieved from: http://www.ssa.gov/OP_Home/ssact/title05/0510.htm.

Somers, Cheryl R. and Amy T. Surmann. 2004. "Adolescents' Preferences for Source of Sex Education." *Child Study Journal* 34(1):47–59.

Tolman, Deborah L. and Sara I. McClelland. 2011. "Normative Sexuality Development in Adolescence: A Decade in Review, 2000–2009." *Journal of Research on Adolescence* 21(1):242–55.

Trenholm, Christopher, Barbara Devaney, Ken Fortson, Lisa Quay, Justin Wheeler, and Melissa Clark. 2007. *Impacts of Four Title V, Section 510 Abstinence Education Programs*. Princeton, NJ: Mathematica Policy Research, Inc.

True Love Waits Project. n.d. *True Love Waits Pledge*. Retrieved from: http://www.lifeway.com/n/product-family/true-love-waits/

True Love Waits Project History. n.d. *True Love Waits Project*. Retrieved from: http://www.lifeway.com/History/True-Love-Waits/c/N-1z0zq7rZ1z13wiu?intcmp=TLWMain-Hero-History-20131216

Uecker, Jeremy E., Nicole Angotti, and Mark D. Regnerus. 2008. "Going Most of the Way: 'Technical Virginity' Among American Adolescents." *Social Science Research* 37(4):1200–15.

Underhill, Kristen, Don Operario, and Paul Montgomery. 2007. "Abstinence-only Programs for HIV Infection Prevention in High-income Countries: Systematic Review." *British Medical Journal* 335(7613):248–60.

United Nations, Department of Economic and Social Affairs. 2014. *United Nations Demographic Yearbook, 2013*. New York, NY: United Nations. Retrieved from: http://unstats.un.org/unsd/demographic/products/dyb/dyb2013.htm

van de Bongardt, Daphne, Ellen Reitz, Theo Sandfort, and Maja Dekovic. 2014. "A Meta-Analysis of the Relations Between Three Types of Peer Norms and Adolescent Sexual Behavior." *Personality and Social Psychology Review* 19(3):1–32.

Vivancos, Roberto, Ibrahim Abubakar, Penelope Phillips-Howard, and Paul R. Hunter. 2013. "School-based Sex Education is Associated with Reduced Risky Sexual Behaviour and Sexually Transmitted Infections in Young Adults." *Public Health* 127(1):53–7.

Vrangalova, Zhana, Rachel E. Bukberg, and Gerulf Rieger. 2014. "Birds of a Feather? Not When It Comes to Sexual Permissiveness." *Journal of Social and Personal Relationships* 31(1):93–113.

Wellings, Kaye, Martine Collumbien, Emma Slaymaker, Susheela Singh, Zoé Hodges, Dhaval Patel, and Nathalie Bajos. 2006. "Sexual Behaviour in Context: A Global Perspective." *Lancet* 368:1706–28.

Woody, Jane D., Robin Russel, Henry J. D'Souza, and Jennifer K. Woody. 2000. "Adolescent Non-Coital Sexual Activity: Comparisons of Virgins and Non-Virgins." *Journal of Sex Education and Therapy* 25(4):261–8.

Zimmerman, Jonathan. 2015. *Too Hot to Handle: A Global History of Sex Education*. Princeton, NJ: Princeton University Press.

UNIT III
DEVIANT SEXUAL ACTS

Unit III introduction

Now that we have established a firm footing of what sexual deviance entails, it is now time to explore the world of deviant sex through in-depth investigations of three major areas: sex in public, fetishes, and sex work. In doing so, we will see that both fantasizing about, and engaging in, sexual behaviors that might be labeled as "deviant" are rather common experiences for the most part. In particular, by examining deviant sexual acts, the reader is exposed to a diverse spectrum of sexual deviance and is encouraged to be introspective during the process. Overall, unit III critically challenges the notion that "deviance" rarely occurs and emphasizes the cultural processes that lead to diagnosing something or someone as deviant.

In chapter 9, fantasies about and the actual participation in public sexual deviance are examined. The significance of the historically intense criminal investigation of men who have sex with other men (MSM) in public spaces shapes this chapter's discussion of public sex. First, the question of how "public" and "private" are defined is offered in context of the U.S. Supreme Court cases *Bowers v. Hardwick* (1986) and *Lawrence v. Texas* (2003). Next, Laud Humphreys' *Tearoom Trade: Impersonal Sex in Public Places* (1970) is emphasized and its cultural significance is highlighted. Then, this chapter offers a description of the distinct sexual cultures found within three types of locations where public sex may take place: noncommercial public areas (including public bathrooms/tearooms/cottages and public parks), commercial establishments (including gym locker rooms and bars/clubs/pubs), and sex-on-site-focused establishments (including sex clubs, bathhouses, and backrooms). The cruising practices, solicitation methods for sex, and the actual sexual behaviors that occur in each particular public sex spot are discussed. Reasons for participation in this type of sexual deviance are also offered.

Sexual fantasies and fetishes that exist outside the normative spectrum are so diverse that entire books, magazines, websites, and communities can be found that are dedicated to each one. In chapter 10, just a small sampling of this complex and curious world of sexual deviance is provided and represented by three sometimes overlapping categories: "object"-specific fetishes (podophilia, retifism, agalmatophilia, pygmalion-ism, balloon fetishes, objectophilia, mechaphilia), "animal"-specific fetishes (zoophilia, formicophilia, bestiality, furry fandom, plushies, bronies, cloppers), and Dom/sub role-play (bondage, discipline, sadomasochism). In addition, fetish fashion and fetishes in popular culture are discussed. The purposes that sexual fantasies (and accompanying fetishisms) can serve as well as who these fetishists are (including gender differences in fetishism) are provided. The stigma that fetishists experience is highlighted alongside the commonality of "deviant" sexual fantasies. Overall, this chapter emphasizes the complexity of the world of fetishism.

Finally, chapter 11 emphasizes the buying and selling of sexual services via an in-depth dialogue about sex work. Various forms of prostitution (including street prostitution, escorting, brothel prostitution, and sugar dating) as well as pornography production and performance are both defined and situated within the stigmatized world of sexual deviance. In addition, this chapter explores sex work as it operates in wider cultures today, considering variable attributions of deviance and the allocation of the sex worker dividend. The relationships between pornography, technology, and law are emphasized along with the diversity of the world of pornography (including "porn for women," political porn, queer porn, and feminist porn). By considering a series of occupations that, in spite of their conventionally normalizing characteristics, are still considered one of the most universally deviant behaviors in contemporary society, the reader is encouraged to think about how wider social norms and ideas about deviance continue to shape our real-world engagement of sex work-related issues.

Overall, the third unit of this textbook considers sexual acts that are perceived, labeled, and stigmatized as sexually deviant as well as the actors who participate in them. Furthermore, the formal laws and social sanctions that accompany these sexually deviant acts are critically evaluated as they pertain to processes that shape these experiences as sexually deviant. By situating issues such as public sex, fetishes, and sex work within a socio-cultural context, the multiple layers of deviance and the processes involved in stigmatizing certain kinds of sexual behavior are illuminated.

9

SEX IN PUBLIC

Parking. Petting. Necking. Canoodling. While you may not use these words to describe your sexual escapades, your grandparents (or maybe even your great-grandparents) probably do. This decade-specific language harkens back to a different era, one in which "Lovers' Lanes" flourished and public sex was on the minds of many—teens, parents, and city officials alike. In the 1950s, adults were aghast at the new generation of randy teens that had come onto the scene. And while that may not be all too uncommon (parents are often threatened by the sexualities of each new generation), easy access to automobiles meant that young lovers moved "from front porch to back seat" (Bailey 1998) and began dating in the public sphere. Beyond the typical locations for romance (i.e., movie theaters, ballgames, soda fountains, bowling alleys, and roller skating rinks), "parking and a distinctive petting culture reached their zenith" (Howard 1995:180). Teens were off their parents' chesterfields and davenports and onto the roomy bench seats that large model 1950s sedans typically featured. Their titillating destination for the evening? A secluded "Lovers' Lane" complete with un-surveilled privacy and a beautiful view of the sparkling city lights of Normalsville, USA. The activity? Parking. Petting. Necking. Canoodling. Sexual activities that could not take place at home under the watchful eye of parents but were easily accomplished in the backseat of a 1957 Chevrolet Bel Air.

In 1950s Atlanta, Georgia, the common destination for young lovers was Piedmont Park, a sprawling 189-acre urban public park located about 2 miles northeast of downtown established in the early 1900s. This "Lovers' Lane" was so popular that on weekend nights, cars were parked bumper-to-bumper by 7:30 p.m. (Burns 1953). One might think that the stereotypical sexual conservativeness of the 1950s would have meant that adults generally disapproved of teens "parking" in the park. However, according to prominent Atlanta councilman John A. White, this was not the case:

> A crowded city offers little of that privacy so necessary in the development of romance ... Given the strange chemistry of youth and the goldfish-bowl nature

of modern living, some adjustment in the national mores is inevitable. If young-sters feel bound to stop their cars to further the associations so dear to them, they will do so. Surely it is better for them to pause in city parks than on lonely roads.

(Burns 1953:9–10)

The Atlanta City Council even authorized the parking of courting couples in the city parks in a unanimous vote declaring "Love is Legal in Piedmont Park" (Burns 1953:10) —at least for straight, young couples (see also Howard 1995).

But not all of Atlanta's Bible Belt[1] citizens were comfortable with the idea of youth canoodling unsupervised in the park; therefore, policemen and park supervi-sors were encouraged to patrol the areas for dangerous circumstances. What they found, however, was that the park was not just a popular parking/petting hotspot for straight, young couples. Piedmont Park was also the home to "a thriving, lively homosexual underground that had previously existed outside the purview of most Atlanta residents" (Howard 1995:180).

Who has sex in public?

The world of public sexual deviance is a much different place than it was in the 1950s. Today, we know that "public" sex is a common fantasy. Multiple surveys from both academic and popular culture sources demonstrate interest in this activity. For example, one in eight report fantasizing about having sex in the office, public toilets, or on a deserted beach and over half (57 percent of women and 66 percent of men) indicate that making love openly in a public place is a common fantasy of theirs (Joyal et al. 2015). Public sex fantasies are also relatively common among het-erosexual men in Australia (Smith and Over 1991) and among a mostly (90 percent) heterosexual male sample in Canada: 48 percent of men fantasized about petting with a total stranger in a public place (e.g., metro) and 73 percent indicated that sex with an unknown person was a common fantasy of theirs (Joyal et al. 2015). Among Canadian undergraduate college students, 67 percent of men and 55 percent of women reported thinking about having sex in a public place (Byers et al. 1998). But beyond just thinking about it, many people are actually doing it—in public. For example, a nationally representative study of adult Americans (N = 1,501) found that 57 percent (62 percent men, 51 percent women) have had sex outdoors or in a public place and of those who had not, 6 percent (7 percent men, 4 percent women) fantasized about it (Langer et al. 2004). In Europe, 41 percent of Danes reported having had sex in public and about one in three from Belgium, Germany, Norway, Spain, Switzerland, Sweden, and the United Kingdom also indicated participation in public sex (European Sex Survey 2013) (see Figure 9.1). Heterosexual American college students (N = 899) report an average of at least one public sex experience (defined as sexual activity in a campus restroom, other public restroom, public park, car, locker-room, sauna, or other public or semipublic venue) (Dodge et al. 2004). In a pop-culture survey of 1,000 American adults, 52 percent said they had sex in a public place. They indicated that their top locations for public sex were: parked cars

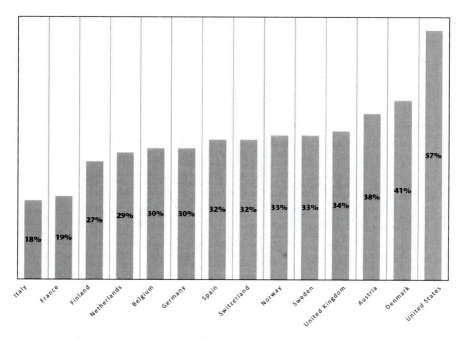

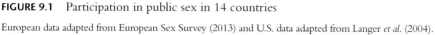

FIGURE 9.1 Participation in public sex in 14 countries

European data adapted from European Sex Survey (2013) and U.S. data adapted from Langer *et al.* (2004).

(80 percent), the woods (55 percent), a park (44 percent), the beach (42 percent), the workplace office (25 percent), public bathrooms (22 percent), movie theatres (16 percent), airplanes (7 percent), churches (5 percent), and taxis (2 percent) (Adamandeve.com 2011). Thus, it is clear that while having sex in public may be labeled a "deviant" activity, it may not be such an uncommon experience.

MSM and public sex

We know that at least some public sex is tolerated, after all the classic image of "Lovers' Lane" in the 1950s is of teenagers petting and parking in popular make-out spots. Contemporary surveys show us that having sex in public is a common fantasy and at least half of Americans and one in three Europeans has done it (in public) at least once (Langer *et al.* 2004; Adamandeve.com 2011; European Sex Survey 2013). But beyond this, we do not know much about the nature of public sex—except among one particular group, men who have sex with other men (MSM).

Starting in the 1950s, there was a police crackdown on clandestine sexual activity taking place in public restrooms (known as tearooms) in the United States. Men having sex with other men in these public locations did not fit in with the mores of 1950s America. As a result, hundreds (if not thousands) of men were arrested on sodomy charges—some spending up to three years in prison for their public toilet trysts (Howard 1995). And while this was not a new activity [scholars note that men have been having sex with other men in public locales since there were public locales (Church *et al.* 1993)], 1950s American norms clearly placed "homosexuality" and sex between men in a category of "deviance." Beyond this, because middle-class, heterosexual teens were now dating in the public sphere, there was heightened awareness of these spaces and the gay men and other MSM who had always been there were now cavorting right alongside straight, young lovers. As a result, these men became the "scapegoats" of "inappropriate" public sex (Howard 1995:168). Their crimes were widely publicized; newspapers even printed the names and addresses of men arrested for having public bathroom sex with other men (Howard 1995). Perhaps not surprisingly, this caught the interest of not only concerned citizens, but also, conscientious sociologists.

The first systematic sociological analysis of sex between men in public restrooms was conducted by American sociologist, Laud Humphreys, in the late 1960s (see Box 9.1). His dissertation research resulted in the publication of a highly controversial book, *Tearoom Trade: Impersonal Sex in Public Places* (1970) that spawned a myriad of subsequent research on this phenomenon (e.g., Ponte 1974; Desroches 1990;

BOX 9.1 LAUD HUMPHREYS AND RESEARCH ETHICS

Native-Oklahoman Laud Humphreys (born Robert Allan Humphreys) was born in Chickasha on October 16, 1930. But you will not find any monuments or statues commemorating this sociology scholar there—or anywhere else. Why? Because after 14 years as an Episcopalian priest in Oklahoma, Colorado, and Kansas, Humphreys decided to pursue his Ph.D. in sociology by studying perhaps one of the most controversial subjects of his time: men having sex with men in public park restrooms known as "tearooms".

After marrying his wife, Nancy, at Tulsa's Trinity Church in 1960, Humphreys bounced around several different parishes and eventually grew particularly interested in sociology (in part because of his work ministering to the gay community as a clergyman over the past several years). In 1965, Humphreys enrolled at Washington University in Saint Louis (a top research institution) where he was supported by his dissertation adviser, Lee Rainwater (born in 1928), to investigate a sexually deviant subculture that had never been studied before: tearoom participants. He produced a detailed ethnographic research project that was eventually published as a book in 1970, but not without controversy. In fact, because he believed that Humphreys had failed to follow university regulations in the protection of human subjects and may have also violated criminal law by viewing acts of sodomy, the university chancellor threatened to revoke his degree. He recommended that he refrain from using his newly earned title of "Doctor" and even contacted the publisher of his forthcoming book to prevent its release (Galliher *et al.* 2004:27). Eventually, Humphreys was cleared of all charges and his degree remained intact but his teaching contract at Washington University was terminated (it is worth noting that this sociology department later permanently disbanded in 1989, perhaps, in part, because of the fragmentation resultant from this controversy). However, Humphreys was quickly hired at Southern Illinois University at Edwardsville (Galliher *et al.* 2004).

Tearoom Trade: Impersonal Sex in Public Places

Humphreys' book *Tearoom Trade: Impersonal Sex in Public Places* immediately caught the attention of the Society for the Study of Social Problems and won the C. Wright Mills Award intended "to recognize outstanding research and writing on critical social issues" (Galliher *et al.* 2004:39). A special British-release edition was also published in 1970 and a German language edition followed in 1974. *Tearoom Trade*'s popularity was no doubt related to Humphreys' meticulous investigation of 19 different men's bathrooms located in five public parks from 1965 to 1968. Beyond providing intimate and rather salacious details about the 120 sex acts he observed, Humphreys (1970) asserted that the men participating in such activities came from diverse social backgrounds and that over half of his subjects were married men with unsuspecting wives at home. How did he know these personal details? Here is where Humphreys' research moved from a study of sexual deviance to a breach in ethical practice.

   After observing sex acts between men in tearooms, Humphreys followed these men out to their cars, wrote down their license plate numbers, had a "friendly policeman" provide their names and addresses, and later came to their homes to interview them under the guise of "market research" (Humphreys 1970:38). Although Humphreys changed his appearance and the interviews occurred more than a year after his observation of sex acts, Humphreys' research has been criticized by sociologists as a major ethical breach in three ways (Warwick 1975:211–12):

*   *Ethical Problem 1.* The researcher took advantage of a relatively powerless group of men to pursue his study. The men in the tearooms could not fight back.
*   *Ethical Problem 2.* His research contributed to the problematic imagery that social scientists are sly tricksters that are not to be trusted. The more widespread this image becomes, the more difficult it will be for any social scientist to carry out studies involving active participants.
*   *Ethical Problem 3.* The use of deception, misrepresentation, and manipulation in social research encourages the same tendencies in other parts of society. Social research involving deception and manipulation ultimately helps produce a society of cynics, liars, and manipulators. It undermines the trust that is essential to a just social order.

Even today, sociologists continue to debate about Humphreys' research ethics in his tearoom research. On the one hand, he was a pioneer in his investigatory methods and brought much needed attention to a group without a voice.

On the other hand, his choice to deceive his respondents and potentially harm them by, for example, revealing their involvement in tearoom trysts to their wives (or at least give the impression that he might do so while interviewing them in their homes), is highly problematic. In the end, the major question that remains is, do the ends justify the means? Did the risk for potential harm outweigh the scholarly contributions of *Tearoom Trade*?

Humphreys himself believed the answer is a resounding "yes" but he admitted to two mistakes in his retrospective ethical assessment published in the second edition of *Tearoom Trade* in 1975: "I am forced to agree with my critics regarding that part of my study in which I traced the license numbers and interviewed respondents in their homes" (Humphreys 1975:230). Even so, Humphreys acknowledges that "there is no reason to believe that any research subjects have suffered because of my efforts" (Humphreys 1975:231). Furthermore, in just a few short years after its initial release, *Tearoom Trade* clearly inspired a great deal of similar research including studies of pornographic bookstore patrons (Karp 1973), "peep show" viewers (Sundholm 1973), and truck stop cruisers (Corzine and Kirby 1977). Thus, Humphreys (and others) view *Tearoom Trade* as within the ethical parameters of social research because its scholarly contribution was significant and it is believed that there was no real harm done to its participants.

Others, however, are not so sure. In fact, *Tearoom Trade* as well as other notable controversial social experiments including the Tuskegee Syphilis Study (1932 to 1972), the Stanford Prison Experiment (1971), the Milgram Experiment (1961) (and others) contributed toward the creation of entities that govern ethical practices in all human subjects research (at Universities, these entities often take the form of an Institutional Review Board). Because of the missteps of our academic forefathers, all modern human subjects research must adhere to the following ethical principles as outlined in *The Belmont Report* (1974) (Moon and Khin-Maung-Gyi 2009:312):

- *Respect for persons.* This principle includes both respect for the autonomy of human subjects and the importance of protecting vulnerable individuals.
- *Beneficence.* More than just promotion of well-being, the duty of beneficence requires that research maximize the benefit-to-harm ratio for individual subjects and for the research program as a whole.
- *Justice.* Justice in research focuses on the duty to assign the burden and benefits of research fairly.

Thus, whatever your opinion of Humphreys' ethics in *Tearoom Trade*, at the very least, his research drew attention to the importance of critically examining ethical practices in human subjects research. Humphreys even taught courses in the qualitative methods of field research/observation that critically addressed these ethical issues. Yet "today Humphreys is routinely condemned in sociology textbooks and held up as a negative role model for how *not* to practice sociology" (Galliher *et al.* 2004:96).

Church *et al.* 1993; Tewksbury 1995). The tearoom was no longer a "gay" secret; now everyone knew about this bathroom behavior—and sociologists wanted to know more. Beyond the increasing scholarly interest in this clandestine activity in the 1970s and 1980s, police and public health officials were particularly focused on MSM in public when the AIDS Crisis began. Not only was bathroom sex between men illegal and deviant, it could also be deadly. As a result, public sex was policed more so than ever before. Police set up sting operations in tearooms and raided other known locales for public sex between men including gay bathhouses and public parks. This "close-the-baths/police-the-parks approach to AIDS prevention" (Leap 1999a:2) continued to keep MSM in the watchful eye of the police and public citizenry ["this also explains why 'sex in public places' is so closely associated with male, rather than female identities" (Leap 1999a:11)]. All the while researchers were developing a scholarly body of work about these titillating toilet trysts. Public sex was now a permanent part of the sociological literature.

What is public sex?

Before moving forward in our discussion, we must first consider what is meant by "public sex." First, let us admit that the notion of "public sex" is entirely misleading in the first place because it suggests that there is some clear universal and easy-to-identify way of defining a "public" activity. There is not. So identifying "public sex" is really first and foremost about understanding distinctions between "public" and "private" behaviors.

Public versus private

We all have a colloquial understanding of "public" and "private." For example, "public" typically identifies a location that appears to be "open," "accessible," and "unrestricted," while "private" suggests a location which seems more "sheltered," "secluded," or "protected" (Leap 1999a:9). Generally, a "public" activity is a behavior that takes place outdoors, in the view of others (including passersby), and/or in a facility owned/operated by a municipality or community (e.g., the public library). By contrast, a "private" activity is a behavior that takes place indoors, either alone or with invited others (e.g., friends or family members), and/or in a privately owned dwelling or establishment. Thus, having oral sex in your apartment bedroom is a "private" activity and masturbating at the public library is a "public" activity. The latter is illegal and deviant and the former is legal and normative—at least you may think it is (see Box 9.2). As seen in the challenges to the anti-sodomy laws in the United States, the State has the power to identify what (and who) garners the privilege of "private" status and as a result, the State also identifies what spaces are police-able. This means that while your apartment bedroom may feel "private," if you are engaging in an illegal sex act in there, your bedroom is a public locale (and the scene of a crime). Thus, "'public' and 'private' are also locally constructed and may be applied differently to conditions at different sites" (Leap 1999a:5). So what behaviors become coded as "private" and "public" are entirely socially constructed.

BOX 9.2 SODOMY LAWS IN THE UNITED STATES

It may surprise you to know that prior to 2003, police in many U.S. states could lawfully arrest you if they saw you having oral sex—even in the privacy of your own bedroom. These so-called "sodomy laws" varied in their state-wide definitions but most explicitly outlawed oral and anal sex between both same-sex and heterosexual couplings (some states even prohibited these acts among married couples). All acts of sodomy were illegal in the United States until Illinois became the first to strike down their existing sodomy laws in 1961 and many states followed in subsequent decades (Carpenter 2012). However, federal statutes continued to uphold the rights of individual states to criminalize oral and anal sex between consenting adults until *Lawrence v. Texas* (2003). The complicated history of sodomy laws in the United States illustrates the dynamic relationship between sexual deviance and legal statutes that target particular people and particular types of sex.

Bowers v. Hardwick

The case that initially fundamentally challenged the constitutionality of anti-sodomy laws was *Bowers v. Hardwick* (1986). The events that led up to this Supreme Court Case illustrate the complexity of sodomy laws in general. In August of 1982, Michael Hardwick (1954–1991) was leaving a gay bar in Atlanta, Georgia, when a police officer issued him a ticket for public consumption of alcohol. Hardwick and the police officer engaged in a heated argument in which Hardwick accused the policeman of gay-related harassment. This exchange would not be their last because unfortunately, the officer wrote down the wrong day of the week for the date of the hearing on the ticket he issued to Hardwick. As a result of this minor paperwork mishap, Hardwick went to the hearing on the wrong day. The officer immediately issued a warrant for Hardwick's arrest and even though Hardwick cleared up his "failure to appear" violation with the court (and the warrant was revoked), the same officer with the original (expired) warrant showed up to Hardwick's apartment to arrest him a few weeks later. When the officer approached Hardwick's bedroom (after entering the apartment through the unlocked front door), he peered in through the slightly ajar bedroom door and saw Hardwick engaging in oral sex with another man. The policeman arrested him on the spot and took him to jail where he proceeded to inform his jail cellmates that Hardwick was "in there for c*cksucking" (Cliett 2003:229). Hardwick's original alcohol violation was eventually cleared up (he paid the $50 fine) and the state decided not to press anti-sodomy charges against him. But due to the blatant anti-gay harassment by the policeman who arrested him and his belief that his right to privacy was violated when the officer voyeuristically observed his private consensual sex act, Hardwick decided to sue the state of Georgia and challenge the constitutionality of the anti-sodomy statute that was defined at the time as when a person "performs or submits to any sexual act involving the sex organs of one person and the mouth or anus of another" (Cliett 2003:227). In doing so, Hardwick joined a heterosexual married couple, "John and Mary Doe," who were also plaintiffs in this suit. Both Hardwick and "John and Mary Doe" believed that the anti-sodomy laws violated their constitutional right to engage in consenting sex acts (of oral and anal nature) in the privacy of their own homes (Cliett 2003).

The case made it all the way up to the Supreme Court and what happened there was quite shocking and most definitely reflected stereotypes about both straight and gay people (and straight and gay sex) evident in 1980s American culture. The Supreme Court first determined that "John and Mary Doe" lacked standing to sue because they were not in danger of violating the anti-sodomy statutes in the first place. Why? Because even though the Georgia law clearly prohibited any acts of oral and anal sex between any persons (regardless of sex, gender, or sexual identity), the Justices decided to focus squarely on acts of sodomy between people of the same sex, citing their belief that heterosexuals (and their sex acts) upheld the traditional view of family and sex acts between those of the same sex did not. Thus, *Bowers v. Hardwick* (1986) became a case about sodomy acts between persons of the same sex despite the fact that Georgia anti-sodomy statutes prohibited both heterosexual and same-sex acts of sodomy. Two contested issues dominated the courtroom legal discourse in *Bowers v. Hardwick* (1986): (i) the constitutional right to privacy (which was first established in *Griswold v. Connecticut*, 1965) and (ii) the fundamental right to the due process clause of the Fourteenth Amendment, which prohibits the states from depriving any person of life, liberty, or property, without due process of law. The Supreme Court ultimately ruled (in a close split decision of 5 to 4) that the right to privacy did not extend to people who engaged in same-sex acts of sodomy and no person had a fundamental right to participate in same-sex oral or anal sex. And with that ruling, the states retained their right to criminalize consensual sex acts (of oral and anal nature) between persons of the same sex, even when they took place in the privacy of their own homes (Cliett 2003). Upholding this law meant that participating in "gay" sex was illegal.

Lawrence v. Texas

This ruling would later be aggressively challenged in several cases and eventually overturned—but not until nearly 20 years later in *Lawrence v. Texas* (2003). Another complex set of events led up to this Supreme Court case as well. On September 17, 1998, a false weapons disturbance report [which was later determined to be a jealous friend of Garner's, Robert Royce Eubanks (1958–2000)] was called in to the Harris County Police Department. Officers responding to the call arrived at the apartment of John Geddes Lawrence (1943–2011) in Houston, Texas, and upon their entry into the apartment's bedroom, the officers allegedly observed Lawrence and Tyron(e) Garner (1976–2006) engaged in a consensual sex act. Lawrence and Garner were arrested and convicted of violating the still intact 1973 Texas anti-sodomy law that outlawed oral and anal sex only between persons of the same sex, for which they both paid small fines. Eubanks (the lying whistleblower) was convicted of making a false police report and spent two weeks in jail. Convicted sodomites, Lawrence and Garner filed for motions with the Texas Court of Criminal Appeals to review the case on the grounds of violations of the due process clause of the Fourteenth Amendment and their right to privacy [(similar to *Bowers v. Hardwick* (1986)]. The Texas Court of Criminal Appeals denied their request and a petition was then filed with the U.S. Supreme Court. On June 26, 2003, in *Lawrence v. Texas* (2003), the U.S. Supreme Court (in a 6 to 3 decision) struck down the Texas anti-sodomy law, reversed the Court's 1986 ruling in *Bowers v. Hardwick*, and invalidated all remaining state sodomy laws in 14 states [Alabama, Florida, Idaho, Kansas, Louisiana, Michigan, Mississippi, Missouri (statewide), North Carolina, Oklahoma, South Carolina, Texas, Utah, and Virginia]. This ruling secured the rights of all consenting adults to participate in sex acts (including oral and anal sex), protected all persons' constitutional rights to privacy, and secured the fundamental right to due process guaranteed by the Fourteenth Amendment of the United States Constitution (Carpenter 2012).

Beyond Lawrence

Beyond the reversal of federal and state anti-sodomy statutes in *Lawrence v. Texas* (2003), in 2014, the U.S. military repealed its existing ban on consensual acts of sodomy found in Article 125 of the Uniform Code of Military Justice (Vergun 2014). However, even in the aftermath of *Lawrence v. Texas* (2003), some states continue to keep statutes on the books that ban acts of sodomy. In fact, as of 2015, of the 14 states that still had intact anti-sodomy laws at the time of *Lawrence v. Texas* (2003), only Alabama (2014), Montana (2013), and Virginia (2014) have actually repealed their anti-sodomy laws in the more than ten years since the Supreme Court decision. Despite the necessity to do so, these remaining states claim that the difficulty in rewriting their anti-sodomy laws (many of which entwine both consensual sodomy and aggravated sodomy into one statute) makes the task nearly unsurmountable (USA Today 2014). Thus, despite the victories of *Lawrence v. Texas* (2003), in reality, anti-sodomy laws remain on the books.

Sodomy laws and deviance

Overall, the continued existence and federal repeal of anti-sodomy laws in the United States illustrate the complex relationship between the law and sexual deviance. For the better part of the twentieth century, participation in "gay" sex was illegal and in some states, anyone (including heterosexuals) could go to jail for participating in oral sex—even in the privacy of their own home. These anti-sodomy laws socialized the general public to believe that some types of sex are normative and acceptable (i.e., penile-vaginal intercourse) and other types of sex are deviant and illegal (i.e., oral and anal sex). Beyond this, the right to privacy (and the right to have certain types of sex in private) was called into question and gay men were particularly at risk. In both *Bowers v. Hardwick* (1986) and *Lawrence v. Texas* (2003), sex was taking place in bedrooms of private dwellings, yet the right to privacy was not granted to these men, quite the contrary. It took a Supreme Court decision to repeal the anti-sodomy laws and secure the right to privacy and the right to life and liberty for consenting adults to be legally granted the right to participate in same-sex oral and anal sex. Even so, the anti-sodomy laws are a reminder of the interference of the State in our sex lives and the unique ability of the State to define sexual norms and deviance.

Defining public sex and public sex locations

Although it is impossible to pin down a precise description of "public sex" because it is a culturally embedded construct, *public sex* can be defined as any sexual activity that occurs in a space identified by cultural norms as communal, shared, municipal, and/or open to all citizens.

Beyond this, there are a variety of spaces in which public sex can occur. These include:

- Sex activities taking place in *noncommercial public areas*, such as a public bathroom (tearoom/cottage), highway rest areas, truck stops, parking lots, alleyways, street corners, bus terminals, parks, beaches, the woods, the docks, cemeteries, etc.
- Sex activities taking place in *commercial establishments* such as health club saunas, gym locker rooms, movie houses/cinemas, or bars/clubs/pubs, etc.
- Sex activities taking place in *sex-on-site-focused establishments* such as sex clubs (i.e., fetish clubs, swingers clubs, etc.), bathhouses, backrooms at adult bookstores, sex shops, or bars/clubs whose primary purpose is to provide opportunities for sex. (Note this does not include "sex for sale" locations such as brothels.[2])

Finding one of these public sex areas is easier than you think. In fact, there are multiple websites and mobile-device applications that offer directories of local parks, tearooms, health clubs, and bathhouses with "public sex" reputations (and some are even GPS-enabled so you can easily see the cruising locations nearest to you on your mobile device, see Box 9.3 later in this chapter). Often, public sex is about more than just the sex act. Part of the experience of public sex is "cruising" for it. *Cruising* is the practice of seeking out others for sex in unexpected locales, a sort of adult "hide and seek" behavior that has its own set of norms and cultural scripts depending on where it is happening. While cruising can take place anywhere, particular techniques are practiced in order to "play the game" correctly (Hollister 1999). These cruising practices will be discussed further later in this chapter.

Public sex locales

While public sex can occur in various locations (i.e., noncommercial public areas, commercial establishments, and sex-on-site-focused establishments), each offers a "distinct sexual culture" that dictates the cruising methods, solicitation methods for sex, and the actual sexual behaviors that are appropriate in each particular sex spot (Flowers *et al.* 2000:73). Not just a mere geographical location, public sex areas are "locales" that feature their own cultures, complete with established norms and deviance (Flowers *et al.* 2000). Below, these distinct sexual cultures are described.

Sex in noncommercial public areas

As noted earlier in this chapter, sex in noncommercial public areas includes sex activities in places such as public bathrooms (tearooms/cottages) or public parks. You may be thinking, "hey wait . . . I've been to the park and I've never seen anyone having sex there!" And you are probably right. So how do we know that sex takes place in these types of noncommercial public areas and why have you not seen it? First, we know this happens because both official reports (from police officers) and unofficial reports (from researchers and participants) tell us so. Second, you probably have never witnessed these activities because even though these are "public" locations, there are certain characteristics that make them prime locales for public sex between men and unlikely spots for you to happen upon without prior knowledge that this, in fact, is a popular location for this type of behavior. For example, even though you have been to a public park, you probably have not ventured deep into a wooded/treed area to find a dilapidated bathroom complete with sex-laden graffiti, no stall doors, and a glory hole. And even if you did, you probably decided not to use the facilities and hightailed it out of there (unless, of course, you were there cruising for tearoom sex). Overall, public-sex-oriented noncommercial public areas, such as tearooms, only attract certain kinds of people for particular reasons; cruisers need only ask themselves "why else could he be there?" to identify a potential sex partner (Hollister 1999:60).

Tearooms and tearoom sex

Public restrooms that are popular locales for public sex between men, known as "tearooms" in America and "cottages" in the UK, have been the subject of sociological research since Humphreys' infamous book was published in 1970. And while such research has been around for decades, scholars continue to find similar patterns when investigating these bathroom behaviors. Indeed, Humphreys contends that "the basic rules of the game—and the profile of the players—are applicable to any place in the United States" (1970:21). For example, in his research and analysis that took place from 1965 to 1968, Humphreys (1970) observed 120 sexual acts in 19 different men's bathrooms located in five public parks in a city of two million people. In doing so, he identified eight key features of popular public park tearooms:

- Location
  - Away from park recreational areas such as playgrounds (offers little public visibility of the structure itself).
  - Near an access road (allows for a getaway car to be parked nearby).
- Structural features
  - A squeaky door into the facility (helps to identify when someone is approaching).
  - Explicit "straightforward" and "functional" graffiti [because men are too busy to spend the time making "creative types of graffiti" (Humphreys 1970:9)].
  - Lack of stall doors.
  - Glory holes (a hole in the partition between the toilet stalls that allows for sex acts to take place between stalls or allows for viewing others).
- People
  - The women's side of the restroom is seldom (if ever) used.
  - The only people in the tearoom (or nearby) are men.

Because of these key features, these particular public restrooms are easily recognized by those who wish to engage in sex and they are seldom happened upon by anyone else (see also Desroches 1990; Hollister 1999).

Furthermore, there are distinct cultural norms within tearooms. For example, part of the appeal of the tearoom is the availability of easy, fast, reliable, anonymous sex. Because of this, there are certain "rules" that tearoom participants must abide by. The first is: no talking. Silence during interactions is key to privacy and anonymity. Signaling a "willingness to play" is done through gestures and behaviors such as showing an erect penis and pseudo-masturbation (Humphreys 1970:63). The second is: impersonality. These sex acts should not lead to any emotional connections in the tearoom or elsewhere; the sex that takes place in tearooms is impersonal. Sometimes men do not even see each another at all while engaging in a sex act (via a glory hole), and thus, sex partners remain somewhat invisible. As a result, men involved in tearoom sex are rarely emotionally involved with their tearoom sexual partners, but they may become attached to the experience of tearoom sex or even the actual structure itself. For example, Humphreys (1970) found that one tearoom participant developed a sentimental attachment to the tearoom he frequented for sex:

> That was the greatest place in the park. Do you know what my roommate did last Christmas, after they tore the place down? He took a wreath, sprayed it with black paint, and laid it on top of the snow—right where that corner stall had stood . . . He was really broken up!
>
> *(Humphreys 1970:14)*

Clearly the physical locale of the tearoom meant more to this person than the actual people with whom he engaged in sex acts with. And this could be due to the nature of the sex acts themselves. Tearoom sex is quick and impersonal. For example, Humphreys (1970) observed that sometimes there could be up to three sex acts taking place in one tearoom in a span of only 30 minutes. In another study inspired by Humphreys' work, one particular tearoom was found to be very active: 35 men entered and left in a span of three hours, with each man spending an average of only 15 minutes in there (Ponte 1974). Furthermore, most men who visit public bathrooms for sex do so either on a regular or daily basis, some even visiting multiple locales in a single week as frequent "regulars" (Humphreys 1970; Desroches 1990; Church et al. 1993). In addition, there is wide diversity in sexual behaviors that take place in tearooms ranging from watching the sex that is taking place, to masturbating, to anal sex. However, the most common activities in tearoom sex are those involving rather impersonal sex acts including masturbation (either solo or with a partner) and giving/receiving fellatio. In contrast, more personal sex acts, such as kissing and anal sex, have been found to be less common (Humphreys 1970; Church et al. 1993) (see Figure 9.2). In particular, four roles in tearoom sex have been identified (Desroches 1990; Humphreys 1970):

- *Players*. Men who participate in sex acts within tearooms.
- *Lookouts* (*Watchqueens*). Men who are watching sex acts for voyeuristic pleasure or just waiting their turn to participate as a player (their primary role also serves to alert players to approaching agents of social control such as policemen).

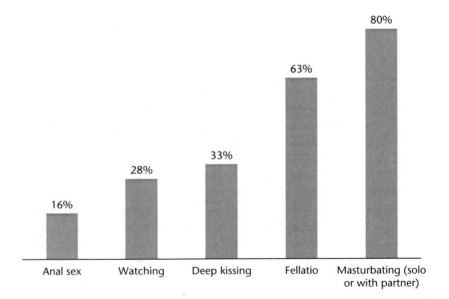

FIGURE 9.2 Top five sex activities in tearooms

Data adapted from Church et al. (1993).

Humphreys describes the watchqueen role as "a man who is situated at the door or windows from which he may observe the means of access to the restroom. When someone approaches, he coughs. He nods when the coast is clear or if he recognizes an entering party as a regular" (Humphreys (1970:27). However, the legitimacy of the watchqueen role has been called into question. In *Tearoom Trade*, Humphreys (1970) claimed that he served as the tearoom's "lookout" and did not participate in any sex acts himself. But after visiting the same park restrooms where Humphreys conducted his tearoom investigations, researchers determined that "Laud probably could not have collected his observations while serving as a watchqueen" (Galliher *et al.* 2004:29). Furthermore, later research attempting to replicate Humphreys' infamous study has not found any evidence of a purely non-sexual watchqueen role in tearoom sex (Desroches 1990). Thus, it is generally believed that Humphreys was, in fact, a tearoom sex participant and the watchqueen role was invented by Humphreys to cover up his clandestine activities. This may have been partially confirmed later by Humphreys himself when he claimed that he was "both academically and personally knowledgeable about tearooms" (Galliher *et al.* 2004:80).

- *Straights*. Men who do not participate in the action but leave tearooms quickly or transition into another role.
- *Teenagers* (*Chickens*). Youths who either want to enlist in tearoom sex or harass other tearoom participants (*toughs*) (sometimes chickens are hustling for payment for tearoom sex participation).

These behavioral distinctions are not mutually exclusive nor are they stable roles; for example, men can be both voyeurs and masturbators in the tearoom. Thus, "role drift" can occur during a single encounter (Humphreys 1970:56) and as result, tearoom sex is quite diverse.

Another significant characteristic of tearoom sex is the participants themselves (see Figure 9.3). Overall, men who visit tearooms are highly likely to identify as heterosexual, in fact, most studies have found that over half of tearoom participants are married to women (Humphreys 1970; Desroches 1990; Moore 1995). This means that even though they are having sex with other men, perhaps as a quick stop off on their drive home from work, they identify as heterosexual because most are married with children (Humphreys 1970; Hollister 1999). Perhaps these men are "closeted" (and are attempting to hide their gay identity from their families) or perhaps these men may not even consider themselves to be gay, as one tearoom sex participant said "no I'm not gay! I never *gave* blow jobs" (Desroches 1990:97). Either way, most tearoom participants are not active in gay subculture. They are not your usual gay bar clientele and that is precisely why they use the tearoom for sex. Unlike at gay bars, for example, there is no standard of physical appearance for sex in tearooms; men of all racial, social, educational, and physical characteristics take part in tearoom sex (Humphreys 1970; Desroches 1990). The tearoom offers these men (who are mostly closeted or otherwise not-gay identified) a place to go for instant access to no-strings-attached sex where nobody will notice them, they will just be "some guy strolling in the park."

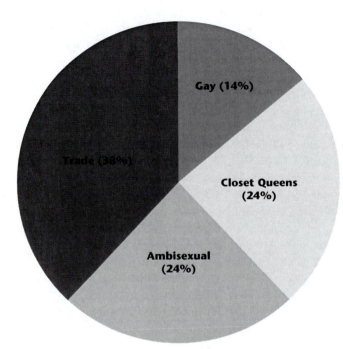

FIGURE 9.3 Humphreys' (1970) typology of tearoom participants

Trade: married men who are not interested in male sexual contact necessarily, just use tearooms as an easy way to reach orgasm.

Ambisexuals: married men who they think of themselves as bisexual and are interested in more exotic types of sex such as anal sex and group sex.

Closet Queens: unmarried men who are very cautious in tearoom encounters who wish to remain closeted.

Gay: unmarried men locked into gay subculture, "the most 'truly' gay of all participant types" (Humphreys 1970:122), and the least representative overall of the tearoom participant population.

Sex in the public park

The park: an idyllic setting with lush gardens, flowers, beautiful sunsets, and some-times ... sex. Some public parks are known locales for public sex between men and they may be especially attractive as "the fantasy of having sex out-of-doors is ... particularly strong for gay men because for so long, sex had to be confined to rooms and behind the closet door" (Bergman 1999:109). Thus, the park allows for sexual freedom and as we will see, it too has its own unique culture—distinct from other public sex hot spots.

Public park sex (outside of tearooms in public parks) most often takes place in wooded areas or behind bushes and in the cover of night. Similar to tearooms, men cruise public parks in search of easily accessible impersonal sexual encounters: "In the park, you go there for one reason ... just straight, lustful, animalistic sex" (Flowers et al. 2000:74). Public park sex interactions involve minimal conversation and solicitation for sex occurs through eye contact, body language, and subtle forms of touching (Tewksbury 1996; Flowers *et al.* 1999; Somlai *et al.* 2001). Casual park sex allows for anonymity and the relative ease of access to multiple sexual partners (Flowers *et al.* 1999, 2000). The sex behaviors within the park more often include fellatio as opposed to anal sex (Somlai *et al.* 2001). In these ways, the rules of tearoom sex and public park sex are similar. However, what differs is the opportunity to move through the park in pursuit of sexual encounters. Sometimes it is like playing a game of adult hide-and-seek or chase:

> The rules of the "chase" game are fairly simple. If you make initial contact with someone that you are interested in, you either follow him or position yourself so that he can easily follow you . . . To be followed is to be complimented.
>
> *(Tewksbury 1996:15)*

The majority of men who cruise public parks for sex fit the profile of most tearoom sex participants: they are overwhelmingly self-identified heterosexuals with traditionally hetero-masculine or even hypermasculine presentations of self and they are there for one reason only: impersonal quick sex (Tewksbury 1996). Anonymity is desired and park sex allows for such forms of secrecy (Somlai *et al.* 2001). Beyond this, park sex between MSM may be more likely among straight-identified men than gay-identified men because cruising public parks is sometimes stigmatized in the gay community (Tewksbury 1996; see also Ponte 1974). Even so, some gay men may hit the park after the gay bars close if they are more "desperate" to find a partner (and their standards have fallen) (Flowers *et al.* 2000:75; see also Hollister 1999). Overall, however, whether gay- or straight-identified, sex in the public park is different than sex at home: "what is understood or sanctioned in the park is very different from what is understood or sanctioned in the bedroom" (Flowers *et al.* 1999:493). Men cruising for sex in public parks understand that this space has its own unique culture that is "outside the parameters of normal social and sexual conduct: its dark interior is characterized as filled with exciting and dangerous possibilities" (Flowers *et al.* 1999:493).

Sex in commercial establishments

Another place that public sex occurs is in commercial establishments such as health club saunas, gym locker rooms, and bars/clubs/pubs. We have all been to these types of places, but similar to tearooms and certain public parks, you will only find sex happening here if you know how to look for it. Thus, the unique sexual cultures within commercial establishments offer yet another option for public sex. But because these spaces are not outdoors and they are privately owned, they differ from noncommercial public areas and so does the public sex that takes place within them.

Sex at the gym

A gym (or health club) is a space that offers amenities such as free weights, basket-ball/volleyball courts, treadmills, etc., along with spaces for dressing and bathing such as locker rooms, saunas, and showers. Usually, gyms require memberships, which makes these spaces not "public" (in the sense that you have to pay to be a part of them) but because money is typically the only requirement for joining a gym, the gym is a certain type of "public" space open to people with the ability to pay to join and to those who have the time to go.

Sometimes certain gyms get a reputation as a locale for sex between men (and there are also "gay gyms" that cater to gay men specifically, see below). Sex at the gym usually takes place in bathing areas such as the showers or saunas. Similar to sex between men in noncommercial public areas, sex at the gym is a quick no-strings-attached activity with minimal verbal interaction. The rules and sexual behaviors are also similar to those that occur in tearooms and public parks with body language (including eye contact) utilized as the primary means to solicit sex and most sexual activity involving masturbation and oral sex (anal sex is uncommon). What differs, however, is the foreplay. Unlike public restrooms and parks, the gym is a space for working out, flexing muscles, lifting weights, and sometimes the occasional need for "spotting" (supporting another person during a particular exercise, typically when lifting large amounts of weight). Beyond this, form-fitting clothing is commonplace at the gym and so is public nudity in the locker rooms and the showers/saunas. As a result, men are judged by their physique and only the most attractive men with perfectly sculpted bodies are solicited for sex in gyms. This is in stark contrast to tearoom and park sex in which physical appearance is seemingly unimportant. As a result, the culture of gym sex between men is one of hyper-appearance-focused interactions (Alvarez 2008).

Similar to sex in public parks and tearooms, most men who have sex in gym locker rooms and saunas are not gay-identified, they are just "guys who like having sex with other guys" (Leap 1999b:124) (with the exception of sex in gay gyms, see below). Sexual encounters in the gym may be especially common among straight-identified men because theses spaces may be amongst the only locales that they feel they can be sexual with other men (Alvarez 2008). However, gym sex differs from public park and tearoom sex in that it is indoors in a membership-only space and thus, more "private" in some ways. For example, the type of men that go to the gym for sex would never go to a park or other outdoor cruising areas:

> Such places are too visible, too open, too unprotected, too dangerous ... anyone can see what you are doing when you are there. The health club is more enclosed, more protected, and more secure, so there is no reason to worry about discovery: people respect each other's privacy, and they leave each other alone.
> *(Leap 1999b:126)*

Thus, privacy and secrecy are important in both noncommercial public area sex and gym sex, but for those men who go to the gym for sex, the locker rooms offer more safety than the park restroom.

In addition to "straight" gyms where the majority of patrons are heterosexual, the "gay gym" (that caters specifically to gay male clientele) has recently emerged in many American metropolises. Men's interest in cultivating and eroticizing sculpted muscles and a graceful athletic body with Olympian potential, however, is not new (think back to ancient Greece where nude male athletes were revered and adult men competed for the sexual companionship of the most beautiful, chiseled, and athletic boys as discussed in chapter 7). Ancient nude (and homoerotic) athletic physiques etched into marble (see for example, Image 9.1) now serve as models for the contemporary ideal male body. In fact, "the gay muscle boy is fast becoming the mainstream male ideal" (Alvarez 2008:90). The gym is how you got there then and it is how you get there now.

In the 1960s, the first identifiable American gay gym (where the majority of patrons were gay men) opened up in the West Village in New York City and was

IMAGE 9.1   Discobolus (discus thrower) by Myron

Replica of the lost Greek sculpture (circa 460 to 450 B.C.E.) representing the male athletic ideal.
© Shutterstock, Carmen Ruiz

followed by a handful of gyms in the gayborhoods of San Francisco and Los Angeles (i.e., the Castro District and West Hollywood) in the 1970s. Soon after, gay gyms became increasingly popular alongside the 1970s successes of gay bathhouses (discussed later in this chapter): "now that they could freely look at naked bodies [in the gay bathhouses], the preference was for nice ripped ones ... the body started becoming the currency of gay culture, and the muscular and gym-built body quickly became its Ben Franklin" (Alvarez 2008:102). In fact, the glamorization and sexualization of the gym-built body is a prominent feature of most contemporary gay men's lives. For example, in a worldwide survey of 5,576 gay and bisexual men, the majority (78 percent) said they feel pressured to exercise in order to meet the muscular and fit body image standards of gay culture (Alvarez 2008:85). Thus, gay gyms provide a space to cultivate this highly sought-after physique.

Beyond a space for lifting weights, sculpting the body, and exercising, gay gyms have their own culture: "in urban gay America, the gym is now an extension of gay social (and sometimes professional, recreational, and political) life" (Alvarez 2008:10). In fact, between the hours of 4 pm and 8 pm, the San Francisco gay gyms are much busier than the local gay bars—the gay gyms have become the home to the new gay "happy hour" (Alvarez 2008:94). Furthermore, many gay men say they go the gym to look for potential dating partners and to cruise for sex (25 percent and 31 percent respectively indicated as such in a worldwide survey of 5,576 gay and bisexual men). And sex in gay gyms is not all that uncommon. Close to half (41 percent) of gay and bisexual men in a global study indicated that they participated in sex at the gym and only 26 percent reported that they think it is "not okay" to do so (Alvarez 2008). Sex at the gay gym largely follows the same rules and patterns as sex at the "straight" gym: voyeurism and exhibitionism are common and "sex in the locker room never leaves the locker room ... totally no strings attached" (Alvarez 2008:266). The difference is that gay gyms cater to gay men, and thus, both the supply and demand for sex are higher: "sex is available to men who want it ... [they] partake *because they can*" (Alvarez 2008:266). Thus, gay gym sex comes with its own mores and patterns unique to this particular locale.

Sex in bars/clubs/pubs

Bars/clubs/pubs are spaces where people imbibe alcoholic beverages, enjoy the company of others, sometimes dance to loud music, and search for dating (or sex) partners. In contrast to noncommercial public areas, the bar is a very public and very appearance-focused space, as one cruiser notes: "if you want to be picky, go to a gay bar" (Couture 2008:84). Appropriate clothing and friendly "flirty" behavior is a must in order to be successful in finding a sexual partner. The norms in bars/clubs/pubs involve dancing, buying drinks for potential partners, and sometimes, a considerable amount of chit chat (Flowers *et al.* 2000). While "hooking up" is common at bars, actually having sex in these public establishments is less common. As a result, when sex activities do occur in these types of spaces, it is typically hidden (such as in a dark corner) away from public view.

The type of people going to gay bars to find sex are likely to be comfortable being seen there, thus, most are openly gay or bisexual and interested in the social and image-conscious setting that most gay bars have. In a typical gay bar, men surveille other men frequently—some searching for sex and others hoping to find romance. Unlike tearooms, public parks, and gyms, the social atmosphere of the gay bar necessitates conversation and courtesy—at least for the most part (see Box 9.3). The norms within gay bars highlight the importance of self-presentation, self-control, and peer surveillance, and thus, limit the access of many straight-identified men searching for sex with other men (Flowers *et al.* 2000). As a result, sex in bars/clubs/pubs is unique, it occurs in a conversational atmosphere with social exchanges, pleasantries, drinking, dancing, and flirting.

BOX 9.3 CRUISING WITH TECHNOLOGY

The process of searching for sex partners, hook-ups, and dating companions has experienced a wave of change since smartphones put technology into the palms of our hands. While there are an assortment of methods available, mobile apps that utilize geosocial networking are likely the most significant innovation, which are akin to "cruising." Geosocial networking apps use your mobile device's geographic services to connect you with local people or events that match your interests. Through the magic of geosocial networking, your physical location (and the physical location of others who might be potential hook-ups) are displayed in one convenient location—your mobile device. Basically, your phone does the "cruising" for you by alerting you to people in the area that you might want to seek out.

Take, for example, Grindr. Grindr is a geosocial networking mobile device app geared towards men interested in men. Initially released in 2009, Grindr quickly became one of the largest and most popular mobile apps for men seeking other men. It touts itself as "the world's biggest mobile network of guys" and they may be right. With two million daily users in close to 200 countries around the globe, cruising for sex has never been easier. The goal of Grindr is to offer men an uncomplicated way to meet guys while "on the go." Unlike other dating/hook-up sites that require detailed profiles, Grindr simply uses your mobile device's location-based services to show you the guys in close proximity to you who are also on Grindr. How does it work? Simply download the app, give yourself a profile name (if you want), upload a photo (also optional), and answer a couple of questions about yourself and your interests (not required). You even have the option of self-selecting into *Grindr Tribes* by classifying yourself as the following:

- Bear: heavy, large-framed, strong and hairy man who is ruggedly masculine.
- Clean-cut: man who is impeccably dressed with a perfectly coiffed short haircut and a clean shaven face.

- Daddy: older, distinguished man with salt-and-pepper or fully gray/white hair and/or beard.
- Discreet: closeted man who is private/secretive about his interest in other men.
- Geek: highly intellectual man who is academically inclined.
- Jock: muscular man who is strong, fit, and athletic.
- Leather: man with a fondness for leather gear and sometimes an interest in SM.
- Otter: hairy man who is smaller in frame than a bear.
- Poz: man who has embraced his HIV positive status.
- Rugged: buff, masculine man who has just the right amount of scruff.
- Trans: person who transgresses dichotomous gender binaries.
- Twink: young-looking, slim boyish man with a hairless face/body and a smooth flawless complexion.

After you have made your selections, you are ready to cruise through the grid of photos of other Grindr users available through the app, all conveniently arranged from guys closest to you ("zero feet away") to those much further away (provided in feet, miles or kilometers). Grindr users' photos are clickable: when tapping on a picture, a brief profile for that user will be displayed, as well as the option to chat, send pictures, and share one's location (grindr.com). And with that, cruising is now clicking.

The popularity of apps such as Grindr and other online dating/hook-up sites has increased dramatically and this has also changed perspectives about this type of internet-based relationship behavior. For example, in a 2013 national survey (N = 2, 252), researchers found that 11 percent of all American adults and 38 percent of those "single and looking" for a partner have used online dating sites or mobile dating apps compared to a scant 3 percent in 2008. In addition, 23 percent indicated that they met their spouse or long-term relationship partner through these types of sites. Perhaps because more people are doing it, attitudes toward meeting partners online have become considerably more favorable. For example, compared to attitudes in 2005, people in 2013 were much more likely to view online dating as a good way to meet people and they were less likely to view online dating as a "desperate" behavior (see Figure 9.4). Thus, the proliferation of online dating sites and mobile dating apps has been accompanied by a shift in attitudes as well. What was perhaps once viewed as deviant may now be much more acceptable—especially among certain groups. The typical "online dater" is between 25 and 44 years old, college educated, and resides in an urban or suburban area. More men than women use online dating sites and mobile dating apps [and this may be especially true for LGBTQ people because their potential dating pools are smaller and the aid of online dating methods makes the process of finding partners especially useful for these groups as well as others with smaller dating pools such as elderly people, single moms, etc., who may have minimal options for meeting people within their immediate geographic

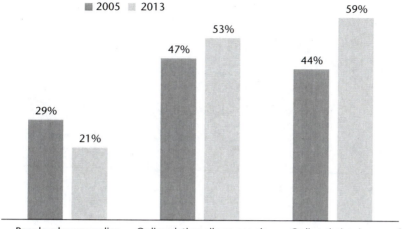

FIGURE 9.4 Attitudes toward online dating in 2005 and 2013
Data adapted from Smith and Duggan (2013).

location or social circle (see Rosenfeld and Thomas 2012)]. Thus, online dating sites and mobile dating apps have not only changed how people "cruise" for partners, but also how people view cruising behavior in general (Smith and Duggan 2013).

Hundreds of location-based dating/hook-up apps currently populate the mobile device market, some specific to MSM and others for straight people, bi-curious people, etc. The relationship between technology and cruising shapes the dating world in ways that continue to offer new perspectives about deviance. While meeting up with a stranger in a tearoom in the 1950s was viewed as a highly deviant (and illegal) activity, today's online cruising marketplace is so easily accessible—it seems like everybody is doing it. Loading instantly on your mobile device, profiles await complete with photos . . . all available at the "tap" of your finger.

Sex-on-site-focused establishments

Another option for public sex is within a sex-on-site-focused establishment such as a bathhouse, a sex club (i.e., fetish club, swingers club, etc.), or the backroom at an adult bookstore or sex shop whose primary purpose is to provide opportunities for sex. Sex is expected in these types of public establishments, in fact, it is so normative that most have amenities to aid in various sex practices (see Figure 9.5). Even so, each offers a unique sexual culture that shapes the experiences of men searching for sex with other men in these establishments.

(a) 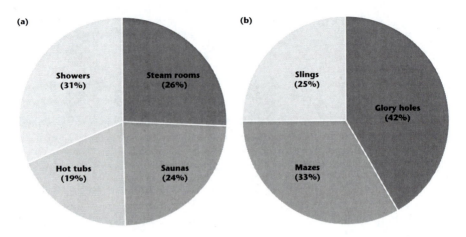 (b)

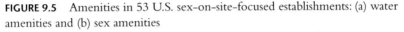

FIGURE 9.5 Amenities in 53 U.S. sex-on-site-focused establishments: (a) water amenities and (b) sex amenities

Data adapted from Woods *et al.* (2010).

Sex in gay bathhouses

Records of people meeting for sex in the public baths from early antiquity show us that bathing and sex have always been a common duo (see chapter 7). However, it was not until the late 1800s that commercial bathing establishments (with saunas, showers, whirlpools, etc.) were designed to specifically appeal to men looking for sex with other men. In the U.S., these gay bathhouses emerged in a time when all sex acts between men were illegal, and thus, some men sought out places to meet each other that felt "safer" than the public parks and tearooms. These so-called "safety zones" allowed men to engage in sex acts with other men with "a minimal threat of violence, blackmail, loss of employment, arrest, imprisonment, and humiliation" (Bérubé 2003:34). Even so, because sex between men was illegal, early gay bathhouses were subject to police raids by vice squads (see Box 9.4). However, today, modern gay bathhouses offer MSM with a relatively "safe" option for anonymous sex.

Modern gay bathhouses exist in most large metropolises and even some medium-sized cities in multiple parts of the world. They are not too hard to find (a quick internet search is all you need) because "bathhouses are the gay community's best worst-kept secret" (Couture 2008:2). Some gay bathhouses are in non-descript buildings and others advertise with rainbows and neon lights; but the set-up is similar.

BOX 9.4 LEGAL ISSUES IN BATHHOUSES

Early American twentieth century gay bathhouses were establishments that skirted the law. At the time, all sex acts between men were illegal in the U.S.

and because these types of behaviors were happening in gay bathhouses, they were in fact, harboring criminals. As a result, police sometimes took it upon themselves to crack down on these establishments. Vice squads set up 24-hour watches, plainclothes officers conducted sting operations, and many gay bathhouse patrons were arrested. For example, the first U.S. bathhouse raid occurred in 1903 in New York City when officers descended upon the Ariston Hotel Baths and arrested 26 men, 12 of whom were charged with sodomy and seven of whom received sentences ranging from four to 20 years in prison (Myers 2013). This was just the first in a stream of gay bathhouse raids by police officers that would occur over the next 50 years (Bérubé 2003).

However, in 1976, California passed the "Consenting Adult Sex Bill" and this made gay bathhouses (and the sex that took place within them) legal for the first time. This was a huge victory for gay bathhouse patrons and business owners in California. Unfortunately, just two years later in 1978, police raided the Liberty Baths in San Francisco and arrested three patrons for "lewd conduct in a public place" (Bérubé 2003:39). Thankfully, the District Attorney's office soon dropped the charges against them, noting MSM's right to engage in sex acts at bathhouses because "there's no question [the Liberty Baths] was a private place" (Bérubé 2003:39). (Note that this issue would come up yet again in *Bowers v. Hardwick*, 1986, and *Lawrence v. Texas*, 2003, see Box 9.2).

When the AIDS Epidemic hit in the 1980s, however, gay bathhouses were once again targeted. In 1984, San Francisco became the first city where gay bathhouses and other sex locales for sex between men were closed because they were "fostering disease and death" by allowing indiscriminate sexual contacts that could lead to HIV/AIDS, according to the city's Public Health Director. In all, 14 of San Francisco's 30 bathhouses/sex clubs/adult bookstores were closed by court order in October of 1984 sending a strong message to its patrons and to society that these places were not only deviant, but also dangerous (*New York Times* 1984). However, just five days later, six clubs challenged the court order and reopened under the Superior Court's new set of strict requirements that included (Collier 1985):

- Removal of doors to individual rooms and cubicles.
- Prohibition of the use of private rooms on the premises.
- Hiring of one employee for every 20 patrons to survey the entire premises every 20 minutes so that sexual activity could be closely monitored.
- Ejection of all patrons found to be engaging in "risky" sexual activity (defined by the San Francisco AIDS Foundation as sex acts with multiple partners that involve the exchange of bodily fluids without condoms).
- Safer-sex education for all patrons.

Although some bathhouses attempted to operate within these restrictive rules, most succumbed to either economic stresses or the continuing legal pressures of the city ordinances and eventually closed in the 1980s. As a result, gay bathhouses suffered greatly during this time in the United States.

In contrast, however, the 1981 gay bathhouse raids in Toronto, where a total of 304 men were arrested, did *not* result in the closure of bathhouses in Canada. In fact, the Toronto bathhouse raids mobilized the gay community to protest against police targeting of bathhouses. As a result of their efforts, the city of Toronto's official investigation into the matter strongly condemned the police for their bigoted behavior and secured "the right of men to engage in consensual sex in private" (Bérubé 2003:44). Furthermore, government and community-based HIV/AIDS prevention initiatives were instituted in all Canadian gay bathhouses (which we still see today) (Haubrich *et al.* 2004). Overall, the Toronto bathhouse raids are often remembered as "the 'turning point' in Canadian gay political history [because they created] a powerful, organized, politically aware gay community" that continues to thrive (Bérubé 2003:45).

Today, the hundreds of gay bathhouses currently in operation are legal establishments and the sex that takes place within them is protected in the United States under *Lawrence v. Texas* (2003). In addition, the vast amount of gay bathhouses and other sex-on-site-focused establishments promote safer sex practices by offering condoms and educational resources. In fact, a study of 53 MSM sex-on-site-focused establishments revealed that all locations provided free condoms (available at the front desk and distributed throughout public areas and in private rooms), and nearly all displayed educational posters and had informational pamphlets available for patrons. Some even offered outreach programs, counseling services, and special events geared toward HIV prevention. Almost all promoted testing for HIV and other STIs (including syphilis, gonorrhea, chlamydia, and hepatitis) and three out of four had on-site HIV testing available in their venues (Woods *et al.* 2010). Thus, the legal troubles of gay bathhouse owners and patrons have been largely ameliorated and in their place is a culture of consensual sex practices with an emphasis on HIV/STI prevention.

Upon entry you proceed to the check-in counter (which is usually behind security glass or bars), show your ID and/or membership card (not always required), make your selections from the options available (which is often choosing to rent a private room if you want one), pay a fee (typically admittance for six to eight hours max) and then then the clerk will buzz you through the second (inner) security door. At that point you head to the locker room, disrobe, and don a towel around your waist (Tattleman 1999; Haubrich *et al.* 2004; Couture 2008). Then, it is time to start cruising.

There are three types of cruising for sex partners happening in most gay bath-houses designed to appeal to varying patrons' predilections:

- *Wet cruising*: Looking for sex in a "wet" water-related space such as a shower, spa, whirlpool, swimming pool, or bathtub (from which *bath*houses got their namesake). Solicitations for sex often come in the form of eye contact and/or presentation or manual stimulation of the genitals, although some talking is permitted. Individuals choose to engage in sex acts here because they enjoy being on display and having others watch or even join in: "the wet area is often a good place to cruise if you like your sex public, in that there may be lots of people around and enough light for them to see" (Couture 2008:4).
- *Dark room cruising*: Looking for sex in areas of complete darkness. In these darkened spaces, individuals cannot see their sex partners and touch is the key sensation for solicitation and response: "one can touch any body one chooses" (Tattleman 1999:89). There is no talking. For some men, the darkroom is the key attraction of a bathhouse because here, "the game of cruising and the meat market of attractiveness status are suspended: men who lack good looks – or the confidence to withstand repeated rejection – are judged by different criteria" (Richters 2007:287).
- *Room cruising*: Looking for sex in rentable rooms available for six to eight hours at a time. Rooms in gay bathhouses are typically tiny, functional spaces with a bed and a small bedside table. They are lined up in a row similar to a prison cell block. Solicitation methods for room sex involve cruising up and down the "cell block" and peeking into rooms for an invitation in. Room inhabitants may make eye-contact or sexual gestures to alert passersby of their interests. Room cruising is the most discriminatory type of sex experience in the gay bathhouse. Typically, men who prefer room cruising are more particular about who they have sex with: "cruising rooms give you the maximum amount of control over who you allow to enter your room and the maximum variety of what type of sex you can have" (Couture 2008:13). In comparison to the wet and dark areas of the gay bathhouse, rooms offer a more sanitary space that gives men more options for intimacy and diversity in sexual positions (e.g., anal sex is most common in rooms and less common in other gay bathhouse areas).

Beyond, wet/dark areas and rooms for rent, some gay bathhouses have outdoor-fantasy spaces, such as glory hole booths designed to replicate tearooms and darkened mazes to imitate the park/woods. Gay bathhouses can also be a social environment for men to chit-chat with one another (however, typically this type of friendly conversation only happens in the bar/café area of the bathhouse). Some even offer holiday parties that can be especially comforting to those men who do not have families to celebrate with (Bérubé 2003). Indeed, gay bathhouses are popular because they offer patrons easy access to anonymous sex as well as for some, "an oasis of free-dom and homosexual camaraderie" (Bérubé 2003:37). For most, the sense of personal safety, privacy, and protection from bigots and police harassment (especially in comparison to other anonymous sex locales, such as parks and public bathrooms) are significant draws to gay bathhouses (Bérubé 2003; Haubrich *et al.* 2004).

In all gay bathhouse cruising experiences, there are six important rules to keep in mind: (i) no means no!; (ii) always be polite and subtle in your advances and rejections; (iii) wait to be invited; (iv) try not to interfere with other people's comfort or activities; (v) everyone has the right to stop at any time; and (vi) do not go every single night (Couture 2008; Gray *et al.* n.d.). Consent and safety are paramount here but unlike the tearoom where mum's the word and daily visits are common, the gay bathhouse is a more social place and frequent "regulars" are frowned upon. Men who visit gay bathhouses may have an interest in public sex and/or they may simply enjoy easy access to impersonal sex with other men. They may be gay-identified or not. Thus, the gay bathhouse is its own unique social institution, "the baths offer everything you need: safety and security, as well as anonymity and a private room" (Couture 2008:74). It is a safety zone where you can escape the world with your own fantasies but "when it is time to get dressed ... one's 'street' identity returns all too quickly" (Tattleman 1999:91).

Sex in sex clubs

A *sex club* is a sex-on-site-focused establishment designed for people who want to have sex with other people (patrons) they meet at the club. Often, sex clubs cater to specific sexual interests such as fetishes (leather, bondage, SM, etc., see more in chapter 10), "swinging" (couples who like to incorporate other people/couples into their sexual relationship), and certain types of people (transgender people, bisexual women, gay men, etc.). Similar to gay bathhouses, sex clubs typically require an admission fee or cover charge and some require a membership to enter. Because sex clubs are specifically designed to gratify a particular sexual interest or type of people, they vary dramatically in their structural features, rules, common sex behaviors, and patrons (Richters 2007).

The very thing that makes sex clubs different from other sex-on-site-focused establishments is their uniqueness. They may be likened to an "adult" theme park with a variety of titillating "rides" complete with theatrical and whimsical settings that set the stage for sex (Richters 2007). For example, the Australian sex club HeadQuarters whose slogan is "Sydney's Ultimate Playground for Men" offers a wide range of activities across four floors that include a social lounge area and three levels of sex play space complete with 11 themed areas for public cruising and group sex (see Table 9.1), private lockable cubicles (for sex between two or three people), as well as specialized rooms available for rent (the sling room that has a leather sex-aid harness and the mirror room for katoptronophiliacs who enjoy having sex in front of mirrors). Their weekly line-up includes featured events such as Naked Monday and Blackout Friday (the entire club is darkened). The rules are clearly posted and adhered to by all HeadQuarters staff and patrons. They include a minimum age (18) and a maximum length of stay (12 hours followed by 12-hour non-return period). Beyond this, safe sex is emphasized (lube and condoms are

TABLE 9.1 HeadQuarters themed areas

Design-themed areas	
Jail	Designed like the county jail, an open room with jail door and padded bench
Alcatraz	Designed like a large prison-type complex with open barred walls and two lockable rooms
The Beat	Designed to mimic the outdoor "beats" of Australia (e.g., public toilets, public parks, beaches), complete with glory holes
Workman's Retreat	Designed to mimic a construction zone with yellow/black tape and divided areas with an open public sling
Sex-act themed areas	
Pig Pen	Open area with a public sling on a stage
Dark Room	Darkened play room
Porn Room	Room offering pornography viewing with bench seating and a divided play space
Lunch Shed	Porn room with bench seating and an open play space
Glory Hole Avenue	An open "street" of glory holes in a row
SUK Station	Open-style glory hole area
Water Sports Room	Large space with bathtub and showers open for public viewing

Adapted from HeadQuarters.com.au.

supplied free in all cubicles and play areas and tighter or larger size condoms as well as dental dams are also available on request) and HeadQuarters follows the local community health organization's recommended code of practice.[3] It is a legitimate business establishment by all accounts; they even offer a reward points program and a student discount. The variety of sexual spaces offered by HeadQuarters illustrates the diversity in sex club clientele. While most sex club patrons are interested in public sex, they may also have concerns about safety. At HeadQuarters (and other similar sex clubs) men can get the thrill of a glory hole at a tearoom without actually going to a tearoom by visiting "Glory Hole Avenue." They can have sex on display in the view of others (i.e., in public)—but in a "private" club. In this way, sex clubs mimic other public sex environments while also providing their own unique sexual spaces (Richters 2007).

Sex in backrooms

Another type of sex-on-site-focused establishment is located within commercial businesses, specifically in the backrooms. Typically, only certain types of commercial establishments have dedicated sex-on-site backroom spaces. These include "adult"-themed businesses such as porn shops, sex toy shops, and adult bookstores. Most often, the entrance to the backroom is in a back alleyway (you have to know it is there to find it) and the majority of business patrons are likely to be unaware of the backroom space (Richters 2007). Entrance fees are normative and backrooms are small, dark, and utilitarian: it is an area where people go to "take care of business" (Leap 1999b:119). Similar to other public sex locales, the backroom is a space of "raw sexuality" (Leap 1999b:132). Talking is minimal and anonymity is paramount. Individual booths with glory holes in between them are a common feature of sex-on-site backroom spaces. However, unlike more expensive sex-on-site-focused establishments such as bathhouses and sex clubs that offer multiple amenities to their patrons, the backroom is not luxurious; in fact, some describe them as "dirty, sticky places" (Richters 2007:281). As a result, the backroom attracts a more "working class" patron in comparison to most bathhouses and sex clubs (Richters 2007:281).

In contrast to noncommercial public area sex in tearooms and public parks, sex in backrooms is more protected. Because the entrances are discreet, most can enter backrooms without any onlookers knowing that a public sex encounter is about to ensue. Furthermore, because the sex shops themselves are typically not "gay"-themed, men seen entering such businesses can avoid being labeled as "gay" (Richters 2007:279). Thus, the type of men who frequent backrooms for sex may not be gay-identified and may just be looking for quick anonymous sex without the risk of detection. And backrooms provide just that: an "enclosed, regulated, sex-positive environment where men are able to pursue male-centered erotic interests without fears of discovery, harassment, or retaliation" (Leap 1999b:135). Furthermore, there is no standard of appearance in the backroom. Men who may feel unattractive or who do not feel comfortable with their bodies on display (as in the case of most bathhouse and sex club sex) may be more likely to prefer backrooms to other sex-on-site-focused establishments (Richters 2007). Thus, similar to other public sex locales, backrooms offer men easy access to impersonal sex. They differ, however, in their unique culture and individualized clientele.

Why public sex?

Public sex offers a host of diverse impersonal sexual experiences but beyond this, sex in public can be risky, dangerous, and exciting. Those who enjoy the thrill of being watched and those who like watching others are also likely to enjoy public sex. MSM who participate in tearoom sex offer diverse reasons for their involvement (see Figure 9.6) but nearly all indicate that tearoom sex is satisfying and most enjoy having sex in the "open air" (i.e., outdoors). They also report that the excitement/thrill of public sex as well as the accompanying anonymity and lack of commitment are also major reasons why they enjoy sex in public restrooms (Church et al. 1993).

It is likely that all of these reasons build upon one another and offer MSM who enjoy public sex overlapping incentives to continue to partake in this form of sexual deviance. For example, the sexual satisfaction of public sex may be directly derived from the excitement of not knowing who your next sexual partner (or partners) will be. As one public park sex participant notes:

> In the park it is totally spontaneous, totally unplanned and, that is the thrill of it, the fact that you don't know what is going to happen. You don't know whether you are going to be having sex with one person or with six people.
> *(Flowers et al. 2000:77)*

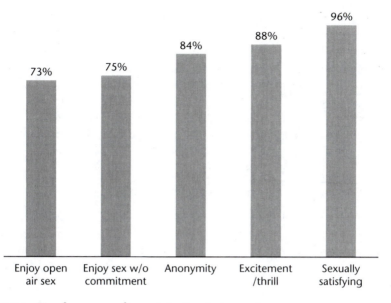

FIGURE 9.6   Top five reasons for participation in tearoom sex

Data adapted from Church *et al.* (1993).

Thus, the "unpredictable nature" of public sex adds to the thrill and satisfaction of this experience (Flowers *et al.* 2000:78).

Because they offer a more protected and social space for impersonal sex, reasons for participating in sex at sex-on-site-focused establishments differ from those reasons offered for engaging in noncommercial public area sex in tearooms and public parks. For example, an educational pamphlet about sex venues issued by the leading LGBTQ health organization in Australia offers a number of reasons why men visit sex-on-site-focused establishments (Gray *et al.* n.d.:3):

- For no-strings-attached casual sex.
- As a way to relax, wind down, de-stress.
- To have a wank.
- To socialize.
- To meet someone to go home and have sex with.
- As an alternative to beats (outdoor park/beach cruising) that is legal and safe from violence.
- To have sex somewhere that has condoms, lube, and HIV information freely available.
- As a way to meet new friends, a f*ck buddy, or a boyfriend.
- As part of a big night out or party weekend.
- To explore sex outside a relationship—either individually or together.
- To explore different sexual scenes such as SM, rubber, or leather.
- To explore new and alternative sexual practices like fisting and group sex.

- As an alternative to meeting people in gay pubs and clubs.
- As a way for guys who are not 'out' to have discreet sex.

Overall, public sex offers its own set of enticements that differ from "private" sexual encounters. Whether it be the thrill and danger of doing something deviant or the option to enjoy sex outdoors, having sex in public is a phenomenon that intrigues many. It is anonymous and readily available. Reasons for participation are as diverse as the men who engage in public sex—a veritable range of sexual deviance and deviants.

Comparing public sex locales and their participants

In this chapter we have learned about the individual sexual cultures within various types of public sex locales. And while there are certainly similarities between them, they also differ in unique ways. Some evoke the thrill of danger of discovery (i.e., tearooms and public parks) while others supply a variety of sexual amenities (i.e., sex clubs). Each offers a different type of sex with a different range of men, as one tearoom and bathhouse patron stated "you go to the baths to have sex with gays. You go to the tearooms to have sex with men" (Califia 2000:26). Whatever the particular enticement is, public sex is quite popular among MSM: estimates indicate that between 25 and 50 percent of gay men participate in public sex (Frankis and Flowers 2005). Although this experience is relatively common, the popularity of the type of location for public sex varies from season to season and by city and country. For example, public parks and tearooms are most frequented when the weather is nice, such as in the spring and fall (Humphreys 1970; Flowers et al. 2000). And while tearooms were found to be more popular than bathhouses in one American study (Binson et al. 2001), the park/woods was the most popular public sex locale among men in a Dutch sample (de Wit et al. 1997). Openly gay men are more likely to patronize gay bars, bathhouses, and sex clubs while closeted or non-gay-identified men are more likely to frequent tearooms, public parks, and backrooms.

The deviance of public sex is entwined with many social and sexual mores. Sex is "supposed to be" a private affair and sexual escapades in public are viewed as deviant (and in many cases, illegal). But beyond this, sex between men has been targeted as especially deviant and the crackdown on public sex between men accompanied the deviance discourse that has placed gay men (and MSM in general) on the social margins. In fact, many men who participate in tearoom sex put on a "breastplate of righteousness" (a protective shield of superiority) in which they deny their involvement in MSM behavior and insist that they are straight (Humphreys 1975:135; see also Desroches 1990). Furthermore, it should be noted that while this chapter focused on public sex between men, anyone of any sexual or gender identity can engage in public sex in any of the spaces discussed in this chapter. And while public sex between men has been highly deviantized, virtually all public sex is viewed as deviant no matter who is engaging in it. Thus, public sex (and especially public sex between men) is a deviant behavior.

Notes

1 "Bible Belt" traditionally refers to the band of highly religious states (in particular, states with a high concentration of fundamentalist Christians) clustered in the southeastern part of the United States.
2 Sometimes "hustlers" (men selling sex) work in public sex areas (Desroches 1990; Couture 2008).
3 The AIDS Council of New South Wales (ACON) Code of Practice aims to maximize the health and well-being of both patrons and staff in sex-on-site establishments and minimize the risk of communicable diseases. The main principles emphasize the right to practice safe and consensual sex, the right to information about safe sex, and the right to be treated with respect (see more on the ACON website www.avp.acon.org.au).

References

Adamandeve.com. 2011, November 14. "Adamandeve.Com Finds Most Americans Have Sex In Public!" Retrieved from: http://www.adameve.com/pressroom.aspx?id=press-550
Alvarez, Eric. 2008. *Muscle Boys: Gay Gym Culture*. New York, NY: Routledge.
Bailey, Beth. 1998. *From Front Porch to Back Seat: Courtship in Twentieth Century America*. Baltimore, MD: Johns Hopkins University Press.
Bergman, David. 1999. "Beauty and the Beach: Representing Fire Island." Pp. 95–114 in *Public Sex/Gay Space*, edited by William Leap. New York, NY: Columbia University Press.
Bérubé, Allan. 2003. "The History of Gay Bathhouses." *Journal of Homosexuality* 44(3–4):33–53.
Binson, Diane, William J. Woods, Lance Pollack, Jay Paul, Ron Stall, and Joseph A. Catania. 2001. "Differential HIV Risk in Bathhouses and Public Cruising Areas." *American Journal of Public Health* 91(9):1482–6.
Bowers v. Hardwick, 478 U.S. 186 (1986).
Burns, Olive Ann. 1953, December 27. "Love is Legal in Piedmont Park." *Atlanta Journal and Constitution Magazine* 8–10.
Byers, E. Sandra, Christine Purdon, and David A. Clark. 1998. "Sexual Intrusive Thoughts of College Students." *The Journal of Sex Research* 35(4):359–69.
Califia, Pat. 2000. *Public Sex: The Culture of Radical Sex*, Second Edition. San Francisco, CA: Cleis Press.
Carpenter, Dale. 2012. *Flagrant Conduct: The Story of Lawrence V. Texas: How a Bedroom Arrest Decriminalized Gay Americans*. New York, NY: W. W. Norton & Company.
Church, J., J. Green, S. Vearnals, and P. Keogh. 1993. "Investigation of Motivational and Behavioural Factors Influencing Men Who Have Sex With Other Men in Public Toilets (Cottaging)." *AIDS Care: Psychological and Socio-medical Aspects of AIDS/HIV* 5(3):337–46.
Cliett, C. Ray. 2003. "How a Note or a Grope Can be Justification for the Killing of a Homosexual. An Analysis of the Effects of the Supreme Court's Views on Homosexuals, African-Americans and Women." *Criminal and Civil Confinement* 29:219–54.
Collier, Stephen. 1985. "Preventing the Spread of AIDS by Restricting Sexual Conduct in Gay Bathhouses: A Constitutional Analysis." *Golden Gate University Law Review* 15:301–30.
Corzine, Jay and Richard Kirby. 1977. "Cruising the Truckers: Sexual Encounters in a Highway Rest Area." *Urban Life* 6:171–92.
Couture, Joseph. 2008. *Peek: Inside the Private World of Public Sex*. New York, NY: Haworth Press.
de Wit, John, Ernest de Vroome, Theo Sandfort, and Godfried van Griensven. 1997. "Homosexual Encounters in Different Venues." *International Journal of STD & AIDS* 8:130–4.
Desroches, Frederick. 1990. "Tearoom Trade: A Research Update." *Qualitative Sociology* 13(1):39–61.

Dodge, Brian, Michael Reece, Sara L. Cole, and Theo G. M. Sandfort. 2004. "Sexual Compulsivity Among Heterosexual College Students." *The Journal of Sex Research* 41(4):343–50.

European Sex Survey. 2013. "European Sex Survey." *YouGov*. Retrieved from: http://cdn. yougov.com/cumulus_uploads/document/mkyaii2h6k/YouGov-Survey-European-Omnibus-Sex-Research-130621.pdf

Flowers, Paul, Graham Hart, and Claire Marriott. 1999. "Constructing Sexual Health: Gay Men and 'Risk' in the Context of a Public Sex Environment." *Journal of Health Psychology* 4(4):483–95.

Flowers, Paul, Claire Marriott, and Graham Hart. 2000. "The Bars, the Bogs, and the Bushes': The Impact of Locale on Sexual Cultures." *Culture, Health & Sexuality* 2(1):69–86.

Frankis, Jamie and Paul Flowers. 2005. "Men Who Have Sex With Men (MSM) in Public Sex Environments (PSES): A Systematic Review of Quantitative Literature." *AIDS Care* 17(3):273–88.

Galliher, John, Wayne Brekhus, and David P. Keys. 2004. *Laud Humphreys: Prophet of Homosexuality and Sociology*. Madison, WI: University of Wisconsin Press.

Gray, Brad, Fred Rainey, Amanda James, David McGuigan, Jonathan Bollan, and David McInnes. n.d. *When You're Hot, You're Hot: An Easy Guide to What You Always Wanted to Know About Sex Venues but were Afraid to Ask!* Distributed by the AIDS Council of New South Wales (ACON)

Grindr.com. (n.d.). www.grindr.com (Accessed June 2015).

Griswold v. Connecticut, 381 U.S. 479 (1965).

HeadQuarters.com.au. (n.d.). www.headquarters.com.au (Accessed June 2015).

Haubrich, Dennis J., Ted Myers, Liviana Calzavara, Karen Ryder, and Wendy Medved. 2004. "Gay and Bisexual Men's Experiences of Bathhouse Culture and Sex: 'Looking for Love in All the Wrong Places.'" *Culture, Health & Sexuality* 6(1):19–29.

Hollister, John. 1999. "A Highway Rest Area as a Socially Reproducible Site." Pp. 55–70 in *Public Sex/Gay Space*, edited by William Leap. New York, NY: Columbia University Press.

Howard, John. 1995. "The Library, the Park, and the Pervert: Public Space and Homosexual Encounter in Post-World War II Atlanta." *Radical History Review* 62:166–87.

Humphreys, Laud. 1970. *Tearoom Trade: Impersonal Sex in Public Places*. New York, NY: Aldine Publishing.

Humphreys, Laud. 1975. "Retrospect: Ethical Issues in Social Research." Pp. 223–32 in *Tearoom Trade: Impersonal Sex in Public Places* by Laud Humphreys. New York, NY: Aldine Publishing.

Joyal, Christian C., Amélie Cossette, and Vanessa Lapierre. 2015. "What Exactly Is an Unusual Sexual Fantasy?" *The Journal of Sexual Medicine* 12(2):328–40.

Karp, David. 1973. "Hiding in Pornographic Bookstores: A Reconsideration of the Nature of Urban Anonymity." *Urban Life* 1:427–51.

Langer, Gary, Cheryl Arnedt, and Dalia Sussman. 2004, October 21. "The American Sex Survey: A Peek Beneath the Sheets." *ABC News Primetime Live Poll* Retrieved from: http://abcnews.go.com/images/Politics/959a1AmericanSexSurvey.pdf

Lawrence v. Texas, 539 U.S. 558 (2003).

Leap, William. 1999a. "Introduction." Pp. 1–23. In *Public Sex/Gay Space*, edited by William Leap. New York, NY: Columbia University Press.

Leap, William. 1999b. "Sex in 'Private' Places: Gender, Erotics, and Detachment in Two Urban Locales." Pp. 115–40 in *Public Sex/Gay Space*, edited by William Leap. New York, NY: Columbia University Press.

Moon, Margaret R. and Felix Khin-Maung-Gyi. 2009. "The History and Role of Institutional Review Boards." *American Medical Association Journal of Ethics* 11(4):311–21.

Moore, Clive. 1995. "Poofs in The Park: Documenting Gay 'Beats' in Queensland, Australia." *GLQ* 2:319–39.

Myers, JoAnne. 2013. *Historical Dictionary of the Lesbian and Gay Liberation Movements.* Lanham, MD: Scarecrow Press, Inc.

New York Times. 1984, October 10. "14 San Francisco Sex Clubs Told to Close to Curb AIDS." Retrieved from: http://www.nytimes.com/1984/10/10/us/14-san-francisco-sex-clubs-told-to-close-to-curb-aids.html

Ponte, Meredith R. 1974. "Life in a Parking Lot: An Ethnography of a Homosexual Drive-In." Pp. 7–29 in *Deviance: Field Studies and Self-Disclosures*, edited by J. Jacobs. Palo Alto, CA: National Books.

Richters, Juliet. 2007. "Through a Hole in a Wall: Setting and Interaction in Sex-On-Premises Venues." *Sexualities* 10(3):275–97.

Rosenfeld, Michael and Rueben Thomas. 2012. "Searching For a Mate: The Rise of the Internet as a Social Intermediary." *American Sociological Review* 77(4):523–47.

Smith, Aaron and Maeve Duggan. 2013, October 21. "Online Dating & Relationships." *Pew Research Center: Internet, Science & Tech.* Retrieved from: http://www.pewinternet.org/2013/10/21/online-dating-relationships/

Smith, David and Ray Over. 1991. "Male Sexual Fantasy: Multidimensionality in Content." *Behaviour Research and Therapy* 29(3):267–75.

Somlai, Anton, S. Kalichman, and A. Bagnall. 2001. "HIV Risk Behaviour among Men Who Have Sex with Men in Public Sex Environments: An Ecological Evaluation." *AIDS Care* 13(4):503–14.

Sundholm, Charles. 1973. "The Pornographic Arcade: Ethnographic Notes on Moral Men in Immoral Places." *Urban Life* 2:85–104.

Tattleman, Ira. 1999. "Speaking to the Gay Bathhouse: Communicating in Sexually Charged Spaces." Pp. 71–94 in *Public Sex/Gay Space*, edited by William Leap. New York, NY: Columbia University Press.

Tewksbury, Richard. 1995. "Adventures in the Erotic Oasis: Sex and Danger in Men's Same-Sex, Public Sexual Encounters." *The Journal of Men's Studies* 4(1):9–24.

Tewksbury, Richard. 1996. "Cruising for Sex in Public Places: The Structure and Language of Men's Hidden, Erotic Worlds." *Deviant Behavior* 17(1):1–19.

USA Today. 2014, April 21. "12 States Still Ban Sodomy a Decade after Court Ruling." Retrieved from: http://www.usatoday.com/story/news/nation/2014/04/21/12-states-ban-sodomy-a-decade-after-court-ruling/7981025/

Vergun, David. 2014, January 8. "New Law Brings Changes to Uniform Code of Military Justice." *United States Department of Defense.* Retrieved from: http://www.defense.gov/news/newsarticle.aspx?id=121444

Warwick, Donald. 1975. "Tearoom Trade: Means and Ends in Social Research." Pp. 191–212 in *Tearoom Trade: Impersonal Sex in Public Places* by Laud Humphreys. New York, NY: Aldine Publishing.

Woods, William, Jason Euren, Lance M. Pollack, and Diane Binson. 2010. "HIV Prevention in Gay Bathhouses and Sex Clubs across the United States." *Journal of Acquired Immune Deficiency Syndromes* 55(Supplement 2):S88–S90.

10

FETISHES

Ponygirls • Niche-Kink Internet Communities • Balloon Popping Fetish
• Fat Admirers & Feeders • Cartoon Animal Sex • Robots, Cyborgs & Future
Sex • Messy Fun • Rampaging Giantesses • Bug-Crushing Freaks • Body
Inflation • AND HUNDREDS OF DEVIANTS, PERVERTS & WEIRDOS.
Cover of Deviant Desires: Incredibly Strange Sex, *Gates (2000)*

Acts of sexual deviance are as varied as humans are and because of this, the sheer
diversity in sexuality can be quite overwhelming to the scholar and student alike.
Before the world wide web became the host of our assorted predilections, evidence
of "unusual" sexual affinities primarily existed in books written for psychiatrists
listing them as sexual "paraphilias," "dysfunctions," or "diseases." All the while, of
course, these deviant interests have been (and continue to be) thriving in our sex
lives—although mostly in secret. However, with the ability to connect with others
now easier (and faster) than ever before, we are learning more and more about
fantasies and fetishes that were once hidden from most:

> The internet has transformed deviants' lives, enabling them to come out of
> the closet and to band together in small groups with shared erotic aesthetics.
> *(Gates 2000:6)*

Millions of people have suddenly gained access to previously unavailable information about non-conformist sex … Deviants with the most obscure and
specific kinks—who always thought they were alone in the world—can now
communicate with likeminded people. Our old monolithic view of human
sexuality as a bunch of normals (us) vs. abnormals (them), is being replaced by
a far richer picture of the human sexual imagination as a vast, complex web of
images and cultural narratives that we can disassemble and reassemble in thrill-
ing new forms. Many people—both vanilla[1] and deviant—are finding that

their desires are becoming more flexible, evolving, and morphing in ways that open up fresh possibilities for sharing intimacy ... They are reinventing and reinterpreting the familiar to give it erotic power. They are actively creating their own sexual entertainment and sharing real information about how to safely pursue their deviant desires.

(Gates 2000: 11)

Sexual fantasies and fetishes that exist outside the normative spectrum are so diverse that entire books, magazines, websites, and communities can be found that are dedicated to each one. And because of this, literally *anything* can be fetishized. From elbows to elbow macaroni, you name it, *somebody* has fetishized and fantasized about it. In this chapter, just a small sampling of this complex and curious world of sexual deviance is provided. You may have some negative responses to some of these behaviors (such as disgust or nausea) or you may find some of them titillating and exciting. Whatever your feelings about the wide range of sexual fetish play that you will learn about here and likely elsewhere, it is important to remember that sexuality is personal and as long as it's consensual, it deserves respect. Beyond this, by opening our minds to these "unusual" sex practices, we can learn more about others and more about ourselves.

Defining "fetish"

We often hear the term "fetish" bandied about but pinning down a precise definition for this concept is another task altogether. The word "fetish" derives from the Portuguese word *feitiço* that means "magic" or "spell." Fifteenth-century European colonialists used this term to "describe the objects, charms, and dolls used as talismans by many of the African tribes they encountered" (Bramwell 2007:13). Today, the term "fetish" evokes diverse, imaginative, and vibrant imagery: "fetishism is a world full of costume, rules, drama, color, game-playing, excitement, emotion, and exploration" (Bramwell 2007:47).

But what exactly is a fetish? In general, people with fetishes are sexually aroused by objects, body parts, or situations that are not typically considered to be sexual. In other words, so-called fetishists (who partake in fetishism/fetish play) are "individuals for whom unusual props, costumes, stories, and playacting are the primary, if not exclusive focus of their sexual excitement" (Gates 2000:8). Furthermore, fetishism exists along a graded continuum of intensities. Having a slight preference for certain kinds of sexual stimuli is relatively common and the term "fetish" is not appropriate for these normative sexual affinities. Rather, *strong* preferences for certain kinds of sexual stimuli, the *requirement* of such preferences for arousal and performance, and even the *replacement of* sex partners by such preferences better encapsulate the degrees (low, moderate, high) of sexual fetishism as seen in Figure 10.1. For the extreme paraphilic fetishist "the fetish object has become even more arousing than the actual erotic target that it represents and is now more or less *required* for sexual gratification" (Bering 2013:117).

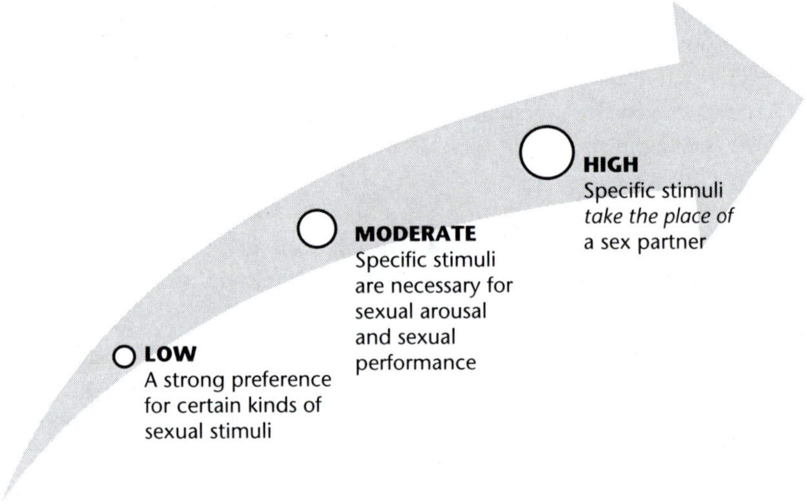

FIGURE 10.1 Sexual fetishism graded continuum of intensities
Adapted from Gebhard (1969).

Historically, various sexual desires have been categorized as "deviant" and diag-nosed as mental illnesses according to the recommendations of the *Diagnostic and Statistical Manual of Mental Disorders* (DSM) (the most widely cited resource in North America utilized to classify and diagnose mental illness). Today, the most current edition of the DSM recognizes that most people with non-normative sex-ual interests do not have a mental disorder and recommends that only those who meet specific criteria should be considered as exhibiting signs of a paraphilic disor-der, those who:

- have an atypical[2] focus of sexual arousal (as manifested by fantasies, urges, or behaviors) and an arousal pattern that is recurrent, intense, and persists for at least six months;
- feel clinically significant distress or impairment in social, occupational, or other important areas of functioning; and/or
- have a sexual desire or behavior that involves another person's psychological distress, injury, or death, or a desire for sexual behaviors involving unwilling persons or persons unable to give legal consent.

In other words, as long as the sexual fetish does not cause distress/harm to the fetish-ist or the object of his/her fetish play, people who participate in unusual sex practices should not be diagnosed with mental disorders simply because of their enjoyment of "strange" sex. Currently there are eight specified paraphilic disorders included in the DSM (see Table 10.1). And while many may have interests in, for example, sexual masochism, only those who experience significant distress or impairment in their lives—socially or occupationally—because of their behavior should be viewed as

TABLE 10.1 DSM paraphilic disorders

Exhibitionistic disorder	Sexual arousal from the exposure of one's genitals to an unsuspecting person.
Fetishistic disorder	Sexual arousal from the use of nonliving objects or a highly specific focus on non-genital body part(s). Note: The fetish objects are not devices specifically designed for the purpose of tactile genital stimulation (e.g., vibrator).
Frotteuristic disorder	Sexual arousal from touching or rubbing against a nonconsenting person.
Pedophilic disorder	Sexual arousal from sexual activity with a prepubescent child or children (generally age 13 years or younger).
Sexual masochism disorder	Sexual arousal from the act of being humiliated, beaten, bound, or otherwise made to suffer.
Sexual sadism disorder	Sexual arousal from physical or psychological suffering of another person.
Transvestic disorder	Sexual arousal from cross-dressing (wearing clothing items typically associated with the opposite sex).
Voyeuristic disorder	Sexual arousal from observing an unsuspecting person who is naked, in the process of disrobing, or engaging in sexual activity.

In addition to these categories, there are two residual categories intended to be used when there is an atypical sexual focus that is not covered by one of the eight specific types of paraphilic disorders: other specified paraphilic disorder and unspecified paraphilic disorder (First 2014).

exhibiting signs of mental illness (DSM-5 Fact Sheet 2013). Put simply, the mere presence of atypical sexual arousal patterns is not evidence of psychopathology[3] (First 2014). This is a vast revision to previous versions of the DSM that have considered behaviors such as "homosexuality" as evidence of mental illness. Even so, the power of the DSM to shape our perspectives about sexual deviance should not go unrecognized or unquestioned (for more, revisit chapter 3, Box 3.6).

Overall, fetishes challenge sexual mores. They go against "traditional" sexual patterns, "disturb the dominant orders of sex" (Terry 2010:34), and reshape eroticism by offering alternative sexual practices: "in fetish play, things are different: pain is expressed as love, humiliation as respect; genders are mixed, and roles are inverted" (Bramwell 2007:14). And they may not be all that uncommon. For example, in a European Sex Survey (2013) of 14,371 men and women from 13 different countries, respondents indicated a wide range of involvement in two types of fetish play (see Figure 10.2). Between 7 percent and 15 percent reported filming/photographing themselves having sex and between 2 percent and 14 percent indicated dressing up in costume while having sex. Related, in a Canadian study with 1,516 participants, 32 percent of women and 44 percent of men described fantasies about being photographed or filmed during sex (Joyal et al. 2015). In an American study with 2,765 respondents, 6 percent of women and 11 percent of men indicated experiences with sexual fetishes and a small number (between 1 percent and 2 percent) actually preferred to achieve orgasm through fetish play (Janus and Janus 1993). Thus, fetish play is certainly happening across the globe.

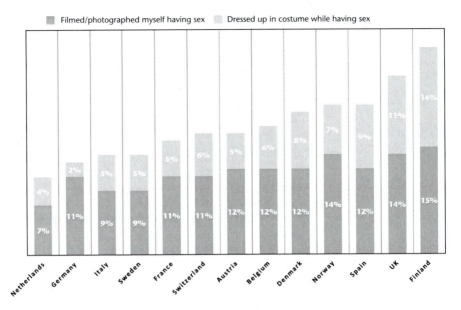

■ Filmed/photographed myself having sex   ▨ Dressed up in costume while having sex

FIGURE 10.2   Sexual fetishes in 13 European countries

Data adapted from European Sex Survey (2013).

Furthermore, fantasizing about fetish play is a far more common experience. In one of the largest studies on sexual fantasies ever undertaken with more than 20,000 American and British respondents, 96 percent of men and 90 percent of women indicated that they had sexual fantasies (Kahr 2008). For example, nearly two-thirds of men indicated that they had voyeuristic fantasies about watching someone undress without him or her knowing and fantasies about group sex (polyiterophilia) and threesomes (triolism) were also common among men (47 percent) and women (36 percent) in a Canadian study with 1,516 participants (Joyal *et al.* 2015). By contrast, fantasies about having sex with animals (bestiality) and urine (urophilia) were far less common (see Figure 10.3). Thus, thinking about "unusual" sex is happening more frequently than participation in deviant sexual behavior. Even so, it is clear that fetish play is a part of many people's sex lives in some form or another.

Fetishes

One of the first easily accessible educational resources about fetishes was written by American sexologist Brenda Love (born in 1950) in 1992. To the 1990s fetish-curious reader, her *Encyclopedia of Unusual Sex Practices* was inviting. Emblazoned across the front cover is the tagline: "More than 750 entries and 150 original illustrations on the world's strangest sex activities" (Love 1992). Prior to the internet, this might have been one of the only resources available to learn about wide ranges of sexual diversity. The book jacket further entices its reader by noting: "everyone wants to know what others are doing behind closed doors. This is the book to

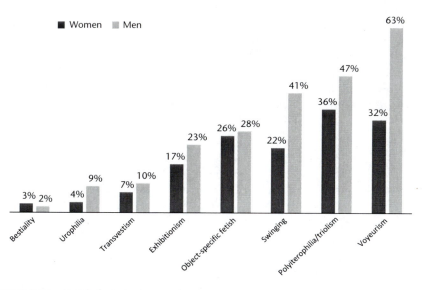

FIGURE 10.3 Fetish fantasies by gender

Data adapted from Joyal *et al.* (2015).

satisfy that curiosity" (Love 1992). But this "holy bible" of sexual fetishes has been replaced by thousands of fetish websites available at our fingertips. The proliferation of the internet has made fetish play highly accessible, and as a result, the diversity in fetishism is overwhelming. An encyclopedia with 750 entries such as Love's (1992) is only the tip of the iceberg when it comes to sexual fetishes and beyond— new fetishes are "invented" every day. Thus, it is impossible to offer an exhaustive listing of all types of fetish-play in any single resource: "even the most comprehensive taxonomy of sexual deviance can't always foresee all the bizarre ways in which paraphilias can possibly materialize, and sometimes it's unclear how a particular expression of sexual deviance should be labeled" (Bering 2013:120). Below, just a few examples from this fascinating and sometimes disturbing world are offered to illustrate this diversity. Although they are loosely divided into three categories ("object"-specific, "animal"-specific, and role-play) many are related to one another (e.g., pony play can be both an "animal"-specific and a role-play fetish). As a result, fetishism can involve any number of predilections and sometimes many at the same time. Remember, as we take this journey into perhaps some of the strangest sexual desires yet, respect for consensual sexual diversity is paramount.

"Object"-specific fetishes

Fetishes that are object-specific sexualize a particular item or "thing." This can include human-related "objects" such as body parts in the case of partialism toward the feet (i.e., podophilia) or objects that are designed to cover human body parts such as shoes (i.e., retifism) and sometimes both. In fact, "many fetishists are attracted to *both* the body part and its covering" (Steele 1996:107). Some object-specific fetishists sexualize objects that resemble the human form such as statues and sex dolls (i.e., agalmatophilia). Still others find sexual pleasure in completely inanimate objects such as balloons (i.e., balloon fetish) or buildings and monuments including the Eiffel Tower (objectophilia). As with all examinations of fetish play, literally *any* object can be fetishized. Below, just a small sampling of object-specific fetishes is offered to highlight this diversity.

Podophilia and retifism

When one hears the word "fetish," the term "foot fetish" is a frequent accompaniment. Foot fetishes involve the eroticization of feet, toes, the arches of the feet, the crevasses between the toes, the heels, etc. Basically any form of intense sexual arousal from feet is known as podophilia. Podophiliacs can indulge their predilection at foot fetish clubs (similar to a strip clubs) where you can pay foot models to participate in foot worship, trampling, tickling, foot smelling, and foot domination.[4] Related to podophilia is retifism, or sexual arousal from shoes. These sexual affinities can be related to one another. For example, part of sexualizing the foot itself might be seeing it in a sexy shoe. Some fetish websites even sell mannequin feet (and shoes) to appeal to podophiliacs who want their very own pair to have and to hold. Thus, sometimes these "object"-specific fetishes involve both the shoe and the foot inside it.

While any footwear can be arousing, the so-called "kinky boot" (often black patent leather, knee high or thigh high, with buttons, laces, zippers, and other embellishments) is frequently eroticized because it has historically been associated with sex workers and dominatrices (Steele 1996:34). In addition, the term "fuck me shoes" has been applied to very high stiletto-heeled pumps, platforms, strappy sandals, etc. (Steele 1996:110). These shoes are eroticized in contemporary women's fashion (i.e., most "sexy" imagery of women includes high-heeled shoes) and many describe how high heels emphasize the legs as well as posture in arousing ways (altocalciphilia is the specific attraction to high-heeled shoes). Extremely high-heeled shoes (more than 8 inches) often inhibit the wearer's movement, such as in the case of the ballet fetish shoe/boot designed to force the wearer's feet almost *en pointe*, like those of a ballerina, with the aid of thin, spiked heels (see Image 10.1). Although some people can walk in them, at best, most can only hobble. This restriction of movement combined with constriction of the foot itself is sometimes described as a form of bondage that is erotic for some (Steele 1996; see also Gebhard 1969). For others, seeing their partner in this type of footwear can also be about power and domination. Still others find the shoe itself to be erotic. And while many shoe fetishists gravitate toward women's high heels, some fetishize other types of footwear including motorcycle boots, riding boots, and even cowboy boots complete with spurs. Indeed, an entire online community, known as the "Foot Fraternity," exists that is dedicated to men who appreciate the erotic dimension of the male bare foot, sneakers, shoes, boots, socks, footgear, etc., and receives over a million website "hits" every two months (Weinberg *et al.* 1995; Gaines, n.d.).

IMAGE 10.1   Ballet fetish boot

Black patent ballet fetish boot with 8-inch spiked heel designed to force the wearer's feet almost *en pointe*, like those of a ballerina. ©Shutterstock, F.Schmidt

Overall, the eroticization of shoes can be about the association of certain types of footwear with certain activities (i.e., horseback riding or sex work) or it can be about the experience of wearing or seeing others wear the actual shoe itself. It can be about feet or about the sexual pleasures feet can bring. Whatever the reason, foot/shoe fetishes are varied:

> Whether they're in stockings, fishnets, white ankle socks, boots, heels, slippers, bare, arched, relaxed, manicured, clean, unwashed, or even a bit whiffy, feet are the undisputed champions of the fetish world. They can be licked, fondled, kissed, tickled, smelled, praised, sucked, or even used to "massage" the genitals for the delights of a "footjob."
>
> *(Bramwell 2007:58)*

Agalmatophilia and pygmalionism

Have you ever seen a mannequin in a department store that was so life-like that you imagined it coming to life? Have you ever imagined what it might be like to be sexually involved with a perfect human sculpture? If so, you may have stumbled upon a specific type of fetish fantasy. Sexual arousal from a statue, mannequin or doll, known as agalmatophilia, can take on many forms. For example, an 1877 case describes a gardener who fell in love with a statue of the Venus de Milo and attempted to have sex with it (Krafft-Ebing 1886). Other instances of agalmatophilia involve humans taking on the role of a statue by remaining perfectly still or gradually coming to life during a sex act (Ellis 1942). A related fetish, pygmalionism (from the Greek mythological story of Pygmalion who fell in love with an ivory statue of a "perfect woman" that he sculpted), denotes love for an object of one's own creation (sometimes also described as "statue love" although agalmatophilia is a more accurate term for those fetishizing statues).

The use of human–like figures for sexual or erotic purposes dates back to the seventeenth century when sailors created makeshift masturbatory dolls out of sewn cloth or old clothes, referred to as *dames de voyage*, for sexual release on long voyages. Because women were generally considered "bad luck" onboard ships and most trips abroad lasted several months, *dames de voyage* were considered to be an acceptable option to relieve sexual frustration and were certainly preferable to same-sex sexual behavior (Ferguson 2010:16). The commercial sale of erotic dolls, however, is a much more modern phenomenon. For example, one of the earliest advertisements for a custom sex doll made to fit customer specifications appears in a 1902 Paris circular:

> The body in action moves like a living being, pressing, embracing, changing position at will by a simple pressure … the complete apparatus, guaranteed against breakage, man or woman, 3000 francs … This apparatus can [also] be fitted with a phonographic attachment, recording and speaking at will.
>
> *(Cary 1922:50)*

While evidence of statue- and doll-love exists throughout recorded history, the modern sex doll has reshaped agalmatophilia in surprising ways. Cheap, inflatable "blow up" vinyl sex dolls with crude genitalia (typically given as gag gifts at bachelor/bachelorette parties) first appeared on the market in the 1970s (Ferguson 2010). Today, the most sophisticated sex dolls are made of silicone and they are highly realistic featuring fully articulated skeletons and flesh-like skin (see Box 10.1). Currently over 250 silicone sex doll manufacturers exist in several countries including China, Germany, France, Japan, Russia, the United Kingdom, and the United States. This multimillion dollar industry has also spawned a myriad of sex doll love-related activities including:

- Doll porn movies and magazines.
- Doll swinger parties.

- Doll artistic photography.
- Doll escort services.
- Doll brothels (hourly rental).

BOX 10.1 THE DOLLS

The world of sex dolls has come a long way since inflatable blow up dolls hit the market in the 1970s (Ferguson 2010; see Image 10.2a). Today's modern sex doll is made of flesh-like silicone and is equipped with an articulated skeleton including moveable joints (see Image 10.2b). In addition, most modern sex dolls are fully customizable to the customer's specifications, which can include:

- Interchangeable faces with various options including eye-color and makeup styles.
- Body types and breast sizes (options for artificial milk glands).
- Genitalia types (labia size/shape, penis size/shape, testicles size/shape, and transgender dolls).
- Mouths, lips, and automatic tongues with various movement capabilities.
- Automated toes for stimulation.
- Eyes equipped with video recording devices.
- Vocal reactions to genital penetration.
- Simulated breathing and heart beats.
- Automated pulse that can be felt at the wrist.
- Fantasy dolls resembling Japanese Anime, aliens, and other sci-fi creations.

Weighing between 40 and 120 pounds, these hyper-realistic, life-sized dolls sell for anywhere between $3,500 to $10,000+ (USD). Although that is a hefty

(a)    (b)

IMAGE 10.2   Sex dolls
Inflatable novelty blow up sex doll (a) juxtaposed with a realistic sex doll (b).
© Shutterstock, Maffi, Laurin Rinder

price to pay for a sex novelty, this highly lucrative market with hundreds of international manufacturers has a diverse global customer base.

One such manufacturer, Abyss Creations, creates one of the world's most well-known sex dolls, the RealDoll. Founded in 1996 and based in San Marcos, California, Abyss Creations has partnerships in 11 other countries: Australia, Canada, China, Germany, Italy, Russia, Spain, Singapore, Switzerland, Turkey, and the United Kingdom. Their media presence is unavoidable. Their website provides customer testimonials as well as studio photos and the U.S. RealDoll factory has been showcased in various documentaries and television specials. RealDolls themselves have been produced for both movie and television series appearances.

Their current line-up includes female RealDolls in both the classic model and an upgraded newer and more expensive version, RealDoll 2. Introduced in 2009, RealDoll 2 features removable inserts for the mouth and vagina and interchangeable faces that attach by magnets instead of Velcro. Originally, RealDoll options were limited. In fact, the founder Matt McMullen did not originally set out to make sex dolls but after posting images online of a realistic poseable mannequin he created, he got many requests about making his artistic model into a sexually functional doll, so he decided to give it a try. He initially only took ten online orders for $5,000 each and created the details in the first dolls' hands and feet using his wife as a model (Ferguson 2010). Today, the current options for the female RealDolls are extensive (see Table 10.2).

Beyond this extensive list of options for female RealDolls, you can select a pre-configured model (the most popular of which are Olivia and Brooklyn with the curviest body type available), which some prefer to do because you can view detailed photographs of these dolls on their website prior to ordering (all sales are final so this might be a safer option for many). If you prefer to have your doll designed to look similar to your wife, your ex-girlfriend, your mom, or even a celebrity, you can email the company a photo and the designers will do their best to create your human-inspired RealDoll from their available options (just allow 16 weeks for production). Or if you prefer (and your bank account is abundant) you can even have your lover come into the factory for a 3D scanning to be made into a fully customized RealDoll. What's more, Abyss Creations has partnered with Wicked Pictures, an adult film production company, to offer completely realistic representations of the Wicked Girls including the first two models, Jessica Drake and Alectra Blue. The Wicked RealDolls are created using the latest cutting-edge technology designed to replicate every detail of these actresses, from digital scanning to silicone casting of fine details such as skin texture on the hands and feet. As noted on their website: "Order your own Wicked RealDoll today, and have a porn star ready and waiting for you every night!" (RealDoll.com).

The male RealDolls are not nearly as advanced as the female RealDolls. In fact, in 2007, only headless torsos with no arms and legs were available for

TABLE 10.2 Female RealDoll options

Face/head (interchangeable)	12 Face designs	4 Full head designs	Cosmetics options: eye shadow, eye liner, lip color
Eye and eyebrows	Eye color options: light blue, blue, blue grey, teal green, green, hazel green, hazel, light brown, brown	Eyebrow options: human hair available in four colors	Also available: eye veins (for more realistic eyes)
Hair	Color options: light blonde, medium blonde, strawberry, red, cinnamon, auburn, light brown, brunette, black	15 Hairstyle options from short bobs to very long	Also available: custom bright pink highlights and wigs
Skin	Color options: fair, medium, light tan, tanned, cocoa	Also available: freckles (face and/or body) and tan lines	Also available: human hair patches in five colors
Body	Height range: 4'10" to 5'7" Waist range: 23" to 26" Hips range: 32" to 39" Dress size range: Size 0 to Size 12 Weight range: 78 pounds to 112 pounds	Most popular type: Body D • Height: 5'6" • Weight: 95 pounds • Bust: 36" (DD cup) • Waist: 24" • Hips: 38" • Dress size: 5 • Shoe size: 8 US • Gel implants in buttocks	*Manufacturers' note:* Although we receive many special requests for larger dolls, we cannot make a very buxom or voluptuous doll because they would be prohibitively heavy and difficult for most people to use
Nipples	Color options: standard, black, pink, chestnut, brown, tan, coffee, blush, light brown, light red, peach	20 nipple textures from standard, perky, puffy, to XXL puffy	Other options: customized areola and nipple diameters
Breasts and buttocks	32A to 38DD	Optional gel implants for buttocks	

(Continued)

TABLE 10.2 Continued

Genitals and pubic hair	12 Insertable labia styles (removable or permanent)	Pubic hair styles: shaved, trimmed, full, natural	Manufacturers' note: All labia inserts are the same inside (ribbed and nubby). The inside dimension is 7" deep by 2" in diameter and stretches to 12" deep by 4" in diameter
Feet	Shoe Size Range: Size 5–9 (US)	Six toenail polish color options	Manufacturers' note: Feet are available for purchase separately
Piercings and other embellishments	Piercing options: clitoris, belly button, nipple(s), lower lip, nose, ears, ear pluqs (gauged at size zero), ear cartilage	Jeweled eyebrows	Manufacturers' note: RealDoll flesh is pierce-able and piercings will become permanent after a few days if owners choose to pierce on their own
Fantasy options	Special colors: blue, green, red skintones	Accessories: vampire fangs, elf ears	

Adapted from RealDoll.com.

those who had interests in bodies with penises. The first full male RealDoll "Charlie" was retired in 2008 and the current options for the male RealDoll 2 can be seen in Table 10.3.

Because so many more custom options are available for female RealDolls, it is clear that they are significantly more popular than male RealDolls. Furthermore, a quick browse of the photography on the RealDoll website reveals an obvious difference in the marketing styles of the male RealDoll as compared to the female RealDoll. The preconfigured models of the female RealDolls are overwhelmingly presented in sexualized, erotic poses. In fact, the female RealDolls are nearly always fully or at least partially nude. In contrast, the preconfigured male RealDolls are depicted in non-sexualized poses such as reading a book, wearing a business suit, or relaxing on a recliner with a magazine. This suggests that the female RealDoll may be objectified as a "sex object" more so than the male RealDoll. Indeed, the female sex doll has a long erotic

TABLE 10.3 Male RealDoll options

Body types	Muscular build	Runner build
	• Height: 5'11"	• Height: 5'8"
	• Weight: 123 pounds	• Weight: 115 pounds
	• Chest: 40"	• Chest: 36"
	• Waist: 30"	• Waist: 28.5"
	• Shirt size: M to L	• Shirt size: S to M
	• Pants: 32W to 32L	• Pants: 29W to 30L
	• Shoe size: 9.5 US	• Shoe size: 9.5 US
Heads and hair (interchangeable)	3 Face options Facial hair options: clean shaven or 5 o'clock shadow	Hair options: shaved head, blonde, brunette, red, black Also available: wigs
Skin	Color options: fair, medium, light tan, tanned, cocoa	Also available: freckles (face only) and human hair patches in five colors
Eyes/eyebrows	Eye color options: light blue, blue, blue grey, teal green, green, hazel green, hazel, light brown, brown	Other options: eye veins (for more realistic eyes) and human hair eyebrows (available in four colors)
Penis and pubic hair	Length Range: 5.5" to 11" Circumference range: 5.25" to 7" Diameter range: 1.75" to 2.5" Pubic hair style: shaved, trim, full	Other options: permanent or detachable penis

Adapted from RealDoll.com.

history and by most accounts, the male sex doll is a relatively new phenomenon (Ferguson 2010; Smith 2013). Perhaps female sex dolls have secured their home in the current erotic marketplace to a greater degree than male sex dolls due to a higher demand for their presence. Currently, the interest in, and demand for, sex dolls is strongly preferential toward the female-bodied.

But as we have learned, there is more to sex than just "male" and "female." Customers interested in transgender options can select from the following configurations for the female RealDoll:

- A detachable penis with testicles eliminating the vagina, which allows you to change to different size penis attachments.
- A permanently attached penis with testicles but no vagina.
- A permanently attached penis without testicles and with an intact vagina.

Beyond these options, if you do not want a "whole" RealDoll, you can purchase torsos with genitalia (bottoms-up male/female torso with no head, arms or legs; flat back male/female torso with no head, arms or legs; complete flat back male/female torso with head but no arms or legs) or lingerie busts without genitalia (with head and breasts but no arms and legs). Additional eyes, teeth, tongues, eyelashes, oral inserts, labia inserts, penis attachments, and interchangeable faces are also available. Furthermore, RealDoll sells a variety of accessories including costumes, wigs, doll stands (tripods), sex toys, and even repair and cleaning kits to keep your RealDoll fresh and exciting (RealDolls typically only last 5 to 7 years so proper maintenance is a must). Overall, the diversity and customizability that RealDoll offers with its product line show that this company has done its homework to appeal to its customers' interests.

Beyond the RealDoll and its similar counterparts, recently, more robot-like dolls (sometimes called sex androids) have entered the marketplace. These dolls have integrated computer software that enables them to respond to vocal commands and facial recognition (and do so with various personality types). For example, New Jersey-based company True Companion LLC introduced the world's first female sex robot Roxxxy in 2010 (in development since 2001) who has five programmable personalities:

- Frigid Farrah – she is reserved and shy.
- Wild Wendy – she is outgoing and adventurous.
- S&M Susan – she is ready to provide your pain/pleasure fantasies.
- Young Yoko – she is oh so young (barely 18) and waiting for you to teach her.
- Mature Martha – she is very experienced and would like to teach you!

Furthermore, Roxxxy has a heartbeat and a circulatory system that helps heat the inside of her body. The male version, Rocky, is also available with similar options. Both Rocky and Roxxxy are truly interactive sex dolls that can carry on simple conversations. They can talk to you about football, shopping, and even the stock market and can do so in English, Spanish, German, and Japanese (truecompanion.com). With such innovative hi-tech options currently available for sex with dolls and robots, who knows what the future will hold?

With so many opportunities to participate in doll-love either with your very own lover or with a by-the-hour rental, it is clear that agalmatophilia is at an all-time historic high.

The vast majority of doll owners are middle-aged, single, heterosexual men[5] who purchase "female" dolls. Although the primary function of these dolls is ostensibly sexual in nature, doll owners have described varying purposes for their purchases (Ferguson 2010; Valverde 2012):

- Sexual gratification and stimulation.
- A masturbation tool.
- Companionship.

- Emotional attachment.
- A life partner/wife.
- Enhance/supplement sex activities with a human partner.
- Novelty item purchase.
- Artistic value (especially for photography).
- Training purposes (especially for medical field training).

Beyond this, doll owners report that sex dolls enhance their quality of life. They can be viewed as therapeutic devices to relieve suffering from depression, anxiety, grief, sexual dysfunction, and/or intimacy issues. Doll owners with physical disabilities and/or mobility issues might find sex with dolls more pleasurable due to their pliability (Ferguson 2010; Valverde 2012). Some may view their doll as a "synthetic" person with humanlike qualities, such as American doll owner Davecat (born in 1973), whose story was featured on the American television series *My Strange Addiction*, who "treats his life-size doll like a human wife. He eats meals with her, shops for her, dresses her and is convinced she returns the same type of affection" (Bolicki and Cutlip 2011). Other doll owners may just see their dolls as a substitute for human companionship as American Gordon Griggs (born in 1967) describes:

> I don't like being around people at all now ... the less human contact I have the happier I am ... I feel safer and more secure knowing that I will never waste my time and money on another human female that just wants to use me.
>
> *(Laslocky 2005)*

While some doll owners appear to relish their relationship with their synthetic lovers, others describe varying degrees of depression, loneliness, shyness, and distrust in others as well as guilt, shame, or embarrassment about their doll ownership (Valverde 2012). Fear of rejection and/or the desire to have power and control over an inanimate object may drive some to engage in agalmatophilia while others who struggle with human attachment or who are looking for a safe way to express sexual fantasies may seek out doll relationships.

Whatever the reason to partake in agalmatophilia fetish play, sex dolls offer an interesting alternative to human sexual contact. They carry no diseases (when cleaned appropriately) and pose virtually no risk of physical harm to their users. The mass availability of sex dolls could even potentially reduce the demand for human sex trafficking and forced prostitution. With the first truly interactive android-like sex doll unveiled in 2010 (Roxxxy, see Box 10.1) a futuristic sci-fi-like world of agalmatophilia sex might not be so far away, as some researchers predict:

> In 2050, Amsterdam's red light district will be all about android prostitutes who are clean of sexual transmitted diseases, not smuggled in from Eastern Europe and forced into slavery. Android prostitutes will be both aesthetically pleasing and able to provide guaranteed performance and stimulation.
>
> *(Yeoman and Mars 2011:366)*

Balloon fetishists

Remember all those bright-colored latex balloons that float around at birthday parties, carnivals, amusement parks, and other nostalgic childhood events? For most people, balloons hold a special place in our hearts and remind us of celebrations and happiness. But for some people, balloons are more than simple party decorations. Typically known as looners (but also sometimes balloonatics), people with a passion for collecting, fondling, inflating, and popping balloons represent a fetish play category that entwines balloons and sex in various ways (Gates 2000; Bramwell 2007; Lewis 2014).

Unlike many other types of fetish play, balloon fetishes only came along relatively recently. Latex party balloons hit the American market in the 1930s and foil balloons arrived in the 1970s. Alongside the emerging toy technology of party balloons, balloon fetishes began to develop. One of the first organizations for balloon fetishists was established in 1976. Balloon Buddies appeals to "adult men and women who enjoy discussing the erotic appeal of toy balloons, sharing photos and videos, having local get-togethers all over the world, and talking about balloon sex, balloon girls, balloon erotica . . . straight [and] gay balloon fetishes" (Balloonbuddies. com). Hundreds of websites dedicated to balloon fetishism exist along with countless movies, erotic novels, and other pornographic materials designed to appeal to looners. The Balloon Buddies website even offers various balloons for purchase including 16 to 18 inch "looneynudes" balloons in 25 colors that feature white-line drawings of bikini-clad women with erotic phrases such as "Don't Stop 'till it Pops!!!" or "Blown to the Max!" (Balloonbuddies.com).

Who are these balloon fetishists? According to a global survey with 298 respondents, the majority of looners are men aged 18 to 39 who are in heterosexual relationships. For most, their interest in balloons began at a young age, and for many, balloon fetishism coincided with their sexual development between approximately 11 and 16 years of age. About 28 percent report engaging in balloon sexual play as a regular part of their relationship and 8 percent indicated that their sexual partner is also a balloon enthusiast. While the majority of those surveyed were currently in a relationship, 65 percent of respondents said they would not give up their balloon play if asked to by a partner because they considered balloon fetishism to be "an integral part of their identity" (Lewis 2014:5). There are many ways that looners incorporate balloons into their sexual lives, which include (Gates 2000; Lewis 2014):

- Sexual interaction (masturbation, rubbing or riding to climax).
- Watching others play with balloons.
- Inflating (some describe the process of blowing up balloons as resembling fellatio).
- Watching inflation (some describe the inflation of balloons as akin to the rising of the erect penis or engorgement of the labia).
- Popping ("the allure is focused on the lead up to, then the moment the balloon pops, which coincides with the peak of their excitement and release" Lewis 2014:7).

- Sitting and bouncing.
- Cuddling, hugging, or otherwise touching.
- Stuffing into clothing.

Sometimes poppers are distinguished from non-poppers (although most research shows that the majority of balloon fetishists enjoy both popper and non-popper play depending on their mood, setting, and play partner) (Gates 2000; Lewis 2014). Poppers enjoy the anticipation of the "pop" (similar to the experience of winding a jack-in-the-box). They find both the "adrenaline rush surrounding the moment when and if the balloon pops" and the sound to be sexually titillating (Lewis 2014:7). As one looner describes, "as it gets tighter, I like the squeak and the crackling sound it makes right before it pops. Some balloons go 'bang,' 'boom,' 'snap,' and even 'poof,' depending on the size and tightness" (Gates 2000:91). Some common methods of popping include sitting, bouncing, riding, squeezing, or stomping on the balloon, as well as using objects to pop the balloon such as long fingernails, needles, safety pins, stiletto heels, or even cigarettes. By contrast, non-poppers are careful never to pop or damage a balloon and may prefer more gentle forms of balloon play such as stroking or caressing them. Most enjoy the company of many balloons in a single sitting, sometimes blowing up over 100 at a time and filling an entire room (some even have special rooms in their houses called "balloon rooms" specifically designated for this activity) (Lewis 2014:10).

The balloons themselves are, of course, an integral part of looners' lives. A global survey of looners found that balloon fetishists rated size, durability and bounce as their top three most important balloon attributes (see Figure 10.4). Most looners prefer large, resilient, and bouncy balloons because "there is more to hold on to and enjoy – and, for those who enjoy popping, larger balloons make a louder bang" (Lewis 2014:9). As far as color partiality goes, red was the winner with 16 percent of looners indicating a preference for red balloons followed by clear (12 percent), and yellow (11 percent) (Lewis 2014). The classic red balloon[6] is perhaps so highly revered because it evokes memories of the most critically acclaimed short film of all time, the Oscar-winning 1956 French fantasy featurette, *The Red Balloon*, which is a story about little boy and his friendship with a big, red balloon[7] (Lamorisse 1956). Similarly, yellow balloons also evoke pleasant childhood memories including their nostalgic association with yellow raincoats and yellow rubber duckies. In contrast, a preference for clear balloons seems to be purely practical in that clear balloons allow the looner to see the features of people's bodies when pressed against them or held in front of them (Lewis 2014).

For some balloon fetishists, their sexual preferences for balloons can be alienating. For example, in a global survey of looners, 33 percent indicated that their balloon fetish play was a purely solo activity, stating lonely and isolating comments such as "I've never had sex with women; my only sex life is with my balloons" or "I've chosen for balloons to replace a human relationship and honestly, I can't see that ever changing" (Lewis 2014:4). Furthermore, most do not reveal their balloon predilections to their family or friends. Perhaps looners prefer to be secretive about

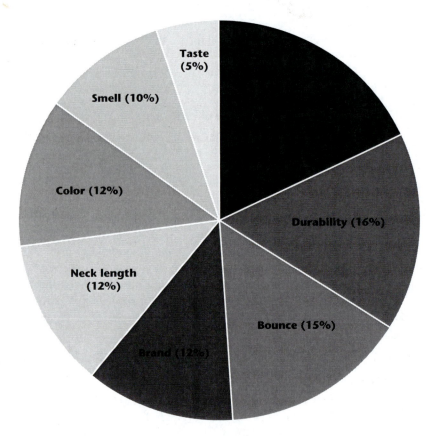

FIGURE 10.4 Looners' preferred balloon attributes

Data adapted from Lewis (2014).

their balloon fetish because they feel others will not understand their desires or worse, that they will be viewed as pedophiles or perverts. Indeed, there is a common misperception that a sexual interest in balloons is somehow directly related to an unnatural or unhealthy interest in children (Lewis 2014). As a result, balloon fetishism exists on the outskirts of sexual deviance. Indeed, "everyone knows about shoe fetishes and leather fetishes—but a balloon is a terribly embarrassing fetish object to have" (Gates 2000:75).

Objectophilia/objectum sexuality

Our daily lives are filled with relationships with objects. For example, most of us use a toothbrush every morning. We sometimes even wake up yearning for the satisfaction of a clean, fresh mouth following a morning brushing ritual. But few of us develop a sexual attraction to such mundane inanimate objects. For objectophiles, also known as objectum sexuals (OS), objects, structures, buildings, monuments, machines, vehicles, electronics, musical instruments, etc., become the subject of their emotional, romantic, and/or sexual desires. In other words, "the object *is* the erotic target" (Bering 2013:117). Some even describe their particular affinity not as fetish (some even take offense to the association of objectophilia with fetishism), but rather as a sexual *orientation* toward objects (Marsh 2010; Terry 2010).

Loving objects is not a new phenomenon. There is historical evidence of romantic attachments to objects in poetry, literature, and art. For example, in *The Hunchback of Notre Dame* (Hugo 1917) Quasimodo clearly had a loving attachment to the cathedral bells:

> What he loved best of all in that material edifice, that which awakened his soul and set the poor wings fluttering that lay so sadly folded when in that dreary dungeon, what brought him nearest to happiness, was the bells. He loved them, fondled them, talked to them, understood them. From the carillon in the transept steeple to the great bell over the central doorway, they all shared in his affection.
>
> *(Hugo 1917, Book IV:19).*

Quasimodo even named his favorite of the cathedral bells, "Marie," who is described as "his best beloved" (Hugo 1917, Book IV:20). Although we see such evidence of loving objects in fantasy, one of the first "real life" publicized instances of objectophilia occurred on June 17, 1979, when a Swedish woman by the name of Eija-Ritta Berliner-Mauer (or "Mrs. Berlin Wall") married the Berlin Wall (she has also been in relationships with a guillotine and a red fence, "Röda Staketet," which is now the icon of Objectùm-Sexuality Internationale). Eija-Ritta coined the term "objectum-sexuality" in the 1970s, and in 1996, she created the first website dedicated to objectum sexuality followed by an internet discussion group in 1999. Since then, Oliver Arndt from Germany and Erika Eiffel from America have built the largest known network of objectum-sexuals through their organization "Objectùm-Sexuality Internationale" designed to educate people about objectum sexuality and offer a global network of support for objectum sexuals (objectum-sexuality.org, published in English, Swedish, French, German, and Japanese). Objectum sexuals have been featured in various media outlets including a handful of documentaries and daytime talk shows. Unfortunately, however, these media appearances are often followed by a torrent of insulting comments (Marsh 2010). Objectum sexuals are perhaps one of the most misunderstood sexually deviant groups of modern times.

Objectum sexuals have loving relationships with objects instead of people. While that alone is certainly unusual, the way objectophiles talk about their relationships is similar to the way most of us describe our feelings about our human romantic partners. Take for example, American Erika Eiffel (formerly Erika Naisho prior to her marriage to the Tower). She is a world champion archer, who used to be in love with her archery bow, Lance, who she was initially attracted to "because of his looks" (Peakman 2013:387) and has also been in relationships with a Japanese sword "Tracie," the Berlin Wall, and the Golden Gate Bridge (Terry 2010). She even married the Eiffel Tower, who she describes as the "Grand Madame of Paris," in a public ceremony on April 8, 2007, where she "lifted her trench coat demurely, straddled one of the Eiffel Tower's massive steel foundations, and sealed the coital deal" by pressing into the structure (Bering 2013:118) (although she later stated in an interview that the director staged this interaction, see Eiffel, n.d. and Terry 2010). Erika describes her relationship with Lance, who she won two world championships with, as passionate and loving:

> My relationship [with Lance] was fantastic, simply put. My bow and I were inseparable and it showed in our ability to connect and perform. There was an energy flow between us that seemed to allow a unification, woman and object, to create a merged being. Though it has since ended, I am forever grateful that we maintained such an amazing relationship for nearly 10 years and as a result I have become a different and better person today.
>
> *(Eiffel n.d.)*

And Erika is not alone. Other objectophiles have publicly discussed their relationships. Englishwoman, Amanda Whittaker, is currently in love with the Statue of Liberty, which she affectionately nicknamed "Libby." Since falling in love with her in 2007, she has visited Libby regularly and while they are apart, she spends time accumulating figurines and other collectibles associated with the Statue of Liberty (Burke 2014). Canadian Val Theroux (who is one of the only public objectophiles who is currently married to another human man), takes an annual 7,000-mile round trip from Canada to England to visit her lover, an Oak tree in Brockenhurst, in the New Forest, Hampshire, who she describes as her "soulmate." During her visits, she wakes up early in the morning so she can be alone with him; she hugs him and stands with her back against him. Her husband of 40 years, John, jokingly describes the Oak as his wife's "tree lover" and seems to support their relationship. When she cannot be with her tree partner in person, Val stays in touch by viewing him on Google Earth (Hanlon 2012).

A subcategory of objectum sexuality, mechasexuality or mechaphilia, is sexual attraction to machines such as bicycles, motor vehicles, trains, helicopters, and airplanes. Objectophile and mechaphile Amy Wolfe has been in love with a roller coaster, a church organ "Paul," the Empire State Building, and the most tragic of all: the World Trade Center [following its 2001 demise, she "grieved her loss ... as one would a love" (Peakman 2013:388)]. She vowed to marry the Pennsylvanian roller coaster "1001 Nachts" in 2009 and change her last name to "Weber" (the manufacturer of the ride) stating: "I love him as much as women love their husbands and know we'll be together forever" (Otto 2009). Amy travels 160 miles, ten times per year to visit her husband and while they are apart, she carries around bolts she took from him and sleeps with a picture of the rollercoaster above her bed to feel closer to him (Otto 2009). A British man by the pseudonym "George" had an erotic relationship with a British-model Austin Metro car. He would masturbate multiple times a day both in and around the car as well as while looking at photographs of the car (De Silva and Pernet 1992). American Edward Smith claims that he has had over 1,000 sexual partners (but only one of them was actually human). He is now in a committed relationship with a white Volkswagen Beetle he calls "Vanilla" (Burke 2014). Then there is Adam:

> My name is Adam, and I'm in a relationship with my 1997 Saturn SW1 Station Wagon, Nina. We're so close emotionally and spiritually that I honestly consider her my wife ... Perhaps that vehicle is as much of a vessel for a soul as my body is a vessel for mine.
>
> *(Adam 2011)*

It is clear that objectophiles feel that their loving relationships with objects are akin to other human + human romances (or maybe even *better* than human relationships). They display a wide range of emotions and deep connections with their lovers (Marsh 2010). Some objectophiles are able to have their object-lovers in their homes (and some even live *in* them) while others, especially those in love with public monuments, view photos, online videos, and websites, create scaled-down models or sculptures, and express themselves through their own paintings, drawings, stories, poems, websites, films, and music to feel close with their lovers. Erika Eiffel even has tattoos of two of her partners including the Golden Gate Bridge and her wife, the Eiffel Tower (Marsh 2010).

As far as the "sex" goes, most prefer to use the word "intimacy" to describe this part of their object love. For example, referring to his sexual interest in a soundboard, one objectophile states: "We are very intimate in the bedroom, we spend a lot of time in bed together, but my pants usually stay on. Our intimacy is very above-the-waist, i.e. kissing, hugging, licking, etc." (Marsh 2010). Another man describes what he enjoys about his sexual relationship with common everyday fisheye buttons:

> [I] sew them onto clothes and straps which I wear on my genitals during masturbation ... The shape, texture, design, plastic material used, colours, the way the light works at a number of different depths (surface, internally), the feel on my fingers, lips. The plasticness [sic] against the material they are attached to. The coldness against my skin. The feeling of power they have for me. The control that comes from their perfection.
>
> *(Marsh 2010)*

Objectophiles' abilities to feel emotionally and intimately connected to their object-lovers set them apart from other fetishists. They emphasize "compassionate, empathic, spiritual, and sensual attachment this it is reciprocated with their object of desire" (Terry 2010:48). Some are even animists who believe that these objects have a spiritual essence or "soul." Although much is not understood about objectum sexuality, some research has found a high instance of Asperger's Syndrome (an autism spectrum disorder that is characterized by significant difficulties in social interaction) among objectophiles as well as the presence of sensory integration issues, ADD, ADHD, executive function issues, pervasive developmental disorders, depression, post-traumatic stress, Tourette syndrome, trauma, and abuse[8] (Marsh 2010; Terry 2010). Yet other objectum sexuals report none of these disorders or traumatic experiences (Marsh 2010).

Although nearly all objectum sexuals express emotional and sexual satisfaction with their orientation to objects, objectophilia is a difficult affinity to have. Objectophiles describe problems related to their love of objects such as human abuse (or total destruction) of their beloved objects and the inability to be publicly affectionate with them. However, the biggest obstacle objectophiles experience is a lack of acceptance by society, though most have been aware of their sexual attraction to objects since childhood, as Erika Eiffel describes in an interview:

> Indeed, there is a period of awakening for an OS person. In most cases, the deeper feelings for objects develop at the onset of puberty. As with other sexual minorities, a degree of societal oppression may cause some OS individuals to go against the grain and come out in later years.
>
> *(Eiffel n.d.)*

The majority of society does not see legitimacy in objectum sexuality. This lack of understanding can be particularly stressful for objectum sexuals who crave approval, as one objectophile stated: "I want people to accept me. I want to be able to take my lovers to the movies like anybody else. I want the public to accept us like [the] majority have homosexuals" (Marsh 2010). The plight of the objectum sexual is difficult because, as one objectophile notes: "[we want to] be free to express our love for our partners in the same way as anybody else would" (Marsh 2010).

Overall, objectophiles are diverse. Some have specific interests in transportation while others have sexualized technological devices, structures, or both (see Figure 10.5). Some sense gender in objects and some have gender preferences if they do sense an object's gender but others do not. They identify as heterosexual, gay/lesbian, bisexual, pansexual, and asexual. Some objectophiles have not had a human sexual relationship and would never consider it, some have had sexual human relationships in the past, and a small number are in human and object relationships concurrently. Some identify as polyamorous and have ongoing relationships with multiple objects at one time while others have a preference for monogamy. Most objectophiles feel a great deal of reciprocity from their object-lovers and/or "energy" from the objects they love and nearly all have sexual feelings as well as an emotional attraction to objects. For objectum sexuals, relationships with objects feel natural and appropriate. As one objectophile notes: "They are real. They are complex. They are no less and no more of value than other romantic relationships" (Marsh 2010). As so eloquently stated by one objectum sexual: "all feelings should be accepted and respected, no matter whom or what they are for" (Marsh 2010).

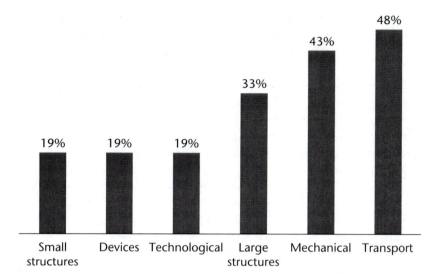

FIGURE 10.5   Objectophiles' object preferences

Data adapted from Marsh (2010).

Small structures: furniture, fences, stairs, ladders; devices: instruments, sporting equipment, work tools; technological: radios, TVs, computers; large structures: buildings, bridges, towers, walls, rail tracks; mechanical: machines, appliances; transport: automobiles, trains, aircraft, bikes, boats.

"Animal"-specific fetishes

Fetishizing animals and animal-like things is yet another area of sexual deviance that is rather diverse. For example, some develop a sexual fondness for animals (zoophilia) or a particular species of animal (avisodomy: sex with birds), some people enjoy the feel of small insects and creatures creeping and crawling on their bodies (formicophilia), still others actually engage in sex acts with non-human animals (bestiality). Some prefer to take their "animal"-specific fetish into the world of fantasy and embody their animal through costume (furry fandom) or sexualize stuffed toy animals (plushies). Some even go so far as to glamorize particular cartoon manifestations of animals, such as the case of adult fans of *My Little Pony* (bronies), only some of whom sexualize these animated horses (cloppers). Most of us have an adverse reaction to the sexualization of animals and animal-like things. There are many issues at play here: visceral gut responses to animal-human sex and the condemnation of such behavior, concern for the potential harm (and lack of consent) of the animal who is sexually targeted (see Box 10.2), as well as fear that sexual deviants who fetishize animals may escalate to hurting humans. Furthermore, in the fantasy world, the undeniable association of furry costumes, stuffed animals, and *My Little Pony* with children means that many see these fetishists as pedophilic (if not fully, at least marginally). Overall, the animal-specific world of fetishes is a complicated terrain. Acting out some of these fantasies can be illegal (in the case of bestiality in some states and countries) but for the majority, acting out animal-specific fetishes is legal, and if not, there is always zoophilic pornography.

BOX 10.2 HUMANS HAVING SEX WITH ANIMALS: CONSENT, HARM, AND ANIMAL CRUELTY

While there are many reasons that people and laws condemn humans who have sex with animals, one major argument against bestiality deals with consent, harm, and animal cruelty. Human sex with animals can be viewed as cruel and harmful because most would agree that animals cannot give consent [although zoophiles would argue the exact opposite (Williams and Weinberg 2003)]. What often follows this argument, however, is that animals do not consent to be slaughtered to become our food, so why can we not sexually pleasure an animal? Zoophiles would surely be quick to point out that bringing an animal to the point of orgasm is certainly more humane than slaughtering it to be eaten. But most simply do not agree with this notion. Even so, when animal-human sex cases come into the courts, the gray area within bestiality is often revealed.

For example, take the case of Robert Melia, a Moorestown, New Jersey, (suspended) police officer who was accused of sticking his penis into the mouths of five calves in rural Southampton in 2006. Although there was no doubt that the incident occurred (there is video footage of it), a Superior Court judge dismissed the charges of animal cruelty on his belief that a grand jury could not infer whether the cows had been "tormented" or "puzzled" by the situation. Burlington County Assistant Prosecutor Kevin Morgan disagreed proclaiming "I think any reasonable juror could infer that a man's penis in the mouth of a calf is torment . . . It's a crime against nature." And even though the owner of the cows was "very upset" by the incident and the judge agreed that Melia's actions were "disgusting," the judge ultimately did not believe that this behavior fit within the parameters of animal cruelty (Nark 2009).

Conversely, there is the case of Rodell Vereen, a South Carolina man who was arrested for having sex with a horse in 2009 while still on probation for having sex with *the same* horse in 2007. Barbara Kenly, the horse's owner, became suspicious when her 21-year-old female horse, Sugar, began acting strange and getting infections. After setting up a surveillance camera in the barn, Vereen was caught on camera having sex with Sugar. Vereen apologized to Kenly and told the court that he was off his medication (he indicated that he had "mental problems"). Ultimately, Vereen pled guilty to horse buggery, was sentenced to three years in prison, and is now required to register as a sex offender (Associated Press 2009).

These two cases show us that when humans are caught having sex with animals and the law intervenes, questions of consent, harm, and animal cruelty become paramount; however, there is no agreement about how to go about establishing a basis for any of these factors in animal-human sex acts. While a New Jersey judge decided that the calves were "unharmed" by Melia's penis in their mouths, a South Carolina judge ruled that Vereen's vaginal sex

with a horse necessitated a three-year prison sentence and a sex offender classification. Can animals consent to sex with humans? Are animals harmed by
sex with humans? Is it "cruel" for humans to engage in sex with animals?
There is no universal way to answer these questions. Most likely, an animal's
non-consent could be better established than consent. For example, if an animal fights back physically (through kicking, head butting, etc.) or must be tied
down for the human to complete the sex act, these could be signs of non-
consent (but not always, some animals routinely kick while mating). Potentially, harm could be established through physical markings on the animal
(bruising, tearing, etc.), although these markings may or may not indicate
injury. Animal cruelty is also a difficult case to make because the "humane"
treatment of animals is a debatable concept (although most agree that concern for animal welfare minimizes unnecessary pain and suffering of animals).
So a zoophile who has sex with an animal would claim that he/she did not
harm the animal, that the animal consented (perhaps through eye contact
and non-verbal cues), and that this was a humane and pleasurable interaction
for both parties. On the other hand, another might view the same human-
animal sex act as harmful, non-consensual, and inhumane due to any number
of arguments (it is disgusting, it is a crime against nature, etc.).

So amidst all this gray, how do we make sense of our strong aversion to
animal-human sex, and for that matter, other kinds of deviant sex? You may
be inclined to rely on "emotionally fueled tautologies" such as "it's wrong
because it's just nasty" or "you shouldn't do it because it's creepy" (Bering
2013:31). In a nutshell, this is "the disgust factor:" a powerful feeling that can
undermine our social intelligence and can even work as "a visceral engine of
hate" (such as in the commonly used defense for hurting/targeting deviants,
"he attacked him because he was *blinded by hate*") (Bering 2013:34). Disgust
is likely at the core of our attitudes toward animal-human sex and other forms
of sexual deviance because after all, "sex can be gross. And deviant sex, almost
by definition, is bound to gross out more people than normal sex" (Bering
2013:34). However, it is important to remember that even if we see something as "disgusting," that does not necessarily "justify the ravages of inequity
and oppression on the lives of sexual deviants themselves" (Bering 2013:34).
And while there are laws in place that make human-animal sex illegal in some
locations, having a fetish or affinity for sex with animals is never illegal.

Zoophilia and bestiality

Humans have always relied upon animals for food, as hunting partners, and as companions. But "man's best friend" has also been a sexual partner for some. Zoophiles
are those that have romantic and sexual feelings toward animals. While some engage
in sex acts with animals, most zoophiles see themselves as separate from bestialists
whose sexual interest in animals is purely based on physical gratification. By contrast,

zoophiles demonstrate "concern for the animal's welfare and pleasure and an emphasis on consent in the pursuit of sexual gratification" (Williams and Weinberg 2003:526). As one self-identified zoophile notes:

> A bestialist only has sex with an animal no matter what the cost for the animal is and the sole purpose of getting their jollies … my relationship with animals is a loving one in which sex is an extension of that love as it is with humans, and I do not have sex with a horse unless it consents.
>
> *(Williams and Weinberg 2003:526)*

Thus, for the zoophile, consent and minimizing harm are essential components of their sexual relationships with animals (how they define consent varies from person to person and animal to animal). For bestialists, sexual gratification is paramount. And then there are people who receive sexual gratification from purposeful cruelty to animals (zoosadists) who are the group whose animal-sexual interests are most likely to escalate to further criminal behavior.[9]

Sexualizing animals is not a modern phenomenon. Animal-human sex acts can be found in art, poetry, and literature throughout history. Some ancient Greek myths even glorify such behaviors. Although attitudes toward animal-human sex have varied throughout time, strong religious convictions in both the Torah and the Bible depict bestiality as unnatural and sinful. As a result, by the year 1000 C.E., humans suspected of bestiality were brought before the courts alongside their animal partners in crime and if found guilty, *both* were hanged or burned for their sins. Thus, during the Middle Ages, most animals[10] were deemed to be criminally culpable in tandem with their human sex partners. Punishment by death for bestiality was common until the 1800s and was then replaced by life imprisonment. Part of the concern about animal-human sex during this time was an emerging fear of "hybrids," or in other words, the fear that a child would be born who would be half animal, half human. The corruption of the human race via bestiality was certainly a very real concern for the better part of 100 years (Peakman 2013). But curiously, alongside this panic, we began to see human-animal love stories emerging in popular media such as *Beauty and the Beast* (de Beaumont 1756), *The Jungle Book* (Kipling 1920 [1894]), and even much later after hybrids were no longer a realistic concern, *King Kong* (Cooper and Schoedsack 1933). Thus, human + animal sexualization is (and always will be) present in society.

However, sexualizing animals is a relatively uncommon form of sexual deviance. For example, Kinsey's research in the 1940s to 1950s found evidence of bestiality in only 8 percent of men and 3.5 percent of women (Kinsey *et al.* 1948, 1953). In a modern Canadian study with 1,516 participants, only 2 percent of men and 3 percent of women reported fantasizing about having sex with an animal (Joyal *et al.* 2015) (see Figure 10.3 earlier in this chapter). Even so, public attention (and outrage) toward bestiality and zoophilia is ever present. For example, in the 1990s, American George Willard married his pony "Pixel" and even wrote a book in which he defended the rights of zoophiles entitled *The Horseman: Obsessions of a*

Zoophile (Matthews 1994). His story made the media circuit and most responded with pure disgust. In addition, animal rights groups have publicly attacked bestialists claiming that any sexual contact between humans and animals constitutes animal cruelty and should be punished (Beirne 2000). Most agree with this stance. For example, in the United States, the vast majority of states have laws criminalizing sex with animals. Some designate these behaviors as misdemeanors with minimal jail time and small fines and others define sex acts with animals as felonies with up to 50 year prison sentences. Thus, zoophilic pornography might be the only legal sexual outlet for those with sexual interests in animals in some places. As a result, "zoophiles operate within a cultural tradition that strongly condemns their behavior with animals as a transgression of a well-marked species boundary" (Williams and Weinberg 2003:524).

Who are these condemned sexual deviants? Some zoophiles are attracted to only specific breeds of a particular animal while others are less finicky in their species choice of sexual partners. Nearly all indicate that their sexual attraction to animals includes aesthetic characteristics such as posture, sleekness, and coat texture, as well as their behavioral qualities such as strength and power (especially when describing male animals) and grace and beauty (especially when describing female animals). Some are exclusive in their sexual practices with animals while others are married or have human sexual relationships as well as animal ones. Some prefer exclusively male or female animals and some prefer both. They self-identify as heterosexual, gay/lesbian, and bisexual. Interestingly, one study with 114 zoophile men found a relationship between the participants' sexual identity and the sex of the animals they were sexually interested in. For example, among self-identified heterosexual zoophile men, 70 percent indicated strong sexual feelings toward female animals. Most become aware of their sexual interests in animals at an early age and begin having sex with them in their teenage years. In fact, the main reason why most zoophiles continue to engage in sex with animals is because they find it to be pleasurable (Williams and Weinberg 2003).

Sexual relationships with animals include behaviors such as performing/receiving oral-genital sex, performing/receiving vaginal or anal sex, and masturbating the animal by hand. Zoophiles differ in their sexual preferences, especially depending on the size of the animal involved. Most commonly zoophile animal lovers are equines (i.e., horses, burros, donkeys) or dogs but there have also been reports of zoophile love with cats, cows, goats, sheep, chickens, dolphins, pigs, monkeys, and even smaller animals such as frogs and mice (however this sexual experience is more likely among formicophiles who enjoy small creatures crawling all over the body[11]). But zoophile animal love is about more than just sex for most. For example, in a study with over 100 zoophile men, the vast majority claimed that their relationships with animals were emotionally deep and almost all said they had been in love with an animal partner. Most even indicated that sex was more satisfying with animals and that they preferred sex with animals over human sex. As one zoophile notes: "I find the company of animals more pleasing than that of humans—there's less stress, fighting . . . Love with an animal is how love should be—a lot less complicated with no strings attached" (Williams and Weinberg 2003:531).

Furries and furry fandom

Remember going to theme parks when you were young where you would get to see your favorite "real life" cartoon characters dressed up in furry costumes? You may have even been so excited to see Mickey Mouse or Strawberry Shortcake that you ran up and gave him or her a hug. For most, this type of experience with an adult dressed up in a fur costume is nostalgic. For furries, this can be much more. Furries are interested in anthropomorphism (the ascription of human traits to animals) and/or zoomorphism (the ascription of animal traits to humans) (Plante et al. 2015). They often participate in furry fandom, a subculture of people interested in dressing up in full costumes known as "fursuits" or similar accessories (tails, collars, or partial fursuits that usually consist of a head, tail, hands, and/or feet) inspired by real animals (such as cat, lion, wolf, fox, dog, etc.), mythical animals (such as dragons, werewolves, and unicorns), and even specific cartoon characters such as ponies from *My Little Pony* (as in the case of bronies). Nearly all furries develop "fursonas" (read furry + persona), which often include a name, species type, color, personality, character history, and special abilities (Plante et al. 2015). Although most do not see their furry fandom as a fetish, some furries, but not all, even bring their fursonas into their sex lives (Lewis 2010).

Furry fandom is a relatively new phenomenon. Most accounts suggest that it started in the early 1980s and emerged out of science fiction fandom in which people enjoy dressing up as characters from their favorite sci-fi movies, books, etc. Throughout the 1980s, furries connected with one another through furry fanzines (magazines dedicated to furry fandom produced by fans) and in January of 1989, the first furry convention "ConFurence Zero" was held in Costa Mesa, California. Although attendance was low in 1989 (only 65 people were at ConFurence Zero), today the world's largest furry convention, "Anthrocon," draws over 5,000 furries annually. Currently, multiple websites, internet communities, online role-play virtual worlds, and forums exist to support furry fandom. There is even furry erotica to appeal to those with sexual interests in furry fandom.

Most furries are young white men aged 23 to 26 but women and older men also participate in furry fandom. Most are single and a sizeable amount still live at home with their parents (Plante et al. 2015). They describe themselves as heterosexual, gay/lesbian, bisexual, asexual, pansexual, omnisexual, and polyamorous (Gerbasi et al. 2008; Plante et al. 2015). Because furry lifestyles are necessarily sexually fluid (i.e., furries have both "real world" and fursona sexualities), furry fandom can allow furries to explore potentially stigmatizing aspects of their sexualities within a safe space (Plante et al. 2015). Furries identify either fully or partially with their fursona. For example, in the first-ever published study of furry fandom with 217 furry-identified respondents (187 men and 30 women), about half (46 percent) indicated that they did not consider themselves to be fully human and of that group, 41 percent indicated that they would become 0 percent human if they could (Gerbasi *et al.* 2008:214). Most (81 percent) reported "sharing characteristics in common with" their furry animal and about one-fourth of furries described "a persistent feeling of discomfort" about their human body and feeling like a "non-human species trapped in a human body" (Gerbasi *et al.* 2008:214). Furthermore, nearly half believed they were born with a mystical connection to their furry animal (Gerbasi *et al.* 2008). Thus, it is clear that for most, furry fandom is more than just a hobby, it is an identity (Lewis 2010).

The majority of furries connect to furry culture in their teenage years coinciding with pubertal development and a sizeable amount of furries incorporate their furry fandom into their sex lives in either a minor or major way. For example, a large percentage (96 percent of men furries and 78 percent of women furries) view furry pornography and some even engage in online sexual role-play (34 percent of men furries and 21 percent of women furries). However, most furries do not see sexuality as the defining motivator of their involvement in furry fandom (Plante *et al.* 2015). Even so, the sexual component of furry fandom is so well-developed that there is special lingo to describe the sex acts that take place between furries. For example, "yiffing" is a slang term used by the furry community to indicate fursuit sexual encounters (both virtual and real life) such as petting, hugging, and "scritching" (light scratching and grooming). Some furries even have their fursuits designed with specialized openings to allow for penetrative sex acts to occur while donning their fursuits.

In a related fetish, plushies eroticize children's stuffed animals or puppets and sometimes engage in sex acts with them, as one plushophile notes: "In Plush We Thrust" (Gates 2000:224). And this can go even further, as in the case of cloppers. Cloppers are a specialized group of bronies (adult furry fans of *My Little Pony: Friendship is Magic*[12]) who sexualize the ponies in various ways and enjoy erotic *My Little Pony* art. Bronies comprise a sizable minority of furries [about 20 percent (Plante *et al.* 2015] but because of their association with a children's cartoon (and more specifically a *girls'* cartoon and toy genre) bronies (and especially cloppers) are highly stigmatized even within the furry community (Jones 2015).

Furries, plushies, bronies, and cloppers find a home in online communities, online role-playing virtual worlds, and large conferences such as Anthrocon and BronyCon. In fact, most view the personal and social relationships that they cultivate through furry fandom as their main influence for continuing the furry lifestyle. Because there is a high incidence of Asperger's syndrome within the furry community, furries may be particularly likely to use their fantasy lifestyle to both escape from stigmatizing experiences and other undesirable aspects of their daily lives as well as to motivate themselves or "to cope with failure, as a means of self-expression, or as a form of recreation" (Plante *et al.* 2015:122).

Overall, furries are imaginative but also quite unconventional (Gerbasi *et al.* 2008). They are graphic artists, photographers, writers, and poets. They are also spiritual; many even have a deep reverence for nature and believe in magic and mysticism (Gerbasi *et al.* 2008; Plante *et al.* 2015). Their interest in "furry" forms of sex represents a form of sexual deviance that is misunderstood and highly stigmatized, especially because of its association with children's themes (i.e., furry costumes, stuffed animals, and *My Little Pony*). Even so, for most furries, furry fandom is a positive and rewarding social experience that allows them to explore fantasy and sexual diversity.

Role-play fetishes

Nurse and patient, schoolgirl/boy and teacher, cop and criminal, mistress/master and slave, French maid and "dirty" home owner, prisoner and warden: each of these represents a role-play scenario. But more than just a game of dress-up, these role-play scenarios are often about power and control. Sexual role-play typically involves an arrangement whereby one partner is dominant, the "Dom" (or for women: "Domme" or "Femdom"), and the other is submissive, the "sub." What is often misunderstood about the Dom/sub arrangement (also referred to as D/s) is that the sub has the most power because he/she controls the activities that take place. D/s role-play fetishes can include any number of arrangements from puppy training [teaching the sub to follow commands such "obey," "sit," or "heel" (Bramwell 2007:42)] and pony play (saddling up the sub like a horse and grooming, training, and sometimes riding him/her), to forniphilia (turning the sub into a piece of human furniture, see Image 10.3) to those focused exclusively on bondage and discipline (BD) and/or pain and sensuality (sadomasochism) and even total power

IMAGE 10.3 Forniphilia

Human woman behaving as a piece of furniture. ©Shutterstock, jwblinn exchange (a 24/7 D/s relationship) (Lewis 2010). Sometimes the Dom even controls the shape of the sub's body through tight-lacing (an extreme form of continuous corseting whereby the waist can be shrunk overtime to an unnaturally small size, such as 13 inches in the case of the Guinness World Record holder,[13] see Image 10.4a), feeding (a fat admirer feeder's fetish is derived from watching extremely obese women eat copious amounts of food, sometimes over long periods of time to the point where the woman becomes immobile at 800 pounds or more) or in ancient practices such as foot binding (see Image 10.4b) (Steele 1996; Gates 2000; Lewis 2010). Whatever character or activity D/s participants choose to take on, all responsible role-play fetishists follow the standards of safe, sane, and consensual (see Box 10.3).

SM by Samantha A. Wallace

SM is a "collection of activities that involve the mutually consensual and conscious use, among two or more people, of pain, power, perceptions about power, or any combination thereof, for psychological, emotional, or sensory pleasure" (Newmahr 2011:18). SM practices may or may not include bondage and discipline (BD), thus, the more commonly used acronym "BDSM" encompasses behaviors outside SM. Socially, SM and BDSM terms may be used to reference the same players, but the acts that constitute each realm vary.

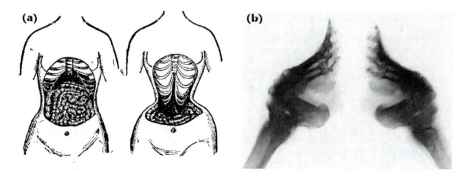

IMAGE 10.4   Two historical examples of the effects of extreme bondage

Image (a) illustrates a 1903 depiction of a normal woman's internal anatomy contrasted with the predicted effects of continuous long-term corseting on the internal organs and bones. While most Victorian women wore corsets, the majority did not wear them continuously. Today, continuous corseting is called "tight-lacing" and is an extreme form of body play. Image (b) is an X-ray of a Chinese woman's bound feet (circa 1890 to 1923). Foot binding was the practice of applying painfully tight bandages to the feet of young girls to prevent further growth and to ultimately cultivate a beautiful, erotic, but broken and mangled extremely tiny foot (the ideal foot was 4 inches in length). Originating in the tenth century, foot binding was popular for several centuries in ancient China but was banned in 1912 (the last case of footbinding was reported in 1957) (Ko 2007). Today, foot bondage is most often temporary, as in the case of the ballet fetish boot (see Image 10.1).
©Shutterstock, Everett Historical

BOX 10.3 SAFE, SANE, AND CONSENSUAL

Samantha A. Wallace

The SM ethos of *safe, sane, and consensual* creates a safe, controlled environment for players to experience pleasure that separates SM play from sex and violence (Fedoroff 2008).

- *Safe* is being knowledgeable about the techniques and safety involved in SM play as well as the potential risks involved with specific types of SM play. Bound by ritual and education, players practice safety by learning to properly perform SM acts, avoiding violence and preventing serious injury (Newmahr 2011). This is particularly important because SM exists in a spectrum where edgier and riskier play requires more evolved learning (Lindemann 2011).
- *Sane* is being of sound mind and knowing the difference between fantasy and reality (Gates 2000).
- *Consensual* is agreeing upon, recognizing, and respecting the limits imposed by SM players. For example, utilizing a *safeword* in a scene.

Being educated, being safe, and knowing risks involved, players consent to SM play, alleviating any notions of coercion. These principles not only shape the practices of SM play, but also operate as a formal set of normative values within the SM community such that violators of this ethos are stigmatized as undesirable partners (Lindemann 2011). Overall, the safe, sane, consensual ethos serves to prevent harm to other players and secure voluntary pleasurable power exchanges.

SM experiences are often highly ritualized and codified by both standards and language. Beyond the principles outlined in Box 10.3, SM involves *players* (those participating) in *play* (SM behaviors) occurring in the context of a *scene* (ritualized pleasurable exchanges between players bounded by hard and soft limits). The activities to take place are mutually and consensually agreed upon between players prior to scenes (Pitagora 2013). For example, within a scene, players have a *safeword* that immediately ends a scene of play, creating trust between players and setting boundaries (Faccio *et al.* 2014). The safeword is an example of a *hard limit*, an absolutely unsurpassable boundary, compared to a *soft limit*, a boundary that can be pushed (Newmahr 2011). Players are further differentiated as *tops* (those that seize power or control) and *bottoms* (those that relinquish power to another); however, pain/power imbalances may not always be concurrently present in SM (Apostolides 1999). For Doms, having absolute control over another can be a source of pleasure while for subs, relinquishing power in these interactions derives considerable pleasure. Ultimately, a bottom (sub) player holds the most power in a scene because he/she sets the boundaries in relation to his/her mental, emotional, and physical limits (Newmahr 2011).

Although psychological literature suggests that people who participate in SM behaviors are doing so to cope with trauma experiences (e.g., Abrams and Stefan 2012), sociological explanations suggest that SM can serve as an outlet for those who seek pain/pleasure experiences. In particular, SM can provide a safe space for players to experience and exert control upon another. Because SM can be considered "make-believe" role-play, such behaviors can be transformative and spiritually fulfilling (Buenting 2003) and may also serve therapeutic purposes for some where other traditional therapies may fall short (Lindemann 2011). Overall, SM creates pleasurable exchanges between players, often using power exchanges and imbalances.

To most SM players, their behaviors are nonpathological. And although the DSM does not categorize interests in sadomasochism as evidence of mental illness unless they cause distress/harm to the fetishist or the object of his/her fetish play (DSM-5 Fact Sheet 2013), the outsider looking in may see these types of behaviors as especially sexually deviant. Indeed, most do not view sadomasochism or pain/pleasure experiences as "normal" sexual behaviors (Janus and Janus 1993). Even so, amongst a wide range of fetishistic behaviors, those involving SM-related activities such as spanking and the use of restraints and nipple clamps are viewed as more acceptable when compared to other fetishes such as agalmatophilia and furry sex (see Figure 10.7 later in this chapter). Furthermore, fantasizing about pain/pleasure experiences is relatively normal. For example, in a Canadian study with 1,516 participants, over half fantasized about being dominated sexually, and being spanked, whipped, or tied up (or being the Dom in this type of experience) were also common fantasies among men and women (see Figure 10.6). Thus, the deviance of SM play is built from social attitudes that stigmatize the pain/pleasure matrix but fantasizing about such activities is a rather normative experience.

Summarizing fetishes

In this chapter we have learned about a variety of fetishes including those from the realms of "object"-specific and "animal"-specific as well as the world of role-play. We have learned about the diverse practices associated with these types of fetish play as well as who these fetishists are. But there are so many more fetishes out there including (see also Box 10.4):

> Shoes, feet, trampling, long fingernails/toe nails, stockings, pantyhose, mouths, tongues, teeth, dentistry, smoking, noses, nasal mucus, sneezing, hair, hairlessness, adult nursing, fat admirers, fat feeders, body inflation, pregnancy, height, age difference, smells, sounds, tastes, tickling, pain, defilement, soiling, vomit, spitting, sweat, tears, urine, feces, flatulence, blood, vampirism, menstrual blood, disability, amputees, casts, blind play, rubber, fur, leather, silk, masks, glasses, diapers, infantilism, human cows, cannibal fantasy, vorarephilia somnophilia, necrophilia, giantness, palm size women, pony play, puppy play, medical

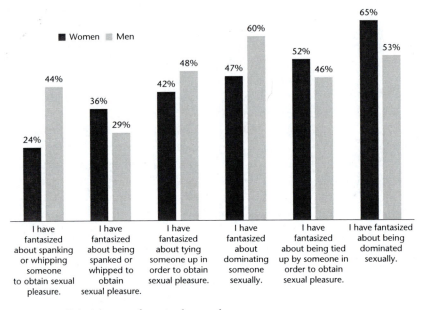

FIGURE 10.6 Pain/pleasure fantasies by gender

Data adapted from Joyal *et al.* (2015).

fetish, urethral play, catheter play, speculum play, vacuum pumping, prostate massage, deliberate clitoral enhancement, enemas, inflatables, balloons, wet and messy play, robbery, erotic asphyxiation, sexual arousal from weaponry, ravishment, arousal from crime, anal play, ass worship, bug chasers, objects, structures, statues, dolls, robots, zoophilia, insects, crush fetish, furry fandom, soft toys, voyeurism, exhibitionism, dogging, frotteurism, mirrors, transvestic fetishism, autogynephilia, transsexualism, domination, submission, total power exchange, consensual nonconsensuality, training, collaring for commitment, femdom, forced feminization, lift and carry, CFNM, hand over mouth, erotic sexual control, milking, facesitting, smothering, cuckholding, financial domination, erotic humiliation, sadomasochism, breast bondage, bondage furniture and fittings, collars, crucifixion bondage, chains, cuffs, hair bondage, predicament bondage, nose hooks, rope bondage, suspension bondage, mummification bondage, discipline, spanking, corner time, whipping, flogging, caning, chastity play, erotic control, forced orgasm, orgasm denial, clamps, sensory deprivation, blindfolds, hoods, abrasions, cock rings, caging, fetish clothing.

(Lewis 2010:viii–xiii)

Fetishes out of the bedroom

The majority of fetish play is a "private" affair. But sometimes fetishes extend beyond the parameters of the four walls you may call home and out into the "real" world. This can be in fetish-focused establishments such as clubs and dungeons or even in everyday

BOX 10.4 LIST OF PARAPHILIAS

Acrotomophilia: arousal to amputees.

Actirasty: arousal to the sun's rays.

Anasteemaphilia: arousal to a fantasy person of extreme stature, either a giant or an extremely tiny person.

Apotemnophilia: arousal to oneself as an amputee.

Autogynephilia: arousal to oneself [men only] in the form of a woman.

Chasmophilia: arousal to small spaces.

Climacophilia: arousal to falling down stairs.

Coprophilia: arousal to feces, being defecated on or defecating on others.

Cratophilia: arousal to displays of strength.

Dendrophilia: arousal to trees.

Ephebophilia: arousal to older adolescents, approximately aged 15 to 19.

Gerontophilia: arousal to the elderly.

Hebephilia: arousal to pubescent adolescents, approximately aged 11 to 14.

Katoptronophilia: arousal to mirrors, especially sex in front of mirrors.

Knismolagnia: arousal to tickling.

Lithophilia: arousal to stones and rocks.

Melissaphilia: arousal to bees, wasps and other stinging insects.

Nasolingus: arousal to sucking on a person's nose.

Nebulophilia: arousal to fog.

Necrophilia: arousal to corpses.

Partialism: arousal to a body part other than the reproductive organs, e.g., elbows.

Pedophilia: arousal to prepubescent children, approximately aged 10 and under.

Podophilia: arousal to feet.

Psellismophilia: arousal to stuttering.

Psychrophilia: arousal to being cold and watching others who are cold.

Pteronphilia: arousal to being tickled by feathers.

Pubephilia: arousal to pubic hair.

Pygophilia: arousal to buttocks.

Pyrophilia: arousal to fire and fire starting.

Savantophilia: arousal to the cognitively impaired or developmentally delayed.

Stygiophilia: arousal to the thought of hellfire and damnation.

Urophilia: arousal to urine, being urinated on or urinating on others.

Vorarephilia: arousal to being eaten or to eating another person's body parts.

Xylophilia: arousal to wood.

life. Fetishists of all types have annual conferences, balls, and festivals such as the leather/fetish/SM-focused San Francisco Folsom Street Fair, hosted by the Sisters of Perpetual Indulgence (see Box 10.5), which draws more than 400,000 visitors annually and yes, clothing is optional on these 13 city blocks because "nude is not lewd" for the duration of the fair (Folsomstreetfair.com). Today, fetishists have more public visibility than ever before and although there is still a strong stigma attached to these types of sex play, the strong social presence of these communities suggests a lessening negativity toward at least some of these groups.

BOX 10.5 THE SISTERS OF PERPETUAL INDULGENCE

Sister Libby Rayshun

The Sisters of Perpetual Indulgence is a non-profit organization dedicated to promoting human rights, respect for diversity, and spiritual enlightenment. It all started on Easter Sunday in 1979 in San Francisco, California. Three gay men decided to do something a little different one day and throw on some nun's habits and parade down the streets of The Castro District (a lively gay neighborhood in the heart of San Francisco). The response to their appearance was so powerful that they eventually decided to found The Sisters of Perpetual Indulgence. Dressed as campy nuns with white painted faces and exaggerated colorful make-up and outrageous accessories (see Image 10.5), the Sisters use humor to combat bigotry while providing social and charitable outreach to the global LGBTQ community.

During the early 1980s, they produced the world's first HIV/AIDS benefit and also published *Play Fair!*, the first HIV/AIDS educational pamphlet to use sex-positive language, practical advice, and humor to discuss safer-sex issues (*Play Fair!* was re-issued in 1999 and updated to be all gender inclusive). In 1992, the Sisters formed an alliance that still exists today with other organizations in an effort to host the Folsom Street Fair, one of the world's largest fetish festivals. The Sisters have a strong presence at many LGBTQ events and their cheerful painted faces and comical nun's habits remind us to see the humor in sex and to feel joyful and confident about our identities (Stein *et al.* 2012).

Today, the Sisters have grown into an internationally recognized non-profit organization that has over 35 separate chapters in most major cities of the United States, as well as Europe, Australia, and parts of South America (Qetesh 2015). Inclusive of members of all gender and sexual identities, the Sisters take public vows to promulgate universal joy, to expiate stigmatic guilt, and to serve their respective communities through outreach and charitable work. Overall, the sisters utilize camp humor and their creative, shocking, and comical appearances to draw attention to issues affecting the LGBTQ community to create awareness and social change.

IMAGE 10.5   Sister of Perpetual Indulgence
Sister Mora Lee Wong pictured here manning the gates and security check points at the
Folsom Street Fair in San Francisco, CA (USA) in 2013. Image used with permission from
Sister Mora Lee Wong.

Fetish clubs/dungeons

Some might venture out to a fetish club or a sex dungeon to meet up with others
and/or find partners with similar sexual interests. Others might enjoy fetish clubs
because they typically have a variety of equipment available that most cannot
afford to have in their homes. For example, at a SM fetish club, you might find
St. Andrews crosses (an apparatus that provides restraining points for ankles,
wrists, and waist), spanking benches, whipping posts, cages, slings, suspension
and bondage hooks, and various SM gadgets (but often it is B.Y.O.B.G.: bring
your own bondage gear) such as steel/leather handcuffs, leg spreaders, bondage
tape, plastic wrap, paddles, riding crops, floggers, bullwhips, ball gags, muzzle
gags, blindfolds, latex masks, collars and leashes, dildos, vibrators, strap-ons, cock

rings, butt plugs, nipple clamps, and straightjackets. Overall, these establishments can be appealing to SM fetishists as well as exhibitionists and voyeurs who enjoy public sex experiences.

Fetish fashion

Fetish fashion is a catch-all term used to describe various clothing styles associated with fetishes. You might see fetish fashion worn in fetish sex clubs ranging from full-body latex suits to black leather hobble skirts and ballet fetish boots or even people walking around entirely nude except for nipple and cock rings. But you might also see people donning fetish gear in their daily lives. Fetishes change over time and thus, so does fetish fashion. For example, "The Victorians went crazy over silk and velvet when these were rare textiles. As quickly as new substances are manufactured, somebody eroticizes them" (Califia 2000:205). Today's fetish fashion can be divided into three categories:

- *Lace.* Anything lacey, fluffy, frilly, or fuzzy fits into this category. Textiles such as velvet, satin, silk, and taffeta as well as feathers and fur are popular fetish accessory textures. "Lace" fetish-gear consists of lingerie, corsets, stockings, garter belts, fishnets, gloves, slips, teddies, petticoats, and even full period costumes.
- *Leather.* Historically the link between sex and leather has been primarily associated with leathermen's attire (see Box 10.6) but really anything made of leather can fit into this category. Leather's companionship with cowboys and bikers (in the form of chaps, boots, pants, vests, hats, etc.) drives the sexual eroticism of leather and it can also be seen in combination with metal (such as in the case of 1960s to 1970s "punk" style with studded dog collars, chains, and extreme facial/sexual piercings and its continuation with 1980s "goths" and 1990s/2000s "emos"). Many aspects of leather can be sexually arousing including the "sight, smell, feel, creak [sounds leather makes while walking/rubbing] ... as well as the aura of sexuality that comes from wearing it" (Lewis 2010:152).
- *Latex/Rubber.* Anything made of latex, rubber, PVC, neoprene, or any other "wet-look" manmade material that is smooth, shiny, and constrictive fits into this category. This can include full body rubber suits, masks, pants, corsets, gloves, and catsuits (see Image 10.6). Some enjoy the sounds latex/rubber makes when rubbed and even the smell but the main appeal is its restrictive quality, it "embraces, constrains, enforces posture and yet can create a strict and commanding presence in the person who wears it" (Califia 2000:201). Latex/rubber is even more restrictive than leather because it is an unbreathable material. The wet-like slick surface can also be a sexual aid: "it turns your whole body into a lubricating erogenous surface" (Steele 1996:153).

One thing nearly all fetish fashion items have in common is color: "black is a uniquely powerful color—abstract, pure, mysterious" (Steele 1996:190). People might choose to wear fetish-associated clothing in public or semi-public (at fetish clubs, conventions, balls, etc.) for practical reasons such as to advertise to others that

BOX 10.6 LEATHERMEN

Trenton M. Haltom

Gay and bisexual men who fetishize leather apparel and/or accessories are often referred to as "leathermen." This community first emerged when military servicemen had difficulties assimilating back into mainstream society after the Second World War. For these men, their time in the service allowed them to explore their homosocial desires and when the war ended, they mourned the loss of their same-sex friendships and sexual relationships they had cultivated while serving overseas. Looking for camaraderie, they found comfort in small niche motorcycle communities that embraced leather. But beyond motorcycles and leather gear, the men who rode the bikes were both outlaws and icons of the ideal hyper-masculine sexual man (Hennen 2008). This image of danger and rebellious masculinity was attractive to gay and bisexual ex-military men seeking a new masculine identity and as a result, these men "began to invest leather with a certain erotic power intimately tied to the way it signaled masculinity" while simultaneously distancing themselves from effeminacy (Hennen 2008:140; Lahti 1998). Quickly, leather gear became a symbol of sexual interest in other men, but because of the raw masculinity that leather evokes, leather (and the sex that came with it) shaped a new form of masculinized gay identity among leathermen (Harris 1997).

The ideal leatherman was popularized through famous images produced by artists such as Tom of Finland[1] who set the standard for the "quintessential leatherman replete with bulging chest, thighs, and cock" (Tyburczy 2014:278). An entire subculture emerged that allowed gay and bisexual men to be both masculine *and* interested in those of the same sex. By donning leather gear, leathermen broadcast their sexual interests in sadomasochism, bondage, and disciplinary sex acts sometimes known as "leathersex" (Hennen 2008). Those in the leather community, however, may also extend their sexual interests to include rubber and sports-related gear such as jock straps, jerseys, sneakers, and tube socks (Tyburczy 2014). However, not all leathermen have interests in sexual kink, some simply like to wear leather.

Leathermen are sometimes distinguished as "Old Guard" and "New Guard." The post-WWII "Old Guard" leathermen typically connect strongly with the military history of leather culture and promote formality, hierarchy, discipline, and respect within their code of conduct (Townsend 1972 [2000]; Weal 2010). These traditions are valorized within the so-called "leather bible:" *The Leatherman's Handbook* (Townsend 1972 [2000]). The "New Guard" leathermen are amongst the most recent evolution of leather culture (emerging in the 1990s). Most see New Guard as less rigid and more inclusive. For example, New Guard leather culture includes lesbian and bisexual women and even heterosexuals (Califia 2000). As a result, there is sometimes contention between New and Old Guard leathermen. Even so, the leather community's diversity is apparent.

Wearing leather can be transformative, it can evoke solidarity among the alienated, it can be a symbol of self-expression and sexual exploration, and it can be a spiritual experience (Harris 1997). Overall, the leather community represents much more than leather-clad motorcycle men. For leathermen, leather is a way of life.

Notes

[1]The works of Finnish cartoonist Touko Laaksonen (1920–1991) known as "Tom of Finland" depict sexualized (often semi-nude) hyper-masculine muscular men in leather gear. His sexually graphic drawings of working class men (such as sailors, policemen, bikers, lumberjacks, construction workers, cowboys, and farm hands) were first circulated through physique magazines in the 1950s, and in the 1970s, Tom of Finland's collective works (of which there are more than 3,500 drawings) were popularized in art exhibitions in the United States. Today, his art represents a sense of nostalgia for how far the modern gay movement has come. By emphasizing bulging muscles and raw masculinity in the context of same-sex sexuality, Tom of Finland's drawings were amongst the first visible symbols of gay culture that opposed the stereotypes of gay men as passive, prissy, and weak. Overall, his art depicted gay men not as effeminate, but rather as hyper-masculine confident and sexual beings. And in doing so, Tom of Finland single-handedly offered a more empowering and affirmative gay icon (Lahti 2008).

they are interested in a particular form of fetish play (i.e., wearing leather chaps to show association with the leather community) or to actually participate in fetish play (i.e., a sub wearing a dog collar[14] and being led by his/her Dom on a leash). Either way, it is sexually titillating: "fetish fashion draws attention to the sexual aspects of the body, while simultaneously restricting access to it" (Steele 1996:193). But beyond this, fetish fashion is often a bold statement. In particular, some women wear fetish fashion to convey strength and power: "the sex-and-power 'bad girl' image is part of the appeal of fetish fashion for women" (Steele 1996:44). Fetish fashion can even be a statement of defiance: "the growing popularity of fetish fashions within the wider culture is directly related to the charisma of deviance. Evil, rebellion, danger, and pleasure exert a powerful emotional appeal" (Steele 1996:193).

Why fetishism?

Now that we have learned about a variety of fetishes and their manifestations, you may be asking yourself one big question: *WHY?* Why do some people eroticize balloons while others get their jollies from women's breasts? Some link fetishisms to childhood abuse and severe trauma. Others blame "porn, the Devil, bad parents, poor role models, our sexually repressed culture, or the psychiatrists" (Bering 2013:165-166). Some particularly horrific violent sex criminals have histories of fetishism but most fetishists are not (and never will be) violent criminals (however, some are, see Box 10.7). The simple truth is: "nobody chooses

IMAGE 10.6 Woman in a latex bodysuit

Woman in a full latex bodysuit and gas mask. ©Shutterstock, DoctorKan

their own sexual triggers and there is no single cause for any particular sexual variation" (Gates 2000:9).

While we cannot know exactly why certain people have certain types of sexual fetishes, we can know a little about what purposes sexual fantasies (and accompanying fetishisms) can serve. For example, in one of the largest-ever international studies of sexual fantasies based on responses from 20,153 British and American individuals, nearly all (90 percent of women and 96 percent of men) fantasized about sex and they indicated various reasons why they did (Kahr 2008:356–7):

- Fantasies help me to relieve boredom.
- Fantasies cheer me up when I am depressed.

BOX 10.7 SEX CRIMINALS AND FETISHISM

While it is certainly true that most fetishists are not violent criminals who seek to hurt and torture people against their will, some people do fit this profile. For example, American serial killer Ted Bundy (1946–1989), who started out as a voyeurist "peeping" in the windows of unsuspecting women and watching them undress, escalated to rape, torture, murder, and necrophilia (see more in chapter 6, Box 6.2). Other prolific serial killers have co-existing fetishisms and horrifying violent tendencies such as American serial killer Jeffrey Dahmer (1960–1994), who was a rapist and murderer as well as a necrophiliac, cannibalist, and vorarephiliac. There are also links between various fetishes, crime, and nonconsensual violence such as:

- Zoosadism and violent behavior directed toward humans including rape and murder (Johnson and Becker 1997).
- Sexual sadism, voyeurism, and exhibitionism and violent crimes including rape and murder (Woodworth *et al.* 2013).
- Agalmatophilia and sadism (Ferguson 2010; Smith 2013). Sex doll repairman, Slade Fiero, has described several instances where RealDolls have been brutalized and "hacked to pieces" (Ferguson 2010:128).
- Agalmatophilia and necrophilia[1] (Ferguson 2010). Necrophiles are interested in corpses because they desire control over an "eternally silent, submissive, and obedient sex partner" and for some, the sex doll can function as "the fresh corpse of a beautiful deceased woman" (Ferguson 2010:136).

However, even among sex criminals, fetishisms are not universal. For example, while a large percentage (between 74 and 85 percent) of sex offenders have sexual paraphilic disorders, not all do (Dunsieth *et al.* 2004; Woodworth *et al.* 2013). Thus, not all fetishists are sex criminals and not all sex criminals are fetishists. Of course, there are some fetishes that are illegal (for the most part) such as exhibitionism, voyeurism, and frotteurism (see Table 10.1 for descriptions of these paraphilias). But there are *legal* ways to partake in such fetishisms. For example, in Japan, there are actually clubs designed to appeal to frotteurists often mimicking crowded areas such as subway cars and busy shopping centers (frottage has become such a large problem in Japan that the subway system now includes "women-only" trains). In addition, fetish pornography, sex clubs, and online role-playing communities can all be utilized to engage in exhibitionism and voyeurism (as well as other fetishes) safely and legally. However, there are some behavioral patterns that suggest links between fetishism and current or future criminal behavior. Specifically, fetishistic behavior is most likely to lead to hurting others against their will when (Kahr 2008:418–9):

- The fetishistic person treats people as objects, violates the object of his/her desire's bodily boundaries and shows no concern for him/her.

- The fetishistic behaviors are compulsive and repetitive. No amount of threat or legal injunction can prevent the person from engaging in the activity.
- The fetish-oriented behavior is predominantly used to release pent-up sexual anxieties (not to develop intimacy) and/or used to express hatred.

Overall, fetishes can sometimes be related to nonconsensual violence but there is not a perfect overlap between fetishistic behavior and sex offending. As a result, when understanding the relationships between sex crime and fetishes, one should consider how the fetishist manages his/her sexual deviance and what other behavioral patterns coexist. More about sex crime and criminals is provided in unit IV.

Notes

[1]Agalmatophilia has also been linked to other fetishes including those associated with lactation, amputation, pregnancy, the elderly, children, and bestiality (Ferguson 2010; Smith 2013). Matt McMullen, the owner and creator of RealDoll, frequently receive requests for "unusual" dolls and does not typically entertain them, he notes: "one chap even wanted a replica of a canine. He offered me $50,000 to do it . . . but I just couldn't" (Smith 2013:249).

- Fantasies allow me to perform acts that I cannot do in real life.
- Fantasies permit me to have sex with people whom I would not or could not have sex with in real life.
- Fantasies permit me to explore different sexual thoughts and activities.
- My partner becomes more attractive to me in my fantasies.
- Fantasies help me to become aroused with my partner or partners.
- I cannot help myself. The fantasies just pop into my mind.
- Fantasies are preferable to actual sexual experiences.
- Fantasies make the outside world go away.

Thus, the functions of sexual fantasy vary from wish fulfillment to indulgence in masochism and/or sadism, discharge of aggression, and avoidance of painful reality, to self-comfort, mastery of trauma, and equilibration of the self (Kahr 2008).

Who are fetishists?

For the most part, fetishists are normal everyday Joes/Janes/Zanes. As noted in Box 10.7, while some fetishists are horrific violent sex criminals, most fetishists are not. Even if they have violent or criminal tendencies, they may choose to responsibly indulge in their fetishes through fetish-oriented pornography or online role-playing sex games, or even hire sex workers to safely act out their fantasies. Overall, fetishists are just like you and me. In fact, they *are* you and me.

And their backgrounds, personalities, and attitudes are just as diverse as most groupings of individuals.

One rather common pattern is that there are more men fetishists than women fetishists. In fact, many of the fetishes discussed in this chapter are more often found among men than women. There are several reasons why this might be the case. It could be that men actually have more fetishistic tendencies than women do, thus, there is a "real" gender difference in fetishism. Related, biological arguments suggest that because males typically have more testosterone than females (which increases libido), men are more likely to have focused and specific sexual urges that might lead to fetishistic activities (Gates 2000). Conversely, many have argued that sex/gender differences in fetishisms may be less about biology and more about culture:

- Compared to men, women are more concerned with impression management and they may fear that engaging in deviant sex might lead to stigmatization so they avoid it altogether (Gates 2000).
- Many cultural scripts cultivate diverse sexual exploration among men (consider the pornography industry's wide appeal to men) while women are more likely to close off or shut down their sexual interests in general, especially if they think they are somehow strange, unusual, or even frightening (Gates 2000).
- Because men are socialized to view their sexual performances as both imperative to their relationships and to their masculine selves, they are more likely to visit sex clinics/psychiatrists to assist them with their "unusual" sexual interests. In contrast, as women do not have to be aroused to engage in a sex act, they may accept their lack of sexual satisfaction at face value rather than looking more deeply in to their non-normative sexual desires (Gates 2000).
- Compared to men, women are less likely to even be aware of their own fetish affinities. For example, in a study of female sexual arousal, even though many women experienced vasocongestion (engorged labia and lubrication) in response to sexual stimuli, they did not indicate sexual arousal when prompted. Put succinctly, "genital arousal does not correspond to a woman's stated sexual interests in the way that it does for men" (Chivers and Bailey 2005:115).
- The current methods of assessing fetishes among men and women are inadequate (Chivers et al. 2010).

Overall, we simply know more about men's experiences with fetishes (and how to understand them) than we do women's. Cultural scripts and gendered socialization processes generate sex differences in fetishisms but as the internet brings more women "out of the closet" and into the world of fetishism, we are seeing shifts toward parity (Gates 2000). For example, one study of college students found that in just a ten-year period, the gender gap in the variety of sexual fantasies that men and women reported decreased significantly (Hsu et al. 1994). Fetishists are a diverse and complicated group of individuals and because what is described as a "fetish" and what is "normal" varies by location, time, and space, *anyone* can be labeled as a fetishist.

Perceptions of fetishists and "us" versus "them" mentalities

Many people view fetishists as "socially wrong" or even worse, as violent perverts who should be quarantined away from us "normals:"

> We tend to assume that anyone who has weird sex is some kind of criminal, or at the very least, crazy and out of control. We believe that sexual compulsions rule deviants' lives, as if non-conformist sexual thoughts ... automatically lead to addiction and criminal behavior.
>
> *(Gates 2000:6)*

For example, when asked to rate their attitudes toward 132 sexual behaviors using a feeling thermometer (from 1 = cold to 10 = warm), only a handful were rated positively (such as vaginal intercourse, oral sex, sensual massage, and foreplay), while the vast majority of sex acts inquired about were rated particularly negatively (lowest rated behaviors include arousal from vomit and feces). Of particular interest, respondents rated many of the fetishes described in detail in the current chapter. As seen in Figure 10.7, people were moderately accepting of role-play and SM-oriented behaviors (restraints, spanking, nipple clamps), less accepting of retifism and podophila,

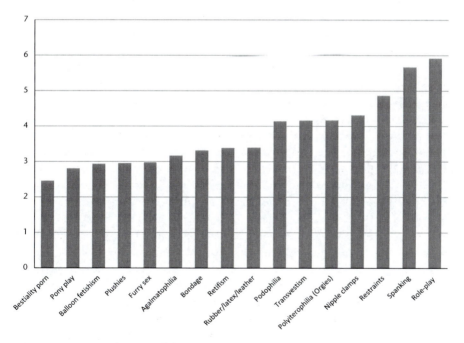

FIGURE 10.7 Attitudes toward fetishes

Respondents rated their attitudes toward fetish behaviors using a feeling thermometer (from 1 = cold to 10 = warm). Data adapted from Reysen *et al.* (2015).

and least accepting of agalmatophilia, furry sex, plushies, balloon fetishism, pony play, and porn depicting bestiality (Reysen *et al.* 2015).

Such attitudinal data clearly indicates that most people have a very narrow perception of what "appropriate" sex entails. In turn, we stigmatize a wide variety of sexual behaviors that we believe are outside of the norm. We even justify this stigmatization process by claiming that acts of sexual deviance are wrong because they are "destructive to society" (Bering 2013:32). Our laws reflect this pattern by utilizing a "better-safe-than-sorry principle" when it comes to regulating sexual deviance (Bering 2013:31). Many sexual behaviors that may or may not be actually harmful are outlawed because "we especially want to protect the most vulnerable members of our society—children, animals, the elderly, the disabled—so we err on the side of extreme caution, even if it means occasionally getting it wrong about the actual harm that they face" (Bering 2013:31) (see also Box 10.2 earlier in this chapter). As a result, sexual deviants are stigmatized and sometimes criminalized while the rest of "us" are not.

However, when we look more closely at these issues, the dividing line between "us" and "them" becomes virtually non-existent. For example, in an examination of the prevalence of 55 sex fantasies in 1,516 Canadian men and women, only five fantasies were found to be "uncommon" (meaning less than 10 percent reported interest in the behavior), these included transvestism, urophilia (active/passive), bestiality, and pedophilia. Thus, among a wide range of sexual fantasies, some of which are considered to be "normal" (such as oral sex) and some of which are considered to be "deviant" (such as being tied up) only five were found to be rare (Joyal *et al.* 2015). Furthermore, another study found that even if an individual is not initially sexually interested in certain behaviors/people, in the "heat of the moment" many things that may have once been viewed as disgusting and deviant become enticing and titillating. In this particular social experiment, 35 straight American college men were asked to masturbate almost to the point of climax and then asked to evaluate the attractiveness of twenty different sexual stimuli. Their evaluations were compared to another "control" group of men who rated the same stimuli, however, they were in a non-aroused state. The results were astonishing. The aroused men rated 18 of the 20 sexual stimuli as significantly more attractive than the non-aroused men (see Figure 10.8). For example, the most extreme difference between the groups was regarding anal sex where the non-aroused men rated their interest in anal sex on a scale from 1 to 100 at 46 compared to the aroused men who rated their interest in anal sex at 71. In other words, many things, even deviant ones, "become more attractive under the influence of arousal" (Ariely and Loewenstein 2006:95). Overall, these findings demonstrate that although we may think of ourselves as sexually "normal," certain conditions can significantly shift our sexual predilections. Thus, the majority of us are sexually deviant—at least in our fantasies if not beyond.

Fetishes and deviance

Humans have always had a wide spectrum of sexual desire but because cultural patterns reject certain forms of sexuality while simultaneously supporting others, the fear of being stigmatized and deviantized "continues to discourage people from creatively exploring other erotic possibilities" (Gates 2000:8). In other words, the distress

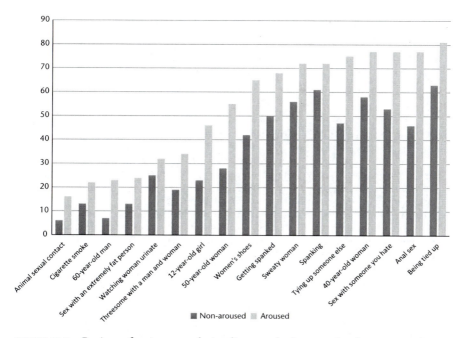

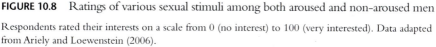

FIGURE 10.8 Ratings of various sexual stimuli among both aroused and non-aroused men

Respondents rated their interests on a scale from 0 (no interest) to 100 (very interested). Data adapted from Ariely and Loewenstein (2006).

of being thought of as a "sexual deviant" keeps certain people (and behaviors) closeted. However, today more and more deviants are coming out of the closet and online communities are supporting their journeys. Still, most people continue to feel uncomfortable about fetishism. Even so, it is important to remember that the label of "fetishist" comes from an entirely arbitrary place. For example, according to the classification of mental health disorders at the time, 75 percent of the men in Kinsey's research (1948, 1953) could have been labeled as "sex deviants" (Bering 2013:89). Overall, the world of fetishism is complex:

> Fetishism evokes images of "kinky" sex, involving an abnormal attraction to items of clothing such as high-heeled shoes and tightly laced corsets, or body parts like feet and hair ... but the stereotype of fetishism as a "picturesque" sexual deviation is too simplistic.
>
> (Steele 1996:9)

Fetish play and fetishists are varied. But more than just an exploration of diversity, understanding fetishism is also about empathy and respect. In closing, consider The Foot Fraternity's (a foot fetish-themed organization) statement of purpose:

> To ignore or belittle those who differ from a "norm" can make a person feel depressed, worthless or alone ... Whatever your fetish, if between consenting

adults, is just fine and very normal for you. The approval of all who come here is the fraternal brotherhood that we all seek. You are NOT alone in your desires and how wonderful that you have found a place to be your TRUE self.

(footfraternityfilms.com)

Notes

1 Gates uses the word "vanilla" rather than relying on the word "normal" to describe non-kinky sex (Gates 2000:8).
2 The DSM-5 first defines "normal" foci of sexual arousal as sexual interest in genital stimulation or preparatory fondling with phenotypically normal, physically mature, consenting human partners, and then defines "atypical" foci of sexual arousal as intense and persistent sexual interest in anything else (First 2014:198).
3 The significance of the DSM in court cases involving sex offenders in North America should not be understated. For example, "the presence of a DSM diagnosis, particularly a paraphilic disorder, is almost always key evidence in sexually violent predator civil commitment adjudications" because DSM diagnoses are widely recognized as clinically valid (First 2014:191).
4 For example, see Foot Worship Party: New York City, www.footworshipparties.com.
5 Only one study could be located that included women who owned sex dolls. Although the sample was extremely small (N = 6) compared to the male sex doll owners (N = 55), the six female sex doll owners reported a significantly higher quality of life, lower rates of depression, and were more likely to be married or in a relationship (Valverde 2012).
6 The 1983 song "99 Luftballoons" by the German band Nena (released in 1984 in English with slightly different lyrics as "99 *Red* Balloons") is generally acknowledged as the looners' anthem (Lewis 2010:201).
7 *The Red Balloon* features a little boy (Pascal) who discovers a large helium-filled, extremely spherical, red balloon on his way to school one morning. The balloon proceeds to follow him wherever he goes including through the streets of Paris and even into his classroom at school. When he encounters a gang of bullies who are envious of the balloon and the boy's newfound friendship with it, they destroy it. The ending of the film is somewhat magical as all the other balloons in Paris arrive and cluster together to take Pascal on a balloon ride over the city. *The Red Balloon* has a music score but almost no dialogue, which adds to its ethereal and fantasy-like feeling. *The Red Balloon* won several awards including the Palme d'Or for short films at the 1956 Cannes Film Festival and it is the only short film to win the Academy Award for Best Writing (Original Screenplay).
8 Objectophiles with histories of personal abuse and/or trauma may feel a deep connection with historical "State" objects that have come to symbolize violence, war, and destruction. For example, Erika Eiffel, who experienced childhood neglect and was sexually assaulted as a child and as an adult, has had a long-term relationship with the Berlin Wall whose dismantled remains now stand as a sordid reminder of shame for most, but for Erika, the battered, beaten wall is a symbol of strength, and she connects to the personal history of struggle that the Berlin Wall has experienced (Terry 2010).
9 Research shows that many serial killers demonstrated their violent tendencies in the form of cruelty to animals (zoosadism) during childhood (Johnson and Becker 1997).
10 There is at least one odd case that stands out against this norm. Frenchman, Jacques Ferron, was tried and hanged in 1750 for copulation with a jenny (female donkey). But unlike other animals of her time (who would have been burned or hanged along with their human sex partner), this particular donkey "was so beloved by the community that she instead was given her own separate trial" in which witnesses testified that they had never "seen her exhibit even the slightest sign of promiscuity" (Bering 2013:28). What's more, prior to the trial, a certificate was produced that affirmed the donkey's "virtuous reputation" (Bering 2013:28). Ultimately, the donkey was acquitted on the grounds that "she'd quite clearly been raped" (Bering 2013:28). Other similar historical cases have not been located but because the court

magistrates often destroyed all legal documents pertaining to shameful acts such as bestiality, the majority of sexually deviant case proceedings have been lost (Peakman 2013).

11 For example, one Sri Lankan man was sexually excited by ants, cockroaches, snails, and frogs crawling over his thighs, nipples, testicles, and anus and even biting the head of his penis (Dewaraja and Money 1986).

12 In the 1980s, the toy company Hasbro created a range of plastic toy ponies, known as *My Little Pony*, which quickly became popular amongst young girls. Unlike other toy ponies, these "were distinguished by the colour of their coats, manes and 'cutie marks', a unique image displayed on their flanks and representative of their distinctive personalities" (Jones 2015:120). The newest version of these toys, Generation 4, is based on the 2010 cartoon incarnation *My Little Pony: Friendship is Magic* (Jones 2015). Nearly all bronies are fans of this new version of the ponies.

13 Ethel Granger of Peterborough, England, reduced her waist from a natural 23 inches to an unnatural 13 inches by tight-lacing (wearing her corset 24 hours a day) from 1928 to her death in 1982 taking only brief breaks during pregnancies, per her obstetrician's recommendations (and much to the dismay of her husband). She started tight-lacing because her dominant husband found it to be sexually arousing but she also enjoyed the feel of the corset. Granger still holds the Guinness World Records title of "the world's smallest waist" (Steele 1996:81).

14 In contrast to this type of fetish play, "collaring" is a process whereby the Dom offers a collar to his sub (sometimes in a formal ceremony) in order to affirm their relationship (akin to an engagement ring) (Lewis 2010:288).

References

Abrams, Mike and Simona Stefan. 2012. "Sexual Abuse and Masochism in Women: Etiology and Treatment." *Journal of Cognitive and Behavioral Psychotherapies* 12(2):231–9.

Adam. 2011. "An Introspective View of Objectùm-Sexuality." *Expressions*. Objectùm-Sexuality Internationale. Retrieved from http://www.objectum-sexuality.org/

Apostolides, Marianne. 1999. "The Pleasure of the Pain: Why Some People Need S&M." *Psychology Today* September/October: 60–5.

Ariely, Dan and George Loewenstein. 2006. "The Heat of the Moment: The Effect of Sexual Arousal on Sexual Decision Making." *Journal of Behavioral Decision Making* 19:87–98.

Associated Press. 2009, November 2. "South Carolina Man, Rodell Vereen, Gets 3 Years for Horse Buggery." *NY Daily News*. Retrieved from: http://www.nydailynews.com/news/national/south-carolina-man-rodell-vereen-3-years-horse-buggery-article-1.413319

Balloonbuddies.com. n.d. "Home Page." Retrieved from: http://www.balloonbuddies.com/

Beirne, Piers. 2000. "Rethinking Bestiality: Towards a Concept of Interspecies Sexual Assault." Pp. 313–31 in *Companion Animals and Us: Exploring the Relationships between People and Pets*, edited by Anthony L. Podberscek, Elizabeth S. Paul, and James A. Serpell. New York, NY: Routledge.

Bering, Jessie. 2013. *PERV: The Sexual Deviant in All of Us*. New York, NY: Scientific American/ Farrar, Straus and Giroux.

Buenting, Julianne. 2003. "Rehearsing Vulnerability: BDSM as Transformative Ritual." *Chicago Theological Seminary Register* 93(1):39–49.

Bolicki, Jason and Melissa Cutlip. [Producers]. 2011, January 26. "Episode 8" of *My Strange Addiction* [Television series]. United States: Discovery-The Learning Channel.

Bramwell, David. 2007. *Fetish*. New York, NY: DK Publishing.

Burke, Sarah. 2014, June 1. "10 People Who are In Love with Inanimate Objects." *The Richest*. Retrieved from: http://www.therichest.com/rich-list/10-people-who-are-in-love-with-inanimate-objects/?view=all

Califia, Pat. 2000. *Public Sex: The Culture of Radical Sex*, Second Edition. San Francisco, CA: Cleis Press.

Cary, Henry. 1922. *Erotic Contrivances: Appliances Attached To, or Used In Place Of, The Sexual Organs*. Chicago, IL: Privately printed.

Chivers, Meredith and J. Michael Bailey. 2005. "A Sex Difference in Features that Elicit Genital Response." *Biological Psychology* 70:115–20.

Chivers, Meredith, Michael C. Seto, Martin L. Lalumière, Ellen Laan, and Teresa Grimbos. 2010. "Agreement of Self-Reported and Genital Measures of Sexual Arousal in Men and Women: A Meta-Analysis." *Archives of Sexual Behavior* 39:5–56.

Cooper, Merian and Ernest Schoedsack [directors]. 1933. *King Kong*. RKO Radio Pictures.

de Beaumont, Jeanne-Marie LePrince. 1756. *Beauty and the Beast*. London: Forgotten Books.

De Silva, Padmal and Amanda Pernet. 1992. "Pollution in 'Metroland': An Unusual Paraphilia in a Shy Young Man." *Sexual and Marital Therapy* 7(3):301–6.

Dewaraja, Ratnin and John Money. 1986. "Transcultural Sexology: Formicophilia, A Newly Named Paraphilia in a Young Buddhist Male." *Journal of Sex & Marital Therapy* 12(2):139–45.

Dunsieth, Neal, Erik Nelson, Lori Brusman-Lovins, Jeff Holcomb, DeAnna Beckman, Jeffrey Welge, David Roby, Purcell Taylor, Cesar, Soutullo, and Susan McElroy. 2004. "Psychiatric and Legal Features of 113 Men Convicted of Sexual Offenses." *Journal of Clinical Psychiatry* 65(3):293–300.

DSM-5 Fact Sheet. 2013. *Paraphilic Disorders*. American Psychiatric Association Publishing. Retrieved from: http://www.dsm5.org/Documents/Paraphilic%20Disorders%20Fact%20Sheet.pdf

Eiffel, Erika. n.d. "FAQ about OS from Erika Eiffel." *Objectùm-Sexuality Internationale*. Retrieved from: http://www.objectum-sexuality.org/

Ellis, Havelock. 1942. *Studies in the Psychology of Sex* (Vol. I). New York, NY: Random House.

European Sex Survey. 2013. "European Sex Survey." *YouGov*. Retrieved from: http://cdn.yougov.com/cumulus_uploads/document/mkyaii2h6k/YouGov-Survey-European-Omnibus-Sex-Research-130621.pdf

Faccio, Elena, Claudia Casini, and Sabrina Cipolletta. 2014. "Forbidden Games: The Construction of Sexuality and Sexual Pleasure by BDSM 'Players.'" *Culture, Health & Sexuality* 16(7):752–64.

Fedoroff, J. Paul. 2008. "Sadism, Sadomasochism, Sex, and Violence." *The Canadian Journal of Psychiatry* 53(10):637–46.

Ferguson, Anthony. 2010. *The Sex Doll: A History*. London: McFarland and Company, Inc.

First, Michael. 2014. "DSM-5 and Paraphilic Disorders." *The Journal of the American Academy of Psychiatry and the Law* 42:191–201.

Folsomstreetfair.com. n.d. "FAQs." *Folsom Street Fair*. Retrieved from: http://www.folsomstreetfair.com

Footfraternityfilms.com. n.d. "Home Page." Retrieved from: http://www.footfraternityfilms.com

Gaines, Doug. n.d. "Doug Gaines and the Foot Fetish Fraternity." *The Foot Fraternity*. Retrieved from: http://www.footfraternityfilms.com/about-dug-gaines.php

Gates, Katharine. 2000. *Deviant Desires: Incredibly Strange Sex*. New York, NY: Juno Books.

Gebhard, Paul. 1969. "Fetishism and Sadomasochism." Pp. 71–80 in *Dynamics of Deviant Sexuality*, edited by Jules H. Masserman. New York, NY: Grune & Stratton.

Gerbasi, Kathleen C., Nicholas Paolone, Justin Higner, Laura L. Scaletta, Penny L. Bernstein, Samuel Conway, and Adam Privitera. 2008. "Furries from A to Z (Anthropomorphism to Zoomorphism)." *Society and Animals* 16:197–222.

Hanlon, Chris. 2012, May 20. "Barking Mad for a Tree." *Daily Mail*. Retrieved from: http://www.dailymail.co.uk/news/article-2147210/Trunk-burnin-love-Canadian-woman-barking-mad-oak-tree-travels-7-000-miles-year-with.html

Harris, Daniel. 1997. *The Rise and Fall of Gay Culture*. New York, NY: Hyperion.

Hennen, Peter. 2008. *Faeries, Bears, and Leathermen: Men in Community Queering the Masculine*. Chicago, IL: University of Chicago Press.

Hsu, Bing, Arthur Kling, Christopher Kessler, Kory Knapke, Pamela Diefenbach, and James E. Elias. 1994. "Gender Differences in Sexual Fantasy and Behavior in a College Population: A Ten-Year Replication." *Journal of Sex & Marital Therapy* 20(2):103–18.

Hugo, Victor Marie. 1917. *Notre Dame de Paris*. Vol. XII. Harvard Classics Shelf of Fiction. New York, NY: P.F. Collier & Son. Retrieved from: http://www.bartleby.com/312/0403.html

Janus, Samuel and Cynthia Janus. 1993. *The Janus Report on Sexual Behavior*. New York, NY: John Wiley & Sons, Inc.

Johnson, Bradley and Judith Becker. 1997. "Natural Born Killers? The Development of the Sexually Sadistic Serial Killer." *Journal of the American Academy of Psychiatry and the Law* 25(3):335–48.

Jones, Bethan. 2015. "*My Little Pony*, Tolerance is Magic: Gender Policing and Brony Anti-Fandom." *Journal of Popular Television* 3(1):119–25.

Joyal, Christian C., Amélie Cossette, and Vanessa Lapierre. 2015. "What Exactly Is an Unusual Sexual Fantasy?" *The Journal of Sexual Medicine* 12(2):328–40.

Kahr, Brett. 2008. *Who's Been Sleeping in Your Head? The Secret World of Sexual Fantasies*. New York, NY: Basic Books.

Kinsey, Alfred, Wardell Pomeroy, and Clyde Martin. 1948. *Sexual Behavior in the Human Male*. Philadelphia, PA: W.B. Saunders Company.

Kinsey, Alfred, Wardell Pomeroy, Clyde Martin, and Paul Gebhard. 1953. *Sexual Behavior in the Human Female*. Philadelphia, PA: W.B. Saunders Company.

Kipling, Rudyard. 1920 [1894]. *The Jungle Book*. New York, NY: The Century Co.

Ko, Alice. 2007. *Cinderella's Sisters: A Revisionist History of Footbinding*. Berkeley, CA: University of California Press.

Krafft-Ebing, Von R. 1886. *Psychopathia Sexualis*. Stuttgart: Verglag Von Ferdinand Enke.

Lahti, Martti. 1998. "Dressing Up in Power: Tom of Finland and Gay Male Body Politics." *Journal of Homosexuality* 35(3-4):185–205.

Lamorisse, Albert [director]. 1956. *The Red Balloon*. France: Films Montsouris.

Laslocky, Meghan. 2005, October 11. "Just like a Woman." *Salon*. Retrieved from: http://www.salon.com/life/feature/2005/10/11/real_dolls/index3.html

Lewis, Angela. 2010. *My Other Self: Sexual Fantasies, Fetishes, and Kinks*. Brisbane: Book Pal.

Lewis, Angela. 2014. "Blown Up and Ready to Pop: A Global Survey of Balloon Fetishism." *Counselling Australia* 14(2):1–11.

Lindemann, Danielle J. 2011. "BDSM as Therapy?" *Sexualities* 14(2):151–72.

Love, Brenda. 1992. *Encyclopedia of Unusual Sex Practices*. Fort Lee, NJ: Barricade Books, Inc.

Marsh, Amy. 2010. "Love among the Objectum Sexuals." *Electronic Journal of Human Sexuality* 13. Retrieved from: http://www.ejhs.org/volume13/ObjSexuals.htm

Matthews, Mark. 1994. *The Horseman: Obsessions of a Zoophile*. Amherst, NY: Prometheus Books.

Nark, Jason. 2009, September 25. "Animal-Cruelty Charges Dropped against Burlington County Cop." *Philly News*. Retrieved from: http://articles.philly.com/2009-09-24/news/24986953_1_animal-cruelty-cows-videos

Newmahr, Staci. 2011. *Playing on the Edge: Sadomasochism, Risk, and Intimacy*. Bloomington, IN: Indiana University Press.

Otto, Sasjkia. 2009, August 5. "Woman getting married to fairground ride." *The Telegraph* Retrieved from: http://www.telegraph.co.uk/news/newstopics/howaboutthat/5972632/Woman-getting-married-to-fairground-ride.html

Peakman, Julie. 2013. *The Pleasure's All Mine: A History of Perverse Sex*. London: Reaktion Books.

Plante, Courtney, Sharon Roberts, Stephen Reysen, and Kathy Gerbasi. 2015. "'By the Numbers': Comparing Furries and Related Fandoms." Pp. 106–26 in *Furries Among Us: Essays on Furries by the Most Prominent Members of the Fandom*, edited by Thurston Howl. Nashville, TN: A Thurston Howl Publications Book.

Pitagora, Dulcinea. 2013. "Consent vs. Coercion: BDSM Interactions Highlight a Fine but Immutable Line." *The New School Psychology Bulletin* 10(1):27–36.

Qetesh, Sister. 2015. *World Orders*. Retrieved from: http://thesisters.org/world-orders

RealDoll.com. n.d. *RealDoll*. www.realdoll.com

Reysen, Stephen, Jennifer Shaw, and Thomas Brooks. 2015. "Heterosexual Missionary as the Sexual Default and Stigmatization of Perceived Infrequent Sexual Activities." *Advances in Social Sciences Research Journal* 2(5):93–104.

Smith, Marquard. 2013. *The Erotic Doll: A Modern Fetish*. New Haven, CT: Yale University Press.

Steele, Valerie. 1996. *Fetish: Fashion, Sex, and Power*. New York, NY: Oxford University Press.

Stein, Sister Phyllis, Catalyst, Sister Kitty, and PHB, Sister Vicious. 2012. *Sisters of Perpetual Indulgence: Sistory*. Retrieved from: http://www.thesisters.org/index.php/sistory

Terry, Jennifer. 2010. "Loving Objects." *Trans-humanities* 2(1):33–75.

Townsend, Larry. 1972 [2000]. *The Leatherman's Handbook*. Los Angeles, CA: L. T. Publications.

Tyburczy, Jennifer. 2014. "Leather Anatomy: Cripping Homonormativity at International Mr. Leather." *Journal of Literary Cultural Disability Studies* 8(3):275–93.

Valverde, Sarah. 2012. *The Modern Sex Doll-Owner: A Descriptive Analysis*. (Unpublished Master's thesis). Pomona, CA: The Department of Psychology and Child Development. California State Polytechnic University.

Weal, John D. 2010. *The Leatherman's Protocol Handbook: A Handbook on "Old Guard" Rituals, Traditions and Protocols*. Las Vegas, NV: The Nazca Plains Corporation.

Weinberg, Martin, Collin J. Williams, and Cassandra Calhan. 1995. "'If the Shoe Fits …': Exploring Male Homosexual Foot Fetishism." *The Journal of Sex Research* 32(1):17–27.

Williams, Colin and Martin Weinberg. 2003. "Zoophilia in Men: A Study of Sexual Interest in Animals." *Archives of Sexual Behavior* 32(6):523–35.

Woodworth, Michael, Tabatha Freimuth, Erin L. Hutton, Tara Carpenter, Ava D. Agar, and Matt Logan. 2013. "High-risk Sexual Offenders: An Examination of Sexual Fantasy, Sexual Paraphilia, Psychopathy, and Offence Characteristics." *International Journal of Law and Psychiatry* 36:144–56.

Yeoman, Ian and Michelle Mars. 2011. "Robots, Men and Sex Tourism." *Futures* 44:365–71.

11

SEX WORK

Chauntelle A. Tibbals

[S]ociety is made up of a vast array of communities and experiences—and though you don't have to like them all, all of them are significant pieces comprising the whole of humanity. As such, all of them are worthy of respectful consideration.

Chauntelle A. Tibbals, Exposure: A Sociologist Explores Sex, Society, and Adult Entertainment *(2015a:159)*

What is sex work?

Sex means many different things to many different people—physical satisfaction, spiritual actualization, community connection, and intense preoccupation (debilitating or otherwise) are only a few. And for some people, sex is work. Not "work" as in a chore, but "work" as in a job. *Sex work* is a generic term for any commercial sexual service, performance, or product given in exchange for compensation. Sex work includes, but is not limited to, various forms of prostitution, exotic dance, phone sex, and pornography (Weitzer 2000). In addition, people who work "behind the scenes" in some form of sex trade but are not necessarily engaging in sex-related labor are *also* sex workers. As such, for example, people who work in sales at an adult novelty (sex toy) company and people who work in management at a brothel are in an occupational class similar to escorts and porn performers—all of these workers participate in the generation and commercial exchange of sex-related goods and services. This is not to suggest that a person working in a "behind the scenes" sex work occupation will have experiences coincident with that of a worker performing sex-related labor. It is, however, to suggest that the stigma of sex work is strong enough to afford all workers some measure of the sex worker dividend. An inverse of the patriarchal dividend [the societal advantages given to men/maleness/masculinity that maintain an unequal gender order (Connell and Pearse 2014)], the *sex worker dividend* encompasses the overall negative treatment and stigma afforded to people working in the sex trade. Presumptions about sexuality, morality, intelligence, health, and general quality of personhood drive the sex worker dividend and generally locate sex workers in a place of societal disadvantage. The sex worker dividend is not allocated equally to all persons in the sex trade – a prominent porn performer, a street walking prostitute, and an office worker at a webcam network will not receive identical negative treatment. But unlike most dividends, the sex worker dividend is not a conventionally advantageous bonus. It is allocated to workers in proportion with a community's perception of deviance regarding sex work and frequently manifests as shaming, marginalization, disempowering charity or "savior" efforts, and/or othering from those outside the sex work industry (Tibbals 2013a).

Modern technological advancements have expanded what is included under the rubric of sex work. Today, in addition to prostitution, exotic dance, and phone sex, sex work also includes web camming, as well as working as a sexual health and/or intimacy expert—or "sexpert" —among other occupations (see Boxes 11.1 and 11.2). Further, many other long-standing but previously infrequently discussed occupations are now key dimensions of the sex work industry and lexicon (e.g., working as a professional dominatrix, sexual submissive, or sexual surrogate).

BOX 11.1 WHAT IS WEB CAMMING?

Web camming is a relatively new type of sex work that merges the adult entertainment industry with innovative technology. On the surface, it is a very simple concept: online video-enhanced chatting between a customer and a model. But in today's social world, web camming is complicated by issues of gender and technology, as well as by attributions of "sexual deviance" from various communities.

The general structure of cam work is not unlike other forms of virtual social interactions. Interested customers browse network websites containing hundreds-to-thousands of model profiles. They can then chat with a model online and, if both parties are amenable, "take them private" for a paid one-on-one video exchange. The fees are pre-set and are either processed as a flat rate in advance or by the minute. What happens "in private [chat]" can vary from a viewer-guided sexual performance to a simple conversation, depending on a customer's wants and a model's comfort. It is common for models to develop "regulars" and, like other sex workers in different occupations (e.g., exotic dancers or escorts), they may have a group of customers who visit them online frequently.

Web cam work is legal, a status largely contingent upon the fact that no actual physical sexual contact with customers is exchanged for money. In fact, on some networks, customers purchase virtual coins or tokens, which are then exchanged for time spent with a model online. This system adds an additional layer of distance from a "money for sex" scenario. Further, when compared to some forms of sex work, web camming is considered relatively physically safe. This is largely because, if conventions and norms are being followed, models never directly interact with customers in person for a sexual or social exchange. When conducted through a host network, as most are, models' interactions with clients are monitored very heavily. This is done both to protect models from things such as harassment and privacy violations, as well as to ensure models and customers are not violating a network's terms of service. This includes not communicating outside the network (the exchange of personal email addresses or phone numbers, for example, is generally forbidden, as is meeting in person).

As an occupation, working as a web cam model comes with many benefits. Workers act as their own supervisors, set their own hours, and generally work from home. Camming can also be quite lucrative as a form of primary or supplemental income. Further, unlike other forms of sex work, cam work does not discriminate in terms of gender identity, aesthetics, age, or any other characteristic—anyone of legal working age can register with a network and get on cam.

But camming also comes with many challenges. Cam models do not generally receive much occupational training. Most networks offer basic coaching, but the real learning is done on-the-job and, from a model's first moment on cam, the work can be very intense. Cam models are also exposed to some very real occupational hazards, from the risk of customers stealing webcam time ["capping" is the unwanted filming and sharing/selling of cam model erotic performances (Jones 2015:565)] and potential online/virtual abuse from customers to the tedium of working without the camaraderie of coworkers. Payment for time spent on cam is also not guaranteed. Models are only paid for time spent in private chat and in special events or shows, as well as via tips. As such, a model can spend hours online but if they cannot secure a customer via private chat, they will not obtain any payment for their time working. It is worth noting though that this payment structure is not unlike other forms of sales and commission-based work. Labor difficulties in this respect are not unique.

Though the labor processes of cam modeling and porn performance are distinctive, those with limited understanding of sex work often conflate the two. The recent trend of porn performers also working on cam augments this confusion. As such, cam models receive a fair measure of the sex worker dividend, and many go to great lengths to keep their work private. This is becoming increasingly difficult, however, as web camming's popularity is rising steadily, making it the current growth industry in adult entertainment and in sex work overall.

BOX 11.2 WHAT IS A "SEXPERT"?

Recall from chapter 8 that sexual health education in the United States varies widely with some teenagers exposed to abstinence-only curriculum and most receiving limited information about condoms and contraception. As a result, many Americans are under-educated about sexual health issues. Sexperts are sexual health educators that have emerged in direct response to these gaps in our understanding who seek to enhance sexual health knowledge and awareness for everyone throughout the life course.

Sexperts are widely varied. Some are conventionally trained educators and therapists; others are skilled in alternative institutions and/or draw from a wealth of community activism and lived experience. In many instances, sexperts connect with particular communities and their unique needs. For example, Joan Price, an "advocate for ageless sexuality," writes and speaks about senior sex (Price 2014). Multi-media pleasure advocate Sunny Megatron is a BDSM expert and the host of Showtime's "SEX with Sunny Megatron" program (SunnyMegatron.com). Conner Habib is an author, porn performer, and sex workers' rights advocate, as well as a frequently cited expert on LGBTQ sex (ConnerHabib.com). These people, as well as many other sex education experts, work to connect sex-related information with relevant communities.

Sometimes sexperts develop educational materials in the form of adult instructional films. Different from conventional porn in which the intended purpose is fantasy-based and has nothing to do with education, adult instructionals are made with input from educators, experts, and/or sex work professionals. An average adult instructional is not dissimilar from any other sort of how-to video—a detailed description followed by a demonstration and Q&A. Topics range from relatively basic how-tos (e.g., foreplay and oral sex) to life course and body-related topics (e.g., plus-size sex and sex during pregnancy), as well as more "deviant" sexual behaviors (e.g., BDSM) (Tibbals 2015b). Through their pragmatic approach, adult instructional films provide viewers with a sort of tacit permission to explore what may be relatively edgy sex adventures with the guidance of experienced professionals.

Educational institutions are also beginning to see the value in sex education coming from sexpert contemporaries. Many universities even train student peer educators as sexperts. Dartmouth University's sexual health peer advisors, for example, respond to student requests for education regarding reproductive health, healthy sexuality, sexual identity, body image, sexual orientation, sexual decision-making, abstinence, sexual pleasure, contraception, STI prevention, consent, and communication (Dartmouth.edu). Similar programs exist at other universities in American colleges (e.g., Boston University, University of Alabama, University of Kentucky, University of Michigan, University of Nevada, University of Oklahoma), in Canada (e.g., University of Calgary, University of Montreal), and elsewhere (e.g. University of Melbourne).

Beyond this, internet resources can also provide invaluable sexual health information, especially for young people who do not have access to accurate in-home or at-school sex education. For example, since 1998, *Scarleteen* has provided free high-quality sex education to millions of young people around the world. Their user-friendly website offers "inclusive, comprehensive, and smart sexuality information and help for teens and 20s" (Scarleteen.com). *Go Ask Alice!* is another educational website supported by a team of Columbia University health professionals. Its Q&A format provides readers with "reliable, accurate, accessible, culturally competent information and a range of thoughtful perspectives so that they can make responsible decisions concerning their health and well-being" (GoAskAlice.com). This is especially significant because most teenagers surf the web in search of accurate facts about sex [especially LGBTQ teens (see Mitchell *et al.* 2014)] and although there are plenty of websites with fallacies out there, resources such as *Scarleteen* and *Go Ask Alice!* receive millions of hits each year and arm teens with helpful and accurate sexual health information.

Overall, human sexuality is varied and diverse. And because porn is frequently misappropriated as "educational," in many ways, both sexperts and adult instructionals function as a sort of sexual exploration bridge—a way to dip your toe into something you may be interested in and test the waters without actually engaging in the behavior (yet) (Tibbals 2015b). As such, though no one sex educator will meet the needs of all communities' norms and values, sexperts are providing a valuable service and filling gaps in our understanding left otherwise unattended.

But in spite of the overall expansion of sex work and increasingly public mainstream discussions about sex workers' lived experiences (e.g., Kobola 2015), allocation of the sex worker dividend via shaming, discrimination, criminalization, and more is still rampant. For example, California public school teacher, Stacie Halas, was terminated from her job in 2013 when co-workers and underage students found out she worked in pornography in the past (they were searching through archived online clips). Although Halas was a board-certified teacher, the fact that she performed in 11 totally legal porn scenes nearly ten years prior (2005 to 2006) was enough to get her fired due to "dishonesty," "immorality," and her "inability to be a role model" (Romero 2013). Not surprisingly, as a former sex worker, Halas bore the brunt of the stigma. At no point were parents prosecuted for allowing minors to access adult content, nor were her co-workers shamed for viewing her "immoral" work. In another example, three-time Olympian distance runner, Suzy Favor Hamilton, was outed as a Nevada escort in 2012. In her 2015 memoir *Fast Girl*, she describes the vitriolic shaming she experienced, expresses a desire to humanize escorts, and hopes people can "forgive her" for her past. Because of their participation in sex work, both Halas and Hamilton received negative treatment, bearing the stigmatizing effects of the sex worker dividend. Halas' and Hamilton's stories speak to two dimensions of sex work that have consistently been considered the most notoriously deviant iterations of sex work—prostitution and pornography. We will now consider both as sexually deviant behaviors in greater depth.

What is prostitution?

Prostitution is a broad and general term that attempts to capture a number of sex work phenomena involving the exchange of an individual's intimate time or services for a sum of money or other form of compensation. Services can range from overtly physically sexual to companionship and emotional intimacy. Forms of compensation can vary from money and material goods to intangible recompense, such as references or mentorship. Depending on the community or culture, some forms of prostitution are legal, others are explicitly defined by law as illegal, and some are illegal but overlooked by authorities in certain instances. Further, some forms of prostitution are sanctioned socially and morally more so than criminally.

Prostitution is one of the most intensely contested forms of sex work. Scholars, activists, and workers themselves have debated about both the individual meanings of sex work and its wider social implications at length (e.g., Jenness 1990; Weitzer 2000). For example, you have certainly heard the adage "the oldest profession"—though it may seem like a small thing, this saying is referring to prostitution as actual *work*—an occupation. Since the 1960s, sex worker activists have argued for prostitution to be understood as an occupation akin to any other form of labor or skill. In this view, workers choose to engage in their occupation, making conscious decisions that do not involve coercion or victimization. Others argue that prostitution is, at very its core, exploitation. As such, there can be no work, worker choice, or worker autonomy. The entire situation is predicated on structural inequalities related to labor, sexualities, and gender. And between these polar "sex work as work" and "sex work as exploitation" perspectives are a wealth of gray areas (Jenness 1990; Matthew 2008; see also, chapter 7).

Hierarchies and unequal allocations of privilege operate within every subculture and social group, including prostitution. As such, issues of choice and autonomy as well as those related to labor opportunity become more complex. For example, a socio-economically disadvantaged person electing to work as a prostitute may have different issues shaping his/her choices relative to a person with more economic resources. Further, some forms of prostitution are more lucrative than others and wider social institutions and norms heavily influence access to these forms and workspaces. These issues, however, are not unique to prostitution or sex work. Inequalities related to access and choice can be seen in every other occupation or career. In this respect, prostitution is simply a microcosmic reflection of wider social inequalities, making issues of choice and coercion more complex (Weitzer 2005).

Stigma and other issues related to sexual deviance are also at play in considerations of sex work and prostitution. Regardless of one's personal feelings about sex work, all classes of prostitutes—from the most advantaged to the most at-risk— must live in the wider world, a space that notoriously, historically, and currently shames and stigmatizes sex-related labor. As such, when sex workers seek social and medical services, attempt to transition out of sex work, or simply want to pay their rent, interactions are shaped by variable perspectives on deviance (Weitzer 2005).

One point to make clear when considering different types of prostitution is that it is in no way akin to sex trafficking. Sex trafficking involves overt coercion, from kidnapping to abuse to imprisonment, and forced sexual labor. In discussions of sex work, even a choice made from a position of extreme disadvantage is not the same thing as being sex trafficked or held in sexual servitude. Some discussions conflate these phenomena, however, it is important to point out that sex positive considerations of prostitution do not equate any form of choice with coercion or force (Weitzer 2007).

There are several different occupational categories and classes under the umbrella of prostitution. Let us consider a few different types in greater detail (see Table 11.1).

TABLE 11.1 Prostitution types and characteristics

	Business location	Fees/services	Risk of harm to worker	Sex worker dividend
Street prostitution	Public or semi-public areas such as streets, alleys, cars	Low prices charged typically for specific sex act(s)	Little protection from police and high potential of exploitation from pimps and clients	High stigma
Escorting	Private premises such as hotels and residences often prearranged online	Moderate to high prices charged often for an experience that involves time and companionship	Clients can be vetted online or through a supervisor which reduces risk of harm and exploitation	Moderate stigma
Brothel prostitution	Brothels	Moderate to high prices charged typically for specific sex act(s)	High level of protection from supervisors and very low potential of harm or exploitation from clients	Moderate stigma
Sugar dating	Private premises such as hotels and residences often prearranged online	Moderate to high prices charged for a long-term relationship that involves time and companionship, mimicking common dating practices	Clients can be vetted online or through a supervisor that reduces risk of harm and exploitation	Moderate to low stigma

Street prostitution

Generally, the image that is conjured when thinking about prostitution within the context of commercial sex is "street prostitution" – most often a woman worker in a public space connecting with a clientele comprised primarily of men. Though this image is not inaccurate, it is only a portion of what constitutes street prostitution. Sometimes street prostitution occurs on roadways, highways, and in alleyways but other times cities and citizens actively shape the ways street prostitution works.

The legality of street prostitution varies widely across (and often within) cultures— from illegal and unregulated to illegal yet permissible to legal in certain forms. For example, consider the Dutch phenomenon of regulated street prostitution in designated areas called *tippelzones* (derived from the Dutch word *tippelen* meaning street-walking). In this instance, prostitution is legal; however, many behaviors frequently associated with street prostitution are illegal or considered a public nuisance—loitering, noise, and vehicles "kerb crawling" (cruising in search of a desirable worker). In response to these issues, as well as in an effort to provide medical and social services to workers and more clearly distinguish instances of prostitution from sex trafficking, the Dutch designated nine tippelzones across the Netherlands specifically for picking up prostitutes, exchanging sexual services, and for workers seeking care. Tippelzones consist of a "pickup" area designed to mimic a street corner setting, a "service" area with parking stalls where sex acts take place, and a "living room" where workers can rest and receive amenities such as clean needles, condoms, and medical assistance, as well as counseling services (van Soomeren 2004). This pragmatic approach, however, ultimately resulted in a "diabolical dilemma" in which police and care workers were pitted against one another (van Soomeren 2004:11). Police argued that the tippelzones had become a breeding ground for crime and illegal sex trafficking (despite the fact that evidence indicates that tippelzones actually decrease crime, see Bisschop *et al.* 2015) and care workers argued that closing the tippelzones would only result in a scattering of prostitution throughout the city, thereby dispersing and masking dangers and problems associated with street prostitution (van Soomeren 2004). Ultimately, most Dutch tippelzones were shut down but a few remain open for "kerb crawling" (Bisschop *et al.* 2015).

In today's world, however, street prostitution is becoming less and less literal as people can now "pick up" prostitutes via online services. For example, Rentboy. com, which was closed by the U.S. federal government in 2015, allowed men to search through worker profiles in the hopes of finding an appealing match. The terms of the client-worker exchange, including locations, sex acts, and fees, were negotiated in advance of ever meeting face-to-face. And although Rentboy.com is no longer operating, similar sites such as Rentmen.com (which is based in the Netherlands) offer comparable services (Murphy 2015). This type of scenario represents a gray area in distinguishing prostitution from higher-end escorting.

Escorting

Though differentiating between the two is often somewhat difficult, escorting is generally considered to be a higher-end form of prostitution. Often, escorting is privately arranged and does not involve the public cruising and perusal that prostitution frequently does. Escorts are generally paid more than prostitutes, often for an experience (as compared to a prescribed sex act) that involves time and companionship. Sometimes described as "the girlfriend experience," this is the hallmark of escorting, distinguishing it from prostitution. Escorting is also less haphazard than street prostitution. Clients can be vetted through an online network or supervisor (e.g., a madam) or via in-advance interpersonal exchanges or even background and credit checks. Consequently, escorting is generally physically safer for the worker, as well as socially safer for the client. These dimensions augment escorting's occupational prestige, elevating it above conventional prostitution, especially in terms of working with high profile and celebrity clientele (Tibbals 2015d).

Brothel prostitution

A brothel is a place of business where people come specifically to purchase sexual services from prostitutes. Akin to a salon where stylists rent monthly chair space or a strip club where dancers pay a fee to the club at the end of a shift, prostitutes often pay a "house fee" for a room in a brothel and split some percentage of their earnings with the venue itself. Brothel prostitution in the U.S. is a good illustration of the debate between decriminalization and regulation.

The *decriminalization* view holds that prostitution is work akin to any other sort of labor. As such, it should neither be illegal nor should it be regulated in any sort of special or excessive manner. In the decriminalization view, special regulation is simply a veiled strategy for rights infringement and continued social marginalization. *Regulation*, on the other hand, monitors workers' health and finances and requires registration with the state. Brothel prostitution in the U.S. state of Nevada represents the sort of intense regulation while decriminalization is more akin to prostitution in the Netherlands (Mullin 2015).

In the U.S., prostitution is only legal in Nevada in certain rural counties with a population below a certain amount. As such, brothel prostitution is illegal in, for example, Clark County where the city of Las Vegas is located. In order to work in a Nevada brothel, prostitutes must obtain a work card and undergo regular health checks. Condoms, or some form of STI preventative barrier protection, must be used during all work–client interactions (Albert 2002).

Though at first glance, brothel regulation may seem beneficial to the worker, advocates for full decriminalization object for the following reasons:

- The licensing requirements create a permanent record, which can lead to discrimination, either in the future or if one is outed as a current brothel prostitute. This taps into concerns of moral sanctioning, often in spite of legal status.
- Although prostitutes undergo legal and health background checks, outside informal inspections done immediately in advance of a sexual exchange, their customers do not. Regulations like this are designed to protect customers from prostitutes, while providing little protection for prostitutes from customers.

- The significant power differential existing between a brothel owner and a highly regulated prostitute creates a workplace environment of marked inequality. Prostitutes have very little influence over their working conditions, while business owners are able to negotiate the system with more autonomy.

Workers are often caught between positions of decriminalization and regulation, with activists and advocates pointing out inequalities while workers labor within the existing system (Mullin 2015).

Sugar dating

Sugar dating, wherein a "sugar baby" receives patronage from a "sugar daddy" or "sugar momma," also operates in an interesting gray area between prostitution and more conventional understandings of dating. Previously informal and obscure, sugar dating has received a lot of attention in recent years due to the development of several online networks and a resulting sugar dating industry (Miller 2011/2012).

Consider *Seeking Arrangement*, currently one of the most prominent networks facilitating sugar relationships. People interested in having a sugar patron create a site profile, while those interested in finding a sugar baby browse for a connection. Mutually interested parties then set forth the terms of their relationship, including what is expected from the sugar baby in exchange for defined compensation from the sugar patron. This can be anything from trips and gifts to an allowance, networking opportunities and mentorship, or bill payment. According to *Seeking Arrangement*, this structure allows both parties to clarify and set goals and expectations before entering a relationship, increasing the possibility of success (seekingarrangement.com).

Absent from the formality of the network, sugar dating is not too unlike conventional dating—parties come to a relationship with different resources and expectations, and each parties' ability and willingness to meet said expectations contribute to its success. Sugar dating, however, requires those resources and expectations be articulated at the outset, which marks a significant divergence from conventional dating. As such, in an interesting twist, sugar dating is often categorized as sexual and social deviance. Sugar dating is unique in the sense that its tendency to highlight and amplify norms, rather than break them, contribute to its deviance (Miller 2011/2012).

Clients of prostitutes

Prostitution crosses all genders and sexual identities. Men seek cisgender women, trans women, and other men, as shaped by their sexual desires and social environment. Occasionally, often due to social and psychological pressures, we see high-profile powerful people seeking out sex workers directly counter to their publically touted personas. American conservative career pastor, Ted Haggard, is an especially egregious example. Haggard, who led millions of evangelical Christians worldwide from his home church in Colorado Springs, CO, repeatedly condemned "homosexual" sex from the pulpit. All the while he was secretly engaging in same-sex sexual behavior with at least one hired sex worker (Mike Jones) and even a 20-year-old man who he met at church (CNN 2009). Politicians, conservative activists, and celebrities are frequently publicly shamed for their involvement with sex workers, but at the same time, sex workers offer these powerful people an important escape from their high-profile lives. In general, hiring a sex worker for companionship and/or sexual release gives people options for power exchanges, sexual diversity, and exploration. In these ways, sex workers are a sort of pressure relief system for social and cultural inconsistencies (Tibbals 2015d). These experiences are attractive to celebrities and laypeople alike and they are rapidly becoming more appealing to wider audiences. In fact, today more so than at any time in recent history, the number of women paying for sex is drastically increasing (Dickson 2015).

While most people think that prostitution is a service specifically for men (indeed, clients of prostitutes are colloquially described as "johns"), women also patronize sex workers—and they are doing so at increasing rates. For example, at Sheri's Ranch (a brothel located in Pahrump, Nevada), the number of single women and women involved in couples purchasing brothel sex has been steadily climbing in recent years. In fact, estimates indicate that about 15 percent of the sex parties at Sheri's Ranch involve women clients. Furthermore, in the United Kingdom, the number of men escorts advertising to women potential clients tripled from 2010 to 2015 (Dickson 2015). Overall, those who hire sex workers are as diverse as sex workers themselves.

What is pornography?

Written descriptions, still images, and filmic representations of sexual activity designed to incite erotic emotions and behaviors are generally considered *pornography*. Many additional social and subjective elements factor into the real-world manifestations of pornography, however, rendering it considerably more complex than this definition would suggest. The current landscape of pornography mostly exists online and the vast majority of popular pornographic websites are tube sites offering free clips of erotic content (see Figure 11.1).

Pornography, technology, and law

Advancements in technology and shifting laws have shaped adult entertainment significantly throughout history, and both have limited and expanded where and how erotic content can be created and accessed. For example, in the past 150 years, U.S. laws have changed from restricting "obscene" texts and imagery judged to be "corrupt" (i.e., the Hicklin Test) to a three-pronged criterion for obscenity based on community standards (i.e., the Miller Test) (see chapter 7, footnote 1). Indeed, such regimented canons had a profound effect on obscenity prosecutions for the better part of a century (from the 1850s to the 1990s).

Interestingly, although the adult film industry began to take shape in the 1960s (see more in chapter 7), porn production was technically illegal in the U.S. until the 1980s. In 1983, adult film director and producer, Harold Freeman, hired five women to perform in one of his films and was subsequently arrested, charged with, and convicted on five counts of pandering. Freeman appealed his conviction,

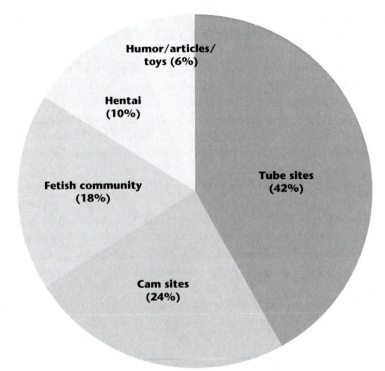

FIGURE 11.1   Top 50 Alexa-ranked adult websites by category

Alexa, a leading provider of free global web metrics, organizes websites into "adult" categories. The Alexa (2015) ranked top 50 "adult" websites were organized into the following categories: tube sites (those with video clips), cam sites (those with cam/chat focus), fetish community (social networking, viewer submitted art, erotic fiction), Hentai (Japanese anime/manga), and humor/articles/toys (Ebaumsworld, Playboy, AdamandEve).

arguing that he had paid these women for their performances in his film, not for the purpose of his own sexual arousal or gratification. In *California v Freeman* (1989), Freeman's conviction was reversed and this Supreme Court case effectively legalized adult film production in the state of California. Today, U.S. porn production is only legal in California and New Hampshire.

Legal regulation of pornographic content has impacted cultures differently. For example, in Japan, cultural norms and obscenity regulations have resulted in the proliferation of uniquely Japanese erotica. Because showing pubic hair and anal penetration was once obscene, producers and consumers sought out content that circumnavigated regulation. As such, many unique fetishes and sub-genres began to flourish. These include *bukkake* (a depiction wherein a number of men ejaculate on a woman or another man), *tentacle erotica* (amalgamates horror, science fiction, and bestiality, while skirting penetration regulations), and content designating children as sexual objects (e.g., *lolicon*, animated porn featuring prepubescent and adolescent girls). In 2014, Japan outlawed possession of sexually explicit content featuring children (production and sale of such content was made illegal in 1999); however, animated and drawn content was not included in this ruling. As a result, we continue to see *Hentai* (Japanese comics featuring drawn pornographic content) featuring explicit sexual scenes of children (Hellmann 2014).

Technology has operated in conjunction with law to further limit, as well as grant, consumer access to adult content. For example, when film viewing was limited to projector technology, people had to travel to "red light districts" (areas zoned specifically for sex-related commercial businesses) if they wanted to view porn. But as discussed in chapter 7, videocassette recorder (VCR) technology began to change all of that in 1975. Though initially limited to the wealthy, close to 90 percent of all households in the U.S. owned a VCR by 1990 and porn viewing shifted from predominantly public to private (Tibbals 2013b). The internet would mark another significant shift.

During the 1980s, a series of technological advancements began to impart everyday-use practicality on existing computer technology and the "world wide web project" was announced in 1991. Three years later, Netscape released its first browser and what is commonly understood today as the internet was born (Tibbals 2013b). A handful of people saw the internet's potential for marketing and distributing adult content immediately, including former exotic dancer turned figure model and softcore porn performer, Danni Ashe. In the 1990s, Ashe built the overwhelmingly successful website "Danni's Hard Drive," a softcore collection of model biographies, FAQs, and various other "fun features" centered on a picture-enhanced model- and adult-website directory. Ashe's website grossed over $2.5 million (USD) in 1997 and $6.5 million (USD) in 2001 (she sold the company in 2004 and now works as a photographer in Arizona). "Danni's Hard Drive" was the first website of its kind and Ashe is commonly credited with presenting consumers with an even more private way to access adult material. She is often described as a pioneer in woman-centered pornography production. Women like Ashe "are not simply content to go with the online flow [of pornography], but are determined to use the technology to shape the face of sex and to create a new category of erotica that appeals to women" (Perdue 2002:175–6).

Following early sites such as "Danni's Hard Drive," subsequent adult content in the virtual world has caused some concern around issues of obscenity and sexuality. Because the U.S. legal parameters regarding pornography are still based on the Miller Test (*Miller v. California* 1973), what constitutes *online* "community standards" is somewhat vague. As a result, "obscenity" (in a legal sense) is extremely difficult to identify. Furthermore, piracy-based online tube sites now command a lion's share of internet porn traffic. Though factual statistics describing the phenomenon do not exist, the porn industry hit extremely difficult financial times in 2008. Many businesses closed and many performers were left without work as the public became more and more convinced that porn was not a commodity worth paying for. The industry has still not recovered financially and estimates commonly touted about its net worth are both inaccurate and off mark (Tibbals 2015a).

For those outside the adult entertainment industry, porn may seem like one monolithic entity—a collection of similar producers creating one uniform product. The adult industry, however, is in actuality a microcosm akin to any other subculture.

Adult content is created by social actors—culturally and socially aware people with families, friends, interests outside of work, and "real" lives—for consumption by other social actors. As such, porn production works in a synergistic relationship with wider society, engaging themes and happenings relevant to the wider culture. Wider social forces shape the adult industry, but the industry also has its own unique norms and culture. The community itself is widely varied—different people and entities producing different content, in many forms, to be distributed across an array of channels. And like every other commercial industry, the porn business has "big players," niche areas, industry-specific services, and industry-specific issues (Tibbals 2015a). Let us now consider some of the hallmarks of modern pornography and the adult entertainment industry today.

Pornography content

Adult content is very diverse, even in its earliest forms. You can see sex depictions often considered "deviant" in discussions today featured prominently in classic porn films produced in the U.S. For example, *Deep Throat* (1972) contains a depiction of anal sex while *The Devil in Miss Jones* (1973) showcases a vaginal-anal double penetration scene (Tibbals 2010).

Adult content also reflects wider social interests. For example, Kim Kardashian-West's "celebrity sex tape," *Kim Kardashian, Superstar,* for which she contracted with adult content producers Vivid Entertainment in 2007, has only grown in popularity in recent years, corresponding with the Kardashian family's continued rise in cultural prominence (Doll 2010). Further, the practice of being directly inspired by wider cultural narratives morphed into a full-blown porn production parody craze, which reached an acme point around 2010 to 2011. Producers would spoof or dramatically render everything from classic television (2010's *Twilight Zone Porn Parody*) and comic books (2010's *Batman XXX: A Porn Parody*) to celebrity meltdowns and cartoons (2009's *Hustler's Untrue Hollywood Stories: Lindsay Lohan* and 2011's *Simpsons: The XXX Parody*) (Tibbals 2014).

You can also see evidence of social and cultural evolutions reflected in adult content. For example, *Behind the Green Door* (1972), which depicts an audience watching a live sex show, showcases racial, age, and body diversity during the audience's orgy sequence, while simultaneously relying on extremely problematic depictions of race as a key part of the sex show/narrative. In another instance, racist language used freely in films such as *New Wave Hookers 2* (1991) is now relegated to race-play sub-genres, wherein certain types of language have highly charged alternate meanings (see for examples films featuring performer/director Shane Diesel) (Tibbals 2010).

Today, porn is often divided into categories that include gonzo, feature films, and online clips. Let us consider each in more detail.

Gonzo

Gonzo is a porn content production form characterized by the presence of a "talking camera," wherein the person recording a particular sequence or scene is also playing an active, integral role in the on-screen action. For example, a person behind the camera may be giving directions or making comments to performers in the midst of a sex scene. These interactions then become part of the final product. Gonzo porn is generally only loosely scripted, and it does not require the same level of preparation as, for example, most feature-length productions. Consequently, although there is certainly some variability, gonzo porn is relatively inexpensive to make. This enables producers to more effectively meet market demands for new material. It is important to note that gonzo is not a rough sex content genre, though it is often misconstrued as such by media and anti-porn activists (Tibbals 2014).

Feature films

Quite different from gonzo porn are "feature" productions. Features include sex depictions couched within an overarching plot and/or a developing narrative. Akin to conventional Hollywood film and television, adult content features span the gamut—from comedies and dramas, to miniseries and serials. Further, also akin to Hollywood productions and every other form of narrative text, adult content and adult content producers do not operate in a social or cultural vacuum. Porn and broader social culture shift and evolve within the context of a symbiotic relation-ship, reacting to, and interacting with, one another. It is not surprising then that wider social narratives and trends are reflected in adult content. In today's adult industry, people are producing fewer and fewer feature length narrative projects. This is due largely to economic concerns, as well as shifts in consumer tastes (Tibbals 2014).

Online clips

One significant web-based adult content form is the single scene "clip"—pre-produced scenes that are sold for streaming and/or downloadable consumption, often on tube sites. There are many web spaces that focus on the online distribu-tion of pre-produced single scenes. For example, on Clips4Sale.com, a producer can upload his/her content and benefit from the site's significant consumer traffic. Anyone may post to Clips4Sale, although the site mostly caters to newer producers and industry amateurs. Revenues are split between the content owner(s) and the site itself. Sites such as Clips4Sale allow producers to build a fan base with minimal distribution overheads (Tibbals 2014).

Porn genre and culture

In terms of sexual expression, there is really nothing new under the sun. As over-viewed in chapter 7, ancient carvings showcase group sex. Erotic domination and servitude have been described in classic literature. Queer sex is a hallmark of the civilized world. Our awareness of variable sexual proclivities, however, shift over time. As a result, mainstream culture actively shapes pornography, and thus, differ-ent porn content genres shift in their popularity. For example, although practices associated with bondage, discipline, sadism, and masochism (BDSM) have been around forever and well-developed online and real world communities congregate around its practice, wider mainstream culture went through a veritable trend cycle with BDSM-related sexual proclivities in 2015. Via the popular *Fifty Shades* book series and the film release of *Fifty Shades of Grey*, which feature explicitly erotic scenes involving BDSM, people who were not BDSM practitioners in any capacity found themselves acutely aware of a "new" sexual fetish (Green 2015). The adult industry responded to the public's interest in kind with themed sex toys, including the branded *Fifty Shades of Grey* Official Collection from UK-based sex toy manufacturer Lovehoney, and a slew of spin-off content titles including the multi-part *A Couples Guide to 50 Shades* from Exquisite films. In addition, as our wider cultural understanding of transgender experiences develops, so too does erotic content featuring transgender performers. And in a world where body acceptance is becoming the norm, so also is content featuring BBW (big beautiful woman) performers. Thus, while porn genres featuring transgender and BBW performers (as well as BDSM) have been popular with particular "niche" consumers for decades, the current landscape of pornography is significantly more inclusive and diverse than ever before (Tibbals 2014).

Clearly, porn content genres vary in their popularity, ebbing and flowing in part with the cultural tide. Within the context of the contemporary adult entertainment industry, there are several noteworthy genres and distribution forms shaping the content we see. Let us take a moment to consider a few of these in greater detail.

"Porn for women"

In a medium that is almost invariably linked to the male gaze, the idea of "porn for women" is somewhat counterintuitive. Women, however, have always been involved in adult content production and, for better and for worse, have always been consumers of erotic material in various forms (Wischhover 2015). Thus, creating pornographic erotica that satisfies a broader range of viewers' needs only makes sense. Starting in the 1980s, performer turned director, Candida Royalle, pioneered porn from a woman's perspective via her company Femme Productions (see Box 11.3). Royalle was not alone, however, and many women became more involved in creating various, more nuanced forms of erotica—particularly, content that was relatively softcore, with less emphasis on showcasing penetration. Alongside these approaches, there were women directing porn, including former performers who are more conventionally hardcore such as Jewel De'Nyle and Shane Diesel. Like Royalle's work, this more typical porn was also shot by (and created for) women; however, the marked difference in style and tone showcased the variability in women's erotic proclivities and perspectives (Milne 2005). As such, while both groups focus on women as porn creators and consumers, the tension created between (allegedly) nuanced softcore and (allegedly) more typical hardcore houses a debate in the "porn for women" spectrum, with invested parties arguing over what sorts of content are truly "for women."

In reality, there is no one universal "women's view." Women enjoy an endless variety of sexual expression, tenors, and activities. If a woman is interested in the content and/or if those responsible for its production are women who feel compelled by women's views, it is all "porn for women." But the debate continues to this day, often conflating "romance porn"—things such as Wicked Pictures' *Passions* series, a line of narrative films engaging conventionally "romantic" storylines and softer sex depictions, with "porn for women," the implications of which include notions that only women are interested in romance. Even so, in today's industry, the spaced carved out by Royalle is still going strong and pornography "for women" and really, "for anyone," is encompassing of diverse desires more so than ever before.

Political porn

While most adult content is primarily focused on the sexual, some adult content also incorporates a significant measure of the political—content that is concerned

---

BOX 11.3 CANDIDA ROYALLE, PORN PIONEER

Candida Royalle (1950–2015) pioneered "porn for women" in the 1980s. She helped shape the landscape of contemporary erotica, both as a media form and as a modern workplace. Royalle began working as a porn performer in 1975 and acted in approximately 70 films during her years in front of the camera before deciding that she belonged behind it. In 1984, Royalle created Femme Productions, the first adult production studio to be owned solely by a woman and to produce films from a woman's perspective. In all, Royalle directed 19 films via Femme Productions, each of them designed to challenge porn's narrative status quo. She asserted there was a space for her unique vision, setting the stage for myriad perspectives we see in adult content production today—because if there was room for the viewpoint of one woman, then certainly there was room for the viewpoints of others. And though the idea of women working in porn may still seem outlandish to some, the fact remains that women work in every occupation, at every level, in front of the camera and behind it, in adult entertainment. This is due in part to the barriers Royalle broke via her own career. And her influence was not limited to porn production. Other ventures included adult novelty development, writing, and documentary filmmaking (Kernes 2015).

Royalle's work showed us there was space for nuance and variability, both in erotic expression specifically and in the creative arts in general. She did this in the face of significant opposition from the wider culture—not, by her own words, opposition from the adult industry. Her work served to augment gender equity and sex positivity in society, creating space for a wider range of sexual expression. Although she passed away in 2015 after struggling for years with recurrent bouts of ovarian cancer, her legacy remains in the world of women's empowerment in adult entertainment (Tibbals 2015c).

with everything from behind-the-scenes labor issues to authentic expression in the final product. In terms of genres, feminist and queer content are doing this most frequently in contemporary adult content production. And though the two are not necessarily mutually exclusive—queer porn is often quite feminist and vice versa—for the sake of discussion, let us consider them one at a time here.

Queer porn. Reclaimed and highly charged, the term "queer" is both a descriptor of sexual identity and a radical political positionality. The word "queer" originally meant strange or unusual, but somewhere around 1900, it morphed into a slur against gay men and perceived sexual deviance. The term was eventually reappropriated, however, and now refers to individuals who identify beyond gender binaries (for example, something other than men or women) and/or heteronormative categorizations (for example, something other than cisgender heterosexual) (Tibbals 2015a; see more in chapter 5). These multi-faceted meanings apply to queer porn content as well. Generally, queer porn features performers of various gender and sexual identities intermixing and exploring genres in ways infrequently seen in other sexually explicit content. Also political, queer porn seeks to present a level of sexuality and identity authenticity (allegedly) absent from most other adult content (Tibbals 2015a).

Aside from the fact that both depict sex scenarios and both often feature performers of various gender and sexual identities, queer porn is almost entirely distinct from what is colloquially known as "tranny" or "shemale" content (hereafter referred to as TS porn). TS porn scenes generally feature at least one trans performer who is undergoing a male-to-female (MtF) transition. TS performers are generally partnered with cisgender men and/or other MtF TS performers, though a slight increase in cisgender women performers working in TS scenes has occurred over the past few years. Unlike queer porn, however, TS content mirrors mainstream adult content production in both form and function and is very rarely overtly political (Tibbals 2015a).

Feminist porn. Often conflated with "porn for women," feminist porn is commonly discussed and frequently debated today, but the genre itself never comes with a clear-cut definition besides that it engages with a feminist dialogue in some way. Indeed, feminist porn has been described as "a self-identified genre and social movement with no one articulated definition" (Tibbals 2014:133). In spite of this ambiguity, the defining tenets of a feminist porn production include an ethical workplace and authenticity for the performers, including authentic sexual expression coupled with an authentic rendering of their image that they feel connected with. Interestingly though, many mainstream porn sets claim to be ethical spaces tapping into authentic sexual expression. Questions related to mainstream porn's capacity to also be feminist are often raised in trade shows and in the feminist porn blogosphere. For example, porn actors' abilities to authentically represent feminism during porn performances are frequently called into question at adult industry trade shows (Tibbals 2015a). To make this even more complicated, many producers and performers reject the attribution of their work as "feminist" while creating content that seems decidedly feminist (Noelle 2016). Thus, in general, "feminist" porn is currently struggling with issues similar to feminism overall—the (impossible) desire to establish and define one "correct" form of feminist expression and, consequently, the capacity to juxtapose and evaluate the feminisms of others.

Queer porn and feminist porn are often, but not always, one and the same. Both seek to showcase the complexities and diversity of erotic expression, while simultaneously engaging erotica as a cultural artifact and tool for social change. As such, for better and for worse, both genres are inextricably linked with the wider queer and feminist social movements.

Thinking about pornography and its meanings

All texts and visual images are polysemic, holding multiple meanings contingent upon time, space, culture, the individual viewer, and more. Further, sexual desire is extremely subjective. As such, universal conceptualizations of erotic and/or sexually stimulating content do not exist. All sexual representations have the potential to be considered banal, artistic, erotic, pornographic, and/or obscene. It is not surprising then that explicit erotic media and the meanings embedded within pornographic depictions of women, men, and sex have been fodder for divisive debates amongst, and between, scholars, politicians, and activists for decades (Tibbals 2010).

Given the potential for a wide variety of meanings, it is important to consider all texts and media within a comparative cultural and historical framework. Pornography's almost inherent volatility makes considering it in context especially important. Pornography and produced erotic stimulation can come in many forms—written, auditory, photographic and drawn, and in some form of moving imagery. As time has passed and technology has evolved, we have seen peeps (short loops of sexual content), conventional movie form, and by-scene and short clips on the internet. Today, you can watch live sex shows or custom order a specific type of short film. Down to casting the performers, you can be your own pornographic director. When considering adult content in any form, it is important to be mindful of the spaces where variability can arise, as well as the consequent bias inherent in any analysis.

Porn and reality

Porn is not real. At least, porn is not real in the sense that it is a literal reflection of reality. Like any other media—a Hollywood film, a bestselling book, or a story on the evening news—porn is crafted. A concept, maybe a script, a director and a crew, lights and makeup, performers, and post-production processing (among many other things) are all elements in creating fantasy visions of various sexual encounters. Sometimes porn may attempt to recreate an actual social or historical happening, and sometimes porn may take inspiration from existing cultural artifacts, but, in the end, it is all just smoke and mirrors.

But, although porn is not real, its creation most certainly involves real people. Real people make porn, and porn performers are real humans who engage in some form of physical sexual performance with other real humans, and they all agree to work with one another before the cameras start rolling. At least, in professional adult content production they do. Unfortunately, porn production and labor are still very mysterious to the wider world and they are often considered unworthy topics for serious consideration by researchers and thinkers in contemporary society. This dynamic feeds into a system that ignores workers' concerns and allows the general population to misappropriate and misuse porn in myriad ways.

Thinking about sex work

Although in many ways we seem to understand the basics of sex work and erotic expression—be it regarding the commercial exchange of sex-related labor or the idea that different people find different representations of sex titillating—wider social norms and ideas about deviance continue to shape our real-world engagement of sex work-related issues. As such, variable preoccupation with evaluating others' desires and life choices sustains continued allocation of the sex worker dividend which, rather than facilitating social and/or psychological growth and development, marginalizes workers and distracts from personal and social issues that may need greater attention. Though we may understand the nuts-and-bolts of sex work, our real-world daily engagement of this vibrant, diverse, and significant part of our social world needs an enhanced critical approach.

References

Albert, Alexa. 2002. *Brothel: Mustang Ranch and Its Women*. New York, NY: Ballantine Books.

Alexa. 2015. *Top Sites In: All Categories > Adult*. Retrieved from: http://www.alexa.com/topsites/category/Top/Adult (accessed November 3, 2015).

Bisschop, Paul, Steven Kastoryano, and Bas van der Klaauw. 2015. *Street Prostitution Zones and Crime*. Discussion Paper No. 9038. Institute for the Study of Labor (IZA).

California v Freeman (488 US 1311; 1989).

CNN. 2009, January 30. "Disgraced Pastor Haggard Admits Second Relationship with Man." *CNN*. Retrieved from: http://www.cnn.com/2009/US/01/29/lkl.ted.haggard/

Connell, Raewyn and Rebecca Pearse. 2014. *Gender: In World Perspective*. Cambridge: Polity Press.

ConnerHabib.com. n.d. *Conner Habib's Blog*. Retrieved from: https://www.connerhabib.com

Dartmouth.edu. n.d. "Sexperts." *Student Wellness Center at Dartmouth University*. Retrieved from: https://www.dartmouth.edu/~healthed/groups/sexperts/

Dickson, E.J. 2015, May 27. "Why are More Women than Ever Paying for Sex?" *DailyDot* Retrieved from: http://www.dailydot.com/lifestyle/women-buying-sex-escorts/

Doll, Darci. 2010. "Celebrity Sex Tapes." Pp. 105–16 in *Porn: Philosophy for Everyone*, edited by Dave Monroe. Oxford: Wiley-Blackwell.

Goaskalice.com. n.d. "Go Ask Alice." *Columbia University*. Retrieved from: http://goaskalice.com/

Green, Emma. 2015, February 10. "Consent Isn't Enough: The Troubling Sex of *Fifty Shades*." Retrieved from: http://www.theatlantic.com/entertainment/archive/2015/02/consent-isnt-enough-in-fifty-shades-of-grey/385267/

Hamilton, Suzy Favor. 2015. *Fast Girl: A Life Spent Running from Madness*. New York, NY: Dey Street Books.

Hellmann, Melissa. 2014, June 18. "Japan Finally Bans Child Pornography." *Time*. Retrieved from: http://time.com/2892728/japan-finally-bans-child-pornography/

Jenness, Valerie. 1990. "From Sex as Sin to Sex as Work: COYOTE and the Reorganization of Prostitution as a Social Problem." *Social Problems* 37(3):403–20.

Jones, Angela. 2015. "Sex Work in a Digital Era." *Sociology Compass* 9(7):558–70.

Kernes, Mark. 2015, September 7. "Famed Actress/Director Candida Royalle Passes." *AVN*. Retrieved from: http://business.avn.com/articles/video/Famed-Actress-Director-Candida-Royalle-Passes-606042.html

Kobola, Frank. 2015, August 13. "Sex Worker Answers All Your Questions About What It's Like to Work at a Legal Brothel." *Cosmopolitan*. Retrieved from: http://www.cosmopolitan.com/sex-love/news/a44814/sex-worker-answers-all-your-questions-about-what-its-like-to-work-at-a-legal-brothel/

Matthew, Roger. 2008. "Prostitution Myths." Pp. 21–42 in *Prostitution, Politics, and Policy*. New York, NY: Routledge-Cavendish.

Miller, Alex. 2011/2012. "Sugar Dating: A New Take on an Old Issue." *Buffalo Journal of Gender Law & Social Policy* 20:33–68.

Miller v. California, 413 U.S. 15 (1973).

Milne, Carly. 2005. *Naked Ambition: Women Who Are Changing Pornography*. New York, NY: Carroll & Graf.

Mitchell, Kimberly, Michele Ybarra, Josephine Korchmaros, and Joseph Kosciw. 2014. "Accessing Sexual Health Information Online: Use, Motivations and Consequences for Youth with Different Sexual Orientations." *Health Education Research* 29(1):147–57.

Mullin, Frankie. 2015, October 19. "The Difference Between Decriminalisation and Legalisation of Sex Work." *Newstatesman*. Retrieved from: http://www.newstatesman.com/politics/feminism/2015/10/difference-between-decriminalisation-and-legalisation-sex-work

Murphy, Tim. 2015, September 25. "What Did Busting Rentboy.com Do to the Hustler Economy? 6 Rentboys Tell All." *New York Magazine*. Retrieved from: http://nymag.com/daily/intelligencer/2015/09/six-rentboys-on-hustling-after-rentboycom.html

Noelle, Nica. 2016, February 2. "Do I Make Feminist Porn?" *Huffington Post*. Retrieved from: http://www.huffingtonpost.com/nica-noelle/do-i-make-feminist-porn_b_3002905.html

Perdue, Lewis. 2002. "How the Internet is Shaping Sex." Pp. 151–68 in *EroticaBiz: How Sex Shaped the Internet*. Lincoln, NE: iUniverse, inc.

Price, Joan. 2014. *The Ultimate Guide to Sex After Fifty: How to Maintain – or Regain – a Spicy, Satisfying Sex Life*. Berkeley, CA: Cleis Press.

Romero, Dennis. 2013, January 16. "Stacie Halas' Porn Career Was Discovered By Two Other Districts, State Panel Says." *LA Weekly*. Retrieved from: http://www.laweekly.com/news/stacie-halas-porn-career-was-discovered-by-two-other-districts-state-panel-says-4172750

Scarleteen.com. n.d. *Scarleteen*. Retrieved from: http://scarleteen.com

Seekingarrangement.com. n.d. "Seeking Arrangement." Retrieved from: http://seekingarrangement.com

SunnyMegatron.com. n.d. *SunnyMegatron*. Retrieved from: http://www.sunnymegatron.com

Tibbals, Chauntelle Anne. 2010. "From 'The Devil in Miss Jones' to 'DMJ6' – Power, Inequality, and Consistency in the Content of US Adult Films." *Sexualities* 13:625–44.

Tibbals, Chauntelle Anne. 2013a. "Sex Work, Office Work – Women Working Behind the Scenes in the US Adult Film Industry." *Gender, Work & Organization* 20(1):20–35.

Tibbals, Chauntelle Anne. 2013b. "When Law Moves Quicker Than Culture – Key Jurisprudential Regulations Shaping the US Adult Content Production Industry." *The Scholar: St. Mary's Law Review on Race and Social Justice* 15:213–59.

Tibbals, Chauntelle Anne. 2014. "Gonzo, Trannys, and Teens – Current Trends in Adult Content Production." *Porn Studies* 1(1-2):127–35.

Tibbals, Chauntelle Anne. 2015a. *Exposure: A Sociologist Explores Sex, Society, and Adult Entertainment.* Austin, TX: Greenleaf Press.

Tibbals, Chauntelle Anne. 2015b, June 8. "Hardcore Sex Ed Videos are the Sexiest Sex Ed of All." *Playboy.* Retrieved from: http://www.playboy.com/articles/hardcore-sex-education

Tibbals, Chauntelle Anne. 2015c, September 8. "RIP, Candida Royalle, Pioneering Adult Film Actress and Producer." *UpRoxx.* Retrieved from: http://uproxx.com/filmdrunk/2015/09/porn-pioneer-candida-royalle-dead/

Tibbals, Chauntelle Anne. 2015d, November 2. "A Sex Worker Tells Us about Her Celebrity Hook-Ups." *Playboy.* Retrieved from: http://www.playboy.com/articles/escort-sex-celebrity

van Soomeren, Paul. 2004. "Design Against Kerb-Crawling: Tippelzones (Vice Zones) – European Experiences in Displacement." *Proceedings of the 9th Annual International Crime Prevention through Environmental Design (CPTED) Conference,* September 13–16, 2004.

Weitzer, Ronald. 2000. "Why We Need More Research on Sex Work." Pp. 1–13 in *Sex for Sale: Prostitution, Pornography, and the Sex Industry,* edited by Ronald Weitzer. New York, NY: Routledge.

Weitzer, Ronald. 2005. "New Directions in Research on Prostitution." *Crime, Law & Social Change* 43:211–35.

Weitzer, Ronald. 2007. "The Social Construction of Sex Trafficking: Ideology and Institutionalization of a Moral Crusade." *Politics & Society* 35(3):447–75.

Wischhover, Cheryl. 2015, September 3. "How I Started Making Porn Women Actually Like." *Cosmopolitan.* Retrieved from: http://www.cosmopolitan.com/sex-love/news/a45823/how-i-started-making-porn-women-actually-like/

UNIT IV
SEX CRIMES AND CRIMINALS

Unit IV introduction

At this point we must now turn our attention to perhaps the most difficult subject area in our journey into a deeper understanding of sexual deviance: sex crimes and criminals. Discussing sex crime is particularly challenging because all of us have some familiarity with unwanted sexual contact, whether it be through our own experiences or through those we are close to. As a result, this final unit requires keen sensitivity and heightened awareness of your own feelings. Recall the recommended steps of self-care for reading this textbook offered in chapter 1, Figure 1.2. Remember to check in with yourself while reading, assess your feelings, and seek additional help if needed.

In chapter 12, a framework for understanding rape and sexual assault is provided. First, rape and consent are defined in both legal and social contexts. Second, the complexities involved in estimating rape prevalence are discussed in terms of barriers to reporting rape and the limitations of existing data sets, including how the victim-perpetrator relationship affects these issues. Next, prominent cultural misconceptions about rape (i.e., rape myths) and their effects are considered as they contribute to the cultural complexities regarding rape and sexual assault. Illustrative examples including the role of alcohol in rape, college culture and rape, women who rape, and rape in prisons and in the military are offered. In addition, the cultural dialogue regarding "legitimate" and "blameworthy" victims is analyzed and discussed. Understandings of motivations of men who rape (i.e., power and control) and rape survivors' experiences, including survivor empowerment, are provided. The conclusion of this chapter considers strategies for change by focusing on language choices and bystander intervention. The goal of this chapter is to encourage the reader to carefully consider the cultural and legal complexities that comprise sexual assault and to begin a conversation about reducing sexual violence, responding to survivors of rape, and creating a global cultural shift away from rape-prone environments.

Chapter 13 discusses the nature of sex crimes against children. Specifically, pedophilia, hebephilia, incest, and child sexual abuse in sex-related media (CSAM), including artificially generated CSAM and sexting, are defined and described. Next, this chapter examines the grooming and luring techniques of child sex offenders, including how the internet has shaped, changed, and influenced the sexual exploitation of children and the difficulties facing law enforcement with prosecuting offenders. Finally, the short- and long-term gendered effects of childhood sexual abuse are discussed.

Finally, in chapter 14, we turn our attention to criminals—in particular those labeled as "sex offenders"—by examining how this deviant label and status affects both societal perspectives about sex offenders and how this highly stigmatized identity relates to particularly harsh treatment by the criminal justice system both while sex offenders are in the prison system and post-prison release (e.g., community notification, restricting where sex offenders live, chemical/surgical castration, and electronic monitoring). The social consequences associated with the "sex offender" label (including employment, housing, victimization) as well as sex offender treatment (i.e., cognitive behavioral therapy, chemical and surgical castration) and its relationship to recidivism are also discussed. Finally, the reader is encouraged to consider, why are we so punitive?

Above all, the content in the remainder of this textbook is likely to evoke intense emotions and may even be particularly disturbing and problematic to some readers. As we learn about some of the darkest and most terrifying forms of sexual deviance (including rape, forced sexual contact, and child molestation) it is important to think about why and how these crimes continue to exist in society. With careful attention to the sociological complexities involved in sex crimes, we can begin to dismantle the socially constructed layers of power that surround these horrific events.

12

RAPE AND SEXUAL ASSAULT

The carnal knowledge[1] of a female forcibly and against her will. What does this convoluted phrase refer to? From 1929 to 2012, this is how the United States Federal Bureau of Investigation defined the crime of "forcible rape" (Federal Bureau of Investigation 2004:19). Obviously grossly limited, rape in the eyes of the most sophisticated law enforcement agency in the United States was a crime that could only be perpetrated against a woman, and only if she was forced to engage in penile-vaginal intercourse. This narrow definition effectively told men that they could not be recognized as victims of rape nor could any person who experienced unwanted oral or anal penetration. Unfortunately, the inadequacy of the FBI's interpretation of the crime of rape is just one example in a stream of misunderstood facts about rape and sexual assault. And while the FBI has now updated their definition to be more inclusive (rape is: "penetration, no matter how slight, of the vagina or anus with any body part or object, or oral penetration by a sex organ of another person, without the consent of the victim"), most people continue to be misinformed about the nuances and intricacies of this all-too common crime (Bierie and Davis-Siegel 2015).

Specifically, this chapter includes discussions of defining rape, estimations of rape prevalence and reporting rape, the victim–perpetrator relationship, rape myths and their effects, situational factors affecting rape recognition and reporting, motivations of men who rape, and rape survivors. The conclusion of this chapter considers strategies for change. The wide scope of this chapter is intended to offer a framework for understanding rape and sexual assault. But this is just a starting point; to stay truly informed about this complicated crime requires continual engagement with cultural discussions of sex and sexuality.

Defining rape

The difficulties in defining rape lie within vast cultural variations in the sociological constructions of gender, sex, and power. Therefore, any discussion of rape "definitions" is necessarily cultural and sociological. For example, in a study with over 300 women and men from Chicago, Philadelphia, and San Francisco comparing attitudes toward different behaviors and whether or not they constituted rape, there were obvious gender differences. Specifically, women were significantly more likely than men to define particular acts as rape (Gordon and Riger 1991) (see Figure 12.1). In addition, although they are certainly aware of the specificities of the ways rape is *legally* defined, when police officers are asked how they *personally* define rape when dealing with victims and criminals, some emphasize lack of consent while others emphasize the use of force in their definitions of rape (Campbell and Johnson 1997). Beyond this, within the U.S., each individual state has its own laws about rape and sexual assault and rape laws also vary globally. For example, in Israel, rape is defined solely as the violation of the woman's "sex organ" while in Oklahoma (USA) and Ireland, rape includes crimes against men and women (see Table 12.1).

Legal definitions of rape are important to examine because they can have a very real impact on how rape is understood from both a legal standpoint and a cultural one. For example, as noted in the beginning of this chapter, the FBI only recently redefined rape from the antiquated and specious phrase "carnal knowledge" to a more inclusive "penetration without consent" (to paraphrase). And this change only came about as a result of successful lobbying by the "Rape is Rape" campaign that was promoted by *Ms.* magazine[2] and a Change.org[3] petition that generated more

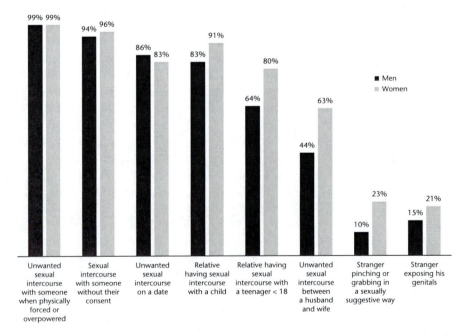

FIGURE 12.1   Is it rape? Men and women define acts as rape

Data adapted from Gordon and Riger (1991).

TABLE 12.1 Rape Laws in Oklahoma, Israel, and Ireland

Oklahoma (USA)	Israel	Ireland
Rape in the First Degree	Rape	Rape
Rape is vaginal or anal penetration by force, violence, threat of force, violence accompanied by apparent power of execution, or if the victim is: • impaired (either because of mental illness, intoxicated by a narcotic or anesthetic agent, or any other unsoundness of mind); • unconscious of the nature of the act and this fact is known to the perpetrator; • under the age of 14 and the perpetrator is over the age of 18. Any sexual penetration, however slight, is sufficient to complete the crime of rape.	Rape has occurred if a person introduces any part of the body or any object into the woman's sex organ: • without her freely given consent; • with the woman's consent, which was obtained by deceit in respect of the identity of the person or the nature of the act; • when the woman is a minor below age 14, even with her consent; • by exploiting the woman's state of unconsciousness or other condition that prevents her from giving her free consent; • by exploiting the fact that she is mentally ill or deficient, if—because of her illness or mental deficiency—her consent to intercourse did not constitute free consent.	Rape is assault upon a person (either male or female) that includes (a) penetration (however slight) of the anus or mouth by the penis, or (b) penetration (however slight) of the vagina by any object held or manipulated by another person.
Okla. Stat. Ann. tit. 21, § 1114	Penal Law 5737–1977, Article Five: Sex Offenses, Rape 345 (a)	Criminal Law (Rape) (Amendment) Act 1990

than 150,000 emails to the FBI demanding the definition be updated (Terkel 2012). Beyond a simple change in wording, this redefinition has had a huge impact on U.S. official rape statistics. For example, analyzing data from 6,328 law enforcement agencies, 2013 FBI data show that the new rape definition resulted in a substantial increase in rape reports. Specifically, there were 11,256 incidents that would have been missed under the old definition of rape—in other words, there was a staggering 41.7 percent increase in rape reports in 2013 as a result of the new rape definition (Federal Bureau of Investigation 2014) (see Figure 12.2). Overall, broadening the scope of the previously narrow definition of rape allows the FBI to capture data about male victims, acts of sodomy, penetration by any object or body part, and offenses in which physical force is not involved.

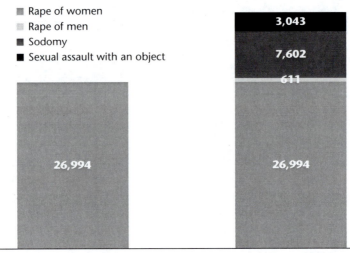

FIGURE 12.2 Annual rape estimates based on old and revised FBI definitions

Data adapted from an FBI (2014) report describing NIBRS 2013 data from 6,328 law enforcement agencies.

While most of us do not sit around analyzing FBI statistics, we do look to legal and law enforcement entities to understand crime. If the law tells us that a crime has occurred, we pay attention, we respond, and we take it seriously. If legal jurisdiction does not apply to a matter, we are less likely to conceptualize a particular act as a "crime." As a result, our cultural presumptions about what constitutes "rape" changes along with state and federal laws (although not always at the same point in time). In effect, there is a reciprocal relationship between legal and cultural definitions of rape. This is especially important when it comes to recognizing rape (and rape victims) that do not fit within prominent cultural stereotypes (e.g., rape of men, see Box 12.1).

While there is a great deal of global variance in the legal parameters of rape (some countries do not even have laws against unwanted sexual intercourse, especially in the context of marriage), the majority emphasize penetration (vaginal, anal, or oral penetration by an object or body part) without consent (see discussion below). Some laws also specify age parameters (e.g., persons under a certain age cannot legally consent to sex, see Box 12.2) and the coercive environment of the crime (e.g., prisons, see later in this chapter).

Overall, there is no simple or universal way to define rape. However, for the purposes of this textbook, "rape" is defined as:

> Any unwanted sexual acts (including vaginal, anal, or oral penetration by an object or body part and being made to penetrate others) committed without consent and/or against a person's will, obtained by force, or threat of force, intimidation, or when a person is unable to consent.

BOX 12.1 MEN AS VICTIMS OF UNWANTED SEX

The dominant cultural stereotypes surrounding rape almost always conceptualize men as perpetrators and women as victims; however, sexual violence is much more complex (Stemple and Meyer 2014). In fact, the National Intimate Partner and Sexual Violence Survey (NISVS 2011) of 18,049 American adults found that in the past year, the number of women who reported being raped was nearly identical to the number of cases where men were forced or coerced to sexually penetrate another person. This striking finding—that men and women reported similar rates of unwanted penetrative sex in a 12-month period—is clear evidence that gender differences in "rape" experiences are not nearly as robust as our cultural stereotypes would lead us to believe. Compared to women, men also reported a similar frequency of experiences with unwanted sexual contact (unwanted sexual experiences involving touch but not sexual penetration) although sexual coercion (unwanted sexual penetration that occurs after a person is pressured in a nonphysical way) was more common among women compared to men (see Figure 12.3). Thus, the realities of rape do not match the cultural stereotype of women as the sole victims of unwanted penetrative sex.

What is more, when we look at the gender of the perpetrators of these crimes, we continue to see trends that do not fit normative conceptualizations of rape. While the majority of women indicated that they were victimized by men in the cases of rape (98.1 percent indicated a male perpetrator) as well as sexual coercion and unwanted sexual contact (92.5 percent indicated a male perpetrator), men also reported that they were victimized by men in the case of rape (93.3 percent indicated a male perpetrator). Thus, the majority of rape perpetrators are men (whether the victim is a man or a woman). However, men overwhelming report being victimized by a woman in the cases of being made to penetrate (79.2 percent indicate a female perpetrator) and sexual coercion (83.6 percent indicate a female perpetrator) while unwanted sexual contact appears to be more evenly split (53.1 percent indicate a female perpetrator) (see Figure 12.4). Thus, these data show that the crime of rape is most often perpetrated by men but when examining other sexual victimization experiences among men, namely being made to penetrate and sexual coercion, women are more likely to be perpetrators of sexual violence against men. Overall, it is clear that men are certainly not the sole perpetrators of sexual violence.

As we can see, for the most part, our stereotypes about unwanted sex do not fit with the reality of these crimes. But beyond simple inaccuracies in the raw numbers, there are two major problems with the prevailing "men as perpetrators and women as victims" rape paradigm. First, this way of thinking obscures any unwanted sex that occurs outside of this conceptualization. In other words, culturally, we do not perceive men as victims or women as

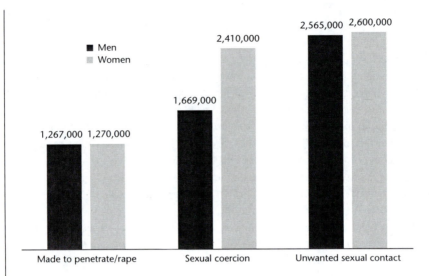

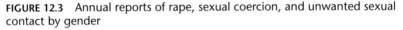

FIGURE 12.3 Annual reports of rape, sexual coercion, and unwanted sexual contact by gender

Data adapted from NISVS (2011) incident reports. Estimates are based on incidents taking place in the last 12 months and are rounded to the nearest 1,000. The cell sizes for "Made to penetrate" (women) and "Rape" (men) were too small to provide a reliable estimate. Here, "Made to penetrate" (men) and "Rape" (women) are presented side-by-side for ease of comparison.

Notes about NISVS: Rape is defined as any completed or attempted unwanted vaginal, oral, or anal penetration by penis, fingers, and/or object through the use of physical force (such as being pinned or held down, or by the use of violence) or threats to physically harm and includes times when the victim was drunk, high, drugged, or passed out and unable to consent.

Being made to penetrate someone else includes times when the victim was made to, or there was an attempt to make them, sexually penetrate someone without the victim's consent because the victim was physically forced (such as being pinned or held down, or by the use of violence) or threatened with physical harm, or when the victim was drunk, high, drugged, or passed out and unable to consent. Among women, this behavior reflects a female being made to orally penetrate another's vagina or anus. Among men, this includes being made to orally penetrate another's vagina or anus; vaginally, anally, and/or orally penetrating another using one's own penis; or being made to receive oral sex.

Sexual coercion is defined as unwanted sexual penetration (vaginal, oral, or anal sex) that occurs after a person is pressured in a nonphysical way that includes being worn down by someone who repeatedly asked for sex or showed they were unhappy; feeling pressured by being lied to, being told promises that were untrue, having someone threaten to end a relationship or spread rumors; and sexual pressure due to someone using their influence or authority.

Unwanted sexual contact is defined as unwanted sexual experiences involving touch but not sexual penetration, such as being kissed in a sexual way, or having sexual body parts fondled or grabbed.

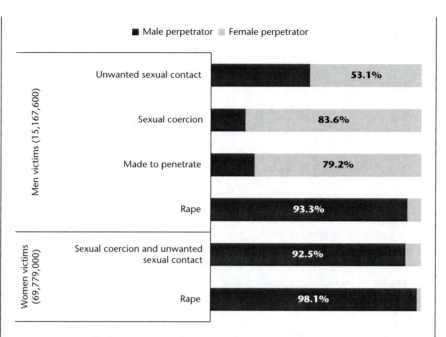

■ Male perpetrator ▨ Female perpetrator

FIGURE 12.4 Lifetime reports of unwanted sex by gender of victim and perpetrator

Data adapted from NISVS (2011). Estimates are based on lifetime reports. The cell sizes for "Made to penetrate" (women) were too small to provide a reliable estimate and the NISVS collapsed the categories of sexual coercion and unwanted sexual contact when providing data about the gender of the perpetrator for women victims (thus, they are combined here). See notes for Figure 12.3 for NISVS definitions of all unwanted sex acts.

perpetrators of sex crimes (even though the data clearly show that this does frequently occur). In this way, we delegitimize male victims and ignore female perpetrators of sex crimes; thus, a significant amount of unwanted sex goes unrecognized by the victims themselves because it does not fit within the dominant cultural stereotypes about rape. Second, because formalized law is a reflection of culture, some law enforcement agencies continue to use outdated definitions of sexual victimization that reflect the "men as perpetrators and women as victims" rape paradigm. As a result, men are often formally excluded from being "rape" victims in the eyes of the law. When a sex crime does occur where the victim is a man and/or the offender is a woman, there is a high likelihood that this crime will go unreported and if it is, it is also likely that the victim will be met with disbelief (Stemple and Meyer 2014). Overall, there is an overwhelming lack of concern for male victims built from the damaging, harmful stereotype that sex crimes are solely perpetrated by men against women.

BOX 12.2 AGE OF CONSENT

Most cultures view sex between adults and children as deviant. What varies, however, is the social construction of "child" status. Historically, the definitive distinction between "child" and "adult" was puberty. But as we learned in chapter 8, the relatively recent invention of the concept of "adolescence" has shifted our understandings of the divisions between childhood and adulthood. Now we recognize the time following puberty until adulthood as a period where teens need supervision and protection, and this is especially the case when it comes to sex. Legal statutes typically identify such protections with an "age of consent," which is the age at which a person is considered to be legally competent to consent to sexual acts, and is thus, the minimum age that a person is legally permitted to engage in sexual activity. The purpose of these laws is to protect teens and children from harmful sexual encounters. In the majority of jurisdictions around the world, laws define the age of consent between 12 and 18 years of age with most countries falling in the 16 to 18 age range. Age of consent is a relatively universal concept and nearly all cultures identify some legal protection against sex with children (Aggrawal 2009). In addition, as of recently, some Western countries have actually *raised* their ages of consent. For example, in 2008, Canada raised their age of consent from 14 to 16 and in Spain, the age of consent was raised from 13 to 16 in 2015 (Miller *et al.* 2010; Greenberg 2015).

However, as with most legal statutes, there are exceptions to the "age of consent" rule. These include:

- *Close-in-age exceptions.* Some jurisdictions allow minors under the age of consent to engage in sexual acts if their partner is close in age to them. For example, in Canada, the age of consent is 16, but there are two close-in-age exceptions: 14- and 15-year-olds are permitted to engage in sexual activity with individuals not more than five years older and 12- and 13-year-olds are permitted to engage in sexual activity with individuals not more not more than two years older (Miller *et al.* 2010). In other situations, a precise number of years is not provided but rather implied. For example, in Slovenia, the age of consent is 15, but the crime of "Sexual Assault on a Person below the Age of Fifteen Years" requires that there is "a marked discrepancy between the maturity of the perpetrator and that of the victim" (Penal Code of the Republic of Slovenia).
- *Gender and age exceptions.* There are also sometimes different ages of consent based on gender. For example, in Papua New Guinea, the age of consent for penile-vaginal sex is 16 for young women but only 14 for young men (and anal sex is illegal in all cases). By contrast in Indonesia, the age of consent is 16 for young women but 19 for young men (Aggrawal 2009).

- *Marriage exceptions.* According to most legal statutes, age of consent laws do not apply if the parties are legally married to each other. So, for example, while the age of consent is 16 in Finland, if a minor under the age of 16 obtains special permission to marry, he/she can legally have sex with his/her spouse. Furthermore, in Afghanistan, Iran, Pakistan, Qatar, Saudi Arabia, Sudan, and Yemen, all sexual activity outside of marriage is illegal. As a result, in these jurisdictions, the *de facto* age of consent is the minimum marriageable age. So in Afghanistan this means that young men must be at least 18 and young women at least 16 years old to marry (and thus, legally have sex with each other). However, some countries, such as Yemen and Saudi Arabia, do not have legal statutes identifying minimum marriageable age and thus, there is no legally defined age of consent (Aggrawal 2009).
- *Same-sex sexual activity exceptions.* In some jurisdictions, the age of consent for same-sex sexual activity is higher than the age of consent for opposite-sex sexual activity. For example, in Chile, the age of consent for opposite-sex sexual activity is 14 but the age of consent for same-sex sexual activity is 18. However, there are still many countries where all same-sex sexual activity is illegal regardless of age (Aggrawal 2009).
- *Position of authority/trust exceptions.* Some legal statutes raise the age of consent when a person is in a position of authority or trust such as teacher, coach, babysitter, or pastor. For example, in Colorado (USA), the age of consent is 17, but if a sexual partner is in a position of authority or trust, the age of consent is 18.
- *Sex work exceptions.* In many jurisdictions, the minimum age of consent to participate in noncommercial sex is differs from the minimum age to legally participate in sex work such as prostitution and pornography. For example, in the Netherlands, the age of consent is 16 but prostitutes must be at least 18 and in the city of Amsterdam, 21 is the minimum age for prostitution (Rodriguez 2013). In addition, in the United States, under federal law it is a crime to film or photograph minors under the age of 18 engaged in sexual acts regardless of statewide age of consent laws (see more in chapter 13).

Beyond legal statutes, there are also cultural understandings of "age of consent." In other words, although laws dictate parameters surrounding sex and age, sexual activity certainly occurs outside of these restrictions and it is not always viewed highly negatively. This is because there is no "magic" age that we can all agree upon where teens turn into rational forward-thinking adults who understand their sexual-decision making, and thus, will not be harmed when engaging in a sex act. In fact, some adults do not ever reach such a hypothetical "magic" age. As a result, we are left to adhere to the laws while understanding that there are exceptions (both legal and social) to the age of consent rules.

In tandem with this, it is essential to define "consent." As with "rape," "consent" is also a culturally defined concept. There are both legal and social ways to identify consent, although consent is rarely explicitly defined in either context. In fact, most of the time, there are not established parameters in place to identify whether consent has or has not taken place, people merely presume the presence or absence of consent based on cultural cues (Beres 2007). Thus, as with rape, there is no simple or universal way to define consent. Overall, however, consent involves four major components (see Figure 12.5):

- *Mental willingness and desire.* A mental willingness and desire to engage in a particular activity are necessary components of consent. However, both willingness and desire are complicated by cultural stereotypes. For example, within heterosexual relationships, the normative sexual script suggests that men should initiate sexual activity while women must either refuse or accept the invitation. In this context, men are perceived as "ready, willing, and able" and women must decide if they want to comply. This leaves little space for men to contemplate their willingness and suggests that women's desire is dependent on men's initiative behavior. This also neglects to recognize same-sex sexual behavior and sex with multiple partners (Beres 2007). As a result, cultural and social scripts surrounding willingness and desire are necessarily embedded within the context of consent.

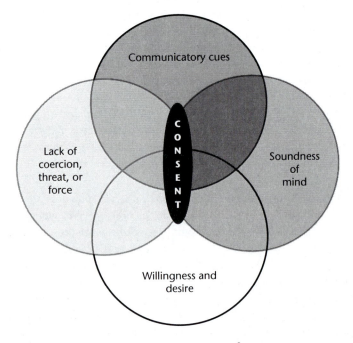

FIGURE 12.5 Four necessary components of consent

- *Communicatory cues.* Communicating willingness and/or desire is a second necessary component of consent. Communicatory cues include both nonverbal and verbal signals that should ideally be discussed and agreed upon by the participants prior to sexual activity. In addition, communicatory cues should be expressed both before and during sexual activity as a continual process of agreement to convey consent. In general, nonverbal signals (e.g., kissing and kissing back, touching and touching back) have been found to be used more frequently than verbal signals (e.g., saying "yes" or "I want you") to communicate consent by both men and women in heterosexual and same-sex sexual encounters (Hickman and Muehlenhard 1999; Beres *et al.* 2004). As with other issues related to consent, communicatory cues are culturally and situationally variant constructs. What signals "yes" in one situation may not in another.
- *Without coercion, threat, or force or under duress.* Consent must take place without coercion, threat, or force or under duress. However, what is defined as coercive or threatening behavior varies. For example, in the U.S. prison system, there are laws that protect those who are in a vulnerable position (i.e., prisoners) from those who are in a position of power over them (i.e., guards, wardens) because any sex acts occurring between them are perceived as inherently coercive. Thus, "coercive" also has cultural and situational variance.
- *Soundness of mind.* All parties involved must be of sound mind to consent to sexual activity. Impairments to soundness of mind include intoxication (via alcohol, drugs, or other mind-altering substances), being asleep, as well as not being of mental capacity to consent, which includes impairment by mental illness and not being of appropriate age to consent (see Box 12.2).

Thus, for the purposes of this textbook, "consent" is defined as:

> A process of agreement to engage in a certain activity at a certain time and place with a particular person or persons without coercion, threat, or force made by persons of sound mind that involves mental willingness and desire and ongoing communicatory cues both before and during sexual activity.

Estimations of rape prevalence and reporting rape

Because rape is such a complicated and culturally defined crime, it is impossible to know the exact number of rapes that occur in a particular society. Criminologists sometimes describe the amount of unreported or undiscovered crime as the "dark figure of crime" and this is especially significant for rape as it is a crime that is frequently not reported to law enforcement agencies. Thus, in order to estimate rape prevalence in the United States, there are two major types of data that can be utilized, each with their own advantages and disadvantages: official measures of crime and unofficial measures of crime. Official measures of crime are collected by reports from law enforcement agencies while unofficial measures of crime are collected from self-reports, typically from victims and criminals themselves, although the NCVS does both (see Table 12.2).

It is especially important to consider the source of data when attempting to estimate the prevalence of rape because the way rape is defined and the method by which rape is reported can strongly effect the estimated rape prevalence. For example, according to official measures of crime in 2012, there were anywhere between 84,376 (UCR) to 346,860 (NCVS) rapes in the United States depending on what data source you use. And unofficial self-report measures of rape are almost always significantly higher. For example, a self-report survey conducted by the CDC estimates there were over 2.5 million rapes in the U.S. in 2010 alone (NISVS 2011).

There are two main reasons why there are such wide variations in rape prevalence estimates. The first is related to reporting to official law enforcement authorities. When rape prevalence estimates only rely on official reports of rape, they are most definitely gross underestimates [it is estimated that only 2 percent of official rape reports are false allegations (Lisak *et al.* 2010)]. This is because the vast majority of rape victims (NCVS estimates suggest 65 percent or higher) do not report to official agencies. Some reasons why victims do not report their rape to law enforcement authorities include:

- *Lack of recognition of rape*

    ○ Do not believe that what happened is actually "rape" (either in a legal or cultural sense).
    ○ Do not think they will be believed.
    ○ Feel it is not important enough to report.
    ○ Do not feel the perpetrator meant to harm them.

- *Emotional responses*

    ○ Embarrassment or shame about the assault.
    ○ Guilt or self-blame about the assault.
    ○ Do not want anyone to know this happened.
    ○ Friendly, loving, or otherwise positive emotions directed toward the perpetrator.
    ○ Placing the needs of others (e.g., children) above the desire to report.

- *Perceived negative social repercussions of reporting*

    ○ Fear the negative stigma attached to being labeled and viewed as a rape victim.
    ○ Fear retaliation/reprisal from the perpetrator(s) or from their friends/family.
    ○ Fear being ostracized from their family, social, or religious group.
    ○ Do not want to get the perpetrator in trouble.

- *Perceived negative legal repercussions of reporting*

    ○ Believe that going through the reporting experience with law enforcement officials might be too traumatic or damaging.

TABLE 12.2 Major sources of crime data in the United States

Official measures of crime			Unofficial measures of crime
Federal Bureau of Investigations' Uniform Crime Reports (UCR)	Federal Bureau of Investigations' National Incident-Based Reporting System (NIBRS)	Bureau of Justice Statistics' National Crime Victimization Survey (NCVS)	Self-report surveys
(1929–Present) Collects count information about crimes reported to law enforcement authorities (~18,000 agencies)	(1989–Present) Collects detailed incident level information about crimes reported to law enforcement authorities (~5,000 agencies)	(1973–Present) Collects detailed information about crimes (both reported and not reported to law enforcement) through interviews with all household members at least 12 years old in a nationally representative sample of approximately 90,000 households two times per year (~160,000 persons)	n/a Collects targeted crime information specific to the goals of the researcher or research institute
Advantages: Provides a reliable count of crimes that are likely to be reported to police (i.e., murder, robbery)	*Advantages:* Provides detailed information about reported crimes (i.e., victim characteristics, injuries, weapons used, location)	*Advantages:* Provides detailed information about victim's experiences and includes crimes not reported to law enforcement	*Advantages:* Provides detailed information about any crime, criminal, or victim experiences the researcher is interested in
Limitations: • Limited to only crimes reported to law enforcement • Only provides a count of crime incidents • Reports only the most serious crime committed in a single incident • Not all states require municipalities to report data to the FBI	*Limitations:* • Limited to only crimes reported to law enforcement • Only a sampling of law enforcement agencies participate • Not all states require municipalities to report data to the FBI	*Limitations:* • Limited to those residing in households and those over the age of 12 • Respondents may be reluctant to disclose their victimization during an interview that takes place in the home within earshot of other family members	*Limitations:* • Limited to only respondents who are willing to participate • Only a sampling of respondents participate • Funding is often limited for self-report survey research

- Believe that they cannot provide enough evidence to prove that an unwanted sex act occurred (i.e., the burden of proof is on the victim).
- Fear that past sexual experiences will be revealed as a result of legal procedures. Although, in many places such as Australia, Canada, and the United States, "rape shield laws" protect victims by limiting the admission of evidence of past sexual experiences in criminal proceedings.
- Fear being punished for other infractions that took place during the rape such as underage drinking or illicit drug use.
- Do not think that anything will be done about it even if they do report.

- *Utilization of non-law enforcement based responses*

  - Decided to deal with it on their own (i.e., it was a personal matter).
  - Decided to report to another source (friend, counselor, teacher, social worker, etc.).

The second reason why there is such diversity in rape prevalence estimates is related to the way "rape" is defined. Because definitions of sexual violence vary between institutions and cross-culturally, when unwanted sexual experiences occur, sometimes they meet the legal parameters for "rape" but sometimes they do not. For example, most laws define "rape" as penetration without consent. However, this definition most often does not recognize situations in which a man was "made to penetrate" another. In addition, culturally, certain unwanted sexual experiences are viewed as rape but others are not (even if they do meet the legal parameters of "rape"). For example, although a drunk person cannot legally give consent, when unwanted sexual experiences occur between drunk people, many do not interpret that as rape (even though it is). By contrast, when cultural norms shift and people begin to recognize, for example, that being raped by somebody you know is common, more rapes of this type will be reported because they meet the cultural stereotype about what "rape" is (Orcutt and Faison 1988). Thus, both legal and cultural definitions define rape in a certain way. As a result, when looking to understand rape prevalence, it is important to recognize that the rape statistics we have are limited by stereotypes about rape that inform both legal and social recognition of certain unwanted sexual experiences as rape.

In summary, precise estimates of overall rape prevalence in a particular society are impossible to come by. There is near universal agreement that rape is an underreported crime and this is further complicated by varying legal and cultural definitions of rape. In addition, when attempting to ascertain an estimate of rape prevalence, it depends on what types of populations are surveyed (i.e., prison populations differ from non-incarcerated adult populations). Overall, most U.S. studies show that **approximately 20 percent of American women (1 in 5)** and **6 percent of American men (1 in 16) will experience rape at some point in their lives** (NISVS 2011). This translates to millions of victims each year. While an exact number is unknown, researchers are confident that rape is an all too common experience.

The victim-perpetrator relationship

The vast majority of sexual violence in the United States occurs between people that know each other. Contrary to the sensationalized rape scenario where a weapon-wielding stranger assaults an unknown victim in a dark alley in a blitz attack and leaves the victim for dead (a scenario that has been popularized in movies and other media but is relatively uncommon), most rapes involve intimate partners and acquaintances. In fact, only a small percentage involve strangers (only 12 percent of women victims indicate being raped by a stranger and only 8 percent of men report being made to penetrate by a stranger) (see Figure 12.6) (NISVS 2011).

The dynamics of the victim-perpetrator relationship are important to recognize because they affect how unwanted sexual experiences are perceived. For example, because acquaintance rape necessarily involves someone known to the victim, victims may be reluctant to conceptualize their unwanted sexual experience as "rape." Furthermore, even if they do see their unwanted sexual experience as "rape," they may not want to risk ruining a friendship or alienation from a social group by reporting it. Beyond this, "acquaintances" can also include colleagues, classmates, dorm mates, or other persons that the victim may be likely to come into contact with again. Thus, victims may choose to avoid confronting the issue in fear of future problematic encounters with an acquaintance.

Victims who are raped by their current or former intimate partners or spouses may also be less inclined to report and/or recognize their victimization because they may feel romantically, emotionally, and/or sexually attached to the perpetrator. This can mean that they do not view their unwanted sexual experiences as rape and/or that the perpetrator did not mean to harm them or even that it is part of their "wifely" or "husbandly" duty to supply sex to their partners at their request. They may also be financially bound to them, they may reside in the same home as them, and they may have children in the home with them. Other situations involving rape among relatives (i.e., incestuous rape) can also be complicated by similar factors.

Additional elements of the victim-perpetrator relationship that can affect both recognition and reporting of unwanted sexual experiences include when the perpetrator is in a position of power or authority over the victim. This can involve situations such as teachers, coaches, religious officials, bosses, and supervisors, as well as parents or older siblings, cousins, and other relatives. Positions of power typically involve trust and authority. Thus, when victims are raped by those in a position of power over them, they experience violations of trust as well as threats to their social relationship with the perpetrator.

Overall, the social dynamics within an unwanted sexual experience most often involve people that know each other and who are of similar age (Spivak 2011). As a result, both the way rape is conceptualized and the ways victims respond to it are affected. Furthermore, because cultural stereotypes convey messages about rape that are directly related to the victim-perpetrator relationship, certain unwanted sexual experiences are more likely to be both socially and legally perceived as rape.

FIGURE 12.6 (a) Women's lifetime reports of rape by victim–perpetrator relationship; (b) men's lifetime reports of being made to penetrate by victim–perpetrator relationship

Data adapted from NISVS (2011). The victim–perpetrator relationship is based on respondents' reports of their relationship at the time the perpetrator first committed any violence against them. Due to the possibility of multiple perpetrators, combined percentages may exceed 100 percent. The cell sizes for men "being made to penetrate" by a person of authority or family member were too small to provide a reliable estimate, thus, they are not included. For comparison purposes, "rape" (women) is presented alongside "being made to penetrate" (men). The majority of male victims of rape indicated being raped by an acquaintance (52.4 percent) and a much smaller percentage indicated being raped by a stranger (15.1 percent) (data not shown). See notes for Figure 12.3 for NISVS definitions of all unwanted sex acts.

Notes: Intimate partner includes both current and former intimate partners.

Acquaintance includes, for example: friends, neighbors, family friends, first date, someone briefly known, and people not known well.

Stranger includes anyone not known to the victim prior to the crime.

Family member includes immediate and extended family members.

Person of authority includes, for example: manager, supervisor, superior in command, teacher, professor, coach, clergy, doctor, therapist, and caregiver.

"Legitimate" and "blameworthy" victims

Although the fact that the majority of rape victims know their assailants is well-documented in statistical reports and social science research, prominent cultural misconceptions about rape (i.e., *rape myths*) continue to blame victims who are raped by known perpetrators (or deny that they even are rape victims) while sympathizing with victims whose rape experiences fit the blitz attack stranger rape scenario described above. This creates a system whereby only *some* people are conceived of as "legitimate" rape victims and others are viewed as "blameworthy" or not even seen as victims at all. The victims that are most likely to be viewed as "legitimate" and most likely to garner sympathy from society, police, and the courts are those that fit within our cultural stereotypes about both what a rape is and who a rape victim is. These include (Karmen 2012:294):

- Victim is a woman.
- Perpetrator is a man (an unknown stranger).
- At the time of the attack, the victim was engaged in a "wholesome" non-sexual activity (no drugs or alcohol involved) and wearing appropriate (non-risqué) attire.
- Blitz attack with weapon.
- Victim clearly articulated "no" by physically fighting back and screaming/yelling.
- Eyewitnesses hear and see the attack and provide identical accounts of the events.
- Clear bodily evidence of attack (bruising, bleeding, etc.).
- Victim immediately reports to the police and other officials.

The list of qualifications of a "legitimate" rape can even be longer than this. For example, if the victim is a bisexual woman, she is less likely to be believed and more at risk for sexual violence than a straight woman (see Box 12.3). Thus, changing, adding to, or deleting from this list affects social judgements about the rape and ultimately raises questions about both the legitimacy of the rape itself and the blameworthiness of the victim. So where does that leave those who do not fit within these restrictive parameters? Overall, due to their own qualities and/or the circumstances of the rape, certain types of victims are perceived (and may perceive themselves) as either "legitimate" or "blameworthy." For example, compared to victims of stranger and acquaintance rape, victims who are raped while on a romantic date are blamed significantly more harshly (Newcombe *et al.* 2008). This means that rape victims that are somehow outside of our societal perceptions of what rapes and rape victims should be like are:

- More likely to be seen as more blameworthy.
- Less likely to be perceived as rape victims.
- Less likely to see themselves as victims.

BOX 12.3 LESBIAN, GAY, AND BISEXUAL PEOPLE AS VICTIMS OF UNWANTED SEX

Most often, dominant cultural stereotypes surrounding rape conceptualize a heterosexual arrangement whereby men are perpetrators and women are victims; however, as we learned in Box 12.1 earlier in this chapter, the reality of sex crime is significantly more multifarious. When considering sexual identity, we continue to see the complexities within the dynamics of unwanted sex. The National Intimate Partner and Sexual Violence Survey (NISVS 2013) found that both gender and sexual identity affect a person's likelihood of experiencing sexual violence. For example, based on their representative sample of American adults that included 1,209 (7 percent) lesbian, gay, and bisexual respondents, 46.1 percent of bisexual women report being raped in their lifetime—over twice that of straight-identified women and close to 3.5 times that of lesbian women. Furthermore, gay men are significantly more likely to experience unwanted sexual contact when compared to bisexual men and three times more likely when compared to straight men (see Figure 12.7).

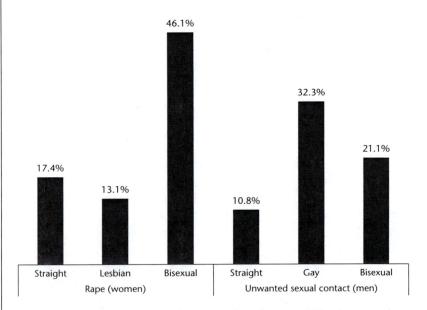

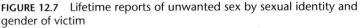

FIGURE 12.7 Lifetime reports of unwanted sex by sexual identity and gender of victim

Data adapted from NISVS (2013). The cell sizes for "Rape" (gay, bisexual, and straight men) were too small to provide a reliable estimate, thus, for comparison purposes the "Rape" (lesbian, bisexual, and straight women) data are presented alongside "Unwanted sexual contact" (gay, bisexual, and straight men). See notes for Figure 12.3 for NISVS definitions of all unwanted sex acts.

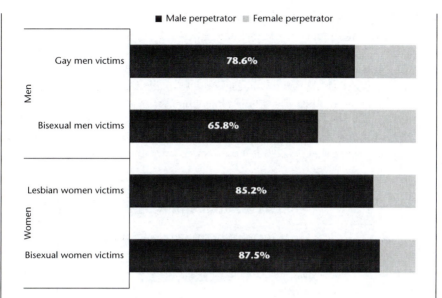

FIGURE 12.8 Lifetime reports of sexual coercion and unwanted sexual contact by sexual identity and gender of victim and gender of perpetrator

Data adapted from NISVS (2013). Estimates are based on lifetime reports of "sexual coercion" and "unwanted sexual contact" (combined). Rape reports for lesbian women, gay men, and bisexual men were too small to calculate a reliable estimate; for bisexual women, 98.3 percent indicated being raped by a man. See notes for Figure 12.3 for NISVS definitions of all unwanted sex acts.

These findings show that heterosexual women are actually *less* likely to be victims of rape when compared to bisexual women and gay men are *more* likely than straight and bisexual men to be victims of unwanted sexual contact. Thus, as seen before in Box 12.1, the realities of rape do not match cultural stereotypes.

Furthermore, when we look at the gender of the perpetrators of these crimes, we find that men are overwhelmingly more likely than women to commit acts of unwanted sexual contact against both gay and bisexual men as well as lesbian and bisexual women (see Figure 12.8). These findings show us that sex crimes are not solely heterosexual in nature.

Overall, our stereotypes about unwanted sex do not match the reality of sex crimes. But as noted before, this is more than just a numerical inaccuracy. When we fail to recognize that sex crimes can be perpetrated by women against gay men, for example, we fall into the same trap of delegitimizing men victims and ignoring women perpetrators of sex crimes. This contributes to a lack of both cultural and legal recognition of unwanted sex that does not fit within the dominant cultural stereotypes about rape. Consequently, all men and non-heterosexual women are often both formally and informally excluded from being recognized as "rape" victims.

- Less likely to see their assailants as rapists.
- Less likely to report to officials (see Figure 12.9).

Unfortunately, nearly all (if not all) rape situations exist outside of the restrictive qualifiers outlined above. That is because the blitz attack stranger rape scenario is an "ideal type," or in other words, an abstract but clear, readily identifiable exemplar of a situation or concept that is unlikely to ever exist in reality but offers a methodological tool for descriptive purposes (Weber 1922 [1978]). The problem lies in the fact that many believe that "ideal type" rapes and rape victims actually do exist.

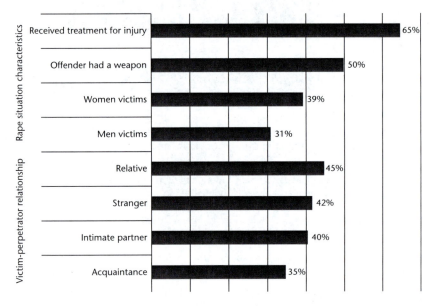

FIGURE 12.9 Percentage of victims who reported their rape to the police by rape situation characteristics and victim–perpetrator relationship

Data adapted from the NCVS 2000 to 2013.

Rape
- Unlawful vaginal, anal, or oral penetration of a person against the will of the victim, with use or threatened use of psychological coercion and/or physical force.

Rape situation characteristics
- Received treatment for physical injuries: the respondent is asked if they received any medical care for their injuries including being treated at the scene, at home, at a medical office, or at another location.
- Offender had a weapon: the respondent is asked if the offender had a weapon. Weapons include items such as guns, knives, and other objects that are used as weapons (for example, rocks, clubs, etc.).

Victim-perpetrator relationship
- Relative: includes parents or stepparents, children or stepchildren, brothers or sisters, and other relatives.
- Stranger: this is anyone not previously known by the victim.
- Intimate partner: includes spouses and ex-spouses, boyfriends and girlfriends, and ex-boyfriends and ex-girlfriends.
- Acquaintance: includes friends or former friends, roommates or boarders, schoolmates, neighbors, people at work, and other known non-relatives.

Putting this all together means that the vast majority of rape victims (who we know are raped by someone they know) exist outside of the "ideal type," and thus, most rape victims are not viewed as "legitimate" victims. Because of these misconceptions, nearly all rape victims are judged harshly, especially the further away from the "ideal type" they are.

Rape myths and their effects

Supporting and maintaining a rape "ideal type" that resembles the blitz attack stranger rape scenario is, in essence, buying into rape myths. There are literally thousands of rape myths floating around in contemporary culture—some of which continue to be bandied about and some of which have (thankfully) been laid to rest. Rape myths were first explicitly defined and measured in the 1980s as "prejudicial, stereotyped, or false beliefs about rape, rape victims, and rapists" (Burt 1980:217). These misconceptions about rape can be clustered into the following groups: deceit/disbelief, victim precipitation/responsibility, just-world perspectives, force and resistance requirements, and perpetrator sympathy (see Table 12.3).

TABLE 12.3 Rape myths

Deceit/disbelief	Victim precipitation/ responsibility	Just-world perspectives	Force and resistance requirements	Perpetrator sympathy
She/he lied.	She/he asked for it.	He/she got what she deserved.	Rape requires a weapon.	He/she didn't mean to do it.
She/he is just trying to get back at someone.	Dressing/acting in a provocative way is an invitation to rape.	Rape only happens to certain kinds of people.	Rape requires physical force and physical resistance.	He/she just couldn't control his/her urges.
Many so-called rape victims actually just had sex and changed their minds afterwards.	If the victim is drinking/using drugs, he/she is responsible for subsequent rape.	Rape simply does not happen to good people.	Because of their superior strength, it is impossible for a woman to rape a man.	It's my fault because I led him/her on.
It wasn't really rape.	If the victim becomes aroused, he/she wanted it.	There are no innocent victims.	Any person can successfully resist rape if he/she really wants to.	He/she loves me/cares about me.

Partially adapted from Payne *et al.* (1999).

Because cultural stereotypes often depict men (especially straight men) as strong, sexual, and masculine beings, there are also myths that are specific to men as rape victims such as:

- *Disbelief*
  - A man cannot be raped.
  - An adult male is too big and too strong to be overpowered and forced into sex.
  - A "real" man should be able to protect himself from sexual assault.
  - Men are in a constant state of readiness to accept any sexual opportunity so they cannot be raped.

- *Minimizing trauma*
  - Most men who are raped are not very upset by the incident.
  - Most men who are raped do not need counseling after the incident.
  - Men are less negatively affected by sexual assault than women.

- *Sexuality/masculinity*
  - Men who are raped by other women are "lucky."
  - Men who are raped by other men are weak and emasculate.
  - Men who are raped by other men must be gay.

These types of rape myths perpetuate damaging stereotypes that deny, minimize, and distort male experiences with rape (Struckman-Johnson and Struckman-Johnson 1992).

Other victim-specific rape myths include stereotypes about LGBTQ people as both hypersexual and more deserving of rape. Indeed, non-heterosexual people in general are thought to be more blameworthy and their sexual assaults are viewed as less serious than those against heterosexual people (Davies 2002). Because LGBTQ people are significantly more likely than straight and cisgender people to experience rape and overall lifetime victimization (Balsam *et al.* 2005; Stotzer 2008); such rape myths that delegitimize LGBTQ people's experiences with sexual assault are particularly problematic.

Rape myth believers

Almost all extant research finds that compared to women, men are more accepting of rape myths (including when rape myths are about men as victims) (see Figure 12.10). In addition, rape myth believers are likely to:

- accept traditional gender stereotypes (e.g., a woman's place is in the home; men should be strong, aggressive and masculine);
- accept interpersonal violence in general and sexual aggression/coercion;
- hold hostile attitudes toward women in general;

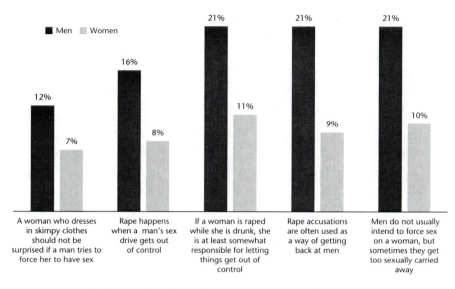

FIGURE 12.10   College students' belief in rape myths by gender

Rape myths are from the Illinois Rape Myth Acceptance Scale (Payne *et al.* 1999). Response data adapted from a survey of college students (N = 1,940) described in Worthen and Baker (2014). Only the rape myths with greater than 10 percent agreement (by men) are reported here.

- support oppressive belief systems including racism, sexism, heterosexism, classism, ageism, anti-feminism, and religious intolerance;
- blame the victim in rape situations;
- diminish the seriousness of rape;
- sexually assault others.

Overall, rape myth acceptance is related to both specific attitudes toward rape and victims as well as larger social constructs of social conservatism and the acceptance of violence (Newcombe *et al.* 2008; Suarez and Gadalla 2010). Furthermore, compared to those who do not support rape myths, rape myth believers are more likely to sexually assault others (Abbey *et al.* 1998).

(Dys)Functions and effects of rape myths

The continued presence of rape myths in contemporary culture suggests that they serve some function or more specifically, dysfunction that perpetuates falsities surrounding rape. In particular, rape myths:

- deny or minimize injuries associated with rape;
- blame victims for their own victimization;
- absolve the perpetrator from responsibility;
- perpetuate sexual aggression; and
- protect non-victims from feeling vulnerable.

Thus, rape myths distort the realities of rape and simultaneously deviantize rape victims (Burt 1980; Payne *et al.* 1999). The effects of this can be far reaching. Beyond hurting rape victims themselves by delegitimizing their victimization, rape myth acceptance can have consequences in the criminal justice system. Specifically, potential jurors who support rape myths are more likely to perceive accused rape perpetrators as innocent and are more likely to agree with victim-blaming statements (Gray 2006; Newcombe *et al.* 2008). Furthermore, when police officers endorse rape myths, they deem victims with certain characteristics (e.g., a virgin, a teacher) as more credible than others (e.g., a man, a sex worker) (Page 2010). As a result, buying into false stereotypes about rape can be particularly damaging to rape victims and can also affect rape recognition and reporting.

Situational factors affecting rape recognition and reporting

Because rape occurs within a particular culture with its own set of norms (including rape myths) and laws, unwanted sex experiences are interpreted in differential ways. This can be further exacerbated by the social context and situational factors involved. For example, the presence of alcohol and/or drugs can shift the ways a rape is interpreted and consequently, the social and legal recognition of unwanted sexual experiences in general. In addition, particular populations such as college students, military members, and prisoners have unique cultures that shape the recognition and reporting of rape. Below, these situational factors are examined.

Alcohol and drugs

The colloquial phrase "date rape drug" refers to a drug that is used to facilitate unwanted sexual activity. In addition to alcohol, often these colorless, odorless, and tasteless drugs are given to a victim unbeknownst to him or her (such as mixed in with a beverage) and have a sedative, hypnotic, dissociative, and/or amnesiac effect. The most commonly used drugs to facilitate unwanted sexual activity are:

- *Alcohol*: By far, alcohol is the most frequently used drug to facilitate unwanted sexual activity. Estimates indicate that approximately half of all rapes in the United States involve alcohol (Kilpatrick *et al.* 2007). Because many people willingly imbibe alcoholic beverages, perpetrators of unwanted sexual activity are able to encourage their victims to drink enough alcohol to become incapacitated and even lose consciousness.
- *GHB (gamma hydroxybutyric acid)*: A clear, colorless, odorless liquid that acts on the central nervous system as a depressant and has similar effects to anesthesia including unconsciousness. It can easily be made by anyone with novice chemistry skills using commonly available ingredients. It acts quickly and aggressively: effects show within 15 minutes of ingestion and last for three to six hours if taken without alcohol and 36 to 72 hours when taken with alcohol.

Street names for GHB include "easy lay, liquid ecstasy, liquid x, clear x, and liquid dream" (Badiye and Gupta 2012:161).

- *Rohypnol (flunitrazepam)*: A benzodiazepine pill (easily ground into powder) that produces a sedative effect, amnesia, muscle relaxation, and a slowing of psychomotor responses. It is available as a prescription medication most commonly used as a pre-operative anesthetic or a strong sleeping aid. Sedation occurs quickly (approximately ten minutes after ingestion) and reaches its peak after eight hours when it can render a person totally unconscious. It lasts for several hours and can cause periods of memory loss (blackouts). When Rohypnol is used in the facilitation of unwanted sex it is commonly described as "roofies" (Badiye and Gupta 2012:162).
- *Ketamine (ketamine hydrochloride)*: A liquid drug that acts as dissociative anesthetic rendering the user fully aware of but uncomfortably detached from all bodily sensations. It is commonly used by veterinarians for procedures with animals and sometimes used as an anesthetic or to treat pain and depression in humans. It takes effect quickly, within ten minutes of ingestion, and lasts for several hours. Street names for ketamine include "special K, super K, OK, KO, kid rock" (Badiye and Gupta 2012:162).

When alcohol and/or drugs are involved in any sexual activity, the issue of consent should be called into question because when people are incapacitated, they are unable to provide consent. Most legal statutes note that if a person is unconscious or somehow not fully aware of the sex act that is happening (via the administration of alcohol, narcotics, anesthetics, or some other means), he/she is unable to legally provide consent to engage in *any* sexual activity. In other words, *drunk and/or otherwise incapacitated people cannot consent to sex*. Thus, having sex while under the influence of alcohol and/or drugs can often be legally defined as rape. However, there are many reasons why such behavior is not recognized as rape:

- Victim believes it is his/her fault because he/she was too drunk/high.
- Perpetrator believes it is the *victim's* fault because he/she was too drunk/high.
- The perpetrator believes it is *not* his/her fault because he/she was too drunk/high.
- Victim does not remember the sex act.
- Perpetrator does not remember the sex act.
- Victims/perpetrators are unaware that drunk and/or otherwise incapacitated people cannot consent to sex.

Furthermore, when the victim "willingly" became incapacitated by drinking alcohol and/or taking drugs, he/she may feel especially culpable. And even when victims are "slipped" drugs in their drinks, victims sometimes feel responsible for taking drinks from friends (or strangers) or even being at parties or other social situations in which these types of activities can occur. As a result, much drug- and alcohol-facilitated unwanted sexual activity goes both unrecognized and unreported.

For example, in a U.S. study of 441 rape victims who did not report the incident to the police, reasons for not reporting varied by the context in which the rape occurred (see Figure 12.11). Compared to victims of rapes that involved the use or threat of force (but no drugs or alcohol), victims of drug- and alcohol-facilitated rape were more likely to choose not to report due to belief the act was not a crime, a lack of proof that the incident occurred, and a belief it was not serious enough to report. By contrast, victims of forced rape were more likely not to report because of fear of reprisal from the perpetrator (Cohn *et al.* 2013). Overall, alcohol- and drug-related unwanted sexual experiences are common but are both under-recognized and under-reported due to the presumption that partaking in alcohol and/or drug use is somehow an indicator of willingness, desire, or even consent to engage in sex. It is not.

College context

College campuses are unique social entities. They are most often comprised of primarily young people in their early twenties who are discovering themselves in an environment that offers a host of new experiences that contribute to shifts in lifestyle, attitudes, and exposure to new ideas. Part of the college experience is social. Meeting new friends and cultivating romantic partnerships has long been

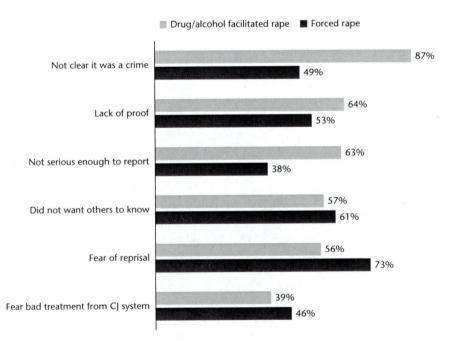

FIGURE 12.11 Reasons for not reporting rape to police by rape context

Data adapted from Cohn *et al.* (2013).

thought to be a significant part of student life. Within the current social scene at colleges, however, there is a "hook-up" culture that creates a space where casual sex is normative and expected. In fact, a new sexual script within college culture has reversed the traditional order of dating: sex happens first and then you *may* decide to go on a date. Beyond this, college is a time for sexual experimentation for many, and this can mean diverse and plentiful sexual experiences (Bogle 2008).

Within this world of youth, sexuality, and personal discovery, many students view college as a time to "have fun," "let loose," and "party" (Bogle 2008:51). As a result, the typical American college experience includes partying, drinking alcohol, and having casual sex. Indeed, 78 percent of American college students indicate that they have "hooked up" at least once and 80 percent of students drink alcohol on a regular basis (Bogle 2008:85; NIAAA 2015). This creates an environment where risky behaviors are not only perceived as normative, but also, they are easy to come by. As a result, two related issues have been highlighted as important concerns on college campuses: binge drinking and sexual assault. The media regularly draws attention to this by pulling headlines from organizations such as the U.S. National Institute on Alcohol Abuse and Alcoholism (NIAAA 2015) that finds:

- About 40 percent of college students binge drink regularly (consume four to five drinks in about two hours).
- Nineteen percent of college students meet the criteria for an alcohol use disorder, but only 5 percent seek treatment.
- Each year, an estimated 860,000 college students drive under the influence of alcohol and 1,825 college students die from alcohol-related injuries.
- Each year, an estimated 400,000 college students have unprotected sex, more than 100,000 students report having been too intoxicated to know if they consented to having sex, and an additional 97,000 students are victims of alcohol-related sexual assault or rape.

These alarming statistics shed light on the seriousness of these issues and also support initiatives including campus alcohol education and rape prevention programs. In addition, because of the increased media attention and university response to both binge drinking and sexual assault on campus, there is a generalized awareness about these issues among college students. This is especially important because college women in particular are at elevated risk for sexual assault.

Estimating rape prevalence on college campuses

As noted above, it is impossible to know the exact number of sexual assaults that take place anywhere, and that includes college campuses. However, there are two sources of data that are often examined when attempting to understand college rape in the United States. The first is the University's official report of crimes on campus generated as a result of the 1990 Jeanne Clery[4] Disclosure of Campus Security Policy and Campus Crime Statistics Act (or Clery Act for short) that requires all U.S. colleges and universities (approximately 7,500 in total of which nearly 4,000 are four-year institutions) to disclose statistics about crime on or near their campuses in annual security reports by gathering crime data from campus security authorities (such as campus police, coaches, and campus housing directors[5]). While the initiatives behind the Clery Act are noble, the actual data generated from them are less than encouraging. For example, from 2011 to 2013, nearly half (45 percent) of residential four-year colleges nationwide reported *zero* sexual assaults and 71 percent reported three or fewer *total* campus sexual assaults (Psychguides.com). These numbers are obviously gross underestimates of campus rape.

The second source of data about campus sexual assault is generated from self-reports of crime gathered from surveys of college students about their experiences. One of these, the Association of American Universities Campus Climate Survey on Sexual Assault and Sexual Misconduct (AAUCCS) provides a detailed overview of various types of sexual assault experienced by university students using data gathered from over 150,000 students enrolled in 27 universities[6] in the United States (Cantor *et al.* 2015a).

- *College sexual assault prevalence*

  The AAUCCS defines "nonconsensual sexual contact" as:

  ○ Sexual penetration (including oral sex): when someone puts a penis, fingers, or object inside someone else's vagina or anus; when someone's mouth or tongue makes contact with someone else's genitals.
  ○ Sexual touching: kissing, touching someone's breast, chest, crotch, groin or buttocks, grabbing, groping or rubbing against another in a sexual way, even if the touching is over the other's clothes.

  Achieved by/when:

  ○ Physical force: holding the victim down, pinning the victim's arms, hitting or kicking, or using or threatening to use a weapon.
  ○ Incapacitation: a victim is unable to provide consent or stop what is happening because he/she is passed out, asleep, or incapacitated due to drugs or alcohol.
  ○ Coercion: threatening serious non-physical harm or promising rewards for compliance.
  ○ Non-active agreement: without active, ongoing voluntary agreement.

Among these college students, about one in four women (23.6 percent) and one in 17 men (5.8 percent) experienced nonconsensual sexual contact since entering college. Among those who identified as transgender, genderqueer, nonconforming, questioning, or as something not listed on the survey (TGQN), nearly one in three (27.8 percent) experienced nonconsensual sexual contact since entering college. The prevalence varied by type of nonconsensual sexual contact (penetration or sexual touching) and tactic (physical force, incapacitation, coercion, or non-active agreement). As seen in Figure 12.12, nonconsensual sexual touching was more common than nonconsensual sexual penetration and physical force was most common for both types of nonconsensual sexual contact. In addition, bisexual women were significantly more likely than any other group to experience physically forced or incapacitated nonconsensual sexual contact during college while straight men were least likely to have these types of experiences (see Figure 12.13).

- *Rape incident characteristics[7]*
  Among college women victims of nonconsensual penetration by force or incapacitation, nearly all (~80 percent) knew the perpetrator (who was a man in 98 to 99 percent of incidents). In addition, a sizeable majority (67 to 88 percent) indicated that the sexual assault happened while they were voluntarily drinking alcohol and 65 to 77 percent indicated the offender was also drinking. Disturbingly, 26 to 41 percent of college women victims were passed out for all or part of the incident. Most sexual assaults occurred at a place of residence (e.g., dorm, apartment, etc.) and 22 percent took place at a fraternity or sorority house. In fact, attending fraternity parties is significantly associated with college women's likelihood of being the victim of incapacitated sexual assault (Krebs *et al.* 2007) (see Box 12.4). The majority of women experienced emotional difficulties following the assault while only a small percentage had physical injuries (4 to 13 percent).
  Among college men that are victims of nonconsensual sexual touching by force, over half (61 to 72 percent) knew the perpetrator (who was a woman in 61 percent of the cases), about half (44 percent) indicated that the sexual assault happened while they were voluntarily drinking alcohol and 74 percent indicated the offender was also drinking. Most sexual assaults occurred at a place of residence (e.g., dorm, apartment, etc.). The vast majority (81 to 89 percent) indicated that they did not experience emotional difficulties or physical injuries following the assault.
- *Harassment,[8] intimate partner violence,[9] and stalking[10] prevalence*
  Harassment was common for undergraduate students (62 percent of women, 43 percent of men, and 75 percent of TGQN people report experiencing harassment since entering college). In contrast, intimate partner violence (IPV) and stalking were less common (13 percent of women, 9 percent of men, and 23 percent of TGQN people report experiencing IPV since entering college; 7 percent of women, 2 percent of men, and 12 percent of TGQN people report experiencing stalking since entering college). Compared to straight students, LGBTQ students are more likely to report these types of experiences.
- *Reporting*
  Most college victims of nonconsensual sexual contact told someone close to them such as a friend or family member about the incident, although few

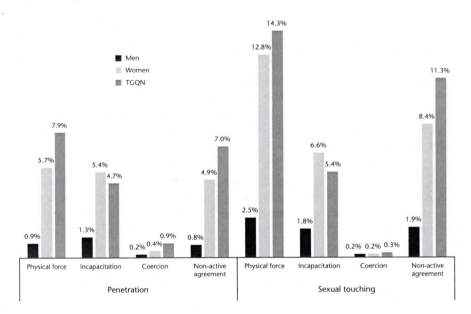

FIGURE 12.12 Nonconsensual sexual contact among undergraduates since entering college by tactic and gender

Data adapted from Cantor *et al.* (2015a).

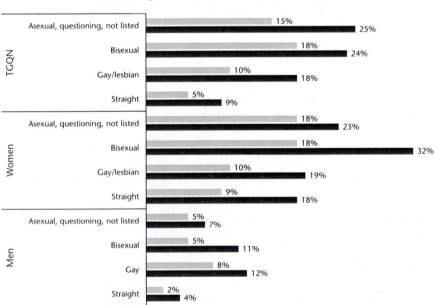

FIGURE 12.13 Nonconsensual sexual contact among students since entering college by sexual identity and gender

Data adapted from Cantor *et al.* (2015a).

BOX 12.4 COLLEGE GREEK CULTURE AND RAPE

Studies consistently show that compared to non-Greek students, sorority women are more likely to be victims of rape and fraternity men are more likely to perpetuate sexual violence (e.g., Copenhaver and Grauerholz 1991). In particular, fraternities are often accused of perpetuating sexual scripts that frame men as sexual aggressors and women as sexual prey (Martin and Hummer 1989). These patterns were largely solidified in the 1980s and 1990s when several scholarly investigations revealed a horrifying picture of misogyny and violent rape within Greek party culture. For example, Peggy Reeves Sanday's book *Fraternity Gang Rape* (1990) exposed the practice of "gang banging" whereby fraternity men would line up and take turns having sex with the same woman who was often too heavily intoxicated to consent (Sanday 1990:1). Not only was this a commonplace occurrence at college fraternity parties, but also, "abuse of women [was] a means to renew fraternal bonds and assert power as a brotherhood" (Sanday 1990:14). Similarly, another widely publicized 1980s study found that "rape is especially probable in fraternities because of the kinds of organizations they are, the kinds of members they have, the practices their members engage in, and a virtual absence of university or community oversight" (Martin and Hummer 1989:459). Furthermore, as we have already discussed, alcohol plays a major role in college campus sexual assault and this is especially true in Greek culture. Alcohol abuse is normative among fraternity men and as a result, Greek life is characterized by binge drinking and partying. Some fraternity men even shrewdly use alcohol as a tool to gain sexual access to women, getting them so drunk (or sometimes spiking their drinks with various incapacitating drugs) that they cannot consent and then preying on their vulnerability (Martin and Hummer 1989; Sanday 1990).

Today, a more contemporary analysis of nearly 30 extant studies with thousands of fraternity men found that fraternities continue to promulgate sexual violence via norms (i.e., rape myth acceptance and hyper-heteromasculinity) and support sexually aggressive behaviors. Indeed, an investigation of almost 5,000 fraternity men revealed that fraternity membership is significantly associated with the perpetration of sexual violence (Murnen and Kohlman 2007). Together, collective research over the past several decades continues to identify fraternities as environments that socially construct attitudes promoting the rape of women, often via the use of alcohol.

However, although there is ample evidence to indicate that *some* fraternities actively cultivate and condone rape-prone environments, certainly *not all* of Greek culture can be painted with such a broad and sweeping generalization. In other words, not all fraternities throw parties that create atmospheres conducive to sexual violence. In fact, it is more reasonable to assume that there is great diversity among Greek cultures ranging from predominately white upper class membership to racial/ethnic fraternities (e.g., Asian American,

Latin American, and Native American), fraternities with religious identification (e.g., Catholic, Jewish, Evangelical Christian), and gay and bisexual social fraternities (Worthen 2011). Fraternity norms can include problematic expressions of masculinity that support the sexual victimization of women but they can also cultivate "productive masculinities" that promote healthy and socially responsible expressions of masculinity (Harris and Harper 2014:706):

- Problematic expressions of masculinity found in fraternities

    o *Hyper-heteromasculinity*: valuing masculinity, toughness, aggression, competition, athleticism, and male dominance while devaluing femininity, women, non-heterosexuality, passivity, and weakness.
    o *Alcohol abuse*: valuing binge drinking, drunkenness, and the use of alcohol to inhibit others, especially women, while devaluing non-drinkers and soberness.
    o *Sexual dominance over women*: valuing sexual prowess over women, high numbers of casual sex partners, and the sexual objectification of women while devaluing virginity, abstinence, egalitarianism, and committed relationships.
    o *Superiority/elitism*: valuing high social status, wealth, and material possessions while devaluing those perceived of as lesser in social standing.
    o *In-group loyalty*: valuing obedience to the group, trust, dedication, and secrecy while devaluing those outside of the fraternity.

- Productive masculinity found in fraternities

    o *Friendship/bonding*: valuing care, concern, thoughtfulness and life-long friendship among brothers.
    o *Leadership*: valuing successful, responsible, and ethical representation of the fraternity among its leaders who also model productive masculinity and integrity.
    o *Growth/maturity*: valuing learning, growing, and maturing among fraternity brothers and actively challenging stereotypes about fraternities (i.e., disrupting sexism, heterosexism, elitism, and racism).
    o *Accountability*: valuing a system of accountability that enforces a shared set of morals/ethics among fraternity men.

Overall, there is no denying the link between college Greek culture and sexual violence. Nearly all studies consistently demonstrate that fraternities promulgate sexual violence (Murnen and Kohlman 2007). But blaming Greek letter organizations for the issue of rape on campus misses the larger complicating factors of alcohol, binge drinking, and campus hook-up culture that exist both within and out of Greek culture. Thus, when considering rape in college environments it is essential to consider how both Greek-specific and larger collegial norms influence sexual violence on campus.

(5 to 26 percent) reported to a campus program such as a university health center, counseling center, campus police, etc. Women and TGQN-identified victims were more likely to report than men and those experiencing penetration by force were nearly two times more likely to report than those experiencing penetration by incapacitation. The top two reasons that students did not report their sexual assault were (i) they did not think it was serious enough to report and (ii) they felt embarrassed, ashamed, or that it would be too emotionally difficult.

Overall, sexual assault is not an uncommon experience for college students. Furthermore, the relationship between alcohol and nonconsensual sexual contact is pervasive and insidious. As a result, it is important to consider the role of alcohol in college rape.

The role of alcohol in college rape

As noted earlier in this chapter, alcohol can have multiplicative effects on rape recognition and perpetration. While anyone of any age can drink alcohol, alcohol use and abuse are most common among young people and particularly those who are college-aged (18 to 25) and those who are actually enrolled in college. For example, one college study found that 85 percent of college men and women drink alcohol, about half get drunk at least once a month, and 21 percent are drunk or high when they have sex (Krebs *et al.* 2007). Furthermore, alcohol plays a major role in the campus hook-up culture. Most college students believe that drinking alcohol makes it easier to find casual sex partners but also results in hooking up with people they would otherwise reject (i.e., "beer goggles") and/or going farther (or too far) sexually than they would if they were sober (Bogle 2008:64). Because alcohol is often involved in college sexual experiences, the risk of alcohol-related rape in college is high. Indeed, most research indicates that the majority of both victims and perpetrators of college sexual assault had been drinking alcohol prior to the assault and in many cases, both parties were drunk at the time of the incident (Abbey *et al.* 2004; Krebs *et al.* 2007; Cantor *et al.* 2015a). And *when people are drunk, they cannot consent to sex* (see Box 12.5). Within campus party culture, norms and expectations about drinking actually contribute to the likelihood of unwanted sexual encounters (Abbey *et al.* 2004). As seen in Table 12.4, college environments socialize people to have certain expectations about people who drink alcohol and about alcohol's effects. These types of expectations can lead to situations with increased risk factors for rape perpetration and victimization.

Alcohol can also affect how nonconsensual sexual experiences are perceived. For example, in a U.S. college study of nearly 7,000 students, when women's experiences met the definitions of rape provided, overall, only 28 percent perceived their sexual assault as "rape." Not surprisingly, a significantly lower percentage of incapacitated sexual assault victims (25 percent) perceived their sexual assault as "rape" compared to 40 percent of the physically forced victims. This difference fits in line

TABLE 12.4 The role of alcohol in campus party culture rape

Alcohol expectations	Diminished assessment abilities	Aftermath
About people who drink alcohol • People who drink alcohol like to "party" and like to have sex • People who drink alcohol are promiscuous *About alcohol's effects* • Alcohol is an aphrodisiac that increases sexual desire and abilities • Drinking alcohol makes you feel more sexual and less inhibited → **Drinking** →	*About sexual cues* • Alcohol increases the likelihood of misinterpretations *About risk* • Alcohol reduces the ability to assess risk *Diminished communication abilities* • Alcohol decreases mental, verbal, and physical capacities • Alcohol enhances difficulties in communicating desire or disinterest → **Rape** →	*Justification* Perpetrator believes that drinking alcohol is justification for engaging in socially inappropriate behavior *Responsibility* Victim takes responsibility for victimization because he/she was drinking alcohol *Future expectations* Unwanted sex is viewed as a normative outcome of alcohol use

Partially adapted from Abbey *et al.* (2004).

BOX 12.5 COLLEGE STUDENT DEFINITIONS OF CONSENT

As discussed earlier in this chapter, consent involves four components: communicatory cues, willingness and desire, soundness of mind, and the lack of coercion, threat, or force. However, campus party cultures that normalize traditional heterosexual scripts and alcohol use affect the ways each of these elements of consent is perceived. Thus, college students must learn to successfully navigate campus environments and understand how consent is constructed within them.

College students define consent simply as "an agreement to have sex" (Jozkowski *et al.* 2014:909) and communicate consent through combinations of communicatory cues that include nonverbal behaviors (body language, eye contact, flirting behavior, kissing, touching, caressing, hugging, removal of clothing) and verbal behaviors (asking if partner wants to have sex, asking about getting a condom or other sex aid, saying "yes"). Furthermore, college students conceptualize their willingness to engage in sex by evaluating their own feelings that include readiness (feeling ready, sure, and wanting to engage in sex), physiological responses (being aroused, turned on), and safety/comfort (feeling secure, protected, safe, respected, and in control) (Jozkowski and Wiersma 2015). In general, these consent definitions and behaviors are similar to those found in non-college populations (Hickman and Muehlenhard 1999; Beres *et al.* 2004) although college student perceptions of consent, especially in heterosexual encounters, are especially marked by norms that prioritize college men's sexual pleasure and diminish the importance of women's sexual pleasure (Jozkowski and Peterson 2013).

Campus party culture norms further shape college student definitions of consent and specifically affect the "soundness of mind" component of consent. In general, drinking any alcohol results in some impairment. As such, scholars note "examining consent under the influence of alcohol seems rather contradictory—how could someone give consent if they are intoxicated? After all, sex with an individual who is too intoxicated to give consent is sexual assault" (Jozkowski and Wiersma 2015:6). That being said, college students do have sexual experiences after drinking alcohol that they would describe as agreed upon and wanted. However, research shows that having sex after drinking alcohol reduces feelings of safety and comfort and overall readiness to have sex (Jozkowski and Wiersma 2015) as well as women's perceived quality of sexual experiences (Jozkowski 2013). Thus, even though sex and drinking alcohol are common co-occurrences on college campuses, they often lead to an overall negative and disappointing sexual experience. Beyond this, alcohol has a significant impact on the likelihood of unwanted sexual experiences (see Table 12.4) and the likelihood of forceful, aggressive, and even violent sex (Abbey *et al.* 2004).

Overall, college students define consent in ways that are similar to non-college populations. However, traditional heterosexual scripts whereby men are expected to be initiators of sexual activity and women are expected to be gatekeepers are commonplace among heterosexual college students. In addition, the normalcy of drinking and partying in college means that many college students are often navigating the complexities involved with the potentially dangerous combination of sex and alcohol. As a result, it is imperative for college students to consider:

- How do I define consent?
- How do those around me define consent?
- How do I convey my own consent to participate in a sexual encounter?
- How do I expect my partners to convey consent to participate in a sexual encounter?
- How does drinking/drug use affect consent in my life?
- Why is consent important?

with the ideas described earlier in this chapter, whereby those who are victims of a rape that fits the "blitz attack stranger rape scenario" (i.e., there is physical force and/or violence) are more likely to perceive their assault as rape and victims who believe they are somehow responsible for their victimization because they were drinking are less likely to perceive their assault as rape. Similarly, while 2.5 percent of college men indicated that they had actually perpetrated a sexual assault [this number is likely a gross underestimate, other studies suggest about a quarter of college men have perpetrated sexual assault (see Abbey *et al.* 1998)], none of these men considered what happened to be rape, even when penetration occurred. This is likely due to the fact that more than 80 percent of the perpetrators indicated that they had been drinking and that the victim was also drinking before the incident occurred (Krebs *et al.* 2007). Thus, both victims and perpetrators are less likely to perceive a sexual assault as "rape" when there is alcohol involved due to stereotypes and misconceptions about what a "rape" actually entails.

Overall, college students are at a particular risk for involvement in unwanted sex. Due to norms about alcohol and sex that are perpetuated by campus party culture, when unwanted sexual experiences do occur in these environments, they are often ignored, downplayed, or worse—somehow justified as a legitimate consequence of drinking alcohol. Thus, campus rape is frequently under-recognized and under-reported.

Military context

Armed forces and other military organizations have their own unique social and legal systems. In recent years, sexual assault in the U.S. Military has been critically examined.

The concern about these issues came to a precipice in the 1990s when two sex scandals were widely publicized. The first included 140 U.S. Navy and Marine Corps aviation officers who allegedly sexually assaulted 83 women and seven men at the 35th Annual Tailhook Association Symposium, in 1991, in Las Vegas, Nevada. The most salacious of these events has been described as a "gauntlet" that was formed on the third floor of the conference hotel and included two lines of military men, one on each side of the hallway, who would fondle and grope women who were passing through the hallway to get to their hotel rooms. After much dispute about what actually happened, 14 admirals and almost 300 naval aviators were disciplined as a result of the Tailhook events. Five years later, dozens of Army women trainees at Aberdeen Proving Ground in Maryland claimed they had been subjected to sexual harassment, forcible rape, and sodomy by their drill sergeants. The Army responded by setting up a worldwide telephone hotline for military members to report sexual misconduct that yielded over 8,000 calls, many of them anonymous (Browne 2007). Other allegations of military sexual assault came in 2003 when 12 percent of the women who graduated from the Air Force Academy in Colorado reported that they were victims of rape or attempted rape while at the Academy and an additional 70 percent experienced sexual harassment, of which 22 percent were pressured to perform sexual favors (Schemo 2003).

In the wake of these events, the military has made significant changes. Sensitivity training that focuses on sexual harassment is now required in all branches of the U.S. military and the Uniform Code of Military Justice Article 120 was updated in 2007 to reflect the crimes of "rape, sexual assault, and other sexual misconduct." In addition, since 1995, the Department of Defense (DoD) has conducted an annual survey to understand sexual assault in the military. In 2012, 6 percent of active-duty women and 1.2 percent of active-duty men experienced unwanted sexual contact while serving in the past year (30 percent women and 6 percent men indicated they experienced unwanted sexual contact prior to entering the military). Over half (57 percent) of women's experiences and 15 percent of men's experiences included attempted or completed vaginal intercourse, anal, or oral sex. Of the four branches (Army, Navy, Air Force, Marines), women in the Marine Corps and men in the Navy reported the most unwanted sexual contact. The vast majority (~70 percent) of these unwanted sexual experiences occurred at a military installation during work hours and for women, nearly all (94 percent) perpetrators were men, but for men, perpetrators included both men and women. Women's unwanted sexual experiences were more likely to involve alcohol (47 percent) and use of force (50 percent) compared to men's (19 percent and 22 percent, respectively). Surprisingly, the vast majority did not consider requesting a transfer or leaving the military as a result of experiencing unwanted sexual contact, but perhaps unsurprisingly, 66 percent of women and 76 percent of men did not report the incident to any official authorities. For women, nearly half indicated that they did not report because they did not think it was important enough to report and they did not think that they would be believed (Rock 2013).

Overall, the sexual assault of military women has only recently been critically addressed in the military context. Prior to the 1970s, very few women were even in the military and overt gender bias was a normal part of military life. In fact, historically, some service branches required women to attend make-up and etiquette classes in their training regimens (Segal 1978). Today, women comprise about 15 percent of the active-duty U.S. military with the highest percentages in the Air Force and the Navy. However, despite women's integration into the armed forces, close to a quarter of a million military jobs remain closed to women (mainly in infantry and armor units) (Tilghman 2015). Because women in the armed forces are now more likely to be assaulted by a fellow soldier than killed in combat (Ellison 2011), issues of sexual assault in the military are necessarily entwined with the military's pro-masculine culture that values toughness, brute strength, control, and domination. Military culture has historically allowed (or turned a blind eye to) women's sexual harassment and assault during military service (Sadler *et al.* 2001) and the sexual assault of military men is even less recognized. The extreme power differentials between officers and cadets coupled with the intense stronghold the military has on shaping relationship dynamics further complicates military sex crimes. Thus, when understanding soldier rape, it is important to consider the promasculine hierarchical military culture that can significantly reduce the likelihood of both recognizing and reporting rape.

Prison context

Much like the military, prisons have their own unique cultures and social dynamics. While prisoners have always been victims of sexual assault, the instigation of the U.S. Prison Rape[11] Elimination Act of 2003 (PREA) shifted more awareness toward sexual victimization in American prisons. Under the mandates of PREA, sexual victimization reports in all federal and state prisons, military prisons and a representative sample of jail jurisdictions, privately operated jails and prisons, and jails holding adults in Native American territories are regularly investigated. In 2011, this included facilities housing a total of 1.97 million inmates who indicated 8,068 allegations of sexual victimization of which only 10 percent were substantiated based on follow-up investigation. Of these, the majority (61 percent) involved unwanted vaginal, anal, oral, or object penetrative sex acts instigated by another inmate (43 percent) or staff member (57 percent) (Rantala *et al.* 2014). Overall, women prisoners report more sexual victimization than men prisoners (14.2 percent of incarcerated women report sexual victimization compared to 7.4 percent of incarcerated men) and women prisoners are significantly more likely to be sexually victimized by other inmates while more men prisoners report staff sexual misconduct (Stemple and Meyer 2014).

Prisons are necessarily spaces of power imbalances. Prisoners are required to abide by the rules of the prison and often have minimal power to resist victimization from prison guards, wardens, and other officials. The abuse of such power in the prison context, however, is complicated by the fact that prisoners themselves are sometimes perceived as either lacking in rights to safety because they have already broken the law (thus, it is ok to sexually assault them) and/or as somehow "working the system" by actively engaging in sex acts with officials. Thus, when sex acts between prison officials and inmates occur, they may not be perceived as sex crimes. In addition, when inmates sexually assault each other, these crimes may go unrecognized. Even if reported, prison officials may again perceive the inmates as somehow deserving of rape or may also believe them to by lying to try and gain special treatment or accommodations. Whether the offender is another inmate or a prison official, prison sex is illegal. However, the recognition and reporting of prison rape is necessarily complicated by the inherent power differentials that comprise prison culture. As a result, current PREA national standards focus on prevention, training and education, screening for risk of sexual victimization and abusiveness, responsiveness, and discipline, as well as medical and psychological care for incarcerated victims of sexual violence (Singer 2013).

Summarizing the situational factors in rape recognition and reporting

Overall, cultural norms as well as the involvement of alcohol and/or drugs affect how unwanted sexual experiences are perceived. Certain environments cultivate gender norms and power differentials that can inculcate rape-prone attitudes. In addition, both victims and perpetrators come to understand and define rape as it relates to their own social and cultural experiences. As a result, both the recognition and reporting of rape are shaped by situational context and this is especially obvious when comparing college, military, and prison cultures.

Motivations of men who rape

It is certainly challenging to think about why someone might want to hurt another person and in the case of sex crimes, this is especially complicated by norms that shape how rape and sexual assault are recognized and reported. One way to begin to understand the crime of rape is to learn about rapists themselves. To do so, criminologists offer discussions about what motivates men to sexually victimize others by emphasizing power dynamics and the desire for control and also considering how sexual fantasy and arousal may be related to rape.

Men who rape: power and control

Rape is most often not about sex. Rather rapists use sex as a tool to assert their desire for power and control. In doing so, their need to dominate emotionally and physically becomes entwined with their erotic desires and sexual victimization becomes a rapist's most accessible means to achieve such goals. In particular, criminologists have identified four types of men who rape, all of whom have entangled sex with control, power, and anger (Groth 1979):

- A *power reassurance rapist* feels sexually, physically, and emotionally inadequate and uses forced sex as a means to achieve or elevate strength, authority, and virility.

He uses only enough force to achieve power over the victim and may even believe that the victim is "enjoying" the rape due to his attempt to demonstrate his sexual prowess. The power reassurance rapist's ultimate desire is to validate his importance and rape constitutes his attempt to demonstrate power and sexual conquest. He derives the most satisfaction from his ability to overpower the victim rather than from sexual pleasure.

- A *power assertive rapist* believes he is entitled to sexual access to others. He asserts his power over the victim through brute force and physical beatings during the sexual assault. The power assertive rapist's ultimate desire is to express his virility and rape constitutes his definitive expression of dominance. He derives the most satisfaction from his assertion of power rather than from sexual pleasure.
- *Anger retaliation rapists* become overwhelmed by feelings of anger and rage, often in a "spur of the moment" physically forceful and aggressive manner. The victim is overpowered, beaten, humiliated, and degraded during the sexual assault. The anger retaliation rapist's ultimate desire is to hurt and debase his victim and rape constitutes his definitive expression of anger. He derives the most satisfaction from his discharge of anger rather than from sexual pleasure.
- *Sadistic rapists* derive sexual and emotional pleasure from inflicting pain and suffering on others. The victim is brutalized and tortured often in a ritualistic manner in accordance with the sadistic rapists' sexually violent fantasies. The sadistic rapist's ultimate desire is to instill fear and terror in his victim and rape constitutes his definitive expression of sexual torment. He derives the most satisfaction from torturing his victim rather than from sexual pleasure. Sadistic rape is the most likely to escalate to murder.

There is much support for this typology. In his study of more than 500 rapists, Groth (1979) found that control and domination were driving forces behind forcible rape and that rapists use sex as a weapon to express power and anger. Another study with 132 incarcerated American prisoners who were found guilty of forcible sexual intercourse (52 percent had multiple rape convictions), convicted rapists indicated that their primary goals for committing rape were revenge/punishment and an overall desire to exert control or power over their victims. In addition, rapists frequently described feelings of anger and hatred and indicated violence as a leading factor in their motivation to commit rape (Hale 1997). Thus, it can be concluded that rapists' desire for control over others is a significant component of sexual violence and forcing submission brings a sense of power and importance to rapists. For rapists, erotic desire is linked to power, control, and often, violence.

Men who think about rape: sexual fantasy and arousal

The consensus of existing research tells us that men who rape use sex as a tool to demonstrate their power and take control over others. By examining rapists, we can learn about how those who have already committed acts of sexual violence describe their crimes and their motivations to commit them. What is missing from this story is men who *think* about rape but who do not commit acts of sexual violence. This is especially important because compared to actual rapists, many more men think about rape, become aroused by thinking about rape, and have sexual fantasies about rape. In fact, between 22 and 31 percent of men have fantasies about forced sex and nearly one-fourth (23 percent) of men have fantasies about sexually abusing a person who is drunk, asleep, or unconscious (Joyal *et al.* 2015). The difference between rapists and those that fantasize about rape is that thinking about rape is not illegal and it does not necessarily hurt anyone. Men who think about rape (but do not actually rape others) may also be more inclined to look to legal and safe means to explore their interests in sexual violence (such as viewing violent pornography or hiring sex workers who allow more hardcore sexual experiences).

Even so, the line between thinking about rape and actually committing rape is hazy at best. In addition, certain factors may influence men who might otherwise not commit rape to engage in acts of nonconsensual sex. As we've already discussed previously in this chapter, approximately half of all rapes in the United States involve alcohol (Kilpatrick *et al.* 2007). Drinking alcohol can result in diminished capacities to read sexual cues and can enhance difficulties in communicating disinterest (see Table 12.4 earlier in this chapter). As a result, alcohol can increase the chances of sexual violence. In addition, an individuals' state of arousal may also affect the likelihood of nonconsensual sex. For example, in a study of 35 heterosexual American college men, compared to those who were not in an aroused state, men who were in an aroused state (almost to the point of climax) indicated a higher likelihood of engaging in rape-conducive behaviors. Specifically, to increase their chances of having sex with a woman, aroused men were significantly more likely to indicate that they would slip her a drug, to keep trying to have sex after she says "no," to tell a woman they love her, and to encourage her to drink alcohol (see Figure 12.14). Thus, aroused men were disturbingly more likely to participate in highly problematic, misleading, and illegal behaviors with the ultimate goal of increasing their chances of having sex. Thus, contextual factors such as drunkenness and/or being aroused may increase the likelihood of rape fantasies turning into real-life nonconsensual sex.

Overall, men who rape are motivated by power and control and they have entwined their desires for dominance with erotic pleasure. However, understanding rapists' motivations to commit acts of sexual violence necessarily entails a critical consideration of deviance and sexuality. To some degree, most Western cultural gender norms dictate that men *should be* powerful, assertive, and even dominant and this is also an expected norm within many romantic and sexual relationships. Rapists, however, forcefully victimize others in their desire for control while non-rapists may negotiate power dynamics in a consensual manner. Thus, rapists are deviant criminals, but it remains unclear, for example, how those with rape fantasies fit into our understandings of deviance and sexuality, especially because nearly one-third of men fantasize about forced sex (Joyal *et al.* 2015). This is further complicated by the lack of existing information about women who rape (see Box 12.6) and the many

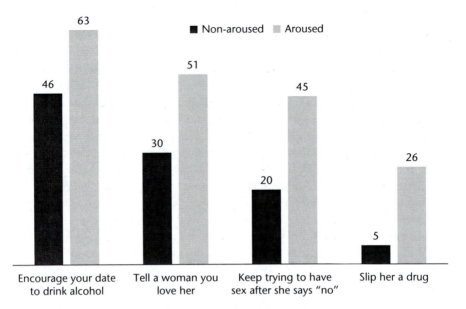

FIGURE 12.14 Ratings of rape-conducive behaviors among both aroused and non-aroused men

Respondents rated their interests in participating in these behaviors to increase their chances of having sex on a scale from 0 (no interest) to 100 (very interested). Data adapted from Ariely and Loewenstein (2006).

complexities involved in recognizing and reporting rape highlighted throughout this chapter. As a result, when examining the motives of men who rape, it is not enough to simply explore the disturbing desires of a subset of sexual deviants, but rather we must think about understanding how broader social norms shape sexual deviance.

Rape survivors

The effects of sexual victimization are far reaching. Beyond the physical, psychological, and social effects of rape, survivors of sex crimes are sometimes judged, blamed, and stigmatized. But not all experiences following sex crime are universal. Factors that may affect recovery from sexual victimization include the personal history, age, and interpersonal attributions the survivor makes concerning the cause of rape as well as the existence of strong social support networks. In addition, men and women survivors cope differently with rape trauma and are viewed differently by society. Below, both survivors' experiences after victimization and society's response to survivors are discussed.

Physical, psychological, and social effects of rape

Physical effects of rape can include bodily harm as well as genital injuries, gynecological complications, erectile difficulties, sexually transmitted infections, cervical

BOX 12.6 WOMEN WHO RAPE

The vast majority of research about rapists focuses exclusively on men who rape. The paucity of research about women who rape is due to cultural norms that suggest that it is too absurd to imagine women as rapists and that women who rape are so rare that their crimes are of little criminological significance. Such erroneous beliefs have had detrimental consequences ranging from lack of research about victims of sexual abuse by women and even the total denial of the existence of women rapists. Today, we know that sex offenses committed by women have been grossly under-estimated both officially and culturally. Part of this inaccuracy has to do with the fact that compared to men who rape, women sex offenders are more likely to attack children (specifically their own children or children they are caring for) and as a result, most of their acts of sexual abuse are disguised within a situation of care (i.e., bathing, dressing, etc.) so they remain unrecognized and undiscovered. Thus, compared to men who rape, women who rape are more likely to have younger victims and their crimes are more likely to go unnoticed because of our stereotypes about who rapes and what a rape looks like. As a result, women who rape are especially impervious to apprehension. Not only do they not fit our stereotype about rapists, they are also more easily able to hide their victimization because we expect women and mothers to have close relationships with children (Colson *et al.* 2013) (see more in chapter 13).

There is also the complicated case of attractive young adult women who rape teenage boys. These crimes are increasingly popularized in media and because there is a "perceived absence of malice" from both the adult woman offender and the teenage boy victim, women who rape teenage boys are continually under-recognized as "rapists" and are often subject to very lenient legal punishments (Hayes and Carpenter 2013:164). Because men, and perhaps especially teenage boys, are perceived to be naturally more sexually aggressive when compared to women, "it is difficult to perceive men as sexually reluctant or as victims of sexual coercion or assault" (Hayes and Carpenter 2013:170). Furthermore, when women rape adults, their crimes continue to disrupt stereotypes about rape (i.e., the false belief that a woman cannot rape a man or there are no women rapists) and as a result, women who rape continue to be under-recognized.

Who are women rapists?

According to a systematic analysis of 6,293 women sex offenders, the majority of women who sexually abuse others have personal histories of childhood sexual abuse and victimization, and a significant number suffer from psychiatric disorders. Compared to men sex offenders, more women sex offenders "come from families where incest is rife, and where physical, sexual and psychological violence is the rule, often passed down from one generation to the next for many years" (Colson *et al.* 2013:112). Contrary to popular belief, most women rapists are not coerced by another male offender into sexually abusing others and a significant percentage of women rapists use physical violence to enact sexual assault. Women who rape teens and adults also fit these profiles and challenge our belief that women are naturally caring, nurturing, sexually passive, nonviolent, and unable to rape (Colson *et al.* 2013).

Overall, cultural stereotypes obscure women rapists and as a result, sex crimes perpetrated by women are under-recognized by social and legal entities. Furthermore, victims of sex crimes perpetrated by women may be less likely to recognize their experiences as rape (or the perpetrator as a rapist) because of dominant cultural norms that shape rape as a crime perpetrated by men against women and further norms that suggest that women cannot be rapists. As a result, sex crimes perpetrated by women are under-reported and women rapists are often undetected.

cancer, chronic pain, gastrointestinal disorders, migraines, and other problems. Psychological effects include both immediate and chronic difficulties. In the immediate aftermath of rape, survivors can experience shock, denial, fear, confusion, acute anxiety, guilt, shame, helplessness, fearfulness, nervousness, anger, vengefulness, and rage, as well as symptoms of post-traumatic stress disorder (PTSD) including emotional detachment, sleep disturbances, and flashbacks. Chronic or more long-term psychological consequences of rape include depression, anxiety disorders, PTSD, suicide ideation, damaged self-image, and low self-esteem. Anyone close to the survivor may also experience psychological difficulties such as anger, denial, confusion, or rage as a response to the trauma of rape of a loved one or friend.

Rape survivors may also experience interpersonal difficulties such as distrust of others, emotional detachment, strained relationships with family, friends, and intimate partners, diminished interest or avoidance of sex, social withdrawal, and isolation or ostracism from family or community. Some survivors might attempt to cope with their victimization through engaging in high-risk behaviors such as alcohol and substance abuse, risky sexual behavior, criminal behavior, unhealthy diet-related behaviors (such as fasting, vomiting, abusing diet pills, or intentionally overeating), self-mutilation, and angry/violent outbursts (CDC 2015).

Gender differences in the effects of rape

Men and women rape survivors often cope differently. Compared to men, women survivors are more likely to experience self-blame (both immediately post-assault and long-term) and they are more likely to withdraw socially (Ullman and Filipas 2005). Women are also more likely to be fearful of rape and are more likely to use precautionary strategies to avoid situations that they perceive as potentially danger-ous (i.e., avoid going out alone at night, avoid eye contact with others on the street) (Gordon and Riger 1991). However, women survivors are also more likely to dis-close their abuse to others and they are more likely to receive positive and support-ive responses to their disclosure when compared to men survivors (Ullman and Filipas 2005).

Responding to survivors

Survivors of rape can experience a mixture of societal judgement and stigma as well as self-blame following their disclosure of victimization. Our cultural ste-reotypes build into these negative social reactions (recall our discussion of rape myths earlier in this chapter). For example, women are more likely to be believed when they disclose rape while men are more likely to be met with skepticism (Ullman and Filipas 2005). Ideally, social reactions to rape disclosure should include listening to the victim, believing the victim, and validating his/her experiences in a non-judgmental way. Offering additional emotional or social support can also be especially helpful (Ullman 2010). It is especially prob-lematic to force or strongly encourage survivors to report their victimization to authorities (a survivor's decision to report or not to report should always be respected).

Survivor empowerment

Beyond the negative and damaging effects of sex crime, rape survivors can become empowered. They can find comfort in disclosing their experiences to other survi-vors (Ullman 2010) and they can find value in sharing their stories with large groups such as in the case of the worldwide initiative, Take Back the Night (TBTN). TBTN is a non-profit global organization with the mission of ending sexual violence. TBTN events typically consist of a rally followed by a march and often a speak-out with personal stories and/or a candlelight vigil. Hundreds of TBTN events are held in over 30 countries annually and occur on college cam-puses, in major metropolitan areas, on military bases, and even in high schools, all with the purpose of promoting awareness about sexual violence and providing survivors with a platform to share their stories (takebackthenight.org).

Strategies for change

Throughout this chapter we have learned that rape and consent are complicated by cultural norms and power differentials that shape attitudes toward gender, sex, sexuality, and sexual violence. We have considered how to define rape and under-stand the reporting and prevalence of rape, we have reviewed how stereotypes inform attitudes toward rape victims and perpetrators, and we have discussed why men rape and how survivors respond to sexual assault. Now it is time to consider how we can change things.

Language, conversations, and dialogue

Our personal choices regarding the language we use can make a difference in changing attitudes and cultural perspectives that dismiss rape and cultivate sexual violence. For example, linguistic research has found that the English language includes over 200 words for a "sexually promiscuous" woman and only about 20 for a sexually promiscuous man (Stanley 1977). This frequent portrayal of women as sexual objects supports a "language of rape" and a cultural acceptance of rape in general (Benedict 1995:103). It also obscures men as victims and reifies stereotypes that blame women victims of rape and encourages men to be sexually aggressive. What is more, because language is an everyday experience, most of us are unaware of how powerful it is. Thus, "the language of rape is insidious, used unconsciously, quickly, and carelessly" (Benedict 1995:104). Changes to our personal language (i.e., avoiding negative and damaging language that disparages women and promotes sexual violence) can shift not only our own thinking about these issues, but also, how this can affect others around us.

Beyond changing the words we use to talk about gender, sex, sexuality, and sexual violence, we can also encourage conversations about such issues. For example, talking about rape as a social problem and as a real issue that affects many people's lives can open up a dialogue that encourages self-reflection. In addition, talking to our intimate partners about sex, especially consent, can help cultivate an environment of sex positivity and more pleasurable and satisfying sexual encounters. We can also support a constructive and critical conversation about rape and sexual violence via other outlets such as social media.

Bystander intervention and education

Another way to support a cultural shift away from sexual violence is to encourage bystanders to intervene when they hear problematic statements or see dangerous situations. This is especially important because, as discussed in Box 12.7, horrific crimes are sometimes met with bystander apathy. For example, the AAUCCS found that the vast majority (77 percent) of college students did not intervene when they witnessed a drunk person headed for a sexual encounter and over half (54.5 percent) did nothing when they saw someone acting in a sexually violent or harassing manner (Cantor et al. 2015a). But bystanders can intervene in many important ways (see Table 12.5). In addition, issues such as bystander intervention can be systematically addressed through educational programing. Encouraging policies and programs that require awareness, sensitivity, and education about gender, sex, sexuality, and sexual violence can contribute to real change (Banyard et al. 2007).

BOX 12.7 KITTY GENOVESE AND THE BYSTANDER EFFECT

In 1964, Queens New York City residents observed the gruesome rape and stabbing murder of 28-year-old Catherine "Kitty" Genovese. Two weeks later, a *New York Times* article with the attention-grabbing headline "37 Who Saw Murder Didn't Call the Police" reported that the attack took over half an hour, that the assailant left and returned multiple times to attack the victim, and that the neighbors, most of whom could see or hear the attack happening from their apartment windows, chose not to call the police. A few witnesses later told the police why they did not intervene (Gansberg 1964):

- "I didn't want to get involved."
- "We thought it was a lover's quarrel."
- "Frankly, we were afraid."
- "I don't know."
- "I was tired."

Although it has generally been concluded that there were some inaccuracies in the initial *New York Times* coverage of this vicious attack (for example, it is speculated that a few witnesses *did* call the police during the attack and there is skepticism that there were in fact "37" apathetic onlookers) and perhaps because Genovese is often depicted as an innocent victim (the events of her attack align well with the "blitz attack with a weapon" scenario described earlier in this chapter), Genovese's murder has become "a kind of modern day parable—the antonym of the parable of the good Samaritan" (Manning *et al.* 2007:555). It provides a cautionary tale about danger, victim culpability, apathy, and the diffusion of responsibility and it also carved the path for the construction of the social psychology concept, the bystander effect, sometimes even described as "Genovese syndrome."

The *bystander effect* refers to the phenomenon whereby individuals are more likely to help when alone than when in the company of others. Specifically, people are less likely to intervene when there are multiple bystanders, the presumption being that somebody else will do it. The bystander effect has been documented in social psychological research and evidence shows that educational programs designed to teach bystanders how to actively intervene in risky situations (before and during acts of sexual violence) have positive results on increasing the likelihood of bystander intervention and preventing sexual violence (e.g., Banyard *et al.* 2007).

Concluding remarks

Rape is a serious social problem that affects everyone. The cultural and legal complexities that comprise sexual assault make it especially nefarious. Through careful

TABLE 12.5 Methods of bystander intervention to prevent sexual assault

Everyday	At parties (with alcohol)	In intimate settings
Personally avoid using sexist language, telling sexist jokes, and disparaging victims of sexual violence.	Check in with my friend who looks drunk when s/he goes to a room with someone else at a party.	Understand how my intimate partner(s) define and communicate willingness, desire, and consent.
Express concern or challenge a family member or friend who is using sexist language, telling sexist jokes, and disparaging victims of sexual violence.	Say something to my friend who is taking a drunk person back to a room at (or away from) a party.	Ask for verbal consent when I am intimate with my partner, even if we are in a long-term relationship.
Refuse to participate in activities where bodies and attractiveness are ranked, rated, or displayed in a disrespectful manner.	Confront a friend who has had sex with someone who was passed out.	Stop sexual activity when asked to, even if I am already sexually aroused.
Promote an active dialogue with friends and family about the realities of sexual violence and how to make socially responsible choices.	Confront a friend if I hear rumors that s/he forced sex on someone. Confront a friend who plans to give someone alcohol/drugs to get sex. Avoid drinking to excess and have a plan if I do.	Stop having sex with a partner if s/he says to stop, even if it started consensually. Decide not to have sex with a partner if s/he is drunk. Keep an open dialogue with my intimate partner(s).

Partially adapted from McMahon *et al.* (2011).

consideration of the sociological significance of rape, we can arm ourselves with the educational tools necessary to begin a conversation about reducing sexual violence, responding to survivors of rape, and creating a global cultural shift away from rape-prone environments.

Notes

1 Carnal knowledge is an archaic euphemism for sexual intercourse derived from Biblical language. The FBI adopted this phrase and defined "carnal knowledge" as "the slightest penetration of the sexual organ of a female (vagina) by the sexual organ of the male (penis)" (Federal Bureau of Investigation 2004:19).

2 *Ms.* magazine is an American liberal feminist magazine that was co-founded by well-known feminists Gloria Steinem and Dorothy Pitman Hughes in 1971.

3 Change.org is a website operated by Change.org, Inc., an American-based company that provides a platform for individuals to construct online petitions and garner online signatures to support their causes. Founded in 2007, Change.org petitions have a significant global presence with more than 100 million active daily users.

4 Jeanne Clery was a 19-year-old college student who was raped and murdered in her campus dormitory, Stoughton Hall, at Lehigh University in Bethlehem, Pennsylvania, by Josoph M. Henry, another student, in 1986. Although Henry was put to death by electric chair, Jeanne's parents argued that, had the University's crime record been made available to the public, Jeanne would not have attended. The Clery family's activism ultimately led to the federal statute known as the "Clery Act."

5 Only licensed mental-health and pastoral counselors are explicitly exempt from Clery reporting requirements.
6 The universities that participated in the AAUCCS were: Brown University, California Institute of Technology, Case Western Reserve University, Columbia University, Cornell University, Harvard University, Iowa State University, Michigan State University, The Ohio State University, Purdue University, Texas A&M University, The University of Arizona, University of Florida, University of Michigan, University of Minnesota-Twin Cities, University of Missouri-Columbia, The University of North Carolina at Chapel Hill, University of Oregon, University of Pennsylvania, University of Pittsburgh, University of Southern California, The University of Texas at Austin, University of Virginia, The University of Wisconsin-Madison, Washington University in St. Louis, Yale University, and Dartmouth College.
7 The rape incident report data here are from the Iowa State University report (Cantor *et al.* 2015b). AAUCCS aggregate data from the 27 universities were not yet released at the time of publication of this textbook.
8 Sexual harassment was defined as behaviors that interfered with the victim's academic or professional performances, limited the victim's ability to participate in an academic program, or created an intimidating, hostile or offensive social, academic, or work environment. Examples include sexual or crude remarks or jokes (in person or via social media) that were insulting or offensive, persistent requests to go out on a date, and inappropriate comments regarding the body.
9 IPV was measured as experiences within a partnered relationship that involved controlling, threatening, physically aggressive, and/or violent behaviors.
10 Stalking was measured as experiences that made the victim afraid for his/her personal safety that involved unwanted phone calls, emails, voice, text or instant messages and/or being spied on, watched, or followed.
11 Although "prison rape" is the official title of this act, the act encompasses all forms of sexual victimization of incarcerated individuals (Singer 2013:5).

References

Abbey, Antonia, Pam McAuslan, and Lisa Ross. 1998. "Sexual Assault Perpetration by College Men: The Role of Alcohol, Misperception of Sexual Intent, and Sexual Beliefs and Experiences." *Journal of Social and Clinical Psychology* 17:167–95.
Abbey, Antonia, Tina Zawackia, Philip O. Bucka, A. Monique Clinton, and Pam McAuslan. 2004. "Sexual Assault and Alcohol Consumption: What Do We Know about their Relationship and What Types of Research are Still Needed?" *Aggression and Violent Behavior* 9:271–303.
Aggrawal, Anil. 2009. *Forensic and Medico-legal Aspects of Sexual Crimes and Unusual Sexual Practices.* Boca Raton, FL: Taylor and Francis.
Ariely, Dan and George Loewenstein. 2006. "The Heat of the Moment: The Effect of Sexual Arousal on Sexual Decision Making." *Journal of Behavioral Decision Making* 19:87–98.
Badiye, Ashish and Mansi Gupta. 2012. "ROHYPNOL®: A Review on Abuse as Date Rape Drug." *Helix* 3:161–4.
Balsam, Kimberly F., Esther D. Rothblum, and Theodore P. Beauchaine. 2005. "Victimization Over the Life Span: A Comparison of Lesbian, Gay, Bisexual, and Heterosexual Siblings." *Journal of Consulting and Clinical Psychology* 7(3):477–87.
Banyard, Victoria, Mary Moynihan, and Elizabeth Plante. 2007. "Sexual Violence Prevention through Bystander Education: An Experimental Evaluation." *Journal of Community Psychology* 35(4):463–81.
Benedict, Helen. 1995. "The Language of Rape." Pp. 101–5 in *Transforming a Rape Culture*, edited by Emilie Buchwald, Pamela Fletcher, and Martha Roth. Minneapolis, MN: Milkweed Editions.

Beres, Melanie. 2007. "'Spontaneous' Sexual Consent: An Analysis of Sexual Consent Literature." *Feminism Psychology* 17(1):93–108.

Beres, Melanie, Edward Herold, and Scott Maitland. 2004. "Sexual Consent Behaviors in Same-Sex Relationships." *Archives of Sexual Behavior* 33(5):475–86.

Bierie, David M. and James C. Davis-Siegel. 2015. "Measurement Matters: Comparing Old and New Definitions of Rape in Federal Statistical Reporting." *Sexual Abuse: A Journal of Research and Treatment* 27(5):443–59.

Bogle, Kathleen. 2008. *Hooking Up: Sex, Dating, and Relationships on Campus.* New York, NY: NYU Press.

Browne, Kingsley. 2007. "Military Sex Scandals from Tailhook to the Present: The Cure can be Worse than the Disease." *Duke Journal of Gender Law & Policy* 14:749–89.

Burt, Martha. 1980. "Cultural Myths and Supports for Rape." *Journal of Personality and Social Psychology* 38(2):217–30.

CDC. 2015. "Sexual Violence: Consequences." Centers for Disease Control. Retrieved from: http://www.cdc.gov/violenceprevention/sexualviolence/consequences.html

Campbell, Rebecca and Camille Johnson. 1997. "Police Officers' Perceptions of Rape: Is there Consistency between State Law and Individual Beliefs?" *Journal of Interpersonal Violence* 12(2):255–74.

Cantor, David, Bonnie Fisher, Susan Chibnall, Reanne Townsend, Hyunshik Lee, Carol Bruce, and Gail Thomas. 2015a. *Report on the AAU Campus Climate Survey on Sexual Assault and Sexual Misconduct.* Rockville, MD: Westat.

Cantor, David, Bonnie Fisher, Susan Chibnall, Carol Bruce, Reanne Townsend, Gail Thomas and Hyunshik Lee. 2015b. *Report on the AAU Campus Climate Survey on Sexual Assault and Sexual Misconduct: Iowa State University.* Rockville, MD: Westat.

Cohn, Amy, Heidi Zinzow, Heidi Resnick, and Dean Kilpatrick. 2013. "Correlates of Reasons for Not Reporting Rape to Police: Results From a National Telephone Household Probability Sample of Women With Forcible or Drug-or-Alcohol Facilitated/Incapacitated Rape." *Journal of Interpersonal Violence* 28(3):455–73.

Colson, Marie-Helene, Laurent Boyer, Karine Baumstarck, and Anderson D. Loundou. 2013. "Female Sex Offenders: A Challenge to Certain Paradigmes. Meta-Analyses." *Sexologies* 22(4):109–17.

Copenhaver, Stacey and Elizabeth Grauerholz. 1991. "Sexual Victimization Among Sorority Women: Exploring the Link Between Sexual Violence and Institutional Practices." *Sex Roles* 24(1/2):31–41.

Davies, Michelle. 2002. "Male Sexual Assault Victims: A Selective Review of the Literature and Implications for Support Services." *Aggression and Violent Behavior* 7(3):203–14.

Ellison, Jesse. 2011, April 3. "The Military's Secret Shame." *Newsweek.* Retrieved from: http://www.newsweek.com/2011/04/03/the-military-s-secret-shame.html.

Federal Bureau of Investigation. 2004. *Uniform Crime Reporting Handbook.* Retrieved from: http://www2.fbi.gov/ucr/handbook/ucrhandbook04.pdf

Federal Bureau of Investigation. 2014. *Rape Addendum: Uniform Crime Reporting Program Changes Definition of Rape.* Retrieved from: https://www.fbi.gov/about-us/cjis/ucr/crime-in-the-u.s/2013/crime-in-the-u.s.-2013/rape-addendum/rape_addendum_final.pdf

Gansberg, Martin. 1964, March 27. "37 Who Saw Murder Didn't Call the Police." *New York Times.* Retrieved from: http://www.nytimes.com/1964/03/27/37-who-saw-murder-didnt-call-the-police.html?_r=0

Gordon, Margaret and Stephanie Riger. 1991. *The Female Fear: The Social Cost of Rape.* Urbana, IL: University of Illinois Press.

Gray, Jacqueline. 2006. "Rape Myth Beliefs and Prejudiced Instructions: Effects on Decisions of Guilt in a Case of Date Rape." *Legal and Criminological Psychology* 11:75–80.

Greenberg, Alissa. 2015, July 24. "Spain Has Finally Made It Illegal for 14-Year-Olds to Get Married." *Time*. Retrieved from: http://time.com/3970710/spain-marriage-age-of-consent-europe/.

Groth, A. Nicholas. 1979. *Men Who Rape*. New York, NY: Plenum Press.

Hale, Robert. 1997. "Motives of Reward Among Men Who Rape." *American Journal of Criminal Justice* 22(1):101–19.

Harris, Frank and Shaun R. Harper. 2014. "Beyond Bad Behaving Brothers: Productive Performances of Masculinities among College Fraternity Men." *International Journal of Qualitative Studies in Education* 27(6):703–23.

Hayes, Sharon and Belinda Carpenter. 2013. "'Social Moralities and Discursive Constructions of Female Sex Offenders." *Sexualities* 16(1/2):159–79.

Hickman, Susan and Charlene Muehlenhard. 1999. "'By the Semi-Mystical Appearance of a Condom': How Young Women and Men Communicate Sexual Consent in Heterosexual Situations." *The Journal of Sex Research* 36:258–72.

Joyal, Christian C., Amélie Cossette, and Vanessa Lapierre. 2015. "What Exactly Is an Unusual Sexual Fantasy?" *The Journal of Sexual Medicine* 12(2):328–40.

Jozkowski, Kristen. 2013. "The Influence of Consent on College Students' Perceptions of the Quality of Sexual Intercourse at Last Event." *International Journal of Sexual Health* 25:260–72.

Jozkowski, Kristen and Zoë Peterson. 2013. "College Students and Sexual Consent: Unique Insights." *Journal of Sex Research* 50(6):517–23.

Jozkowski, Kristen and Jacquelyn Wiersma. 2015. "Does Drinking Alcohol Prior to Sexual Activity Influence College Students' Consent?" *International Journal of Sexual Health* 27(2):156–74.

Jozkowski, Kristen, Zoë Peterson, Stephanie Sanders, Barbara Dennis, and Michael Reece. 2014. "Gender Differences in Heterosexual College Students' Conceptualizations and Indicators of Sexual Consent: Implications for Contemporary Sexual Assault Prevention Education." *The Journal of Sex Research* 51(8):904–16.

Karmen, Andrew. 2012. *Crime Victims: An Introduction to Victimology*. Belmont, CA: Wadsworth Publishing.

Kilpatrick, Dean, Heidi Resnick, Kenneth Ruggiero, Lauren Conoscenti, and Jenna McCauley. 2007. *Drug-facilitated, Incapacitated, and Forcible Rape: A National Study*. The National Institute of Justice [NIJ 219181]. Washington, D.C.: U.S. Department of Justice.

Krebs, Christopher, Christine Lindquist, Tara Warner, Bonnie Fisher, and Sandra Martin. 2007. *The Campus Sexual Assault (CSA) Study Final Report*. The National Institute of Justice [NIJ 2004-WG-BX-0010]. Washington, D.C.: U.S. Department of Justice.

Lisak, David, Lori Gardinier, Sarah C. Nicks, and Ashley M. Cote. 2010. "False Allegations of Sexual Assault: An Analysis of Ten Years of Reported Cases." *Violence Against Women* 16(12):1318–34.

McMahon, Sarah, Judy Postmus, and Ruth Koenick. 2011. "Engaging Bystanders: A Primary Prevention Approach to Sexual Violence on Campus." *Journal of College Student Development* 15(1):115–30.

Manning, Rachel, Mark Levine, and Alan Collins. 2007. "The Kitty Genovese Murder and the Social Psychology of Helping: The Parable of the 38 Witnesses." *American Psychologist* 62(6):555–62.

Martin, Patricia Yancey and Robert A. Hummer. 1989. "Fraternities and Rape on Campus." *Gender and Society* 3(4):457–73.

Miller, Bonnie, David Cox, and Elizabeth Saewyc. 2010. "Age of Sexual Consent Law in Canada: Population-Based Evidence for Law and Policy." *The Canadian Journal of Human Sexuality* 19(3):105–19.

Murnen, Sarah and Marla Kohlman. 2007. "Athletic Participation, Fraternity Membership, and Sexual Aggression Among College Men: A Meta-Analytic Review." *Sex Roles* 57:145–57.

Newcombe, Peter, Julie van den Eynde, Diane Hafner, and Lesley Jolly. 2008. "Attributions of Responsibility for Rape: Differences Across Familiarity of Situation, Gender, and Acceptance of Rape Myths." *Journal of Applied Social Psychology* 38(7):1736–54.

NIAAA. 2015, April. "College Drinking Factsheet." *National Institute on Alcohol Abuse and Alcoholism*. Retrieved from: http://pubs.niaaa.nih.gov/publications/CollegeFactSheet/CollegeFactSheet.pdf

NISVS. 2011. The National Intimate Partner and Sexual Violence Survey: 2010. *National Center for Injury Prevention and Control*. Retrieved from: http://www.cdc.gov/ViolencePrevention/pdf/NISVS_Report2010-a.pdf

NISVS. 2013. The National Intimate Partner and Sexual Violence Survey, 2010: Findings on Victimization by Sexual Orientation. *National Center for Injury Prevention and Control*. Retrieved from http://www.cdc.gov/violenceprevention/pdf/nisvs_sofindings.pdf.

Orcutt, James and Rebecca Faison 1988. "Sex-Role Attitude Change and Reporting of Rape victimization 1973–1985." *The Sociological Quarterly* 29(4):589–604.

Page, Amy. 2010. "True Colors: Police Officers and Rape Myth Acceptance." *Feminist Criminology* 5(4):315–34.

Payne, Diana, Kimberly Lonsway, and Louise Fitzgerald. 1999. "Rape Myth Acceptance: Exploration of Its Structure and Its Measurement Using the Illinois Rape Myth Acceptance Scale." *Journal of Research in Personality* 33:27–68.

Penal Code of the Republic of Slovenia. "Sexual Assault on a Person below the Age of Fifteen Years." *Republic of Slovenia Legislation* Article 183/1.

PsychGuides.com. n.d. "Sexual Assaults on Campus." Retrieved from: http://www.psychguides.com/interact/sexual-assaults-on-campus/.

Rantala, Ramona, Jessica Rexroat, and Allen Beck. 2014. "Survey of Sexual Violence in Adult Correctional Facilities, 2009–11, Statistical Tables." *U.S. Department of Justice, Office of Justice Programs*. Washington, D.C.: Bureau of Justice Statistics.

Rock, Lindsay. 2013. *2012 Workplace and Gender Relations Survey of Active Duty Members: Survey Note No. 2013–007*. Alexandria, VA: DMDC.

Rodriguez, Cecilia. 2013, March 1. "Reforming Prostitution in Amsterdam Includes a Business Plan and Business Hours." *Forbes*. Retrieved from: http://www.forbes.com/sites/ceciliarodriguez/2013/03/01/reforming-prostitution-in-amsterdam-includes-a-business-plan-and-business-hours/.

Sadler, Anne, Brenda Booth, Brian Cook, James Torner, and Bradley Doebbeling. 2001. "The Military Environment: Risk Factors for Women's Non-Fatal Assaults." *Journal of Occupational Environmental Medicine* 43:325–34.

Sanday, Peggy Reeves. 1990. *Fraternity Gang Rape: Sex, Brotherhood, and Privilege on Campus*. New York, NY: NYU Press.

Schemo, Diana. 2003, August 29. "Rate of Rape at Academy Is Put at 12% in Survey." *The New York Times*. Retrieved from: http://www.nytimes.com/2003/08/29/national/29ACAD.html?th

Segal, Mady. 1978. "Women in the Military: Research and Policy Issues." *Youth and Society* 10:101–26.

Singer, Michael. 2013. *Prison Rape: An American Institution?* Santa Barbara, CA: Praeger.

Spivak, Andrew. 2011. *Sexual Violence: Beyond the Feminist-Evolutionary Debate*. El Paso, TX: LFB.

Stanley, Julia P. 1977. "Paradigmatic Woman: The Prostitute." Pp. 303–21 in *Papers in Language Variation*, edited by David L. Shores and Carole Hines. Tuscaloosa, AL: University of Alabama Press.

Stemple, Lara and Illan Meyer. 2014. "The Sexual Victimization of Men in America: New Data Challenge Old Assumptions." *American Journal of Public Health* 104(6):e19–e26.

Stotzer, Rebecca. 2008. "Violence Against Transgender People: A Review of United States Data." *Aggression and Violent Behavior* 14:170–9.

Struckman-Johnson, Cindy and David Struckman-Johnson. 1992. "Acceptance of Male Rape Myths Among College Men and Women." *Sex Roles* 27(3/4):85–100.

Suarez, Eliana, and Tahany M. Gadalla. 2010. "Stop Blaming the Victim: A Meta-Analysis on Rape Myths." *Journal of Interpersonal Violence* 25(11): 2010–35.

Terkel, Amanda. 2012, January 6. "Eric Holder Expands FBI's Narrow, Outdated Definition of Rape." *Huffington Post*. Retrieved from: http://www.huffingtonpost.com/2012/01/06/eric-holderfbi-rape_n_1189145.html

Tilghman, Andrew. 2015, June 21. "Women in Combat Units: Final Decision Due." *Military Times*. Retrieved from: http://www.militarytimes.com/story/military/pentagon/2015/06/21/women-in-combat-final-phase/28930521/

Ullman, Sarah. 2010. *Talking about Sexual Assault: Society's Response to Survivors*. Washington, D.C.: APA.

Ullman, Sarah and Henrietta Filipas 2005. "Gender Differences in Social Reactions to Abuse Disclosures, Post-Abuse Coping, and PTSD of Child Sexual Abuse Survivors." *Child Abuse & Neglect* 29(7):767–82.

Weber, Max. 1922 [1978]. *Economy and Society*. Berkley, CA: University of California Press.

Worthen, Meredith G. F. 2011. "Fraternities." Pp. 297–301 in *The Encyclopedia of Social Networks*, edited by George A. Barnett. Sage Reference Publications.

Worthen, Meredith G. F. and S. Abby Baker. 2014. "Consent is Sexy? University Student Reactions to a Mandatory Online Sexual Misconduct Training Program." *Sexual Assault Report* 17(5):65–75.

13

SEX CRIMES AGAINST CHILDREN

Melissa S. Jones

On Friday, July 20, 1994, seven-year-old Megan Kanka spent the day riding her bike around her neighborhood in Mercerville, New Jersey. Across the street from Megan lived Jesse T. Timmendequas, a 33-year-old twice-convicted sex offender. Timmendequas lured Megan into his house by offering to show her a puppy. He took her into his bedroom where he attempted to sexually assault her. Megan screamed and tried to escape but Timmedequas would not let her. After raping her, he slammed her head into a dresser, put two plastic bags over her head, and strangled her to death with his belt. He put her body into a wooden toy box, placed the box in his truck, and took it to the nearby Mercer County Park. In the woods at the park, Timmedequas sexually assaulted Megan again before dumping her body. The next day, at police headquarters, Timmedequas confessed to Megan's murder and took law enforcement to the dumpsite. Evidence, including bloodstains, hair, and fiber samples, as well as a bite mark matching Megan's teeth on Timmedequas' hand, led to his conviction of kidnapping, four counts of aggravated sexual assault, and two counts of felony murder (Goodman 1997).

This chapter reviews sex crimes against children. Specifically, pedophilia, hebephilia, incest, and child sexual abuse in sex-related media (CSAM) are defined, described, and discussed. We also examine the grooming and luring techniques of sex offenders, including how the internet has shaped, changed, and influenced the sexual exploitation of children and the difficulties facing law enforcement when prosecuting offenders. We conclude with a discussion of the short- and long-term gendered effects of childhood sexual abuse.

Defining pedophilia and hebephilia

Most of us tend to learn about sex crimes against children through the media, and consequently, given the nature of media reporting, we mostly learn about violent, predatory, and astonishing crimes. But in reality, cases such as the murder of Megan Kanka are the exceptions rather than the rule and few sex crimes against children involve homicide, brutality, sexual mutilation, or significant bodily injury (Sheldon and Howitt 2007). Nonetheless, sex crimes against children typically evoke horrifying, sickening, and nightmarish thoughts and feelings. However, before we begin to discuss the traits, techniques, and explanations for sex crimes against children, we need to first define pedophilia and hebephilia.

Pedophilia is a sexual attraction to prepubescent children approximately 10 years of age and younger, as indicated by persistent and recurrent sexual thoughts, fantasies, urges, and arousal (Seto 2008). A pedophile then, is an adult or older adolescent at least 16 years of age who has sexual attraction to prepubescent children. Pedophilic behavior usually begins in the late teenage years but sometimes pedophiles begin acting on their sexual interest in children later in life. *Hebephilia* is a sexual attraction to pubescent children, approximately aged 11 to 14, whose bodies show discrete signs of puberty (e.g., some pubic and/or underarm hair, signs of breast development) (Glueck 1955). The majority of this chapter is concerned with pedophilia. Pedophiles may engage in a variety of contact and noncontact sexual acts with children that can include (Seto 2008; Holmes and Holmes 2009; Zilney and Zilney 2009; Rufo 2012):

- Masturbating in the company or presence of a child.
- Exposing or revealing themselves to a child (exhibitionism).
- Looking at naked children without their knowledge (voyeurism).
- Sexually related contact with children via the phone or internet.
- Fondling or "playful" behavior to touch a child inappropriately.
- Taking a child's clothes off.
- Oral contact with the child's vagina, anus, or mouth or forcing the child to engage in oral sex acts in some other manner.
- Penetration of the child's vagina, anus, or mouth or forcing the child to penetrate.
- Viewing/watching child sexual abuse in sex-related media (CSAM).

In addition, pedophiles often masturbate when they fantasize about children. It is important to note that the words "pedophile" and "child molester" are often presented as synonymous in the media. Technically, however this is incorrect. If a person who has sexual interest in a child acts upon these illicit desires (e.g., touching or fondling a child), that would indeed fall under the category of child molester. However, some individuals with pedophilic tendencies are able to keep their sexual impulses in the realm of thought and fantasy. Thus, some pedophiles become child molesters and some do not (Zilney and Zilney 2009; Rufo 2012).

Characteristics of pedophiles

Most individuals who engage in pedophilia are heterosexual married men and contrary to the media's portrayal of pedophiles, the majority of perpetrators are known to their victims. According to official data collected by the FBI's National Incident-Based Reporting System (NIBRS), 92 percent of sexually victimized children under the age of 12 knew their offender (Finkelhor and Shattuck 2012). And while society views pedophilia as extremely deviant, it may be more common than one would like to think. For example, in a study with close to 200 college undergraduate men, a surprisingly high percentage sexualized children. Specifically, 21 percent of college men reported sexual attraction to prepubescent children, 9 percent described sexual fantasies involving children, 5 percent admitted to having masturbated to fantasies, and 7 percent indicated that they would have sex with a child if they could not be detected or punished. These sexual interests in children were associated with experiencing childhood abuse (physical and sexual abuse), self-reported likelihood of raping a woman, high numbers of sex partners, sexual conflicts, and general attitudes supportive of sexual dominance over women (Briere and Runtz 1989). Thus, sexual interest in children may be more common than we think but it is likely related to other negative life experiences and problematic attitudes.

Pedophile types

Pedophiles are not all alike. Specifically, they differ in their victim preferences, types of preferred sexual activities, and motivations. Situational offenders do *not* usually have sexual preferences for children. Instead, they engage in sex with children for a variety of reasons. For example, a regressed offender, who lacks poor coping skills or suffers from low self-esteem, may turn to children as a sexual substitute for a preferred similarly-aged sex partner. In contrast, preferential offenders have definite sexual attractions to children. These individuals have sexual fantasies and enjoy erotic imagery focusing on children, and have specific gender and age preferences for their victims. For example, a seduction offender engages children in sexual activity by "seducing" them through grooming them with attention, affection, and gifts. This grooming/seduction process gradually lowers the child's sexual inhibitions (Terry and Tallon 2004). Other types of child sex offenders are described in Table 13.1.

Women pedophiles

The topic of women committing sex crimes against children has not generally received much attention until recently. There was a time when it was believed that women simply could not be pedophiles (Chow and Choy 2002). As a result, most studies about pedophiles focus on men offenders. However, research suggests that women are offenders, on average, in 15 to 20 percent of all substantiated child sexual abuse cases reported to child protective services in the United States (McLeod 2015) and most researchers agree that this is likely a gross underestimate (see chapter 12, Box 12.6).

Overall, most convicted women sex offenders are young, between the ages of 21 and 35, and compared to men sex offenders, they are more likely to come from abusive homes and have experienced sexual abuse as children and teens. Many also

TABLE 13.1 The FBI's typology of child sex offenders and factors associated with pedophilia

Type of offender	Characteristics of offenders	Associated factors
Situational offenders		
Regressed	Offenders have poor coping skills, target victims who are easily accessible, and abuse children as a substitute for adult relationships.	Blockage
Inadequate	Offenders are socially insecure, have low self-esteem, and view relationships with children as their only sexual outlet.	Blockage
Morally indiscriminate	Offenders tend to use children for their own interests, including sexual.	Disinhibition
Sexually indiscriminate	Offenders are primarily interested in sexual experimentation and abuse children out of boredom.	Disinhibition
Preferential offenders		
Seductive	Offenders "court" children and give them affection, love, and gifts in order to carry on a "relationship."	Emotional congruence; Sexual arousal
Fixated	Offenders have poor psychosocial development, desire affection from children, and are compulsively attracted to children.	Emotional congruence; Sexual arousal
Sadistic	Offenders are aggressive, sexually enticed by violence, target stranger victims, and are extremely dangerous.	Sexual arousal

Data adapted from Finkelhor and Araji (1986) and Terry and Tallon (2004).

have a personal history of alcohol and/or related drug use, depression, anxiety, personality disorders, coping difficulties, and often struggle with both intimate and interpersonal relationships with similarly-aged peers (Vandiver and Kercher 2004; Strickland 2008; Rufo 2012; Colson *et al.* 2013). The majority commit offenses against children they know (either their own or those they are caring for) and because of this, they can easily hide their abusive behaviors within their nurturing and caregiving responsibilities. Women sex offenders typically fit into the following categories (Vandiver and Kercher 2004; Rufo 2012):

* A mother who victimizes her own children.
* A woman who victimizes a family relative (other than her own child).
* A woman who holds a position of authority (e.g., teacher, coach) over the victim.

- A woman who has caregiving responsibilities (e.g., nanny, babysitter) over the victim.
- A woman who sexually abuses others along with a domineering male partner.

Factors associated with pedophilia

There are four key factors associated with sexual interest in children: emotional congruence, sexual arousal, blockage, and disinhibition (Finkelhor and Araji 1986).

- *Emotional congruence.* Pedophiles may choose children for sexual partners because they share an emotional congruence with children. They are not just immature, but generally have low self-esteem and little efficacy in their adult social relationships. Some psychological theories have suggested that pedophiles have arrested psychological development, in that they experience themselves as children, they have childish emotions, and accordingly wish to connect intimately with children (Seto 2008). Moreover, relating to children is fitting because it provides feelings of being powerful and in control (Araji and Finkelhor 1985; Holmes and Holmes 2009). Within the FBI Typology (see Table 13.1), both fixated and seductive child sex offenders likely feel emotional congruence with their victims.
- *Sexual arousal.* Pedophiles may be sexually aroused by children because they experienced early or frequent exposure to sex during childhood or early adolescence (Seto 2008). This may come in the form of observing others engaging in sexual activities, viewing sexual materials, such as pornography, and experiencing sexual abuse. Because of these early experiences with and/or exposure to sex in childhood, men and women may remain attracted to children when they become older (Durkin and Hundersmarck 2008; Rufo 2012; Colson *et al.* 2013). Biological factors, such as brain development, neurochemistry, and neurostructure have also been found to be associated with adult sexual arousal to children (Sheldon and Howitt 2007; Rufo 2012). Preferential offenders, including seductive, fixated, and sadistic pedophiles, are likely sexually aroused by their victims (see Table 13.1).
- *Blockage.* Pedophiles may be blocked from making appropriate adjustments to having sex with similarly-aged peers. These blocks may include: fear of adults, traumatic sexual experiences with adults, and inadequate social skills. Moreover, they may also experience marital disturbances, such as divorce or separation that disrupt their competence in adult relationships (Finkelhor and Araji 1986; Seto 2008). Inadequate and regressed child sex offenders are likely experiencing blockage (see Table 13.1).
- *Disinhibition.* Pedophiles may not have developed inhibitions against having sex with children. Disinhibition can result from poor socialization patterns, certain personality traits (e.g., impulse disorders, lack of empathy, poor risk assessment), or can occur as a result of situational factors, such as drug/alcohol use or intoxication (Seto 2008). Morally and sexually indiscriminate pedophiles feel disinhibited about engaging in adult-child sex (see Table 13.1).

Grooming techniques

Pedophiles often target specific types of children, especially those who have poor relationships with their parents and lack close friendships, because they are most vulnerable to victimization (Craven *et al.* 2006). After a vulnerable child has been identified, pedophiles participate in *sexual grooming*—a three-part process to facilitate child abuse whereby they prepare:

- themselves (self-grooming through personal justifications of their desire for sex with children, see Box 13.1);
- the environment [gain "legitimate" access to the child through establishing social relationships with those individuals who provide the closest access to the child (Craven *et al.* 2006; Rufo 2012)]; and
- the child (gain the child's trust and compliance in order to maintain the child's secrecy and ultimately avoid discovery).

Although all three parts of the sexual grooming process are often necessary to aid in sexual abuse of children, grooming the child is the most commonly recognized form of sexual grooming and often the most time-consuming because it involves the gradual process of sexualizing the offender–child relationship (van Dam 2001). The offender may start desensitizing the child to touching by beginning with various forms of non-sexual touching, such as tickling. Conversations between the offender and child may become progressively more sexual over time and the offender may introduce sexually graphic imagery (such as pornography or CSAM) to further sexualize their relationship (Finkelhor 1984). Through this process, the child is encouraged to think about his/her sexual relationship with the offender as "special" but "secretive." In doing so, the child is discouraged from telling anyone about the sexual behaviors that take place between them. In addition, offenders will often employ bribes (e.g., gifts, extra privileges) and/or threats (e.g., hurt parents, hurt pets) to encourage compliance in sexual behaviors. Sometimes, the offender convinces the child that he/she is actually responsible for the victimization (Craven *et al.* 2006; Rufo 2012).

The internet as a luring technique

Sometimes, pedophiles find victims via online interactions. Through chat rooms, social media, and instant messaging, pedophiles can meet children and develop online social relationships. A similar sexual grooming process is employed, although this one is virtual—at least until they meet in person. Some pedophiles choose to lure/groom their victims in this way because the internet provides anonymity. Offenders can provide fake names, misrepresent their age, and even change their appearance by sending fake pictures to children or adolescents to whom they may chat with online. Fundamentally, the internet allows offenders to keep their true identity a secret (Sheldon and Howitt 2007; Rufo 2012) although many are overt

BOX 13.1 NORTH AMERICAN MAN/BOY LOVE ASSOCIATION (NAMBLA) AND TECHNIQUES OF NEUTRALIZATION

Established in 1978, the North American Man/Boy Love Association (NAMBLA) is a political, civil rights, and educational organization that advocates and promotes adult sexual behaviors with children, specifically men and boys. Members of NAMBLA are socially stigmatized because their beliefs about sex with children deviate substantially from expected, acceptable, and normative beliefs by the wider society. As such, they are motivated to reduce or eschew their stigmatization by engaging in behaviors that promote, justify, or in some way normalize their deviance in relation to larger societal expectations and beliefs. They do so in various ways, many of which fit with the Techniques of Neutralization (Sykes and Matza 1957) outlined in chapter 3.

Specifically, NAMBLA members attempt to neutralize their deviant interests in adult-child sex in four ways (DeYoung 2015):

- *Denial of injury.* NAMBLA argues that adult-child sexual relationships cause no harm or injury but instead, have benefits and advantages for children that include helping children get in touch with their own sexuality and rescuing children off of the streets to bring them into a home filled with love. In addition, NAMBLA suggests that even if children experience harm, it is not from the adults they are having sex with, but rather it is the harm caused by the general public who disparages their behavior. To support their claims, NAMBLA even publishes accounts from children that describe the benefits they received from their sexual encounter with an adult.
- *Denial of victim.* NAMBLA uses the technique of "denial of victim" to conceptually transform the thought of children as "victims of sexual abuse" into willing partners in adult-child sex. Noticeably, the main issue here is the concept of consent and the age at which a person can freely and intelligently make sexual decisions. NAMBLA does not offer an explanation as to how, for example, a 5-year-old might be able to consent to a sex act with an adult.
- *Condemnation of condemners.* This strategy redirects the disapproval of a particular form of deviance back onto the wider society. NAMBLA "condemns the condemners" by publishing pieces that denounce professionals in the fields of child sexual abuse, the criminal justice system, and mental health systems.
- *Appeal to higher loyalties.* NAMBLA suggests that the "higher loyalty" that comes from adult-child sex is the sexual liberation of children from what they characterize as the "repressive bonds of society." They argue that children should be awarded the sexual freedom to develop into "full human beings," which includes having sex with adults.

> In addition to these strategies, NAMBLA has also attempted to incorporate goals, beliefs, and values of other non-stigmatized organizations into its social welfare concerns for sexism, ageism, racism, among others (DeYoung 2015).
>
> Overall, NAMBLA recognizes their deviant status in society and to counteract it (and continue to support adult-child sex), they engage in neutralizing techniques that attempt to justify and normalize their sexual interests in children. This is also part of self-grooming, whereby pedophiles mentally convince themselves that their sexual interests in children are not harmful or problematic. In doing so, these techniques of neutralization serve to assist NAMBLA members and pedophiles with preparing for the sexual abuse of children.

about their age and explicit about their sexual interests. For example, in a study of 51 convicted internet-initiated sex offenders, only 17.6 percent lied about their age and 51 percent used sexually explicit conversations to locate a sexually active teen and determine if they were willing to have sex with an adult (Briggs *et al.* 2011). The internet also creates opportunities to lure multiple victims at a time. If a sex offender is unable to interest a child in exchanging images, or perhaps eventually meeting face-to-face, he can easily move on to another child (O'Donnell and Milner 2007). Overall, some pedophiles see the internet as an important resource in luring and sexually grooming their victims.

Incest

Intrafamilial child sexual abuse has been increasingly recognized as a serious problem. Incestuous relationships include sexual activity with a child by a family member in a position of trust and authority over the child as well as sexual relationships between adult family members (Rufo 2012). According to official reports from the FBI's NIBRS, 48 percent of sexually victimized children under the age of 12 are victimized by a family member (Finkelhor and Shattuck 2012). Adult-child incestuous relationships tend to last significantly longer than extra-familial adult-child sexually abusive relationships in part because they are easily hidden (family members often have ubiquitous access to familial children). The most commonly reported cases of incest involve father-daughter and stepfather-stepdaughter relationships, and as a result, this is the most frequently investigated incestuous dyad. There are five types of incestuous fathers who abuse their daughters identified in previous research (Williams and Finkelhor 1990):

- *Sexually preoccupied.* These men have a clear and conscious sexual interest in their daughter, often from an early age. They generally begin to molest their daughter when she is young, usually prior to age 6. These fathers commit extensive abusive acts over a long period of time and are more likely to penetrate their victims. They have often experienced intense abuse and mal-treatment during their own childhood.

- *Adolescent regressives.* These men have a conscious sexual interest in their daughter, but they tend not to act on their interests until their daughter reaches puberty.
- *Instrumental sexual gratifiers.* These men do not experience sexual arousal specifically from their daughter, but instead use their daughter for sexual gratification while fantasizing about another partner. They tend to have feelings of guilt and remorse for their actions and their abusive activity tends to be infrequent.
- *Emotionally dependent.* These men are often extremely lonely and depressed. Although sexual arousal may not be the primary aspect of intimacy with their daughter, the abuse seems to satisfy specific pressing needs for closeness and comfort. They tend to romanticize the quality of their relationships with their daughters.
- *Angry retaliators.* The primary focus of the sexual abuse of their daughter is in response to anger toward the mother of their daughter for neglect, abandonment, and presumed or actual infidelity.

Although father-daughter incest is the most commonly reported type of incestuous relationship, brother-sister incest may also be common, but is likely underreported. This is because these incestuous relationships are often viewed as benign and within the context of "normal" or "acceptable" sexual play or exploration; however, research has shown that penetration is much more frequent in brother-sister incestuous relationships (73 percent) when compared to stepfather-daughter (27.3 percent) or father-daughter (34.8 percent) incest (Cyr *et al.* 2002). Because brother-sister incestuous relationships are more likely to be viewed as "normal" or at least "acceptable," they are less likely to be viewed as rape, incest, or sexually inappropriate behavior and as a result, they go both unrecognized and unreported. In contrast, father-daughter incest is a near universal social taboo. This type of incestuous arrangement not only fits our stereotypes about rape (adult male assaulting a young helpless girl), but also, these types of rapes may be more likely to result in pregnancies, and as a result, others (such as friends, teachers, concerned family members) may be more likely to recognize and label the abuse. Furthermore, other types of incest (e.g., mother-son, cousin-cousin, aunt-nephew) are overwhelmingly under-researched and underreported and as a result, much about incest (including its prevalence) is unknown.

Child sexual abuse in sex-related media

Under Federal Law 18 U.S.C.§2256, "child pornography" is defined as any visual depiction, including any photograph, film, video, or picture that involves a minor (under age 18) engaging in sexually explicit conduct. These types of sexual exploitation materials involving minors are considered to be illegal in the vast majority of countries around the world, including the United States. The term "child pornography" that is used to describe these materials is highly problematic (see Box

13.2). Thus, throughout this chapter the term CSAM will be used when referring to these materials.

Traditionally, CSAM was produced and distributed in the form of print photographs and magazines to cater to adults with sexual interests in children. But with advancements in technology, CSAM can be generated in a variety of formats including digital photographs, online clips, film, and text images that can be downloaded, shared, and transmitted via internet-enabled devices (see Boxes 13.3 and 13.4). Since the advent of the internet, it is easier now than ever before for CSAM users to create, access, and share CSAM images worldwide at the simple click of a mouse. CSAM

BOX 13.2 "CHILD PORNOGRAPHY" AND CSAM: LANGUAGE, AND THE PERPETUATION OF CRIME AND MARGINALIZATION

Chauntelle A. Tibbals

As we have learned, ideas about deviance are variable and subjective—what is reprehensible and illegal to one may be ordinary practice to another. There are some occurrences, however, that come close to being universally deviant. Media captures of child sexual exploitation, or what is commonly referred to as "child pornography" (also, "CP"), are one such thing. Unfortunately, discussing sex crimes against minors via phrases such as "CP" and "child pornography" serves to perpetuate crime and marginalization because of one key issue: "child pornography" does not exist.

Graphic depictions of child sexual abuse in sex-related media (CSAM) involving persons under the age of 18 exist and are highly illegal in the United States and elsewhere. Pornography, on the other hand, is a legal enterprise, made for and featuring consenting adults. Professionally produced erotic content made in the U.S. does not include models or performers who are under the age of 18. The phrases "CP" and "child pornography" thus connect the sexual abuse of minors (illegal) with porn production in the U.S. (legal). This type of sensationalist language serves to distract from the very real issue of child sexual exploitation and further stigmatize and marginalize sex workers working as porn performers (Tibbals 2015). Thus, CSAM is a preferable term to describe these illicit representations of child sexual abuse and sex-related media.

In summary, porn is a legal enterprise and a labor negotiation between consenting adults. The use of "porn" in conjunction with illegal enterprises related to privacy violations, entrapment, coercion, and revenge muddies the issues in a similar manner. It augments harm experienced by survivors of illegal activity, while enhancing the stigma and marginalization experienced by sex workers working in the adult entertainment industry. The issue of language is especially significant here: while "child pornography" does not exist, CSAM is a very real, criminal, and horrific enterprise.

images are distributed using websites, email, internet chat rooms, and instant messaging—and this is happening at alarming rates. For example, the UK-based Internet Watch Foundation, a hotline system that actively monitors the internet for illegal material, received close to 50,000 reports from the public about images that were believed to be CSAM in 2014 alone—26 percent (12,180 images) of which were identified as CSAM and featured highly disturbing content:

- 80 percent of the children appeared to be aged 10 years or younger and 4 percent of children appeared to be aged 2 years or younger.
- 43 percent of the images showed sexual activity between adults and children including rape or sexual torture.
- 30 percent of the images involved non-penetrative sexual activity.
- 80 percent of the images were of girl victims, 10 percent of the images were of boy victims, and 7 percent contained images of both genders (Internet Watch Foundation 2014).

BOX 13.3 ARTIFICIALLY GENERATED CSAM

Artificially generated CSAM includes media (i.e., images, clips, etc.) that is:

- age-regressed (modified images of non-minor teenagers or adults made to look younger and more child-like);
- drawn (drawings or animations that depict sexual acts involving children); and
- fully computer-generated (virtually constructed images of children, such as avatars, in sexualized poses and/or engaging in sex acts).

Laws concerning artificially generated CSAM vary by country. In the United States, this type of media is considered legal as long as a digital or computer image is "distinguishable" from a real child (18 U.S.C. §2252, 18 U.S.C. §2252A, and 18 U.S.C. §2256). However, certain jurisdictions in Australia and the European Union take a zero-tolerance approach to CSAM and any media—whether drawn, fully computer generated, or something else—is deemed to be illegal if it depicts any representation of a child engaged in real or simulated explicit sexual activities or any representation of the sexual parts of a child for primarily sexual purposes (United Nations Convention of the Rights of Children, Article 2C, 2007). In other places such as Japan, drawn erotica featuring children as sexual objects (e.g., *lolicon*, animated porn featuring prepubescent and adolescent girls) is entirely legal. Thus, the world of CSAM has become overwhelmingly complex with the introduction of technologies that allow for the creation of artificially generated images of sexualized children.

BOX 13.4 SEXTING

Cell phones and other hand-held mobile devices have created a new form of sexual deviance: sexting. *Sexting* involves sending, receiving, and/or forwarding sexually explicit messages, clips, or images via an internet-enabled device. How prevalent is sexting in the United States? Results from a 2008 survey of 1,280 teens (ages 13 to 19) and young adults (ages 20 to 26) indicated that 20 percent of all teens and 33 percent of all young adults have "sexted" nude or semi-nude images of themselves to others. Moreover, 39 percent of all teens and 59 percent of all young adults have sent sexually suggestive messages (Sex and Tech 2008). Thus, sexting is both a new and popular activity.

Sexting in general is legal in the United States if all parties involved are over the age of 18, and the process takes place with their knowledge and consent. However, when sexting involves minors, felony charges can follow. For example, under U.S. Federal Law, it is a crime to knowingly produce, distribute, receive, or possess with intent to distribute, visual media that depicts a minor engaging in sexually explicit conduct and is obscene (Federal Law 18 U.S.C.§2252).

How often are Americans arrested for sexting? According to a nationally representative sample of sexting arrest cases from 2008-9, illegal sexting is an all-too common activity and varies as follows (Wolak *et al.* 2012a):

* 62 percent of sexting arrests involved an adult as a recipient of a youth's sexual image.
* 36 percent of sexting arrests involved a youth distributing an image with the intent to harm (e.g., extort, sexual abuse, maliciousness) or reckless misuse (e.g., creating or distributing images without the knowledge or against the will of the minor who was pictured).
* 18 percent of sexting arrests involved adolescents sending images of themselves to flirt, find romantic partners, experiment with sex, and get attention from peers.

The penalties for sexting also differed. While 45 percent of the adults who received a sexual image of a child were required to register as a sex offender as a result of their illegal participation in sexting, only 5 percent of youth who distributed an image with the intent to do harm or reckless misuse were similarly punished. And of the teens that were sexting to "flirt," none were required to join the sex offender registry (Wolak *et al.* 2012a). Thus, it appears that while sending, receiving, and/or forwarding sexually explicit images of minors is illegal for everyone, adults who participate in this activity are more harshly punished and deviantized.

Even though sexting is a rather common occurrence, it is widely considered to be sexually deviant if minors are involved. But cellphones and other internet-enabled devices have made sexting a very easy and very appealing practice—some teens even find sexting to be a fun and titillating practice. As a result, the potential for committing an act of sexual deviance is high—especially for teens.

Characteristics of CSAM users

In 2009, 3,791 arrests were made in the United States for CSAM possession. Based on these arrests, CSAM offenders are primarily white (91 percent), older than 25 (74 percent), and typically employed (73 percent), while two-thirds are single (67 percent), a third are married/and or living with a partner (33 percent), and a quarter are living with a minor child (25 percent) (Wolak *et al.* 2012b). In addition, CSAM users often have difficulties such as:

- Interpersonal problems (e.g., marital discord, loneliness, insecure attachment).
- Health-related problems (e.g., long-term illness or injuries, mental health problems, substance abuse problems).
- Sexual frustrations or dissatisfactions (e.g., lack of desired sexual experiences, not able to live out preferred fantasies, not feeling close to their partner during sex).
- Work-related problems (e.g., unemployment, overworked, financial difficulties).
- Low self-esteem and poor self-image.
- Physical and/or sexual abuse in childhood.
- Neglect, family instability, and problematic parenting during childhood.

But as we have learned, there are various overlapping characteristics associated with non-familial pedophilia and incest and this is also the case for CSAM users. The reason for this overlap is that those who are "hands on" in their sexual abuse of children are also likely to view illicit sexual images of children on the internet. In particular, three distinctive groups of pedophiles have been identified: (i) internet-only, (ii) contact-only, and (iii) mixed. Although all three groups share similar developmental histories, contact-only pedophiles have the highest rates of childhood physical and sexual abuse while internet-only pedophiles have the lowest rates. Behavioral and emotional problems, such as truancy, running away, criminal activities, substance abuse, and aggression towards others are comparable across all three groups. In addition, childhood neglect and parent absenteeism are also common experiences but mixed pedophiles are most likely to have spent time in institutions such as foster care, group homes, and juvenile detention centers (see Figure 13.1) (Sheldon and Howitt 2007).

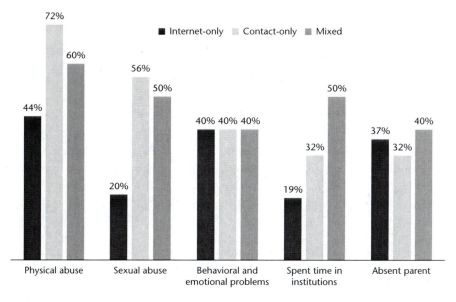

FIGURE 13.1   Childhood experiences of child sex offenders by type (internet–only, contact–only, or mixed)

Data adapted from Sheldon and Howitt (2007).

CSAM user types

Knowing the different ways in which CSAM offenses are committed is vitally important in understanding the scope of the problem of sexual exploitation of children. Overall, nine types of CSAM users have been identified by extant research (Krone 2004):

- *Browser*: these individuals come across CSAM unintentionally, usually through spam, but then decide to watch/save it.
- *Private fantasy*: these individuals create their own text or digital images for private use.
- *Trawler*: these individuals actively seek free CSAM using internet search engines.
- *Non-secure collector*: these individuals collect (purchase, download) and/or exchange CSAM from sources on the internet or in chat rooms that do not impose security barriers.
- *Secure-collector*: these individuals use security barriers to collect/exchange CSAM.
- *Groomer*: these individuals initiate contact with a child on the internet with the intention of establishing a sexual relationship involving cybersex and/or physical sex.
- *Physical abuser*: these individuals physically sexually abuse children they meet online.

- *Producer:* these individuals record/photograph the physical sexual abuse of children they meet online, creating CSAM to collect/exchange.
- *Distributors:* these individuals distribute CSAM and may or may not have a sexual interest in children themselves.

Prosecuting CSAM users

Since the arrival of the internet, identifying and prosecuting CSAM users has been a difficult task for law enforcement and other officials. The internet is a free-flowing global system with no fixed physical location or central point of control; thus, there is no way of imposing order on content, including the exchange and retrieval of information (O'Donnell and Milner 2007). The sheer size of the internet, the rate of technological innovation and rapid change, the lack of any boundaries to its expansion, as well as its disregard for national borders makes it a daunting environment for law enforcement. Moreover, definitions of CSAM vary internationally—different jurisdictions have different laws concerning CSAM (Sheldon and Howitt 2007). As a result, these characteristics allow for a much greater volume of undetected criminal activity than ever before and law enforcement officials face the overwhelming task of trying to identify both CSAM users and victims (O'Donnell and Milner 2007).

Although the internet provides a super-highway for the exchange and distribution of CSAM, law enforcement has responded in a variety of ways. Specialized CSAM units have been created in federal agencies, such as the FBI, U.S. Postal Inspection Services, and U.S. Bureau of Immigration and Customs Enforcement. The U.S. Department of Justice has also funded task forces and specialized training programs to help investigate CSAM. Moreover, the National Center for Missing & Exploited Children has set up the CyberTipline to encourage reporting and investigation of CSAM and other online threats to children (Wolak *et al.* 2003). International organizations, such as the International Association of Internet Hotlines (INHOPE), Virtual Global Task Force (VGT), and the Internet Watch Foundation also provide hotlines for reporting CSAM. Overall, while the task of eliminating CSAM is virtually insurmountable, many people have dedicated their lives to this endeavor.

Survivors of child sexual abuse

Children who experience sexual abuse may encounter a range of short- and long-term effects including nightmares, flashbacks, depression, loneliness, guilt, shame, blame, anger, low self-esteem, loss of control, an inability to concentrate, a continual sense of fear or panic, posttraumatic stress disorder (PTSD), as well as a lack of trust in others and withdrawal from normal or daily activities (Durkin and Hundersmarck 2008; Holmes and Holmes 2009; Rufo 2012). Childhood sexual abuse can also be associated with a range of negative outcomes in adulthood including mental health problems (e.g., depression, PTSD, suicide attempts), alcohol/drug abuse, difficulties with interpersonal relationships, physical health problems (e.g., obesity, health disease, cancer), and criminal involvement including perpetrating familial abuse (Roberts *et al.* 2004; Felitti *et al.* 1998; Durkin and Hundersmarck 2008; Widom *et al.* 2008).

Gender differences in the effects of child sexual abuse

Boys and girls often cope differently with their sexual abuse. Boys are likely to externalize their feelings in relation to their victimization through acting out aggressively and/or violently toward others. Boys are also likely to experience anger, rage, powerlessness, and feelings of revenge as a result of their victimization. They fear being identified as "unmanly" or ashamed because they were unable to protect themselves and if molested by a man, they sometimes experience concerns about their sexual identity. If sexually abused by a woman, boys may be reluctant to report because of the erroneous belief that a woman cannot rape a man (recall our discussion of rape myths in chapter 12). Compared to boys, girls are more likely to internalize their responses to victimization through depression, alcohol/drug abuse, and self-injury. Girls are also likely to experience sadness, self-blame, guilt, and shame. While boys are likely to minimize their abuse, girls are more often blamed for their abuse yet girls are much more likely than boys to be believed (Sheldon and Howitt 2007; Holmes and Holmes 2009; Rufo 2012).

Summarizing sex crimes against children

In this chapter we have learned that sex crimes against children can take on many forms and that child sex offenders themselves vary in their motivations and criminal patterns. Furthermore, we have learned that the internet has created tremendous opportunities for CSAM, which continues to be an obstacle faced by law enforcement. The deviance of sex crimes against children is undeniable and yet the complexities involving the contemporary landscape of technology and sex crime (e.g., sexting, CSAM) has further complicated the ways these crimes are recognized and deviantized. Even so, one group retains the ultimate embodiment of deviant criminal—sex offenders. In the next chapter, we will examine how this group is labeled, stigmatized, and treated in both the criminal justice system and wider society.

References

Araji, Sharon and David Finkelhor. 1985. "Explanations of Pedophilia: Review of Empirical Research." *Journal of the American Academy of Psychiatry Law* 13(1):17–37.

Briere, John and Marsha Runtz. 1989. "University Males' Sexual Interests in Children: Predicting Potential Indices of 'Pedophilia' in a Nonforensic Sample." *Child Abuse & Neglect* 13: 65–75.

Briggs, Peter, Walter T. Simon, and Stacy Simonsen. 2011. "An Exploratory Study of Internet-Initiated Sexual Offenses and the Chat Room Sex Offender: Has the Internet

Enabled a New Typology of Sex Offender?" *Sexual Abuse: A Journal of Research and Treatment* 23(1):72–91.

Chow, Eva and Alberto L. Choy. 2002. "Clinical Characteristics and Treatment Response to SSRI in a Female Pedophile." *Archives of Sexual Behavior* 31(2):211–15.

Colson, Marie-Helene, Laurent Boyer, Karine Baumstarck, and Anderson D. Loundou. 2013. "Female Sex Offenders: A Challenge to Certain Paradigmes. Meta-Analyses." *Sexologies* 22(4):109–17.

Craven, Samantha, Sarah Brown, and Elizabeth Gilchrist. 2006. "Sexual Grooming of Children: Review of Literature and Theoretical Considerations." *Journal of Sexual Aggression* 12(3):287–99.

Cyr, Mireille, John Wright, Perre McDuff, and Alain Perron. 2002. "Intrafamilial Sexual Abuse: Brother-Sister Incest Does Not Differ From Father-Daughter and Stepfather-Stepdaughter Incest." *Child Abuse & Neglect* 26(9):957–73.

DeYoung, Mary. 2015. "The World According to NAMBLA: Accounting for Deviance." *Journal of Sociology & Social Welfare* 16(1):111–26.

Durkin, Keith F. and Steven Hundersmarck. 2008. "Pedophiles and Child Molesters." Pp. 144–50 in *Extreme Deviance*, edited by Erich Goode and Vail D. Angus. Thousand Oaks, CA: Pine Forge Press.

Felitti, Vincent J., Robert F. Anda, Dale Nordenberg, David F. Williamson, Alison M. Spitz, Valerie Edwards, Mary P. Koss, and James S. Marks. 1998. "Relationship of Childhood Abuse and Household Dysfunction to Many of the Leading Causes of Death in Adults: the Adverse Childhood Experience (ACE) Study." *American Journal of Preventative Medicine* 14(4):245–58.

Finkelhor, David. 1984. *Child Sexual Abuse: New Theory and Research*. New York, NY: Free Press.

Finkelhor, David and Sharon Araji. 1986. "Explanations of Pedophilia: A Four Factor Model" *The Journal of Sex Research* 22(2):145–61.

Finkelhor, David and Anne Shattuck. 2012. *Characteristics of Crimes Against Juveniles*. Durham, NH: Crimes Against Children Research Center.

Glueck, Bernard. 1955. *Final Report: Research Project for the Study and Treatment of Persons Convicted of Crimes Involving Sexual Aberrations, June 1952 to June 1955*. New York, NY: New York State Department of Mental Hygiene.

Goodman, John. 1997. "Details Convey Horror of Megan's Death." Latimes.com, May 6. Retrieved from: http://articles.latimes.com/1997-05-06/news/mn-55980_1_megankanka.

Holmes, Stephen T. and Ronald M. Holmes. 2009. *Sex Crimes: Patterns and Behavior*, Third Edition. Thousand Oaks, CA: Sage.

Internet Watch Foundation. 2014. "Operational Trends 2014: Overview." Retrieved from: https://www.iwf.org.uk/resources/trends

Krone, Tony. 2004. "A Typology of Online Child Pornography Offending." *Trends & Issues in Crime and Criminal Justice* 279:267–80.

McLeod, David A. 2015. "Female Offenders in Child Sexual Abuse Cases: A National Picture." *Journal of Child Sexual Abuse* 24(1):97–114.

O'Donnell, Ian and Claire Milner. 2007. *Child Pornography: Crime, Computers, and Society*. Portland, OR: Willan Publishing.

Roberts, Ron, Tom O'Conner, Judy Dunn, and Jean Golding. 2004. "The Effects of Child Sexual Abuse in Later Family Life; Mental Health, Parenting and Adjustment of Offspring." *Child Abuse & Neglect* 28(5):525–45.

Rufo, Ronald A. 2012. *Sexual Predators Amongst Us*. Boca Raton, FL: CRC Press.

Seto, Michael C. 2008. *Pedophilia and Sexual Offending Against Children: Theory Assessment and Intervention*. Washington, D.C: American Psychological Association.

Sex and Tech. 2008. "Sex and Tech: Results from a Survey of Teens and Young Adults." Washington, DC: The National Campaign to Prevent Teen and Unplanned Pregnancy.

Sheldon, Kerry and Dennis Howitt. 2007. *Sex Offenders and the Internet.* West Sussex: John Wiley & Sons.

Strickland, Susan M. 2008. "Female Sex Offenders: Exploring Issues of Personality, Trauma, and Cognitive Distortions." *Journal of Interpersonal Violence* 23(4):474–89.

Sykes, Gresham M. and David Mazta. 1957. "Techniques of Neutralization: A Theory of Delinquency." *American Sociological Review* 22(6):664–70.

Terry, Karen J. and Jennifer A. Tallon. 2004. "Child Sexual Abuse: A Review of the Literature." The Nature and Scope of the Problem of Sexual Abuse of Minors by Priests and Deacons, 1950–2002. Washington, D.C.: United States Conference of Catholic Bishops.

Tibbals, Chauntelle. 2015. *Exposure: A Sociologist Explores Sex, Society, and Adult Entertainment.* Austin, TX: Greenleaf Book Group Press.

van Dam, Carla. 2001. *Identifying Child Molesters: Preventing Child Sexual Abuse by Recognizing the Patterns of the Offenders.* Binghamton, NY: Haworth Press.

vandiver, Donna M. and Glen Kercher. 2004. "Offender and Victim Characteristics of Registered Female Sexual Offenders in Texas: A Proposed Typology of Female Sexual Offenders." *Sexual Abuse: A Journal of Research and Treatment* 16(2):121–37.

Widom, Cathy Spatz, Sally J. Czaja, and Mary Ann Dutton. 2008. "Childhood Victimization and Lifetime Revictimization." *Child Abuse & Neglect* 32(8):785–96.

Williams, Linda Meyer and David Finkelhor. 1990. "The Characteristics of Incestuous Fathers: A Review of Recent Studies." Pp. 231–55 in *Handbook of Sexual Assault: Issues, Theories, and Treatment of the Offender,* edited by William Lamont Marshall, D. R. Laws, and Howard E. Barbaree. New York, NY: Plenum Press.

Wolak, Janis, Kimberly J. Mitchell, and David Finkelhor. 2003. *Internet Sex Crimes Against Minors: The Response of Law Enforcement.* National Center for Missing and Exploited Children.

Wolak, Janis, David Finkelhor, and Kimberly J. Mitchell. 2012a. "How Often Are Teens Arrested for Sexting: Data From a National Sample of Police Cases." *Pediatrics* 129(1):4–12.

Wolak, Janis, David Finkelhor, and Kimberly J. Mitchell. 2012b. *Trends in Arrests for Child Pornography Possession: The Third National Juvenile Online Victimization Study (NJOV-3).* Durham, NH: Crimes Against Children Research Center.

U.S. Code, Title 18, Part 1, Chapter 110, section 2252 (2000).

U.S. Code, Title 18, Part 1, Chapter 110, section 2252A (2000).

U.S. Code, Title 18, Part 1, Chapter 110, section 2256 (2000).

United Nations Convention of the Rights of Children, Article 2C (2007).

Zilney, Laura J. and Zilney Lisa Anne. 2009. *Perverts and Predators: The Making of Sexual Offending Laws.* Lanham, MD: Rowman & Littlefield.

14

SEX OFFENDERS AND SOCIETY

In July 1947, J. Edgar Hoover (1895–1972), the first Director of the Federal Bureau of Investigation of the United States, published an article in *American Magazine* titled "How safe is your daughter?" In it, he warned American citizens of the acute dangers at hand:

> The most rapidly increasing type of crime is that perpetrated by degenerate sex offenders ... Should wild beasts break out of circus cages, a whole city would be mobilized instantly. But depraved human beings, more savage than beasts, are permitted to rove America almost at will.
>
> *(Hoover 1947:32)*

Hoover's warning sent a wave of panic through parents everywhere: child molesters were viewed as the ultimate embodiment of pure evil and drastic measures should be taken to lock them up. The idea of "stranger danger" was also promoted at this time (Jenkins 1998:56). Parents were encouraged to protect their children from unknown unsavory characters and to keep children off the streets, but unfortunately, this guidance was often misplaced because, as discussed in chapter 13, the majority of sex crimes against children are committed by someone known to the child, not a stranger. All too quickly a moral panic broke out and citizens became squarely focused on child sexual predators as the scapegoat for all that was wrong with America and this continues to shape current discourse about sex crimes today (recall the discussion of moral panics in chapter 2).

Since then, America has continued to be tough on all those who commit sex crimes, whether or not they committed an offense against a child. In fact, sex offenders are considered to be one of the most abhorred types of criminals both in and out of prison (Sapp and Vaughn 1990). This chapter examines how this deviant label and status affects both societal perspectives about sex offenders and how this highly stigmatized identity relates to particularly harsh treatment by the criminal justice system.

The sex offender label and general societal attitudes

The label "sex offender" can be applied to anyone who has been convicted of a crime that is sexual in nature. This includes child molesters, rapists, and those convicted of other crimes such as public urination, bestiality, and indecent exposure. Thus, the term "sex offender" is quite broad and encompasses a diverse group of individuals. In general, however, most people see sex offenders as a monolithic group of criminals who are insatiable sexual predators out to harm the vulnerable (e.g., children, women, and elderly people). In addition, the majority view sex offenders as deserving of severe punishment for their crimes (i.e., lengthy prison time, mandatory castration, and even capital punishment) and when/if released, in need of an extraordinary amount of supervision (Levenson *et al.* 2007). Despite the facts that in comparison to other types of offenders (e.g., those who commit drug offenses and theft), sex offenders have lower rates of re-arrest for sex offenses and their recidivism rates can be significantly reduced through participation in treatment programs (Mann *et al.* 2010; Kim *et al.* 2016), the general attitude toward sex offenders is that they are not amenable to change (Griffin and West 2006). Indeed, sex offenders are viewed as "the lowest of the low" (Griffin and West 2006:143) and they are frequently viewed as undeserving of basic human rights both in and out of the criminal justice system.

Sex offenders in prison

Although not all sex offenders receive prison sentences, because of the general societal interest in highly punitive punishment for sex criminals, many do serve time in prisons. While incarcerated, these "outcasts among outcasts" [i.e., those inmates who are stigmatized within prisons (Åkerström 1986:1)] face the greatest animosity among all prisoners and are generally seen as worthless degenerates by both prison staff and other inmates. Indeed, within the prison status hierarchy of inmates, sex offenders (rapists, murderer-rapists, incest offenders, and child molesters) possess the lowest social status, ranking significantly lower than drug offenders, robbers, burglars, murderers, and assaultive criminals in terms of social acceptance within penal institutions. Furthermore, those who commit sex offenses against children are viewed especially harshly. Due to their negative social stigma within prison, child sex offenders are at high risk for harassment and physical assault by other inmates and sometimes prison staff. As a result, child sex offenders are often placed into administrative segregation/protective custody arrangements in which they are sequestered from other inmates in separate cell blocks or single cell units and given alternative eating and recreational schedules. In these ways, the low status of the incarcerated sex offender can lead to victimization and isolation (Åkerström 1986; Sapp and Vaughn 1990). For the outsider looking in, this may seem like a perfectly acceptable punishment; however, such differential treatment can lead to especially problematic consequences that are both directly and indirectly related to public safety.

Continued legal punishments of sex offenders post-prison release

Although sex offenders are more likely to spend time in prison when compared to other violent offenders, the vast majority are released back into the community (Kong et al. 2003). While all ex-convicts suffer difficulties when reintegrating back into society, sex offenders can arguably face more complex barriers to reintegration. Even after serving time in prison as punishment for their crimes, sex offenders continue to be regulated and monitored by the criminal justice system. In particular, many countries have laws requiring sex offenders to keep their home addresses in national databases to monitor their whereabouts. Argentina, Australia, Bermuda, Canada, France, Germany, Ireland, Jamaica, Kenya, South Africa, South Korea, Taiwan, Trinidad and Tobago, the United Kingdom, and the United States all have sex offender registries, however, only a few countries (the United States and South Korea) have national sex offender registries that are publicly accessible (in other countries, sex offender registries are only accessible by law enforcement officials). In the United States and South Korea, sex offender registries are available through public websites that include information such as a photo, list of convictions, and a home address. These websites are also searchable by name, address, zip code, and/or city/town/county. For example, established in 2000, the South Korean sex offender registry includes (SMART 2014):

- Name (both in Korean and Chinese characters)
- Resident registration number
- Home address
- Occupation, job position, and work address
- Photograph, physical description, and age
- Car registration number
- Case number, name of the crime, and summary of case facts
- Date of conviction and sentence imposed

In the U.S., sex offender registration began to take shape in the 1990s with the 1994 Jacob Wetterling[1] Crimes Against Children and Sexually Violent Offender Registration Act that required states to keep registries of sex offenders' information on file for law enforcement purposes. In 1996, Megan's[2] Law made this sex offender information public under certain circumstances. In 2006, Dru's[3] Law helped to create the National Sex Offender Public Website (NSOPW) to provide the public with access to sex offender data nationwide. In addition, Title 1 of the Adam Walsh[4] Child Protection and Safety Act of 2006 outlined the Sex Offender Registration and Notification Act (SORNA) that included a three-tiered classification system based on the type and number of sex offense convictions an individual has:

- *Tier 3 offenders* are those who have committed crimes such as aggravated sexual assault, aggravated sexual abuse, sexual contact with children below the age of 13, non-parental kidnapping of minors, and attempts or conspiracies to commit such offenses. Offenders classified as Tier 3 are presumably at the highest risk for recidivism and must register as a sex offender for life and notify law enforcement of their whereabouts four times per year.
- *Tier 2 offenders* are those who have committed offenses such as sex trafficking, coercion and enticement, transportation with intent to engage in criminal sexual activity, using a minor in a sexual performance, soliciting a minor for prostitution, or producing or distributing CSAM materials (i.e., illicit pornographic material). Offenders classified as Tier 2 are at moderate risk for recidivism and must register as a sex offender for 25 years and notify law enforcement of their whereabouts twice yearly.
- *Tier 1 offenders* are those who have committed offenses that do not fit into the other tiers, these may include misdemeanor offenses such as voyeurism, indecent exposure, public urination, and possession of CSAM materials. Offenders classified as Tier 1 are considered to be low risk and must register as a sex offender for 15 years and notify law enforcement of their whereabouts once per year (Zgoba *et al.* 2015).

Thus, beyond the "sex offender" label, the three-tiered American system outlines the perceived severity of the crime and the SORNA requirements for those convicted of sex crimes. Thus, American sex offenders are labeled with both the generalized status of "sex offender" and a tiered status (1, 2, or 3) which further contributes to the stigma that they experience.

In addition to being listed in a national sex offender registry, sex offenders can also face additional legal consequences for their crimes *after* their release from prison that include:

- GPS tracking devices worn by offenders (typically in the form of an "ankle bracelet") to monitor their whereabouts.
- Driver's licenses with "SEX OFFENDER" imprinted on them.
- Risk of felony prosecution for failure to fully comply with state or national sex offender registration requirements.
- Submission of blood or saliva for purposes of maintaining a DNA database.
- Forced surgical or chemical castration.
- International travel restrictions and firearm ownership restrictions.
- Community notification of residency in the form of internet postings, newspaper ads, police visits, yard signs, bumper stickers, paper flyer postings/mailings, automated telephone calls, and/or community notification meetings.

Thus, the criminal justice system continues to formally impose punishments to sex offenders after completing their prison sentences. These continued penalties post-prison release serve not only to castigate sex offenders, but they also have negative consequences in larger society.

The "sex offender" label and its social consequences

Being labeled a "sex offender" can have many negative consequences including:

- *Employment restrictions.* Those with sex offender convictions are limited in their job opportunities. Even places that hire ex-convicts often refuse to hire sex offenders. For many, low-paid unskilled labor is the only option for legitimate means of employment, and thus, illegitimate means can become compulsory for survival.
- *Housing restrictions.* Residency restrictions for convicted sex offenders are common in most jurisdictions. Many outline prohibitions for living within 2,000 feet of a school or park. This means that in many cities, sex offenders are forced into homelessness.
- *Victimization.* In locations where sex offenders must register and/or notify their community of their residency, they run the risk of victimization from "concerned" community members.
- *Loss of relationships.* Many sex offenders indicate that their conviction results in strained relationships with family and friends. Social isolation among sex offenders is common.

Overall, the most common problems reported by sex offenders are difficulties in securing housing and employment as well as harassment and social isolation. These problems are not surprising, however, given that the "sex offender" label follows an individual through his/her personal documents that are often needed to process job and housing applications. Harassment is also not an unexpected consequence of sex offenders' lives, especially in the case of community notification practices in place in the United States that alert community members (either via websites, yard signs, and other means) as to the home addresses of sex offenders. Thus, when community members learn that a sex offender lives in their neighborhood, they can become fearful or enraged, and as a result, they may harass, victimize, or discriminate against them. Some may see these types of volatile interpersonal exchanges as legitimate, utilizing a "he got what was coming to him" justification. But what many people do not recognize is that this type of treatment actually exacerbates the problem. Sex offenders who are continually victimized by both the criminal justice system and community members can become increasingly isolated and frustrated, which can lead to a decreased likelihood of successful reintegration back into society and may also increase the chances of recidivism (Tewksbury 2005; Zilney and Zilney 2009).

In particular, many of the social consequences related to the "sex offender" label can increase the likelihood of reoffending because they both stigmatize and alienate sex offenders (Tewksbury 2005). For example, when sex offenders cannot find legitimate avenues for employment, they may seek out illegitimate means to survive and this, in turn, may result in further collaboration with other convicted criminals. When sex offenders cannot find housing (which is increasingly difficult due to the housing restrictions for sex offenders), they may be forced into homelessness and may live amongst other convicted felons who cannot find housing. Even if they have a job and a place to live, sex offenders may withdraw from social situations out of shame and embarrassment and/or fear of being verbally or physically harassed for their sex offender status. As a result, they may either actively remove themselves or may be forced out of social support networks, and thus, they may become totally isolated or may build relationships with other sex offenders who have been similarly publicly shunned. Being homeless, unemployed, and socially isolated can cause an immense amount of stress on any person, but for sex offenders who are already a highly stigmatized group, these circumstances can not only lead to distress, but may also lead to reoffending. Coupled with the likelihood that sex offenders are both angry with society and the criminal justice system for their poor treatment and the likelihood that they are connecting with other sex offenders (via blocked opportunities for employment, housing, and pro-social networking), sex offenders are at an especially high risk for recidivism.

Sex offender treatment and recidivism

Although sex offenders face significant social barriers when reintegrating back into society, they are also likely to benefit from treatment programs. In fact, compared to other types of criminals, sex offenders are less likely to reoffend and studies show that recidivism can be dramatically reduced following treatment (Mann *et al.* 2010; Kim *et al.* 2016). Below, types of treatment and recidivism are reviewed.

Types of treatment

Cognitive behavioral therapy

The most common practices used in sex offender treatment programs in the United States and Canada involve cognitive behavioral therapy. Cognitive behavioral therapy is designed to address thoughts and beliefs (the cognitive focus) as well as behaviors and actions (the behavioral focus). The cognitive focus encourages offenders to understand and confront their own attitudes that have contributed to their dysfunctional thinking. The behavioral focus allows offenders to examine how their own actions and surroundings have contributed to their dysfunctional behavior. Collectively, through cognitive behavioral therapy, offenders consider how their own perspectives (attitudes, beliefs, thinking patterns) have contributed to their own rationalizations for their dysfunctional behaviors. This approach helps sex offenders to develop competencies to control their dysfunctional sexual impulses, evaluate internal and external risks (and triggers) that may lead to problematic situations, and to learn new skills to maintain appropriate behaviors. Overall, treatment programs focused on cognitive behavioral therapy "include various strategies that focus on correcting thoughts, feelings, and behaviors that promote inappropriate behaviors and replacing them with self-directed behavioral skills that maintain prosocial beliefs and behaviors" (Kim *et al.* 2016:106).

Medical treatment

Although used less frequently than therapeutic methods, sometimes psychotherapy treatment can be replaced or augmented by medical interventions that are designed to lower testosterone levels in the hope of reducing the sex drive (including aggressive and impulsive sexual urges) and/or inhibiting the ability to become sexually aroused. The two most common methods include:

- *Androgen deprivation treatment* that involves the use of anti-androgen drugs to reduce and control androgen hormones (specifically testosterone). Because most male recipients undergoing androgen deprivation have difficulties achieving erections, this is also sometimes referred to as *chemical castration*.
- *Surgical castration* is the irreversible removal of the testes that results in a severe reduction in testosterone levels and a reduced likelihood of achieving erections.

Although somewhat controversial, some U.S. states (about 20 percent) and a few other countries (e.g., Czech Republic, Poland) have laws that allow the use of chemical or surgical castration of sex offenders either in lieu of prison time or for a reduction in prison time. Some even have laws that require castration (either chemical or surgical) as a condition of release back into the community (e.g., Canada) or as mandatory continued punishment for repeat sex offenders (in the U.S., California and Florida) (Rice and Harris 2011). Although sometimes sex offenders voluntarily choose to undergo castration to help curb their deviant sexual desires and/or spend less time incarcerated, critics, including the American Civil Liberties Union (ACLU), see mandatory castration as a violation of the Eighth Amendment prohibition of cruel and unusual punishment (Gimino 1997). Furthermore, because the effects of both methods of castration can be reversed with the use of injectable testosterone, their long-term effectiveness is often called into question. Similarly, male sex offenders need not assault others with their erect penises (consider oral- or object-assault), thus "without changing the sexual attitudes and behaviors that resulted in the offense in the first place, sexual offending is still possible for a castrated male" (Zilney and Zilney 2009:163).

Treatment and recidivism

According to a large-scale analysis with close to 35,000 sex offenders, sex offender treatment results in a 22 percent overall reduction in recidivism. That is to say that sex offenders who partake in treatment programs are significantly less likely to reoffend when compared to sex offenders who do not. However, the effects vary. Specifically, sex offender treatment programs are more effective for adolescents when compared to adults. In addition, surgical castration reduces recidivism at nearly double the rate of chemical castration methods while psychological treatments, including cognitive behavioral therapy, are less effective than both chemical and surgical medical interventions. The use of multiple treatment methods, for example androgen deprivation in conjunction with cognitive behavioral therapy, is perhaps the most effective intervention plan to prevent future sex crime (Kim *et al.* 2016). Overall, sex offender treatment reduces the likelihood of reoffending but such interventions do not eliminate recidivism altogether—no treatment methods are 100 percent effective.

Why are we so punitive?

We have now learned that many societies have multiple layers of punishment for sex offenders both within prisons and post-prison release via registration, community notification, and other requirements. In general, sex offenders are viewed more negatively and stigmatized at higher rates when compared to other types of criminals even though they are less likely to recidivate and more likely to respond positively to treatment programs (Tewksbury 2005; Mann *et al.* 2010; Kim *et al.* 2016). Why?

Most people are scared of sex offenders. They think that they are out to harm everyone—especially the vulnerable (e.g., children, women, and elderly populations). In addition, public perceptions about sex offenders are often misguided by media misrepresentations and cultural misconceptions (see Table 14.1). This is perhaps why most people support practices such as community notification, restricting where sex offenders live, chemical castration, and electronic monitoring of sex offenders. Interestingly, research also indicates that even if scientific evidence showed that these strategies were ineffective at reducing recidivism, the vast majority would still support them (Levenson *et al.* 2007).

In particular, however, the fears, anxieties, and overall punitively focused responses to sex offenders are largely built on moral panics associated with child sexual predators (Jenkins 1998). Indeed, the goals of sex offender registration and notification systems are often decidedly focused on helping people protect their children from sex crimes (consider the U.S. laws that restrict sex offender housing near schools and parks *because* they are areas commonly inhabited by children). Similarly, many existing U.S. sex offender laws were both inspired by and named after children who were victimized (e.g., Jacob Wetterling Act,[1] Megan's Law,[2] Adam Walsh Act,[4] AMBER Alert,[5] Jessica Lunsford Act[6]). Thus, a "protect the children" theme underlies the majority of sex offender punishment practices—not unlike Hoover's (1947) message laced with fear tactics noted at the start of this chapter. And while it is certain that we should, in fact, "protect the children," this mentality has resulted in extremely harsh sex offender legislation that has shaped a culture of fear and misinformation about sex crimes in general.

TABLE 14.1 Common myths and realities about sex offenders

Myth	Reality
Sex offenders have the highest recidivism rates of all criminals.	Compared to other types of criminals, sex offenders have amongst the lowest recidivism rates.
Sex offenders do not respond to treatment.	Sex offender treatment results in a significant reduction in recidivism.
The myth of stranger danger: children are at great risk from predators who lurk in schoolyards and playgrounds.	Child victims of sex crimes are most likely victimized by somebody they know.

Adapted from Levenson *et al.* (2007).

"Protect the children" – but at what costs?

Sex offenders are one of the most detested types of criminals (Sapp and Vaughn 1990). Part of the reason why most cultures perceive sex offenders as reprehensible, heinous, and violent is related to an overarching desire to "protect the children" from all threats—and sex offenders are universally recognized as dangerous criminals. Deemed as "sexual psychopaths" in the 1930s, sex offenders (and those thought to be at risk for sexual compulsivity) were involuntarily committed to psychiatric facilities for an indefinite amount of time based on the belief that sex offenders are driven by uncontrollable impulses (Zilney and Zilney 2009:71). Today, we see that sex offenders continue to be outcast as social deviants and we continue to view them as the ultimate embodiment of evil. Thus, we overwhelmingly support the harsh punishments doled out to them (Levenson *et al.* 2007). But there are social costs (and very real risks) associated with these punitive actions including:

- *Increasing the likelihood of recidivism among sex offenders.* Because sex offenders are often limited in their access to employment, housing, and pro-social relationships, they face many debilitating barriers to reintegration and many lack the support to successfully reform themselves into law-abiding citizens. Reoffending is likely when negotiating such challenges.
- *Cultivating a false sense of security in society.* Because we are aware of the many legal protections forced upon sex offenders in society, we may have the false impression that we are "safe." For example, we may think our children are "safe" because sex offenders are precluded from living nearby schools and parks in many jurisdictions. But these types of housing laws typically do not prevent sex offenders from living next door to families with children. Even if we are able to learn that we live in a neighborhood that is "pedophile free" (via national sex offender registry website maps or even neighborhood signs as seen in Image 14.1), this masks the realities that child sex offenders can have multiple victims before they are caught. Thus, in relying on the harsh penalties

enforced on sex offenders by the criminal justice system, citizens may be cultivating a false sense of security.

- *Perpetuating the false "stranger danger" myth in society.* Because many sex offender laws and punishments are designed to "protect the children" from strangers lurking in parks or observing school children, the public is misinformed about the actualities of sex crimes against children. In reality, children are most likely to be sexually assaulted by someone they know including relatives, neighbors, and babysitters (people who are highly unlikely to be restricted in their movement by laws designed to prevent sex offenders from access to children). As a result, both the laws and societal norms that continue to indicate that "strangers" are the most "dangerous," perpetuate false myths about sex crimes against children that obstruct our abilities to protect the children from the *real* threats—those who are closest to our kids.

Overall, the repugnancy of sex offenders is indisputable. Their status as both an "ex-convict" and a "sex offender" follows them through many negative social experiences and secures their deviant place in society. Because most are released from prison, however, the general public places many restrictions on sex offenders including, but not limited to, registration, community notification, and continued monitoring practices post-prison release. But all this comes with social costs and

IMAGE 14.1   "Pedophile Free Zones"

Sign proclaiming "Pedophile Free Zones" in the city of Wapello, Iowa (USA). By Bill Whittaker, Wikimedia Commons, CC BY-SA 3.0 (2009).

risks, making the complexities of sex offenders in society an all too commonly dismissed social problem.

Notes

1   In 1989, Jacob Wetterling was kidnapped by an unknown assailant (Daniel James Heinrich became a person of interest in this case in November 2015) from his hometown of St. Joseph, Minnesota, at the age of 11. His whereabouts are unknown. In 1994, the Jacob Wetterling Act was passed in his honor.
2   In 1994, Megan Kanka was raped and murdered at the age of 7 by her neighbor, Jesse Timmendequas, who was a twice-convicted sex offender. Timmendequas was originally sentenced to death but his sentence was commuted to life in prison without the possibility of parole when the New Jersey Legislature abolished the state's death penalty in 2007. In 1996, Megan's Law was passed in her honor.
3   In 2003, Dru Sjodin was murdered by a convicted sex offender, Alfonso Rodriguez Jr., at the age of 22 in Minnesota. Rodriguez was sentenced to death in 2006 and remains on death row. In 2006, Dru's Law was passed in her honor.
4   In 1981, Adam Walsh was abducted from a Sears department store and murdered at the age of 6 by Ottis Toole, who died in prison in 1996 (although he was never convicted for this crime, the police closed the Adam Walsh murder case in 2008 believing Toole to be the killer). His father, John Walsh, became an advocate for victims of violent crimes and the host of the television program, *America's Most Wanted* (1988–2012). In 1994, the Code Adam program for helping lost children in department stores was established and named in Adam's memory. In 2006, The Adam Walsh Child Protection and Safety Act was passed in his honor.
5   In 1996, Amber Hagerman was kidnapped and murdered in Texas at the age of 9. Her murderer was never found. The AMBER (America's Missing: Broadcast Emergency Response) Alert system was developed in her honor in 1996 in the U.S. and is utilized in Australia, Europe, Canada, Malaysia, and Mexico. The system provides repeated broadcasts via television, radio, highway notification signs, and text messages about child abductions and perpetrator details in an effort to garner tips from the public.
6   In 2005, Jessica Lunsford was raped and murdered by a registered sex offender, John E. Couey, at the age of 9. Couey was sentenced to death but died in prison in 2009. The Jessica Lunsford Act was passed in Florida in 2005 and requires a 25-year mandatory minimum sentence for offenders convicted of sexual assault upon a child under the age of 12 and lifetime electronic surveillance upon release.

References

Åkerström, Malin. 1986. "Outcasts in Prison: The Cases of Informers and Sex Offenders." *Deviant Behavior* 7(1):1–12.

Gimino, Peter. 1997. "Mandatory Chemical Castration for Perpetrators of Sex Offenses Against Children: Following California's Lead." *Pepperdine Law Review* 25:67–105.

Griffin, Michael and Desirée West. 2006. "The Lowest of the Low? Addressing the Disparity Between Community View, Public Policy, and Treatment Effectiveness for Sex Offenders." *Law & Psychology Review* 30:143–69.

Hoover, J. Edgar. 1947. "How Safe is Your Daughter?" *American Magazine* 144:32–3, 102–4.

Jenkins, Philip. 1998. *Moral Panic: Changing Concepts of the Child Molester in Modern America.* New Haven, CT: Yale University Press.

Kim, Bitna, Peter J. Benekos, and Alida V. Merlo. 2016. "Sex Offender Recidivism Revisited: Review of Recent Meta-analyses on the Effects of Sex Offender Treatment." *Trauma, Violence & Abuse* 17(1):105–17.

Kong, Rebecca, Holly Johnson, Sara Beattie, and Andrea Cardillo. 2003. "Sexual offences in Canada." *Juristat* 23(6):1–26.

Levenson, Jill, Yolanda Brannon, Timothy Fortney, and Juanita Baker. 2007. "Public Perceptions about Sex Offenders and Community Protection Policies." *Analyses of Social Issues and Public Policy* 7(1):1–25.

Mann, Ruth, Karl Hanson, and David Thornton. 2010. "Assessing Risk for Sexual Recidivism: Some Proposals on the Nature of Psychologically Meaningful Risk Factors." *Sexual Abuse: A Journal of Research and Treatment* 22(2):191–217.

Rice, Marnie and Grant Harris. 2011. "Is Androgen Deprivation Therapy Effective in the Treatment of Sex Offenders?" *Psychology, Public Policy, and Law* 17(2):315–32.

Sapp, Allen D. and Michael S. Vaughn. 1990. "The Social Status of Adult and Juvenile Sex Offenders in Prison: An Analysis of the Importation Model." *Journal of Police and Criminal Psychology* 6(2):1–6.

SMART. 2014. *Global Overview of Sex Offender Registration and Notification Systems.* SMART. Retrieved from: http://www.smart.gov/pdfs/GlobalOverview.pdf

Tewksbury, Richard. 2005. "Collateral Consequences of Sex Offender Registration. *Journal of Contemporary Criminal Justice* 21(1):67–81.

Zgoba, Kristen, Michael Miner, Jill Levenson, Raymond Knight, Elizabeth Letourneau, and David Thornton. 2015. "The Adam Walsh Act: An Examination of Sex Offender Risk Classification Systems." *Sexual Abuse: A Journal of Research and Treatment*, doi: 10.1177/1079063215569543.

Zilney, Laura and Lisa Zilney. 2009. *Perverts and Predators: The Making of Sexual Offending Laws.* New York, NY: Rowman and Littlefield.

15
CONCLUDING REMARKS

> It's not easy, but digging into the darkest corners of our sexual nature (that is to say our 'perversions') can expose what keeps us from making real moral progress whenever the issues of equality and sexual diversity arise. With each defensive layer we remove, the rats therein will flee at the daylight falling at their feet, and the opportunity to eradicate such a pestilence of fear and ignorance makes the excavation of our species's lascivious soul worth our getting a little dirty along the way.
>
> *Jessie Bering,* PERV: The Sexual Deviant in All of Us *(2013:6–7)*

We started out with the basics: *what is deviance? what is sex? what is gender? what theoretical and historical insights can help us understand these things?* Then, with the groundwork laid, we delved into the world of sexual deviance learning about public sex, fetishes, and sex work. In discovering the ins and outs of this complicated sexual terrain, both the deviance and the normalities of sexual diversity were revealed. Next, we traveled to the darker side of sexual deviance by investigating sex crimes and criminals. The alarming incidence of rape and sexual assault was embedded in a conversation about gender, power, relationships, and myths. In discussing how cultural scripts and situational contexts contribute to rape, the realities of sexual assault were explicated. Finally, we considered social responses to sex offenders in society and how their presence as "sexual predators amongst us" perpetuates a culture of fear and misunderstanding.

In this process, you may have felt excited, disgusted, inspired, uncomfortable, and sometimes—to put it simply—confused. You may have asked yourself, *how can I make sense of all of these various forms of sexuality? Why are some sexual experiences thought to be normative and some judged to be deviant?* In other words: *what is the point?*

While I fully believe that each and every reader of this text will connect differently with the material—some will hear their own stories told here, some will have their morals, religious values, and sex lives challenged, still others will feel empowered with their newly expanded knowledge of sexual diversity—I offer some final take-home points to ponder:

- Deviance is neither inherently bad, nor good, it is a social construct.
- Sexual deviants, then, are also neither inherently bad, nor good, but rather the socially constructed stigmas attached to certain people, behaviors, and identities categorize them as such.
- Sexual deviants are just like you and me—in fact they *are* you and me.
- Sex crimes—including rape, child molestation, and incest—are most likely committed by persons known to the perpetrator. "Stranger danger" is mostly a myth.
- Sexual deviance is complex, diverse, and universal.

In all, we learned about deviance. But we learned about more than that. We learned to see deviance as "a badge of pride," "as a sign of defiance against the forces of sexual conformity" (Gates 2000:8), and as a stigmatized label that is built from cultural stereotypes. We integrated theories of crime, deviance, and gender to better understand the sociological constructions of sex and sexuality, and in doing so, we saw that sexual deviance is all around us. In short, we learned:

> Sex is never just about sexual acts. Those acts are always embedded within structures of meaning. Marriage, religion, science, and the law are frameworks that organize meanings of sex … In different times and places, sex acts and the environments in which they occur take on specific meanings. While there is always a set of dominant beliefs, individuals and groups develop other ideas and practices, sometimes in opposition to, and sometimes appropriating aspects of, the dominant structures … From the matrix of deviance—itself derived from sexual norms—[come] new forms of sexual normativity … deviance reveals that the only stability is the fact of change.
>
> *(Crawford 2007:189–90)*

Back when I was a student, I hoped for an undergraduate classroom experience where we learned about sex, sexuality, and sex crime in terms of how these issues were socially constructed and how they impacted my life and the lives of others. I wrote this textbook to help fulfill my own educational experience and in doing so, I hope I have contributed to yours. Thinking back to the beginning of this journey, I presented you with an opportunity to critically examine the ways societies construct sex and sexuality. In doing so, I contended that expanding our knowledge about sexual deviance can create a space for self-reflection and can help establish a new way of thinking about stigmatized people and behaviors. I invited you to learn, to think, and to evolve: to arm yourself with knowledge and awareness. By shining the light onto some very "dark" issues—some of which are decidedly abhorrent, some that are becoming much more mainstream, and still others that are still very misunderstood—it is my sincere hope that you have been challenged, reassured, titillated, and inspired along this journey and that you will continue to critically question sexual deviance in your own lives and within larger global conversations about crime, sex, gender, sexuality, and power.

References

Bering, Jessie. 2013. *PERV: The Sexual Deviant in All of Us*. New York, NY: Scientific American/Farrar, Straus and Giroux.

Crawford, Katherine. 2007. *European Sexualities: 1400–1800*. New York, NY: Cambridge University Press.

Gates, Katharine. 2000. *Deviant Desires: Incredibly Strange Sex*. New York, NY: Juno Books.

GLOSSARY

Achieved stigma: a stigma derived from conduct and/or individual contribution.

Adam Walsh Child Protection and Safety Act (2006): U.S. law that outlined the Sex Offender Registration and Notification Act (SORNA), which includes a three-tiered classification system based on the type and number of sex offense convictions an individual has. Learn more about Adam in chapter 14, footnote 4.

Age-crime curve: a depiction of the age distribution of crime that plots the age of the offender and a particular criminal act against one another.

Agender: a label for those who think of themselves as without gender, genderless or gender neutral.

AIDS epidemic: a label applied to the period in time (from 1981 to 1992) in which nearly a quarter of a million Americans were diagnosed with HIV, and diseases related to complications from HIV/AIDS claimed the lives of more than 90 percent of these people.

Anger retaliation rapist: is overwhelmed by feelings of anger and rage and responds by overpowering, beating, and humiliating his victim during sexual assault.

Anomie: from Durkheim (1893, 1897), social instability that emerges from normlessness caused by the modernization of society.

Bisexual: a label for those who are sexually, romantically, physically, and/or emotionally attracted to both men and women.

BDSM: umbrella term for practices that include bondage and discipline (BD) and sadomasochism (SM).

Brothel prostitution: a form of sex work that takes place in brothels where people come specifically to purchase sexual services from prostitutes.

Bukkake: a form of Japanese erotica wherein a number of men ejaculate on a woman or another man.

Bystander effect: the phenomenon whereby individuals are more likely to help when alone than when in the company of others (also referred to as "Genovese syndrome").

Chicago School: school of early criminology that arose in the early twentieth century and shifted the focus of criminology away from individual characteristics to the examination of ecological and social structures.

Cisnormativity: the assumption that it is "normal" to be *cisgender*.

Cisgender: a label for individuals who have a match between their sex assigned at birth, their bodies, and their personal gender identity.

Classical School: school of early criminology that emphasized free will as part of the causes of criminal behavior and deterrence as an effective prevention mechanism.

Clery Act (1990): the Jeanne Clery Disclosure of Campus Security Policy and Campus Crime Statistics Act, or Clery Act for short, requires all U.S. colleges and universities to disclose statistics about crime on or near their campuses in annual security reports by gathering crime data from campus security authorities. Learn more about Jeanne in chapter 12, footnote 4.

Consent: a process of agreement to engage in a certain activity at a certain time and place with a particular person or persons without coercion, threat, or force made by persons of sound mind that involves mental willingness and desire and ongoing communicatory cues both before and during sexual activity.

Contagious Diseases (CD) Acts of 1864, 1866, and 1869: in the United Kingdom, the CD Acts effectively required any woman believed to be a prostitute to be subjected to compulsory examinations for venereal disease.

Comfort women: name given to the hundreds of thousands of women from Korea, Taiwan, China, the Philippines, Indonesia, and other countries that were forced into prostitution by the Japanese military during WWII.

Compulsory heterosexuality: whereby "heterosexuality is presumed as a 'sexual preference' of 'most women,' either implicitly or explicitly" (Rich 1980: 633).

Comstock Act of 1873: the Comstock Act made it illegal to use the U.S. Postal Service to transport any "obscene" materials.

Counterculture: a subgroup whose values and norms are at odds with the dominant culture.

Courtesan: a professionally trained female performer who entertained men with music and dance but also provided sexual pleasure; especially common in ancient China.

Courtesy stigma: from Goffman (1963), where individuals are stigmatized simply for being close to a stigmatized individual.

Covering: from Goffman (1963), effort to conceal stigma through reducing visibility and obtrusiveness of a stigmatizing quality.

COYOTE (Call Off Your Old Tired Ethics): one of the first and most well-known groups advocating for prostitutes' rights in the United States, founded by former prostitute Margo St. James in 1973.

Crime/criminal deviance: violation of formally enacted law.

Criminology: investigates the causes, consequences, and prevention of criminal behavior (formal violations of laws) in both the individual and society.

Cruising: the practice of seeking out others for sex in unexpected locales.

CSAM: graphic depictions of child sexual abuse in sex-related media involving persons under the age of 18.

Cultural genitals/genitalia: a description of a situation whereby an individual's masculine and feminine performances and displays dictate a particular gender and it is only a presumption that such behaviors "match" an individual's biological genitals.

Cultural relativism: a perspective that recognizes that "although for every culture some moral judgements are valid, no moral judgement is universally valid. Every moral judgment is culturally relative" (Tilley 2000: 505).

Date rape drug: a drug that is used to facilitate unwanted sexual activity.

Deviance: the sociological field that investigates non-normative beliefs, behaviors and identities in efforts to understand how norms are created, reinforced, and violated in a particular society. Deviance is an ever changing social construct that is both culturally and temporally relative to norms in a particular society.

Deviance admiration: from Heckert and Heckert (2002), underconformity to norms that carries an extremely positive connotation.

Deviance fascination: underconformity to norms that carries a somewhat positive connotation.

Double living: from Goffman (1963), a strategy whereby individuals keep their deviance secret from one class of persons while systematically exposing themselves as deviant to other classes of persons.

Dru's Law (2006): helped to create the U.S. National Sex Offender Public Website (NSOPW) to provide the public with access to sex offender data nationwide. Learn more about Dru in chapter 14, footnote 3.

Escorting: a higher-end form of sex work that involves payment for a sexual experience (as compared to a prescribed sex act).

Existential stigma: a stigma derived from a condition which the target either did not cause or over which he has little control.

Feminist porn: a political porn genre that engages with feminist dialogue.

Fetishes/fetishism: people with fetishes are sexually aroused by objects, body parts, or situations that are not often considered sexual.

Folk devils: the scapegoats; they are the groups who are blamed for the shortcomings (and deviance) in a particular society.

Folkways: everyday norms based on manners, customs, and decorum.

Gay: label for those who are sexually, romantically, physically, and/or emotionally attracted to members of the same gender as themselves.

Gay bathhouse: commercial establishments (typically with saunas, showers, whirlpools, etc.) designed to appeal to men looking for sex with other men.

Gender: a social construct that is related to the ways a culture organizes people and labels characteristics and visual cues into dichotomous identities of "men" and "women." Often gender is described as distinct from *sex* (see glossary: *sex*).

Genderqueer: a label for individuals who perceive and/or describe their gender identity as neither man nor woman, or as between or beyond genders, or as some combination of multiple genders.

Gender nonconformity prejudice: differential treatment and/or negative attitudes toward individuals whose gender expression does not follow traditional stereotypical gender roles and/or norms.

Glory hole: a hole in the partition between the toilet stalls in a public restroom that allows for sex acts to take place and/or allows for viewing others through the hole.

Gonzo: a porn content production form characterized by the presence of a "talking camera," wherein the person recording a particular sequence or scene is also playing an active, integral role in the on-screen action.

Hebephilia: sexual attraction to pubescent children, approximately aged 11 to 14, whose bodies show discrete signs of puberty.

Hentai: a form of Japanese erotica featuring drawn pornographic content.

Heteromasculinity: a type of masculinity that is closely entwined with the stereotypes associated with men and heterosexuality.

Heteronormativity: the assumption that it is "normal" to be heterosexual. Heteronormativity is produced through the presumptions that heterosexuality, gender performance, and gender identity follow from biological genitalia.

Heterosexism: the bias that heterosexuality is "the only way to be" and those that are not heterosexual are somehow "wrong."

Heterosexual: a label for those who are sexually, romantically, physically, and/or emotionally attracted to those identifying in the opposite gender identity category as themselves.

Hijra: a third gender category ascribed to those in South Asian cultures who are typically born and identified as male based on the appearance of their genitalia who are deemed to have mystical powers.

HIV/AIDS: human immunodeficiency virus/acquired immunodeficiency syndrome.

Homophobia: fear and dislike of homosexuality.

Homosexual/homosexuality: an outdated (sometimes pejoratively used) term to describe those who have romantic, sexual, emotional, intellectual, and/or spiritual attraction to those of the same sex and/or gender identity. See Box 4.2 in chapter 4.

Jacob Wetterling Act (1994): the Jacob Wetterling Crimes Against Children and Sexually Violent Offender Registration Act required U.S. states to keep registries of sex offenders' information on file for law enforcement purposes. Learn more about Jacob in chapter 14, footnote 1.

Lesbian: typically, a label for women who are sexually, romantically, physically, and/or emotionally attracted to other women.

LGBTQ: acronym that represents lesbian, gay, bisexual, trans, and queer-identified people and/or communities.

Lolicon: a form of Hentai Japanese erotica featuring prepubescent and adolescent girls.

Looking-glass self: from Cooley (1902), our interpretation of our own self concept is based on how we think others perceive us.

Lord Campbell's Act: also known as the Obscene Publications Act of 1857, United Kingdom Act that determined that any material found to be "obscene" could be destroyed by a magistrate or justice of the peace.

Marxism: a perspective that emphasizes class struggle and societal conflict to critique capitalism and argue for social change. The Social Conflict Approach emerged out of this tradition.

Master status: a defining characteristic of an individual.

Mechanical solidarity: from Durkheim (1893), a form of social solidarity exhibited in small primitive societies where people feel connected through their homogeneity (e.g., they have similar work, educational, and religious experiences).

Megan's Law (1996): U.S. law that made sex offender information available to the public under certain circumstances. Learn more about Megan in chapter 14, footnote 2.

Middle Assyrian Law (MAL) 40: dated to 1115 to 1077 B.C.E., a law that legislated the practice of veiling to only certain types of women and in doing so, effectively created a hierarchical rank order system for the social status of women related to their sexual histories.

Moral entrepreneur: individuals and groups who crusade to combat what they see as social evils and work to eradicate or convert deviants to their ways of acting and thinking.

Moral panic: from Cohen (1972), a condition, episode, person, or group of persons emerges to become defined as a threat to societal values and interests; its nature is presented in a stylized and stereotypical fashion by the mass media; the moral barricades are manned by editors, bishops, politicians and other right-thinking people; socially accredited experts pronounce their diagnoses and solutions; ways of coping are evolved or (more often) resorted to; the condition then disappears, submerges or deteriorates and becomes more visible.

Mores: norms about moral values.

MSM: men who have sex with men.

Negative deviance: underconformity or nonconformity to norms that carries a negative connotation.

Norms: established standards of behavior and beliefs maintained by a particular society.

Onanism: all non-procreative sexual activity; rooted in the Biblical story of Onan who resorted to "spilling his seed on the ground" (*Genesis* 38: 7–10) instead of impregnating his dead brother's wife.

Organic solidarity: from Durkheim (1893), a form of social solidarity that emerges when societal demands require specializations in the workplace and societies depend on complementarities between people (rather than similarities) to strengthen society.

Panopticon: an idealized institutional building designed by Jeremy Bentham in 1791 to promote constant surveillance so that chains and other restraints become entirely superfluous.

Paragraph 175: a provision of the German Criminal Code active from 1871 to 1994 that criminalized acts of sodomy. Both East and West Germany continued to enforce Paragraph 175 until it was amended in 1968/9 to include only sodomy acts engaged in with minors and it was fully repealed in 1994 upon the reunification of Germany.

Pederasty: (derived from Greek meaning "boy-love"), in ancient Greece, a social system in which mutual loving relationships between adult men and teenage boys were socially sanctioned and normalized.

Pedophilia: a sexual attraction to prepubescent children approximately 10 years of age and younger.

Political porn: a porn genre that engages a dialogue about politicized issues, examples: queer porn and feminist porn.

Polygamy: when a married person has more than one spouse at the same time.

Pornography: written descriptions, still images, and filmic representations of sexual activity designed to incite erotic emotions and behaviors.

Positive deviance: overconformity to norms that carries a positive connotation.

Positivist School: school of early criminology whose theorists believed individual characteristics pre-determine criminal behavior..

Power assertive rapist: believes he is entitled to sexual access to others and asserts his power over the victim through brute force and physical beatings during sexual assault.

Power reassurance rapist: feels sexually, physically, and emotionally inadequate and uses forced sex as a means to achieve or elevate strength, authority, and virility.

PREA (2003): U.S. Prison Rape Elimination Act mandates sexual victimization reports in all federal and state prisons, military prisons and a representative sample of jail jurisdictions, privately operated jails and prisons, and jails holding adults in Native American territories.

Primary deviance: from Lemert (1951), a behavior that departs from a social norm yet causes no long-term consequences for the offender.

Prostitution: a form of sex work involving sexual activities for the exchange of money, goods, or services.

Public sex: any sexual activity that occurs in a space identified by cultural norms as communal, shared, municipal, and/or open to all citizens.

Queer: a descriptor of sexual identity and/or a radical political positionality that encompasses acceptance of sexual diversity. Queer people identify beyond gender binaries (for example, something other than men or women) and/or heteronormative categorizations (for example, something other than cisgender heterosexual). (Note: "queer" can also be used as a derogatory slang word.)

Queer porn: a political porn genre that features performers of various gender and sexual identities in efforts to present sexuality and identity authenticity. Distinct from TS porn.

Rape: any unwanted sexual acts (including vaginal, anal or oral penetration by an object or body part and being made to penetrate others) committed without consent and/or against a person's will, obtained by force, or threat of force, intimidation, or when a person is unable to consent.

Rape myths: prominent cultural misconceptions about rape.

Rate-busting: from Heckert and Heckert (2002), overconformity to norms that carries a negative connotation.

Sadistic rapist: derives sexual and emotional pleasure from inflicting pain and suffering on others through brutal and ritualized torture in accordance with sexually violent fantasies.

Secondary deviance: from Lemert (1951), a violation of social norms that results in a realignment of an individual's self-concept either with the deviance itself or with a subgroup that is considered deviant in relation to the social norms. Secondary deviance often leads to a permanent label from external observers.

Sex (identity): typically confined to the labels of "male" or "female" based on biological markers such as the external appearances of genitalia and to a lesser extent, chromosomes.

Sex club: a business establishment whose primary purpose is to provide opportunities for sex.

Sexology: the scientific study of human sexuality.

Sex offender: a label applied to anyone who has been convicted of a crime that is sexual in nature.

Sexting: sending, receiving, and/or forwarding of sexually explicit messages, clips, or images via an internet-enabled device.

Sex trafficking: the transportation of humans for the purposes of involvement in forced sexual labor that can include coercion, kidnapping, abuse, and imprisonment.

Sex work: a generic term for any commercial sexual service, performance, or product given in exchange for compensation. Sex work includes, but is not limited to, various forms of prostitution, exotic dance, phone sex, and pornography.

Sex worker dividend: a societal construct that supports and maintains the overall negative treatment and stigmatization of people working in the sex trade.

Sexual deviance: sexual behaviors and identities perceived as deviant in a particular society.

Sexual diversity: an umbrella term for the wide spectrum of sexual behaviors and identities that exist in society.

Sexual grooming: a three-part process whereby a person prepares themselves, the environment, and the child to facilitate the sexual abuse of this child.

Sexual identity: an individual's self-identification of his/her romantic, sexual, emotional, intellectual, and/or spiritual attraction to others based on the ways a culture organizes people and labels characteristics and visual cues into socially constructed identities; sometimes also described as a sexual orientation or sexual preference.

Sexual prejudice: from Herek (2000, 2004), a negative attitudinal evaluation of an individual because of her/ his sexual orientation that is based on emotional, cognitive, and behavioral information.

Sexual socialization: the process in which adolescents learn about sex and how to be sexual individuals from their social contexts.

SM: a collection of activities that involve the mutually consensual and conscious use, of pain, power, perceptions about power, or any combination thereof, for psychological, emotional, or sensory pleasure (from Newmahr 2011).

Social deviance: violation of a cultural norm.

Social Conflict Approach: a macro-level approach to understanding society that highlights power and conflict through considering large social structures as they relate to both the causes and solutions to social inequality.

Stigma: from Goffman (1963), an attribute that is deeply discrediting.

Street prostitution: a form of sex work that commonly takes place in public or semi-public areas such as streets, alleys, and cars and involves the exchange of sex acts for remuneration.

Structural Functionalist Approach: this macro-level approach to understanding society highlights all existing parts of society as integral and functional to its continued survival.

Sugar dating: a practice wherein a "sugar baby" receives patronage from a "sugar daddy" or "sugar momma" typically prearranged at the outset of the relationship.

Swinging: a practice whereby a couple incorporates other people/couples into their sexual relationship.

Symbolic interactionism: this micro-level approach to understanding society supports the belief that "reality" is a social construct developed through human interaction and modified through interpretation.

Tearooms: public restrooms that are known locales for public sex between men (also known as cottages).

Tentacle erotica: a form of Japanese erotica and Hentai that amalgamates horror, science fiction, and bestiality, while skirting penetration regulations.

Tertiary deviance: from Kitsuse (1980), tertiary deviance refers to "the deviant's confrontation, assessment, and rejection of the negative identity imbedded in secondary deviation, and the transformation of that identity into a positive and viable self-conception" (Kitsuse 1980: 9). Through tertiary deviance, individuals celebrate their "deviant" identities.

Tippelzone: areas in the Netherlands outside of the city center designated specifically for picking up prostitutes, exchanging sexual services, and for seeking care.

Trans*: an umbrella term for anyone in the transgender community.

Transgender: a label for individuals who do not have a match between the sex they were assigned at birth, their bodies, and their personal gender identity.

Trans woman: transgender individuals who have transitioned or are currently transition- ing from having male/man sex and/or gender characteristics to having female/ woman sex and/or gender characteristics (also described as male-to-female or MtF individuals).

Trans man: transgender individuals who have transitioned or are currently transitioning from hav- ing female/woman sex and/or gender characteristics to having male/man sex and/or gender characteristics, (also described as female-to-male or FtM individuals).

Tribal stigma: from Goffman (1963), stigmas associated with race, nationality, or religion (these may be transmitted through family lineages).

TS porn: a porn genre that features transgender performers but is not political in motivation or content. Distinct from queer porn.

Two-spirit people: individuals in North American Native American communities who occupy a third gender category. They are sometimes described as simultaneously embodying both a masculine and a feminine spirit. Two-spirit people often receive a spiritual calling to transform into the third gender category; as two-spirits, their status is typically associated with mystical powers and fortune-telling abilities.

WHISPER (Women Hurt in Systems of Prostitution Engaged in Revolt): prostitutes' rights activism group that emerged in the early 1980s whose primary objective is the total and complete abolition of prostitution.

*Note: Many fetish definitions are not provided in this glossary. See chapter 10 for definitions of a variety of paraphilias. In particular, see Table 10.1 and Box 10.4.

References

Cohen, Stanley. 1972. *Folk Devils and Moral Panics.* London: Routledge.

Cooley, Charles Horton. 1902. *Human Nature and the Social Order.* New York, NY: Scribner's.

Durkheim, Émile. 1997 [1893]. *The Division of Labor in Society*. New York, NY: Free Press.

Durkheim, Émile. 1951 [1897]. *Suicide: A Study in Sociology.* New York, NY: Free Press.

Goffman, Erving. 1963. *Stigma: Notes on the Management of Spoiled Identity*. Englewood Cliffs, NJ: Prentice-Hall.

Heckert, Alex and Druann Maria Heckert. 2002. "A New Typology of Deviance: Integrating Normative and Reactivist Definitions of Deviance." *Deviant Behavior* 23: 449–79.

Herek, Gregory. 2000. "The Psychology of Sexual Prejudice." *Current Directions in Psychological Science* 9: 19–22.

Herek, Gregory. 2004. "Beyond Homophobia: Thinking about Sexual Prejudice and Stigma in the Twenty-First Century." *Sexuality Research & Social Policy* 1: 6–24.

Kitsuse, John. 1980. "Coming Out All Over: Deviants and the Politics of Social Problems." *Social Problems* 28: 1–13.

Lemert, Edwin. 1951. *Social Pathology.* New York, NY: McGraw-Hill.

Newmahr, Staci. 2011. *Playing on the Edge: Sadomasochism, Risk, and Intimacy.* Bloomington, IN: Indiana University Press.

Rich, Adrienne. 1980. "Compulsory Heterosexuality and Lesbian Existence." *Signs* 5(4): 631–60.

Tilley, John. 2000. "Cultural Relativism." *Human Rights Quarterly* 22(2): 501–47.

INDEX